SEVENTH EDITION

Writing That Works

Communicating Effectively on the Job

Walter E. Oliu

U.S. Nuclear Regulatory Commission

Charles T. Brusaw

NCR Corporation (retired)

Gerald J. Alred

University of Wisconsin–Milwaukee

Bedford/St. Martin's

Boston ◆ New York

For Bedford/St. Martin's

Developmental Editor: Ellen Thibault
Senior Editor, Publishing Services: Douglas Bell
Production Supervisor: Joe Ford
Project Management: Books By Design, Inc.
Marketing Manager: Richard Cadman
Text Design: Claire Seng-Niemoeller
Cover Design: Zenobia Rivetna
Cover Photo: Lisette LeBow/Superstock
Composition: Pine Tree Composition, Inc.
Printing and Binding: Haddon Craftsmen, an RR Donnelley & Sons Company

President: Charles H. Christensen
Editorial Director: Joan E. Feinberg
Editor in Chief: Karen S. Henry
Director of Marketing: Karen R. Melton
Director of Editing, Design, and Production: Marcia Cohen
Manager, Publishing Services: Emily Berleth

Library of Congress Control Number: 00–106402

Manufactured in the United States of America.

6   5   4   3   2   1
f   e   d   c   b   a

For information, write: Bedford/St. Martin's, 75 Arlington Street, Boston, MA 02116
(617-399-4000)

ISBN: 0-312-25629-9

Acknowledgments

Figures 7–3, 7–8, and 7–9: Instructions without an illustration, "Cleaning Inside of Grill"; a warning in a set of instructions, "Warning"; and a caution in a set of instructions, "Safety Precautions"; all adapted from "Char-Broil Use and Care Manual for LP Gas Grills" from "Char-Broil Use and Care Manual." Adapted and reprinted with the permission of W. C. Bradley Company.

Acknowledgments and copyrights are continued at the back of the book on pages 887–888, which constitute an extension of the copyright page.

Chapter 8: Principles of Business Correspondence

Chapter 9: Types of Business Correspondence

Chapter 10: Informal Reports

Chapter 11: Researching Your Subject

Chapter 12: Designing Effective Documents and Visuals

Writing That Works

Communicating Effectively on the Job

Preface

Writing That Works, Seventh Edition, continues to address the communications needs for students of varied academic backgrounds and occupational interests whose jobs will, or already do, require these skills. Each chapter provides clear, thorough explanations; abundant and realistic examples drawn from a wide range of occupations; and carefully structured exercises and writing assignments. The text is unusually comprehensive, and probably few instructors will wish to assign every chapter. We have, therefore, built into the book sufficient flexibility to enable instructors to choose the sections they consider most important for any particular class. (In addition, among the supplemental materials offered at our companion Web site at http://www.bedfordstmartins.com/writingthatworks is a suggested syllabus for a 16-week course.) At the same time, we feel that this text is inclusive enough to serve as a reference tool for students long after the course is over, because no course can possibly cover all the writing concerns students will encounter once they are actually on the job.

■ New to This Edition

A More Accessible Book

- A **fresh design** features wider pages, annotated and hand-corrected examples, and a realistic presentation of model documents. A handy **list of figures and model documents** on the inside front cover allows readers to quickly find the more than 250 model business documents included in the seventh edition.

- **New ESL Tips** throughout the text highlight specific writing advice for nonnative speakers.

- **New Writer's Checklists**—two in each chapter—provide concise writing advice. (ESL Tips and Writer's Checklists are listed at the back of the book for easy reference.)

More Advice for Writing at Work

- A new section called **Writing for the Web**—focused on considerations of audience, Web style, the presentation of long documents, and the use of keywords and hyperlinks—offers students expert advice for meeting the demands of the type of writing required by many entry-level jobs as more companies develop their presence on the Web.

- **Expanded coverage of presentations** with plenty of new examples and new information on using presentation software such as Power Point™ helps students prepare and deliver seamless presentations.

- **New entry-level Voices from the Workplace** complement the experienced voices in each chapter and offer experiences and advice from young adults (many of whom are recent graduates) who are new to the workplace.

- **A new case study in Chapter 1** takes students step by step through the persuasive writing process. In this contemporary scenario, an employee drafts, writes, and revises until she produces a memo that convinces her boss to consider a new policy.

- **Two Meeting the Deadline sections** provide practical guidelines for tackling time-sensitive business proposals and memos on the job.

More Writing Practice Than Any Book of Its Kind

- **More model documents**—over 250 in the seventh edition—offer students more examples of business writing than competing texts and are easy to find using the model documents list on the book's inside front cover.

- **More writing assignments**—twice as many as any other business-writing text—include new and expanded end-of-chapter exercises, individual and collaborative in-class activities, research projects, and Web projects that provide students with ample opportunity to apply the principles introduced in each chapter. Additional online cases are provided at the text's companion Web site (as are suggestions for instructors in responding to student writing for each online case and each assignment in the book).

More Information on Using Technology

- **A fully revised research chapter** provides more advice for library and online research and includes a step-by-step search of the catalog of an online university library, solid guidelines for evaluating online sources, and examples of pages from the Web evaluated and annotated by the authors. This chapter offers current Modern Language Association (MLA) documentation models and now includes American Psychological Association (APA) documentation models for a wide range of sources. Practical workplace technology includes **updated email coverage** and information on etiquette and the appropriate use and management of email, with plentiful examples.

- **New information on creating electronic résumés** and finding employment resources on the Web (with additional resources at the companion Web site) provides students with indispensable advice for the job search.

- A **new section on Web-page design** offers advice for planning a Web site—from its navigation and links to its graphics and typography—with information on home-page and site layout.

- A **new section called Preparing Forms for the Web** shows students how to plan and create information-gathering forms at Web sites.

- A **revised Electronic Office appendix** offers an updated guide for using electronic tools and the Internet during the writing process.

A New Companion Web Site

A new companion Web site at http://www.bedfordstmartins.com/writingthatworks features practical resources for instructors and students—organized for easy access by both chapter and category. (See the inside back cover for a look at the site's home page.)

Student Resources

- **Finding a Job or Internship**—a section that takes students step-by-step through the search process—includes Web resources, interview tips, sample résumés, and correspondence.

- **Online cases** help students use the Web to practice skills covered in each chapter.

- **Model documents** of business writing offer samples of correspondence, reports, résumés, and more.

- **Chapter Exercises, In-Class Activities, Research Projects,** and **Web Projects** from the text are provided in electronic format with Web links.

- **Writer's Checklists, Chapter Summaries,** and **Digital Shortcuts** from the text are provided in electronic format.

Instructor Resources

Our expanded, **online instructor's manual** offers:

- Course goals and teaching tips with sample syllabi
- Concise overviews and teaching strategies for each chapter
- Responses to Online Cases
- Responses to Chapter Exercises, In-Class Activities, Research Projects, and Web Projects
- Handouts offering assignments, tips, and model documents
- Bibliographies and additional online resources

■ Organization and Coverage

For the seventh edition we have retained and refined the three-part organization of the text—an organization designed to facilitate both the teaching and learning of various types of writing. Part One is an introduction to the writing process. The six chapters in this part guide the student through all the steps of the process—planning, organizing, writing (including a separate chapter on how to highlight key ideas), and revising—with special emphasis on the questions a writer must ask when approaching any writing task: What is my purpose in writing? For whom is the writing intended? How much information must I include? Have I used plain language? By page 52 the student is familiar with the most common organizational patterns; by page 81 he or she has been introduced to the elements of writing an effective first draft. And by page 167 the student has studied the ways of achieving emphasis in writing—use of the active and passive voices, subordination, word order, and introductory words and phrases. Chapter 6, "Collaborative Writing," provides detailed guidance, including advice for collaborating through electronic communications, and exercises for this widely used practice in most job settings.

Part Two—Chapters 7 through 16—looks at the writing process at work, considering in particular the various kinds of on-the-job writing and the strategies appropriate to each one. Chapter 7, "Instructions and Other Writing Strategies," presents the range of rhetorical applications for specific purposes that should be part of every writer's basic equipment: creating instructions (whether for colleagues on the job or for a technical manual), explaining a process, describing information, defining terms and concepts, explaining cause and effect, and persuading readers—whether on the printed page or on the Web screen. Each rhetorical application is illustrated by one or more job-related examples. New to this edition is a section called Writing for the Web, a unique form of communication, the importance of which is growing as companies post increasing amounts of information at their internal and public Web sites. Chapter 8, "Principles of Business Correspondence," focuses on the importance of goodwill and the "you" viewpoint and covers typical letter and memo formats—both printed and electronic. The workplace increasingly offers far more options for communicating with customers and coworkers than letters and memos. Because each option has unique advantages for specific kinds of audiences and messages, we have included a section called Selecting the Appropriate Medium that discusses the salient characteristics of letters, memos, email, faxes, telephone calls, voice-mail messages, face-to-face meetings, and videoconferences. Chapter 8 also provides expanded treatment of email, the workplace communications medium that has grown the fastest over the last several years. Coverage includes guidance on the appropriate writing style for email messages, including netiquette, and the privacy implications of this medium. Chapter 8 ends with a comprehensive section on international correspondence.

Chapter 9, "Types of Business Correspondence," covers the most widely used forms of business communication and groups them into two categories: Types of

Routine and Positive Messages, such as acknowledgment letters, cover letters (or transmittal letters), inquiries, responses, recommendations, and sales and promotional messages; and Sensitive and Negative Messages, such as refusals, complaints, adjustments, resignations, and collections letters.

We have thoroughly revised Chapter 11, "Researching Your Subject," so that it provides more advice on online research and includes a step-by-step search of the catalog of an online university library and more information on evaluating online sources. This material is balanced with up-to-date coverage of library research and the importance of the research librarian as a resource. In addition to MLA documentation style coverage—with models for a variety of print and nonprint sources—Chapter 11 now includes coverage of the APA documentation style with plenty of models. This chapter also offers information on additional research techniques relevant to report writing, including interviews, questionnaires, and first-hand observation.

Writing That Works continues to cover the major types of formal and informal reports, offering updated tips and sample documents. Chapter 10, "Informal Reports," covers trouble reports, investigative reports, progress and periodic reports, trip reports, and test reports; Chapter 13, "Formal Reports," discusses all parts of the formal report and features a new, annotated sample report. A revised Chapter 12, "Designing Effective Documents and Visuals," is divided into two main parts, beginning with Creating Documents, a section that offers expanded information on document layout and design, Web-page layout and design, and the creation of forms—for both print and the Web. The Creating Visuals section of the chapter presents practical but essential information on how to design illustrations—tables, graphs, drawings, charts, maps, and photographs—and integrate them with text as well as advice for how to use graphics to communicate with an increasingly international business audience.

Chapter 14, "Proposals," covers both internal proposals and external, or sales, proposals (both solicited and unsolicited). Comprehensive examples of both internal and external proposals are provided. Also new to this edition is the section called Meeting the Deadline: The Time-Sensitive Proposal that describes how to approach a task common to many firms: effective proposal writing under a pressing deadline.

Chapter 15, "Presentations and Meetings," discusses the preparation and delivery of oral presentations, including expanded coverage of presentation software such as PowerPoint™ with plenty of examples, and includes information about effective listening and a section about conducting productive meetings.

Chapter 16, "Finding a Job," is a practical, step-by-step guide to finding employment, with special emphasis on preparing effective résumés, letters of application, and follow-up letters. Plenty of sample résumés—several prepared for electronic submission—are provided both for students with little or no job experience and for those with a great deal of experience.

Finally, Part Three of *Writing That Works* is a highly accessible Writer's Guide, presenting important supplemental tools for the writer. Section A provides focused coverage of word processing as an aid to the writing process. This section features guidelines for using this technology to maximum effect for capturing ideas, revising text, and formatting and printing well-designed written documents. Section A also includes an overview of how the components that make up the Internet function to facilitate the sharing of information from sources throughout the world. The section concludes with a concise look at the useful role that faxes continue to play in the workplace.

Section B provides instructional material on spelling and vocabulary building, while Section C is a comprehensive handbook of grammar, punctuation, and mechanics. The handbook is based on materials drawn from our *Handbook of Technical Writing* and *Business Writer's Handbook,* both published by Bedford/St. Martin's. In an effort to make the handbook section of this book as useful and accessible as possible, we have cross-referenced it with Chapter 4 on revising. Section D of the Writer's Guide includes expanded help for speakers of English as a Second Language. Section D rounds out coverage — that begins with Writing International Correspondence in Chapter 8 and Using Graphics to Communicate Internationally in Chapter 12 — and emphasizes the importance of international communications in a global economy. The Writer's Guide is linked by cross-references that appear throughout the text.

Other reference features of this edition include the handy new list of model documents printed on the book's inside front cover, as well as a list with page references facing the inside back cover of the Writer's Checklists, Digital Shortcuts, and ESL Tips that are included throughout the text.

Writing That Works is accompanied by helpful instructors' resources, provided at the instructors' area of our new companion Web site at http://www.bedfordstmartins.com/writingthatworks. These resources were prepared by Lisa-Anne Culp of Oglethorpe University, Suzanne Karberg of Purdue University, Candy Henry of Pennsylvania State University, and Kate Williams of Oglethorpe University. They provide Chapter Overviews and teaching strategies, suggestions for responding to student writing assignments in the text, additional assignment models of business writing, and more.

■ Acknowledgments

We are grateful to Lisa-Anne Culp of Oglethorpe University for her thoughtful work on past editions of the *Instructor's Manual* and her work on this book's companion Web site, as well as for the sample letter she provided for Writing International Correspondence in Chapter 8. We are grateful to Candy Henry of Pennsylvania State University for her online cases, expert ESL advice, and the numerous student assignments that she contributed. We are grateful to Sandra Petrulionis and her students, Susan Litzinger and Eric Shoop, of Pennsylvania State University for the formal report and informal proposal included in this edition. We are grateful to Sandy Fuhr, research librarian at Gustavus Adolphus College for her valuable contributions to Chapter 11, "Researching Your Subject," and to Kate Bishop of the *Smithsonian Magazine* for her work on the writing-for-the-Web section. We are also grateful to Suzanne Karberg of Purdue University for her work in providing practical student assignments for each chapter, and also to the numerous instructors who contributed their class-tested material: Luann Okel Adams, Mid-State Technical College; Margaret Armstrong, Old Dominion University; Phyllis Bunn, Delta State University; Elizabeth Coughlin, DePaul University; and Linda Van Buskirk, Cornell University. In addition, we also wish to thank the following instructors who have substantially strengthened this edition by generously sharing their helpful comments and recommendations for the seventh edition:

John L. Allison, Morehead State University

Janel Bloch, Iowa State University

Kathryn Browning, Mesabi Range Community and Technical College

Judith M. Buddenbaum, Colorado State University

Susan Corey, California Lutheran University

Joyce R. Durham, University of Dayton

Ron Ebest, University of Missouri–St. Louis

Tim Giles, Georgia Southern University

Gregory D. Horn, Southwest Virginia Community College

Priscilla Kanet, Clemson University

Patricia W. Kato, Chattanooga State

George Littleton, Auburn University

Jim Mastro, National University

Susan Mueller, University of Missouri–St. Louis

Gary Dean Patterson, California State University–San Bernardino

Patricia D. Reed, California State University–San Bernardino

Sue Roth, Trident Technical College

Stuart Selber, Pennsylvania State University

Lynn Setzer, North Carolina State University

Barbara Weaver, Clemson University

We also wish to thank the following on-the-job professionals from a variety of fields who so thoughtfully shared their experiences of writing and communicating in the workplace:

James Bates, U.S. Department of Housing and Urban Development

Kate Bishop, *Smithsonian Magazine*

Steve Bramlage, Vectren Energy of Ohio

Kevin Buckley, Office of Massachusetts State Senator Brian P. Lees

Sheree Crute, *Heart and Soul* Magazine

Corey Ann Eaton, First Union Brokerage Services, Inc.

Cara Feinberg, *The American Prospect*

Nicole Gallagher, ABC News

Paul Greenspan, TIS Worldwide

Joanna Honig, Hill and Knowlton

Terry Kalna, ISL United States, Inc.

Dan Krick, Iams Company

Susan U. Ladwig, Medical College of Wisconsin

Molly Lawless, JuniorNet

Colleen McDonough, Hobart and William Smith Colleges

Susan McLaughlin, The Seldi Group

Chris Meeker, AMT Capital Management

Rachel O'Malley, iCast

Sherri Pfennig, University of Wisconsin–Milwaukee

Joseph Rappaport, Office of the Public Advocate, City of New York

Priya Ratneshwar, Bedford/St. Martin's

Samuel Rosenbaum, Adams, Harkness, & Hill

Jessica Salo, RAD Employment Services, Inc.

Diane Schumacher, Eskie Adventures

Rebecca Dellinger Shugart, Data Processing Services (DPS), Inc.

Christopher Smith, SquashBusters

Nancy Spain, Empire Blue Cross and Blue Shield

Jonathan Spiegel, The Foundation Center

Adam Thompson, *The Denver Post*

Larrell Walters, Lytton Electronics

Mary Warren, Argonne National Laboratory

Macie Whittington, Amdahl Corporation

We are also greatly indebted to the leadership of Bedford/St Martin's, beginning with Charles Christensen, President; Joan Feinberg, Editorial Director; and Karen Henry, Editor in Chief, for helping us to re-imagine our approach to key facets of this edition and for their unstinting support throughout the revision process. We are pleased to acknowledge the unfailingly helpful and timely assistance of Sara Eaton, Editorial Assistant, of Bedford/St. Martin's. Finally, we were especially fortunate to work with Ellen Thibault, our Developmental Editor at Bedford/St. Martin's, who set a new standard of excellence for her thoughtful guidance, creative coordination, and indispensable presence from conception to completion of work on this edition.

Walter E. Oliu
Charles T. Brusaw
Gerald J. Alred

Brief Contents

Contents

| PART ONE | The Writing Process | 1 |

Chapter 8   Principles of Business Correspondence   265

Chapter 9   **Types of Business Correspondence**   325

Chapter 16 | **Finding a Job** | 683

Determining the Best Job for You   683

Preparing an Effective Résumé   689

Doing Well in the Interview   709

Sending Follow-Up Correspondence   713

Writing a Job Description   713

PART THREE   Writer's Guide   727

The Writing Process

In Part One, you will learn techniques for developing, drafting, and revising letters, memos, and a wide array of other on-the-job writing tasks. Using these strategies will help you produce clearly written, well-organized documents, because effective on-the-job writing always reflects the writer's attention to the work that goes on before the finished memo or letter emerges from the printer.

- ◆ **Determining Audience and Purpose.** Chapters 1 through 3 provide discussion and exercises to help you clearly define your reader's needs and the message you intend your document to convey.

- ◆ **Brainstorming and Gathering Information.** Chapter 1 includes detailed examples and discussion of methods you can use to generate ideas and collect and begin to organize information.

- ◆ **Outlining.** Chapter 2 describes how you can organize your information into an outline that is appropriate to your purpose and audience. It also offers examples of a wide range of outline styles.

- ◆ **Drafting.** Chapter 3 discusses and offers examples of the process through which writers turn an outline into a successful rough draft.

- ◆ **Revising.** Chapters 4 and 5 describe the kinds of problems you need to evaluate when you revise a draft. You will learn how to review a draft to see how well it communicates to its intended audience; to emphasize key ideas; to check information for factual accuracy; to consider the ethical implications of your writing; to scrutinize language for grammatical correctness, consistency, and preciseness; and to proofread for punctuation and spelling.

- ◆ **Collaboration.** Chapter 6, which closes Part One, discusses the importance of the writing strategies learned in Chapters 1 through 5 to collaborative writing projects on the job, whether you are a member of a collaborative writing team or the team leader.

Within the chapters of Part One, you will find Writer's Checklists that provide concise writing advice; ESL Tips that offer writing help to non-native speakers of English; and Digital Shortcuts that offer brief tips for using technology to help you organize, write, and revise your drafts.

1 Getting Started

Christine Thomas was aware of a potential opportunity at HVS Accounting Services, where she worked as the company's Systems Administrator. The company was prospering. In just the past year, Harriet Sullivan, the president and founder of the small company, hired five new employees to handle the increasing workload of tax preparation, financial planning, and investments services. HVS now had 12 full-time employees, about half of whom commuted over an hour each way. The company had also lost several prospective employees because they did not wish to spend two or more hours a day driving to and from work.

For the past several months, Christine had carefully reviewed several management magazines and Web sites about the benefits of telecommuting for companies and their employees. Companies that offered this option to their employees had a happier workforce, less absenteeism, and greater productivity per employee. Such a program would also benefit the local community by reducing traffic congestion and air pollution.

So, with all the information in hand and confident of the value of her suggestion, Christine wrote an email message to Harriet Sullivan (see Figure 1–1, page 5). Two days later, Christine received the following terse return email from Harriet: "Not right for HVS." Christine was not only disappointed but also puzzled. She knew that her suggestion was timely and reasonable because she had checked all the facts before writing the email. Yet she had failed to convince Harriet Sullivan.

■ Using a Systematic Approach to Writing

In writing her email message, Christine Thomas committed the most common of all mistakes made by people who write on their jobs: She lost sight of the purpose of her message and overlooked the needs of her reader. Christine had been so convinced of the rightness of her suggestion that she forgot that her reader was not familiar with the information her research had produced and could not see the situation from her perspective. Had she kept her primary purpose and her reader clearly in mind, Christine would then have been able to generate ideas, establish her scope, and organize her ideas in a way that ultimately might have achieved her objective.

The last three steps are important: Even with her reader and her purpose clearly in mind, Christine would still not have been ready to write her email to

Harriet. She would simply have established a framework in which to develop her message. Some writers, once they have identified their purpose and their reader, don't know what to do next and stare at a blank computer screen or page waiting for inspiration.

A systematic approach helps writers over this hurdle. Before beginning to write, careful writers not only identify their purpose and reader but think seriously about the content of their writing and about how to organize and present it.

Voices from the Workplace

Sheree Crute, *Heart and Soul* Magazine

Sheree Crute is an editor-at-large for *Heart and Soul* Magazine, a women's health magazine published by Black Entertainment Television, Inc., and a freelance editor and writer for Rodale Press, *Consumer Reports on Health,* and other publications. *Heart and Soul* is a bimonthly publication that presents sophisticated information on health and fitness that is of particular interest to African American women. In addition to her responsibilities of editing some of the magazine's features, as well as other parts of the magazine, Sheree writes every day.

Understanding and writing to her audience is crucial. Sheree says: "Before you pick up a pen or flip on the computer to write, make sure you understand the reader you are trying to reach. You cannot produce information that's on target if you are unsure of the interests or needs of your audience. *Heart and Soul* readers want their health information delivered in a succinct and accessible way. They want news they can use—and bring into their daily lives. For this type of reporting, it doesn't matter how eloquent you are—if you don't understand your audience's needs, you will never be heard or understood."

Entry-Level
Colleen McDonough, Hobart and William Smith Colleges

Colleen McDonough is the assistant director of Annual Giving at Hobart and William Smith Colleges. As a fund-raiser, Colleen is called upon not only to express enthusiasm for her alma mater but also to persuade other alumni to contribute to the Colleges.

Colleen says: "Having excellent writing skills is essential to succeeding in a job like mine where I deal with people and their individual concerns every day. Persuasive writing skills are easy to develop, but difficult to fine-tune. I must know how to address different audiences. I have to remember that the similarity between alumni groups is often only that they have graduated from the same school. Era of attendance, current age, race, politics, gender, and geographic location also come into play. Needless to say, the scope of my writing has to have quite a range; soliciting support from a man who graduated in 1955 would take quite a different angle than when addressing a group of 23-year-old women. Having the ability to convey facts, be persuasive, and be flexible enough to craft the same basic thoughts in different ways to appeal to different groups are valuable skills which come with much practice and dedication."

Visit Hobart and William Smith Colleges online at http://www.hws.edu.

Figure 1–1
Christine Thomas'
Email to Harriet
Sullivan

To: Harriet V. Sullivan, President
From: Christine Thomas, Systems Administrator
Attch.:
Subject: Telecommuting and HVS Accounting Services

I believe that HVS Accounting would benefit greatly if we permitted our employees to telecommute one or more days a week. There are a growing number of companies, large and small, that permit employees to perform company work at home on a schedule they jointly agree to. The companies can communicate with these employees during the work day in a variety of ways — telephone, email, and fax.

There are many advantages to such a policy that would help HVS and our employees. Employees would save the time and expense necessary to commute every day. They would also suffer less stress and be in a better frame of mind to tackle their work. This would result in greater worker productivity. Finally, our community would benefit because fewer commuter cars on the road means reduced traffic congestion and cleaner air.

Please consider my suggestion that we permit our employees the opportunity to perform their HVS work at home one or more days a week.

================================
Christine Thomas, Systems Administrator
HVS Accounting Services
1226 W. Kenyon Road, Urbana, IL 61801
(217) 328-9955 Fax: (217) 328-9956
cthomas@hvs.com
http://www.hvs.com
================================

This process involves first listing all the ideas and facts the writer might wish to include, then refining the list by examining each item in it from the perspectives of reader and purpose, and finally organizing the resulting list in a way that satisfies the writer's primary purpose and the reader's needs.

WRITER'S CHECKLIST: Using a Systematic Approach to Writing

Complete each of the following steps before beginning to compose any important document:

- ☐ Determine your purpose.
- ☐ Determine your reader's needs.
- ☐ Generate, gather, and record ideas and facts.
- ☐ Establish the scope of coverage for your topic.
- ☐ Organize your ideas.

Determine Your Purpose

Everything you write is written for a purpose. You want your reader to know, to believe, or to be able to do something when he or she has finished reading what you have written. Determining your purpose is the first step in preparing to write; unless you know what you hope to accomplish by your writing, you cannot know what information should be presented.

Purpose, then, gives direction to your writing. The more precisely you can state your primary purpose at the outset, the more successful your writing is likely to be. (You may also have a secondary purpose, such as to motivate or reassure.) Christine Thomas might have said that her purpose was "to allow HVS employees to telecommute"—but permitting employees to telecommute was the *result* she wanted, not the precise purpose of her memo. Further thought would have led Christine to recognize the more specific goals of the email itself.

To make sure that your purpose is precise, put it in writing. In most cases, you can use the following formula to guide you:

■   My primary purpose is to _____ so that my readers _____ .

Using this formula, Christine Thomas might have come up with the following statement of purpose:

■   My primary purpose is to explain the advantages of telecommuting so that my reader, Harriet Sullivan, will be persuaded that the idea has enough merit for the company and its employees that she will permit it at least for a trial period.

With this statement of purpose, Christine would have recognized that her purpose was more complicated than it had at first appeared and that she would have to present persuasive evidence to be effective.

Determine Your Reader's Needs

Remember that your job as a writer is to express your ideas so clearly that your readers cannot misinterpret them and that an important element of the purpose formula is the phrase "so that my reader. . .". Simply identifying the response you would like is very different from actually achieving it. Although a purpose statement addresses a problem from the writer's point of view, the reader's needs must also be taken into account. Yet writers often forget that they have readers and they write essentially to themselves, focusing solely on their own purposes.

After you have stated your purpose, ask yourself, "Who is my reader?" Often you will know the answer. For example, if you are writing a memo to your boss attempting to convince him or her to fund a project, you know who your reader is. In another situation, however, you might be writing a letter to someone you do not know in another company. In this case, you would try to imagine your reader, taking into consideration what you know about that company, your reader's position in the company or department, and your reader's responsibilities regarding the topic you are writing about. You could not know what your reader's needs were until you knew at least this much about him or her.

Obviously, when you know enough about your reader that you can actually picture him or her responding to what you have written, you have an advantage. However, even when you know your reader very well, a little reflection is necessary. Without careful thought, Christine Thomas might have answered the question "Who is my reader?" from only one point of view:

■ My reader is Harriet Sullivan, and she's been my boss for six years. We've worked together since she founded the company, so she'll no doubt understand that I have her best interests in mind.

Had Christine carefully analyzed Harriet as the reader of her email, she would have considered Harriet's role in the company, her lack of familiarity with the topic, and her anxiety about taking such a step. Bearing these concerns in mind, Christine might have answered the question differently.

■ My reader is Harriet Sullivan, president of HVS Accounting Services. Harriet founded HVS six years ago with modest savings and a substantial loan. Cautious, industrious, and a stickler for detail, Harriet has built HVS into a sound business and is now beginning to see some return on her investment. Harriet is also a hands-on executive. She puts in long hours at the office and is in frequent contact by email and telephone

---

WRITER'S CHECKLIST: Determining Your Purpose and Your Reader's Needs

Try to answer each of the following questions in as much detail as possible to help focus on your reader's needs in relation to your subject. This process is helpful for all types of writing but will be especially important for longer, more complex tasks.

- ☐ What do you want your reader to know, believe, or be able to do after reading your writing?
- ☐ Have you narrowed your topic to best focus on what you want your reader to know?
- ☐ Who is your reader?
- ☐ What are your reader's needs in relation to the subject?
- ☐ What does your reader know about the subject?
- ☐ Do you have more than one reader?
- ☐ Do your multiple readers have different levels of knowledge about your subject?

intercom with the staff. In addition to a regularly scheduled staff meeting every Wednesday, she holds informal meetings several times a week. She also values computer technology and is purchasing laptop computers for the accountants and financial analysts to help them as they visit clients around the metropolitan area.

Generate, Gather, and Record Ideas and Facts

When you have determined your purpose and analyzed your reader's needs, you must decide what information will satisfy the demands of both. There are several techniques you can use for gathering and recording information.

Brainstorm

A good way to start generating ideas and gathering information is to interview yourself so that you can tap into your own knowledge and experience. You may find that you already have enough information to get started. This technique, commonly known as brainstorming, may also suggest additional ways of obtaining information.

To begin, create a list containing as many ideas as you can think of about the general subject of the document you plan to write and jot them down as they occur to you. (Keep in mind that this type of research may be performed especially effectively by a group of writers or project team members.) Jot down what you know and, if possible, where you learned of it, using a dry-erase board, a computer, a pad of paper, or notecards. (Notecards are especially useful if you are working alone because they can be easily shuffled and rearranged.) If you use a computer, turn the monitor brightness down and type as many ideas as you can think of. (Keeping the screen dark will prevent you from criticizing your thoughts too soon — before you run out of fresh ideas.) Then turn the screen brightness up and review and group ideas as described in the following paragraphs.

For every idea noted, ask yourself the following questions, as expressed in a short poem by Rudyard Kipling:

> I keep six honest serving-men
> (They taught me all I knew);
> Their names are What and Why and When
> And How and Where and Who.

Reporters and other writers have long used these questions as a guide to make sure they have answered the questions their readers are likely to have about a particular story: What happened? Why did it happen? When did it happen? How did it happen? Where did it happen? Who was involved? Rarely will you be able to apply all these questions to any single on-the-job writing situation, but the range of information they cover can be useful in helping to start your thinking.

Once you have assembled a list of ideas, examine each item and decide whether it contributes to your purpose or satisfies your reader's needs. Then mark the item with a *P* for purpose or an *R* for reader. Some items will satisfy both your purpose and your reader, others will appear to satisfy only one, and still others will appear to have nothing to do with either. Often you will mark an item first with one letter and then see that the other applies as well. The order in which you write down the letters will indicate whether you consider the item to be more important for your purpose or for your reader.

When you have finished marking your list, cross out any item that is not marked. Be sure to reconsider an unmarked item from the perspectives of both your purpose and your reader, making certain that the item fits neither before eliminating it. Ideally, you will have a comprehensive list of items beside which you have placed both a *P* and an *R,* although many items will no doubt belong more to one category than to the other, and you may find that some will belong exclusively to one or the other. The more common ground your purpose and your reader's needs share, the more effective your writing will be.

As you review the items on your list, you will find that those items relating clearly to both your purpose and your reader's needs are easiest to work with. Items that your reader might need but that would get in the way of your purpose are trickier. Harriet Sullivan, for example, needs to know that after the program begins, she will not have direct oversight of employees working at home. She's a "hands-on" manager and this break with her customary practice will be difficult for Harriet to accept. Christine, on the other hand, would be reluctant to mention this fact because it appears to undermine her purpose. However, to reconcile Harriet's interests and her own, Christine would have to point out this implication of the program.

Turning a writer's list of ideas into a reader's list of information should be neither difficult nor mysterious; thoroughness is the key. Christine Thomas, for example, might have generated the well-balanced list shown in Figure 1–2, using one or more of the methods described here. Such a list will give you a tentative idea of the content of the project. It will probably be sketchy or missing information, but that's actually helpful in showing where additional research is needed. It will also give you a framework for where to integrate the details of the additional research.

Use Other Sources of Information

Brainstorming may not produce all the information you need. Christine, for example, read about this new way of working by reviewing trade journals and Web sites in the field. To get enough information to meet your reader's needs, you may need to conduct formal, systematic research into your subject. In such cases, you should have some idea of how thoroughly you will cover your subject. To consult the appropriate sources, you will have to know how much detail is required. If you know what you are looking for and where to find it, research presents few problems.

The library provides books, articles, reference works, and other written material for your research. A personal interview with an expert can provide you with up-to-date information not readily available in printed material. The Internet,

**Figure 1–2
Brainstorming List:
Items for Telecom-
muting Proposal**

ITEMS FOR TELECOMMUTING PROPOSAL

R   Harriet needs to see benefits of new practice
P   Current commutes too long
RP Employee morale down because of long commutes
R   Good feature for recruiting and keeping skilled staff
R   Productivity gains
P   Saves employees time and money
R   ~~Eliminate need for current office space?~~
R   Done elsewhere?
P   Need for additional equipment — computers, phones, faxes?
R   Costs of additional technology
R   Do on trial basis
R   Is home work space OK?
R   Need to establish home working hours
P   ~~Advantages to community~~
P   Benefits to employees of avoiding long commutes
P   Benefits to community of fewer auto commuters
R   Advantages to customers?
PR Benefits to employees with special needs
P   ~~Employee isolation~~
P   Is this a program for everyone?
R   Management can't look in on workers — not physically in office
P   Not all jobs lend themselves to telecommuting
R   What about staff meetings?
R   What about meetings with clients?
R   What about taking confidential information home?
R   How can Harriet assess employee productivity?
R   ~~Danger of losing employee loyalty?~~
R   What's in it for HVS?
R   Will employees be distracted at home?
RP Does program apply to all HVS employees?
R   ~~Will those not in program resent those who are?~~
R   How will work be coordinated among employees?

used carefully, provides access to vast amounts of information from commercial, educational, governmental, and other sources. A questionnaire permits you to obtain the views of a group of people without taking the time and expense necessary for numerous personal interviews. These different sources of information are discussed in detail in Chapter 11, "Researching Your Subject."

Establish the Scope of Coverage for Your Topic

SCOPE = DETAIL

Having refined your list of ideas and facts, you must review it once again to establish your scope. Your scope is the degree of detail you decide is necessary to cover each item in your list; and, as before, you must consider this aspect of preparation in terms of your purpose and your reader's needs. This step is really a refinement of the previous one: As you contemplate each item, ask yourself, "How much information should I include to support my purpose? To satisfy my reader's needs? Have I omitted only unnecessary information that gets in the way of meeting my purpose and my reader's needs?" Often you will find that you are omitting important facts or figures and will have to research your subject further to come up with them. At other times, you will find that your list is cluttered with unnecessary detail.

Had Christine Thomas drawn up the list shown in Figure 1–2 and then reviewed it to establish her scope, she would have discovered that some of the items on her list needed detailed information to satisfy her reader's concerns. Entries such as "Costs of additional technology" would tell her that she had to either provide detailed figures for this equipment or explain why no additional costs are necessary. However, other items requiring more detail might be more difficult to identify: "How can Harriet assess employee productivity?" indicates Christine's sense that evaluating productivity would present a cost-conscious person like Harriet with a challenge. She would want to know how this could be done effectively. Figure 1–3 shows the list in Figure 1–2 after the scope has been established.

Be careful when establishing your scope. Writers who have much knowledge of a subject tend to unload information on readers who have no time or need to wade through a boring catalog of topics or a mass of details to get to the point. Understand, too, that establishing your scope in the classroom may be different from doing so on the job. The scope of topics for classroom assignments must often be limited because of accessibility of information, the goals of the course, or other learning objectives. Consider these limitations as part of the purpose of an assignment. In whatever context you establish the scope of your writing, always be guided by your purpose and your reader's needs.

Organize Your Ideas

Once you have established your scope, you should have a list of the ideas and facts to be included in your writing. Examine this list and look for relationships among the items in it. Group the related ideas and arrange them under headings — short phrases that identify the kind of items in each group. As you group the related ideas, consider the following questions: Is the time sequence among items important? If so, organize them chronologically. Do you need to compare the features of one item with those of one or more other items? Organize accordingly. Should you present the most important information first or, instead, build a case that ends with the most important information? Organize items by decreasing order of importance or by increasing order of importance, respectively. As you assemble and

Figure 1–3 Brief
Outlining Notes
for Telecommuting
Email

POINTS TO COVER

Good feature for recruiting and keeping skilled staff

Productivity gains — note industry data

Saves employees time and money

Our competitors permit telecommuting

Costs of additional technology and types needed — although HVS is set up well right now

Do on trial basis — recommend three months, two days per week

Need to establish home working hours

Advantages to community — less congestion and pollution

Advantages to customers — maybe?

Benefits to employees with special needs — two HVS employees can use now!

Employee morale down because of long commutes

Management can't look in on workers — not physically in office

Not all jobs lend themselves to telecommuting — such as receptionist

Scheduling staff and client meetings

Need to protect confidential information when home

Show how Harriet can assess employee productivity

Possible danger of losing employee loyalty?

Address possibility that employees will be distracted at home

arrange the groups of ideas, rework the items in your groups; add, delete, and move ideas around until you feel that you have the best possible organization.

As she prepared to organize her information, Christine thought again about Harriet as her reader. Harriet is a practical businessperson concerned about money and wary of change. Christine realizes that she must organize her ideas first to convince Harriet of the advantages of such a program before going on to point out the potential disadvantages from Harriet's perspective. Figure 1–4 shows Christine's organization of the list in Figure 1–3. To organize larger and more complex subjects, a more formal outline is often helpful. Chapter 2 discusses outlining techniques in detail.

From these groups of items, presented in the order shown, Christine can now write a rough draft and polish it into a final form that not only will achieve its purpose but also will demonstrate Christine's skill and effectiveness to her boss.

■ Writing for Success

Soon after she received the disappointing response to her email, Christine found the courage to step into Harriet's office. Christine explained, "I've really investigated the situation, and I'm sure my suggestion would be in our best interests.

Figure 1–4 Revised Notes for Telecommuting Email

1. **Company Benefits**

   - Productivity gains
   - Done elsewhere—by competitors
   - Advantages to customers?
   - Special-needs employees
   - Do on trial basis only—low risk
   - Worker recruitment and retention

2. **Company Concerns**

   - Need for additional equipment
   - Need to establish home working space and hours
   - Employee isolation?
   - Not for all jobs/employees
   - Can't observe workers firsthand
   - Staff meetings
   - Client meetings
   - Confidential information
   - Assessing productivity
   - Employee loyalty
   - Distractions at home
   - Coordinating work

3. **Employee Benefits**

   - Help special-needs employees
   - Improve morale—less time on the road
   - Save time and expenses

4. **Community Benefits**

   - Less air pollution and traffic congestion

Perhaps if I gave you more information, you'd reconsider my suggestion." Harriet thought for a moment and then said, "All right. Give me the major benefits and any associated disadvantages and costs by next Monday. If they are convincing, I'll meet with you and Fred Sadowski, our Controller, as soon as I get the chance. And, by the way, give me the information in a memo. An email is too informal for what you're suggesting. Also, I don't want to have to read the material on my computer screen." Christine Thomas left Harriet Sullivan's office both relieved and determined that this time she would convince Harriet.

After writing a statement of purpose; determining the general needs of her reader; generating, gathering, and recording ideas and facts; and establishing her scope, Christine organized the items she wanted to cover and wrote the rough draft of her memo (Figure 1–5). Note that this first draft is less concerned with

Figure 1–5
Rough Draft
of Telecom-
muting Memo

HVS Accounting Services

Date: May 9, 20--   **Draft**
To: Harriet V. Sullivan, President
From: Christine Thomas, Systems Administrator
Subject: Telecommuting and HVS Accounting Services

I believe that HVS Accounting Services and its employees would benefit if we permit our professional staff to telecommute two days a week. Telecommuting is becoming increasingly common throughout the United States. I suggest that we try the program for three months. That would give us a trial basis. I suggest that we begin on September 1. That would be before our busy end-of-year and winter tax preparation period.

There are a lot of advantages to HVS from such a program. The biggest advantage is that employee productivity could increase. I looked at a dozen trade journal articles and they show average gains of from 15 to 30 percent. I spoke with other financial services companies at monthly Accounting Society meetings. They mention gains in the 20 to 30 percent range. We need to pull even with the competition. This would also benefit our employees. They save time and money on the days they work at home. They also wind up being less frazzled. Employees say that the time savings and better frame of mind are two reasons why they can better focus on their jobs. Also, the competition is doing it. They say they have an easier time recruiting and keeping employees. This is an important option that we can offer to our employees. The current job market is very competitive.

The program would also be good for Bill Mayhue and Mabel Chong. Bill is having a hip replacement next month. He will be away from the office for up to six weeks. Part of this time away could be used productively if he's allowed to work at home. Mabel's baby is due in September. Mabel plans to spend three months at home after the birth. Instead of losing their services, we would all mutually benefit. This would be a great boost for employee morale, too.

Will the program work in practice? One key issue is keeping track of employees working away from the office. HVS currently has details on staff productivity by billable hours. This system would apply to work-at-home employees. I will work with Fred Sadowski to set up and maintain measurable goals for those in the program. We would then review these goals in the middle and at the end of the three-month trial period with you.

I believe that Mondays and Fridays would be ideal work-at-home days. That would leave Tuesday through Thursday as core business days. Keeping in touch with employees at home will not be difficult. Everybody has a telephone. Our staff also has

Figure 1–5
(continued)

page 2

home desktop computers with Internet access. They also have fax machines and printers. Several also have small copiers. HVS has secure electronic information exchange. That's how we send and receive confidential client information electronically. Those in the program can be given password access to this information with their current remote-access software. In other words, they can log into and work on their office computer from their home computer. Finally, we can put home email addresses and phone and fax numbers on our internal Web site. We can give that information to clients, also.

Everyone I have spoken with already maintains a home office. So, they have access to private work space at home already. They also believe that they would not lose touch with everyone else at HVS if they're only gone for a day or two a week. Our staff has a proven record of getting the job done. This makes them well suited to a work-at-home program.

creating a coherent, correct, and persuasive memo than it is with getting all the needed information down in a reasonably organized manner.

After writing the draft, Christine put it aside for an afternoon, then reread her work the next morning to discover problems with clarity, coherence, and correctness. (See Chapters 4 and 5 for discussions of specific revision techniques that writers use to evaluate and improve their drafts.) She also emailed the draft to a trusted coworker and asked for suggestions. The coworker said that Christine had obviously researched her subject with care, and that the memo presented the appropriate information about starting the new program, but that Christine needed to do a better job of anticipating some of Harriet's questions. The coworker suggested also that Christine might rephrase and reorganize the memo with a sharper eye for her reader's needs. For instance, she said that Harriet Sullivan would not appreciate being told that Christine will work independently with Fred Sadowski without Harriet's permission. However, Harriet would appreciate reading that the new program would benefit both the company and its employees. Finally, she told Christine that the writing was too choppy because of too many short sentences and needed to be smoothed out. She emailed Christine a marked-up draft (Figure 1–6).

Christine considered the suggestions noted in the text of her draft, reviewed the brainstorming lists she'd written earlier, and then developed her introduction and conclusion and reworked the body of the memo. The extra attention she gave to her reader's needs provided a helpful point of focus she could use to restructure and polish her writing. When she finished her revisions, she proofread her work for mechanical errors and sent the final version of the memo to Harriet Sullivan (Figure 1–7). Note that the content and style of the finished memo reflect the suggestions made by Christine's coworker.

Figure 1–6
Rough Draft
of Telecom-
muting Memo
with
Coworker's
Comments

HVS Accounting Services Memo

Date: May 9, 20--   **Draft**
To: Harriet V. Sullivan, President
From: Christine Thomas, Systems Administrator
Subject: Telecommuting and HVS Accounting Services

[Make subject line more descriptive?]

I believe that HVS Accounting Services and its employees would benefit if we permit our professional staff to telecommute two days a week. Telecommuting is becoming increasingly common throughout the United States. I suggest that we try the program for three months. That would give us a trial basis. I suggest that we begin on September 1. That would be before our busy end-of-year and winter tax preparation period. [Sentences too choppy—smooth out.]

There are a lot of advantages to HVS from such a program. The biggest advantage is that employee productivity could increase. I looked at a dozen trade journal articles and they show average gains of from 15 to 30 percent. [Include list of articles and the publications they appear in?] I spoke with other financial services companies at monthly Accounting Society meetings. They mention gains in the 20 to 30 percent range. We need to pull even with the competition. [Any other reasons??] This would also benefit our employees. They save time and money on the days they work at home. They also wind up being less frazzled. Employees say that the time savings and better frame of mind are two reasons why they can better focus on their jobs. Also, the competition is doing it. They say they have an easier time recruiting and keeping employees. This is an important option that we can offer to our employees. The current job market is very competitive.

The program would also be good for Bill Mayhue and Mabel Chong. Bill is having a hip replacement next month. He will be away from the office for up to six weeks. Part of this time away could be used productively if he's allowed to work at home. Mabel's baby is due in September. Mabel plans to spend three months at home after the birth. Instead of losing their services, we would all mutually benefit. This would be a great boost for employee morale, too.

Will the program work in practice? One key issue is keeping track of employees [Note that staff has well-defined tasks] working away from the office. HVS currently has details on staff productivity by billable hours. This system would apply to work-at-home employees. I will work with Fred Sadowski to set up and maintain measurable goals for those in the program. We would then review these [Don't approach Fred w/o Harriet's permission!] goals in the middle and at the end of the three-month trial period with you. [OK for all jobs at HVS??]

**Figure 1–6
(continued)**

page 2

I believe that Mondays and Fridays would be ideal work-at-home days. That would leave Tuesday through Thursday as core business days. Keeping in touch with employees at home will not be difficult. Everybody has a telephone. Our staff also has home desktop [Long-distance calls?] computers with Internet access. They also have fax machines and printers. Several also have small copiers. [Who pays for paper? Other supplies?] HVS has secure electronic information exchange. That's how we send and receive confidential client information electronically. Those in the program can be given password access to this information with their current remote-access software. In other words, they can log into and work on their office computer from their home computer. Finally, we can put home email addresses and phone and fax numbers on our internal Web site. We can give that information to clients, also. [Any costs to HVS? And will employees mind sharing info?]

Everyone I have spoken with already maintains a home office. So, they have access to private work space at home already. They also believe that they would not lose touch with everyone else at HVS if they're only gone for a day or two a week. Our staff has a proven [Any evidence? How about auditors?] record of getting the job done. This makes them well suited to a work-at-home program.

**Figure 1–7
Final
Telecommut-
ing Memo**

HVS Accounting Services Memo

Date: May 13, 20--
To: Harriet V. Sullivan, President
From: Christine Thomas, Systems Administrator *CT*
Subject: The Advantages of Telecommuting to HVS Accounting Services

I believe that HVS Accounting Services and its employees would benefit if we permit our professional staff to telecommute one or more days a week. Telecommuting is becoming increasingly common throughout the United States for several important reasons. I have researched the topic and talked with colleagues here and among our competitors. This memo presents the results of my findings and proposes that HVS set up a work-at-home program on a three-month trial basis beginning September 1. The trial period would occur well before our busy end-of-year and winter tax preparation period.

*Introduction
to proposing a
new program*

(continued)

Figure 1–7 (continued)

Harriet V. Sullivan   2   May 13, 20--

What Are the Advantages?

Advantages to company

The greatest advantage to HVS is that employee productivity for those in a work-at-home program would very likely increase. I have reviewed a dozen trade journal articles in our field and several Web sites that show average productivity gains of from 15 to 30 percent. In conversations with managers at other financial services companies at monthly Accounting Society meetings, they mention gains in the 20 to 30 percent range. This is an area where I believe that we need to pull even with the competition.

Advantages to employees

There are important advantages to the staff that would also help us to recruit and retain qualified employees. Several of our employees commute over an hour each way daily. Telecommuting would permit them to save time and money on the days they worked at home. They would also be less frazzled on those days. Employees report that the time savings and better frame of mind are two reasons why they can better focus on their jobs. Our competitors note that they have an easier time recruiting and retaining valuable employees when they offer telecommuting as an option. This is an important benefit that we can offer to our employees, especially in the current competitive job market.

The program would also be strongly beneficial to HVS and to two employees in particular: Bill Mayhue and Mabel Chong. Bill is scheduled for a hip replacement in two months and will be away from the office for up to six weeks. Part of this time away could be used productively if he's allowed to work at home. Mabel's baby is due in September. Mabel plans to spend three months at home after the birth and would also be a good candidate for this program. Instead of losing their services for extended periods—and their ongoing contacts with their clients—we would all mutually benefit. This would be a great boost for employee morale, too.

How Will Telecommuting Work at HVS?

Addresses company concerns

Any new program of this kind raises questions about how well it will work in practice. One key issue is keeping track of employees working away from the office. HVS Accounting Services is in an ideal position to benefit from telecommuting. Each member of the professional staff has well-defined tasks in financial and estate planning for families and tax preparation and auditing for families and small businesses. As you know from our monthly reports, HVS currently maintains detailed information that quantifies staff productivity by billable hours. This system would apply equally to work-at-home employees. Also, with your approval, I will work with Fred Sadowski to set up and maintain measurable goals for those in the program. We would then review these goals in the middle and at the end of the three-month trial period with you. Not all jobs at HVS would be suitable for the program. The receptionist, mail staff, several of our temporary employees, and I need to be at the office during business hours, so we would not participate.

Figure 1–7
(continued)

Harriet V. Sullivan   3   May 13, 20--

I believe that Mondays and Fridays would be ideal work-at-home days. That would leave Tuesday through Thursday as core business days for staff meetings, client conferences, and other activities better done at the office. Even on Mondays and Fridays, keeping in touch with employees at home will not be difficult in this electronic era. In addition to telephones, everyone suited for the program already has home desktop computers with Internet access, fax machines, and printers. Several also have small copiers. Essentially, there are no startup expenses for HVS associated with the program. The staff can keep a log of long-distance business calls and bring in their telephone bill monthly for reimbursement. They can also submit receipts for printer paper and other supplies for reimbursement.

Can We Protect Customer Information?

Customer confidentiality would also be protected. HVS has secure electronic information exchange software that allows us to send and receive confidential client information electronically. Those in the program can be given password access to confidential and other client information at home using pcEverywhere, their current remote-access software. In other words, the software allows them to connect to and work on their office computer from their home computer. Finally, I can post the home email addresses and phone and fax numbers for employees in the program on our internal Web site and provide that information to the appropriate clients. I will also program everyone's phone speed-dial feature with the home numbers of participants.

Systematic coverage of program details

Everyone I have spoken with already maintains a home office, so having access to private work space at home is not a hindrance. Having this space also minimizes the possibility of interruptions or other disturbances during the day while still permitting employees to schedule home repair visits rather than having to leave work to meet a repair person, as happens now. The staff also believes that they would not lose touch with everyone else at HVS if they're only gone for a day or two a week. As you know, the auditing staff is periodically away from the office for a week or two at a time at client sites until an audit is completed. Working away from the office is customary to them and causes few disruptions. Finally, everyone in the program would keep the same business hours, minus the commute, of course. Another indirect benefit of telecommuting is that it allows us to help do our part to reduce air pollution and traffic congestion in the area.

Can We Make It Happen?

Our staff has a proven record of getting the job done regardless of where they are working, which I believe makes them well suited to a work-at-home program. I look forward to discussing this option with you at your convenience.

Closing

Christine's story had a happy ending: Harriet was persuaded by Christine's final memo and started the work-at-home program on a trial basis that September.

CHAPTER 1 SUMMARY: Getting Started

Successful writing on the job is the result of careful preparation. The following checklist is based on the information covered in this chapter and contains the steps essential to ensure that your writing assignments—in the classroom and on the job—are adequately planned. Ask yourself the following questions as you plan and draft your document.

☐ Have I determined the purpose of my writing?

☐ Have I considered my reader's needs and perspectives?

☐ Have I established the scope of coverage essential for my purpose and my reader's needs?

☐ Have I gathered and recorded all of the facts and ideas necessary for my scope of coverage?

☐ Have I organized my ideas into related groups and determined the best sequence to link these groups based on my reader's needs?

☐ Have I reviewed my draft for problems with clarity, coherence, and correctness?

☐ Have I revised the draft to emphasize the points most important to my reader?

■ Exercises

1. Using the pattern suggested in this chapter, create a statement of purpose for a memo you could write. Select a problem at your place of employment (past or present) or on your campus—for instance, inadequate parking, poor food services, or lack of tuition reimbursement for job-related courses. Aim your memo at a reader who could make a decision regarding your suggestion. Be sure to give the reader's name and position in your statement of the objective.

2. Using brainstorming, create a list of items for the subject selected for Exercise 1. Try to list 15 to 20 items; don't worry if some seem inappropriate, just keep listing. Mark the items with a *P* for purpose or an *R* for reader.

3. Eliminate the items in your list from Exercise 2 that clearly do not meet the reader's needs or contribute to your objective. Then establish your scope and rewrite the list. Group the items in your revised list from Exercise 2 into three or more categories. Next, arrange the items in each category in sequence.

4. Using the outline created in Exercise 3, write the memo suggesting a solution to the problem.

5. For three of the following topics, or topics of your own choosing, list one possible purpose for a document and then list the kinds of information that would be needed to meet that objective. (Be sure to give *kinds* of information and not *sources* of information.) Because the following topics are broad, you will need to select some particular aspect of the topic that you choose. Be sure to identify your reader.

■ **Topics**

Banking	Office procedures
Computer programming	Personal computers
E-commerce	Photography
Electronics	Printing
Health care	Real estate
Highway construction	Small businesses
The Internet	Sports
Marketing	Television
Music	Welding
Occupations	

The following is an example list:

Subject:	Internet faxing
Reader:	The average computer user
Objective:	To instruct the average computer user on how to set up and send a fax message to a friend, fellow student, coworker, instructor, or someone else
Kinds of information:	Required hardware, Internet access, email address, fax number, location (Web address) of one or more Internet faxing services, detailed instructions on how to send and receive faxes over the Internet

6. Using the techniques described in this chapter, write a memo describing how to perform your job (or a job you've had) for an employee who will be replacing you while you are on vacation. Write two versions of this memo: (1) to an employee hired through a temporary job service from outside the organization and (2) to an employee who works in your department but not in the same job.

7. Prepare a memo for your manager asking for tuition reimbursement to attend this or another course you are taking. Assume that the memo will be sent elsewhere for further approval. Use the course and text descriptions as well as the syllabus as you prepare your memo. Remember that the effectiveness of the memo will depend on how well you are able to help your reader see the value of this course. You may wish to attach supporting material (within reason); this material may not be counted as adding length to your memo. The length of the memo should be two or three double-spaced pages.

8. Using the list of topics in Exercise 5, select a product or service from one of the suggested areas. Write a complaint letter about a problem you, the consumer, have had with this product. Before writing, consider the purpose of your letter, the exact nature of your complaint, the reader you are addressing, and what you want the company to do about the problem or what you think the resolution to the problem should be. Bring your letter to class.

9. Keeping in mind this chapter's discussion of clarifying your purpose before writing, make a list of the five most important features a company or other employer would need to have to make you interested in working for them; be specific. Next, make a list that details what you would want to gain from your work experience.

10. Your boss has asked you to report on the in-house food service vendors that your company uses; however, you feel you do not have enough information to begin your assignment. Make a list of questions to ask your boss to clarify your assignment. Include details about purpose and priorities.

■ In-Class Activities

1. Discuss similarities and differences between writing for the reader in Exercise 6 and writing for the reader in Exercise 7.

2. Discuss the similarities and differences between writing on the job and writing for a general composition class.

3. Divide into groups of four to six students each. For 20 to 25 minutes, brainstorm as a group to develop a collective list of problems that make studying on campus difficult. For the next 15 or so minutes, revise the list, creating two versions. The first list is for a committee from the Dean's office whose assignment it is to make studying on campus easier. The second list is for the residence hall planning committee that is in charge of designing a new dormitory on campus. As you wrap up your session, discuss how the different purposes and audiences affected your lists.

4. Divide into small groups. Choose and recommend a recreational activity for an end-of-semester celebration for the class. Your goal is to find an activity or theme that will please the majority of your classmates. After 20 minutes, each group shares its results with the class. (Select a spokesperson from your group to present your group's ideas.) Discuss the ideas generated by all groups and, if desired, select the best one.

5. Exchange the complaint letter that you wrote for Exercise 8 for that of another student in your class. Using the ideas listed in the chapter summary, score your classmate's letter, allowing 10 points for each of the seven items on the checklist on page 7. Provide your classmate with specific notes on what makes his or her letter successful or offer suggestions on how your classmate might improve the letter.

6. Revise your complaint letter from Exercise 8, based on your exchange in In-Class Activity 5. Exchange letters again, this time with a different classmate. Write a reply to your classmate's complaint letter as if you are the person receiving the complaint.

■ Research Projects

1. Find an article on a subject of interest to you in two different types of publications—for example, a newspaper and a newsmagazine, a magazine such as *Popular Science* and a technical journal, and so on. After you have read the two articles, respond to the following:
   a. Compare the approaches taken in each article toward the intended audience. Look specifically for the presence or absence of technical terms, the kind and number of illustrations used, and the audience's knowledge of the subject.
   b. Create statements of purpose for each article, as if you had been the writer.
   c. Discuss how well the writers met the needs of their readers. (Respond only after you have completed *a and b.*)

2. Using the pattern described in Exercises 1 through 5, prepare a five- to seven-page double-spaced proposal recommending an achievable waste materials recycling program for a specific facility within your college or place of work—for example, a dormitory, an office building, a shop, or a restaurant. Consider recycling wastepaper, glass, cans, and plastic. Estimate the volume of such waste now generated annually at that location, its potential environmental impact (for example, landfill volume), and the steps necessary to implement the program to recycle this waste.

3. Find and interview someone in a position that you imagine holding five years from today. Ask about the amount and type of writing this person does on the job. After the interview, write a memo to your instructor describing what you learned. *Note:* Before you begin, read the section on interviewing in Chapter 11, "Researching Your Subject."

4. Choose a topic of particular interest to you as the subject for a research paper. Using the Writer's Checklist on page 7, you may select any reader and purpose you wish as long as your topic has a business setting. Your instructor may want to approve your topic before you get started. You may interview experts as part of your research; however, you must use at least three different types of sources for your information (journal articles, books, newspapers, etc.) and document all information appropriately (see Chapter 11 for models for documenting works cited).

5. Write a five- to seven-page research paper about the company that you think you would like to work for. (You can use your research from Web Project 4 and your memo from Web Project 5 as the basis of your paper.) Gather and analyze materials from at least three print sources, such as newspaper, magazine, and journal articles, and interviews about the company you've chosen. Based on your research, what are your reasons for wanting to work for this company? Be specific. Document all sources appropriately.

■ Web Projects

1. If you have regular access to the Internet, join the Misc.Writing discussion group (or Usenet). This group comprises new and experienced writers who discuss writing processes—"scholarly, technical, journalistic, artistic, and mere day-to-

day communication." After monitoring the group for a period of time specified by your instructor and investigating the resources at the Web site, send your instructor an email message describing any writing tips learned from the group that you believe will help you.

2. Suppose that the company you work for provides a paid week's vacation package as a reward to the "Employee of the Year." The vacation is for that employee and his or her immediate family. Your boss has asked you to select this year's vacation package. You have a budget of $4,000 and your boss also has asked you to suggest a location that has educational value. Using the Web, compare and contrast different vacation packages and then prepare a memo for your boss outlining your reasons for your recommendation. Keep the Writer's Checklist on page 7 in mind as you write a concise memo to your boss.

3. Once you have selected the vacation package in Web Project 2, research the Web to find out as much as you can about the geographic location you have chosen. Make a list of Web sites that you would forward to the winner of the vacation package to help the employee learn about the place he or she will be visiting. Provide a brief description (no more than two or three sentences) of each site's content. Your description should make clear why these particular sites are helpful.

4. Select a topic from the list provided in Exercise 5 (or choose your own) and think of a product that specifically relates to your topic. (For example, if you choose the topic of personal computers, a related product could be a particular brand of personal computer.) Your goal is to write an advertisement about that product. Using the Web, find as much product information as you can. Brainstorm as you search, building a list of as many different features of the product as possible (for example, some features of a particular brand of personal computer might include memory capacity (random and hard drive), the software it comes with, its affordability, etc.). Use at least four different Web sites and note which information came from which Web site. (Be sure to save the Web address of each site so that you can return to the site and provide formal documentation of these sources if asked to do so by your instructor.)

5. Search the Web to identify three companies from your field that you would like to work for. Write a one-page memo to your instructor explaining why you chose these companies and making a case for the employer that you view as the best match for you. What makes that particular employer more attractive than the others? Be as specific as possible. When preparing your memo, keep in mind the Chapter 1 Summary and the components that you outlined in Exercise 9.

2 Organizing Your Information

When a motion picture is being filmed, the scenes are usually shot out of the sequence in which they will eventually appear. Different shooting locations, actors' schedules, weather conditions, and many other circumstances make shooting out of sequence necessary. If it were not for a skilled film editor, the completed film would be a jumble of randomly shot scenes. The film editor, following the script, carefully splices the film together so that the story moves smoothly and logically from one event to the next, as the screenwriter and director planned. Without a plan, no such order would be possible: The editor would have no guide for organizing the thousands of feet of film.

Organizing a movie and organizing a written document are obviously different tasks, but they have one element in common—both must be planned ahead of time. For a film, planning means creating a script. For a written document, it means organizing the information into a sequence appropriate to the subject, the purpose, and the reader.

■ Outlining

Organizing your information before you write has two important advantages. First, it forces you to reexamine the information you plan to include to be sure that you have sufficient facts and details to satisfy your reader's needs and achieve the purpose of your writing. Second, it forces you to order the information logically, so that your reader understands it as clearly as you do.

The importance of these advantages emerged from a study of the writing habits that separated good from poor writers in a corporate setting. According to the researcher, more than three times the number of good writers as compared with poor writers use a written outline. Whereas none of the good writers denied using an outline or plan for their reports, 36 percent of the poor writers said they never use an outline or plan, either written or mental.[1]

Not every piece of writing benefits from a full-scale outline, of course. For relatively short items, such as memos and letters, you may need only to jot down a

---

[1]Christine Barabas, *Technical Writing in a Corporate Culture: A Study of the Nature of Information* (Norwood, NJ: Ablex Publishing Corp., 1990), p. 188. "Good" and "poor" writers were so classified by their readers within the corporation.

Voices from the Workplace

Steve Bramlage, Vectren Energy of Ohio

Steve Bramlage is Director of Engineering and Central Operations at Vectren Energy of Ohio. He is responsible for the transmission and distribution of natural gas in 17 counties of west central Ohio. In this role, he is accountable for the safe and reliable delivery of energy and must meet all Department of Transportation (DOT) Pipeline Safety as well as the Occupational Safety and Health Administration (OSHA) rules and regulations.

Performing these functions requires Steve to be efficient. Whether he is writing to his operating personnel or to the executive offices, he has learned the value of organization in writing. "If you don't organize your thoughts before you write your draft" he says, "you're sure to end up writing several ineffective versions instead of writing a good, workable draft the first time. In today's business world you never want to work out your organization the hard way—there just isn't time."

Entry-Level
Adam Thompson, the *Denver Post*

Adam Thompson is a sports writer for the *Denver Post*. As a journalist, Adam must think about how to organize the information in his news stories to attract and hold his readers' attention. Adam carefully considers his method of organization; as he says, "a good news story keeps you until the final period."

Journalists often use the Inverse Pyramid theory. "This school of writing, commonly applied in straight Associated Press stories, says that the most important information should go up top, with the rest of the facts placed in descending order of importance." As an alternative, Adam prefers what he refers to as the breadcrumb theory. "I start off with a strong hook. From there, I like to leave a trail of information—or crumbs—doling out my good bits a little at a time throughout the piece to keep the reader biting."

"As you go from highlight to highlight, try to use transition sentences that connect one to the next. It creates a much smoother flow. Save a zinger for the end—to reward the readers or listeners who stayed with you. You want to guide your readers, taking them down the path of your choice—it takes conscious effort to keep your readers interested. Some careful thought about how you place your points takes little time and can make all the difference in the world."

Read the *Denver Post* online at http://www.denverpost.com.

---

few notes to make sure that you haven't left out any important information and that you have arranged the information in a logical order. These notes then guide you as you write the draft. For example, note how Christine Thomas organized her ideas for the memo to Harriet Sullivan in Chapter 1 (see Figure 1–4).

Longer documents generally require more elaborate planning, such as a formal outline. In addition to guiding your first draft, the outline can be circulated for review by your colleagues and superiors. They can easily see in the outline the scope of information you plan to include and the sequence in which it is organized. Their reviews can help you find and fix major problems before you've committed a great deal of time to writing your draft. Any outline, including one you circulate, is tentative and represents your best thinking at that point. It need not be labored over for page after page so that it becomes virtually an end in itself. This chapter introduces conventions for creating simple and complex outlines and provides techniques for verifying that your outline is sound.

Roman Numeral Outline

The most common type of outline emphasizes topics and subtopics by means of Roman numerals, letters, and Arabic numbers in the following sequence of subdivisions:

    I. Major section
       A. First-level subsection
          1. Second-level subsection
             a. Third-level subsection
                1) Fourth-level subsection

Creating a Roman numeral outline permits you to recognize at a glance the relative importance of topics and subtopics within your subject. Your subject will seldom require this many divisions, but dividing it this way allows for a highly detailed outline if one is necessary. Stop at the level at which you can no longer subdivide into two items, keeping the outline balanced so that no parts are much more divided than others. For every Roman *I,* you should have at least a Roman *II.* For every *A,* you should have at least a *B,* and so on.

    When you are ready to write, you should know your topic well enough to be able to identify its major sections. Begin your outline by writing them down. Then consider them carefully to make sure that they represent the logical divisions of the subject. For example, assume that you are writing an article about computers for a company magazine. You might start with the following major sections.

      I. Development of computers
     II. Types of present applications
   III. Future and potential benefits
   IV. Potential benefits to humanity

After a moment's reflection, you might decide that you can combine "present" and "future." A few more moments of thought might convince you that you can also combine "applications" and "benefits." So you might substitute the following two major sections for the original four.

     I. Development of computers
    II. Present and future applications and benefits

You quickly decide, however, that you have put too many topics in your second major section, so you make another effort.

 I. Development of computers
 II. Present applications
III. Future applications

Now you are satisfied that you have appropriately identified the major sections for your topic.

Once you have established your major sections, look for minor divisions within each section. For example, you might first arrive at the following minor divisions within your major sections.

 I. Development of computers
   A. Early efforts not practical
   B. New industry created
 II. Present applications
   A. Business
   B. Social
III. Future applications
   A. Economic
   B. Social

This outline is a start, but it is weak. The minor divisions are too vague to be useful. After considering these weaknesses, you might produce the following revision:

 I. Development of computers
   A. History of computing tools
   B. Development of the computer to a practical size
   C. New industry created around the more compact computer
 II. Present applications
   A. Business applications of the computer
   B. Social, scientific, and technical applications of the computer
III. Future applications
   A. Potential impact of the computer on business and industry
   B. Potential social impact of the computer

Now you are ready to insert any information that you compiled during your research under the appropriate major and minor divisions, as shown in Figure 2–1. When you have finished, you have a complete outline. Even though the outline looks final at this point, you still must check for a number of things. For example, make sure that corresponding divisions present material of equal importance (i.e., that major divisions are equal to one another and minor divisions are equal to one another in importance).

**Figure 2–1
Sample
Outline**

I. Development of computers
   A. History of computing tools
      1. Abacus as first computing tool
      2. First electronic computer patented in 1944
   B. Development of the computer to a practical size
      1. Early computers very large, impractical for commercial use
      2. First electronic computer weighed 3 tons, took 1,500 square feet of floor space
      3. Introduction of transistor in 1958 made computer commercially practical
      4. Introduction and refinement of computer chip improved the size and speed of computers radically
   C. New industry created around the more compact computer
      1. Transition from research phase to commercial-application phase
      2. Corporate competition
   D. The impact of the Internet
      1. Revolutionized global communications with email, newsgroups, online chat rooms
      2. Provides wealth of information for research and education
      3. Creates jobs, businesses, and is revolutionizing commerce and investing, especially in the United States

II. Present applications
   A. Business
      1. Route long-distance telephone calls
      2. Monitor airline reservations
      3. Keep records and aid project management
      4. Communicate by email
   B. Social, scientific, and technical
      1. Prepare weather forecasts
      2. Direct city traffic
      3. Maintain data banks on crime and criminals
      4. Monitor the condition of patients in hospitals
      5. Compare chemical characteristics of drugs
      6. Navigate ships and planes
      7. Monitor the performance of automobile engines

III. Future applications
   A. Potential impact on business and industry
      1. More efficient and effective day-to-day operations
      2. Greater productivity
      3. More leisure time for employees, enhancing the recreation industry
   B. Potential impact on society
      1. Make education and government more effective and efficient
      2. Help find cures for diseases, translate languages, land jetliners without human aid

NOT   II. Present applications
          A. Business
          B. Social, scientific, and technical
          C. Future applications

BUT   II. Present applications
          A. Business
          B. Social, scientific, and technical
     III. Future applications

Subtopics are typically divided into at least two parts, although doing so may not always be possible. A head must be divided into at least two parts if it is to be divided at all.

NOT
SUBDIVIDED
    A. Retailer benefits
      1. Permits direct transfer of purchase price to retailer's account

SUBDIVIDED
    A. Retailer benefits
      1. Permits direct transfer of purchase price to retailer's account
      2. Provides daily printout of vital records

Finally, review your outline for completeness, determining whether you need additional information. If you find that your research is not really complete, return to your sources and dig out the missing material.

Decimal Numbering System Outline

The sample outlines shown to this point use a combination of numbers and letters to differentiate the various levels of information. You could also use a decimal numbering system, such as the following, for your outline.

1. FIRST-LEVEL SECTION
   1.1 Second-level section
   1.2 Second-level section
      1.2.1 Third-level section
      1.2.2 Third-level section
         1.2.2.1 Fourth-level section
         1.2.2.2 Fourth-level section
   1.3 Second-level section
   1.4 Second-level section
      1.4.1 Third-level section
      1.4.2 Third-level section
2. FIRST-LEVEL SECTION

This system should not go beyond the fourth level because the numbers get too cumbersome past that point. In many technical articles and reports, the decimal numbering system is carried over from the outline to the final version of the document for ease of cross-referencing sections. Typical uses for the decimal outline include procedural manuals, mathematical texts, and scientific and technical material of many kinds. For a discussion of how this system applies to formal reports, see Headings in Chapter 13.

Remember that the outline is only a means to an end, not an end in itself. Don't view it as being cast in concrete. Outlines are preliminary by their nature. If you suddenly see a better way to organize your material while you are writing the draft, depart from your outline and follow the better approach. The main purpose of the outline is to bring order and shape to your information *before* you begin to write the draft.

WRITER'S CHECKLIST: Creating an Outline

When you have completed your research and know your topic well enough to write about it, the following tips will help you create a logical outline.

☐ Break a large topic into its major divisions and write them down. Does the sequence fit the method of development you have decided to use? If not, resequence and label the topics with Roman numerals (I, II, III, etc.).

☐ Repeat the same process for each major topic. Break each into its logical subtopics and list them under each major topic. Then sequence the subtopics to fit your method of development and label them with capital letters (A, B, C, etc.).

☐ If necessary, repeat the process for each subtopic, breaking each into its logical sub-subtopics and list them under each subtopic. Sequence them to fit your method of development, and label them with Arabic numbers (1, 2, 3, etc.).

☐ Now go to your notes and key each one to the appropriate place in your outline (placing *II-C* beside any note the topic of which fits the portion of your outline labeled *II-C*).

☐ Merge your notes and your outline, placing every note under the appropriate head, subhead, or sub-subhead in your outline. Then organize the notes under each head in the most logical sequence.

You now have a detailed outline. To convert it to your first draft, put the first head on your computer screen and expand the notes listed under it into sentences and paragraphs.

■ The Influence of Audience and Purpose

The kinds of information and organization that shape your outline will vary according to your purposes for writing and according to the decisions you make about your reader's needs as Christine Thomas learned in Chapter 1. Let us say, for example, that a writer needs to prepare two documents about the Lifemaker System, a home gym that combines ten Nautilus machines into a compact weight-and-cable exercise system. The first document will be a sales brochure directed toward potential purchasers of the Lifemaker; the second document will be a maintenance guide written for customers who have already purchased the system.

The two documents would share the following aspects of audience and purpose:

1. Both documents will describe the design and structure of the Lifemaker System, though they will do so in different ways and for different reasons. Thus, much of the information gathered and used for brainstorming and outlining will be useful for both the sales brochure and the manual.

2. The audience for both the brochure and the manual is composed of nonspecialist readers, so both documents should contain a minimum of technical language and should not use terms that would be accessible only to technicians, engineers, and sales representatives.

3. At the same time, the writer might assume that the audience, whether they are potential or current customers of Lifemaker, will know some things about the design features common to Nautilus-type exercise systems. Descriptions of the exercise equipment for either document, then, need not be spelled out letter by letter, as though the reader had never even heard of it.

In two important ways, however, the documents reflect different purposes:

1. A written statement of purpose for the sales brochure might read as follows: *My primary purpose for writing is to describe the benefits and features of the Lifemaker so that my readers will want to purchase it.* The writer of such a brochure will need to select and organize the information so that it per-

---

DIGITAL SHORTCUTS: Creating an Outline

Using the outline feature of your word-processing software permits you to —

- format your outline automatically
- fill in, rearrange, and update your outline
- experiment with the organization and scope of information

- rearrange sections and subsections far more easily on screen than cutting and taping the paper version
- create alphanumeric or decimal numbering outline styles

suades the reader to purchase the system. The brochure's outline, then, should offer more general comments about the design and structural features of the system and specific comments about the benefits of buying it.

2. A written statement of purpose for the maintenance manual might read as follows: *My primary purpose for writing is to explain the maintenance of the Lifemaker so that my reader knows exactly how to put it together and take care of it.* Because the manual will be directed toward readers who have already purchased the system, the writer will not be concerned with organizing information so that it forms a persuasive argument. Instead, the writer will want to create an outline that will eventually lead to clearly written, step-by-step instructions on how to assemble and maintain the Lifemaker. References to structural features will be very specific and more technical than they would be for the sales brochure. Because the audience is still a nonspecialist one, however, the writer still needs to keep the use of technical terms to a minimum, and might refer in the outline to diagrams that will eventually appear in the manual as clarifying illustrations.

Figure 2–2 shows the outline for the brochure. The outline in Figure 2–2 notes specific design details (cast-iron plates, adjustable cables, 4′ by 7′ size), but the information is organized to support the brochure's persuasive purpose: The Lifemaker is a compact, well-designed, and affordable home gym system. (See Chapters 3 and 4 for drafts and revisions of this sales brochure.)

Because the second document is a maintenance manual, its purpose is to instruct rather than to persuade the reader. As you might guess, the manual's organization would differ from that used for the brochure. Figure 2–3 is an excerpt from the outline for the manual.

This outline follows a step-by-step organization of information (see p. 35), which is an ideal method to use when instruction, rather than persuasion, is the major purpose for writing. In contrast, the outline for the sales brochure uses a general-to-specific sequencing of information (see p. 34), which is more appropriate when the purpose for writing is to persuade the reader via a general argument supported with special details. Thus, although both documents are drawn from the same source and speak to nontechnical audiences, their different purposes call for different methods of organization, as shown by the two different outlines here and the variety of outlines presented in the following section on organizational methods.

■ Methods of Organization

The choice of a method of organization comes naturally for some types of writing. Instructions for operating a piece of machinery are arranged step by step. A trip report usually follows a chronological sequence. When a subject does not lend itself to one particular sequence, you can choose the best sequence, or

Figure 2–2
Sample Outline for
a Brochure (General
to Specific)

Lifemaker: The Compact Affordable Home Gym

I. General benefits of owning Lifemaker
    A. More compact than other systems
    B. Provides better training programs than other systems
    C. Lower-priced and easier to assemble and maintain than other systems

II. Design benefits/features
    A. Multiple stations so two people can work out at the same time
    B. Takes up minimal space (measures only 4′ by 7′)
    C. Designed to work all muscle groups (40 different combinations of exercises)

III. Structural benefits/features—weights
    A. Dual weight stacks that total 200 pounds of cast-iron plates
    B. Adjustable weight stacks with resistance range of 10 to 150 pounds
    C. Varied individual weights with resistance adjustable in 5-, 10-, and 15-pound increments

IV. Structural benefits/features—cables
    A. Adjustable cables that increase tension at stations working strongest muscle groups
    B. Reconfigurable weight stacks (cables permit reconfiguring of weights without dismantling entire system)
    C. Reversible tension (cables can increase/decrease tension in mid-set)

V. Financial and maintenance benefits
    A. More reasonably priced than leading system: $799.99
    B. Two-year guarantee for all parts
    C. Easy maintenance (no oiling or solvents necessary)

combination of sequences, by considering your purpose in writing and your reader's needs. Suppose, for example, that you report on a trip to several offset-printing companies to gather information on the most efficient way to arrange equipment in the printing shop where you work. You would probably organize the report of the trip chronologically, but your description of the various shop layouts, emphasizing the physical locations of the equipment, would be organized spatially. If you went on to make recommendations about the most workable arrangement for your shop, you would present the most efficient arrangement first, the second most efficient arrangement next, and so on. Thus the

**Figure 2–3
Sample Outline
for Instructions
in Manual (Step by
Step)**

Maintaining Your Lifemaker

I. Maintenance and troubleshooting
   A. Inspect and safeguard all parts each time you
      1. Inspect parts for wear
         a. Check cables for fraying
         b. Check weights for cracks
         c. Replace worn parts immediately
      2. Tighten tension on cable #1
         a. Find end of 125″ cable (#43 on diagram)
         b. Turn end of cable clockwise
         c. Thread cable farther into weight tube (#35 on diagram)
      3. Tighten tension on cable #2
         a. Find end of 265″ cable (#46 on diagram)
         b. Turn end of cable clockwise
         c. Thread cable farther into weight tube (#35 on diagram)
      4. Clean parts
         a. Clean with damp cloth
         b. Use nonabrasive detergent
         c. Use no solvents or oils

recommendations portion of the report would be organized according to decreasing order of importance.

Table 2–1 describes the most common ways to organize, or sequence, information in on-the-job writing.

**Table 2–1
Methods-of-
Organization
Chart**

Method	*Description*
Sequential	Consecutive order of steps, not connected to a specific time
Chronological	Sequence of steps or events related to time
Spatial	Description from top to bottom, front to back, etc.
Division and classification	Division into parts and grouping of parts by class
Decreasing order of importance	Order beginning with the most important item and leading to the least important item
Increasing order of importance	Order beginning with the least important item and leading to the most important item
General to specific	Order leading from an overview to a detailed explanation
Specific to general	Order leading from the details of a topic to a broad overview or conclusion
Comparison	Assessment of traits or characteristics of two or more items to determine their relative value

Sequential /INSTRUCTIONAl

In the sequential method of organization, you divide your subject into steps and then present the steps in the order in which they occur. This arrangement is the most effective way to describe the operation of a mechanism, such as a photocopier, or to explain a process, such as cardiopulmonary resuscitation (CPR). Sequencing is also the logical method for writing instructions. For example, the instructions for installing printer software on a desktop computer follow a step-by-step sequence.

To install printer software:

1. Make sure that your printer is plugged in and connected to your computer.
2. Turn your computer ON.

Figure 2–4
Sample Outline
for Sequential
Instructions

Outline

I. Developing
   A. In total darkness, load film on spindle.
   B. Enclose in developing tank.
   C. Do not let film touch tank walls or other film.
   D. Add developing solution.
   E. Turn lights on.
   F. Start timer; set for seven minutes.
   G. Agitate for five seconds, then agitate for five seconds every half-minute.

II. Stopping
   A. Drain developer from tank.
   B. Add stop bath.
   C. Rinse for 30 seconds in stop bath, agitating continually.

III. Fixing
   A. Drain stop bath from tank.
   B. Add fixing solution.
   C. Fix for two to four minutes.
   D. Agitate for five seconds, then agitate for five seconds every half-minute.

IV. Washing
   A. Remove tank top.
   B. Remove film from tank and wash for 30 minutes under running water.

V. Drying
   A. Hang film, placing drip pan beneath.
   B. Sponge gently to remove excess water.
   C. Allow film to dry completely, at room temperature.

3. When you see the "New Hardware Found" screen, insert Printing Software Disk 1 of 3.

4. Follow the instructions on the screen.

The greatest advantage of presenting your information in sequential order is that it is easy for your reader to understand and follow because the sequence of steps in your writing corresponds to the order of the process being described. Sequential and chronological methods of organization overlap because each describes steps in a process. If you were to write instructions for the proper way to process film, for example, you would present the information in a step-by-step sequence (Figures 2–4 and 2–5).

When you present your information in steps, you must carefully consider the needs of your reader. Do not assume that your readers are as familiar with your subject as you are; if they were, they wouldn't need your instructions. Even for a simple process, be sure that you list *all* steps and that you explain in adequate detail how each step is performed. Sometimes you must also indicate the purpose or function of each step.

In some instructions or process descriptions, the steps can be presented in one sequence only. For example, the steps for installing printer software must be carried out in the sequence in which they are listed. In many other instructions or process descriptions, however, the steps can be presented in the sequence that the writer thinks is most effective. The steps in the process by which a company solicits proposals for new equipment, for example, may vary in sequence from the steps a company uses to solicit proposals for services.

Figure 2–5 Sample Sequential Instructions

Processing Film

Developing.   In total darkness, load the film on the spindle and enclose it in the developing tank. Be careful not to allow the film to touch the tank walls or other film. Add the developing solution, turn the lights on, and set the timer for seven minutes. Agitate for five seconds initially and then for five seconds every half-minute.

Stopping.   When the timer sounds, drain the developing solution from the tank and add the stop bath. Agitate continually for 30 seconds.

Fixing.   Drain the stop bath and add the fixing solution. Allow the film to remain in the fixing solution for two to four minutes. Agitate for five seconds initially and then for five seconds every half-minute.

Washing.   Remove the tank top and wash the film for at least 30 minutes under running water.

Drying.   Suspend the film from a hanger to dry. It is generally advisable to place a drip pan below the rack. Sponge the film gently to remove excess water. Allow the film to dry completely.

Chronological /STEPS IN TIME

In a chronological sequence, you focus on the order in which the steps or events occur in time, beginning with the first event, going on to the next event, and so on, until you have reached the last event. Trip reports, work schedules, minutes of meetings, recipes, and certain accident reports are among the types of writing in which information may be organized chronologically.

In the outline and memo shown in Figures 2–6 and 2–7, a retail-store manager describes the steps taken over a one-year period to reduce shoplifting at his store.

Spatial / FLOOR PLAN / LAYOUT /

In a spatial sequence, you describe an object or a process according to the physical arrangement of its features. Depending on the subject, you may describe the features from top to bottom, from side to side, from east to west (or west to east), from inside to outside, and so on. Descriptions of this kind rely mainly on dimension (height, width, length), direction (up, down, north, south), shape (rectangular, square, semicircular), and proportion (one-half, two-thirds). Features are described in relation to one another:

- One end is raised six to eight inches higher than the other end to permit the rain to run off.

Features are also described in relation to their surroundings:

- The lot is located on the east bank of the Kingman River.

**Figure 2–6
Sample Outline
for Chronological
Instructions**

Outline

I. Task force established
   A. Salespeople, buyers, department managers, executives
   B. Four meetings in January and two in March

II. Mark IV Surveillance System
   A. Installed in April
   B. Includes closed-circuit TV
   C. Helps detect suspicious customer patterns

III. Employee training
   A. Held workshops in May and June
   B. Conducted by Security, Inc.

IV. Other steps
   A. Remodeled some areas to improve merchandise visibility
   B. Hired extra security guards for the holidays

**Figure 2–7
Sample Memo
Showing
Chronological
Instructions**

The Rack
Memo

To: Joanna Sanchez, Vice President for Marketing
From: Larry Brown, Manager, Downtown Branch   *LB*
Date: September 9, 20--
Subject: Reducing Shoplifting at the Downtown Store

Over the past year, my staff and I have taken a number of measures to try to reduce the amount of shoplifting in the downtown store. As you know, we've spent much time, effort, and money on the problem, which we hope will be alleviated during the Christmas shopping season. Let me recap the specific steps we have taken.

Task Force
We formed a task force of salespeople, buyers, managers, and executive staff to rec-ommend ways of curtailing shoplifting and methods of implementing our recom-mendations. We met four times during January and twice in March to reach our final recommendations. During the meetings. . . .

Mark IV Surveillance System
In April, we installed a Mark IV System, which uses closed-circuit TV cameras at each exit. The cameras are linked with our security office and are capable of taping signals from all exists simultaneously. The task force felt the Mark IV System might be useful in detecting a pattern of specific individuals entering and leaving the store. This system, which was operational on April 20, has been very helpful in. . . .

Employee Training
During May and June, we held workshops for employees on detecting shoplifters. We used the consulting firm of Security, Inc., which provided not only lectures and tips on spotting shoplifters but also demonstrations of common techniques used to divert store personnel. All those who attended the workshops thought they were quite helpful. . . .

Other Steps Taken
Because the task force determined that certain items were particularly vulnerable to shoplifters, we decided in July to restructure some of the display areas. Our purpose was to make these areas less isolated from the view of clerks and other store per-sonnel and thus less vulnerable. The remodeling, most of which was relatively minor, was completed over the summer months.

For the fall and holiday sales, we have hired extra security guards. These guards, also from Security, Inc., should deter first-time shoplifters, although we know that. . . .

We believe the steps we have taken will substantially reduce theft. Of course, after we've reviewed the figures at the end of the year, the task force intends to meet again in January to assess the effectiveness of the methods we have used. If you need more details, please let me know.

The spatial method of organization is commonly used in descriptions of buildings and laboratory equipment, in proposals for landscape work, in construction-site progress reports, and, in combination with a step-by-step sequence, in many types of instructions.

Figure 2–8 presents an outline and Figure 2–9 a description for a house inspection using a bottom-to-top, clockwise (south to west to north to east) sequence, beginning with the front door.

Division and Classification / *COMPLEX SUBJECTS*

An effective way to organize information about a complex subject is to divide it into manageable parts and then discuss each part separately. You might use this approach, called *division*, to describe a physical object, such as the parts of a fax machine; to examine an organization, such as a company; or to explain the components that make up the Internet global computer network. The emphasis in division is on breaking down a complex whole into a number of like units—because it is easier to consider smaller units and to examine the relationship of each to the other.

If you were a financial planner describing the types of mutual funds available to your investors, you could divide the variety available into three broad categories: money-market funds, bond funds, and stock funds. Although this division is accurate, it is only a first-level grouping of a complex whole. These three can, in turn, be subdivided into additional groups based on investment strategy. The second-level grouping could lead to the following categories:

Money-Market Funds

- taxable money-market funds
- tax-exempt money-market funds

**Figure 2–8
Sample Outline for
Spatial Description**

> **Outline**
>
> I. Ground floor
>   A. Front hall and stairwell
>   B. Dining room
>   C. Kitchen
>   D. Bathroom
>   E. Living room
>
> II. Second floor
>   A. Hallway
>   B. Southwest bedroom
>   C. Northwest bedroom
>   D. Bathroom
>   E. Master bathroom
>   F. Master bedroom

**Figure 2–9
Sample
Spatial
Description**

Interior of a Two-Story, Five-Room House

The front door faces south and opens into a hallway seven feet deep and ten feet wide. At the end of the hallway is the stairwell, which begins on the right-hand (east) side of the hallway, rises five steps to a landing, and reverses direction at the left-hand (west) side of the hallway. To the left (west) of the hallway is the dining room, which measures 15 feet along its southern exposure and ten feet along its western exposure. North of the dining room is the kitchen, which measures ten feet along its western exposure and 15 feet along its northern exposure. East of the kitchen, along the northern side of the house, is a bathroom that measures ten feet (west to east) by five feet. Parallel to the bathroom is a passageway the same size as the bathroom and leading from the kitchen to the living room. The living room (15 feet west to east by 20 feet north to south) occupies the entire eastern end of the floor.

On the second floor, at the top of the stairs is an L-shaped hallway, five feet wide. The base of the L, over the front door, is 15 feet long. The vertical arm of the L is 13 feet long. To the west of the hall is the southwest bedroom, which measures ten feet along its southern exposure and eight feet along its western exposure. Directly to the north, over the kitchen, is the northwest bedroom, which measures 12 feet along its western exposure and ten feet along its northern exposure. To the east, at the end of the hall, is a bathroom, which is five feet wide along the northern side of the house and seven feet long. To the east of this bathroom and also along the northern side of the house is the master bathroom, which is ten feet square and is entered from the master bedroom, which is directly over the living room. Like the living room, the master bedroom measures 15 feet along the northern and southern exposures of the house and 20 feet along the eastern exposure.

Bond Funds

- taxable bond funds
- tax-exempt bond funds
- balanced funds—mix of stocks and bonds

Stock Funds

- balanced funds—mix of stocks and bonds
- equity-income funds
- growth and income funds
- domestic growth funds
- international growth funds
- aggressive growth funds
- small capitalization funds
- specialized funds

Specialized funds can be further subdivided as follows:

Specialized Funds

- communications
- energy

- financial services
- technology
- environmental services
- gold
- worldwide capital goods
- health services
- utilities

After you have divided the variety of mutual funds into accurate categories, you could *classify* them by their degree of relative risk to investors. To do so, you would reorganize your original categories based on the criterion of risk. Depending on how risk is defined, this classification might look as follows:

Low-Risk Funds
- taxable money-market funds
- tax-exempt money-market funds

Low- to Moderate-Risk Funds
- taxable bond funds
- tax-exempt bond funds
- balanced funds
- equity-income funds
- growth and income funds

High-Risk Funds
- domestic growth stock funds
- international growth stock funds
- aggressive growth funds
- small capitalization funds

High- to Very High-Risk Funds
- specialized stock funds

The process by which a subject is classified is similar to the process by which a subject is divided. While division is the separation of a whole into its parts, classification is the grouping of a number of units (such as people, objects, or ideas) into related categories.

When dividing or classifying a subject, you must observe some basic rules of logic. First, divide the subject into its largest number of equal units. The basis for division depends, of course, on your subject and your purpose. If you are describing the *structure* of a four-cycle combustion engine, for example, you might begin by dividing the subject into its major parts—the pistons, the crankshaft, and the housing that contains them. If a more detailed explanation were needed, each of these parts, in turn, might be subdivided into its components. A discussion of the *function* of the same engine, however, would require a different logical basis for the division; such a breakdown would focus on the way combustion engines operate: (1) intake, (2) compression, (3) combustion and expansion, and (4) exhaust.

Once you have established the basis for the division, you must apply and express it consistently. Put each item in only one category, so that items do not overlap categories. An examination of the structure of the combustion engine that listed the battery as a major part would be illogical. Although it is part of the car's ignition system (which starts the engine), the battery is not a part of the engine itself. A discussion of the parts of the ignition system in which the battery is not mentioned would be just as illogical.

An outline provides a clear expression of classification and is especially useful in preparing a breakdown of any subject at several levels. In the following example, two Canadian park rangers classify typical park users according to four categories; the rangers then discuss how to deal with potential rulebreaking by members of each group. The rangers could have classified the visitors in a variety of other ways, of course: as city and country residents, backpackers and drivers of recreational vehicles, U.S. and Canadian citizens, and so on. However, for law-enforcement agents in public parklands, the size of a group and the relationships among its members were the most significant factors (Figures 2–10 and 2–11).

Outline

I. Types of campers
   A. Family groups
   B. Small groups
   C. Large groups
   D. Informal or hostile groups

II. Dealing with groups of campers
   A. Groups A and B
      1. One on one
      2. Courses of action
   B. Groups C and D
      1. Large groups
         a. Make the leader responsible
         b. Course of action
      2. Informal or hostile groups
         a. Make the person who assumes command responsible
         b. Course of action

Figure 2–10
Sample Outline for Division and Classification

**Figure 2–11
Sample Memo
Showing
Division and
Classification**

Memo

To: All Employees
From: Canadian National Park Service, Office of Rangers
Date: June 15, 20--
Subject: Dealing with Campers in Violation of National Park Rules

To respond to campers breaking National Park Rules and Codes for Safety and Conduct, first, recognize the various types of campers. They can be categorized as follows:

   A. Family groups
   B. Small groups (up to six well-acquainted members)
   C. Large groups or conventions (organized, but not always well-acquainted)
   D. Informal or hostile groups (may not have evident leader)

Persons in groups A and B can often be dealt with on a one-to-one basis. For example, suppose a member of the group is picking wildflowers, which is an offense in most of our park areas. Two courses of action are open. You could either issue a warning or charge the person with the offense. In this situation, a warning is preferable to a charge. First, advise the person that this action is an offense, but, more important, explain why. Point out that the flowers are for all to enjoy and that most wildflowers are delicate and die quickly when picked.

For large groups, other approaches may be necessary. Every group has a leader. For a large group or convention, find out who the event organizer is (this is likely to be the person who reserved the campsite). Hold the group's leader responsible for the group's behavior and take action—issue a warning or charge the leader with the offense—according to the guidelines of the National Park Rules and Codes for Safety and Conduct.

For informal or hostile groups, try to determine who the leader is. Observe the group's behavior to learn which person(s) assumes command of the group's actions, and try to deal with that person. Ultimately, it is best to regain control over a group through one or two individuals within the group. In a potentially hostile environment, always request backup of at least one other ranger on duty. Issue a warning or charge the leader or the group with the offense according to the guidelines of the National Park Rules and Codes for Safety and Conduct. If necessary, eject the group from the premises, as outlined in the Codes.

Decreasing Order of Importance /NEWS PAPERS

When you organize your information in decreasing order of importance, you begin with the most important fact or point, then go on to the next most important, and so on, ending with the least important. Newspaper readers are familiar with this sequence of information. The most significant information always ap-

Figure 2–12
Sample Outline
for Decreasing
Order of
Importance

Outline

I. Most qualified candidate: Mildred Bryant, acting chief
   A. Positive factors
      1. Twelve years' experience in claims processing
      2. Thoroughly familiar with section's operations
      3. Strong production record
      4. Continually ranked "outstanding" on job appraisals
   B. Negative factors
      1. Supervisory experience limited to present tenure as acting chief
      2. Lacks college degree required by job description

II. Second most qualified candidate: Michael Bastick, claims coordinator
   A. Positive factors
      1. Able administrator
      2. Seven years' experience in section's operations
      3. Currently enrolled in management-training course
   B. Negative factors
      1. Lacks supervisory experience
      2. Most recent work indirectly related to claims processing

III. Third most qualified candidate: Jane Fine, administrative assistant
   A. Positive factors
      1. Skilled administrator
      2. Three years' experience in claims processing
   B. Negative factors
      1. Lacks broad knowledge of claims procedures
      2. Lacks supervisory experience

pears first in a news story, with related but secondary information completing the story. Minor details go last, where they may be cut to accommodate a last-minute need for column space.

Decreasing order of importance is an especially appropriate method of organization for a report addressed to a busy decision-maker, who may be able to reach a decision after considering only the most important points—and who may not even have time to read the entire report. This sequence of information is useful, too, for a report written for a variety of readers, some of whom may be interested in only the major points and others in all the points. The outline and memo shown in Figures 2–12 and 2–13, respectively, present an example of such an approach.

Increasing Order of Importance /LASTING MEMORY

When you want the most important of several ideas to be freshest in your reader's mind at the end of your writing, organize your information by increasing order of importance. This sequence is useful in argumentative or persuasive writing when

Memo

To: Tawana Shaw, Director, Human Resources Department
From: Frank W. Russo, Chief, Claims Department   *FWR*
Date: November 13, 20--
Subject: Selection of Chief of the Claims Processing Section

The most qualified candidate for chief of the Claims Processing Section is Mildred Bryant, who is at present acting chief of the Claims Processing Section. In her 12 years in the Claims Department, Ms. Bryant has gained wide experience in all facets of the department's operations. She has maintained a consistently high production record and has demonstrated the skills and knowledge that are required for the supervisory duties she is now handling in an acting capacity. Another consideration is that she has continually been rated "outstanding" in all categories of her job-performance appraisals. However, her supervisory experience is limited to her present three-month tenure as acting chief of the section, and she lacks the college degree required by the job description.

Michael Bastick, claims coordinator, my second choice, also has strong potential for the position. An able administrator, he has been with the company for seven years. Further, he is currently enrolled in a management-training course at the university. He is ranked second because he lacks supervisory experience and because his most recent work has been with the department's maintenance and supply components. He would be the best person to take over many of Mildred Bryant's responsibilities if she should be made full-time chief of the Claims Processing Section.

Jane Fine, my third-ranking candidate, has shown herself to be a skilled administrator in her three years with the Claims Processing Section. Despite her obvious potential, she doesn't yet have the breadth of experience in claims processing that would be required of someone responsible for managing the Claims Processing Section. Jane Fine also lacks on-the-job supervisory experience.

you wish to save your strongest points until the end. The sequence begins with the least important point or fact, then moves to the next least important, and builds finally to the most important point at the end. You build your case inductively (reasoning from the particular to the general).

Writing organized by increasing order of importance has the disadvantage of beginning weakly, with the least important information. Your reader may become impatient or distracted before reaching your main point. However, for writing in which the ideas lead, point by point, to an important conclusion, increasing order of importance is an effective method of organization. Reports on

**Figure 2–14
Sample Outline
for Increasing Order
of Importance**

Outline

I. Staffing problem
    A. Too few qualified electronics technicians
    B. New recruiting program necessary

II. Apprentice program
    A. Providing insufficient numbers
    B. Enlistment bonuses tempting the high school graduates into the military services

III. Technical college
    A. Enrollment at area and regional technical colleges up, but fewer students studying electronics
    B. Keen competition from the military services for high school graduates

IV. Military veterans
    A. Relied heavily on veterans in the past
    B. Military reenlistment bonuses have all but removed this source

V. Devise a strategy to compete with the military services

production or personnel goals are often arranged by this method, as are oral presentations. Figures 2–14 and 2–15 present an outline and a memo, respectively, that show the use of increasing order of importance as a method of organization.

General to Specific

In a general-to-specific sequence, you begin your writing with a general statement and then provide facts or examples to develop and support that statement. For example, if you begin a report with the general statement "Companies that diversify are more successful than those that do not," the remainder of the report would offer examples and statistics that prove to your reader that companies that diversify are, in fact, more successful than companies that do not.

A memo or report organized in a general-to-specific sequence discusses only one point. All other information in the memo or report supports the general statement (Figures 2–16 and 2–17).

Examples and data that support the general statements are frequently accompanied by charts and graphs. Guidelines for creating and presenting illustrations are given in Chapter 12.

Specific to General *(GET TO The POINT)*

When you organize information in a specific-to-general sequence, you begin with specific information and build to a general conclusion. The examples, facts, and statistics that you present in your writing support the general conclusion that

Figure 2–15
Sample Memo
Showing
Increasing
Order of
Importance

Memo

To: Phillip Ting, Vice President, Operations
From: Harry Mathews, Human Resources Department   *HM*
Date: May 19, 20--
Subject: Recruiting Qualified Electronics Technicians

As our company continues to expand, and with the planned opening of the Lakeland Facility late next year, we need to increase and refocus our recruiting program to keep our company staffed with qualified electronics technicians. In the past five years, we have relied on our in-house apprentice program and on local and regional technical schools to fill our needs.

Although our in-house apprentice program provided a qualified pool of employees in the past, military enlistment bonuses are tempting graduating high school seniors to join a branch of the military services rather than join our apprentice program or attend the technical schools. This is particularly tempting to graduating high school students because the military services often send them to a technical school free of charge while they are in the service. Even our most vigorous Career Day recruiting at the high schools has yielded disappointing results.

We have also in the past relied on recruiting skilled veterans from all branches of the military services. With the military now offering very attractive reenlistment bonuses, however, this source of technicians has all but disappeared.

I would like to meet with you soon to devise a strategy for competing with the military services' enlistment and reenlistment bonuses.

comes at the end. For example, if your subject were highway safety, you might begin with details of a specific highway accident, go on to generalize about how that accident was similar to many others, and then present recommendations for reducing the probability of such accidents. If your purpose is to persuade a skep-

Figure 2–16
Sample Outline
for General to
Specific (Excerpt)

Outline

The company needs to locate additional suppliers of computer chips because of several related events.

    I. The current supplier is reducing output.
   II. Domestic demand for our laptop computers continues to increase.
  III. We are expanding into the international market.

Locating Additional Computer-Chip Suppliers

On the basis of information presented at the supply meeting on April 14, we recommend that the company locate additional suppliers of computer chips. Several related events make such an action necessary.

General statement

Our current supplier, ABC Electronics, is reducing its output. Specifically, we can expect a reduction of between 800 and 1,000 units per month for the remainder of this fiscal year. The number of units should stabilize at 15,000 units per month thereafter.

Supporting information

Domestic demand for our computers continues to grow. Demand during the current fiscal year is up 25,000 units over the last fiscal year. Sales Department projections for the next five years show that demand should peak next year at 50,000 units and then remain at that figure for at least the following four years.

Finally, our expansion into England and Germany will require additional shipments of 5,000 units per quarter to each country for the remainder of this fiscal year. Sales Department projections put computer sales for each country at double this rate, or 40,000 units in a fiscal year, for the next five years.

Figure 2–17   Sample Report Showing General to Specific (Excerpt)

tical reader by providing specific details, this method is useful because it suspends the general point until your case has been made. This method of organization is somewhat like increasing order of importance in that you carefully build your case and do not actually make your point until the end, as shown in Figures 2–18 and 2–19.

**Figure 2–18
Sample Outline
for Specific
to General**

Outline

I. Study of 4,500 accidents involving nearly 7,200 adult front-seat passengers showed only 20 percent of the vehicles equipped with passenger-side air bags

II. Study shows adult front-seat passengers in vehicles without air bags twice as likely to be killed as those in vehicles with air bags
   A. Children riding as front-seat passengers can be killed by deployment of air bags
   B. Children should ride in back seat

III. Estimated 40 percent of adult front-seat passenger vehicle deaths could be prevented if passenger-side air bags were installed

IV. Survival chances for adults in an accident greater with passenger-side air bags

· Statistic

Specific

Cite
Statistics
First –

General
conclusion

Based on
Statistics

The Facts About Air Bags

Recently, a government agency studied the use of passenger-side air bags in 4,500 accidents involving nearly 7,200 front-seat passengers of the vehicles involved. Nearly all these accidents occurred on routes that had a speed limit of at least 40 mph. Only 20 percent of the adult front-seat passengers were riding in vehicles equipped with passenger-side air bags. Those not riding in vehicles equipped with passenger-side air bags were more than twice as likely to be killed than passengers riding in vehicles that were so equipped.

A conservative estimate is that 40 percent of the adult front-seat passenger vehicle deaths could be prevented if all vehicles came equipped with passenger-side air bags. Children, however, should always ride in the back seat because other studies have indicated that a child can be killed by the deployment of an air bag. If you are an adult front-seat passenger in an accident, your chances of survival are far greater if the vehicle in which you are riding is equipped with a passenger-side air bag.

Figure 2–19   Sample Report Showing Specific to General (Excerpt)

Comparison

When you use comparison as a method of development, you compare the relative merits of the items you are considering. Comparison works well in determining which of two or more items is most suitable for some specific purpose, such as selecting the best product, determining the least-expensive messenger service for your company, or finding the most-qualified job applicant for your job opening.

To be sure that your choice will be the best one, you must determine the basis (or bases) for making your comparison. For example, if you were comparing bids from among contractors for a remodeling project at your company, you most likely would compare such factors as price, previous experience, personnel qualifications, availability at a time convenient for you, or completion date. Once you decide on the bases important to your comparison, you can determine the most effective way to structure your comparison: whole by whole or part by part. In the whole-by-whole method, all the relevant characteristics of one item are discussed before those of the next item are considered. In the part-by-part method, the relevant features of each item are compared one by one. The outline (Figure 2–20) and discussion (Figure 2–21) of typical woodworking glues, organized according to the whole-by-whole method, describe each type of glue and its characteristics before going on to the next type.

As is often the case when the whole-by-whole method is used, the purpose of this comparison is to weigh the advantages and disadvantages of each glue for certain kinds of woodworking. The comparison of woodworking adhesives first focused on the relative strength of the glue, then noted constraints on its use (conditions such as moisture and temperature), and finally discussed clamping.

However, if your purpose were to consider, one at a time, the various characteristics of all the glues, the information might be arranged according to the

Outline

I. White glue
   A. Best for light construction
   B. Weakened by high temperature, moisture, and stress
   C. Takes about 30 minutes to set

II. Aliphatic resin glue
   A. Strong and resistant to moisture
   B. Used at temperatures above 50°F
   C. Takes about 30 minutes to set

III. Plastic resin glue
   A. Strongest of the common wood adhesives
   B. Moisture resistant
   C. Sold in powder form—must be mixed with water
   D. Used in temperatures above 70°F
   E. Takes four to six hours to set

IV. Contact cement
   A. Very strong
   B. Bonds very quickly
   C. Ideal for mounting plastic on wood
   D. Most brands are flammable
   E. Fumes can be harmful if inhaled

Figure 2–20
Sample Outline for Comparison: Whole-by-Whole Method

Figure 2–21
Sample Comparison: Whole-by-Whole Method

Common Woodworking Adhesives

White glue is the most useful all-purpose adhesive for light construction, but it should not be used on projects that will be exposed to moisture, high temperature, or great stress. Wood that is being joined with white glue must remain in a clamp until the glue dries, which will take about 30 minutes.

Aliphatic resin glue has a stronger and more moisture-resistant bond than white glue. It must be used at temperatures above 50 degrees Fahrenheit. The wood should be clamped for about 30 minutes.

Plastic resin glue is the strongest of the common wood adhesives. It is highly moisture resistant—although not completely waterproof. Sold in powdered form, this glue must be mixed with water and used at temperatures above 70 degrees Fahrenheit. It is slow setting and the joint should be clamped for four to six hours.

Contact cement is a very strong adhesive that bonds so quickly it must be used with great care. It is ideal for mounting sheets of plastic laminate on wood. It is also useful for attaching strips of veneer to the edges of plywood. Because this adhesive bonds immediately when two pieces are pressed together, clamping is not necessary, but the parts to be joined must be very carefully aligned before being placed together. Check the label before you work with this adhesive. Most brands are quite flammable and the fumes can be harmful if inhaled. For safety, work in a well-ventilated area, away from flames or heat.

Outline

Rating adhesives by bonding strength, moisture resistance, and setting times.

   I. Bonding strength
      A. Contact cement and plastic resin glues bond very strongly
      B. Aliphatic resin glue bonds moderately strongly
      C. White glue bonds least effectively

  II. Moisture resistance
      A. Plastic resin glue and contact cement are highly resistant to moisture
      B. Aliphatic resin glue is moderately resistant
      C. White glue is least resistant

 III. Setting times
      A. Contact cement dries immediately and requires no clamping
      B. White glue and aliphatic resin glue must be clamped for 30 minutes
      C. Plastic resin glue is strongest and must be clamped for four to six hours

part-by-part method (Figures 2–22 and 2–23). Note that this method of comparison emphasizes the subdivided part or characteristics rather than the main types. Your emphasis can be further highlighted by syntax (word order) and mechanical highlighting (*italics*, **boldface,** or <u>underlining</u>).

Characteristics of Woodworking Adhesives

Woodworking adhesives are rated primarily according to their bonding strength, moisture resistance, and setting times.

Bonding strengths are categorized as very strong, moderately strong, or adequate for use with little stress. Contact cement and plastic resin glue bond very strongly, while aliphatic resin glue bonds moderately strongly. White glue provides a bond that is least resistant to stress.

Moisture resistance of woodworking glues is rated as high, moderate, and low. Plastic resin glue is moderately moisture resistant. Aliphatic resin glue is moderately moisture resistant, and white glue is least moisture resistant.

Setting times for these glues vary from an immediate bond to a four- to-six-hour bond. Contact cement bonds immediately and requires no clamping. Because the bond is immediate, surfaces being joined must be carefully aligned before being placed together. White glue and aliphatic resin glue set in 30 minutes; both require clamping to secure the bond. Plastic resin, the strongest wood glue, sets in four to six hours and also requires clamping.

CHAPTER 2 SUMMARY: Organizing Your Information

Before you begin to write, consider the following questions as you organize your information into a logical sequence.

☐ Will I need a brief list or a full-scale outline to organize my information?

☐ Will I need to circulate the outline to colleagues or superiors?

☐ Is the outline divided into parts and subparts that reflect the logical divisions of the topic?

☐ Will my word-processing software structure the outline automatically?

☐ Does the topic lend itself naturally to one of the following methods of development?

- sequential
- chronological
- spatial
- division and classification
- decreasing order of importance
- increasing order of importance
- general to specific
- specific to general
- comparison

☐ Does the topic need to be organized by more than one method of development?

■ Exercises

1. Create an outline for one of the following topics, organizing it *sequentially*. Using the outline, write a paper of assigned length on the topic.
   a. Preparing a household budget
   b. Tuning a guitar
   c. Setting up a personal computer
   d. Opening an online checking account
   e. Sharpening a chain-saw or lawn-mower blade
   f. Finding an apartment to rent
   g. Repairing a broken window
   h. Applying for a personal loan
   i. Maturing of a monarch butterfly egg to an adult
   j. Changing a baby's diaper
   k. Preparing your favorite meal
   l. Purchasing a product on the Internet
   m. Buying a car (preowned or new)

2. Create an outline for one of the following topics, organizing it by a *chronological* sequence. Using the outline, write a paper of assigned length on the topic.
   a. A report on an accident
   b. Instructions for breeding, raising, and selling puppies or other pets
   c. A description of the life cycle of a typical fruit, from blossom to ripe fruit, in one growing season
   d. A description of the job-search process
   e. A report on the steps involved in completing a research assignment
   f. Instructions for building a campfire
   g. Instructions for performing a particular sport or activity with which you are familiar (focus on a specific aspect of the sport or activity, such as how to swing a golf club properly or how to swim the butterfly stroke, for example)

3. Create an outline for one of the following topics, organizing it in a *spatial* sequence. Using the outline, write a paper of assigned length on the topic. Without relying on illustrations, describe the topic clearly enough so that a classmate, if asked, could create an accurate drawing or diagram based on your description.
   a. The layout of your apartment or of a floor in your home
   b. The layout of the reference room or other area of the school library
   c. The dimensions and pertinent features of the grounds of a public building
   d. The layout of a vegetable or flower garden
   e. The layout of the shop, office, or laboratory where you work
   f. Instructions for disinfecting a hospital room, exterminating insects in a kitchen or other area, or painting or wallpapering a room
   g. The layout of your apartment or home, not as it is, but as you would like it to be

4. Create an outline for one of the following topics, organizing it by a *decreasing-order-of-importance* sequence. Using the outline, write a paper of assigned length on the topic.
   a. Your job qualifications
   b. The advantages to you of living in a particular city or area of the country
   c. The importance of preventive maintenance of a machine or piece of equipment with which you are familiar
   d. The importance of preventive care in one health-related area (diet, exercise, dental care, and so on)
   e. Your own career goal
   f. The advantages of having your paycheck directly deposited into your account, of having savings automatically deducted from your paycheck, or of using online banking
   g. The advantages of recycling
   h. The advantages of owning life insurance
   i. The advantages of carpooling

5. Create an outline for one of the following topics, organizing it by an *increasing-order-of-importance* sequence. Using the outline, write a paper of assigned length on the topic.
   a. The college courses that you believe will be most important to your career (discuss no more than five)
   b. Why smoking should or should not be permitted in restaurants
   c. The advantages of learning to pilot a small airplane

    d. The reasons why you need a pay raise

    e. The advantages of alternatively fueled vehicles

    f. A proposal to change a procedure where you work

6. For this exercise, use a *general-to-specific* sequence. Choose one of the following statements, then support it with pertinent facts, examples, anecdotes, and so on. Outline the information and write a paper of assigned length based on the outline.

    a. Volunteer jobs provide valuable experience in the working world.

    b. For families living within limited means, budgeting is essential.

    c. The mark of a capable administrator is willingness to delegate authority.

    d. Post–high school education or technical training is essential in today's job market.

    e. Ongoing computer education is fundamental in today's workplace.

    f. A sound management training program pays off for companies.

7. For this exercise, use a *specific-to-general* sequence. For one of the following sets of data, study the trends or patterns that are presented, draw your own conclusions, and state the conclusions in a plausible general statement. Outline the information that supports your main point, and write a paper of assigned length based on your outline. Alternatively, as a basis for this exercise you may select other information from lists and tables in current yearbooks, almanacs, or newspapers.

    a. Deaths from motor vehicle accidents in the United States

Year	Number of Deaths
1988	47,087
1989	45,582
1990	44,599
1991	41,508
1992	39,250
1993	40,150
1994	40,716
1995	41,817
1996	42,065
1997	42,013
1998	41,471

Sources: Vehicle Miles of Travel and Licensed Drivers—Federal Highway Administration; Registered Vehicles—R. L. Polk & Co. and Federal Highway Administration; Population—U.S. Bureau of the Census. Compiled by the National Center for Statistics and Analysis. National Highway Traffic Safety Administration, "Traffic Safety Facts 1998: A Compilation of Motor Vehicle Crash Data from the Fatality Analysis Reporting System and the General Estimates System: DOT HS 808 983. Table 2. Washington, D.C., National Highway Traffic Safety Administration, October 1999.

    b. Apartments completed in the United States in buildings with five or more units

Year	Apartments with ≤ 5 Units
1999	291,800
1998	273,900
1997	247,100
1996	251,300
1995	212,400
1994	154,900

Year	Apartments with ≤ 5 Units
1993	124,800
1992	155,200
1991	216,500
1990	294,400

Source: U.S. Census Bureau. U.S. Department of Housing and Urban Development, the U.S. Department of Commerce, and the U.S. Census Bureau. "Housing Completions: April 2000." C22/00-4. Table 1. Washington, D.C. U.S. Government Printing Office, June 2000.

8. Create a topic outline for one of the following topics, organizing it by *division and classification.* Using the outline, write a paper of assigned length on the topic.
   a. Personal Digit Assistants (including pocket PCs)
   b. Conventional and alternative medical therapies
   c. Weight loss strategies and programs
   d. Home exercise equipment
   e. Bicycles (e.g., racing, mountain)
   f. Cameras for home and vacation use
   g. Cable TV channels in your area

9. Create a topic outline for one of the following topics, organizing it by the *comparison* method of development. Using the outline, write a paper of assigned length on the topic.
   a. The features of two or more word processing software programs
   b. The features of two or more spreadsheet software programs
   c. The features of two or more Web publishing programs
   d. Intellectual property laws in the United States (e.g., trade secret law, copyright law, trademark law, and patent law)
   e. Search features of at least five specialized Internet search engines (e.g., Argus Clearinghouse, Health AtoZ, Thomas Legislative Information, Zip Code Lookup)

10. Revise the following list on the advantages and disadvantages of flexible work schedules, eliminating any unrelated notes or repetition and combining any closely related items.
    • Advantageous to working parents
    • More satisfied employees
    • Workers not always available when needed
    • Must have core hours when everyone must be at work
    • Starting time from 7:00 a.m. to 10:00 a.m.
    • Quit any time from 3:00 p.m. to 9:00 p.m.
    • Personal lives easier to schedule
    • Carpooling more difficult
    • Cafeteria hours would have to be expanded
    • Extended work day would increase utility bills
    • Time-zone differences across the country become a potential problem
    • Morning and afternoon people can take advantage of their best hours
    • Daylight saving time
    • Day care made easier
    • Easier for employees to schedule medical appointments

- Employees can take advantage of daylight hours
- Bus schedules
- Greater efficiency
- Employees can work their most productive hours
- Employees are more productive
- Employees gain more control over their lives
- Could result in decreased control by managers and supervisors
- Could produce healthier employees
- Could result in cheating
- Could decrease or eliminate tardiness

11. Prepare an outline for a report to your boss from the list of notes you created in Exercise 8. Identify the method of organization you used in your outline.

12. Using the outline you created in Exercise 10, write a short report to your department manager recommending that flexible hours be adopted by your department.

13. Identify the method of organization that would be most effective for each of the following topics and explain how consideration of audience and purpose might affect your decision.
    a. Instructions for setting the time on a VCR
    b. A police report of the results of a stake out
    c. A report on the different kinds of programs available on prime-time television
    d. A report on the differences among the major computer manufacturers
    e. Instructions for preparing a five-course meal, including recipes
    f. A report on the different types of media coverage of a world event
    g. A report on the results of a governmental election and its importance
    h. Instructions for buying or selling a house

14. The following is a list of topics about which you might write. Determine the best method of organizing each topic: sequential, chronological, spatial, division and classification, decreasing order of importance, increasing order of importance, general to specific, specific to general, or comparison. You will use some of the methods more than once and at least one method not at all. It is possible for a topic to fit more than one method. Be prepared to defend your choice.
    - The process of registering for classes
    - The reasons why yours should be a tobacco-free environment
    - The different types of dogs at the dog show
    - Selecting the job you will accept
    - How to get the job you want
    - The most important room in your house
    - Announcing the winners of a contest
    - The fire-escape route for a building
    - Determining the best computer to buy
    - The nine planets in our solar system
    - The changing educational system in your state

■ In-Class Activities

1. Following is a sample of a poorly developed outline. In small groups and within the time frame allotted by your instructor, revise this outline, following the guidelines included in this chapter. Select a spokesperson from your group who will present your outline to the class.

COMPANY SPORTS

    I. Intercompany sports
        A. Advantages to the company
            1. Publicity
            2. Intercompany relations
        B. Disadvantages
            1. Misplaced emphasis
            2. Athletic participation not available to all employees
    II. Intracompany sports
        A. Wide participation
        B. Physical fitness
        C. Detracts from work
        D. Risks injuries

2. The list in Column A contains both major and minor heads. In small groups and within the time frame allotted by your instructor, select the heads that you feel should be major heads and arrange them in the appropriate sequence. Then select the minor heads that should go under each major head and arrange them in the appropriate sequence. Put each next to the appropriate Roman numeral or capital letter in Column B. Use the following definitions:

CONDUCTION   the transmission of cold or heat *through solid material.*

AIR INFILTRATION   the transmission of cold or heat *through cracks and other open spaces.*

When your group has completed this task, choose a representative who will share your outline with the class.

REPORT ON A PLAN TO REMODEL A FIFTY-YEAR-OLD HOUSE TO MAKE IT MORE ENERGY EFFICIENT

Column A	Column B
I. _____	Insulation
A. _____	Introduction
B. _____	Heat loss through conduction
C. _____	Scope of the report
II. _____	Storm doors and windows
A. _____	The solutions
B. _____	Procedure used to prepare the report
III. _____	Heat loss through air infiltration
A. _____	The problems
B. _____	Weatherstripping
C. _____	Purpose of the report
D. _____	Caulking

3. Rejoin your group (from In-Class Activity 2) and key all the following notes to the topic outline that your group created. Work within the time frame required by your instructor and choose a representative who will present your revised outline to the class. Use the following definitions:

WINDOW SASH: the frame holding the panes of a window

WINDOW CASING: the framework in a wall within which the window sash is set

- Specific costs are not discussed.
- Caulking is a flexible adhesive that is used to insulate against air infiltration.
- Fiberglass (six inches thick) should be installed between the unfinished basement and the floor.
- Recommend a remodeling plan to make the house more energy efficient.
- Window sashes and casings fit loosely.
- The best weatherstripping is the spring-bronze or felt-hair type.
- The cost of insulating is recovered in fuel savings in five years.
- The proposed plan does not specify methods or materials.
- The house will be warmer in winter and cooler in summer.
- Lack of insulation means that much of the heat passes through the walls and ceilings by conduction.
- Caulking should be done after weatherstripping.
- The history of the house was studied.
- Storm windows and doors also reduce conduction through the glass by half.
- The windows and doors were checked for air leaks.
- Weatherstripping is insulating material that is installed around windows and doors in an outside wall to help insulate against air infiltration.
- Each cavity between the studs in the walls should be filled with foam.
- Fuel bills will be lower.
- Doors and windows, made of thin materials, waste vast amounts of heat.
- Eight inches of insulation should be installed in the attic.
- To ensure watertight weatherstripping, windows should be sealed and new window latches installed.
- Caulking provides an airtight seal between the doors and windows and the building materials.
- The report deals with the causes of heat loss and the solutions being recommended to solve the problem.
- The house was built at a time when little insulation was used.
- A storm window or door is an extra window or door in an outside wall to help insulate against air infiltration.
- Insulation is material that resists the conduction of heat and cold. It is installed in attics and walls of the homes.
- Doors do not close tightly.
- Such openings allow cold air to enter and hot air to escape.
- Insulation provides comfort and a pleasant sense of well-being.
- Storm windows and doors should be installed to help reduce air infiltration.
- Conduction through doors and windows is even worse.
- The structure of the building and its foundation were studied.

4. This assignment requires that your instructor (or assigned students) bring to class five common tools, such as a can opener, a pencil sharpener, a level, a hammer, or a wrench. Spend five minutes passing the tools around and outline a narrative description of one or more of the tools, keeping in mind the particular function of the tool(s). Your instructor may suggest that students describing the same tool(s) sit together to have easy access to the tool(s) while preparing the outlines. However, this is not a group project and outlines are to be prepared individually. When finished, exchange your paper for that of a classmate and critique one another's outlines based on whether the outline effectively describes the tool.

5. In small groups, identify the three greatest barriers facing small businesses in the United States today. Your group will have 30 minutes (or a time period allotted by your instructor) to create an outline with these three subheadings. You may outline to the third or fourth level as needed. Choose a spokesperson to briefly present (in three minutes or so) the outline to the class.

6. Create a list of your activities during the last seven days. You may categorize your list in any way that you find useful, such as chronological or categorical. Divide into groups of four to six members and during the next 25 minutes (or time allotted by your instructor), based on your individual lists, create a collective outline for an essay titled, "How the Average College Student Spends Time." At the end of the allotted time, your group must be ready to explain why you chose the method of outline used. Choose a spokesperson from your group to present your outline to the class. (If required by your instructor, your group will then write a draft of the essay outlined.)

■ Research Projects

1. Locate a government, business, or industry report *or* an article in a professional journal in your major field of study. Analyze the organization of information in the report or article, and write an outline that mirrors the organization. Develop the outline to the level of detail of the outline shown on page 29, or to the level of detail specified by your instructor. Then assess the report or article for its use of the methods of organization described in this chapter, citing specific sections or paragraphs in which each method is demonstrated. Finally, describe how the organization of the report or article helped or hindered you in understanding it.

2. Gather and review all sources, notes, and other research material that you have been collecting for your term project or current writing assignment. (At your instructor's discretion, this exercise may be done now or later in the academic term.) Brainstorm for 20 minutes on how to organize the material by writing down as quickly as possible the key points, main ideas, and subtopics that seem most important to you. Don't stop to evaluate the data; simply write the ideas down as fast as you can. Take a break and come back to the list to look for a way to organize the information into a structure that satisfies the internal logic of the topic, your reader's needs, and your purpose. Write an outline and submit it to your instructor. In a transmittal memo to the instructor, explain any gaps in your outline and give an estimate for completion of the remaining stages of the writing project.

3. You are the information and marketing person for a small business. You have been asked to help plan your company's first Web site. For purposes of this project the business may be floral, printing, fabricating, wholesale (you choose the product), or another small business with your instructor's approval. Give your company a name and gather information from at least three print sources about the business in which your company is involved. Draft an outline of the knowledge you have about your company's business and the goods and services it provides. Based on your outline, make a list of what other information consumers would be interested in knowing about your company. (*Note:* This project is continued in Web Projects 3 through 6. Ultimately you will provide your company's graphics designer with an outline and complete information for the site.)

4. Your boss has asked you to interview a successful businessperson of your choice for your company's newsletter. Prepare an outline to use during your 30-minute interview.

5. In 30 to 45 minutes (remember, your expert is a busy person), interview the person you selected for Research Project 4. Use your outline as a guide to the interview. When completed, create a new outline using the information you obtained during the interview.

■ Web Projects

1. Visit five or more credible Web sites and examine the variety of ways that information is organized at each site. Write one to three paragraphs analyzing each site's method of organization—how effective or ineffective is the presentation of information at each site, and how they compare to one another. Write another one to three paragraphs explaining how *other* methods of organization and the use of outlining (as discussed in this chapter) could improve each of these sites. In your narrative, document at least five specific examples from the Web site.

2. Select a current event or news story that interests you. Read about the event or story on at least five credible Web sites (you may want to print out the material that you find). Develop an outline for an essay in which you would compare and contrast the different perspectives on this event that are offered at the different Web sites. What conclusions can you draw about the coverage of this event? Your outline should indicate a clear method of organization. (Be sure to record the URLs of the sites you researched.)

3. This project builds on Research Project 3, in which you were asked to draft an outline for your company's Web site. Search the Internet to locate at least three Web sites relevant to your company's business—these can include sites run by your competitors (be sure to bookmark these sites for later use). Note the different ways that information is organized at these sites. Is a clear style of organization evident? What style of outline might have been used to create each site? Compare the organization of these sites with the organization you have planned for your company's Web site. Why is the organization that you have planned for your site particularly appropriate? Be specific, but brief.

4. This project builds on Research Project 3 and Web Project 3. Using the material you have gathered for Research Project 3 and Web Project 3, consider in more

detail what information should be included at your company's first Web site. What facts about your company will you want to include? What resources do you want to provide for your readers or customers? How should this information be organized? Create an outline for your Web site. You may organize it by decreasing order of importance, or you may choose any method of organizing presented in this chapter that seems logical for your topic. Refer to the sample Web sites you researched as you put together the plan for your company's Web site, and consider what you liked best about these sites and what seemed most effective to you.

5. This project builds on Research Project 3 and Web Projects 3 and 4. Return to the Internet to find the information that you need to complete your outline of information for your company's Web site. Document all sites that you will use in your outline.

6. This project builds on Web Projects 3 through 5. Based on the information you have found on the Web, finalize a detailed outline of your company's first Web site. Your outline should be detailed enough so that the graphic designer will understand what information you wish to include. Sketch a rough map of how you would like the site to look. The layout should make the site's organization obvious.

3 Writing the Draft

I f you have gathered and recorded enough information to meet your purpose, reader's needs, and scope, as described in Chapter 1, and if you have prepared an outline, as described in Chapter 2, you are well prepared to write a rough draft. Yet, for most people, writing the draft remains a chore—if not an obstacle.

One technique experienced writers use to get started is to think of writing a rough draft as simply transcribing and expanding the notes from the outline into paragraphs without worrying about grammar, style, or such mechanical aspects of writing as spelling. Refinement will come with revision, a process discussed in Chapters 4 and 5.

Imagine your typical reader sitting across the desk from you as you explain your topic to him or her. This will make your writing more direct and conversational. If you are writing instructions or procedures, visualize your reader actually performing the actions you are describing. This should help you see the steps your reader must perform and ensure that you provide adequate information. If you are writing a sales letter, think of your arguments from the reader's point of view. Imagine how the features you describe can best be translated into benefits for a prospective customer.

Whatever technique you use, don't worry about a good opening—that can wait until you've constructed your paragraphs. Just start. Concentrate on ideas without attempting to polish or revise. Writing and revising are different activities. Keep writing quickly to achieve unity, coherence, and proportion.

As you write your rough draft, remember that the first rule of good writing is to help your readers. Your function as a writer is to communicate certain information to them. Don't try to impress them with a fancy writing style. Write in a plain and direct style that is comfortable and natural for both you and your readers.

Also keep in mind your reader's level of knowledge of the subject. Doing so not only will help you write directly to them but also will tell you which terms you must define. (Review Chapter 7, "Instructions and Other Writing Strategies," for guidelines on when to define terms.)

Above all, don't wait for inspiration to write the rough draft—treat writing the draft as you would any on-the-job task. The following are tactics that experienced writers use to start, keep moving, and get the job done; you will discover which ones are the most helpful to you.

The most effective way to start and to keep going, however, is to use a good outline as a springboard and a map for your writing. The outline also serves to

Nicole Gallagher, ABC News

Nicole Gallagher is a producer for "World News Tonight with Peter Jennings." As ABC's evening news show, "World News" tries to reach as large and varied an audience as possible. As a producer, Nicole is responsible for every element that goes into the making of a news piece: suggesting the story idea, reporting it, hiring a camera crew to shoot it, writing the script or editing a script written by the correspondent, and supervising the video editing process.

Correspondents are usually responsible for the writing, but it's the producer's duty to make sure that every script is clear and well organized. If a correspondent can't accomplish this, the task falls to the producer. Some stories take weeks to put together, others take months. On particularly busy days, the whole process happens in six hours.

Nicole has had to come up with scripts in much less time. Here's how she gets it done: "I had to write a script about an alleged Timothy McVeigh confession [to the Oklahoma City bombing] that was about to be published in *Playboy* magazine. While I had read the article, I knew little about its significance — I had no idea what the main point was, or why the audience would care. However, it was 5 P.M. and this was to be our lead story. I had ninety minutes — to write it *and* get it on the air. My correspondent and I sat down, grabbed a researcher who was very familiar with the story to check our facts, and plunged in. We wrote the script in 25 minutes, and finished the piece with a minute to spare. The lesson here is: When all else fails, jump right in and start writing. Write everything you know about your topic, without thinking about how it sounds. When it's all down on paper, go back and see what you can organize, shorten, and improve."

For more information about ABC News, visit their Web site at http://www.abcnews.com.

Entry-Level
Jonathan Spiegel, The Foundation Center

Jonathan Spiegel is a fund-raiser for The Foundation Center, a large, national nonprofit organization. Many nonprofit organizations rely on the financial support of charitable foundations (organizations that give money away to nonprofits), and written grant proposals are the primary vehicle through which nonprofits ask foundations for money. The Foundation Center sends out more than 500 of these letter proposals each year, and it is crucial that the letters are both highly persuasive and personalized for each individual reader. From his draft, through the revisions to the final product, Jonathan acknowledges the importance of considering the audience in the writing — of thinking of the subject through his reader's point of view.

"We must always assume that our audience is not familiar with our organization's internal lingo and does not need to know (and may not care) about every detail of what we're doing. So, what exactly does our reader want to know? Because foundations are a diverse bunch, we never know the precise answer to this question, but there are several things that most foundations need to know before they write you a check: What are our organization's recent accomplishments? How about plans for the near future? What is our general mission and significance? How do we carry out that mission? Do we work with other similar organizations to accomplish common goals? Is the work of our organization of interest to the foundation to which we are writing? If we are writing to someone who has previously supported us, the answer to this last question is usually yes; however, we must always restate our case year after year when asking for a renewed gift. Our generic proposal is not a static document; we constantly revise and update the information throughout the year so that it is timely and relevant."

"Getting the money you need to support your organization's cause is not an easy task. As fund-raisers for nonprofits, we need to learn how to write effectively and how to talk to an audience whom we usually don't know and rarely even get to meet. That is part of what makes the job a challenge; at the end of the day, we hope to help a few people — and, in that sense, proposal writing is very rewarding."

To learn more about The Foundation Center, visit their Web site at http://www.fdncenter.org.

group related facts and details. Once these facts are grouped, you are ready to construct unified and coherent paragraphs—the major building blocks of any piece of writing.

■ Developing Confidence

On-the-job writers must deal with the constant pressure of deadlines, causing a great deal of anxiety. Nothing builds a writer's confidence more than adequate preparation. If you haven't done enough research to feel comfortable with the material, for example, you will no doubt face great anxiety—perhaps even "writer's block"—as you begin the draft. Furthermore, if you start without an adequate outline, not only will you face writing anxiety, but you will also be frustrated because you will spend far too much time producing a first draft.

To avoid undermining your confidence, keep in mind that writing and revising are two very different tasks. When you write the draft, consider yourself a writer communicating with your reader; when you revise, then—and only then—become your own toughest critic. One of the several dangers of trying to write something perfectly the first time is that it puts pressure on you—pressure that can become self-defeating. In fact, any attempt to correct or polish your writing only stimulates the internal critic and undermines your ability to complete the draft.

One way to avoid the temptation to revise is to understand that the first draft is necessarily rough and unpolished. Far from criticizing yourself for not being able to write a smooth, readable sentence the first time, you should comfort yourself that it is natural for first drafts to be clumsy and long-winded. So when you write the draft, don't worry about precise word choices, usage, syntax, grammar, or spelling. Instead, concentrate entirely on getting the message down; concentrate on what you are writing, not on how you are writing it.

Once you are prepared and understand that the goal of the first draft is simply to produce a draft, avoid procrastination at all costs. For example, be wary of such diversions as checking the mail, watching the clock, rearranging files, or calling to check an appointment. They may be simply ways of avoiding work. Furthermore, you cannot afford to wait for inspiration; doing so is often an excuse for stalling.

■ Using Time-Management Tactics

Because on-the-job writers must deal not only with constant deadlines but also with several assignments at once, managing time is an essential part of the writing process.

Allocate Your Time

One effective time-management practice is keeping a calendar on your desk or computer that indicates various deadlines for projects, appointments for interviews, and time periods for gathering information. Your daily calendar should also include "writing appointments," times set aside for writing that you must keep (without interruptions) as if you had an appointment with another person.

Within the deadlines set by teachers, managers, and others, set your own short-term, manageable deadlines for completing sections of a draft and other tasks. Concentrating on such subgoals can help you meet the overall deadline, and it can also relieve some of the pressure of writing the draft. Some professional writers think of the completion of subgoals as building a draft one brick at a time.

List these goals, together with your other job tasks; then schedule each task for a specific time. Time-management experts advise working on the most difficult or unpleasant tasks during the time of day when your mind is keenest.

Prepare Your Work Environment

Another useful time-management strategy for writing the draft is to prepare your writing environment and assemble your materials before you begin. Find an isolated place or a method of isolating yourself for writing the draft; then hang out the "Do Not Disturb" sign. Especially when a deadline is in jeopardy, finding a quiet area, away from phones and meetings, can be effective.

Put order into your writing environment by arranging your materials and supplies. Use whatever writing technology (pen and pad, computer, or tape recorder) is most comfortable for you. You may even discover that certain props will help you get started. For example, sitting in a favorite chair, opening computer files, or placing a reference book on your desk may symbolize your commitment to yourself and your work.

Remain Flexible

Start with the outline as a guide, but remember that it is not cast in concrete. Feel free to improve your organization as you work. Consider starting with the easiest or most interesting part just to get moving and build some momentum. You may find that just writing out a statement of your purpose will help you to get started.

Once you are rolling, keep going. You may even wish to write comments to yourself while you are writing the rough draft if that tactic keeps you moving. When you reach landmarks (such as the subgoals described earlier) or feel powerfully tempted to start revising, you may need to take a break. When you do, leave a signpost, such as a printout of an unfinished section or a note in the outline recording the date and time you stopped, so you will not waste time searching for your place when you resume work. When you finish a section, reward yourself with a cup of coffee, a short walk, or another small diversion. Physical activity serves as an excellent break for writers. If possible, avoid immersing yourself in another mental activity while you are on your break. If you are not under mental pressure, you may even discover a solution to a nagging writing problem.

When you resume, reread what you have written up to the point where you stopped so you can recall your frame of mind. Some writers also like to change their writing tools or environment when they resume writing the draft. (For guidelines on writing two types of time-sensitive documents, see Meeting the Deadline: The Time-Sensitive Memo on pages 298–300, and Meeting the Deadline: The Time-Sensitive Proposal on pages 625–627.)

■ Communicating with Your Reader

When writing the draft, focus on communicating with your reader. To communicate effectively, avoid writing about a subject for yourself instead of for your reader, a mistake even experienced writers make. Think of your subject from your reader's perspective. How do you determine that perspective? Begin with Christine Thomas' successful analysis of her reader, Harriet Sullivan, in Chapter 1. Christine asked:

1. What information does my reader need to understand what I'm writing about?
2. What is my reader's basic attitude likely to be toward what I'm writing about?

These questions—which might be rephrased as "What does my reader probably know?" and "What does my reader probably think?"—always repay the effort required to think about them.

Suppose your purpose is to explain your plan for bypassing a malfunctioning piece of equipment that causes periodic production bottlenecks. If your reader were the company's director of the maintenance department, these questions would be easier to answer than if your reader were the president of your company, someone you know only by name and title. In the first case, your reader understands the equipment, the terminology you will use, and the production system. In the second case, your reader is a decision-maker primarily interested in the big picture—the broader implications of these bottlenecks on production schedules and the feasibility of your plan to correct the problem. This reader probably would not know and would not need to know the technical details of the day-to-day operation of your production system and would likely have neither the time nor the inclination to learn them simply to understand your explanation. A memo to the company president would have to focus on the effect of the bottlenecks on production, alternative ways to fix the problem, and estimates of the costs and schedules for each alternative. These issues, rather than a detailed explanation of the problem, are important to a top executive. After reading your explanation, the president would have to decide whether to choose one of several alternatives or some combination of them or to investigate the plan further.

Determine Your Reader's Point of View

Your reader, whether a coworker, a customer, or a company president, is interested in the problem you are addressing more from his or her point of view than from yours. Imagine yourself in your reader's position. One way to do so is to visualize your reader performing a set of activities based on your writing. When you are writing instructions or procedures, think of your reader as an actor in a role performing certain actions. Taken together with what you know about your reader's background, this picture will help you predict your reader's needs and reactions. This process should ensure that all the information your reader needs is clearly stated.

For instance, if you were working for a bicycle manufacturer and your purpose were to write a set of assembly instructions so that people who buy your new model 1050J could get from opening the carton to riding the bicycle with a minimum of frustration, you would have to break down the assembly process into a sensible series of easy-to-follow steps. You would avoid technical language and anticipate questions that your readers would be likely to have. You would make it unnecessary for them to consult other sources to follow your directions. You would not explain the engineering theory that is responsible for the bicycle's unique design; your readers would be more interested in riding the bicycle than in reading such details, however fascinating they might be to you. If you ventured into theory at all, it would be for a specific reason, such as to explain why a particular step in the assembly process had to be completed before the next. You would also include assembly diagrams, a list of parts, and a list of the tools necessary for assembly.

You would approach the situation differently if you were preparing assembly instructions for a bicycle dealer. You could use standard technical terms without defining them, and you would probably reduce the number of steps necessary for assembly by combining related steps because your reader, the dealer, would be familiar with bicycle assembly and would be able to follow a

---

WRITER'S CHECKLIST: Thinking Like Your Reader

Here are some typical questions that readers ask that can help you to anticipate and address their concerns as you plan and write your on-the-job documents.

- ☐ Why do I need to read this document or email message?
  - • To perform a task
  - • To investigate a problem
  - • To make a decision
  - • To schedule a meeting
  - • To prepare for a meeting
  - • To skim it for information only
- ☐ Is there enough information for me to understand the subject?
- ☐ Does the writing get to the point or do I have to wade through blocks of dense text to learn its purpose?

more sophisticated set of instructions. Your reader would not need a list of tools required for assembly; the dealer's shop would no doubt have all the necessary tools, and the dealer would know which ones to use. You might well, in a separate section, include some theoretical detail, too. The dealer could possibly use this information to explain to customers the advantages of your bicycle over a competitor's.

Establish Your Role and Voice as the Writer

Writers must also assume roles. If you are an on-the-job writer, you may need to assume the role of a teacher who guides the reader's learning process. In this case, you must do more than explain—you must anticipate your reader's reactions and growing understanding of the subject. You must be alert to questions that your reader might ask, such as "Why do I need to read this document?" "Is this subject easy to learn?" "How much time must I spend to read it?" and "Where can I find a quick answer to my problem?" By anticipating that the reader will ask such questions, you will be more likely to answer them as you write the draft.

You may discover that readers' interests do not always coincide with their needs. Some readers, for example, would prefer not to read your document at all; however, they are interested in completing a task or solving a problem as quickly as possible. You must demonstrate how your document links the readers' interests with their need to read the document.

As you write the draft, consider which voice your readers should hear. Should it be authoritarian or friendly, formal or accessible, provocative or reassuring— or somewhere in between? Determine the voice you adopt by considering what is appropriate to your specific purpose. The guidelines shown in Figure 3–1 are intended for respiratory care therapists when they assess patients to develop a plan of care. The writer's voice is slightly formal (the guidance is in the imperative mood) yet caring in tone, as befits the subject.

Readers of newsletters, by contrast, may expect a voice that is fast-paced and reportorial. Consider the attention-getting approach in the opening of an article in an employee newsletter (Figure 3–2).

Respiratory Care Plan

1. Let the patient know exactly what is being done.
2. Maintain a good rapport; answer questions the patient may ask to allay fear.
3. Maintain the privacy and dignity of the patient at all times.
4. Be prepared. A stethoscope, a watch with a sweep second hand or a stop-watch, and a pen are basic items essential to this process.
5. Document your findings as soon as time permits; otherwise, you may forget important points.

Figure 3–1
Sample of Formal Voice (in Instructions)

**Figure 3–2
Sample of Con-
versational Voice
(in Employee
Newsletter)**

A number of centuries back, the Roman satirist Persius said, "Your knowing is nothing, unless others know you know." Today at Allen-Bradley, some of our engineers are subscribing to Persius' philosophy. They contend it takes more than the selling of a product for a corporation to enjoy continuing success.

"We must sell our knowledge as well," stresses Don Fitzpatrick, Commercial Chief Engineer. "We've got to get our customers to think of us as knowledge experts."

Write for Multiple Readers

When you write for a group of readers who are similar in background and knowledge—all sales associates, for example, or all security officers—you should picture a typical representative of that group and write directly to that person. Occasionally, however, you may need to write a document for a group of readers with widely different work environments, technical backgrounds, or professional positions. For example, you might write a technical report that would be used by field-service engineers, sales associates, and company executives. In such a situation, you could address each audience separately in clearly identified sections of your document: an executive summary for the executives, an appendix for the service engineers, and the body of the document for the sales associates. (See Chapter 13 for an explanation of the different parts of a formal report.) When you cannot segment your writing this way, determine who your primary reader is, and make certain that you meet all of that reader's needs. Then meet the needs of your other readers only if you can do so without placing a burden on your primary reader.

For example, if your primary reader is an executive and your secondary reader is a technical specialist, you should not include a large amount of technical detail that would obscure the main points for the executive, even though the technical specialist might find such details of interest. Instead, you could include a brief section containing detailed technical information for the specialist without interfering with your message for the executive, especially if you label such a section "Technical Analysis," or something else appropriate.

Figures 3–3 and 3–4 are from a Technical Assessment report that describes the advantages to an organization of acquiring media streaming technology. The first part of the report (Figure 3–3) provides an overview of the topic for policymakers who may be unfamiliar with this technology and its uses. The second part (Figure 3–4) is targeted at technical experts who must understand the hardware and software requirements for the system.

**Figure 3–3
Introduction
to a Technical
Report for
a General
Audience**

Technology Assessment:
Media Streaming Technologies

This report was undertaken to demonstrate how the Office of the Chief Information Officer can improve the distribution of agency information and enhance communications with the staff, the nuclear industry, other federal agencies, the media, and the public by using media streaming technology. This report explains this emerging technology and its advantages to our organization, details the resources necessary to deploy it, and recommends a course of action to achieve these goals.

Media streaming is the receipt of audio and video broadcast media over the Internet at one's desktop computer. The advantages of providing this capability to the agency are threefold:

- Enhance the agency's ability to collaborate with the nuclear industries, the states, other federal agencies, the public, and other agency stakeholders.
- Provide desktop delivery of training, Commission meetings, public meetings at remote locations, staff safety programs, nuclear industry standards, and much else.
- Build partnerships with government and private-sector organizations.

This report provides no single solution to deploying media streaming technology. Agency requirements are not static and will require alternative configurations over time at headquarters and the regional offices.

Accordingly, the coverage includes necessary background information for decision-makers in the following areas:

- Business requirements for and cost of supporting media streaming technology.
- Technology cost alternatives based on a variety of agency program requirements.
- A new internal Web site focusing on media streaming technology to assist management and staff in determining how the technology can be used to improve agency programs and customer relations.

The report's overview of a technology new to an organization is aimed at the broadest possible audience. It is written with the assumption that decision-makers are unfamiliar with media streaming technology (MST) and need an introduction to what it is and what it can do. The section shown in Figure 3–4 occurs later in the report and is clearly aimed at a technical reader familiar with the details of the technology. Note the frequent use of technical terms and acronyms. The author assumes that technical readers in this field will be familiar with them. GIF and JPEG, for example, are abbreviations that refer to common formats for coding and exchanging graphics images on the Internet. This section also refers readers to detailed system cost information in an appendix to this report.

**Figure 3–4
Subsection of
a Technical
Report for a
Technical
Audience**

Architecture Overview

Real System G2 is a client-server application that delivers live and on-demand MST content across TCP/IP networks. The Real System architecture has three main components: Real Server, Real Player, and content publishing tools. Real Server streams live and on-demand Real Audio, Real Video, Real Flash animation, Real Pix (GIF and JPEG images), and Real Text content across the Internet and NGN. Real System G2 supports most other existing media file formats, such as ASF, AVI, JPEG, MPEG, VIV, and WAV. The Real Player is used on client workstations to play the MST content. Real System publishing tools, such as the Real Producer and Real System G2 Authoring Tool, are used to create MST content.

The Real Producer is used to convert audio and video source content into Real Audio and Real Video format. The Real Producer then sends the encoded Real Audio and Real Video content to the Real Server, where it is made available for live or on-demand access. The Real System G2 Authoring Kit is used to create Real Pix and Real Text content. Real System G2 uses Synchronized Multimedia Integration Language to define the layout and integration of various data types into a synchronized multimedia presentation. The MST architecture is described in Appendix A, "Cost Management Strategies."

■ A Sample Rough Draft

Figures 2–2 and 2–3 in Chapter 2 offer examples of outlines written for a sales brochure and an assembly manual for the Lifemaker home gym. Figure 3–5 shows a rough draft for the sales brochure. It follows the gist of the outline and uses many of the drafting techniques discussed in this chapter.

Nevertheless, the draft is quite rough—loosely organized, lacking in transitions and punctuation, ungrammatical, inconsistent in upper- and lowercase letters and point of view, and cluttered with jargon and unnecessary phrases. Still, as drafts go, this one reflects a strong start for the writer. Not only has she followed the basic organization of her outline, but she has managed also to work

---

DIGITAL SHORTCUTS: Writing a Rough Draft

When writing the draft, word-processing software will permit you to

- Record your ideas quickly by entering them as fast as you type.

- Sustain momentum as you write because there's no need to slow down for mechanical concerns such as line and page endings.

- Overcome writer's block by practicing freewriting — typing your thoughts as quickly as you can without stopping to correct mistakes or even to complete sentences.

**Figure 3–5
Rough Draft
of a Sales
Brochure**

Lifemaker: The Compact Exercise System You Can Afford

For opening—say something about how owning a Lifemaker will give you healthy bones and teeth, straighten your hair, improve your love life . . . no . . . Whether you are young or young at heart, male or female, developing well-conditioned muscles will help your body perform better, look better, and help you maintain an ideal level of fitness (Needs work!! Keep going, go back to it later. Get to the muscle of the matter.)

Description: The Lifemaker design more compact than leading competitor's, eliminates hassle and expense of going to health club to work out. The Lifemaker fits easily into small space—4 × 7 ft living room can accommodate the Lifemaker with more ease than many home gym systems, offers more stations and more exercises because of its multiple stations. What's the point I'm making? More compact than many fancy systems, offers 40 + exercises, more than most systems priced at a comparable level—comparably priced and sized systems. OK OK, don't compromise your exercise needs with an overpriced or ineffective system. The integration of an exercise program to suit your lifestyle and budget is possible with Lifemaker.

I'm writing all over the place and I sound like I'm making a coronation speech—don't pick, THINK. Headings, use headings you used in outline.

Cast-Iron Weight Stack

Dual weight stacks total 200 pounds of cast-iron plates. You can arrange stacks to offer a resistance range of 10 to 150 pounds and they are adjustable in 10-pound increments.

Adjustable Cables

Resistance can be increased—no—The unique cable system is engineered to increase resistance at the stations that work the strongest muscle groups. The cables can quickly be redesigned—restructured—reconfigured without taking apart the entire system. Just pulling the center rod permits adding or removing as many plates as needed.

The cable tension is also adjustable within sets to make sure that your muscles get the most resistance from each exercise for maximum efficiency and results.

(*Closing*) Heading? Low Maintenance—Easily Affordable
Best of all, no it's not best of all, think later about transition. . . . The Lifemaker is easy to assemble and requires little maintenance. And at $799.99, it is priced lower than the leading competitor.

Need to emphasize financial perks—mention low-interest monthly payment plan. Lifemaker will fit your back and your budget.

through so-called writer's blocks and to jot down the new idea of emphasizing financial incentives. She can now go on to write a second draft, develop an opening and closing that will help her tighten her focus, and then revise the entire document by using the techniques covered in Chapters 4 and 5. A marked-up version of a later draft of this memo, along with a revision, can be found in Figures 4–2 and 4–3 in Chapter 4.

WRITER'S CHECKLIST: Writing a Rough Draft

Use the following checklist to help you write better rough drafts:

☐ Set up your writing area with the equipment and materials (paper, dictionary, source books) you will need to keep going once you get started. Then hang out the "Do Not Disturb" sign.

☐ Use whatever writing tools, separately or in combination, that are most comfortable for you: pencil, felt-tip pen, or computer.

☐ Remind yourself that you are beginning a *draft* version of your writing project that no one else will read.

☐ Remember the writing projects you have finished in the past—you have completed something before and you will this time.

☐ Give yourself a boost by starting with the section that seems easiest or most interesting to you. Your reader will neither know nor care that you first wrote a section in the middle.

☐ Give yourself a time limit (10 or 15 minutes, for example) in which you write continually, regardless of how good or bad your writing seems to you. The point is to keep moving.

☐ Don't let anything stop you when you are rolling along easily; if you stop and come back, you may not regain the momentum.

☐ Stop writing before you're completely exhausted; when you begin again, you may be able to regain the momentum.

☐ Give yourself a small reward—a short walk, a soft drink, a short chat with a friend, an easy task—after you have finished a section.

☐ Reread what you have written when you return to your writing. Often, seeing what you have written will trigger the frame of mind that was productive.

■ Writing an Opening

As discussed earlier in this chapter, you do not need to begin your draft by writing the opening; however, understanding the purposes of an opening and the strategies for writing one can help you start the draft.

The opening statement of your writing should (1) identify your subject and (2) catch the interest of your reader.

Most readers of on-the-job writing are preoccupied with other business when they begin to read a memo, letter, report, or even an email message; therefore, it is a good idea to catch their interest and focus their attention on the subject you are writing about. Even if your readers are required to read what you've written, catching their interest at the outset will help ensure that they pay close attention to what follows. If you are attempting to persuade your readers, you must catch their interest if your writing is to succeed. The author of the Allen-Bradley newsletter article (see Figure 3–2) did this quite well.

To catch your reader's interest, you first must know your reader's needs (as discussed in Chapter 1). An awareness of those needs will help you to determine which details your reader will find important and thus interesting. Consider the opening from a memo written by a human resources manager to her supervisor (Figure 3–6). This opening not only states the subject of the report but also promises that the writer will offer solutions to a specific problem. Solutions to problems are always of interest to a reader.

Another, less-obvious problem is that of shaping the sales brochure for the Lifemaker home gym. According to the purpose of the memo, the reader is spending too much time and money working out at health clubs or has found home exercise machines oversized or inadequate. The Lifemaker System 40, with its compact design, multiple stations, and affordable payment plan, offers a solution. Thus, an initial revision of the brochure's opening section would not deal with the general benefits of exercise but should state the specific problem and solution as shown in Figure 3–7.

Figure 3–6 Problem-Solution Opening to a Memo

Memo

To: Paul Route, Corporate Relations Director
From: Sondra L. Rivera, Human Resources Manager *SLR*
Date: November 1, 20--
Subject: Decreasing Applications from Local College Graduates

This year only 12 local college graduates have applied for jobs at Benson Tubular Steel. Last year over 30 graduates applied, and the year before 50 applied. This decline in applications is occurring despite increasing enrollments at each school. After talking with several college counselors, I am confident that we can solve the problem of decreasing applications from local colleges.

First, we could resume our advertisements in local student newspapers. . . .

Lifemaker System 40
The Compact, Affordable Home Gym
Designed for Maximum Fitness Conditioning

Home gyms were designed to eliminate the hassle and expense of going to a health club to work out. But most home gyms are too bulky to fit either your home or your budget and do not offer a comprehensive workout program. The Lifemaker System 40 was designed to meet the needs of a limited living space and a limited budget and offers more exercises than the leading home system.

For most types of writing done in offices, shops, and laboratories, openings that simply get to the point are more effective than those that provide detailed background information. Furthermore, the subject of a memo or report is often, by itself, enough to catch the reader's interest. The openings shown in Figures 3–8 through 3–11 are typical; however, do not feel that you must slavishly follow these patterns. Rather, always first consider the purpose of your writing and the needs of your reader and then tailor your opening accordingly. Notice that all these openings get directly to the point; they do not introduce irrelevant subjects or include unnecessary details. They give the readers exactly what they need to focus their attention on what is to follow. (For examples of openings for special types of writing, such as application letters, complaint letters, and formal reports, refer to specific entries in the Index.)

Mr. George T. Whittier
1720 Old Line Road
Thomasbury, WV 26401

Dear Mr. Whittier:

You will be happy to know that we have corrected the error in your bank balance. The new balance shows . . .

William Chang, M.D.
Phelps Building
9003 Shaw Avenue
Parksville, MD 29099

Dear Dr. Chang:

To date, 18 of the 26 specimens you submitted for analysis have been examined. Our preliminary analysis indicates . . .

Progress Report on Rewiring the Sports Arena

The rewiring program at the Sports Arena is continuing ahead of schedule. Although the cost
of certain equipment is higher than our original bid had indicated, we expect to complete the
project without exceeding our budget because the speed with which the project is being
completed will save labor costs.

Work Completed

As of August 15th, we have . . .

Memo

To: Jane T. Meyers, Chief Budget Manager
From: Charles Benson, Assistant to the Director of Human Resources
Date: June 12, 20--
Subject: Budget Estimates for Fiscal Year 20--

The human resources budget estimates for fiscal year 20-- are as follows: . . .

■ Writing a Closing

A closing not only ties your writing together and ends it emphatically but also may make a significant point. A closing may recommend a course of action, offer a value judgment, speculate on the implications of your ideas, make a prediction, or summarize your main points. Even if your closing only states, "If I can be of further help, please call me" or "I would appreciate your comments," you are showing consideration for your reader and thereby gaining your reader's goodwill.

The way you close depends on the purpose of your writing and the needs of your reader. For example, the purpose of the sales brochure for the Lifemaker System 40 is to persuade the reader to purchase the system. The closing, then, could summarize the benefits described throughout the brochure and then cap the summary with a specific financial incentive.

■   Lifemaker, Inc., is offering this state-of-the-art, compact home gym for only $799.99. You can also purchase the Lifemaker System 40 on a monthly payment plan, because we believe that an exercise program should strengthen your back, not flatten your wallet. Call 1–800–933–7800 to talk with us about purchasing a Lifemaker today or visit our Web site for more information at http://www.lifemaker.com.

A document written with a different kind of purpose might be a report studying a company's annual sales; an effective closing for the report might offer a judgment about why sales are up or down. A report for a retail department store about consumer buying trends could end by speculating on the implications of these trends, perhaps even suggesting new product lines that the store might carry in the future. A lengthy report could end with a summary of the main points covered to pull the ideas together for the reader. Figures 3–12 through 3–16 show typical closings paired with the openings previously illustrated to provide a context.

A good closing is concise and ends your writing emphatically, making it sound finished. Any of the methods for closing can be effective, depending on the purpose of your writing and the needs of your reader. Be careful, however, not to close with a cliché or a platitude, such as "While profits have increased with the introduction of this new product, the proof of the pudding is in the eating" or "Please feel free to contact us at your earliest convenience," when the contents don't call for a response of any kind. Also be careful not to introduce a new topic in your closing. A closing should always relate to and reinforce the ideas presented in the opening and body of your writing.

Figure 3–12 Closing That Offers Help: Correspondence

Mr. George T. Whittier
1720 Old Line Road
Thomasbury, WV 26401

Dear Mr. Whittier:

You will be happy to know that we have corrected the error in your bank balance. The new balance shows . . .

Please accept our thanks for your continued business, and let us know if we can be of further help.

Sincerely,

Michael Fosse

Michael Fosse
Branch Manager

Figure 3–13 Closing That Recommends a Response: Progress-Report Letter

William Chang, M.D.
Phelps Building
9003 Shaw Avenue
Parksville, MD 29099

Dear Dr. Chang:

To date, 18 of the 26 specimens you submitted for analysis have been examined. Our preliminary analysis indicates . . .

These results indicate that you may need to alter your testing procedure to eliminate the impurities we found in specimens A through G, and K.

Sincerely,

Marion Lamb

Marion Lamb
Research Assistant

Progress Report on Rewiring the Sports Arena

The rewiring program at the Sports Arena is continuing ahead of schedule. Although the cost of certain equipment is higher than our original bid had indicated, we expect to complete the project without exceeding our budget because the speed with which the project is being completed will save labor costs.

Work Completed

As of August 15th, we have . . .

Although my original estimate on equipment ($20,000) has been exceeded by $2,300, my original labor estimate ($60,000) has been reduced by $3,500. Therefore I will easily stay within the limits of my original bid. In addition, I see no difficulty in having the arena finished in time for the December 23 Christmas program.

Memo

To: Jane T. Meyers, Chief Budget Manager
From: Charles Benson, Assistant to the Director of Human Resources
Date: June 12, 20--
Subject: Budget Estimates for Fiscal Year 20--

The human resources budget estimates for fiscal year 20-- are as follows . . .

Although our estimate calls for a substantially higher budget than in the three previous years, we believe that it is justified because of our need to recruit more information technology professionals.

Figure 3–16
Closing That
Summarizes
the Main
Points: Memo

Memo

To: Paul Route, Corporate Relations Director
From: Sondra L. Rivera, Human Resources Manager *SLR*
Date: November 1, 20--
Subject: Decreasing Applications from Local College Graduates

This year only 12 local college graduates have applied for jobs at Benson Tubular Steel. Last year over 30 graduates applied, and the year before 50 applied. This decline in applications is occurring despite increasing enrollments at each school. After talking with several college counselors, I am confident that we can solve the problem of decreasing applications from local colleges.

First, we could resume our advertisement in local student newspapers . . .

Second, we could restart our co-op program . . .

Third, we could participate in career-day programs . . .

Etc. . . .

As this report has indicated, we could attract more recent graduates by

1. increasing our advertising in local student newspapers
2. resuming our co-op program
3. sending a representative to career-day programs at local colleges and high schools
4. inviting local college instructors to teach in-house courses here in the plant and
5. encouraging our employees to attend evening classes at local colleges.

CHAPTER 3 SUMMARY: Writing the Draft

Gathering the details you need (see Chapter 1) and grouping them in an outline (see Chapter 2) will enable you to write a good rough draft. When writing the draft, remember that your task is to produce only a working document, not a polished piece of writing. Polish will come with revision (see Chapters 4 and 5).

   Use the following guidelines as you write the draft:

☐ Concentrate solely on getting the draft written.

☐ Do not confuse writing with revising; they are different tasks and each requires a different frame of mind.

☐ Avoid revising as you write—do not worry about perfection at this point in the writing process.

☐ Focus on *what* you are writing, not on *how* you are writing.

☐ Allocate your time efficiently.

☐ Prepare a comfortable work environment.

☐ Sustain momentum once you begin writing.

☐ Take brief breaks after reaching certain milestones.

☐ Keep your intended readers actively in mind, visualizing them if possible.

☐ Empathize with your readers, addressing your topic from their point of view.

☐ Role play with yourself as a teacher guiding your readers through your draft.

☐ Consider the voice your readers should hear—concerned, neutral, authoritative.

☐ Write an opening that identifies your subject to focus your reader's attention.

☐ Get to the point first, even when providing essential background information in the opening.

☐ Create closings that reinforce, summarize, or tie together the ideas in the body of your writing.

☐ Do not introduce ideas in the closing that have not been discussed elsewhere in your writing.

■ Exercises

1. Keep a log of your activities while drafting a document. Maintain the log for at least two writing sessions or, if time permits, for as many sessions as it takes to finish the draft. When the document is complete, review the log and write a brief assessment of your drafting process. Consider the following:
   a. Did you stop to revise often while you were drafting? If so, what kind of revision did you do, and what effect did it have on your progress?
   b. Did you find ways to procrastinate? How much did this hinder your progress?
   c. Did you experience interruptions that hindered you?
   d. Did you manage your time well with a workable self-imposed schedule?
   e. Was your writing environment conducive to good writing?
   f. Did you try any suggestions from this chapter?

2. If you have not already started drafting a class assignment, use the following focused freewriting technique to get started. Gather your resource material in a quiet place; your material may include a project plan, an outline, research notes, audience analysis, and so forth. Review your resource material and then focus on your role and voice as the writer who must communicate with a specific audience. To focus your thoughts on the larger needs of your audience, consider the audience in the section Establish Your Role and Voice as the Writer (page 69). After you've thought of the most important thing your audience wants to know, begin a focused freewrite on the subject by using the process described in this exercise. This process works especially well with a computer and a blank screen, but you can also use a pen and a pad of paper.
   a. You will have 15 minutes. Time yourself by setting a timer or alarm or by writing down the time you start and glancing at the clock.
   b. Write for 15 minutes without stopping about the most important thing your audience needs to know about your topic or document. If you are using the computer, turn the monitor brightness down so that you cannot see what you are writing.
   c. Write whatever pops into your head and write as fast as you can. If you can't think of anything to say, just keep writing "I can't think of anything to say" over and over until something else comes into your head.
   d. Don't pause to read what you have written; don't stop to correct or to revise. Just keep going forward.
   e. Don't worry about making mistakes or about writing incomplete sentences or paragraphs; just fill the screen or notepad with as much writing as possible while staying focused on the topic.
   f. When the time is up, finish your last thought and then stop. Take a break, and then come back to read what you've written. Consider the most important point you uncovered in the freewriting and where you need to go next. Focusing on your next point or idea, repeat the process. When done, repeat the process one more time. By now, you should have written several pages.
   g. Let your writing sit for a long period—at least overnight—and then reread what you've written. Write a brief assessment of the technique and turn in your assessment and freewriting to your instructor.

3. Write an opening paragraph for two of the following topics. The audience for each topic is specified in parentheses.

    a. My favorite instructor (to someone nominating him or her for a teaching award)

    b. Ways to improve employee motivation (to the president or head of the organization that employs you)

    c. Ways to improve student advising at your school (to the Dean of Students or someone in an equivalent position)

    d. What to look for in a first apartment (to a friend who is looking)

    e. Important features to consider when purchasing a new automobile, cellular phone, or personal computer (to a friend who is looking)

    f. The advantages of setting up your budget or checking account on your personal computer (to a spendthrift friend)

4. Write a closing for the same topics and readers.

5. With prior approval of your instructor, interview three people who write as a major part of their jobs, such as technical writers, attorneys, professors, managers, and reporters. Ask them about the techniques that they find especially useful in writing their first drafts. As directed by your instructor, report what you learn in writing or present your findings to the class.

6. Using the Lifemaker compact exercise system as your topic (see Figure 3–5), write three different opening paragraphs for a Lifemaker System 40 sales brochure geared toward each of the following audiences (one paragraph for each):
    a. college students
    b. retired persons
    c. industry executives

7. Using the Lifemaker compact exercise system as your topic (see Figure 3–5), write three different closing paragraphs for a Lifemaker System sales brochure geared toward each of the following audiences (one paragraph for each):
    a. college students
    b. retired persons
    c. industry executives

8. Summarize in a list all of the differences you had to be aware of when writing for different audiences and for different purposes in Exercises 6 and 7 (for example, time constraints, mobility constraints, and so forth).

9. For each of the following types of closings, describe a writing situation in which you might use that closing:
    a. polite, but helpful
    b. recommends response
    c. makes a prediction
    d. offers a judgment
    e. summarizes

10. Write a letter to a prospective student who is interested in learning more about your chosen course of study. Assume that this person is from your hometown and is considering the same plan of study and has inquired about specifics of the program. With your audience and purpose in mind, draft a letter that includes an effective opening, specifies important details in the body, and uses an appropriate closing. Use correct business-letter format when preparing your letter. (See Chapter 8 for format.)

11. Assume that your university is planning to exercise the power of eminent domain that was granted by the city council at the time the university was founded. The university is asking to purchase a block next door to the business school. A grocery store, a print shop, a snack shop, and two apartment buildings have all been asked to sell their properties to the university. The property owners feel their businesses would not survive farther from campus. Without knowing any more details, write a letter of support—either for the property owners who do not want to sell or in favor of the university, which feels expansion is necessary. After you have completed your letter, make a list of specific types of information that would have helped you write a more effective letter.

■ In-Class Activities

1. Your instructor has asked you as a class to make a recommendation to the Dean's office asking them not to schedule evening exams beginning after 8:00 P.M. The primary reason for this, according to your instructor, is campus safety. You are encouraged to brainstorm other reasons as well. Divide into small groups, refer to the Writer's Checklist: Thinking Like Your Reader (see page 68) and quickly (in approximately 15 minutes) prepare an outline of what your response as a group should be. During the next 30 minutes, each group will prepare a short memo explaining to the Dean's office why holding evening exams is not a good policy.

2. This activity may be completed in conjunction with In-Class Activity 1 during the same class session or the next class session.

   Have a spokesperson from each group read their group's memo to the class. The class will then vote on which memo to send to the Dean's office or perhaps will vote on the three most effective memos. (Later, the best elements of these memos can be merged into one document.) Then, in your small groups, analyze your own memo comparing it to the ones you heard from your classmates. Was your outline sufficient? Was your memo written for the correct intended reader (see page 67)? As a group, review your role and voice as writer. Did your opening identify your subject and catch the attention of the reader? Did it tie the writing together? Finally, analyze your closing. Discuss as a group what could have made your memo more effective.

3. As a class, discuss the Chapter 3 Summary guidelines on page 82. Be prepared to contribute to the discussion of the tasks on that list that are easy for you and those that are difficult and explain why. Make note of your classmates' comments that may be useful to you.

4. Divide into small groups and make a list of barriers to developing good writing habits. Refer again to the list of guidelines in the Chapter 3 Summary on page 82. As a group, make a list of suggestions for how to remove the barriers and develop good writing habits.

5. Bring to class an advertisement from a magazine for a personal computer, a wristwatch, a cellular phone, a fax machine, a copier, or a similar item. In 45 minutes or less, create an outline and then draft a brief narrative describing the product and its technology. The audience for your narrative is a person who knows nothing about this product.

Or, draft a letter or memo aimed at a particular type of consumer whom you would like to persuade to purchase this product. Begin by assessing your reader and creating a brief outline.

■ Research Projects

1. Research a business or technological advancement that you know nothing about. Narrow your topic to one particular aspect of that field and write a rough draft of a paper entitled "Recent Breakthroughs in _____ (a particular field): _____ (specific breakthrough)." For example, if you chose the field of medical science, your title and subtitle might be "Recent Breakthroughs in Cancer Treatment: The Risks and Benefits of Stem-Cell Research." Analyze the topic and support your analysis with information that you've researched. For example, if you decided to write about stem-cell research (or other current research), your analysis might be that the risks do or do not outweigh the benefits; you would then support your opinion with the findings that persuaded you.
   a. Submit a four- to five-page draft with an outline to your instructor.
   b. Meet with your instructor to discuss his or her suggestions for revision.
   c. Conduct further research if necessary.
   d. Write a second draft and do any further revisions necessary.
   Save this draft, as you will be asked to refer to it at the end of Chapter 4.

2. Gather three sales brochures that promote the same product or service—you may find the brochures on location at retail stores or other businesses, or receive them in the mail (many retail stores and other businesses have direct mailing campaigns).
   a. Write a two- to three-page paper in which you compare and contrast the *opening paragraph* of each brochure.
      • In the first part of your paper, address the following: Do the brochures differ in their purposes? Are they geared toward different audiences? Explain why you believe this is the case, supporting your analysis with examples from the brochures.
      • In the second part of your paper, address the following: Based only on the opening paragraph of each brochure, identify which brochure is your favorite and explain why. Be as specific as possible, supporting your choice with examples from the opening text of that brochure.
   b. Write a two- or three-page paper in which you compare and contrast the *closing paragraph* of each brochure. In your paper, address the questions in Research Project 2a, considering only the closing paragraph of the brochures.

3. Write your own sales brochure. You may use the same general topic you researched in Research Project 2, or you may select a different topic. Refer to the Chapter 3 Summary, remembering the importance of the opening and closing paragraphs. Begin by drafting an outline.

4. Gather samples of correspondence, brief articles, or reports, using books, newspapers, magazines, and materials that you receive in the mail. Find an example of each of the following types of closings:

a. polite, but helpful
b. recommends a response
c. makes a prediction
d. offers a judgment
e. summarizes

Based on the closing, what is the purpose of each writing sample that you have collected? What is the target audience for each? Support your conclusions with examples.

5. You have been invited to apply for a semester's paid tuition because of your interest in and dedication to your prospective field of study. All you need to do to apply for the funds is submit a letter describing the diversity of job opportunities in your field. After researching to find different job opportunities in your field, direct a letter to the "Job Diversity, Free Tuition Committee" in the Industrial Relations Department at your university. Include an effective opening, a variety of job possibilities in the body, and an effective closing.

■ Web Projects

1. Locate the Web site of at least three companies you are familiar with, such as Chrysler, Procter & Gamble, IBM, Apple, Dell, The Gap, or any other company of interest to your career. What information does the company's home page provide? For example, take note of the following:
   a. product information
   b. warranty information
   c. sales information for consumers
   d. employment information

   List the common purpose your companies have when providing information on the Internet. Choose one common type of information provided by all three companies—for example, product information at IBM, Apple, and Dell—and write an opening paragraph on that topic for each company.

2. Using the Internet and noting the URL addresses for later use, prepare an outline and write a draft of a report on a particular aspect of the U.S. 2000 Census. You may begin your search with the Census Bureau URL http://www.census.gov.

3. Using the Internet and noting the URL addresses for later use, prepare an outline and write a draft of a report on a particular project being carried out by a U.S. government agency. Or, write about specific research of a particular topic of interest that relates to a government agency. For example, you may want to write about the latest food recalls from the U.S. Department of Agriculture. You may begin your search with the U.S. government agency listing URL http://www.Lib.lsu.edu/gov/fedgov.html.

4. Using the Internet and noting the URL addresses for later use, research an individual in your field of professional interest whom you admire. Gather specific information that you find helpful—particularly any advice that the individual may have about writing on the job, giving presentations, or some other specific aspect of their work. What have you learned that may be helpful to you and your career?

Draft a paper in which you briefly describe that person's professional achievements; explain the relevance of those achievements to you; and detail the useful advice or information that you have gathered during your research. How might you apply this advice or information to your own career?

5. Using the Internet and noting the URL addresses for later use, find at least three companies who hire business or technical writers. For example, what companies in the area of medicine, technology, or advertising hire writers? What kinds of documents or other materials do writers for these companies produce? How would the information covered in Chapter 3 apply to the writing required by these companies? (To better answer this question, perhaps search the companies' Web sites for documents produced by their professional writers.) Prepare a brief draft of your reply.

4 Revising for Essentials

One of the enduring legends of American history is that President Abraham Lincoln wrote the Gettysburg Address as he made the train trip from Washington, D.C., to Gettysburg. The address is a remarkable accomplishment, even for a writer as gifted as Lincoln. It is the eloquent testimony of a leader with a powerful intellect and a compassionate heart.

The facts of how the Gettysburg Address was composed do not support the legend, however. Lincoln actually worked on the address for weeks and revised the draft many times.[1] What Lincoln was doing on the train to Gettysburg was nothing more than what any of us must do before our writing is finally acceptable: He was revising. What is remarkable about the address is that Lincoln made so many revisions of a speech of well under 300 words. Obviously, he wanted it to fit the occasion for which it was intended, and he knew that something written hastily and without reflection would not satisfy his purpose and audience.

This principle is as true for anyone who writes on the job (which, of course, is what the president was doing) as it was for Lincoln. Unlike the Gettysburg Address, however, most on-the-job writing should not strive for oratorical elegance; the more natural a piece of writing sounds to the reader, the more effort the writer has probably put into revising it.

■ Strategies

Have you ever found after writing a first draft that you knew it wasn't the best you could do, but that you did not know how to improve it? If your answer is yes, you are not alone. All writers—even professional writers—have the same problem at some time or another.

The problem has a simple explanation. Immediately after you write a rough draft, the ideas are so fresh in your mind that you cannot read the words, sentences, and paragraphs objectively. That is, you cannot sufficiently detach yourself from them to be able to look at the writing critically. To revise effectively, you must be critical. You cannot allow yourself to think, "Because my ideas are good,

---

[1]Tom Burnam, *The Dictionary of Misinformation* (New York: Perennial Library, 1986), pp. 93–94.

Voices from the Workplace

Dan Krick, Iams Company

Dan Krick is an organizational development specialist for the Iams Company, which manufactures pet food at four different plants throughout the United States. Dan is responsible for making sure that all the plant workforces are organized to the best advantage for the company's operations.

Dan writes many reports in his daily work. "I find that the trick is to put as much time as possible between writing the rough draft and revising it," he says. "The errors and awkward sentences seem glaringly obvious after a day or two, but they seem to be invisible immediately after I've written the rough draft."

Visit the Iams Company Web site at http://www.iams.com.

Entry-Level
Cara Feinberg, *The American Prospect*

As an editorial assistant for *The American Prospect* magazine, Cara Feinberg is usually responsible for the behind-the-scenes work: the research and fact checking, the proofreading, the correspondence with authors, and the coordination of projects.

Cara says, "Editing is a delicate process. The editing process usually becomes a balancing act, or a kind of bargaining session in which the editor suggests a change, the author resists the revision, and then, sentence by sentence, the two come to a compromise. Still, the editor has enough distance to spot errors easily or dispense with a wordy sentence without lamenting its demise. It is a cut-and-dry process based on several questions: Is the language precise? Is the work cogent? And, just as importantly in magazine publishing, does it fit within the space allotted?"

The American Prospect is available online at http://www.prospect.org.

the way I've expressed them must also be good." The first step toward effective revision, then, is to develop a critical frame of mind—to become objective.

As professional writers have learned, there are a number of ways to put distance between yourself and your writing and become objective.

1. Allow for a cooling period. Allow a period of time to go by between writing a rough draft and revising it. The ideas will not be as fresh in your mind then, and you can look at the writing itself more objectively. A cooling period of a day or two is best, but, if you are pressed for time, even a few hours will help.

2. Pretend that a stranger has written your draft. Because it is often easier to see faults in the work of others than in your own, pretend that you are revising someone else's draft. If you can look at your writing and ask, "How could I have written that?", you are in the right frame of mind to revise.

3. Revise in passes. Don't try to find everything that is wrong with your draft in only one pass through it. Make multiple passes. Make a first pass, looking at

only one aspect of your writing, such as organization. Then make another pass, looking at a different aspect of your writing, such as the problem of wordiness. Continue to make such passes, looking for different things or different sets of things each time, until you are satisfied with your draft.

4. Be alert for your most frequent problems. Be sure that you are aware of the errors you typically make, and watch for them as you revise. One of the benefits of taking a writing course is learning what your weak points are. Once you know what they are, you should work to overcome them, and searching for them during revision will help you do so.

5. Read aloud. Some people find that reading their rough draft aloud enables them to distance themselves from their writing so they can become more objective about it. Try this technique and see if it works for you. Be careful with this technique, however, because in reading aloud, you may provide meaning with your vocal inflections that is not actually there in the words.

6. Ask someone else to read and criticize your draft. Someone who is fresh to your draft can see it much more objectively than you can and is much more likely to be able to identify problems or problem areas. If your reader has trouble reading your work aloud, or if your reader cannot identify your purpose or your major points, then you'll know you have to revise the draft further.

Of course, you may discover your own methods of becoming objective. One student, for example, finds that she can be more critical if she writes her first draft on yellow paper. Another student creates his first draft on a computer because he cannot be critical when looking at his own handwriting. Some students like to revise with a felt-tip pen; others prefer using colored pencils. Experiment and find out what helps you. The particular methods that work for you are not important. What is important is that you develop some technique for becoming objective about your writing—and then use it.

■ Organization and Content

The more experienced you become as a writer, the more you will tend to view revision as a whole-text task involving changes to the overall structure and content of a piece of writing, as well as changes at the sentence level. The instructions about revising in passes in this chapter emphasize this point by indicating the sequence most commonly used by experienced writers in revising their drafts. They begin with the global issues—organization and scope of coverage—before proceeding to the details of grammar and punctuation.

The easiest way to test the soundness of your organization is to write an outline of your rough draft, a technique most useful for longer drafts but helpful with smaller ones, too. The advantage of doing so is that the outline boils down the blocks of text to the essential ideas and makes the sequence of these ideas easy to

> ### WRITER'S CHECKLIST: Reviewing Your Draft
>
> Use the following checklist to review your draft for these larger issues before proceeding.
>
> ☐ Is the purpose of the document clear?
>
> ☐ Is the information organized in the most effective sequence?
>
> ☐ Does each section follow logically from the one that precedes it?
>
> ☐ Is the scope of coverage adequate?
>
> ☐ Is there too little or too much information?
>
> ☐ Are all the facts, details, and examples relevant to the stated purpose?
>
> ☐ Is the draft written at the appropriate level for the reader?
>
> ☐ Are the main points obvious?
>
> ☐ Are subordinate points related to main points?
>
> ☐ Are contradictory statements resolved or eliminated?
>
> ☐ Do the descriptions and illustrations aid clarity? Are there enough of them?
>
> ☐ Are any recommendations adequately supported by the conclusions?
>
> ☐ Are any topics mentioned in the introduction also addressed in the conclusions?
>
> ☐ Are any topics discussed in the text also addressed in the conclusions?
>
> If the answer to any of these questions is "no," revise until the problem is resolved.

see. Does this outline conform to the outline from which you wrote the draft? It may not because you probably rethought some ideas or added or deleted information as you wrote. If you find a problem with the logic of the sequence or with the amount or type of information included or omitted, revise the outline—and then your draft—to reflect the solution.

A review of the relevant information in Chapters 1, 2, and 3 will be especially helpful as you reassess the effectiveness of your draft when it comes to these larger issues. Review the sections titled Establishing Your Scope and Organizing Your Ideas in Chapter 1. Further evaluate the logic of your organization by reviewing the material in Chapter 2 on testing the difference between major and subordinate ideas. See Chapter 3 for guidance on ensuring that you address the right audience in the right voice. Once you complete this review, you are ready to tackle the smaller, more detailed steps of the process described in the remainder of this chapter.

Chapter 5 describes the final revision stage. This stage encompasses paragraph unity, length, and coherence; knitting together the various components of your draft with a variety of transitional devices; and achieving emphatic writing—emphasizing important ideas and downplaying secondary ideas.

■ Accuracy and Completeness

Above all else, your information must be accurate. Although accuracy is important in all types of writing, it takes on special significance when you write on the job. One misplaced decimal point, for example, can create a staggering budgetary error. Incorrect or imprecise instructions can cause injury to a worker. At the very least, if your writing is not accurate you will quickly lose the confidence of your reader. He or she will be annoyed, for example, if a figure or fact in your writing differs from one in a chart or graph. These kinds of inaccuracies are easily overlooked as you write a first draft, so you must correct them during revision.

Revision is the time to insert any missing facts or ideas. When you finish your draft, check it against your outline. If any of the main ideas or supporting details you listed are missing from your draft, rewrite your sentences and paragraphs as necessary to incorporate the missing information.

In revising your draft for completeness, you may also think of new information that you failed to include when you were preparing and writing your draft. Always carefully consider such new information in the context of your reader and purpose. If the information will help satisfy your reader's need and accomplish the purpose of your writing, by all means add it now. However, if the information—no matter how interesting—does not serve these ends, it has no place in your writing.

DIGITAL SHORTCUTS: Revising Your Draft

You can perform the following revision tasks on screen and print out the results when you are satisfied.

- Print out a double-spaced copy of your draft. Viewed on the screen, it may look more polished than it is. Make notes and revisions on this draft before returning to the computer to enter the corrections.

- Copy or move blocks of text, such as phrases, sentences, paragraphs, or whole pages.

- Use the search and replace command to find and delete inappropriate diction such as *a lot;* wordy phrases such as *that is, there are, the fact that,* and *to be;* and unnecessary helping modifiers or verbs such as *very* and *will.*

- Use the search command to find technical terms and other data that may need further explanation for some readers and define them in the text or in a glossary.

- Use the spellchecker and other specialized programs to identify and correct typographical errors, misspellings, and grammar and diction problems.

- Maintain a file of your most frequently misspelled or misused words and use the search command to check for them in your documents.

■ Effective Sentences

An effective writing style communicates precisely, clearly, and concisely. To create such a style, review each sentence for the presence of several typical problems that can obscure precision, clarity, and conciseness: unconventional sentence structure, fuzzy subjects and verbs, and nominalizations. The normal word order in English is subject-verb-object: *Marketing research improved sales.* The majority of your sentences should follow this pattern, because your readers subconsciously expect that pattern.

An effective sentence also states the *doer* of the action in the subject of the sentence and the *action* in the verb. Although that advice may seem too simple to be necessary, business writing abounds in sentences that do not identify the doer of the action that is being expressed. Consider the following sentence from a training manual:

INCORRECT   This command enables sending the entire message again if an incomplete message transfer occurs.

This sentence contains no subject for the verb *sending.* The reader doesn't know who or what is doing the sending. (*This command* is the subject of *enables,* not *sending.*) Improve such a sentence by providing the missing subject:

CORRECT   This command enables you to send the entire message again if the message is incompletely transferred.

The doer of the action may also be buried someplace other than in the subject:

AMBIGUOUS   Decisions on design and marketing strategy are made at the *managerial level.*

For your style to be effective, you must make sure that the doer of the action is stated in your subject:

CLEAR   *Managers* make the decisions on design and marketing strategy.

CLEAR   *Managers* make design and marketing decisions.

Analyze your draft for *nominalizations,* which occur when you indicate the action of a sentence or clause with a noun (*to perform an audit*) instead of using the verb form of the noun (*to audit*). Although nominalizations are not grammatically wrong, their repeated use makes writing sluggish under the weight of all those formal-sounding nouns and redundant verbs. Whenever a sentence seems particularly fuzzy, look for the action being expressed; if it is expressed

ESL TIPS: Using Common Sentence Patterns

In English, using different sentence patterns helps to keep your reader interested. The five common patterns include the following:

1. **Subject + Verb**
   The meeting + began.
2. **Subject + Verb + Direct Object**
   The chairperson + began + the meeting.
3. **Subject + Verb + Subject Complement** (renames or describes the subject)
   The meeting + was + effective.
4. **Subject + Verb + Indirect Object + Direct Object**
   The secretary + gave + the accountant + the pay schedule.
5. **Subject + Verb + Direct Object + Object Complement** (renames or describes the direct object)
   The chairperson + considered + the merger + a success.

with a noun instead of a verb, try revising the sentence to state the action in a verb:

■   The Legal Department will ~~conduct an investigation of~~ *investigate* the charge.

■ Basics

Grammatical errors, like inaccurate facts or incomplete information, can confuse or irritate readers and cause them to lose confidence in you. Even worse, many of the errors discussed in this chapter are so severe that they can actually alter the meaning of a sentence. Therefore, it is essential that in revising your draft, you check for grammatical correctness.

Following is a summary of common grammatical errors. Each type of error is described briefly here and is then explained in detail in the Handbook section of the Writer's Guide. (See Section C, Handbook of Grammar, Punctuation, and Mechanics, pages 754–865, and Section D, English as a Second Language (ESL), pages 866–886.) If you find it helpful, use the following summary as a checklist for grammatical revisions.

Agreement

Agreement means that the parts of a sentence, like the pieces of a jigsaw puzzle, fit together properly. The following discussion beginning on page 97 points out the types of sentences in which problems of agreement often occur.

ESL TIPS: Determining Word Order

In English, word order is an important signaler of the meaning in a sentence. In the sentences "Jessica called Donald" and "Donald called Jessica," only the word order conveys who is doing the calling and who is getting the call. Here are some helpful generalizations for determining word order in English sentences.

Declarative sentences follow the subject-verb-object/complement word order.

- Edward arrived late this morning.

Interrogative sentences add a question word and invert the subject and the first auxiliary verb (auxiliary verb-subject-main verb-object).

- Will Edward arrive on time?

Adjectives precede nouns.

- *my* book
- *seven* files
- *contented* coworkers
- *angry* chairperson

Adverbs generally can be ordered depending on the other components of the sentence. An adverb is often placed at the end of the sentence.

- Edward arrived *late*.

An adverb should never separate a verb from its object.

immediately
- Edward phoned ~~immediately~~ his boss.

When adverbs of time, manner, and location are present, the adverb of time may appear at the beginning and adverbs of manner at the end of the sentence:

- *Tomorrow,* Edward will arrive *late at his office.*

or the adverbs of manner, location, and time may appear at the end:

- Edward will arrive *late at his office tomorrow.*

Frequency adverbs generally follow *be* or the first auxiliary verb and precede the main verb.

- Vacations are *always* too short.
- Vacations have *always* been assigned on the basis of seniority.
- Vacations *always* fly by too quickly.

Subject-Verb Agreement

A verb must agree with its subject in number. A singular subject requires a singular verb; a plural subject requires a plural verb. Do not let intervening phrases and clauses mislead you. (See Section 3.4.5 of the Writer's Guide.)

■ The *use* of insecticides, fertilizers, and weed killers, although they offer unquestion-

able benefits, often *result* in unfortunate side effects.

[The singular verb, *results,* must agree with the singular subject of the sentence, *use,* not with the plural subject of the preceding clause, *they.*]

Be careful not to make the verb agree with the noun immediately preceding it if that noun is not its subject. This problem is especially likely to occur when a modifying phrase containing a plural noun falls between a singular subject and its verb.

■ Only one of the emergency lights was functioning when the accident occurred.

[The subject is *one,* not *lights.*]

■ The advice of two engineers, one attorney, and three executives was obtained prior to making a commitment.

[The subject is *advice,* not *two engineers, one attorney, and three executives.*]

Words such as *type, part, series,* and *portion* take singular verbs even when such words precede a phrase containing a plural noun.

■ A series of meetings was held to decide the best way to market the new product.

Subjects expressing measurement, weight, mass, or total often take singular verbs even though the subject word is plural. Such subjects are treated as a unit.

■ *Four years is* the normal duration of the apprenticeship program.

ESL TIPS: Forming the Third-Person Singular Present Tense

In English, the third-person singular present tense must end in an *-s* or *-es.* The third-person singular is formed when the subject of the verb is either a singular noun or one of the following pronouns: *he, she,* or *it.*

The pronoun *you* in English is not a third-person pronoun and, therefore, does not require an *-s* or an *-es* on the verb.

■ He *walks* every day.
■ She *does* her homework.
■ You *walk* every day.
■ You *do* your work

However, when such subjects refer to the individual items that make up the unit, a plural verb is required.

■ If you're looking for oil, *three quarts are* on the shelf in the garage.

Similarly, collective subjects take singular verbs when the group is thought of as a unit and plural verbs when the individuals are thought of separately.

■ The *committee* is holding its meeting on Thursday.

[*Committee* is considered a unit.]

■ The *majority are* opposed to delivering their reports at the meeting.

[*Majority* is thought of as made up of separate individuals.]

A relative pronoun (*who, which, that*) may take either a singular or a plural verb depending on whether its antecedent (the noun to which it refers) is singular or plural.

■ He is an *employee* who *takes* work home at night.

■ He is one of those *employees* who *take* work home at night.

A compound subject is composed of two or more elements joined by a conjunction such as *and, or, nor, either . . . or,* or *neither . . . nor.* Usually, when the elements are connected by *and,* the subject is plural and requires a plural verb.

■ Chemistry and finance are prerequisites for this position.

A compound subject with a singular and a plural element joined by *or* or *nor* requires that the verb agree with the element nearest to it.

■ Neither the office manager nor the *accountants were* there.

■ Neither the accountants nor the office *manager was* there.

■ Either they or *I am* going to write the report.

■ Either I or *they are* going to write the report.

Pronoun-Antecedent Number Agreement

A pronoun must agree with its *antecedent,* the noun to which it refers, in number (singular or plural). (See Section 3.2.3a of the Writer's Guide.)

■ Although the typical engine runs well in moderate temperatures, *it* ~~they~~ often stall*s* in extreme cold.

ESL TIPS: Understanding Agreement of Pronouns and Antecedents

If you are a writer of English as a second language, make a special editing pass to check for agreement between pronouns and their antecedents. The following guidelines highlight where English differs from many languages regarding agreement of pronouns and antecedents.

The pronouns *he, she, it, his, hers,* and *its* must agree in gender with their antecedents, not with the words they modify.

INCORRECT	The lawyer won all its cases.
	[*Its* refers to *cases.*]
CORRECT	The *lawyer* won all *her* cases.
	[The pronoun *her* agrees with *lawyer.*]

Each and *every* take singular pronouns, even in compound antecedents.

- *Each* business has *its* own logo.
- *Every* book and article was included on the list with *its* title and date of publication.

All and *some* can take singular or plural pronouns, depending on whether the noun they modify is a count noun or a mass noun.

- *All* of the chocolate melted; *it* was stored near a furnace.
- *Some* of the prisoners escaped; *they* were left unattended.

A possessive pronoun agrees with the subject (*father*), not the object (*son*).

- The *father* watches *his* son.

The phrase *one of the* . . . takes a singular pronoun even though the noun that follows must be plural. The pronoun refers to *one.*

- *One* of the accountants lost *her* luggage.

The relative pronoun *who* is used for people; *which* and *that* are used for objects.

- The *man who* spoke at the shareholders' meeting is the company's largest investor.
- Mr. Geoff invests heavily in Exxon *stocks, which* have split twice in recent months.
- The boss wants the *folder that* he left on his desk.

Collective nouns rarely end in *-s,* but they take plural pronouns.

- Those *people* are interested only in seeing *their* investment grow.

Some singular nouns end in *-s,* but they take singular pronouns.

- The *United States* asked *its* allies to support the effort.

ESL TIPS: Understanding Agreement of Possessive Pronouns and Antecedents

In many languages, possessive pronouns agree in number and gender with the nouns they modify. In English, however, possessive pronouns agree in number and gender with their antecedents. Check your writing carefully for agreement between a possessive pronoun and the word, phrase, or clause that it refers to.

■ The woman brought ~~his~~ *her* brother a cup of soup.

[*Her* refers to *woman*.]

■ Robert sent ~~her~~ *his* mother flowers on Mother's Day.

[*His* refers to *Robert*.]

Pronoun-Antecedent Gender Agreement

A pronoun must also agree with its antecedent in gender—masculine, feminine, or neuter. (See Section 3.2.2b of the Writer's Guide.)

■ Mr. Lin in the accounting department acknowledges *his* responsibility for the misunderstanding, but Ms. Barkley in the research division should acknowledge *her* responsibility for *it* also.

Consistency of Person and Tense

Much like agreement errors, illogical shifts in person or tense can confuse the reader. You would be confused, for example, if someone wrote to you: "If you show the guard your pass, one will be allowed to enter the gate" (shift in person) or "When the contract was signed, the company submits the drawings" (shift in tense). Your confusion would disappear, however, if the sentences were revised as follows:

■ If you show the guard your pass, you will be allowed to enter the gate.

[consistent use of person]

■ When the contract was signed, the company submitted the drawings.

[consistent use of tense]

Person

Person refers to the forms of a personal pronoun that indicate whether the pronoun represents the speaker, the person spoken to, or the person (or thing) spoken about. If the pronoun represents the speaker, the pronoun is in the *first person*. (See Section 3.2.2a of the Writer's Guide.)

■ *I* could not find the answer in the manual.

If the pronoun represents the person or persons spoken *to,* the pronoun is in the *second person.*

■ *You* are going to be a good supervisor.

If the pronoun represents the person or persons spoken *about,* the pronoun is in the *third person.*

■ *They* received the news calmly.

Identifying pronouns by person helps you avoid illogical shifts from one person to another. A common error is to shift from the third person to the second person.

■ People should spend the morning hours on work requiring mental effort, because *their* ∧

~~your~~ mind ∧ ~~is~~ ∧ *s are* freshest in the morning.

■ Spend the morning hours on work requiring mental effort, because *your* mind is freshest then.

Tense

Tense refers to the forms of a verb that indicate time distinctions. A verb may express past, present, or future time. Be consistent in your use of tense; an unnecessary and illogical change of tense within a sentence confuses the reader. (See Section 3.4.3d of the Writer's Guide.)

ILLOGICAL   Before he *installed* the circuit board, he *cleans* the contacts.

This sentence, for no apparent reason, changes from the past tense (*installed*) to the present tense (*cleans*). To be both correct and logical, the sentence must be written with both verbs in the same tense.

CORRECT   Before he *installed* the circuit board, he *cleans* the contacts.
                                                           ed ∧

CORRECT   Before he *installed* the circuit board, he *cleans* the contacts.
                                    s ∧

The only acceptable change of tense within a sentence records a real change of time.

■ After you *have assembled* Part A [past tense, because the action occurred in the past], *assemble* Part B [present tense, because the action occurs in the present].

Dangling Modifiers

Modifiers are words that describe, explain, or qualify an element in a sentence. They can be adjectives, adverbs, phrases, or clauses. A dangling modifier is a phrase that does not clearly refer to another word or phrase in the sentence. As you will see in the next section, misplaced modifiers can result in ambiguity; dangling modifiers, by contrast, result in illogical sentences. (See Section 4.3.4d of the Writer's Guide.)

ILLOGICAL   While eating lunch in the cafeteria, my computer experienced a power surge and shut down.

Although the idea of a computer eating lunch in a cafeteria is ridiculous, that is what the sentence actually states. With the dangling modifier corrected, the sentence reads as follows:

CORRECT   While *I* was eating lunch in the cafeteria, my computer experienced a power surge and shut down.

Dangling modifiers are often humorous, as in the first example, but they can also cause such confusion that your reader misinterprets the meaning of your sentence completely.

One way to correct a dangling modifier is to add a noun or pronoun for the phrase to modify.

■   After finishing the research,   *we found that*   the job was easy.

[The phrase *after finishing the research* has nothing to modify without the pronoun *we* that tells the reader who finished.]

■   Having evaluated the feasibility of the project, the   *committee unanimously approved the*   centralized plan. ~~was unanimously approved.~~

[The noun *committee* tells the reader who approved the plan.]

■   As I was keeping busy,   *I felt that*   the afternoon passed swiftly.

[Who was keeping busy?]

A dangling modifier can also be corrected by making the phrase a clause.

ILLOGICAL   After finishing the research [phrase], the job was easy.

CORRECT   *After we finished the research* [clause], the job was easy.

ILLOGICAL   Having evaluated the feasibility of the project [phrase], the centralized plan was unanimously approved.

CORRECT   *Once the committee had evaluated the feasibility of the project* [clause], the centralized plan was unanimously approved.

ILLOGICAL	Keeping busy [phrase], the afternoon passed swiftly.
CORRECT	*Because I kept busy* [clause], the afternoon passed swiftly.

Misplaced Modifiers

Another source of ambiguity occurs in the placement of modifiers. The simple modifiers most likely to create ambiguity are *only, almost, just, hardly, even,* and *barely.* When you use one of these terms in a sentence, be sure that it modifies the word or element that you had intended it to. In most cases, place the modifier directly in front of the word it is supposed to qualify. (See Section 4.3.4d of the Writer's Guide for a more extensive discussion of modifiers.)

■   Katrina Lloyd was the *only* engineer at Flagstead Industries.

[The sentence says that Flagstead has one engineer, and she is Katrina Lloyd.]

■   Katrina Lloyd was *only* the engineer at Flagstead Industries.

[The sentence says that Katrina Lloyd holds a position at Flagstead no higher than that of engineer.]

■   Anna Jimenez *almost* wrote $1 million in insurance policies last month.

[The sentence says that although Anna Jimenez came close to writing $1 million in insurance policies, she didn't actually do so.]

■   Anna Jimenez wrote *almost* $1 million in insurance policies last month.

[The sentence says that Anna Jimenez wrote nearly $1 million in insurance policies last month—a very different matter.]

Misplaced phrases can also cause problems. As with simple modifiers, place phrases near the words they modify. Note the two meanings possible when the phrase is shifted in the following sentences:

■   The equipment *without the accessories* sold the best.

[Different types of equipment were available, some with and some without accessories.]

■   The equipment sold the best *without the accessories.*

[One type of equipment was available, and the accessories were optional.]

Either of these sentences could be correct, of course, depending on the meaning the writer intends.

A third type of misplaced modifier is a *misplaced clause.* To avoid confusion, clauses should also be placed as close as possible to the words they modify.

CONFUSED	We sent the brochure to four local firms *that had three-color illustrations.*
CLEAR	We sent the brochure *that had three-color illustrations* to four local firms.

A different kind of ambiguous modifier is the squinting modifier—a modifier that could be interpreted as qualifying either the sentence element before it or the sentence element following it.

■   We agreed *on the next day* to make the adjustments.

The reader doesn't know which of the following possible interpretations the writer intended.

MEANING 1   *On the next day* we agreed to make the adjustments.

MEANING 2   We agreed to make the adjustments *on the next day*.

Sentence Problems

A number of errors can make a sentence ungrammatical. The most common such errors are sentence fragments, run-on sentences, and sentences with comma errors.

Fragments

A sentence that is missing an essential part (*subject* or *predicate*) is called a *sentence fragment*. (See Section 4.3.4c of the Writer's Guide.)

SENTENCE   He quit his job.

                   [*He* is the subject; *quit his job* is the predicate.]

FRAGMENT   And left for Australia.

                   [The subject is missing.]

Having a subject and a predicate does not automatically make a group of words a sentence, however; the word group must also make an independent statement. *If I work* is a fragment because the subordinating conjunction *if* turns the statement into a dependent clause.

ESL TIPS: Understanding the Basic Requirements for a Sentence

■ A sentence must start with a capital letter.
■ A sentence must end with a period, a question mark, or an exclamation point.
■ A sentence must have a subject.
■ A sentence must have a verb.
■ A sentence must express an idea that can stand on its own (called the main or independent clause).
■ A sentence must conform to subject-verb-object word order (or inverted word order for questions or emphasis).

ESL TIPS: Understanding the Subject of a Sentence

In English, every sentence, *except* commands, must have an explicit subject.

> *He established*
> ■ *Ozzie* worked fast. ~~Established~~ the parameters for the project.
>   ^
>
> [*He* is the subject.]

In commands, the subject *you* is understood and is used only for emphasis.

> ■ Wait!
>
> [*You* is understood.]

> ■ Show up at the airport at 6:30 tomorrow morning.
>
> [*You* is understood.]

> ■ *You* do your homework, young man.
>
> [parent to child]

The subject of a sentence can be a noun (*the office*), a pronoun (*he*), a noun clause (*what the manager reported*), a gerund (*working*), or an infinitive (*to attend*).

> ■ *The office* was closed because of Martin Luther King Day.
> ■ *He* offered to work on the project over the weekend to meet the deadline.
> ■ *What the manager reported* did not agree with the director's report.
> ■ *Working* late made the employees angry.
> ■ *To attend* the conference was a wonderful opportunity.

The subject of an English sentence may be a noun or a pronoun but not both at the same time.

INCORRECT   *The meeting it* was adjourned.

CORRECT   *The meeting* was adjourned.
             or
             It was adjourned.

If you move the subject from its normal position (subject-verb-object), English often requires you to replace the subject with an expletive (*there, it*). In this construction, the verb agrees with the subject that follows it.

> ■ *There are* two files on the desk.
>
> [The subject is *files*.]

> ■ *It is* presumptuous for me to speak for Jim.
>
> [The subject is *to speak for Jim*.]

(continued)

> ## ESL TIPS (continued)
>
> Time, distance, weather, temperature, and environmental expressions use *it* as their subject.
>
> - *It* is ten o'clock.
> - *It* is ten miles down the road.
> - *It* never snows in Florida.
> - *It* is very hot in Jorge's office.
> - *It* gets very stuffy in here very quickly.

Sentence fragments are often introduced by relative pronouns (such as *who, whom, whose, which,* and *that*) or subordinating conjunctions (such as *although, because, if, when,* and *while*). The presence of any one of these words should alert you to the fact that what follows is a dependent clause, not a sentence, and must be combined with a main clause.

SENTENCE FOLLOWED BY FRAGMENT	The new manager instituted several new procedures. *Many of which* are impractical.
	[*Many of which* must be linked to *procedures.*]
SENTENCE	The new manager instituted several new procedures, many of which are impractical.

A sentence must contain a main, or finite, verb. *Verbals,* which are forms derived from verbs but different in function, do not perform the function of a main verb. (See Section 3.4.2b of the Writer's Guide.) The following examples are sentence fragments because they do not contain main verbs.

FRAGMENT	*Providing* all employees with hospitalization insurance.
SENTENCE	The company provides all employees with hospitalization insurance.
FRAGMENT	*To work* a 40-hour week.
SENTENCE	The new contract requires all employees to work a 40-hour week.
FRAGMENT	The customer *waiting* to see you.
SENTENCE	The customer waiting to see you is from the Labatronics Corporation.

Fragments usually reflect incomplete and sometimes confused thinking. The most common type of fragment is the careless addition of an afterthought.

SENTENCE FOLLOWED BY FRAGMENT	These are my coworkers. A fine group of people.
SENTENCE	My coworkers are a fine group of people.

Run-on Sentences

A *run-on sentence,* sometimes called a *fused sentence,* is made up of two or more independent clauses (sentence elements that contain a subject and a predicate and could stand alone as complete sentences) not separated by punctuation. (See Section 4.3.4b of the Writer's Guide.)

INCORRECT   The new manager instituted several new procedures some were impractical.

Run-on sentences can be corrected in the following ways:

1. Create two separate sentences.

CORRECT   The new manager instituted several new procedures. Some were impractical.

2. Join the two clauses with a semicolon if they are closely related.

CORRECT   The new manager instituted several new procedures; some were impractical.

3. Join the clauses with a comma and a coordinating conjunction.

CORRECT   The new manager instituted several new procedures, but some were impractical.

4. Subordinate one clause to the other.

CORRECT   The new manager instituted several new procedures, some of which were impractical.

5. Join the two clauses with a conjunctive adverb preceded by a semicolon and followed by a comma.

CORRECT   The new manager instituted several new procedures; however, some were impractical.

■ Preciseness

The following sign once hung on the wall of a restaurant.

CUSTOMERS WHO THINK OUR WAITERS ARE RUDE
SHOULD SEE THE MANAGER

After several days, the sign was removed because customers continued to chuckle at the sign's unintended suggestion: that the manager was even ruder than the waiters.

In the case of the sign, of course, the customers understood the point that the restaurant owner had wanted to make. However, in many types of job-related communication—a report or a letter, for instance—the reader may have difficulty deciding which of several possible meanings the writer had intended to convey. When a sentence (or a passage) can be interpreted in two or more ways and the writer has given the reader no clear basis for choosing from among the alternatives, the writing is ambiguous. Such lack of preciseness is a common source of miscommunication in on-the-job writing.

ESL TIPS: Understanding the Importance of Directness

The writing style in English is direct and linear, which means the writer gets to the main point as quickly as possible, supports the point with specific evidence, and provides a clear transition to move smoothly to the next point. Direct writing can be achieved by using precise words, simple sentence structure, and clear explanations. Each word in a sentence should have a specific purpose. By following the direct strategy, the writer presents the information in an easy-to-understand format and acknowledges the importance of the reader's time.

Precise writing is so clear that your reader should have no difficulty understanding exactly what you want to say. In checking for precision, look for three likely trouble spots that may lead to misinterpretation by your reader: faulty comparisons, unclear pronoun reference, and imprecise word choice.

Faulty Comparisons

When you make a comparison, be sure that your reader understands what is being compared.

FAULTY   Ms. Jones values rigid quality-control standards more than Mr. Johnson.

            [Does Ms. Jones value the standards more than she values Mr. Johnson, or does she value the standards more than Mr. Johnson values them?]

CORRECT   Ms. Jones values rigid quality-control standards more than Mr. Johnson does.

When you compare two persons, things, or ideas, be sure they are elements that can logically be compared with each other.

FAULTY	The *accounting textbook* is more difficult to read than *office management.*
	[A textbook cannot logically be compared with a field of study.]
CORRECT	The *accounting textbook* is more difficult to read than the *office management textbook.*

Unclear Pronoun Reference

A *pronoun* is a word that is used as a substitute for a noun. The noun for which the pronoun substitutes is called its *antecedent.* Using a pronoun to replace a noun eliminates the monotonous repetition of the noun. When you use a pronoun, though, be sure that your reader knows which noun the pronoun refers to. If you do not clearly indicate what word, or group of words, a pronoun stands for, your reader may be uncertain of your meaning. When you revise your sentences to correct unclear pronoun references, look especially for three types of errors: ambiguous reference, general (or broad) reference, and hidden reference. (For a further discussion of pronoun reference, see Section 3.2.3b of the Writer's Guide.)

In an ambiguous reference, there is uncertainty as to which of two or more nouns a pronoun is referring.

AMBIGUOUS	Studs and thick treads make snow tires effective. *They* are installed with an air gun.
	[*What* are installed with an air gun—studs, treads, or snow tires? The reader can only guess.]
CLEAR	Studs, which are installed with an air gun, and thick treads make snow tires effective.
	[Now it is clear that only *studs* are installed with an air gun.]
AMBIGUOUS	We made the sale and delivered the product. *It* was a big one.
	[Does *It* refer to the sale or to the product?]
CLEAR	We made the sale, which was a big one, and delivered the product.
	[Now it is clear that the *sale,* not the *product,* was a big one.]
AMBIGUOUS	Jim worked with Tom on the report, but *he* wrote most of it.
	[*Who* wrote most of the report, Tom or Jim?]
CLEAR	Jim worked with Tom on the report, but Tom wrote most of it.
	[Now it is clear that *Tom,* not *Jim,* wrote most of the report.]

In a general (or broad) reference, the pronoun—which is frequently a term such as *this, that, which,* or *it*—does not replace an easily identifiable antecedent. Instead, it refers in a general way to the preceding sentence or clause.

TOO GENERAL	He deals with social problems in his work. *This* helps him in his personal life.
	[The pronoun *This* refers to the entire preceding sentence.]
IMPROVED	Dealing with social problems in his work helps him in his personal life.
TOO GENERAL	Mr. Bacon recently retired, *which* left an opening in the accounting department.
	[The pronoun *which* refers to the entire preceding clause.]
IMPROVED	Mr. Bacon's recent retirement left an opening in the accounting department.
	[Revising the sentence to eliminate the pronoun makes the meaning clear.]

The third cause of unclear pronoun reference is the hidden reference. In sentences that contain a hidden reference, the antecedent of the pronoun is implied but never actually stated.

UNCLEAR	Despite the fact that our tractor division had researched the market thoroughly, we didn't sell *many*.
	[Many what? The pronoun *many* has no stated antecedent in the sentence. The writer assumes that the reader understands that *many* refers to *tractors*.]
IMPROVED	Despite the fact that we had thoroughly researched the market for *tractors*, we didn't sell *many*.
	[Now the pronoun *many* has an antecedent, *tractors*.]
IMPROVED	Despite the fact that our tractor division had researched the market thoroughly, we didn't sell many *tractors*.
	[Revising the sentence so that *many* becomes an adjective modifying *tractors* makes the meaning clear.]

Imprecise Word Choice

As Mark Twain once said, "The difference between the right word and almost the right word is the difference between 'lightning' and 'lightning bug.'" Precision requires that you choose the right word. (See Section B, Part 2, Vocabulary, of the Writer's Guide.)

When you write, be alert to the effect that a word may have on your reader—and try to avoid words that might, by the implications they carry, confuse, distract, or offend your reader. For example, in describing a piece of machinery that your company recently bought, you might refer to the item as *cheap*—meaning inexpensive. However, because cheap often suggests "of poor quality" or "shoddily made," your reader may picture the new piece of equipment as already needing repairs.

In selecting the appropriate word, you will want to keep in mind the context—the setting in which the word appears. Suppose you call the new machine "inexpensive" or "moderately priced." Your reader may ask, "What does the writer mean by inexpensive?" A desktop computer at $2,000 might be inexpensive; a small printing press at $80,000 could also be a good buy. The exact meaning of inexpensive would depend on the context. For readers who are unfamiliar with the cost of heavy machinery, it might be surprising to learn that an $80,000 press was reasonably priced. It would be up to you, the writer, to provide your readers with a context—to let them know, in this case, the relative costs of printing equipment.

The context will also determine whether a word you choose is specific enough. When you use the word *machine,* for instance, you might be thinking of an automobile, a lathe, a cash register, a sewing machine—the variety of mechanical equipment we use is almost endless. *Machine,* in other words, is an imprecise word that must be qualified, or explained, unless you want to refer in a general way to every item included in the category *machine.* If you have a particular kind of machine in mind, then you must use more precise language.

■   *network printers*
   The maintenance contract covers all ~~the machines~~ in Building D.

Depending on the context, you might need to choose a term even more specific than network printers. Figure 4–1 illustrates just how specific a particular context might require you to be. The terminology goes from most general, on the left, to most specific, on the right. Seven levels of specificity are shown; which one would be appropriate depends on your purpose in writing and on the context in which you are using the word.

For example, a person writing a company's annual report might logically use the most general term, *assets,* to refer to all the property and goods owned by the firm: Shareholders would probably not expect a further breakdown. Interoffice memos between the company's accounting and legal departments would appropriately call the firm's holdings *real estate* and *inventory.* To the company's inventory-control department, however, the word *inventory* is much too broad to be useful; a report on inventory might contain the more specific categories *equipment* and *parts in stock.* To the assistant inventory-control manager in charge of equipment, that term is still too general; he or she would speak of several particular

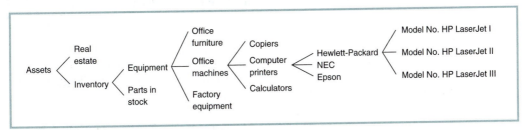

Figure 4–1   Example of Increasing Specificity

kinds of equipment—*office furniture, office machines,* and *factory equipment.* The breakdown of the types of office machines for which the inventory-control assistant is responsible might include *copiers, computer printers,* and *calculators.*

However, even this classification wouldn't be specific enough to enable the company's purchasing department to obtain service contracts for the normal maintenance of its printers. Because the department must deal with different printer manufacturers, printers would have to be listed by brand name: *Hewlett-Packard, NEC,* and *Epson.* The Hewlett-Packard technician who performs the maintenance must go one step further and identify each Hewlett-Packard printer by model number. As Figure 4–1 shows, a term may be sufficiently specific at one of the seven levels—but at the next level it becomes too broad. Your purpose in writing and your intended reader will determine how specific you should be.

Purpose and audience may sometimes require a general rather than a specific term. To include printer model numbers in a company's annual report, a detailed parts list in a sales brochure, or highly technical language in a letter to the accounting department would, of course, be inappropriate. In all the writing you do, you must decide what your purpose is and who your reader will be, and then select a term that is neither too general nor too specific for the context.

Remember that you must sometimes define terms for your reader. Suppose you are making a proposal to your boss, who must pass your proposal along to his or her boss for final approval. You may be using terms that your boss's superior will not recognize because you work with details that will be unfamiliar to someone interested in only the big picture. If you want your proposal to be approved, you should do everything you can to make your ideas readily understandable. In some cases, you may define specific terms; in others, you may prefer to omit specialized terms and write at a more general level.

ESL TIPS: Using a Thesaurus

The English language has many words to express a thing or an idea. Sometimes it is difficult to choose the exact word to best represent a thought, so a thesaurus may be used. A thesaurus is a helpful tool for a writer because it lists numerous words with similar meanings. A word of caution: If you choose a word from a thesaurus, be sure to also check it in a dictionary. Not all words in a given thesaurus entry are exact synonyms of the word you looked up, and therefore will not be correct choices. Remember: simple words are often the best choice.

How you define the terms that need explanation depends on the context. It may often be sufficient to give a brief explanation, in everyday language, of a technical or specialized term.

- The property includes approximately 1,700 feet of waterside (land bordering a body of water).

Or you may find it easiest to provide an extended definition to familiarize readers new to a specialized term.

■ Our Web site's new search engine will permit Boolean searching capabilities. That is, it will permit *and* searches for two or more key words, *or* searches when something is referred to in more than one way, *not* searches to exclude certain terms, and *proximity* searches of terms near other terms in a string of text, like a sentence or title.

Sometimes it may be necessary to provide a formal definition of a word. (See Chapter 7 for a complete discussion of formal definition.) To write such a definition, place the term in a category and show how the term differs from other members of that category.

■ A lease [*term*] is a contract [*category*] that conveys real estate for a specified period of time at a specified rent [*how* a lease *differs from other contracts*].

■ Style

Revising for style means examining the ways you have expressed your ideas. Key stylistic elements include conciseness and precision in your use of language and presenting your information in the appropriate point of view.

Conciseness

Conciseness is freedom from unnecessary words. The more concise your writing, the more effective it will be. Wordiness, as well as stilted or pretentious language, can place a barrier between writer and reader by making your ideas difficult to understand. You can achieve conciseness by eliminating words that do not contribute to your meaning and expressions that are too fancy or obscure. Do not confuse a short sentence with a concise one; long or short, a wordy sentence is always less readable because of the extra load it carries. As you revise your writing, be particularly alert for three types of wordiness: *redundancy,* or the use of words that only repeat the meaning of something already stated (*round circle* is an example of redundancy); *padded phrases,* which express in several words an idea that could easily be said in one (*due to the fact that* for *because* is an example of a padded phrase); and *affectation,* the senseless inflation of language to make a message sound more important than it really is (*peruse the text* for *read a book* is an example of affectation).

Redundancy

When a modifying word, phrase, or clause adds no new information to what a sentence already says, the modifier is redundant.

■ To complete the circuit, join the wires ~~together~~ with solder.

    [The word *together* repeats the thought contained in the word *join.*]

■ Contemporary students ~~today~~ consider work experience to be as valuable as class-room attendance.

[The word *today* repeats the thought expressed by the word *contemporary.*]

■ Our imported products ~~which come from abroad,~~ all have limited warranties.

[Because all *imported products* are manufactured *abroad,* the clause is not needed.]

■ We moved the storage cases into the empty warehouse ~~which had nothing in it.~~

[An *empty* warehouse is understood to have nothing in it.]

When they are selected carefully, modifiers—whether adjectives, adverbs, prepositional phrases, or subordinate clauses—can make the words they describe vivid and specific. Modifiers to avoid are those that simply repeat the idea contained in the word they modify. Study the following list of redundant expressions to sharpen your ability to spot this kind of wordiness.

blue ~~in color~~

to resume ~~again~~

square ~~in shape~~

brief ~~in duration~~

to plan ~~ahead~~

tall ~~high-rise~~

basic ~~essentials~~

small ~~in size~~

descended ~~down~~

to attach ~~together~~

visible ~~to the eye~~

to cooperate ~~together~~

Padded Phrases

When an idea that could be stated in one word is buried in an expression that takes several words—and is no clearer than the single word—a padded phrase results.

■ The contractor will issue regular progress reports *while* ~~during the time that~~ the contract is in effect.

■ I recently met with the city attorney *about* ~~with reference to~~ your case.

■ We missed our deadline *because of* ~~due to the fact that~~ a strike ~~was in progress~~ at the company that manufactures and supplies our parts.

- We cannot accept new clients at ~~the~~ present ~~time~~.

  about
- We have received four complaints ~~in connection with~~ the project.

  To
- ~~In order to~~ meet the deadline, we must work overtime.

- She was thinking ~~in terms~~ of subcontracting much of the work.

There are times, however, when longer wording is desirable to clarify meaning.

- *In terms of* gross sales, the year has been successful; *in terms of* net income, however, it has been discouraging.

Expressions such as these must be evaluated individually. If the expression does not contribute to the meaning of the sentence, use its simpler substitute.

A half-dozen terms are particular villains of wordiness. When they occur, examine your work critically for padded phrases. The words are *case, fact, field, factor, manner,* and *nature.*

  Students often
- ~~In many cases, students~~ profit from writing a term paper.

  [Sometimes it is necessary, when revising a sentence, to shift the location of the modifier.]

- I was not certain ~~of the fact~~ that your cousin is a steelworker.

- I have been interested in ~~the fields of~~ drafting and electronics for several years.

- Speed is also ~~an~~ important ~~factor~~ in the cause of the accident.

  unsafely
- The pallets were stacked ~~in an unsafe manner~~.

  controversial
- The committee seldom considered grievances ~~of a controversial nature~~.

Affectation and Plain Language

Affectation is language that is more technical or showy than necessary to communicate information. It creates a smokescreen that the reader must penetrate to discover the writer's meaning. The following example is all-too-common in job-related writing. A company needs to tell employees about its policy for personal phone calls during the workday.

INFLATED   It is the policy of the company to provide the proper telephonic appa-
LANGUAGE   ratus to enable each employee to conduct the interoffice and intrabusi-
               ness communication necessary to discharge his or her responsibilities;
               however, it is contrary to company practice to permit telephones to be

	utilized for personal employee communications. Coin-operated apparatus in the building lobby may be used for personal communications.
PLAIN LANGUAGE	Your telephone is provided for company business; do not use it for personal calls. Instead, use the pay phones in the lobby for personal calls.

Most people would have to read the first version of the sentence several times before deciphering its message. The meaning of the revised version, which uses direct, simple, and precise language, is evident at a glance.

In recent years, consumer interest groups, lawmakers, and businesses have become concerned about the problem of affectation and legal-sounding language in insurance policies, contracts, government regulations, and other writing. As a result, many states have created "plain English laws," which require that documents be written in clear, understandable language. The federal government also now requires that all its new regulations be written in plain language. The following passages show how "legalese" can be converted into plain language.

INFLATED LANGUAGE	I hereby authorize the above repair work to be done along with the necessary material, and hereby grant you and/or your employees permission to operate the car or truck herein described on streets, highways, or elsewhere for the purpose of testing and/or inspection.
PLAIN LANGUAGE	You have my permission to make repairs listed on this work order and to use the necessary materials. You or your employees may drive my car or truck to test its performance.

In the revised version, notice the absence of the legal-sounding phrases: *I hereby authorize, hereby grant, herein described, the above repair work,* and *and/or.* Notice that when it is translated into straightforward English, the statement gains in clarity what it loses in pomposity. The following example is shown exactly as it appears in company literature given to potential investors.

INFLATED LANGUAGE	NO PERSON HAS BEEN AUTHORIZED TO GIVE ANY INFORMATION OR MAKE ANY REPRESENTATION OTHER THAN THOSE CONTAINED OR INCORPORATED BY REFERENCE IN THIS JOINT PROXY STATEMENT/PROSPECTUS, AND, IF GIVEN OR MADE, SUCH INFORMATION OR REPRESENTATION MUST NOT BE RELIED UPON AS HAVING BEEN AUTHORIZED.
PLAIN LANGUAGE	Rely only on the information contained in this document or that we have referred you to. We have not authorized anyone to provide you with information that is different.

The plain-language version uses everyday words, shorter sentences, and eliminates the hard-to-read capital letters of the original.

In your own writing,

- Avoid obscure and pretentious words (*discharge responsibilities, aforesaid, hereto,* and so on).
- Eliminate trendy words or phrases such as *factoid, infomercial, right-sizing, solution* (used to mean *product*).
- Do not use big, imprecise words as a substitute for simple, well-thought-out language.
- Take a critical look at what you've written to see whether any of the wording should be deflated—replaced with clearer, shorter, down-to-earth words and phrases.

Consider the following example:

INFLATED LANGUAGE	The Model 3211 is a solution that provides the capability of performing the printing and binding functions to produce documents on demand in one effortless, seamless process.
PLAIN LANGUAGE	The Model 3211 can print and bind documents in one integrated process.

The first sentence reads like an important pronouncement. Stripped of its pretentious phrases, however, it is actually a simple statement.

You can also help your readers by eliminating strings of nouns used as modifiers.

INFLATED LANGUAGE	Your *staffing level authorization reassessment* plan should result in a major improvement.
PLAIN LANGUAGE	Your plan to reassess authorizations for staffing levels should result in a major improvement.

In the first example, the noun *plan* is preceded by four modifiers. Such strings, known as *jammed modifiers,* impede the reader, who must wonder when the noun being modified will appear.

Technical Terminology

Technical terms are standard, universally recognized words used in a particular field to refer to specific principles, processes, or devices. Unlike the legalese and overblown language discussed in the previous section, technical terms are useful and sometimes essential in communicating clearly and concisely. For example, the term *divestiture* has a specific, generally understood meaning among readers who are familiar with management strategies. Similarly, the term *logic gate* would be understood by readers who have studied computer science or

> ## WRITER'S CHECKLIST: Avoiding Affectation
>
> If you know the possible reasons for affectation, you will be taking the first step toward avoiding it. The following list addresses the most common reasons for affected writing—review and revise your document if you recognize any of the following in your writing:
>
> ☐ *Impression.* One reason writers use pretentious language is that they wish to impress the reader. Attempts to create an impression begin in school, when students try to impress their teachers with fancy words instead of evidence and logic. Later, an employee may want to impress superiors or clients with how well he or she performs on the job.
>
> ☐ *Insecurity.* Writers who are insecure about their facts, conclusions, or arguments may try to protect themselves with a smokescreen of pretentious words.
>
> ☐ *Imitation.* Perhaps unconsciously, some writers imitate poor writing they see around them. In one company, for example, everyone referred to himself or herself in memos as *the writer* instead of *I*. Each new person who joined the company unthinkingly followed the style until the president of the company noticed the practice and told the employees that they could refer to themselves with the normal *I*.
>
> ☐ *Intimidation.* A few writers, consciously or unconsciously, try to intimidate or overwhelm their readers with words—often to protect themselves from criticism. Such writers seem to feel that the best defense is a good offense.
>
> ☐ *Initiation.* Those who have just completed their training for an occupation often feel that one way to prove their professional membership is to use technical terminology and jargon as much as possible. Usually, after a few years pass and the novice feels respected by coworkers, the impulse for affectation passes. Readers of their writing, however, wish the process did not take so long.
>
> ☐ *Imprecision.* Because a writer is having trouble being precise, he or she may find that an easy solution is to use a vague but trendy, pretentious word. It is easier to say "the policy will have a positive impact upon the department" than to explain precisely how the policy will affect the department, for example.

electrical engineering. If you are certain that all your readers (and potential readers) will understand a technical term, use it to ensure precision. If you are at all uncertain, however, define the term in plain language when you first use it. If your readers are unlikely to understand the concept that a technical term represents, you should explain the concept, perhaps including easy-to-understand examples. Although digressing into an explanation is not as efficient as simply using a technical term, your goal of making your writing easily understandable should be paramount.

Jargon

Jargon is highly specialized technical slang that is unique to an occupational group. If all your readers are members of a particular occupational group, jargon (like technical terminology) may provide a time-saving and efficient means of communicating with them. For example, if you were writing to a computer software developer, you could use the term *interface* and be understood. A computer *interface* is a boundary across which data or information flows (such as a computer screen); an *interface* can also be software that links a computer with the commands or images that allow communication between the computer and its user.

Jargon enters the language for a variety of reasons. Common words that already have established meanings in everyday speech are sometimes applied to new concepts and devices. For example, *access*—a noun meaning the ability to enter, approach, communicate with, or pass to or from—has always been part of our language. However, as a transitive verb meaning to get at something, such as a computer file, *access* should be used only in that context. So although you can access a computer file, you cannot access a novel. Understandably, the developers of new concepts and devices, in their need to name their creations, rarely have time for elegance. This technical shorthand is not a satisfactory substitute for everyday language outside the field in which it is standard.

Yet another type of jargon is used to define occupations euphemistically. Tactfulness dictates that if you are writing to an undertaker and must refer to his occupation, you should use the term *funeral director*. For similar reasons, a garbage collector is frequently called a *sanitation worker*.

A type of jargon that is indefensible is the useless elongation of standard words. Frequently, one hears *analyzation, summarization,* and *notation;* the correct words are *analysis, summary,* and *note.* The additions to such words do not make them mean anything more precise; they make them both incorrect and long-winded.

When jargon becomes so specialized that it applies only to one company or subgroup of an occupation, it is referred to as "shop talk." For example, an automobile manufacturer might produce a "pollution-control valve—Model LV-20." In the department where the device is built, it may be referred to as an "LV-20." Obviously, shop talk is appropriate only for those familiar with its special vocabulary and should be reserved for speech, informal memos, and email messages within a company.

Sexist and Racist Language

Sexist language can be an outgrowth of sexism—the arbitrary stereotyping of men and women in their roles in life. Sexism can breed and reinforce inequality. To avoid sexism in your writing, treat men and women equally, free of assumptions and stereotypes about traditional roles. Not all secretaries, nurses, and elementary school teachers are women any more than all police officers, soldiers, and physicians are men. Our language should reflect this reality. Accordingly, use nonsexist occupational descriptions in your writing.

Change	To
fireman	firefighter
salesman	salesperson
chairman	chair, chairperson
foreman	supervisor
telephone lineman	telephone installer
stewardess/steward	flight attendant
waitress/waiter	server
cameraman	photographer, videographer, camera operator
mailman	letter carrier
manpower	staff, personnel, workers

These guidelines should apply equally to the use of parallel terms to describe men and women.

Change	To
man and wife	husband and wife
Ms. Jones and Bernard Weiss	Ms. Jones and Mr. Weiss, Mary Jones and Bernard Weiss
ladies and men	ladies and gentlemen, men and women

Sexism can also creep into your writing by the unthinking use of male pronouns where a reference could apply equally to a man or a woman.

■   *Everyone* may stay or go as *he* chooses.

One way to avoid this usage is to rewrite the sentence in the plural.

INCORRECT   Every *employee* will have *his* supervisor sign *his* attendance slip.

CORRECT   All *employees* will have *their* supervisors sign *their* attendance slips.

Be careful not to change the pronoun to the plural and leave its antecedent in the singular. The pronoun and its antecedent must always agree.

INCORRECT   An *auditor* can expect to advance on *their* merit.

CORRECT   *Auditors* can expect to advance on *their* merit.

Other possible solutions are to use *his or her* instead of *his* alone or to omit the pronoun completely if it isn't essential to the meaning of the sentence.

INCORRECT	*Everyone* must submit *his* expense report by Monday.
CORRECT	*Everyone* must submit *his or her* expense report by Monday.
CORRECT	*Everyone* must submit *an* expense report by Monday.
CORRECT	All expense reports must be submitted by Monday.

He or she can become monotonous when constantly repeated, and a pronoun cannot always be omitted without changing the meaning of a sentence. The best solution, then, is the first one—to use the plural whenever possible.

Likewise, do not use racial or ethnic stereotyping in your writing. In fact, identifying people by race or ethnicity is simply not relevant in most contexts. Telling readers that a physician is Pakistani or that a professor is African American almost never conveys useful information. Of course, there are contexts in which race or ethnicity matters and should be identified. If you are writing about your firm's hiring practices for an Equal Employment Opportunity Commission report, then the racial composition of the workforce is relevant. If you sell food products and services to regional restaurants, the mix of ethnic cuisines at the restaurants you serve matters greatly to your business. In this case, your correspondence and reports would appropriately reflect this mix.

Point of View

Some writers feel that, especially in job-related writing, it is immodest or inappropriate to use the first-person point of view—that is, to speak of themselves as *I* or *me*. They believe that their material will sound more objective or businesslike if they refer to themselves in the third person (using such terms as *the writer, this technician,* or *this reporter*) or if they use the passive voice. Writing of this sort tends to sound stuffy and unnatural, however. In most cases, your message will be clearer and easier to follow if you speak of yourself in the first person.

■   *I*
     ~~The technician~~ will complete the wiring and test the system at the end of June.

■   *I performed all the*
     ~~The~~ tests described in the attached report ~~were all performed by the writer~~.

Also, in on-the-job writing, avoid the use of *one* as a pronoun because it is inexact, indirect, and pretentious. The use of *one* does not make your writing more objective; it merely makes a statement sound impersonal, almost as if some nameless, formless being, rather than you yourself, were expressing an idea or making a suggestion.

■   *I*
     ~~One~~ can only conclude that the new valves are not effective on the old fire trucks.

> ### ESL TIPS: Understanding the Importance of Stating an Opinion
>
> In some cultures, stating an opinion in writing is considered impolite or unnecessary, but in business writing in the United States, readers expect to see a writer's opinion stated clearly and assertively. The opinion should be supported by specific examples to help the reader understand the writer's point of view.

The use of an impersonal *it is* expression to avoid the pronoun *I* has the same kind of stuffy effect as *the writer* and *one*.

- *I regret*   *we cannot accept*
  ~~It is regrettable~~ that ˄ the material shipped on the 12th ~~is unacceptable~~.

The revised sentence is more direct and suggests that the writer is not trying to avoid responsibility for what he or she has stated.

Some writers, looking for ways to make their work sound more authoritative or more serious, introduce expressions such as *It should be noted that* or *I am inclined to think that* in their writing. Such expressions only add wordiness.

- *The*
  ~~It should be noted that~~ ˄ the gaskets tend to turn brittle after six months in the warehouse.

- I ~~am inclined to~~ think that each manager should attend the meeting to hear the committee's recommendations.

The more natural your writing sounds, the more effectively it will communicate.

◼ Mechanics

Comma Errors

The most common punctuation problem is misuse of the comma. This is understandable because the comma has such a wide variety of uses: It links, it encloses, it separates, and it indicates omissions. (For a complete discussion of the comma, see Section 5.1 of the Writer's Guide. Other marks of punctuation are covered there as well.) The following guidelines will help you to use the comma correctly and effectively.

When two independent clauses are joined with only a comma, the error is known as a comma splice. (See Section 5.1.6a of the Writer's Guide.) Like a run-on sentence, which also contains improperly connected clauses, a comma splice can be corrected in several ways:

1. Join the two clauses with a comma and a coordinating conjunction.
2. Subordinate one clause to the other.
3. Join the two clauses with a semicolon if they are closely related.
4. Join the two clauses with a conjunctive adverb preceded by a semicolon and followed by a comma.
5. Create two separate sentences.

INCORRECT　　　It was 500 miles to the facility, we made arrangements to fly.

　　　　　　　　　[comma splice]

CORRECT　　　It was 500 miles to the facility, so we made arrangements to fly.

　　　　　　　　　[comma plus coordinating conjunction]

CORRECT　　　Because it was 500 miles to the facility, we made arrangements to fly.

　　　　　　　　　[one clause subordinated to the other]

CORRECT　　　It was 500 miles to the facility; we made arrangements to fly.

　　　　　　　　　[semicolon]

CORRECT　　　It was 500 miles to the facility; therefore, we made arrangements to fly.

　　　　　　　　　[semicolon, conjunctive adverb, comma]

CORRECT　　　It was 500 miles to the facility. We made arrangements to fly.

　　　　　　　　　[two sentences]

When correcting a comma splice, be sure that the solution you choose correctly conveys the intended meaning of the original sentence.

Do not place a comma everywhere you pause. Although commas usually signal pauses, *pauses do not necessarily call for commas.* A number of common errors involve placing commas where they do not belong. (See Section 5.1.6b of the Writer's Guide.)

Do not place a comma between a subject and its verb or between a verb and its object.

INCORRECT　　　The cold conditions, made accurate readings difficult.

　　　　　　　　　[The comma incorrectly separates the subject, *conditions,* from its verb, *made.*]

CORRECT　　　The cold conditions made accurate readings difficult.

INCORRECT　　　He has often said, that one company's failure is another's opportunity.

　　　　　　　　　[The comma incorrectly separates the verb, *said,* from its object, *that one company's failure is another's opportunity.*]

CORRECT　　　He has often said that one company's failure is another's opportunity.

Do not place a comma between the two parts of a compound subject or a compound predicate.

INCORRECT
The director of the Engineering Department, and the supervisor of the quality-control section were both opposed to the new schedules.

[The comma incorrectly separates the parts of the compound subject, *director* and *supervisor*.]

CORRECT
The director of the Engineering Department and the supervisor of the quality-control section were both opposed to the new schedules.

INCORRECT
The director of the Engineering Department listed five major objections, and asked that the new schedules be reconsidered.

[The comma incorrectly separates the parts of the compound predicate, *listed five major objections* and *asked that the new schedules be reconsidered.*]

CORRECT
The director of the Engineering Department listed five major objections and asked that the new schedules be reconsidered.

In most cases, do not place a comma after a coordinating conjunction such as *and* or *but*.

INCORRECT
The chairman formally adjourned the meeting, but, the members of the committee continued to argue.

[The word *but* is part of the second clause and should not be separated from it by a comma.]

CORRECT
The chairman formally adjourned the meeting, but the members of the committee continued to argue.

INCORRECT
I argued against the proposal. And, I gave good reasons for my position.

[The word *and* is part of the second sentence and should not be separated from it by a comma.]

CORRECT
I argued against the proposal. And I gave good reasons for my position.

Do not place a comma before the first item in a series or use a comma to separate a final adjective from its noun.

- We are considering a number of new products, such as/handheld PCs, flat panel speakers, and digital cameras.

- It was a fast, simple, inexpensive/process.

Spelling Errors

Use your computer spellchecker as a first step to finding spelling errors. The software will locate misspelled words, repeated words (*the the*), words with numbers instead of letters (*will* with two *1*'s rather than two *l*'s), and common errors in capitalization made during keying (*THere* for *There*). Spellcheckers typically rely on a 100,000- to 200,000-word dictionary to compare against each word of your text.

Although the spellchecker is an important tool for on-screen proofing, it cannot identify whether you meant *their* or *there* in a given context. It recognizes both words as correctly spelled and so will pass over each whenever it occurs, regardless of whether you intended one instead of the other. It will not help you with numbers or the special characters in chemical or mathematical equations. You still must print a paper copy of your document and proof it carefully to catch all keying mistakes. (Section B of the Writer's Guide provides instructions that will strengthen your knowledge of English spelling conventions.)

■ Two Revised Drafts

Figures 4–2 and 4–3 show two drafts of the sales brochure that was outlined and drafted in Chapters 2 and 3. In Figure 4–2, the writer has taken her second draft and, after allowing for a cooling-off period, critiqued her work, using the main points covered in this chapter as her guide. Figure 4–3 shows a revised version of

**Figure 4–2
Draft Sales
Brochure
Marked for
Revision**

The Lifemaker System 40
The Compact, Affordable Home
Gym Designed for Maximum
Fitness Conditioning

Home gyms were designed to eliminate the hassle and expense of going to a health club to work out, but most of them are too bulky and awkward to fit either your budget or your wallet. The Lifemaker System 40 was designed for limted living space, a limited budget, and maximum fitness needs.
sp

Compact Design

too much jargon The Lifemaker's multiple stations provide a technologically sophisticated strength training program, and is architecturally configured for minimal space and maximal efficiency. At 4 fett wide and 7 feet long, your living room can *misplaced modifier*
missing pronoun and verb
sp

(continued)

**Figure 4–2
(continued)**

page 2

easily accommodate the Lifemaker with more ease than many home systems.
At the same time, the Lifemaker offers more stations and more exercises.

Point of view

faulty comparison

Move
this ¶ to
intro-
duction

One need not compromise your exercise needs with an oversied or ineffective system. Our home gym lets you integrate a complete home exercise
system into your available space and your budget.

sp

Cast-Iron Weight Stack

*need direct
object "of
plates"*

agreement

*too vague
"can be
adjusted in
5, 10, 15
pound
increments"*

not
true!!

The dual cast-iron weight stacks totals 200 lbs. Which can be arranged to
offer a resistance range of 10 to 150 pounds. In addition, Lifemaker offers
the only weight system on the market that can be adjusted in multipul
increments.

sp

Adjustable Cables

*missing subject-
verb agreement*

too
much
jargon;
too
vague

The Lifemaker's unique cable system allows quick reconfiguring of the
weight stacks without taking apart the entire system. Just pulling the center
rod and one can add or remove as many plates as you need. The cable tension can also be adjusted to make sure your muscles are working against all
the possible resistance in each exercise to increase reflexor capacity and
resistance ability.

*verb
agreement;
point of
view*

Easy Assembly and Maintenance

sounds
awkward

redundant

You can assemble the Lifemaker yourself in under an hour; we even include
all the tools needed for assembly. The system requires little maintenance and
upkeep; simply check all parts each time you exercise and tighten cable ten-
sions. You can clean the system by wiping all parts with a damp cloth; unlike
most other systems, no special cleaning fluids or oiling is necessary.

*not true!! most systems don't
require special treatment*

Easy Affordability

make more
personal
"is pleased
to offer
you . . ."

Lifemaker, Inc. is offering this state-of-the-art, compact home gym at only
$799.99. All parts carry a two-year guarantee, and replacement parts can be
shipped to you in under 24 hours by calling our 800 number.

*dangling modifier and
sounds wrong — "within
24 hours
of placing
an order."*

add bit
about talking
to service rep

For a limited time, you can also purchase the Lifemaker System 40 on a no-
interest monthly payment plan, because at Lifemaker, Inc., we believe that an
exercise system should strengthen your back, not flatten your wallet.

**Figure 4–3
Final Sales
Brochure**

The Lifemaker System 40
The Compact, Affordable Home Gym
Designed for Maximum Fitness Conditioning

Home gym systems were designed to eliminate the hassle and expense of working out at a health club, but most systems take up too much space and can injure both your budget and your back. The Lifemaker System 40 offers a solution to the problem of oversized, overpriced, and ineffective home gyms, because Lifemaker was designed to fit a limited living space, a limited budget, and maximum fitness requirements. Purchasing a Lifemaker System 40 will let you integrate a complete weight and cable exercise system into your living space and your budget.

Compact Design

The Lifemaker's comprehensive strength-training program is designed to occupy minimal space. The system offers more than 40 exercise combinations, but because it measures only 4 feet wide and 7 feet long, Lifemaker will fit easily into almost any room.

Multiple Stations

Three workout stations let you move through your conditioning program as efficiently as if you owned a roomful of weight and cable machines. In addition, the multiple stations are designed so that two people can work out at the same time.

Cast-Iron Weights

The Lifemaker features dual weight stacks totaling more than 200 pounds of cast-iron plates. The dual stacks offer a resistance range of 10 to 150 pounds; resistance can be adjusted in 5-, 10-, or 15-pound increments.

Adjustable Cables

A unique cable system allows you to reconfigure the dual weight stacks without taking apart the entire system. Simply pull the rod located between the stacks and you can add or remove as many plates as you need for a particular exercise. The cable tension can also be adjusted to increase or decrease the amount of resistance within exercise sets.

Easy Assembly, Easy Maintenance

The Lifemaker System 40 can be assembled in less than an hour; no special tools are needed for assembly. You can maintain the Lifemaker in good condition simply by wiping down the system with a damp cloth; no oiling or scrubbing of parts is ever necessary. All parts carry a two-year guarantee and can be shipped to you within 24 hours of your placing an order.

Easy Affordability

Lifemaker, Inc., is pleased to offer you this state-of-the-art, compact home gym for only $799.99. You can also purchase the Lifemaker on a low-interest monthly payment plan. Call (800) 555-1212 and we will be happy to arrange a plan that works with your financial needs. At Lifemaker, Inc., we believe that owning a home gym system should strengthen your back, not flatten your wallet.

the draft. Notice that the writer has not simply made mechanical, sentence-level corrections to her work. Instead, she used her marginal comments to revise the structure and organization as well as its sentences.

CHAPTER 4 SUMMARY: Revising for Essentials

Use the following revision checklist to help you remember the various aspects of revision that this chapter has covered. Refer to this list both before and after you write the final draft of any document; fix any problems before your reader sees them.

- ☐ Have I allowed a cooling period?
- ☐ Is my content complete and accurate?
- ☐ Does the subject of each sentence accurately identify the doer of the action expressed in the verb?
- ☐ Are all nominalizations eliminated?
- ☐ Do all subjects and verbs agree in number?
- ☐ Do all pronouns and their antecedents agree in number and in gender?
- ☐ Are verb tenses accurate and consistent?
- ☐ Have I eliminated any dangling or misplaced modifiers?
- ☐ Are all sentences complete and properly punctuated?
- ☐ Is the language precise, unambiguous, and free of jargon, sexist language, and ethnic stereotyping?
- ☐ Have I removed all redundancy, padding, and affectation?
- ☐ Is the point of view appropriate and consistent?
- ☐ Have I eliminated all comma errors?
- ☐ Are all the words spelled correctly?

■ Exercises

1. Each of the following sentences contains a faulty comparison. Rewrite each sentence to eliminate the error.
   a. The copier equipment in the direct-mail department operates more efficiently than the customer relations department.
   b. The production manager expressed greater appreciation for the temporary help than the sales manager.
   c. Julia Valenti, the human resources manager, felt that the applicant was better qualified than Charles Crane, the director of administrative services.
2. Each of the following sentences contains a squinting modifier—that is, a modifier that may qualify either of two elements within the sentence. Locate the squinting modifier and rewrite the sentence in two ways.

    a. The transformer that was sparking violently shocked the line operator.

    b. The accountant who was making budget calculations hastily rose from the desk and left the room.

    c. After the committee decided that the work must be completed by Monday, in spite of other commitments, it adjourned immediately.

    d. He planned after the convention to take a short vacation.

3. Each of the following sentences contains an unclear pronoun reference. Rewrite the sentences as necessary to eliminate the errors.

    a. Many members complained that their representatives made decisions secretly without considering them.

    b. The crane operator did not file a safety grievance and does not plan it.

    c. Our company decided to relocate in Grandview Hills, after rejecting Westville and Dale City, which was a difficult decision to make.

    d. Anita has held positions in two insurance companies and in an auto-rental firm, and it should help her in finding a new job.

    e. Ms. Jardina wanted to meet with her assistant, Ms. Sanfredini, but she was unable to do so until after lunch.

    f. If you feel that you would like to become a dental hygienist, by all means take a course in it.

    g. The movie star smashed a bottle of champagne over her stern as she slid gracefully into the sea.

    h. They keep the streets clean in Auburn Hills.

    i. This is the friend of Professor Loup, who lives in Binghamton.

    j. For those of you who have small children and don't know it, we have a nursery downstairs.

    k. We can't recommend that Mr. Sedirko go to Mr. Anderson's office uninvited because he is so unkind.

    l. If washing machines have been tearing your fine linens and laces, let us do it for you by hand.

4. Each of the following sentences contains a faulty pronoun-antecedent agreement. Rewrite each sentence to eliminate the error.

    a. Everyone did their own work.

    b. Either the president or the managers will do their best to help you.

    c. Any customer who writes to us should have their letter answered promptly.

    d. Either of the companies has the right to exercise their option to sell stock.

    e. The engineering staff is moving their facilities on Friday.

    f. One of our sales managers, along with several salespeople, is planning his retirement.

    g. Neither Jackie nor Kim wanted their desk removed.

    h. Either James or Leroy will have their work reviewed next week.

    i. Every customer has a right to expect their inquiries to be treated courteously.

5. Each of the following sentences contains at least one padded phrase. Rewrite each sentence to eliminate such phrases.

    a. We began the project in the month of April.

    b. He opened the conversation with a reference to the subject of inflation.

    c. The field of engineering is a profession that offers great opportunities.

    d. The process was delayed because of the fact that the chemicals were impure.

e. The human resources manager spoke to the printing-plant supervisor with regard to the scheduling of employee vacations.
f. Due to the fact that Monday was a holiday, we will not be able to complete the job until Wednesday.
g. We want to suggest to you that first and foremost you pack each and every basic essential.
h. Final completion of the research investigation study revealed and showed that the UFO is small in size, triangular in shape, and purple in color.
i. I am of the opinion that in the majority of instances the event is held during the month of December.

6. In each of the following sentences, select the correct word or words from the two items in parentheses. In some sentences, the choice involves the correct pronoun; in other sentences, it involves the correct verb. After adjusting for agreement, you may need to revise several sentences further to avoid sexism.
   a. The supervisor asked each employee to decide whether (he/they) wanted to work overtime to finish the project.
   b. Her job during the negotiations (was/were) to observe and then report her observations to the manager.
   c. Our line of products (is/are) sold in the West and in the Midwest.
   d. Neither John nor Peter remembered to submit (his/their) work on time.
   e. The Association of Corporate Employees failed because (they/it) never received full support from the member companies.
   f. Any employee who has not completed (his/their) time sheet must do so now.
   g. A number of beneficial products (has/have) resulted from the experiment.
   h. Anyone in (their/his) right mind can see that these figures are contradictory.
   i. A staff member is held responsible for any errors that (he or she/they) may introduce.

7. Revise the following sentences to correct any errors in agreement. The errors may be in subject-verb agreement or in pronoun-antecedent agreement.
   a. A survey of residents in the selected communities show a large potential market for our product.
   b. After each of the passages are translated, the report is given to the Office of Policy Analysis.
   c. The committee is planning to submit their recommendations before the end of the week.
   d. The course instructs students in the basics of the subject and provides him with hands-on time.
   e. A project engineer must be able to justify the changes they make in a technician's drawing.
   f. Every one of the passengers were waiting in line quietly.
   g. Neither of your responses seem satisfactory.
   h. The report and the letter was on my desk.
   i. Either the report or the letter were on my desk.
   j. Neither the report nor the letter were on my desk.
   k. Both Sara's story and Ben's story sound true.
   l. Neither Sarah's story nor Ben's story sounds true.
   m. Every battery, radio, and antenna are missing.
   n. Everything that was in the garages are gone.
   o. Many a fortune have been made and then lost.

8. Each of the following sentences contains either a dangling modifier or a misplaced modifier. Locate the errors and correct them. Add any necessary words.
   a. An experienced technician, the company was anxious to hire her.
   b. Before taking the training course, it is recommended that each operator read the Safe Operation Manual.
   c. After evaluating the 38 answers, the test was found by the production manager to reveal a serious deficiency.
   d. Hoping to be promoted for her contribution to the project, the vice-president's report represents three months of work.
   e. We purchased the store's inventory that was going out of business.
   f. We are going to install an ergonomic desk chair for our assistant with a rigid back.
   g. Having misunderstood the assignment, my paper got a low grade.
   h. Exhausted after 14 hours of driving, the Denver exit was a welcome sight.
   i. Having stood in the oily marinade for six hours, you are now ready to grill the meat.
   j. Painstakingly repairing the damaged web, I marveled at the spider's skill and patience.
   k. Approaching the Continental Divide, there was a noticeable drop in temperature.
   l. Covered with the grime of centuries, the archaeologists could not decipher the inscription.
   m. To avoid overexposing the picture, a light meter should be used.
   n. Meeting Lou after geology class, he suggested a handball game.
   o. If unable to attend, a call to the reservation clerk would be appreciated.

9. Correct any sentence fragments or run-on sentences in this exercise. Add words and punctuation as necessary.
   a. Judge Ernest Owen rejected the appeal. Eight days after it was made.
   b. You may attend the conference. After you submit your request to the section supervisor.
   c. Nice to have talked to you.
   d. Have a profitable meeting.
   e. You can take the Universal Remote with you. Anywhere you need a remote control!
   f. They bought the graphing calculator for the staff they did not even know how to operate a graphing calculator.
   g. The cost of insuring a small business fleet skyrocketed last year combating that increase has taken on increased importance.
   h. We would like to inspect your car, please contact your authorized dealer immediately.
   i. If the necessary work has already been done or if you no longer own your Volkswagen.
   j. We would very much appreciate your completing the enclosed questionnaire return it in the postage-paid envelope.
   k. Because they know they can save money and time when they shop with us.
   l. Bills are mailed on the 16th of each month, they are payable by the 10th of the next month.
   m. We are happy to grant your request for a credit account with us we welcome you as a charge customer.

    n. Accounts that are payable by the 10th of each month and subject to a finance charge of 1.5 percent if unpaid.

    o. Your credit record, Mr. Deckman, is excellent, therefore, we are happy to welcome you as a charge customer.

    p. A service representative was dispatched immediately he found that the computer had been programmed incorrectly.

    q. As long as you are able to make a rush delivery of pottery to arrive before February 28.

10. The memos shown in Figures 4–4 and 4–5 were drafted by students requesting tuition reimbursement from their employers for a business writing course. They both contain many examples of the kinds of writing problems discussed in this chapter. Revise each, applying the revision guidelines in this chapter.

■ In-Class Activities

1. During the next 15 minutes, correct the comma faults in the following sentences by adding, changing, or deleting words and punctuation as needed. Your instructor may ask you not to use your text or other materials to help you with this exercise. Also, when you complete your task, you may be asked to exchange papers to evaluate the results.

    a. The electric voltage in the line was too high, he dared not risk touching it.

    b. An emergency occurs, another committee is born.

    c. Members may pay their dues immediately, they may choose to have a statement mailed to their homes or offices.

    d. The computer printer has separate drawers for paper, and the toner cartridge.

    e. One should never be ashamed to be somewhat sentimental, for, a certain amount of sentimentality makes a person human.

    f. The new law did not put all computer hackers behind bars, it did make some fearful, though.

    g. The engine overheated, the operator turned it off.

    h. A letter of transmittal for a report may include background information supplementary information or confidential information.

    i. If becoming a supervisor sounds interesting to you you should start to prepare now.

    j. My sister's friend manages a small elegant speciality shop in Hartford.

    k. Whenever you can take some management courses do so.

    l. Should you move to a supervisory job from a technical one you must quickly become people-oriented.

    m. On January 3 20—we shall meet at the Mystic Seaport to discuss the future of fishing in the waters off Cape Cod Massachusetts.

    n. Norma who is the president's assistant is located in room ES 12.

    o. All children especially those aged 6 to 12 fascinate me.

    p. We need two printers for our office in Vance Canada and in Calgary.

2. Each of the following sentences contains a redundant word, phrase, or clause. During the next 15 minutes, rewrite the sentences to eliminate the redundant elements. Your instructor may ask you not to use your text or other materials to help

Figure 4–4
Sample Memo for Revision (a)

Memo

Date: September 11, 20--
To: Harold Wells
From: Norman Hill   *NH*
Subject: Tuition Reimbursement for Business Writing course at Ivy College

Dear Mr. Wells: *↗ elete·*

I seek tuition reimbursement for the course Business Writing at Ivy College. In the time I have been employed at the Springfield Steel Co. as an assistant manager, I believe that my managerial skills could be broaden by participation in this course. This course would increase my communication skills along with the capacity to deal with others more effectively and efficiently. As far as I observe it, it would be in the best interest of the Company if I enrolled in this course.

My enrollment in this course would be advantageous for a number of reasons;

First the course is an adaptation of a work situation. The teacher poses himself not as an teacher, but your manager, the one you write too. He gives the student different situations and teaches the student the right format, whether it's a memo or letter. His grading margin is dependant on whether the manager would be satisfied or not. Included with that he tries to teach the student how to solve each situation with many different methods and technics.

Another reason why the course would valuable is because it would make me more versatile in the position I occupy now. This course would give me a broader range in response letters, reports or article I might be responsible for. Also it will give me the much needed skill to communicate more effectively with the other personnel I don't see.

Next this course could be an asset to the company by the new skill I would possess. It would make me more competent to deal with others in a new formal way not known before, such as formal request and memos.

Also the Business Writing course I would attend could be valuable to employees and future students. Once I learn the proper formats and different styles I will be able to help to broaden others awareness of different formats and styles. Plus I will have the experience of the course and will be able to recommend the course.

My responsibility at Springfield Steel mainly consist of dealing with people on a one to one basis, and referring problems I see in the warehouse to the manager. The efficiency of one's job could be increased by taking this course. It may also install one of the skills one will need to operate at my most efficient point. This course would be good for me as well as the company to create a better manager.

Comm. interpersonal

The classified

versitility

Par. I

Bio -
broaden my

**Figure 4–5
Sample Memo for
Revision (b)**

Memo

Date: September 10, 20--
To: Patrick Alien
From: Henry Jacobs   *HJ*
Subject: Tuition Reimbursement to attend a writing class

As of September 1, 20--, I started my new position as Office Manager. This one requires much more work in the area of writing, such as letters, memos, and reports compared to my old job. Because I feel that I am not doing satisfactory work in these areas of writing, I would like to enroll in a night class at Ivy College to correct my personal judgment on my writing skills. However, I feel that the company should reimburse me the tuition of $203.50 for a number of reasons.

First of all, this writing class will teach me the best and correct way to write memos, outlines, reports, letters, proposals, etc. It will also sharpen my other writing skills. Since not only do many people within the company see my writing but also a large number outside. And I feel this class is necessary to make sure a good job is done. Good writing skills can be impressive to our customers, this writing class will benefit my area of the company.

Second, I feel the tuition should be reimbursed because I am taking my own free time to improve my work as well as my job. There is a lot of homework that includes research for a big formal report. I am doing this for the company and again, I say, this class will benefit my productivity in the company as well as being beneficiary.

Finally, the importance of this writing class is great, but the $203.50 is quite expensive. I feel that since I am doing this for the company, it can be considered as a training or workshop expense. And in turn I will provide you and the company with my best job to benefit it.

As you can see, I have stressed the importance of this writing class as a benefit to our company as well as making my job easier and more productive. I feel this class is a must and tuition should be reimbursed. I will be happy to elaborate more on this at your request.

you with this exercise. Also, when you complete your task, you may be asked to exchange papers to evaluate the results.

a. Our experienced salespeople, who have many years of work behind them, will plan an aggressive advertising campaign to sell the new product.
b. Any two raceway assemblies can be connected together with the plate as shown.

c. The radio announcer kept repeatedly saying, "Buy PDQ brand pretzels!"

d. Dissatisfied employees should give their complaints to the manager who is in charge as supervisor.

e. If you are interested in economics, do not neglect to read the above-mentioned book, which was discussed previously.

3. Let's have some fun with affectation. During the next 15 minutes, try to figure out common proverbs buried in these overwritten substitutes. When you complete your task, you may be asked to exchange papers to evaluate the results.

   EXAMPLE   Everything that coruscates with effulgence is not ipso facto aurous.

   TRANSLATION   Everything that glitters is not gold.

   a. Never calculate the possible number of juvenile poultry until the usual period of incubation has been accomplished.

   b. People who reside in transparent domiciles should not cast geological specimens.

   c. The warm-blooded, feathered, egg-laying vertebrate animal that is among the first invariably comes in the possession of a small, legless, crawling invertebrate animal.

   d. Where there is gaseous evidence of flammable matter, there is an indicated insinuation of incendiary pyrotechnic.

   e. Ornithological specimens of identical plumage tend to congregate in close proximity.

   f. Do not utter loud or passionate vocal expressions because of the accidental overturning of a receptacle containing a whitish nutritive liquid.

   g. Do not traverse a structure erected to afford passage over a waterway prior to the time of drawing nigh to the same.

   h. Hemoglobin is incapable of being extracted from the edible root of brassica rapa.

   i. Deviation from the ordinary or common routine is that which gives zest to the cycle of existence.

   j. A donee would be wise to abolish the habitual casting of glances into the oral cavity of equestrian specimens.

4. Each of the following passages contains unnecessary jargon, padded phrases, and affectation. During the next 20 minutes, revise the passages. Your instructor may ask you not to use your text or other materials to help you with this exercise. Also, when you complete your task, you may be asked to exchange papers to evaluate the results.

   a. With reference to the matter that management has declared to be in the best interest of the furtherance of company-employee relations, the president has been authorized and empowered to grant each and every employee, upon the attainment of 30 years of continued and uninterrupted service to the company, an additional period of vacation that shall be of one week's duration.

   b. I hereby designate Mr. Samson, who has been holding the position and serving in the capacity of assistant technical supervisor, to be named and appointed to the position and function of deputy director of customer relations. In his newly elevated position Mr. Samson will report, in the first instance, directly to the department director — that is, to me.

c. Purchasers of the enclosed substance should carefully and thoroughly follow the instructions provided herein for the use of the substance, and should in no case whatsoever consume, or otherwise partake of, said substance without proceeding in the manner set forth on the accompanying circular of instructions.

5. During the next 15 minutes, examine each underlined word in the following sentences. If the word is incorrect, rewrite the sentence using the correct word. Otherwise, make no changes. Your instructor may ask you not to use your text or other materials to help you with this exercise. Also, when you complete your task, you may be asked to exchange papers to evaluate the results.
   a. His appearance won't have an <u>affect</u> on his ability.
   b. The <u>principle</u> problem is lack of funds.
   c. Buy your envelopes at the <u>stationery</u> store.
   d. The highest achievers are more <u>likely then</u> the others to believe they're responsible for what is good and not good in their lives.
   e. Did the loss <u>effect</u> you personally?
   f. The Miami City <u>Counsel</u> meets Fridays.
   g. I would like to go to <u>they're</u> concert.
   h. <u>Its</u> been a long time since we met as a committee.
   i. We will work on the project <u>thru</u> next Thursday.
   j. He plans to attend <u>irregardless</u> of the consequences.

6. Find a study partner in the class and exchange copies of the rough drafts of an upcoming assignment well in advance of the deadline. Using the revision checklist at the end of this chapter, identify specific areas for improvement or correction. Keep in mind that early drafts naturally contain trouble spots and your job is to help your partner receive a better grade. Return the draft to your partner ahead of the due date so that he or she can incorporate your suggestions.

■ Research Projects

1. Research Project 1 in Chapter 3 asked that you write a rough draft about a business or technological field that, until now, you knew nothing about. Continue to revise the draft using the suggestions on page 128. When revising, remember to
   a. Allow a cooling period.
   b. Pretend a stranger has written your draft.
   c. Revise in passes.
   d. Be alert to your most frequent problems.
   e. Read your draft aloud.
   f. Ask someone else to read and criticize your draft.

   You may also want to keep a journal of your revisions, noting what was easy and what was difficult for you. Your instructor may ask you to submit your journal when you submit your report.

2. Locate at least three of your past academic research papers. These will be reports that have already been evaluated by another instructor for another class. Now, as suggested in this chapter, review each paper with the following components in

mind: organization and content, accuracy and completeness, and effective sentences with correct basic construction. Review the material in this chapter to guide you through your revision process. Using a red pencil, make note of changes you would now suggest in your papers.

3. Interview an instructor whom you admire and respect. It does not matter what that instructor's specialty area is. Ask the instructor what revision process he or she uses when preparing work for class or when writing his or her own correspondence, papers, or proposals. Write a draft of the information gathered in the interview. Include any new information you gained about good writing habits.

4. Write a letter to your state representative asking that attention be given to a matter of concern to you. Use at least three outside sources to supply evidence that a problem exists. Sources may include books, magazines, newspapers, and journal articles. Put your letter aside for at least three days. Revise your letter. Put your letter aside again for at least three days. Revise a second time. Note the changes you have made. Your instructor may ask you to submit all drafts when you submit your letter.

5. Collect at least six articles on the same current event from as many different newspapers as possible. The article may present different aspects of the same event. Using Chapter 4 as your guide, check the articles for the following basics: subject-verb agreement, pronoun-antecedent number agreement, pronoun-antecedent gender agreement, and consistency of tense and person, dangling modifiers, misplaced modifiers, sentence problems such as fragments and run-on sentences. Also check for preciseness, including faulty comparisons, unclear pronoun reference, and imprecise word choice. Finally, review style looking for redundancy, padded phrases, affectation, technical terminology, jargon, and correct spelling. Make a list of the errors you found. Your instructor may ask you to share your list and sources with your classmates.

6. Choose a controversial topic in your field of study. Topics might relate to engineering (legislation and ethics); health professions (continuing education and licensure); environmental sciences (environmentally conscious legislation); health-care administration (managed health-care plans); computer science (laws governing the Internet; censorship); agriculture (genetically engineered products). Once you have selected a topic, research it to discover your own point of view on the subject. Support your point of view with as much evidence as possible. Write a memo to your boss (or instructor) stating why your company or organization (or university) should take a stand in support of your view.

■ Web Projects

1. The Internet has many sites offering English grammar help, rules, and advice. The following two addresses are samples of what is available:

Grammar Slammar http://englishplus.com/grammar/index.html
Lycos Zone Language Arts http://www.lycoszone.com/dir/langarts.html

Explore the Internet to find at least three other Web sites focusing on English grammar. Write a paragraph explaining which of the sites you discover would be helpful to you and why.

2. The Internet has been criticized because the quality of information found on the Web may not be credible. The same may be true for the style of writing used on the Internet. Explore the Internet to find at least one sample of good writing style and one sample of poor writing style on the same subject. What makes that sample good? What makes it poor? Use Chapter 4 as your guide. Prepare a brief report on your findings, supporting your critique with examples from both texts.

3. Research a company on the Web that produces a new high-tech product or another type of innovative product.
   a. Prepare an email to send to that company in which you ask specific questions about features of the product, warranty information, and so on.
   b. Write a traditional business letter addressing the same questions that you asked in your email.
   c. Print a copy of your email and your business letter and then write one or two paragraphs describing the differences and similarities between the two. Address issues such as style, tone, correct English usage, format, and length. For this particular communication, do you think the email or the business letter is more advantageous? Why? Be specific.
   d. Send your email and mail your letter.
   e. Compare the email and business letter replies that you receive from the company, considering the same issues that you addressed when reviewing your own email and letter. Is one reply more detailed or in some way different from the other? Write one or two paragraphs in which you discuss which reply is better and explain why.

4. Precise word choice is a critical component of writing on the job. The wrong word can cost a company thousands of dollars or, sometimes worse, a lost client. Using the Webster Dictionary Reference on the Web, http://www.m-w.com/dictionary.htm, find the following word pairs and note the differences in their meanings: Cement/Concrete, Straw/Hay, Immigrant/Emigrant, Affect/Effect.

5. Find three Web sites concerned with one of the following occupations: fire fighting, health-care occupations, merchandising, retail sales, telephone repair, police work, investment banking, or journalism. Or you may find Web sites with information about flight attendants, waiters or servers, photographers, mail carriers, truck drivers, or other occupations. Review the three sites related to that occupation, checking them for sexist language. (*Note:* Two excellent occupation-related sites to begin your research with are America's Career Infonet, sponsored by the U.S. Department of Labor at http://www.acinet.org/acinet and the Bureau of Labor Statistics *Occupational Handbook* site at http://stats.bls.gov/ocohome.htm.)

5 Revising for Coherence, Emphasis, and Ethics

If you have followed the revision cycle outlined in Chapter 4, you should have a draft that is accurate, logically organized, grammatically correct, and free of all nonessential information. One last revision cycle remains. This time, your goal is to link, unify, and highlight ideas so that your readers can grasp them with a minimum of time and effort.

The basic building blocks of the draft are paragraphs. Effective paragraphs must be unified around a central idea so that every sentence is related to the idea stated in the topic sentence. Paragraphs must be the appropriate length—long enough to develop a central idea but not so long that they overwhelm the reader with too many details. Paragraphs must also be coherent, with all ideas arranged in a logical order, with transitional devices linking sentences and paragraphs throughout the draft so that the reader can follow your reasoning from sentence to sentence and from paragraph to paragraph.

Effective writing highlights the facts and ideas that the writer considers most important and downplays those that the writer considers less important. Writers can make their material more accessible to their readers by revising to achieve emphasis. This chapter provides you with a number of devices that you can use to achieve emphasis—using the active and passive voices, highlighting primary while subordinating secondary ideas, taking advantage of introductory words and phrases, using parallel structure and lists to present ideas that are equal in importance, and using a number of other highlighting techniques.

This chapter will also help you consider the possible ethical implications of these revisions and earlier ones—making sure that you do not use language in ways that could mislead readers or suppress important information that readers should know.

Finally, because it is important to consider the physical appearance of your writing when you submit the finished version, this chapter ends with a set of guidelines to ensure that the appearance of your document reflects the effort that you have put into creating its contents.

Voices from the Workplace

Larrell Walters, Lytton Electronics

Lytton Electronics is a contract manufacturer that populates circuit boards and builds electromechanical assemblies for industrial and commercial control systems. As president, Larrell Walters oversees an operation that includes 210 employees.

Here is what Larrell has learned about the revision process: "I learned early that using the active voice is key for effective business communication," he says. "If I said, 'A and B should be done,' it somehow never seemed to get done, but if I said, 'Engineering should do A and Human Resources should do B,' it never failed to happen. Also, I learned that the use of lists is very important in business communication. A paragraph of sentences is much more dense and difficult to grasp than a succinct list, so your odds of communicating successfully are much better with a list. Further, I learned that properly using transition, parallel structure, and subordination makes revision a pleasant and rewarding effort instead of the chaotic and time-consuming task it used to be."

To find out more about Lytton Electronics, email Larrell Walters at lytlwalt@tcdn.com.

Entry-Level
Jessica Salo, RAD Employment Services, Inc.

Jessica Salo is a human resources coordinator at RAD Employment Services, Inc., a small job-placement firm. As part of a small company, Jessica says she does "a little bit of everything" including writing the company newsletter once a month, writing and proofreading advertisements, and recently co-authoring (with the founder of the company) the company's new Web site. Jessica finds herself revising her own writing, as well as that of others in her office.

Jessica has found that "writing in the workplace is much different than writing for school or even for pleasure." Because effective business writing is concise and straightforward, Jessica admits that she needs to resist her tendency to be "rather verbose." "I have some poetic license when it comes to the newsletter, but more often than not I find myself editing and re-editing my work. In most cases I find that the quickest and clearest way to say something is often the best—even if that means sacrificing sentences I am particularly attached to."

Jessica says that one of the most challenging aspects of writing in the workplace is editing a superior's work. She often edits the work of the president and founder of the company. That proves difficult sometimes, for she often has her own opinions regarding certain passages, ads, or letters. "Compromise and a great deal of tact have become invaluable tools. I have learned that I have to be careful not to let my own style get in the way of what the other writer is trying to accomplish." She has also learned when revising other people's work that "there is a time to stand your ground." Instinct is not to be underestimated when writing or editing. "You must trust yourself at times, doubt yourself at times, and certainly know when to put the red pen down."

> ## ESL TIPS: Writing for Your Reader
>
> What is considered good writing varies from culture to culture. In many cultures, a writer must adapt his or her writing style to fit the needs and expectations of the audience. In North American English, it is the writer's responsibility to make sure that the reader understands the information. Generally, there are two types of writing in terms of reader-writer responsibility.
>
> The first type, which is followed by many non-English speaking cultures, is *writer-based*. In this type of writing, the reader is expected to have a common understanding of the writer's ideas and is responsible for developing the connection between the writer's ideas.
>
> The second type of writing, which is used in North America and in some European cultures, is *reader-based*. In this type of writing, the writer is expected to provide clear, specific details to help the reader's understanding and is responsible for developing the relationship between ideas.

■ Paragraph Unity

Suppose you were responsible for writing the report of a committee examining possible locations for your company's new distribution center in the United States. The part of your outline concerning the way in which the committee narrowed 30 possible locations to three might look like this:

Outline

I. Method Committee Used to Narrow Locations
  A. Considered 30 locations
  B. Eliminated 20 locations because of problems with labor supply, tax structure, and so forth
  C. Narrowed selection to three cities
  D. Visited Chicago, Minneapolis, and Philadelphia
  E. Observations follow in the report

From this group of items, you could write the following paragraph:

Specific example of how locations were narrowed

■ *Topic sentence* → The committee narrowed 30 possible locations for the new distribution center to three. From the 30, 20 possibilities were eliminated almost immediately for reasons ranging from unfavorable tax structures to inadequate labor supplies. Of the remaining ten locations, the committee selected for intensive study the three cities that seemed to offer the best transportation and support facilities: Chicago, Minneapolis, and Philadelphia. The committee then visited these three cities, and its observations on each follow in this report.

Another specific example explaining how the committee decided on the three cities

Concluding thought and transition to the next idea, which will follow in a new paragraph

Because the sentences in the paragraph evolved from the items listed in the outline, every sentence is directly related to one central idea—narrowing the selection of possible locations for the distribution center to three cities. Notice that the paragraph does not contain the committee's final recommendation or the specific advantages of each of the three cities. Those details will follow later in the report. To include such details in this paragraph would make the paragraph stray from its one central idea. In fact, the function of any paragraph is to develop a single thought or idea within a larger piece of writing.

ESL TIPS: Expressing Ideas Directly

In many cultures, it is inappropriate to express strong conclusions too directly, so competent writers do not state their ideas—they hint at them and approach the topic indirectly in as many different ways as possible. Writing around an issue is highly valued in those cultures. In other cultures, competent writers are expected to write in an elaborate style. In North American English, *conciseness, coherence, clarity,* and *cogency* are the four words most often used to express the values assigned to "good" writing. Be brief, make sure your writing holds together, be clear, and say only what is necessary to communicate your message. Of course, no writing style is inherently better than another, but to be a successful writer in any language, you must understand the cultural values that underlie the language in which you are writing.

When every sentence in a paragraph contributes to developing one central idea, the paragraph has unity. If a paragraph contains sentences that do not develop the central idea, it lacks unity. The following is a later paragraph from the report in which possible locations for the new distribution center are evaluated. Does this paragraph have unity?

■   Probably the greatest advantage of Chicago as the location for our new distribution center is its excellent transportation facilities. The city is served by three major railroads. *In fact, Chicago was at one time the hub of cross-country rail transportation.* Chicago is also a major center of the trucking industry, and most of the nation's large freight carriers have terminals there. *We are concerned, however, about the delivery problems that we've had with several truck carriers. We've had far fewer problems with air freight.* Both domestic and international air cargo services are available at O'Hare International Airport. Finally, except in the winter months when the Great Lakes are frozen, Chicago is a seaport, accessible through the St. Lawrence Seaway.

Every sentence in this paragraph should have been about the advantages of Chicago's transportation facilities. The three italicized sentences, however, do not develop that central idea: the sentence about Chicago as the former hub of rail transportation, and the two sentences about delivery problems.

> ## ESL TIPS: Supporting Assertions with Examples
>
> North American readers of English expect a writer's conclusions, opinions, and recommendations to be supported by facts and statistics and are not convinced by extensive use of general analogies or vague metaphors. All assertions need to be supported by clear, specific examples.

Now read the paragraph without the italicized sentences. Each of the remaining sentences is directly related to the central idea, and the paragraph has unity.

■ Probably the greatest advantage of Chicago as the location for our new distribution center is its excellent transportation facilities. The city is served by three major railroads. Chicago is also a major center of the trucking industry, and most of the nation's large freight carriers have terminals there. Both domestic and international air cargo services are available at O'Hare International Airport. Finally, except in the winter months when the Great Lakes are frozen, Chicago is a seaport, accessible through the St. Lawrence Seaway.

One way to make sure that your paragraph has unity is to provide a topic sentence, which is a sentence that clearly states the central idea of that paragraph. If every sentence in the paragraph directly relates to the topic sentence, the paragraph will have unity.

> ## ESL TIPS: Forming and Placing Your Topic Sentence
>
> In North American English writing, readers generally expect the topic sentence to be located at or near the beginning of a paragraph. Paragraphs are structured so they present an idea in the topic sentence and then provide specific examples supporting the idea. The topic sentence must contain two things: the limited subject and the claim about the subject that will be developed in the paragraph.
>
>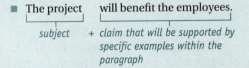
>
> ■ The project   will benefit the employees.
>
>   subject   + claim that will be supported by
>   specific examples within the
>   paragraph

Notice that all the sentences in the following paragraph directly relate to the topic sentence, which is italicized here:

■ *Probably the greatest advantage of Chicago as the location for our new distribution center is its excellent transportation facilities.* The city is served by three major railroads.

Chicago is also a major center of the trucking industry, and most of the nation's large freight carriers have terminals there. Both domestic and international air cargo services are available at O'Hare International Airport. Finally, except in the winter months when the Great Lakes are frozen, Chicago is a seaport, accessible through the St. Lawrence Seaway.

Beginning a paragraph with the topic sentence helps both the writer and the reader. The writer has no difficulty constructing a unified paragraph because every sentence can be measured against the topic sentence and the central idea it expresses. The reader knows immediately what the paragraph is about because the opening sentence states the central idea. Busy readers, especially, appreciate being told at once what a paragraph will deal with. For this reason, topic sentences are usually the first sentences of paragraphs in on-the-job writing.

Occasionally, however, a topic sentence may be placed somewhere other than at the beginning of a paragraph. Placing the topic sentence at the end of a paragraph emphasizes the central idea because all the sentences build up to that idea. Notice how the sentences in the following paragraph lead up to the topic sentence:

■   A study by the Department of Agriculture revealed that insect damage in our region increased from 15 percent to 23 percent between 1997 and 1999. During this past year, many farmers reported a 30-percent increase in insect damage over the previous year. Furthermore, another recent study found that certain destructive insects are migrating north into our area. *Clearly, we should prepare for increased insect damage in the coming year.*

Although a topic sentence placed at the end of a paragraph provides a forceful conclusion, it also makes reading the paragraph more difficult. Especially in on-the-job situations, where time is at a premium, the reader may become irritated at having to plow through details to reach the main point of a paragraph. Therefore, it is best to place topic sentences at the ends of paragraphs only occasionally.

■ Paragraph Length

Paragraph length should be tailored to the reader's convenience. Specifically, a paragraph should help the reader by providing a physical break on the page as well as by signaling a new idea. Long paragraphs can intimidate your reader by failing to provide manageable subdivisions of thought. Overly short paragraphs have a disadvantage, too: They may make it difficult for your reader to see the logical relationships between ideas in your writing. A series of short paragraphs can also sacrifice unity by breaking a single idea into several pieces.

Although there are no fixed rules for the length of paragraphs, paragraphs in on-the-job writing average about 100 words each, with two or three paragraphs to a double-spaced, printed page. Paragraphs in letters tend to be shorter; two- or even one-sentence paragraphs are not unusual in letters. The best advice is that a paragraph should be just long enough to deal adequately with the central idea stated in its topic sentence. A new paragraph should begin whenever the subject changes significantly.

■ Paragraph Coherence

An effective paragraph has not only unity but coherence; that is, it takes the reader logically and smoothly from one sentence to the next. When a paragraph is coherent, the reader clearly recognizes that one sentence or idea leads logically to the next, which in turn leads to the sentence or idea that is next, and so on. Consider the following paragraph. Does each sentence or idea lead logically and clearly to the one that follows?

■   The Lifemaker's cables can be adjusted for too much slack. To adjust the cable attached to the weight stack next to the weight upright, find the end of the 125" cable. Turn the end of the cable clockwise. Thread the cable farther into the weight tube. Turn the cable about an inch counterclockwise.

Because each sentence in the paragraph says something about how to adjust cables on a home-fitness machine, the paragraph has unity. Yet the paragraph does not move as smoothly from one sentence to the next as it could. Nor does the paragraph make as clear as possible how each idea relates to the others. Transitional devices will achieve both these goals.

Transitions between Sentences

Transitional devices are words and phrases that help the reader to move smoothly from one sentence to the next and to see the logical relationships between the sentences. Notice how the simple technique of putting the steps in sequence (see the italicized words and phrases) provides effective transitions between ideas in the sample paragraph:

■   The Lifemaker's cables can be adjusted for too much slack. To adjust the cable attached to the weight stack next to the weight upright, *first* find the end of the 125" cable. *Then,* turn the end of the cable clockwise *in order* to thread it farther into the weight tube. *When you have finished,* turn the cable about an inch counterclockwise.

Now, because the transitional devices provide coherence, the reader can follow the writer's step-by-step instructions easily.

The following list includes other words and phrases that commonly function as transitional devices:

ESL TIPS: Using Coordinating Conjunctions

In many languages, sentences can begin with a conjunction (*and, or, nor, so, yet, but,* and *for*), but in North American English this practice is not as acceptable. English uses these words as coordinating conjunctions to join two complete thoughts (two simple sentences) because they are closely related. A comma is used before the coordinating conjunction to join the two thoughts.

■ The accountant checked the financial documents , *but* he could not find the mistake.

sentence   + *comma and coordinating conjunction + sentence*

To express:	Use:
result	*therefore, as a result, consequently, thus, hence*
example	*for example, for instance, specifically, as an illustration*
comparison	*similarly, likewise*
contrast	*but, yet, still, however, nevertheless, on the other hand*
addition	*moreover, furthermore, also, too, besides, in addition*
time	*now, later, meanwhile, since then, after that, before that time*
sequence	*first, second, third, then, next, finally*

Some of the words and phrases in this list are nearly synonymous but imply somewhat different logical connections. Be sure that the transitional device you choose conveys the precise meaning you intend. Table 5–1 is a list of common transitions.

The use of pronouns, such as *he, she, they,* and *it,* is another transitional device. Because pronouns refer to a person or thing mentioned in a previous sentence, they bind sentences and ideas together. Notice the use of pronouns as transitional devices in the following paragraph:

It *refers to the billing software*

They *refers to the billing staff*

He *refers to Bill Mendena*

■ We have recently discovered a problem with the new billing software. *It* consistently fails to note reimbursement amounts when *it* is generating invoices. The billing staff is concerned that the software poses an administrative nightmare. *They* believe that the software could generate a complete billing cycle without noting any reimbursements that are due to clients. *Bill Mendena,* the billing supervisor, reports that the computer services department does not consider the problem an administrative hazard. *He* has pointed out to me, however, that when the software does not note reimbursements, the billing employees must do a computer search for every client in our current account base. *He* believes that this fact warrants a thorough analysis of the problem.

The repetition of key words and phrases is a transitional device that links sentences and ideas. Notice how repetition of the key words and phrases in the following paragraph moves the paragraph forward:

■ Over the past several months, I have heard complaints about the Merit Award *Program*. Specifically, many employees feel that this *program* should be linked to annual *salary increases*. They believe that *salary increases* would provide a much better incentive than the current $500 to $700 *cash awards* for exceptional service. In addition, these *employees* believe that their supervisors consider the *cash awards* a satisfactory alternative to *salary increases*. Although I don't think this practice is widespread, the fact that the *employees* believe that it is justifies a reevaluation of the Merit Award *Program*.

Table 5–1
Common Transitions

To add information			
also	besides	moreover	furthermore
in addition	finally	next	additionally
first, second, etc.	last		

To give an example or to illustrate a point			
for example	for instance	to illustrate	specifically
in particular	in this case	to demonstrate	notably

To compare or contrast			
on the other hand	on the contrary	likewise	however
although	similarly	nevertheless	meanwhile
whereas			

To prove			
because	moreover	furthermore	besides

To show time			
initially	eventually	during	thereafter
finally	then	later	previously
formerly	first, second, etc.	next	afterwards
at last	before	at the same time	currently

To show sequence			
next	now	finally	simultaneously
first, second, etc.	after	consequently	concurrently
thus	therefore		

To conclude			
in conclusion	therefore	thus	as a result
finally	all in all		

Conjunctions			
and	or	nor	so
yet	for	but	

Transitions between Paragraphs

Transitional devices used to link sentences can also be effective for transitions between paragraphs. The repetition of a key phrase, for example, connects the first paragraph in the following example with the second.

■ Consumers spend more money for plumbing repairs than for any other home repair service. The most common repair that plumbers make is the clearing of drains. Because the kitchen *sink drain* is used more often than any other drain in the home, that is the drain that is most often clogged.

Clearing the *sink drain* yourself is easier than you might expect. You probably have all the tools you need. . . .

ESL TIPS: Using Transitional Words and Expressions

In North American English, transitional words or expressions are used to connect ideas between the main sections of the body of the text or between sentences within a paragraph. Their purpose is to help the reader understand the relationship between two ideas and how the second idea follows logically from the first (see Table 5–1). By using transitional words and phrases, the writer can move the reader smoothly from one idea to the next. Be warned, however, that writers may be tempted to add transitional expressions at the beginnings of every sentence—such overuse of transitions is not necessary and may even make the writing hard to follow. When choosing a transition, remember to check its specific meaning in the dictionary.

Another transitional device for linking paragraphs is to begin a paragraph with a sentence that summarizes the preceding paragraph. In the following excerpt from a report, notice how the first sentence in the second paragraph summarizes the ideas presented in the first paragraph:

■ Each year, forest fires in our region cause untold destruction. For example, wood ashes washed into streams after a fire often kill large numbers of fish. In addition, the destruction of the vegetation along stream banks causes water temperatures to rise, making the stream unfit for several varieties of cold-water fish. Forest fires, moreover, hurt the tourist and recreation business, for vacationers are not likely to visit flame-blackened areas.

These losses, and many other indirect losses caused by forest fires, damage not only the quality of life but also the economy of our region. They also represent a huge drain on the resources and personnel of the Department of Natural Resources. For example, our financial investment last year in fighting forest fires. . . .

Opening sentence summarizes examples from preceding paragraph

If used sparingly, another effective transitional device between paragraphs is to ask a question at the end of one paragraph and answer it at the beginning of the next. This device works well in the following example:

■ Robotics has become an ugly word for many people because it has sometimes meant the displacement of employees from their jobs. But the all-important fact that is so often overlooked is that robotics invariably creates many more jobs than it eliminates. The vast number of people employed in the automobile industry, compared with the number of people who had been employed in the harness-and-carriage-making business, is a classic example. Almost always, the jobs that have been eliminated by robotics have been menial, unskilled jobs, and the people who have been displaced have been forced to increase their skills. The result has been better and higher-paying jobs for many workers. *In view of these facts, is robotics really bad?*

Transition using a question and answer

There is no question that robotics has freed many people from boring and repetitive work. . . .

When you use this transitional device, make sure that the second paragraph does, in fact, answer the question posed in the first. Again, do not use this device too often. Your reader may find it monotonous and gimmicky if it is overdone.

WRITER'S CHECKLIST: Creating Effective Paragraphs

☐ Unify the paragraph around a central idea.

☐ Ensure that every sentence relates to the topic sentence.

☐ Arrange ideas (and sentences) in a logical order.

☐ Use transitional words, phrases, and clauses so readers can follow the logic of your paragraph.

☐ Keep paragraphs at an appropriate length:

  • Long enough to develop your central idea

  • Short enough not to swamp your reader in unnecessary details

---

◼ Achieving Emphasis

Effective writing is also emphatic writing—it highlights the facts and ideas that the writer considers most important and subordinates those of less importance. By focusing the reader's attention on the key elements in a sentence, emphatic writing enables the reader to determine how one fact or idea in a sentence is related to another. Emphatic writing, then, offers writers a powerful means for making their material more accessible to their readers. Writers achieve emphasis through a number of techniques: using the active and passive voice, highlighting primary and subordinating secondary ideas, taking advantage of introductory words and phrases, and creating patterns for ideas that are equal in importance through parallel structure and lists. Other highlighting techniques available to writers include arranging word order, varying sentence length, labeling ideas, and using mechanical devices such as dashes and italics.

Active and Passive Voice

If you were going to relate the information contained in the following two sentences to someone in conversation, which version would you use?

EXAMPLE 1   The complicated equipment is operated skillfully by the x-ray technician.

EXAMPLE 2   The x-ray technician operates the complicated equipment skillfully.

You would probably choose Example 2, because it conveys its message more directly than Example 1. By making the x-ray technician the *actor* (or *doer*) in the sentence, Example 2 readily communicates the fact that it is the technician's initiative that turns the equipment into a working tool. Example 1, in contrast, downplays the role of the operator; the focus of the sentence is on the x-ray equipment as the *receiver* of the action. The technician, though still the performer of the action, appears in a *by* phrase at the end of the sentence, rather than as the subject of the sentence.

What accounts for the difference in "feel" between the two sentences is that Example 2 is in the active voice, while Example 1 is in the passive. A sentence is in the active voice if the subject of the sentence acts; it is in the passive voice if the subject is acted upon.

In general, the active voice is the more emphatic of the two. In active-voice sentences, the reader can move quickly and easily from *actor* (the subject) to *action performed* (the verb) to *receiver of the action* (direct object); in passive-voice sentences, the reader often has to reach the end of the sentence to find out who (or what) performed the action that the subject received.

ACTIVE VOICE   Sheila Cohen *prepared* the layout design for the new pump.

     [The subject—*Sheila Cohen*—acts on *the layout design*—the direct object.]

PASSIVE VOICE   The layout design for the new pump was prepared by Sheila Cohen.

     [The subject—*the layout design*—receives the action.]

Passive-voice sentences tend to be longer than active-voice sentences for two reasons. First, a verb in the active voice often consists of only one word (in this example, *prepared*), whereas a verb in the passive voice always consists of at least two words (*was prepared*). Second, passive-voice sentences tend to be longer because they frequently require a *by someone* or *by something* phrase to complete their meanings. The active-voice version of the Sheila Cohen sentence contains 10 words; the passive-voice version contains 12.

Note the word order and verb forms in these examples:

PASSIVE VOICE   Up to 600,000 printed pages *can be stored* on a CD-ROM disk.

ACTIVE VOICE   A CD-ROM disk *can store* up to 600,000 printed pages.

PASSIVE VOICE   Instructions on how to use the automatic teller *are described* in the brochure.

ACTIVE VOICE   The brochure *describes* how to use the automatic teller.

PASSIVE VOICE	The circuit-breaker switches *are lubricated* by maintenance personnel every three months.
ACTIVE VOICE	Maintenance personnel *lubricate* the circuit-breaker switches every three months.

The chief advantage of the active voice is that by clearly stating who is doing what, it gives the reader information quickly and emphatically. A straightforward style is especially important in writing instructions. Compare the following two versions of a paragraph giving nurses directions for treating a serious burn. The first version is written entirely in the passive voice; the second uses the active.

PASSIVE VOICE	The following action must be taken when a serious burn is treated. Any loose clothing on or near the burn is removed. The injury is covered with a clean dressing, and the area around the burn is washed. Then the dressing is secured with tape. Burned fingers or toes are separated with gauze or cloth so that they are prevented from sticking together. Medication is not applied unless it is prescribed by a doctor.
ACTIVE VOICE	Take the following action when treating a serious burn. Remove any loose clothing on or near the burn. Cover the injury with a clean dressing and wash the area around the burn. Then secure the dressing with tape. Separate burned fingers or toes with gauze or cloth to prevent them from sticking together. Do not apply medication unless a doctor prescribes it.

If you were the nurse who had to follow these instructions, which version would you find easier to read and understand?

Occasionally, of course, the passive voice can be useful. There are times, for example, when the doer of the action is less important than the receiver of the action, and the writer can emphasize the receiver of the action by making it the subject of the sentence.

EFFECTIVE PASSIVE VOICE	The new medical secretary was recommended by several staff doctors.

The important person in this sentence is the medical secretary, not the doctors who made the recommendation. To give the secretary—the receiver of the action—the needed emphasis, the sentence should be written in the passive voice.

The same principle holds true in the sciences for situations where the data are more important than the scientist collecting that data. Laboratory or test reports are good examples of the proper use of the passive voice.

EFFECTIVE PASSIVE VOICE	The test was conducted to identify the soil pH levels at the site.

The passive voice is also useful when the performer of the action either is not known or is not important.

EFFECTIVE PASSIVE VOICE	The valves were soaked in kerosene for 24 hours. [Who soaked them is not important.]
EFFECTIVE PASSIVE VOICE	The wheel was invented thousands of years ago. [Who invented it is not known.]

Consider the same principle at work in a longer passage that describes a process.

EFFECTIVE PASSIVE VOICE	Area strip mining *is used* in regions of flat to gently rolling terrain, such as that found in the Midwest and West. Depending on applicable reclamation laws, the topsoil from the area to be mined may *be removed, stored,* and later *reapplied* as surface material during reclamation of the mined land. Following removal of the topsoil, a trench *is cut* through the overburden to expose the upper surface of the coal to be mined. The length of the cut generally corresponds to the length of the property or of the deposit. The overburden from the first cut *is placed* on the unmined land adjacent to the cut. After the first cut *has been completed,* the coal *is removed* and a second cut *is made* parallel to the first.

If you were to specify a doer in this passage, you might write the operator, referring to the person operating the equipment that performs these tasks. Using the operator in each sentence, however, would soon get monotonous and, finally, pointless. The writer might even want to leave open the possibility of several doers: operators, mining companies, or an industrial society in general. The proper focus of this passage, however, is on what happens and in what sequence, not on who does it. The passive voice is also commonly used when the writer wants to avoid identifying the performer of an action.

EFFECTIVE PASSIVE VOICE	The guilty employee was placed on disciplinary probation. [The writer does not want to say *who* placed the guilty employee on probation.]

As you write—and as you revise—select the voice, active or passive, that is appropriate to your purpose. In most cases you can express your ideas more simply and more emphatically in the active voice, especially if you are writing instructions or making a report in which you intend to emphasize *who did what* (for example, which employee performed which subtask of a large project). If you are describing a complicated piece of equipment, the active voice will probably provide better clarification of how one part interacts with another part. If, however, you are explaining a process in which the *doer* is not known or is not important, the passive voice is likely to be more effective. In whatever kind of writing

> ## ESL TIPS: Forming Verbs in the Passive Voice (Using -*ed*)
>
> Each passive verb must have a form of *to be* and a past participle. With regular verbs, the past participle will have the -*ed* word ending. Sometimes it is difficult to hear these -*ed* endings in spoken English, so be careful to include them in your writing.
>
> ■ The scientists were honored for their discovery.
>
>   *past tense of* to be + *past participle*
>
> ■ The article was written to inform the public.
>
>   *past tense of* to be + *past participle*

you do, be careful to maintain consistency of voice. Avoid making an awkward switch from active to passive (or vice versa), either within a sentence or between sentences.

■ *ten applicants had taken the*
    After the test for admission to the training program ~~had been taken by ten applicants,~~
    each one wrote a brief essay on his or her career plans.

Subordination

Read the following passage.

■ The computer is a calculating device. It was once known as a mechanical brain. It has revolutionized society.

Reading the passage—a group of three short, staccato sentences—is like listening to a series of drumbeats of identical tone. The writing, like the music, is monotonous, because every sentence has the same subject-verb structure. Further, the writing is unemphatic because every idea is given equal weight. The passage can be revised to eliminate the monotonous sentence structure and to stress the most important idea: The computer has revolutionized society.

■ The computer, *a calculating device once known as a mechanical brain,* has revolutionized society.

The key to transforming a series of repetitive, unemphatic sentences is subordination, a technique in which a fact or an idea is subordinated to—that is, shown to be less important than—another fact or idea in the same sentence. You can subordinate an element in a sentence in three basic ways:

- Make it a dependent clause.
- Make it a phrase.
- Make it a single modifier.

With all three methods, the less-important element can be combined with the more-important element to form one unified sentence.

Ways of Subordinating

Clauses. A *subordinate clause* (also called a *dependent clause*) has a subject and a predicate but by itself is not a sentence. Rather, it must be joined to a sentence (called an *independent clause*) by a connecting word. That is, when two sentences are joined by subordination, one sentence becomes the independent clause, and the other sentence, introduced by a connecting word, becomes the dependent clause. The words most commonly used to introduce subordinate clauses are *who, that, which, whom, whose* (relative pronouns) and *after, although, because, before, if, unless, until, when, where, while* (subordinating conjunctions). A few word groups are also used to introduce subordinate clauses—*as soon as, even though, in order that, so that.*

In the following examples, two sentences are turned into one sentence that contains a subordinate clause.

WITHOUT SUBORDINATE CLAUSE	Virginia Kelly has become a lithographer at the Granger Printing Company. She graduated from the Midcity Graphic Arts School last month.
WITH SUBORDINATE CLAUSE	Virginia Kelly, *who graduated from the Midcity Graphic Arts School last month,* has become a lithographer at the Granger Printing Company.
WITHOUT SUBORDINATE CLAUSE	Their credit union has a lower interest rate on auto loans. Our credit union provides a fuller range of services.
WITH SUBORDINATE CLAUSE	*Although their credit union has a lower interest rate on auto loans,* our credit union provides a fuller range of services.

Phrases. A *phrase* is a group of related words that does not have a subject and predicate and that acts as a modifier. In the following groups of two-sentence passages, one sentence is turned into a subordinate phrase that modifies an element in the other sentence.

WITHOUT SUBORDINATE PHRASE	The Beta Corporation now employs 500 people. It was founded ten years ago.
WITH SUBORDINATE PHRASE	The Beta Corporation, *founded ten years ago,* now employs 500 people.

WITHOUT SUBORDINATE PHRASE	Roger Smith is a forest ranger for the State of Michigan. He spoke at the local Kiwanis Club last week.
WITH SUBORDINATE PHRASE	Roger Smith, *a forest ranger for the State of Michigan,* spoke at the local Kiwanis Club last week.

Single modifiers. The *single modifier* may be either a one-word modifier:

■ The file ~~is obsolete. It~~ is taking up valuable storage space.
obsolete

or a compound modifier:

■ The police radio was ~~out of date. It was~~ auctioned to the highest bidder.
out-of-date

Depending on the context of your writing—your subject, your purpose, and your reader—you may find that, in a sentence, one way of subordinating is more effective than another. In general, a subordinate single modifier achieves some emphasis, a subordinate phrase achieves more emphasis, and a subordinate clause achieves the most emphasis of all. In the following example, one idea has been subordinated in three ways.

WITHOUT SUBORDINATION	The landscape designer's report was extensively illustrated. It covered ten pages.
SINGLE MODIFIER	The landscape designer's *ten-page* report was extensively illustrated.
PHRASE	The landscape designer's report, *covering ten pages,* was extensively illustrated.
CLAUSE	The landscape designer's report, *which covered ten pages,* was extensively illustrated.

Subordinating to Achieve Emphasis

Just as you can determine the kind of subordinate element that you think is most appropriate in a given sentence, so you can decide, according to the context in which you are writing, which ideas you should emphasize and which you should subordinate. In the following sets of examples, two sentences have been combined into one, in two different ways. Notice how the emphasis varies in each set.

WITHOUT SUBORDINATION	Blast furnaces are used mainly in the smelting of iron. They are used all over the world.
EMPHASIZES PURPOSE	Blast furnaces, *in use all over the world,* are employed mainly in the smelting of iron.
EMPHASIZES EXTENT	Blast furnaces, *used mainly in the smelting of iron,* are employed all over the world.

WITHOUT SUBORDINATION	The manual explains how to install the gear. It is written for the service technician.
EMPHASIZES PURPOSE	The manual, *written for the service technician,* explains how to install the gear.
EMPHASIZES INTENDED READER	The manual, *which explains how to install the gear,* is written for the service technician.
WITHOUT SUBORDINATION	Henry Ford was a pioneering industrialist. He understood the importance of self-esteem.
EMPHASIZES PIONEERING WORK	Henry Ford, *who understood the importance of self-esteem,* was a pioneering industrialist.
EMPHASIZES SELF-ESTEEM	Henry Ford, *a pioneering industrialist,* understood the importance of self-esteem.

If you wish to emphasize an item in a sentence, place it either at the beginning or at the end of the sentence; if you wish to subordinate an item, place it in the middle of the sentence.

Avoiding Overloaded Sentences

Subordination is a helpful technique that can enable you to write clear and readable sentences, but like many useful devices, it can be overdone. Be especially careful not to pile one subordinating clause on top of another. A sentence that is overloaded with subordination will force your reader to work harder than necessary to understand what you are saying. The following sentence is difficult to read because the bottleneck of subordinate clauses prevents the reader from moving easily from one idea to the next.

TOO MUCH SUBORDINATION	When the two technicians, who had been trained to repair Maurita printers, explained to Erin that the new Maurita 5090 printer, which Erin had told them was not working properly, needed a new part, Erin decided that until the part arrived the department would have its sales letters reproduced by an independent printing supplier.
EFFECTIVE SUBORDINATION	Erin told the two technicians that the new Maurita 5090 printer was not working properly. The technicians, who had been trained to repair Maurita printers, examined the printer and explained to Erin that it needed a new part. Erin decided that until the part arrived, the department would have its sales letters reproduced by an independent printing supplier.

Subordinating everything is as bad as subordinating nothing. For example, study the next three sample paragraphs of a letter from a garage owner to a parts supplier.

TOO LITTLE SUBORDINATION	I am returning the parts you sent me, and I am enclosing the invoice that came with them. You must have confused my order with someone else's. I ordered spark plugs, condensers, and points, and

I received bearings, piston rings, head gaskets, and valve-grinding compound. I don't need these parts, but I need the parts I ordered. Please send them as soon as possible.

TOO MUCH
SUBORDINATION

You must have confused my order with someone else's, because although I ordered spark plugs, condensers, and points, I received bearings, piston rings, head gaskets, and valve-grinding compound; therefore, I am returning the parts you sent me, along with the invoice that came with them, in the hope that you will send me the parts that I need as quickly as possible because this delay has already put me behind schedule.

EFFECTIVE
SUBORDINATION

I am returning the parts you sent me, along with the invoice that came with them, because you must have confused my order with someone else's. Although I ordered spark plugs, condensers, and points, I received bearings, piston rings, head gaskets, and valve-grinding compound. Because I need the parts that I ordered and this mix-up is causing an unexpected delay, please send me the parts that I ordered as quickly as possible.

Introductory Words and Phrases

Another way to achieve emphasis is to begin a sentence with an introductory element—a modifying word or phrase that contains the idea you wish to stress. Such a modifier would normally occur later in the sentence.

- Sales have been good recently.

- *Recently,* sales have been good.

  [Emphasizes the recentness of good sales]

- You must commit yourself to lifetime learning to advance in your career.

- *To advance in your career,* you must commit yourself to lifetime learning.

  [Emphasizes career advancement]

- She found several factual errors while reading the report.

- *While reading the report,* she found several factual errors.

  [Emphasizes the reading of the report]

When you use introductory words and phrases, though, you should watch for two dangers. First, beginning a sentence with a modifying word or phrase may lead you to write a dangling modifier. The first sentence in the following example contains a dangling modifier because the phrase *to advance* cannot logically modify *a commitment to lifetime learning.* The second sentence corrects the error by making it clear that *to advance* modifies the pronoun *you.*

INCORRECT   To advance, a commitment to lifetime learning is required.

CORRECT   To advance, you must commit yourself to lifetime learning.

Second, beginning a sentence with a modifying word or phrase may accidentally change the meaning of the sentence. The first of the following sentences instructs the reader to measure the volume of serum that drips over a time period of 15 seconds. The second sentence instructs the reader to wait 15 seconds before making the measurement—a completely different thought.

■ Measure the volume of serum that drips into the graduated cylinder in 15 seconds.

   [Emphasizes measurement]

■ In 15 seconds, measure the volume of serum that drips into the graduated cylinder.

   [Emphasizes time]

Once again, make sure that your sentences say exactly what you intend them to say.

Parallel Structure

Parallel structure requires that sentence elements—words, phrases, and clauses—that are alike in function be alike in structure as well. In the following example, the three locations in which a cable is laid are all expressed as prepositional phrases.

■ The cable was laid *behind the embankment, under the street,* and *around the building.*

Parallel structure can produce an economy of language, clarify meaning, indicate the equality of related ideas, and, frequently, achieve emphasis. Parallel structure allows your reader to anticipate a series of units within a sentence. The reader realizes, for instance, that the relationship between the second unit (*under the street,* in the example) and the subject (*cable*) is the same as that between the first unit (*behind the embankment*) and the subject. A reader who has sensed the pattern of a sentence can go from one idea to another more quickly and confidently.

Parallel structure can be achieved with words, with phrases, and with clauses. Whether you use words, phrases, or clauses to make a sentence parallel depends, as it does with subordination, on the degree of emphasis you wish to create. In general, words in parallel structure produce some emphasis, phrases produce more emphasis, and clauses produce the most emphasis of all.

PARALLEL WORDS	If you want to earn a satisfactory grade in the receptionist training program, you must be *punctual, courteous,* and *conscientious.*
PARALLEL PHRASES	If you want to earn a satisfactory grade in the receptionist training program, you must recognize the importance *of punctuality, of courtesy,* and *of conscientiousness.*
PARALLEL CLAUSES	If you want to earn a satisfactory grade in the receptionist training program, *you must arrive punctually, you must behave courteously,* and *you must study conscientiously.*

To make the relationship among parallel units clear, repeat the word (or words) that introduces the first unit.

■ The advantage is not in the pay but *in* the greater opportunity.

■ The study of electronics is a necessity and *a* challenge to the technician.

Parallel structure can contribute greatly to the clarity of your writing. However, it is more than just a helpful device—sentences that contain faulty parallel structure are often awkward and difficult to read.

■ Adina Wilson was happy about her assignment and *about* getting *her* a pay raise.

■ Jason advises his employees to work hard and *not to rely* ~~against relying~~ on luck.

■ Check the following items: the dipstick for proper oil level, the gas tank for fuel, the spark plug wire *for proper* attachment, and *the lawn for* ~~that no~~ foreign objects ~~are under or near the mower~~.

Lists

You can also consider using lists to achieve emphasis. Lists break up blocks of dense text and complex sentences, allow key ideas to stand out, and show the relationship of parallel or sequential ideas. Be aware, however, that lists are easier for your readers to understand when they are grammatically parallel. When you use a list of phrases or short sentences, begin each with the same part of speech:

AWKWARD (NOT PARALLEL)	Because expenses for the past month have far exceeded our budget, the business manager has recommended the following reforms: 1. Employees will not use company telephones for personal calls. 2. For any written copy that is not to go out of house, use low-grade yellow paper rather than bond. 3. Make double-sided copies rather than one-sided photocopies of all internal correspondence.
SMOOTH (PARALLEL)	Because expenses for the past month have far exceeded our budget, the business manager has recommended the following reforms: 1. Do not use company phones for personal calls. 2. Use low-grade yellow paper rather than bond for any written copy that is not to go out of house. 3. Make double-sided copies rather than one-sided photocopies of all internal correspondence.

Notice how much more smoothly the revised version reads when all items begin with imperative verbs.

Lists help focus the reader's attention because they stand out from the text around them. Be mindful, however, not to overuse lists in an attempt to avoid writing paragraphs. When a memo, report, or letter consists almost entirely of lists, the reader is unable to distinguish important from unimportant ideas. Further, the information lacks coherence because the reader is forced to connect strings of separate items without the help of transitional ideas. To make sure that the reader understands how a list fits with the surrounding sentences, always provide adequate transition before and after the list.

If you do not wish to indicate the rank or sequence that numbered lists suggest, you can use bullets, as shown in the list of tips in the Writer's Checklist on using lists.

WRITER'S CHECKLIST: Using Lists

☐ List only comparable items.

☐ Use parallel structure throughout.

☐ Use only words, phrases, or short sentences.

☐ Provide adequate transitions before and after lists.

☐ Use bullets when rank or sequence is not important.

☐ Do not overuse lists.

☐ Use numbers when rank or sequence is important.

■ Other Ways to Achieve Emphasis

You can create a feeling of anticipation in your reader by arranging a series of facts or ideas in climactic order. Begin such a series with the least important or lowest-impact idea and end it with the most important or highest-impact one.

■ The hostile takeover of the company will result in some employees being let go, some being downgraded, and some being relocated to different cities.

CLIMACTIC
ORDER
    The hostile takeover of the company will result in some employees being relocated to different cities, some being downgraded, and some being let go.

The writer leads the reader step by step from the disruption of employee relocation to the more serious problem of the downgrading of jobs, and finally to the hostile takeover's most devastating impact on employees, the loss of jobs.

An abrupt change in sentence length can also achieve effective emphasis.

■ We have already reviewed the problems that the accounting department has experienced during the past year. We could continue to examine the causes of our problems and point an accusing finger at all the culprits beyond our control, but in the end it all leads to one simple conclusion: *We must cut costs.*

Sometimes, simply labeling ideas as important creates emphasis.

■ We can do a number of things that will help us to achieve our goal. We can conduct sales contests in the field; in the past, such contests have been quite successful. We can increase our advertising budget and hope for a proportionate increase in sales. We can be prepared to step up production when the increase in sales makes it necessary. But *most important,* we can do everything in our power to make sure that we are producing the best communication equipment on the market.

If you don't overuse them, direct statements such as *most important* should make your reader take particular notice of what follows.

Another kind of direct statement is the warning to your reader that something dangerous is about to follow. Warnings most often appear in instructions, where they may be brought to the reader's attention by a special format—the material may be boxed off, for instance—or by attention-attracting devices such as ALL-CAPITAL letters or a distinctive typeface, such as **boldface** or *italic* type. These features can be used to emphasize important words and phrases in warnings.

WARNING

DO NOT proceed to the next instruction until you have checked to be sure that the equipment has been unplugged. The electrical power generated by this equipment can kill!

Other typographical devices can be used to achieve a certain amount of emphasis. A dash within a sentence, for example, can alert the reader to what follows it. (The dash can be indicated by striking the hyphen twice, with no space between the two.)

■ The job will be done—after we are under contract.

■ The manager pointed out that our conduct could have only one result—dismissal.

Italics can be used occasionally to emphasize a word or phrase.

■ Sales have *not* improved since we started the new procedure.

The problem with devices such as italics and the dash is that they are so easy to use that we tend to rely on them too readily, as in the following examples.

- Sales have *not* improved since we started the new procedure and are not likely to improve unless we initiate a more *aggressive* advertising campaign.

- The rating panel—John Burton, Carol Ramirez, and Pat Nelson—evaluated the three job applicants—Mary Fontana, David Moschella, and Tyrone Braxton—and found them well qualified, but only one person—the company president—can make the final selection—and that will not happen until March.

Overuse of typographical devices may cancel their effectiveness. The reader quickly learns that the writer is using the signals to point out unimportant as well as truly important material.

WRITER'S CHECKLIST: Achieving Emphasis

To highlight your most important facts and ideas, follow these guidelines:

☐ Use the active voice.

☐ Subordinate secondary ideas.

☐ Use introductory words and phrases to stress key ideas.

☐ Use parallel structure to focus attention on how ideas are related.

☐ Use lists (such as this one) to highlight ideas by setting them apart from surrounding text.

☐ Arrange ideas in most-important to least-important order.

☐ Use typographical devices such as *italic,* **boldface,** or underlined text.

☐ Label key ideas as important.

■ Ethical Issues and Revision

When you make the revision choices discussed in this chapter and in Chapter 4, you should be aware of the potential ethical choices involved in some of those decisions. Consider, for example, the discussion in the previous section about how warnings can be emphasized with capital letters and various features such as boldface, increased font size, italics, exclamation marks, and boxed sections. Using language and design to appropriately emphasize a clear danger to readers is a positive ethical choice—and a relatively uncomplicated one.

However, choices may not always be so easy or so clear cut. A writer may struggle, for example, over how to present potential dangers, disadvantages, or limitations while at the same time achieving an objective of promoting a product, an idea, or even the writer himself or herself (as in a letter of application or a résumé). Although professionals should always act ethically, many choices the writer makes depend on the writer's own ethical standards and on the specific circumstances surrounding these choices. Obviously, no textbook can tell you how to act ethically in every situation; however, be aware that the way you express ideas affects readers' perceptions of your ethical stance. Following are some typical ethical dilemmas to watch for and avoid as you revise.[1]

- *Using language that attempts to evade responsibility.* Some writers inappropriately use the passive voice (discussed earlier in this chapter) because they hope to avoid responsibility or obscure an issue, as in the following examples: *several mistakes were made* (who made them?), *it has been decided* (who has decided?), and *the product will be inspected* (who will inspect it?). Although writers sometimes use the passive voice and vague language unintentionally in such constructions, attempts to hide or evade responsibility for past problems or to fulfill future commitments clearly involves an ethical choice.

- *Using language that attempts to mislead readers.* As discussed in Chapter 4, information should be labeled correctly and appropriately. Consider, however, the company document that stated, "a *nominal* charge will be assessed for using our facilities." When clients objected that the charge was very large, the writer pointed out that the word *nominal* means "the named amount" as well as "very small." In this situation, readers had a strong case in charging that the company was attempting to be deceptive. In other circumstances, various abstract words, technical or legal jargon, and euphemisms—when used to mislead readers or to hide a serious or dangerous situation—are unethical, even though technical or legal experts could interpret them as accurate.

- *De-emphasizing or suppressing important information.* As the example of warnings suggests, document design features should be used to highlight information important for readers. Conversely, a writer using a very small typeface or a footnote to de-emphasize a negative feature of a product or service could be perceived as suppressing important information. Likewise, failing to mention disadvantages could easily mislead readers. Even making a list of advantages, where they stand out, and then burying a disadvantage in the middle of a paragraph could unfairly mislead readers.

- *Emphasizing misleading or incorrect information.* In a technique similar to hiding negative information, a writer might be tempted to dramatically highlight a feature or service that readers would find attractive—but the attractive feature or service may be available only with some models of a product or at extra cost. In that case, readers could justifiably object that the writer has given them a false impression in order to sell a product or service, especially if the extra cost or other special conditions were also de-emphasized. This technique is as unsavory as a bait-and-switch tactic,

---

[1]Based on and adapted from "Linking Ethics and Language in the Technical Communications Classroom" by Brenda R. Sims, *Technical Communication Quarterly* 2.3 (Summer 1993): 285–299.

in which one product is advertised but is sold out when customers ask for it. Customers are then directed to more expensive models of the product.

On the job, such ethical dilemmas do not often present themselves as clear-cut choices. To help avoid the ethical problems described here as well as others, ask the following questions as you complete your revision:

- Is the communication honest and truthful?
- Am I acting in my employer's best interest? my client's or the public's best interest? my own best long-term interest?
- What would happen if everybody acted or communicated in this way?
- Am I willing to take responsibility for what the communication says, publicly and privately?
- Does the action or communication violate the rights of any of the people involved?
- Am I ethically consistent in my communications?

Above all, keep in mind that the language choices you make and their ethical implications are important because they influence how readers perceive not only your ethical stance but also the position of the organization for which you work.

■ Physical Appearance

The most thoughtfully prepared, carefully written, and conscientiously revised writing will quickly lose its effect if it has a poor physical appearance. In the classroom or on the job, a sloppy document will invariably lead your reader to assume that the work that went into preparing it was also sloppy. In the classroom, that carelessness will reflect on you; on the job, it can reflect on your employer as well.

Unless your instructor provides other specific instructions, use the following guidelines to give your writing a neat and pleasing appearance:

1. Use good-quality, white bond paper.
2. Make sure your printer produces a clear, dark image.
3. Use at least one-inch margins on all sides of the page.
4. Make sure that the type is not crowded and that ample white space separates sections.

The appropriate physical arrangement or format of specific types of writing such as letters or formal reports is discussed elsewhere in this book. Format guidance for letters and memos appears in Chapter 8 and guidance for formal reports is discussed in Chapter 13.

DIGITAL SHORTCUTS: Laying Out the Page

You can use a variety of word-processing features to improve the layout and other elements affecting the appearance of your text on the page.

- *Page margins.* Page margins, usually preset at one inch on all sides of a page, can be changed for an entire page or for blocks of text within a page.

- *Columns.* Lines of text can be arranged to run across the page from left to right or arranged in two or more columns. The columns feature can also be used for data in tables, membership lists, financial statements, rosters, and the like.

- *Margin alignment.* Text columns can be perfectly aligned in the right margin as well as the left margin.

- *Widows and orphans.* The awkward appearance of stand-alone words and lines of text at the top or bottom of a page can be eliminated automatically.

- *Centering.* Words, lines of text, and blocks of text can be centered between the right and left margins, a feature useful for creating titles, letterheads on stationery, and captions for tables and figures.

- *Line, word, and letter spacing.* The space between lines of text can be adjusted (single-, double-, triple-spaced, etc.) and unnecessary space between words and letters on a line can be eliminated.

- *Headers and footers.* Headers (titles at the top of a page) and footers (titles at the bottom of a page) can be inserted automatically on each page.

- *Type fonts.* The text for letters, reports, manuals, and other types of documents can be printed with a variety of type fonts that you deem appropriate to your purpose and readers. (A font is a complete set of letters, numbers, and other type characters with a distinctive and uniform design.)

- *Type style.* The text may also be printed using a variety of type styles with the basic font chosen. Type-style options include boldface, italic, and underlining to highlight or otherwise create distinctive text.

- *Preview mode.* Preview mode allows you to view a full page of your document on screen exactly as it will look when it is printed before you print it. Using this feature permits you to evaluate the overall look of a page and to correct it if necessary before it is printed. This practice saves time and the expense of printing a paper copy for review.

- *Style sheets.* The format specifications for recurrent documents with a uniform look can be created and saved as a separate file. The file can be called up and automatically applied over and over for subsequent versions of the same kind of document.

◼ Rough and Revised Drafts

Figures 5–1 and 5–2 show rough and revised versions of a letter written to persuade a well-known health specialist to serve as a consultant for a hospital's new outpatient clinic. As you compare the two drafts, note that the writer has not only corrected problems of coherence, clarity, and emphasis, but has also rephrased and shifted sentences so that the persuasive purpose comes through more clearly.

Figure 5–1
Rough Draft
of a Persua-
sive Letter
(with Writer's
Notes)

Morgantown Hospital

211 New Brighton Blvd.
Minneapolis, MN 55413
(612) 378-4000
http://www.morgantownhospital.org

April 2, 20--
Dr. Roberta Landau
Menken Clinical Outreach Center
New Paltz, Minnesota 55112

Dear Dr. Landau:

Overloaded sentences

Wordy introductory phrase

I am writing on behalf of Morgantown Hospital to invite you to serve in the capacity of consultant for the development and implementation of a clinic designed to provide short-term treatment of phobic disorders. Our development team is well-acquainted with your clinical experience with phobias and is familiar as well with your expertise in the area of outpatient services. Our hope is that you will advise our development team on issues of staffing and treatment protocols for the new clinic.

Subordinate reference to experience; distracts from main point

— Not parallel

Needs transition! and change to active voice

Redundant (see intro)

It is our plan currently to design the clinic as a small outpatient division affiliated with Morgantown Hospital. The clinic would be staffed by ten mental-health specialists, all of them board-certified psychologists and CSWs. It would offer short-term treatment for phobic disorders, which we know to be your particular research and clinical interest. The clinical program will include both group and individual therapy. On a monthly basis, specialists will be invited to address the general public about the diagnosis and treatment of phobic disorders.

Transitions within sentences

No — she's not involved in this part

Needs transition

We would ask you to attend a consultant's meeting on June 5, 20--, for which transportation and accommodation will be provided, to review and suggest changes to our current staffing and treatment plan. You will be paid $2,000 for attending the meeting.

Too much information

Yikes! much too abrupt. And add part about bimonthly follow-up visits

If you have questions with reference to the project, please contact me at (612) 378-6168, Mon.–Fri., 8:00 a.m. to 4:30 p.m., or by email at blakoff@ mhosp.org. We look forward to working with you.

Emphasize our desire to work with her

Sincerely,

Benjamin Lakoff

Benjamin Lakoff
Associate, Research and Development

Figure 5–2
Revised
Version of a
Persuasive
Letter

Morgantown Hospital

211 New Brighton Blvd.
Minneapolis MN 55413
(612) 378-4000
http://www.morgantownhospital.org

April 2, 20--
Dr. Roberta Landau
Menken Clinical Outreach Center
New Paltz, Minnesota 55112

Dear Dr. Landau:

Over the past year, Morgantown Hospital has been planning a new outpatient clinic devoted to the diagnosis and treatment of phobic disorders. Currently, our development team is seeking expert advice about optimal ways to organize staff and implement treatment protocols. Because your name was recommended to us as a leading authority on staffing and treatment issues, we would like to invite you to serve as consultant to our phobia clinic project.

A brief description of the project may help to clarify our invitation. The phobia clinic, which is scheduled to open in January 20—, will function as a small outpatient division of Morgantown Hospital and maintain a permanent staff of seven to ten board-certified psychologists and CSWs. Treatment programs will emphasize short-term individual and group therapies for a wide range of phobic disorders.

Your advice on selecting the clinic's staff and organizing its range of treatments would be of great value to our development team. If you agree to work with us on the project, we would ask you to attend a consultant's meeting, scheduled for June 5, 20--, to review and suggest revisions to our current plans for staff and treatments. Following the meeting on June 5, we would ask you to visit the clinic and review its status on a bimonthly basis.

If you decide to work with us on the clinic project, Morgantown Hospital will be happy to pay for your hotel and travel expenses. The hospital also will provide you with a $2,000 honorarium for attending the initial meeting and an annual honorarium of $5,000 for as long as you continue to visit and evaluate the clinic.

We look forward to hearing from you soon. If you have any questions about the clinic and your role in helping us plan it, please call me at (612) 545-6168 or by email at blakoff@mhosp.org.

Sincerely,

Benjamin Lakoff

Benjamin Lakoff
Associate, Research and Development

CHAPTER 5 SUMMARY: Revising for Coherence, Emphasis, and Ethics

When reviewing your draft, ask the following questions to verify that you have used crucial style devices to help readers focus on and grasp your central points and examples.

☐ Does each paragraph develop a single thought or idea within the larger piece of writing?

☐ Does each paragraph have a topic sentence?

☐ Are the sentences in each paragraph related to the paragraph's central idea?

☐ Are paragraphs long enough to adequately explain the paragraph's central idea but not so long as to burden readers with more details than necessary?

☐ Do the sentences in each paragraph contain enough transitional words and phrases so that readers can follow the logical relationship among ideas?

☐ Are sentences in the active voice when the doer of the action should be highlighted?

☐ Are sentences in the passive voice when the doer of the action is unimportant or unknown?

☐ Are secondary ideas subordinated to primary ideas?

☐ Are introductory words and phrases used to achieve emphasis?

☐ Are ideas of equal importance written in parallel structure using words, phrases, clauses, or lists?

☐ Are lists grammatically parallel in structure?

☐ Are other highlighting devices used appropriately?

☐ Do any potential ethical problems need to be resolved?

☐ Is the physical appearance of your final document neat and clean?

■ Exercises

1. Read the following paragraph and then complete the exercises pertaining to it.

   ■ Frequently, department managers and supervisors recruit applicants without working through our corporate human resources office. Our human resources departments at all of our locations across the country have experienced this problem. Recently, the manager of our tool design department met with a graduate of MIT to discuss an opening for a tool designer. The graduate was sent to the human resources department, where she was told that no such position existed. When the tool design manager asked the director of human resources about the matter, the manager learned that the company president had ordered a hiring freeze for two months. I'm sure that our general employment situation will get better. As a result of the manager's failure to work through proper channels, the applicant was not only disappointed but bitter.

    a. Underline the topic sentence of the paragraph.

    b. Cross out any sentences that do not contribute to paragraph unity.

2. The sentences in the following paragraphs have been purposely placed in the wrong order. Rearrange the sentences in each paragraph so that the paragraphs move smoothly and logically from one sentence to the next. Indicate the correct order of the sentences by placing the sentence numbers in the order in which the sentences should appear.

    a. (1) If such improvements could be achieved, the consequences would be significant for many different applications. (2) However, the most challenging technical problem is to achieve substantial increases in the quantities of electrical energy that can be stored per unit weight of the battery. (3) The overall process yields about 70 percent of the electricity originally put into the battery. (4) A storage battery is a relatively efficient way of storing energy.

    b. (1) Each atrium is connected to the ventricle below by a valve that allows blood to flow in only one direction. (2) The two upper chambers are called *atria,* and the two lower chambers are called *ventricles.* (3) The ventricles are also connected by one-way valves to the main outgoing blood vessels. (4) The organ is divided into four chambers. (5) The heart is a fist-sized, heavily muscled organ located approximately in the center of the chest.

    c. (1) It merely shrank the public's wealth and eventually created even more unemployment. (2) So Pericles, who was the boss man of the city-state, took action. (3) However, it was also having a recession. (4) Finally, in order to combat unemployment and the increasing recession, Pericles decided to go to war with Sparta. (5) But all this public spending didn't produce any goods. (6) As part of it, he built some of the greatest architectural wonders of the world. (7) About 500 years before the birth of Christ, Athens was the world center of democratic civilization. (8) For these artistic achievements, the people elected him to the top spot three times. (9) He started a tremendous public-works program.

3. Underline the topic sentence in each of the following paragraphs.

    a. Whether you use a hand mower, a power reel mower, or a rotary power mower to cut your lawn, the blades should be sharp enough to trim the grass cleanly without bruising or tearing the leaves. Both the cutting edge of the bedknife or reel-type mower and the reel blades should be sharp, and the reel should be set firmly against the bedknife. Make any necessary adjustments of the bedknife or of the roller (which determines the height of cut) on a flat surface, such as a concrete walk or floor. Rotary mower blades in particular require frequent sharpening. On most rotary mowers, height of cut is fixed by adjusting the wheels in holes or slots on the mower frame.

    b. One property of material considered for manufacturing processes is hardness. Hardness is the internal resistance of the material to the forcing apart or closing together of its molecules. Another property is ductility, the characteristic of material that permits it to be drawn into a wire. The smaller the diameter of the wire into which the material can be drawn, the greater the ductility. Material may also possess malleability, the property that makes it capable of being rolled or hammered into thin sheets of various shapes. Engineers, in selecting materials to use in manufacturing, must consider the materials' properties before deciding which ones are most desirable for use in production.

c.   People who raise houseplants must periodically replace the soil that serves as the growing medium for most indoor plants. When the soil of plants housed in small pots needs to be replaced, the plant is usually *potted up*—that is, transplanted to a pot of the next larger size. The plant, with its root ball intact, is removed from the small pot, and fresh dirt is piled into the larger container, with space allowed for the root ball. The plant is then carefully inserted into the new soil. For plants already in the largest-sized pots, the indoor gardener may take the plant, along with its root ball, out of the pot, discard the remaining earth, put in a similar amount of fresh dirt, and then return the plant to its original container.

d.   Scientists disagree on what memory is and even on how to describe it. Sometimes it is defined by its duration. Primary memory, the portion of active consciousness that lets you repeat a sentence you just heard, rarely declines with age. Secondary memory, which lasts from a few seconds to a few days and includes things like who borrowed your pen, erodes as we get older. Alternatively, memory can be divided by function: *implicit,* involving learned skills, such as swinging a tennis racquet or speaking French, that become automatic; *semantic,* comprising objective facts, such as the date of the Battle of Hastings, general knowledge, and information independent of context; and *episodic,* concerning specific events defined by time, place, and personal history. Only the last of these three degenerates dramatically over time.

4.   Each of the following pairs of sentences lacks a transition from the first sentence to the second. From the list of transitional devices on page 147, select the most appropriate one for each sentence pair. Then rewrite the sentences as necessary.

a.   Ms. Silvenski arrived at the post office just before closing time. She was not able to mail her package because it had not been wrapped according to post office specifications.

b.   An improperly cut garment will not hang attractively on the wearer. When you sew, you should be sure to lay out and cut your pattern accurately and carefully.

c.   The Doctors Clinic was able to attain its fund-raising goal on time this year. Mercer Street Hospital was forced to extend its fund-raising deadline for three months.

d.   When instructing the new tellers, the branch manager explained how to deal with impatient customers. The personal-banking assistant told the new employees that they should consult her if they had difficulty handling those customers.

e.   There are several reasons why a car may skid on ice. The driver may be going faster than road conditions warrant.

5.   Underline the transitional words and phrases in the following paragraphs.

a.   Homeowners should know where the gutters on their houses are located and should be sure to keep them in good repair, because gutters are vulnerable to various weather conditions. On many houses, gutters are tucked up under or into the eaves, so that they appear as little more than another line or two of trim. As a result, many homeowners are not even aware that their houses have gutters. Unless the gutters are well maintained, however, the thousands of gallons of water that may fall onto the roof of the average house each year can easily damage or weaken the gutters. During the winter months, the weight of snow and ice may pull gutters away from the house or loosen the downspout straps. Clogged and frozen downspouts may also develop seam cracks. When spring comes, these seam cracks sometimes create leaks that may allow heavy rains to flood the yard or the house instead of draining properly into the sewer system. In addition, melting snow that flows freely off the roof may go down the house wall, wetting it sufficiently to cause interior wall damage.

b. The causes of global climate change remain in dispute. Existing theories of climate, atmospheric models, and statistical data are inadequate to provide planners with information on future weather patterns. In the long run, research may lead to more reliable forecasts of climate. For the present, however, planners have no choice but to heed expert judgments about the world's future climate and its effect on agriculture and other sectors of the economy.

6. Bring a document to class that you have written either in this (or another) class or at your job. Under the direction of your instructor, take the following steps:
   a. Circle all the words or phrases that provide transition between each sentence.
   b. If you find two sentences that do not have adequate transition, place an X in the space between them.
   c. For those sentences that seem not to have adequate transition, insert a word, phrase, or clause that will improve the transition.

7. Write an opening paragraph for two of the following topics. The audience for each topic is specified in parentheses.
   a. My favorite instructor (to someone nominating him or her for a teaching award).
   b. Ways to improve employee motivation (to the president or head of the organization that employs you).
   c. Ways to improve student advising at your school (to the dean of students or someone in an equivalent position).
   d. What to look for in a first apartment (to a friend who's looking).
   e. The advantages of budgeting (to a spendthrift friend).

8. Business writing is more forceful if it uses active-voice verbs. Revise the following sentences so that verbs are in the active voice. Add subjects if necessary.
   a. The computers were powered up each day at 7 A.M.
   b. Initial figures for the bid were submitted before the June 1 deadline.
   c. A separate bill from AT&T will be sent to customers who continue to use AT&T as their long-distance carrier.
   d. Substantial sums of money were saved by customers who enrolled early in our stock-option plan.
   e. A significant financial commitment has been made by us to ensure that our customers will be able to take advantage of our discount pricing.

    f.   Smaller-sized automated equipment was ordered so that each manager could have an individual computer.

9. Rewrite the following sentences to eliminate *excessive* subordination.
    a.   The duty officer who was on duty at 3:30 A.M. was the one who took the call that there was a malfunction in the Number 3 generator that had been repaired at approximately 9:00 A.M. the previous morning.
    b.   I have referred your letter that you wrote to us on June 20 to our staff attorney who reviewed it in the light of corporate policy that is pertinent to the issue that you raise.
    c.   Will your presentation that is scheduled for the 12th of next May and that will answer questions submitted in advance be circulated before the 12th to those who will be attending the workshop?

10. Some of the following sentences violate the principle of parallel structure. Identify the incorrect sentences and revise to make them parallel. The sentences may be correctly changed in more than one way.
    a.   We expected to be disappointed and that we would reject the proposal.
    b.   Etiquette is important in social life, and you need it in business too.
    c.   To type fast is one thing, but typing accurately is another.
    d.   Do you prefer filing, typing, or balancing the budget?
    e.   Is your home well heated and with adequate ventilation?
    f.   The mailing notation should not only appear on the original but also on the copies.
    g.   The office has been not only cleaned but also newly decorated.
    h.   Our friends enjoy winter sports like hockey, skiing and to skate.
    i.   Ms. Jory either wants Anna or me to proofread the galleys for our annual report.
    j.   The desk was neither the correct size nor the right model.
    k.   You may either send a check or a money order.
    l.   We are afraid that either the package is lost or stolen.
    m.   Next weekend, we plan to rent a cabin, hire a guide, and hiking through the countryside.
    n.   Mr. Levesque is a well-read and an interesting person.

■ In-Class Activities

1. Choose a topic sentence from the following list and write a paragraph that develops that sentence. Be certain that the paragraph is both unified and coherent; follow the guidelines offered in this chapter. When you are finished writing, divide into groups. Evaluate each paragraph as a group. Use the Writer's Checklist: Creating Effective Paragraphs on page 149 as your evaluation guide. In group discussion, decide which tips are most difficult to follow and why.
    a.   I chose [name your major] because I am interested in [name one skill or task such as "working with numbers" or "helping people"].
    b.   On-the-job writing courses show why the principles of good writing are important.

    c. Working at a part-time (or full-time) job has helped me appreciate my education in three specific ways.

    d. Business ethics today is simply good business.

    e. Job opportunities for employees are created by company growth.

    f. Good management-labor relations and higher productivity are mandatory for the creation of new jobs.

    g. Every successful industrial corporation has at least one bread-and-butter product that sells well year in and year out.

    h. Labor unions are no longer the powerful monoliths they were 50 years ago.

2. Rewrite each of the following sentences so that the verb is in the active voice. Whenever a potential subject is not given in a sentence, supply one as you write. When you have finished your sentences, divide into groups to share and discuss them. Is there much variation in the wording of your sentences? Is the meaning of the sentence affected by the differences in wording? Is a different tone implied?

    a. The entire building was spray-painted by Charles and his brother.

    b. It was assumed by the superintendent that the trip was postponed until next Tuesday.

    c. The completed form should be submitted to Tim Hagen by the 15th of every month.

    d. The fluid should be applied sparingly and should be allowed to dry for eight to ten seconds.

    e. The metropolitan area was defined as groups of counties related by commuting patterns by the researchers.

    f. The machine tool industry was dominated by two companies: Welland Industries and Machine Tools Unlimited.

    g. Their way to raise capital was to set up a limited partnership.

    h. A test of the equipment should be conducted at the vendor's location.

    i. The brochures and notes from the trade show should be gathered and read carefully.

    j. Images are converted into electronic impulses that can be quickly stored, analyzed, and transmitted by computers in electronic photography.

    k. Reducing absenteeism was a way of enhancing productivity, the company president was told.

    l. Two basic types of business loans are offered by the Small Business Administration: guaranty loans made by private lenders and direct SBA loans.

    m. "Will the new tax laws make leasing rather than purchasing equipment more attractive?" was what the distributor recently asked me.

3. Combine each of the following series of short sentences into one unified sentence. Use subordination (1) to indicate how the ideas expressed in the sentence relate to each other, and (2) to emphasize the most important idea or ideas. When you have completed the sentences, exchange papers with a classmate. Mark each subordinate clause and underline the most important idea in your classmate's sentences. When finished, compare your paper to the one you evaluated.

    a. I recorded my speech on a videotape. The videotape can be recorded over. It does not need to be erased.

    b. It rained this morning. The construction crew stayed indoors. Members played a game of hearts. Valdez won.

    c. It had snowed for a week. I like to ski. I was delighted.

    d. He studied autoCAD® at a technical school. He joined his brother's firm as a CAD specialist in 2001.

    e. Thomas Edison was one of America's greatest inventors. Teddy Roosevelt was the twenty-sixth president of the United States. Edison and Roosevelt were friends.

    f. Sales of DVD players were declining. The management of DVDeluxe became worried. The management decided to initiate an online ad campaign.

    g. The technology group had a backlog of work. No one could make updates to the company Web site. The updates are due in two days.

    h. The cost of gasoline has increased. All the suppliers have increased their prices. The suppliers are wholesalers.

    i. Recently a new type of wireless technology was developed by engineers. It is much more effective than those previously used.

    j. Some writers place every idea into a separate sentence. They should try to show the relationships between ideas. To do this, they should reduce unimportant, short sentences to words, phrases, or dependent clauses.

    k. The cost of computer parts has increased. All the wholesale suppliers have increased their prices. Some of them still have a supply of parts purchased at the old price. They may be willing to sell parts to you at the old price to get your business.

4. In the amount of time allotted by your instructor, quickly rewrite the following lists to make them parallel. The first three writers to finish the assignment will write their sentences on the board or on a transparency for the overhead projector so that the class can discuss and approve the revisions.

    a. Carry this emergency equipment in your car during long winter trips:

- Chains for tires and towing
- Snow shovel
- Scraper
- Sand or salt
- A wireless phone
- For minor repairs, a car tool kit
- Flashlight—be sure to check for fresh batteries
- Flares, reflectors
- First-aid kit
- Blankets
- A bottle of water
- Jumper cables are also a good idea

    b. Keep these safety tips in mind as you work on your car:

- Wear safety goggles when working under the hood, especially when dealing with the battery.
- The engine should be operated only in a well-ventilated area.
- Fans and belts are dangerous when moving—you or your clothing could get caught in them.
- Avoid contact with hot metal parts, such as the radiator and the exhaust manifold.

5. Divide into small groups and appoint a recorder in each group. Working as a team, write as many variations as possible for the following sentences making the elements within them parallel in each construction. If desired, after each group is finished, the recorders may share the results from their group with the rest of the class.

   a. The system is large and convenient, and it does not cost very much.
   b. The processor sends either a ready function code or transmits a standby function code.
   c. The log is a record of the problems that have occurred and of the services performed.
   d. The committee feels that the present system has three disadvantages: It causes delay in the distribution of incoming mail, duplicates work, and unnecessary delays are created in the work of several other departments.
   e. In our first list, we inadvertently omitted the seven lathes in room B-101, the four milling machines in room B-117, and from the next room, B-118, we also forgot to include 16 shapers.
   f. This product offers ease of operation, economy, and it is easily available.
   g. The manual gives instructions for operating the machine and to adjust it.
   h. Three of the applicants were given promotions, and transfers were arranged for the other four applicants.
   i. To analyze the data, carry out the following steps: examine all the details carefully, eliminate all the unnecessary details, and a chart showing the flow of work should then be prepared.
   j. We have found that the new system has four disadvantages: too costly to operate, it causes delays, fails to use any of the existing equipment, and it permits only one in-process examination.
   k. The design is simple, inexpensive, and can be used effectively.
   l. Management was slow to recognize the problem and even slower understanding it.

■ Research Projects

1. Find a document (instructions, direct-mail advertising, or other sample) that you believe demonstrates one or more of the four ethical problems discussed in this chapter: using language that attempts to evade responsibility, to mislead readers, to de-emphasize or suppress important information, or to emphasize misleading or incorrect information. As your instructor directs, (1) report what ethical problems you see and describe how the document might be revised to eliminate those problems, and (2) rewrite the samples to eliminate the ethical problems.

2. As you did in Chapter 4, find a study partner in the class and with the approval of your instructor, exchange copies of the rough drafts of an upcoming assignment well in advance of the deadline. Using the chapter summary at the end of this chapter, identify specific areas for improvement. Keep in mind that drafts naturally contain trouble spots and your job is to help your partner receive a better grade. Return the draft to your partner ahead of the due date so that he or she can incorporate your suggestions.

3. Find at least three news articles on the same current event (they may be from print media or well-established news service Web sites). Underline and identify examples of subordinate clauses used to achieve emphasis. Write a brief summary of how this method in news reporting has affected the outcome of the news articles. Include whether you think that the subordination used was effective or if you found examples of too much subordination. Use examples from the articles to explain and support your conclusions.

4. Gather at least three samples of technical writing from printed sources that use lists to convey information in a paragraph. Find at least three samples of technical writing from printed sources that use conventional sentences to convey information in a paragraph. Compare the samples and evaluate whether lists or sentences work better. Revise at least two of your samples from lists to sentences or from sentences to lists and compare the results to the original. Which works better—the original or your revision? Support your conclusion with examples from the sample texts.

5. Find at least three newspaper articles that use climactic order to achieve emphasis. Create a list of facts or ideas from each article, beginning with the least important idea and ending with the most important idea. Explain why you think the author of each article chose this method of organization.

■ Web Projects

1. a. Because ".com" Web sites are often designed with the consumer in mind, they are often written in a persuasive manner. List the names and URLs of at least three ".com" sites—perhaps sites where you have purchased a product online—that contain examples of emphatic writing. Write a brief narrative about your sample sites, noting voice, overloaded sentences, and the use of subordination. Is the writing persuasive? Support your conclusions using examples from the texts at the sites.

   b. Alternatively, government sites, educational sites, and the sites of organizations tend to be more objective. List at least three ".gov," ".edu," or ".org" Web sites that contain examples of emphatic, yet effective, writing. Prepare a brief narrative about your sample sites, noting voice and use of subordination. How does the writing at these sites compare to that at the ".com" sites that you have visited?

2. Internet sites often use lists to convey information in a quickly readable format. Find samples of text from at least five Web sites related to your field of study and occupational interest that contain lists. Print out the lists and note the order of arrangement. Rank the items in the list by order of importance. How accurately and effectively are the lists used to provide information?

3. Language that attempts to evade responsibility or mislead readers leads to ethical dilemmas. Internet sites—especially ".com" sites—often include disclaimers that are supposed to alleviate the authors' responsibility for such dilemmas. Find at least three sites that offer disclaimers. What content at the site do you believe initiated the disclaimer? Write a brief narrative summarizing your findings and citing examples from the text at the sites.

4. The language of advertising—whether communicated in print or on the Web— can be used to de-emphasize or suppress information, or to emphasize misleading or incorrect information. Suppose you have been asked to purchase online a new scanner, printer, fax, or other piece of office equipment for your company. As you look for the best piece of equipment to purchase, preview several different Web sites offering similar products. Because you will want to act in your employer's best interest, make a list of statements that you found at each site that you believe makes that site and its product trustworthy and reliable. Also, list statements at the sites that you believe may misrepresent information. Write a brief summary of your findings and make a recommendation on what site you feel is the best place to make your online purchase. (Be sure to include the site's URL.) If you are interested in reading about the federal laws covering this subject of advertising, visit FindLaw, http://prof.findlaw.com/. See the section covering General Principles of Advertising Review.

5. Your company needs to hire several more employees in the coming months. You are part of a committee that is working with the human resource director to find the best candidates for your company to hire. You have been asked to review three online employment agencies as your company looks for the one to best represent its hiring needs. Select three online employment agencies, make notes about each one, and compare them to one another. Then, in a memo to your boss, recommend one of the employment agencies and explain why you think this agency is the right one for your company. As you prepare your recommendation, refer to the Chapter 5 Summary on page 168 of the text.

6 Collaborative Writing

On the job or in the classroom, no one works in a vacuum. To some degree, everyone must rely on the help of others to do their jobs. No matter what you write or how often you write, you will likely have to collaborate with other people. Collaborative writing involves working with other people as a team to produce a single document, with each member of the team contributing equally to the planning, designing, and writing. It also involves sharing equal responsibility for the end product.

Collaborative writing is generally done for one of three reasons:

1. The project requires expertise or specialization in more than one area.
2. The project benefits from the merging of different perspectives.
3. The size of the project, the time constraints imposed on it, or the importance of the project to your organization requires a team effort.

The larger and more important the document, the more likely it is to be produced collaboratively. Sales proposals, for example, require contributions from many different types of experts (engineers, systems analysts, scientists, financial experts, sales managers, etc.). Formal reports and specifications are among other documents that are commonly written collaboratively. For collaborative writing, the writing process varies only by the addition of a reviewing step; otherwise, the process itself is no different, consisting of planning, researching, writing, reviewing, and revising. Typically, one person then edits the draft, to unify it, and manages the production of the proposal.

■ Advantages and Disadvantages of Collaborative Writing

Collaborative writing can offer many benefits.

1. *Many heads are better than one.* The work that a collaborative writing team produces is normally considerably better than the work any one of its members could have produced alone. Team members lead each other to consider ideas different from those they would have explored individually.

Voices from the Workplace

Joseph G. Rappaport, Office of the Public Advocate, City of New York

Joseph G. Rappaport is transit advisor to Mark Green, New York City's Public Advocate. On any given day, Joe can find himself talking to the press; writing leaflets and investigative reports; and composing letters to transit officials, the governor, or the mayor. Much of the writing Joe produces is written collectively.

Here's Joe's comment on collective writing: "One person here usually takes the lead in getting a letter out the door. I try hard to respond quickly to drafts composed by that person. I always make a concrete suggestion if I don't think a word, a phrase, or a sentence works. There's nothing less helpful than getting a letter marked up with notes that say, 'this doesn't work' and no ideas on what might work better. Quick turnaround and detailed suggestions for revision help the collaborative writing process work smoothly."

To find out more about the Office of the Public Advocate for New York City, visit http://www.publicadvocate.nyc.gov/.

Entry-Level
Rachel O'Malley, iCast

Rachel O'Malley was Associate Movies Editor at iCast, formerly an entertainment Web portal. Rachel built media pages (with film clips, interview bites, movie trailers), updated various main pages, wrote and managed an influx of movie reviews, and occasionally interviewed movie-related celebrities. At iCast, Rachel collaborated with coworkers on Web-page copy and content.

Of her experience, Rachel writes that "the main advantage to writing collaboratively is that it keeps mistakes to a minimum. An extra pair of eyes helps to ensure that the copy on a page, whether it's just a title, review, or interview, is clean and consistent. I usually get a lot of edits during the revision process—which I am grateful for—because sometimes, if you spend a significant amount of time looking at a small piece of your own writing, you can lose perspective; having another writer work with you can only help make the finished product stronger and more appealing to the reader."

2. *Team members provide immediate feedback*—even if it is sometimes contested and debated—which is one of the great advantages of collaborative writing. Fellow team members may detect problems with organization, clarity, logic, and substance—and point them out during reviews. The fact that you may receive multiple responses also makes criticism easier to accept; if three out of three team members offer the same criticism, you can more readily accept it. It's like having your own personal set of critics—but critics who have a personal stake in helping you do a good job.

3. *Team members play devil's advocate for each other;* that is, they take contrary points of view to try to make certain that all important points are covered and that all potential problems have been exposed and resolved.

4. *Team members help each other past the frustrations and stress of writing.* When one team member needs to make a decision, there is always someone to talk it over with.

5. *Team members write more confidently* knowing that their peers will offer constructive criticism—not to find fault but to make the end product better.

6. *Team members develop a greater tolerance of and respect for the opinions of others.* As a team member, you become more aware of and involved in the planning of a document than you would working alone because of the team discussion that takes place during the planning stage. The same is true of reviews and revisions.

The primary disadvantage of collaborative writing is the demand it can place on your time, energy, and ego as a writer. Collaborative writing takes more time and energy than writing alone; and learning to accept criticism of your writing is not always easy.

■ Functions of the Collaborative Writing Team

Writing teams collaborate on every facet of the writing process: (1) planning the document, (2) researching the subject and writing the draft, (3) reviewing the drafts of team members, and (4) revising the draft on the basis of comments from all team members. (Read the section Conducting a Meeting in Chapter 15 before calling your first meeting.)

Planning

The team plans, as a group, as much of the document as is practical. Beyond a certain level, however, the team does not have sufficient command of details to plan realistically at this preliminary stage and must assign detailed planning to individual team members. During the planning stage, the team also produces a schedule for each stage of the project. The agreed-upon schedule should include the due dates for drafts, for team reviews of the drafts, and for revisions. It is important that each team member meet these deadlines, even if the draft submitted is sketchy or not quite as good as desired. The other team members will have the opportunity to comment on the draft and suggest improvements. A deadline missed by one team member may hold up the work of the entire team, so all team members should be familiar with the schedule and submit their drafts and revisions on time.

As part of the planning process, the team should agree on the style guidelines that all team members will follow in writing their drafts. The guidelines should

provide for uniformity and consistency in the writing, which is especially important because different team members are writing separate sections of the same
document. Project style guidelines should address the following issues:

- Levels of headings and their style: all capital letters, all underlined, first
  letter capitalized, or some combination of these
- Preferred capitalization of words in the text
- Reference format (if references are used)
- Abbreviations, acronyms, and symbols
- Spacing and margin guidelines
- Key terms that require hyphenation or that should be written as one word
  (*on site/onsite, on-line/online*)
- Guidelines for handling proprietary, confidential, or classified information
- Format and wording of disclaimers (to satisfy legal or policy require-
  ments)
- Distinction between research sources that must be cited and those that
  need not be cited
- Use of the active voice, the present tense, and the imperative mood in
  most situations

WRITER'S CHECKLIST: Planning a Collaborative Writing Project

☐ Establish guidelines to ensure that all team members are working toward
the same goal and moving in the same direction.

☐ Agree on a standard reference guide for matters of style and format.

☐ Make sure that work assignments are appropriate to each person's particular talents.

☐ Establish a schedule that includes due dates for drafts, for team reviews of
drafts, and for revisions.

Research and Writing

The planning stage is followed by research and writing stages. These are periods
of intense independent activity by the individual team members. At this stage,
you gather information for your assigned segment of the document, create a
master outline of the segment, flesh out the outline by providing the necessary
details, and produce a first draft, using the guidelines discussed in Chapters 2 and
3. Collaboration requires flexibility: The team should not insist that individual

team members slavishly follow the agreed-upon outline if it proves to be inadequate or faulty in one or more areas. When a writer pursues a specific assignment in detail, he or she may find that the general outline for that segment was based on insufficient knowledge and is not desirable, or even possible, as written. Or perhaps during the research process, a writer may discover highly relevant information that is not covered in the team's working outline. In such cases, the writer must have the freedom to alter the outline. If the deviation is great enough, the writer should bring the other team members into the picture before proceeding.

Revise your draft until it is as good as you can make it, following the guidelines in Chapters 4 and 5. Then, by the deadline established for submitting drafts, send copies of the draft to all other team members for their review. You may circulate the draft by hard copy, by email, or online, as described in Digital Shortcuts: Using Email for Collaborative Writing.

DIGITAL SHORTCUTS: Using Email for Collaborative Writing

Email can play a vital role in collaborative writing, allowing writers to exchange their draft documents regardless of whether members of the collaborative group live across the country or overseas. Email encourages members of a collaborative group to communicate more readily with each other, share information, ask questions, and solve problems. Collaborating by email can even make criticism easier to accept or to offer because it is not a face-to-face communication. Email also removes the likelihood of miscommunication that sometimes plagues face-to-face meetings. Although email does not eliminate the need for a group to meet in person, it can reduce the requirement for face-to-face communication.

Using email to send a draft as an attachment enables collaborative team members to solicit feedback electronically and revise the original draft based on the comments received. This process can be repeated for each team member until all sections are in final form and ready for consolidation into the master copy maintained by the team leader. For tips on how to set up a document for electronic review, see Digital Shortcuts: Setting Up a Document for Electronic Review on page 185.

Reviewing

During the review stage, team members assume the role of the reading audience in an attempt to clear up in advance any problems that might arise for that audience—a customer, a senior official in the organization, or the board of directors. Each team member reviews the work of the other team members carefully and critically (but also with sensitivity to the person whose work is being reviewed), checking for problems in content, organization, and style.

Figures 6–1 and 6–2 represent one section of a proposal that was written to persuade a company president to merge the company's profit-sharing plans. The proposal describes the merger process and shows its associated costs. Two collaborative writing team members have worked together to prepare the document. Figure 6–1 shows the second member's initial draft, which describes the merger's benefits and costs, with the first team member's comments on the draft.

**Figure 6–1
A Draft
Section of a
Report with a
Collaborative
Team
Member's
Comments**

Part II. Merger of Plans/Amending and Restating Plans/Applications for Determination Letters

Title is too technical— "Costs/Benefits of Merging"?

We can no longer test the Oakite product services 401(k) Profit Sharing Plan separately for coverage and nondiscrimination because combined, <u>Oakite products and Oakley services have fewer than 50 employees</u>. The merger of the 401(k) Profit Sharing Plans takes care of this problem while reducing the implementation and audit costs. We wil need to amend and restate the new plan to bring it into compliance with tax law 409921-65. *sp*

This is covered in Part I (make this into transition)

Too technical and you need to emphasize <u>benefits</u>.

The cost of merging, amending, restating, and redesigning the surviving 401(k) Profit Sharing Plan and for filing of notices 54-90 and 36-98 and applications 56-98 and 45-98 would be between $18,000 to $25,000.

(cost <u>reduction</u> over 2 years)

Transmittal sheet: Team Member #2 (B. Reisner, Sales Development)

Comments:

Please note marginal comments. Your information sounds correct, but the prospective client will need definitions and explanations for many of the terms and names (notices 54-90 and 36-98) that you're juggling. You should also note in your opening that Part I explains the problems associated with maintaining separate plans. Doing so will give you a better lead into your section than you've got at this point.

Further, you need to break down the specific financial costs and benefits that will result from the merger. You don't need to go into detail here; remember, Section 3 describes the details of the merger process. Simply note specific costs for specific services in a table, and give an estimate of the client's projected financial gain. NOTE: The range for costs is $19,000 to $26,000, not $18,000 to $25,000. CHECK: Can client deduct merger costs from gross profit?

Finally, you should promote our services with more vigor. You're not simply reporting information so that Mr. B. can phone up another company to do the merger—you're talking him into working with Anderson Associates.

Because the entire report will be sent to the client company's president, whose time is limited and who has only a general knowledge of profit-sharing plans and mergers, the reviews must carefully note any parts of the report that are not appropriate for a nonexpert reader.

As Figure 6–1 shows, reviewing a colleague's draft is similar to reviewing your own work: A good reviewer evaluates a document in terms of audience and

Figure 6–2
Revised
Section of
the Draft
Presented in
Figure 6–1

Part II. Benefits and Costs of Merging Current Profit-Sharing Plans

As Part I of this report explains, the separate profit-sharing plans for your two companies, Oakite Products and Oakley Services, can no longer ensure that each employee is assigned the correct number of shares and the correct employer contribution. In addition, administrative costs for maintaining separate plans are high. If you commissioned Anderson Associates to merge the plans, however, adequate tests could be performed to ensure accuracy, and administrative costs would be greatly reduced.

Further, although a merger would require you to make certain changes to your current profit-sharing procedures, Anderson Associates would help you amend and restate the new plan so that it complies with the most recent tax legislation. Anderson Associates will also prepare and file necessary merger documents with the Departments of Taxation and Labor.

The estimated cost for merging, amending, and refiling the profit-sharing plans would be between $19,000 and $26,000. Please see Table 1 for a breakdown of specific costs.

In reality, you would incur no cost if Anderson Associates merged your profit-sharing plans because of reduced administrative costs. According to our estimates, the merger would give you a yearly net reduction of $36,000 in administrative costs. Thus, you would save approximately $11,000 during the first year of administering the plan and at least $36,000 annually after the first year. See Table 2 for a breakdown of net reductions in administrative costs.

WRITER'S CHECKLIST: Reviewing Drafts by Other Writers

The following guidelines will help you review the work of others:

☐ Verify that the content is complete.

☐ Look for any technical errors or for anything that seems technically questionable.

☐ Check to see if the material falls within the predetermined scope of coverage.

☐ See if the details and examples support the main points.

☐ Make sure the draft meets the established purpose of the document.

☐ Check to see if the draft meets the needs of the identified reader.

☐ Look to see if the draft generally follows the agreed-upon outline.

purpose, coherence, emphasis, and correctness. For this reason, the revision strategies you studied in Chapters 4 and 5 will serve as your foundation for collaborative work. Revising collaborative writing is much like revising any other type of writing: The writer mulls over the suggested changes, checks questionable facts, and then reworks the draft. Figure 6–2 shows the same section of the report, revised in response to the team member's comments.

DIGITAL SHORTCUTS: Setting Up a Document for Electronic Review

You have completed a draft and want it reviewed online by other members of your class or by colleagues in your office. Depending on your preference, reviewers can edit and comment on your draft in a number of ways without changing your original document. One way is for reviewers to make tracked changes — edits that are clearly highlighted and that you can accept or reject — to copies that you distribute. Another way is for reviewers to make changes directly to the document — in this case, you set up your document so that it will automatically save each version, along with the original draft, all in one document. Let your reviewers know which method you would like them to use, and send your document as an attachment to an email message or post it in an electronic folder on your school's or company's internal network. When all reviewers return your draft, you can create a revised document by accepting or rejecting their edits (if using the tracked-changes method) or by merging components of reviewers' versions (if using the multiple-versions method).

An important feature that can be used with either of these review options is the Insert Comment feature. To insert comments throughout your document, reviewers can select the text or graphic for comment, click on the **Insert comment** button on the toolbar, and type their comments in a window that opens at the bottom of the screen. The text or graphic that is commented on will be highlighted in color, numbered, and marked with the reviewer's initials. (Note that multiple reviewers can make comments.) You can view each comment by pointing the cursor at the highlighted text or on the reviewer's initials — when you move your cursor over the text or initials, the comments pop up — or you can read the comments at the bottom of your screen. It is important to note that if reviewers suggest particular changes within the Comments area, you will need to manually add any changes that you want to make.

Making Tracked Changes to the Document

The tracked-changes option is convenient because reviewer edits are clearly highlighted and later can be individually accepted or rejected. If you choose this method, you may wish to protect your document by assigning a password that will prevent any changes except for tracked changes and comments, before emailing or posting your draft. Reviewers may add, delete, or move text or graphics and even reformat the document. The software automatically highlights the changes (usually by underlining text changes and permitting you to specify different formatting for other changes) so that you can easily locate reviewer changes when accepting or rejecting them. Using this feature, reviewers may also insert comments. Any changes suggested by reviewers in the Comments area must be added manually.

Making Changes Directly to the Document

Another option is to set up your document so that it will automatically save the original version of your draft as well as each succeeding version edited by your reviewers. (See the instructions or the Help menu for your word-processing software for details about how to enable this feature and use it in conjunction with other options.) When you use this method, all versions of the draft are stored within one document and each version includes the date and name of the person who made the changes. Reviewers can make their edits to the document as if it were their own — adding, deleting, reformatting, or moving text or graphics (there is no automatic highlighting unless tracked changes are selected). When revising your draft, you can compare each version and merge edits as needed. Using this feature, reviewers can also insert comments. Any changes suggested by reviewers in the Comments area must also be added manually by you to your final revision.

The review stage may lead to additional planning. If, for example, a review of the first draft reveals that the original organization for a section was not adequate or correct, or if new information becomes available, the team must return to the planning stage for that segment of the document to incorporate the newer knowledge and understanding.

Revising

The individual writers now read and evaluate the reviews of all other team members and accept or reject the suggested revisions. At this point, you, as a writer, must be careful not to let your ego get in the way of good judgment. You must consider each suggestion objectively on the basis of its merit, rather than simply reacting negatively to criticism of your writing. Writers who are able to accept criticism and use it to produce a better end product participate in the most fruitful kind of collaboration.

■ The Role of Conflict in Collaborative Writing

It is critically important to the quality of the document being produced that the viewpoints of all team members be considered. However, when writers collaborate, conflicts will occur. They may range from a relatively minor difference over a grammatical point (whether to split an infinitive) to a major conflict over the basic approach to the document being written (whether there is too little or too much detail for the intended reader). Regardless of the severity of the conflict, it must be worked through to a conclusion or compromise that all team members can accept, even though all might not *entirely* agree. When the group can tolerate some disharmony and work through conflicting opinions to reach a consensus, its work is enhanced.

WRITER'S CHECKLIST: Working in a Collaborative Group

☐ Know the people on your team and establish a good working rapport with them.

☐ Put the interests of your team ahead of your own.

☐ Think collectively, as a group. Do not regard one person's opinion as more or less important than another's.

☐ Participate constructively in group meetings.

☐ Be an effective listener (see Listening in Chapter 15, page 659).

☐ Be receptive to constructive criticism.

☐ Provide constructive feedback to your coauthors.

☐ Meet your established deadlines.

Although mutual respect among team members is necessary, too much deference can inhibit challenges—and that reduces the team's creativity. You have to be willing to challenge another team member's work, while still being sensitive to that person's ego and feelings. The same rule applies to collaborative writing that applies whenever critical give-and-take occurs: Focus on the problem and how to solve it rather than on the person.

Conflicts over valid issues almost always generate more innovative and creative work than does passive acceptance. However, even though the result of conflict in a peer writing team is usually positive, it can sometimes produce self-doubt or doubt about your fellow team members. Remember that conflict is a natural part of group work. Learn to harness it and turn it into a positive force.

If not managed properly, conflict can produce negative results. Some people may feel defeated, and distrust may develop among team members. Participants may begin to put their own narrow interests ahead of the team goal and cooperation may break down because of resistance among members. In a team that manages conflict well, however, the problems that surface can be resolved early on in the writing process rather than adversely affecting the final document. Not only can conflict provide an opportunity for open communication and a forum for each team member's views, it can also stimulate synergy and creativity and, as a result, lead to better ideas and approaches.

In working through conflict, try to maximize its benefits and minimize its negative effects. First, be sure that everyone involved is aware of areas of agreement, and emphasize those areas in order to establish a positive environment. Then identify differences of opinion and ask why they exist. If differences occur over facts, it is simply a matter of determining which are correct. If it is a problem of different goals, encourage each team member to look at the problem from the other person's perspective. When conflict arises, define the problem, describe the alternate solutions, and select the one solution—or compromise—to achieve the solution that provides all team members and the team with the most benefits.

The following suggestions can help you manage the different aspects of conflict:

- Avoid taking a win-or-lose stand if you are personally involved in the conflict. If you use a win-or-lose approach, your victory will be at the other person's expense. This is not a constructive approach because, by definition, there *must* be a loser. Most conflicts don't start out this way, but when one team member regards a compromise as a personal defeat, a conflict can lead to nonproductive results.

- Avoid accusations, threats, or disparaging comments. Instead, try to emphasize common interests and mutual goals, bearing in mind that conciliation fosters cooperation. Expressing a desire for harmonious relations can have a very disarming effect on an aggressive personality in the group.

- Support your position with facts. Point out the ways that your position could benefit the team's ultimate goal. Show how your position is consistent with precedent, prevailing norms, or accepted standards (if true, of course). Tactfully point out any overlooked disadvantages or logic errors in the other person's point of view. Again, focus on the problem and the solution, not the person.

- Use bargaining strategies to arrive at an exchange of concessions until a compromise is reached. Both parties win through a compromise. Even if you settle for less than you initially wanted, you don't risk losing out altogether as in a win-or-lose struggle. A successful compromise satisfies each participant's minimum needs.

- Use collaboration to resolve conflict. This means each team member accepts the others' goals and all members work to achieve the best outcome for the team. A flexible, exploratory attitude is a prerequisite for collaboration; each team member must understand the others' points of view and determine the group's needs for it to be successful.

DIGITAL SHORTCUTS: Sharing Material in Electronic Files

You don't need to redo work that has already been done. If boilerplate material (policy statements, instructions, procedures, correspondence, or reports created by colleagues) that meets your needs exists in other company documents, copy and paste the information into your document. Be sure to edit the material to make it an exact fit. Borrowing passages from such sources is neither plagiarism nor a violation of copyright since the information is simply being used in a different setting by the organization to which it already belongs. Such passages do not need to be acknowledged when you document other sources of information.

Discuss sources of boilerplate material in group planning meetings and store them in electronic folders or on shared network drives for sharing with other team members. Many companies and organizations post key policy and procedural documents on their internal Web sites where team members and others can view and copy them as necessary.

■ Leading a Collaborative Writing Team

Although the team may designate one person as its leader, that person shares decision-making authority with the other team members while assuming the additional responsibility of coordinating the team's activities, organizing the project, and producing the final product. Leadership can be granted by mutual agreement among team members to one team member or it can be rotated among members if the team produces many documents over time. The teams that collaborate best are composed of members who are professionally competent, who have mutual respect for the abilities of the other members, and who are compatible enough to work together harmoniously toward a common goal.

On a practical level, the team leader's responsibilities will include scheduling and leading meetings, writing and distributing minutes of meetings, and maintaining the master copy of the document during all stages of its development. To make these activities as efficient as possible, the leader should prepare and distribute forms to track the project's status. These forms should include style guidelines mutually agreed to in the project planning meeting, a project schedule, and transmittal sheets to record the status of reviews.

Schedule

All team members must know not only what is expected of them but when it is expected. The schedule provides this information. Schedules come in different formats. Figure 6–3, for example, shows a tabular schedule used for a team project for a business writing class. Figure 6–4 shows a modified bar-chart schedule for the production of a software user's manual that required coordination among the writing, review, and production staffs over a five-month period. Regardless of the format, the schedule must state explicitly who is responsible for what, and when the draft of each section is due.

Review Transmittal Sheet

The team leader should provide review transmittal sheets for writers to attach to each of their drafts, enabling each reviewer to sign off as having reviewed the draft. The review transmittal sheet presents at a glance the status of the project during the review cycle. It also lists in order those who must review the draft, as shown in Figure 6–5. (Remember that as part of a collaborative writing team, you will act as both writer and reviewer.)

**Figure 6–3
Sample Tabular
Schedule**

Project Schedule

January 1:	Assignments
	Introduction—Jeanette
	Theory Section—Jeff
	Methods Section—Scott
February 1:	Sections to coauthors for review
February 15:	Sections returned to coauthors for revision
March 1:	Sections to instructor
March 1:	Assignments
	Tutorial—Jeanette
	Parts List—Jeff
	Appendix—Scott
March 15:	Sections to coauthors for review
April 1:	Sections returned to coauthors for revision
April 15:	Sections to instructor

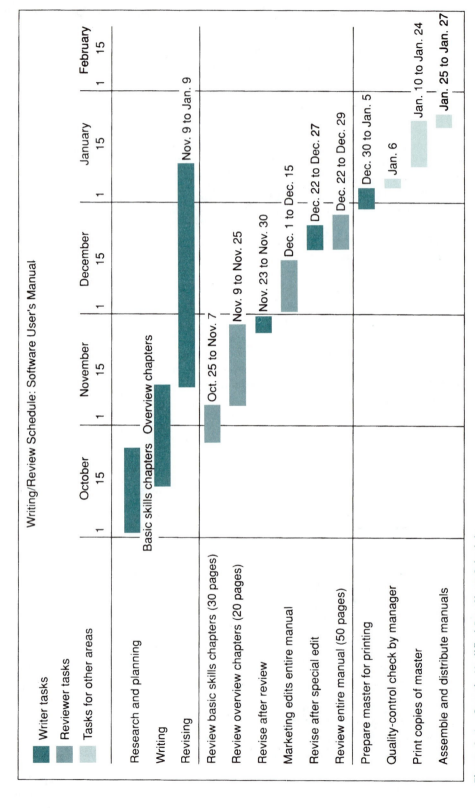

Writing/Review Schedule: Software User's Manual

	October	November	December	January	February
	1 15	1 15	1 15	1 15	1 15

Research and planning

Writing — Basic skills chapters / Overview chapters

Revising — Nov. 9 to Jan. 9

Review basic skills chapters (30 pages) — Oct. 25 to Nov. 7

Review overview chapters (20 pages) — Nov. 9 to Nov. 25

Revise after review — Nov. 23 to Nov. 30

Marketing edits entire manual — Dec. 1 to Dec. 15

Revise after special edit — Dec. 22 to Dec. 27

Review entire manual (50 pages) — Dec. 22 to Dec. 29

Prepare master for printing — Dec. 30 to Jan. 5

Quality-control check by manager — Jan. 6

Print copies of master — Jan. 10 to Jan. 24

Assemble and distribute manuals — Jan. 25 to Jan. 27

Legend:
Writer tasks
Reviewer tasks
Tasks for other areas

Figure 6–4   Sample Modified Bar-Chart Schedule

Review Transmittal Sheet

Project: [Project name]
Author: [Author's name]
Section: [Title of chapter or section]

	Initial	*Date*
Reviewer 1	_____	_____
Reviewer 2	_____	_____
Reviewer 3	_____	_____
Reviewer 4	_____	_____

**Figure 6–5
Review Transmittal
Sheet**

■ Collaborating with Other Departments

In some work settings, writing team leaders arrange for the cooperation of different departments within the organization. For example, the team leader may need to meet with the graphic-arts staff to

- Plan for the creation of graphs, charts, drawings, maps, etc.
- Plan for the document's cover.
- Arrange for photographs to be taken or scanned.

The team leader may meet with the print production staff to

- Inform them of when to expect the manuscript.
- Discuss any special printing requirements, such as color, special bindings, document size, foldout pages, etc.

In addition, the team leader may also need to obtain reviews and approval from other organizations, such as the sales and legal departments.

CHAPTER 6 SUMMARY: Collaborative Writing

Collaborative writing teams can, in many cases, produce a document that is better than one that could be produced by a single writer. Form a collaborative writing team when:

☐ Your project requires specialists in more than one subject area.

☐ Your project would benefit from the merging of different perspectives.

☐ Your project's size, importance, or deadline requires a team effort.

As a member of a collaborative writing team, you are expected to:

☐ Work with others as a team of peers to plan, design, and write a single document.

☐ Provide immediate feedback and advice to fellow team members.

☐ Ensure that all important points are discussed and all problems addressed.

☐ Learn tolerance and respect for the opinions of others.

☐ Research the topics of your assigned section.

☐ Write your draft.

☐ Review the work of other team members.

☐ Revise your draft based on comments from other team members.

☐ Share equal responsibility for the end product.

Collaborative teams require leadership — leadership can be granted by mutual agreement or, if multiple documents are to be produced, it can be shared by rotation. As a team leader, in addition to your responsibilities as a team member, you would be expected to:

☐ Share decision-making authority with other team members.

☐ Coordinate the activity of team members.

☐ Coordinate the production of the final product.

■ Exercises

1. a. Draft a 300- to 500-word summary of Chapter 6. Arrange with a study partner to exchange drafts of your summaries by email. Review one another's work, make suggestions for revision, and return the file by email. Refer to the Digital Shortcuts on pages 182, 185, and 188. Together decide which method you will use to mark the files. Also review Writer's Checklist: Reviewing Drafts by Other Writers on page 184.

   b. Bring a draft of your writing assignment and exchange copies with another student. Read the draft you receive from another student and make comments and suggestions for revision.

2. Schedule a telephone, email, or personal interview with a health-care, agribusiness, business, technology, or industry representative who is part of a collaborative writing team. Remember to keep your interview to no more than 20 to 30 minutes, as the person you will be interviewing is busy. Before the interview, review Chapter 6 to help you prepare a list of questions to ask. You'll want to ask your interviewee about details of the collaborative writing style used by his or her group or company. For example, you might ask how planning meetings are conducted. Does your interviewee collaborate with other specialists or use peer reviews? How are drafts of documents circulated and comments for revision shared? What comments has your interviewee found most helpful during the collaborative writing process? Ask your interviewee to share specific experiences with collaborative writing. Were these experiences positive or negative? Why? Add relevant questions of your own. After the interview is complete, prepare an outline, a draft, and a final report on your findings. Your classmates may benefit from having a copy of all the interview reports. Remember to send the person you interviewed a thank-you letter.

3. Form a collaborative writing team with three or four of your classmates to conduct an evaluation of a restaurant in your area. Assume that your team has been hired by the restaurant's national headquarters after receiving complaints about the service, quality, and cleanliness of the restaurant. Appoint a team leader who will assign specific items for each group member to observe while in the restaurant—for example, the cleanliness of the dining room, linen, silverware, and rest rooms; the attentiveness of service; the quality of food; and so forth. As a collaborative writing effort, summarize your findings in an outline and then create a draft letter addressed to the person who hired your team.

4. Assume that there has been an increased rate of absenteeism in your class recently. Form a collaborative writing team with at least two other classmates to prepare a 300-word report listing the possible causes and solutions to the problem.

5. Form a collaborative writing team with two or three classmates. As a group, choose a product or service and create a company name. Decide on the nature of your business (service, manufacturing, etc.), or the scope and size of your business (international, many branches), and on the client or consumer groups that form the audience for your company's product or service. Develop and design a logo, letterhead, and business card appropriate to your company and clients. Submit your finished products to your instructor.

6. Form collaborative teams with your classmates based on common career interests: agriculture, communications, computer science, engineering, environmental science, health professions, health-care administration, human resources, or other similar groupings. Assume that you have been asked by your university's freshman recruiting team to create a document based on your experience as a student explaining why your campus is a great place to prepare for _____ (the occupational interest you and your team have chosen). The recruiters will use each team's written material as a resource to persuade high school students of the benefits of attending your university. In your group, appoint a team leader and a team recorder, and decide how to organize and write this assignment.

7. Form a collaborative writing group that will meet weekly for the rest of the semester. Your assignment each week is to discuss and write about the new material

you learned in class and the assigned reading that you did that week. Your group will submit a brief, informal memo to your instructor each week that summarizes your group's discussion. Individually, you will also keep a weekly journal that records the group's interactions, activities, conflicts, and progress throughout the semester. Your instructor may ask to review your journal from time to time. In your final journal entry, comment on whether you think your writing group functioned as a productive writing team and analyze why or why not.

8. As a collaborative writing effort, choose three classmates with whom you share similar interests to help you work on one of the following writing assignments: (With the approval of your instructor, your group may substitute another topic as long as each member of the group is familiar with the topic. This assignment should not require outside research to complete.)

   a. Write a report on an extracurricular activity listed in the campus catalog that you and your teammates participate in. Explain the activity and why it is worthwhile. Support your report with details.

   b. Write a report on careers related to your and your teammates' fields of study. Explain the jobs available, the industries they are related to, locations, rate of pay, etc. What is the outlook overall?

   c. Write a report summarizing the computer lab facility your university offers students. As lab users, do you feel that the facility is adequate or in need of improvement? Support your report with details.

   d. Write a report explaining how to operate a piece of equipment that everyone in your group uses at least weekly. Your choice of topic may be operating a kitchen aid, power tool, VCR, or some other more sophisticated item, as long as every member of the group is familiar with the equipment. Evaluate the effectiveness of the equipment and make any suggestions you may have for improving it.

9. Collaborate with a classmate to develop a process that your class can follow to review and comment on each other's written work. After reviewing Chapter 5, create an outline and a rough draft for a plan that facilitates peer feedback in your class. Be sure to highlight the specific benefits of your plan. Your instructor may ask you to share your plan with the rest of the class.

10. Form a collaborative group of no more than six members in which both genders are represented equally. Appoint a group leader and a group recorder. Based on your personal experiences, brainstorm as a group to create a list of gender-related issues that you have encountered as college students. Ideas for your list may include the stereotyping of women and men in regard to expectations of academic performance skills (verbal, mathematical, technological, etc.) or expectations of success in other areas. Use your collaborative lists to generate a brief narrative reporting on current campus gender issues. Include the ideas of each group member. Your instructor may ask your group to share your report with the rest of the class. You may also be asked to write an individual report summarizing the personal interactions of your group during your meetings.

11. Form a collaborative group of no more than four members to develop a study guide for college students. For six weeks, your group will hold a weekly meeting of no more than one hour. Each member will bring to each meeting a brief analysis of his or her previous week's study habits—Which habits were not helpful?

Which were successful? Why? Be as specific as possible. As a team, generate at each meeting a summary of all the members' study habits for that week. In the final week of the project, your team will draft a final report on your findings and recommendations. You may also be asked to individually submit a report analyzing your team's ability to work together productively.

12. Write a brief narrative explaining why collaborative writing experiences are (or are not) a productive part of learning business writing skills. Use your own academic and on-the-job collaborative writing experiences as a basis for your conclusions. Review this chapter before you begin your draft.

■ In-Class Activities

1. An important stage of the collaborative writing process is the planning stage. During planning, it is crucial to establish that all members of the team will work toward the same goal, use the same standard reference guide, meet due dates, and agree on how to enforce the standards that have been established. To give you practice in setting up these guidelines, divide into groups of no more than five members. Assume that your boss has given you a collaborative writing assignment on a topic specific to the company's main product. Your job as a group during the next 30 minutes is to:
   a. Quickly become acquainted with one another's expertise. To do this, ask each person to talk about his or her background for two minutes or less.
   b. Select a team leader.
   c. Decide the time schedule for making initial assignments and submitting drafts, coauthor reviews, and revisions.
   d. Decide what method you will use to enforce the timeline.
   e. Decide what other rules are necessary to ensure the group's success in its mission.

   Remember that unstated policies can lead to confusion about responsibilities. For example, if there is no late penalty for drafts that do not meet the time schedule, the message can be that it is acceptable for them to be late. When your group has discussed project guidelines, the team leader will summarize these policies in a list.

2. Divide into groups of five or fewer members. During the next 15 minutes, make a list of the duties that a collaborative team leader would be responsible for during a collaborative writing project. Next, using no more than 15 minutes, brainstorm a list of qualities needed to lead a collaborative writing team. When you have completed your lists, refer to Leading a Collaborative Writing Team (pages 188–191). In ten minutes or less, decide if your group's list is similar to the suggestions stated in the text. Discuss any differences and decide as a team which of your ideas you would like to share with your class.

3. As is pointed out in this chapter, conflicts over valid issues almost always generate more innovative and creative work than does passive acceptance. To experiment with positive conflict, divide into collaborative groups of five or fewer members. As a team, you will write a recommendation on whether your company

should provide a smokers' lounge. Assume that half of the members of your team are smokers and half are nonsmokers. The smokers on the team claim that the existing nonsmoking lounge is large enough to be divided into two separate areas, while the nonsmokers feel smoking in the building should not be permitted. As a team, spend 45 minutes developing an outline of the pros and cons for both sides of the issue. Here is a suggested schedule for your group to follow:

a. Quickly get to know one another, establishing who is a nonsmoker and who is a smoker.

b. Appoint a team leader.

c. Begin brainstorming your list of pros and cons for first one side of the issue and then the other.

During the next 15 minutes, quickly draft your collaborative outline. It may be helpful, too, if team members review the Writer's Checklist: Working in a Collaborative Group (page 186) during the session.

4. Divide into groups of five or fewer members. Assume that your class will be featured in an upcoming brochure focusing on diverse and talented students who are attracted to your campus. As a team, you have been asked to submit a one-page summary of the individual strengths of your team members. To complete this assignment, follow these steps:

a. Begin by writing a one-page statement about yourself, allowing 30 minutes to complete the task. Ask yourself what special awards or honors you have received. Next, think about what details of your life helped to shape you into the college student you are today. Explain what influences directed you toward your chosen field of study. Tell how long you have known that this was the right choice for you. Describe the mentors who have been important in your life. Talk about your employment experiences and how they fit into your course of study and plans for a career. Focus on any leadership or managerial experiences that have contributed to your personal growth. Your instructor may ask you to share your personal statement with the class.

b. After each member of your group has completed personal statements, spend the next several minutes reading one anothers' papers. Because getting to know one another is important to a team's success, personal statements are a good way for team members to introduce themselves to the group.

c. Appoint a team leader who will coordinate your group as you select and edit a paragraph or two from each paper to complete a collaborative report titled "[your] University Attracts Diverse and Talented Students." Your instructor may ask the team leader to share your group's report with the class.

5. Divide into groups of five or fewer members. Assume that you are a collaborative writing team at a company of 350 employees. Your first job as a team is to write a recommendation to the company president that a cafeteria be added on-site for the company's employees. Appoint a team leader and, for 15 minutes, brainstorm to produce a list of at least five company goals that would be accomplished with an on-site employee cafeteria. Include issues such as time management, employee satisfaction, etc. Next, your team leader will assign each member one of the established goals. Write a paragraph about how the on-site cafeteria will help the company meet the particular goal that you have been assigned. Share your paragraphs with one another and, as a group, make suggestions for revision and a list of the areas that require additional research.

■ Research Projects

1. Form a collaborative team to research and write an owner's manual for one of the following items (or other item of your choice):

   - Power lawn mower
   - Microwave oven
   - VCR
   - DVD
   - cellular or wireless telephone
   - telephone answering machine
   - "palm pilot"
   - ten-speed bicycle

   Your manual should have four distinct sections, each fully developed:

   - Physical Description
   - Theory of Operation
   - Operating Instructions
   - Maintenance Instructions

   Your group must research the broad subject as well as the subject of each individual section of the manual.

2. Meet with your instructor and collaborative team to select a collaborative research and writing project. Potential projects might include the following:

   - A pamphlet or brochure describing what every freshman student should know about basic services available on your campus and how to survive during his or her first year
   - A document explaining how to use a research facility, media resource center, or resources at the library
   - User documentation for software and hardware available to students on campus
   - A pamphlet or brochure describing the job-search information and job-placement centers on your campus
   - A pamphlet or brochure describing the professional organizations available to students (Include information on how a student can become a member)

   Once your group has set up specific project guidelines, divide tasks by assigning the research and writing of report segments either to separate members of the group or to two-person teams. Make certain that every member of the group reads and comments on the first draft of every other member's segment. You should compose a brief introduction and conclusion together—preferably on a computer if one is available to your group.

3. Form a collaborative writing team to research and write a major report for the head of the department responsible for this course, recommending the purchase of a laptop computer, or more than one if you feel more are justified. The computer(s) would be available for students to borrow for class projects.
   a. Your team will be responsible for preparing the following:

      - A memo requesting your instructor's approval for you to undertake the project and to evaluate a specific computer
      - Biweekly progress reports, to start as soon as your team has received project approval and to continue for the duration of the project
      - A formal report of your findings and recommendations

- An oral description of the computer you have researched, presented to the other team members involved with the project
- A report to the other team members engaged in the project on the results of your preliminary evaluation
- The final results of the project, and your recommendations to an evaluation board

b. The deadline dates for submission of these documents are

Proposal: _____

Progress reports: ___(Every two weeks from project approval)___

Final report: _____

Final presentation: _____

c. Each team must (1) prepare and submit a joint (single) copy of the proposal, progress reports, and formal report, and (2) make group oral presentations. Your instructor will award a group mark to each assignment, which all team members will receive.

d. In your proposal, identify the type and brand of computer you will be evaluating, as well as how and where you will gather information on the product (in person at a retail location, on the Internet, etc.). When your team has gathered sufficient information, report to the class during a group presentation. Hand out copies of any printed information you have obtained.

e. As you carry out the project and write your report, consider the following:

- Why the computers are needed (You will have to *persuade* the department head, and anyone else who is likely to be approving the purchase, of their value.)
- The number of computers you think are needed
- How the computers should be kept secure, and how borrowing them would be controlled
- What the total cost will be, for one or for more, and whether an educational discount or quantity discount is available
- Specific features the portable computers should have, such as memory size, operating speed, compatibility with personal computers already installed at the college, and the type of software that should be installed

f. Your group should also consider how much the visual appearance of your report will influence whether your recommendations receive approval. If the department head likes what he or she reads, your report may be attached to his or her budget request to demonstrate why the computers are needed (this is commonly known as "the justification"). Consequently, the quality of your report, both in appearance and in content, can help convince those readers who will approve the expenditure that your request warrants approval.[2]

---

[2]This exercise is adapted, with permission, from "An Integrated Collaborative Writing Project" by Ron S. Blicq, in *Collaborative Technical Writing: Theory and Practice,* ed. Richard Louth and Martin Scott (Hammond, LA: The Association of Teachers and Technical Writing, n.d.), pp. 57–60.

4. Form a collaborative team of three members to research and write a comparative study of three major companies that might hire someone just graduating from your college with a degree in business. Compare such things as size (in number of employees and gross sales), financial condition, geographical location, corporate culture (paternalistic or individualistic, rigidly structured or loosely structured, regular or flexible working hours, etc.), salary, benefits, advancement opportunities, the degree of independence granted to employees, variety of the work, and work environment (noisy or quiet working conditions, etc.). Compare all three companies in every category. At the end of your report, recommend the best company to work for and explain why you chose that one.

   Sources of information could include annual reports, corporate recruiting brochures, discussions with present or former employees, discussions with each company's Human Resources Department, information from the library, the Internet, and so forth.

   Assign one company to each team member, so that only one person is contacting each company, but make certain that all three team members are working from the same set of categories. Collectively decide on the format of your report before you begin your research.

   Each team member should write a rough draft about the company assigned to him or her, and every team member's draft should be submitted to the other two team members for peer review. At a peer review meeting to discuss suggested changes to the rough drafts, the whole team should agree on the content of an introduction and a conclusion and assign one team member to write them. The team leader should then gather the revised parts of the final report from the other team members and combine them, doing any revision necessary to make the parts fit together smoothly.

5. You are a member of a large publications department at a major computer manufacturer. The vice president of your division has learned that a key competitor has decentralized its publications efforts, dispersing small publications groups to each of the various manufacturing plants and making them part of the different engineering or software development departments. You are part of a three-member team appointed by the vice president to visit the publications departments of all the company's major competitors, to determine how they are all organized, and to recommend how your company should do it in the future.

   You and your team will assume that you have each visited a different computer manufacturer and learned how each one handles its publications effort. You must then meet and share what you have learned with your peers and then write a formal report explaining how the other companies publish their documents and recommending how your company should do it.

   Consider the following:
   a. Advantages of a large, centralized publications department

      • The efficiency and economy of a centralized group of technical writers and artists
      • A better career path for technical writers
      • The easy exchange of state-of-the-art knowledge among the writing groups
      • Pride of identity for the writers in having their own department

b.   Advantages of small, dispersed writing groups

- Better control of overall product development by the development department
- Better access to the technical experts for the writers
- Cost savings in the travel budget
- The writers become integrated members of the development teams

c.   Disadvantages of a large, centralized publications department

- The lack of control by the development groups
- The lack of a close rapport with the development teams
- The cost of frequent travel to interview developers and inspect the new products

d.   Disadvantages of small, dispersed writing groups

- Widespread duplication of production effort (writers, artists, printers, etc.)
- Loss of career path for the technical writers
- Loss of a certain degree of professionalism caused by having small, isolated groups of writers scattered throughout the country

■ Web Projects

1. Review the following Web sites: Online Technical Writing: Strategies for Peer-Reviewing and Team-Writing at Austin Community College at http://www.io.com/~hcexres/tcm1603/acchtml/team.html, and the Center for the Study of Work Teams at the University of North Texas at http://www.workteams.unt.edu/. Write a brief narrative citing at least four strategies that you find to be potentially helpful in collaborative writing. Exchange your narrative with that of a classmate, by email, responding to each other's work with comments or suggestions for revision. Refer to page 185 for guidelines to revising online.

2. Several of today's successful companies encourage collaborative writing on the job. Search the Web to learn how such companies advertise their team approach when hiring. Samples include Saturn at http://www.saturncars.com/communication/index3.html, and the Kimberly-Clark Corporation at http://www.kc-careers.com/. Choose a company whose team approach is appealing to you. Prepare an outline listing the kinds of collaborative writing assignments that a writer at this company might encounter. Your outline should cover areas such as product information, warranty information, employment training, management styles, and so forth.

3. Compare the designs and content of the Web sites of three different companies. Examples include Microsoft at http://www.microsoft.com, Disney at http://disney.com, and Merck at http://www.merck.com/. In a brief narrative, suggest the various departments that likely contributed to the construction of the company's Web site, and describe the role that each would play in the design, development, and maintenance of the Web pages.

4. Form collaborative groups of five or fewer members. You have been asked by the Office of Publications at your university to submit a Web page design for your

course. Appoint a team leader to assign each member of the group an area of specialty. Next, ask each specialist to decide the content that would be included in that area. Ask each member of the group to visit at least three course Web pages at your university. Examples include Purdue University at http://www.purdue.edu, Penn State University at http://www.psu.edu, and the University of Wisconsin at http://wisc.edu. Meet as a group to compare notes and then ask for a volunteer from your team to outline the content and draw a representation of how your Web page would look. Your instructor may want you to share your drawing with the rest of the class.

5. Complete one of the following exercises:
   a. You are part of a collaborative team at your company that has been asked to write a recommendation for health-care insurance alternatives for employees. Visit the Web sites of at least three companies to research available options. Sample sites of major U.S. health-insurance companies include Aetna at http://www.aetnaushc.com/, Blue Cross at http://www.bluecares.com/, and Humana at http://www.humana.com/.
   b. You are part of a collaborative team at your company that has been asked to write a recommendation to purchase wireless telephones and services for field representatives. Visit the Web sites of three companies to research available options. Sample sites of major wireless telephone companies include Telephone Support Systems at http://www.telsupsys.com, Bell Atlantic Mobile at http://www.bam.com.wireless/index.htm, and AT&T Wireless Services at http://www.attws.com/general/product_index/main.htm/.

While Part One discussed the principles of effective writing that apply to all on-the-job writing tasks, Part Two focuses on the practical applications of these principles. These applications include writing strategies that are basic to all on-the-job writing and explicit guidelines for writing the most common types of work-related communications: memos, business letters, email messages, instructions, proposals, forms (including Web forms), and a variety of formal and informal reports. The unique features of writing for the Web are also included. Such aids to communication as tables and illustrations, the preparation and delivery of oral presentations, and conducting effective meetings are also covered. Part Two gives extensive treatment to researching your subject, including using the library and the Internet, interviewing, using questionnaires, and making first-hand observations. As you have seen, researching a subject takes place before the first draft is written. However, the chapters on research and on creating tables and illustrations appear in Part Two preceding the chapter on formal reports rather than in Part One, because the comprehensive scope of these chapters is more appropriate to the preparation of formal reports than to many other kinds of job-related writing.

Finally, this part ends with a chapter that puts everything you learned earlier in the text to its first practical test: finding a job appropriate to your education and abilities.

As in Part One, the chapters in Part Two offer Writer's Checklists that provide concise writing advice, ESL Tips for non-native speakers of English, and Digital Shortcuts for using technology for workplace communication.

7 Instructions and Other Writing Strategies

I n Part One, you learned that you must establish a *purpose* in writing before you begin to write. Depending on the kind of material you wish to present, who your reader will be, and how familiar he or she is with your subject, you can determine your purpose and then choose the most effective way to present your material.

In this chapter, we will consider specific types of writing frequently used on the job—explaining how to do something, how something works, or how something happened, or describing how something looks or is planned to look. We will look at both informal (nontechnical) and formal (technical) instructions and discuss the importance of using plain language to write instructions. We will discuss two areas crucial to many types of on-the-job writing: when and how to define terms and concepts that may confuse readers and how to develop credible explanations of why something happened the way that it did. We will also discuss one of the more challenging writing tasks—persuading your reader to accept your point of view or to take a particular action. Finally, because of the increasing demand for Web writing skills in the workplace—and because the Web is a medium that requires a somewhat different approach than writing for print—we will offer a discussion, examples, and guidelines for writing for the Web.

Although this chapter will focus on each type of writing separately, the types are often used in combination, depending on the writer's purpose and audience. For example, many instructions for how to assemble consumer products include descriptions of parts or components, as do instructions for assembling manufactured goods. Investigative and accident reports try to explain why something happened (cause and effect). To adequately explain why something happened, the writer must first focus on what exactly did happen (explaining a process), which frequently requires descriptions of people, places, or equipment (what something looks like now), as well as definitions of terms and concepts important to the explanation. Finally, a skillful integration of these writing elements that accurately presents the evidence will be powerfully persuasive to your readers.

The writing strategies discussed in this chapter should help you, first, to establish your purpose and then to present the information relevant to your purpose in a way that will be clear and convincing to your reader.

Voices from the Workplace

James Bates, U.S. Department of Housing and Urban Development

James Bates is a community builder with the U.S. Department of Housing and Urban Development (HUD) in Buffalo, New York, where he has worked since 1990. As a community builder, James connects HUD's diverse constituency—a group that includes mayors, legislators, the media, developers, banks, homebuyers, and grassroots organizations—with HUD's many community-development programs and services. Working closely with community groups and individual HUD program experts, James helps design comprehensive strategies to reduce homelessness, to respond to natural disasters, and to finance shopping centers and increase home ownership in low-income neighborhoods.

Presenting information clearly by using plain language is essential to James's work as a community builder. When communicating about a specific project with clients, HUD senior management, and technical staff, James considers the content and language of his message carefully, avoiding the temptation to "communicate everything to everyone. . . . I tell people only what is most relevant to them, given their position and level of interest. Managers want to know the bottom line—solutions, recommendations, and actions. Technical staff want to know about resources, process, and timetables. Clients want to know what they are going to get and when they will get it."

Communicating clearly is particularly important when dealing with the public. "Lapsing into 'government speak'" James says, can mean losing "a genuine opportunity to connect with the public, and to get a community to invest in what we are trying to accomplish." This skill connects with another essential requirement of James's job—that he communicate persuasively. Because his job is to build a solid working relationship between individual communities and the programs and services offered by a government organization, James emphasizes the collaboration that is at the heart of HUD's work with communities. "I'd never want a community group to feel that we [HUD] were only present because they had a high concentration of poverty and crime, or appeared to lack the capacity to address community problems. . . . I let people know we are about partnerships and collaboration, and that that is the only way to truly take advantage of the opportunities that exist for the community—jobs, employment, and decent and affordable housing."

Tour the HUD Web site at http://www.hud.gov.

Entry-Level
Rebecca Dellinger Shugart, Data Processing Services (DPS), Inc.

Rebecca Dellinger Shugart is a technical writer for DPS, Inc., a consulting firm of computer professionals. Although the types of writing that Rebecca does at DPS depends on the needs of her clients, she spends most of her time writing policies and procedures for a variety of audiences, functions, and media. Whether writing for a Web page, manual, quick-reference guide, or presentation, Rebecca suggests following three basic writing principles.

First, know your audience. "As writers, our tendency may be to use language we're comfortable with, and syntax that we favor—rather than what will benefit our audience. In order to write for your client or audience, research their needs and write for their ears."

Second, keep your writing simple and use plain language. "When conveying ideas or giving instructions, ask yourself: Will the meaning change if I remove this word, phrase, or sentence? Can I make this piece more concise and understandable by using one three-syllable descriptive word in place of these four one-syllable words?"

Finally, review your writing and ask for input from your colleagues. "During various stages of the writing process—especially when writing instructions—I test them out myself and revise them for logic and clarity. Next I ask a colleague or someone unfamiliar with the project to do the same, and ask them to suggest edits for logic and clarity. The result is always a better, more effective piece of writing."

To find out more about DPS, Inc., visit their Web site at http://www.dps-consults.com.

Instructions

When you tell someone how to perform a specific procedure or task, you are giving instructions. Instructions may indicate how to carry out a particular task in the workplace, perform a procedure (such as recording a television program on your VCR), operate equipment (such as using a spray-paint gun), assemble a product (such as putting together a bicycle), or repair equipment (such as fixing a lawn mower).

How many times have you heard people complain about instructions being unclear or inaccurate? Clear, easy-to-follow instructions can actually build goodwill for your company, both internally and externally. Poor instructions, however, can cause miscommunication and delays in an important project, or, worse, can be directly responsible for an injury, which could result in damage claims and lawsuits. If your instructions are based on clear thinking and careful planning, they should enable your reader to carry out the procedure or task successfully.

Informal Instructions

Employees write many kinds of informal, nontechnical instructions to coworkers every day. These instructions often take the form of an assignment for someone to complete a task and are frequently sent by email. In the email instructions in Figure 7–1, for example, a budget analyst requests data about an office's copier program from the manager of that program to plan for the upcoming fiscal year's budget.

Other informal instructions to a coworker may be geared toward training and may therefore be more detailed. Figure 7–2 is a memo in which a writer outlines a task for her assistant to carry out—the review and preparation of a manuscript. To highlight the importance of this task, the writer chose to communicate her instructions to her assistant by memo rather than by email. In her memo, the writer supplies necessary background information for the project and clearly outlines her assistant's responsibilities. Note the use of headings, the organization of the required tasks, and the straightforward language of the memo.

Figure 7–1
Informal
Employee-to-
Employee
Instructions
(Email)

Subject: Planning Call for FY-- Budget
Date: March 1, 20--
From: Carol Quenten
To: Gene Carruthers

Gene,

We are planning the 20-- budget cycle and I'll need the following information about the copier program.

- Current and projected monthly maintenance charges for each copier and the totals
- Any indication of projected maintenance increases from our vendors
- The number of copiers we lease and the number we own
- The number of copiers we need to replace based on a seven-year life cycle per machine
- The projected costs for replacing our current copiers with networked copiers

Do not include projected toner and paper costs at this time.

Fill in the data on the budget form located on the shared S:\ drive at S:\OCIOO\IMD\copiers. The information is due for my review on 3/15/--. Thanks.

================================
Carol Quenten, Budget Analyst
TechQuest Inc.
119 Trowbridge Rd., Minneapolis, MN 55401
(507) 333-3333 Fax: (507) 333-3334
cquenten@techquest.com
http://www.techquest.com
================================

Formal Instructions

Some instructions are intended to help customers assemble products and comply with requests for information for medical records, credit ratings, and the like. Such instructions tend to be formally written and carefully reviewed before they are used. Figures 7–3 and 7–4 show two sets of relatively simple technical instructions, one without an illustration and one with an illustration.

Parts of Formal Instructions

Most instructions are in four parts: Introduction, Required Equipment and Materials, Procedural Steps, and Conclusion.

Introduction.   For longer instructions, you can use an introduction to provide any needed background information, to state the purpose of the procedure, or to offer a theory of operation to help readers understand why the product works the way it does. Figures 7–5 and 7–6 include an introduction that provides the

Figure 7–2
Informal
Employee-to-
Employee
Instructions
(Memo)

Memo

Date: September 15, 20--
To: Gina Felizolla
Fr: Claire Chin
Re: *P & E International: Import-Export Guide 20--*
        Instructions for manuscript preparation

Gina,

We have received the manuscript for the manual entitled *P & E International: Import-Export Guide 20--* from the author team of Anna Anzaldua and Emmet Ross. In assembling the new manuscript, the authors worked with the first-edition manual—significantly adding to, updating, and reorganizing the contents. I have reviewed and edited the manuscript and would like you to review it as well. Once you have read the manuscript and made any necessary edits, prepare it to be turned over to the production department. Following is an outline of the next steps necessary for this project:

Editorial Tasks

- Read the manuscript for completion and check each page against the table of contents.
- Make sure that all additions and edits are clear and correct.
- Check the special bolded terms against the index manuscript. (See manual page 6-a for an example.)
- Flag with a Post-It note anything that you can't resolve. We can sit down and address any questions together and email remaining questions to the authors.

Manuscript Preparation

Refer to the material on manuscript preparation in the electronic Editorial Assistant notebook (located in our shared file on the neighborhood network). I've included an abbreviated version of those guidelines, based on the good condition of this manuscript.

- Position all manuscript page numbers in the upper-right corner of the page.
- Clearly mark inserted material.
- Circle or strike out running heads.
- Strike out any cross-references to page numbers; replace page numbers with "000" and write "x-ref" beside that line in the right margin. (Please circle "x-ref" and any other instructions that you may indicate in the manuscript—any circled items will not be typeset.)

(continued)

Figure 7–2
(continued)

2   September 15, 20--

- Make all edits legible—anything illegible should be retyped and double-spaced.

Manuscript Turnover

- The manual is being handled in-house by our production department. The production manager of this project is Stacy Cramer, who will be working with the composition staff to produce the bound manual. I will email you Stacy's contact information. Please call her within the next couple of days to introduce yourself and to let her know that you will be working on this project.
- When you turn the manuscript over to production, include the following:
  - A manuscript turnover form and manuscript prep checklist (I've included copies of these with the manuscripts and will help you fill them out.)
  - A turnover memo to Stacy (copied to me) that indicates what material is included, what is still forthcoming, and any special instructions (I have attached samples of turnover memos for your reference.)
  - Two duplicate paper copies and a copy of the manuscript on disk (The material for these manuals comes from two sources—from the first edition of the manuals and from the new disk that the authors have submitted.)

Schedule

- The manuscript is due to our production department on October 15th. Let's meet in one week (on September 22nd at 10 a.m.) to discuss the status of the project.

Thanks, Gina. Let me know if you have any questions about these instructions.

Cleaning Inside of Grill

- Disconnect ignitor wire from ignitor before cleaning grill. Do not mistake brown and black accumulation of grease and smoke for paint. Interiors of gas grills are not painted at factory (and should never be painted).
- Remove grill lid, cooking grate, grease cup, and Drip VapoRISER Bar. Discard old lava rock or briquets. A grease cup must be attached to grease hanger and emptied after each use.
- Apply a strong solution of detergent and water or use grill cleaner from Char-Broil® Certified Grill Parts and Accessories with scrub brush to insides of grill lid and bottom. Rinse and allow to completely air dry.

Figure 7–3   Instructions without an Illustration   *Source:* "Char-Broil Use and Care Manual," Courtesy of W. C. Bradley Company, 1997, Columbus, GA.

Time Counter

The time counter shows the actual time it takes to record a program or play back a segment of a prerecorded tape. It helps locate the beginning or end of programs you taped. The time counter resets to 0:00:00 whenever the tape is ejected from the VCR.

For example, if a 30-minute program was recorded at the beginning of the tape, you would:

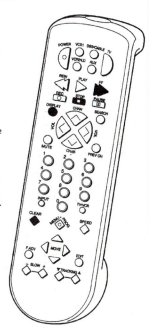

1. Insert the prerecorded tape. Press STOP. Make sure the tape is rewound.

2. Press DISPLAY twice to display only the time counter on the TV screen.

3. Press CLEAR to reset the time counter to 0:00:00.

4. Press FF on remote or turn the shuttle on the VCR clockwise to fast forward the tape until the time counter reads 0:30:00. Press STOP.

   This is the approximate end of the program and you can begin recording at this spot.

5. Press DISPLAY twice to remove the time counter from the screen and return to the normal displays.

Figure 7–4   Instructions with an Illustration   *Source:* "VR542 User's Guide," Courtesy of Thompson Consumer Electronics, Inc., 1995, Indianapolis, IN.

When using one of the basic hookups, the TV•VCR button lets you switch between the picture coming from the VCR or the picture from the TV channel. This button lets you record a program on the VCR while watching another channel on the TV.

Introduction

A. Press VCR1 to set the remote to control the VCR.
B. Press TV•VCR to see the picture from the VCR. The VCR indicator lights in the display panel.
C. Press CHANNEL up or down on the VCR or CHAN on VCR's remote to change channels on the VCR. The channel number changes in the display panel.
D. Press TV•VCR to see the TV channels. The VCR indicator does not light in the display panel. Change channels using the TV's remote.
E. Return the TV to the VCR viewing channel—CH3 or CH4.
F. Press VCR1, then TV•VCR to switch back to the picture from the VCR.

Instructions

Figure 7–5   Introduction That Provides the Purpose of the Instructions   *Source:* "VR542 User's Guide," Courtesy of Thompson Consumer Electronics, Inc., 1995, Indianapolis, IN.

Introduction

COMMERCIAL▶▶ADVANCE™ is a patented technology that detects and marks most commercials on your tape for any recording that is more than 15 minutes long. During playback, the VCR automatically skips the detected commercial segments or you can choose to manually skip them. This feature reduces three minutes of commercials into approximately 8–12 seconds of fast forwarding in the SLP mode. You can select a background of blue or see the video as the commercials are skipped.

After recording, the VCR rewinds the tape and determines where the commercials are located. It then marks the beginning and end of the detected commercial segments and returns the tape to the end of the recording. *It does not erase the commercials from the tape.*

Instructions

1. Press MENU•PROG to display the VCR MAIN MENU.
2. Press 6 to display the PREFERENCES menu.
3. Make sure CF Marking is set to ON. If not, press 5.

Figure 7–6   Introduction That Provides a Theory of Operation   *Source:* "VR542 User's Guide," Courtesy of Thompson Consumer Electronics, Inc., 1995, Indianapolis, IN.

purpose of the instructions and an introduction that gives the theory of operation, respectively.

Required Equipment and Materials.   If special tools, materials, or equipment will be needed to perform your instructions, inform your readers at the outset— don't let them get well into the procedure and then learn about such requirements. Provide a well-labeled section that tells them clearly what they need before they begin the procedure. Figure 7–7 demonstrates the tools and equipment needed for the set of instructions that follow it.

Procedural Steps.   The procedural steps are the sequential steps involved in the operation. Review the section on sequential organization in Chapter 2 (page 36) for a full discussion of this method of development.

Conclusion.   A brief set of instructions can simply end with the last step in the procedure. For longer and more involved instructions, a conclusion may help your readers feel assured and confident about completing the job successfully.

■   Congratulations on successfully assembling your gas grill. With proper care, it will serve you well for many years to come.

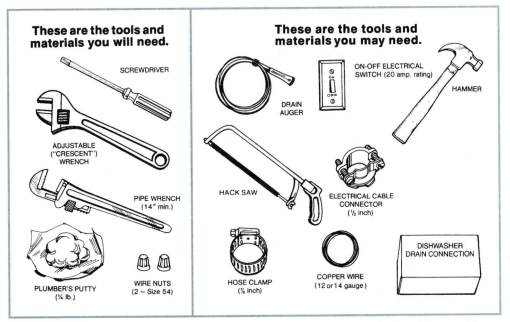

Figure 7–7 Illustration of Required Tools and Equipment *Source:* "Installation of Kenmore Waste Disposers," Courtesy of Sears, Roebuck and Company, 1997, Hoffman Estates, Il.

■ Writing Instructions

To write instructions successfully, you must assess the needs of your reader, write directly to your reader, learn how to perform the operation yourself, organize the instructions, include warnings and cautions, use illustrations wherever they would be helpful, and test the instructions when you have finished them.

Assess Your Reader's Needs

Learn your reader's level of knowledge and experience, and try to put yourself in your reader's position. Is your reader skilled in the kind of task for which you are writing instructions? If your reader is knowledgeable about the subject, you might feel free to use fairly specialized vocabulary. However, if your reader has little or no knowledge of the subject, you should use simple, everyday language — avoiding specialized terms as much as possible.

Write Directly to Your Reader

The clearest and simplest instructions are those written as commands. Your instructions will be easier to follow and less wordy if you address each sentence directly to your reader, in the imperative mood and the active voice.

INDIRECT	The operator should close the access lid.
	[indicative mood, passive voice]
DIRECT	Close the access lid.
	[imperative mood, active voice]

Although instructions should be concise, do not try to achieve conciseness by leaving out needed words such as articles (*a, an, the*), pronouns (*you, this, these*), and verbs. Doing so will certainly shorten sentences, but sentences that have been shortened this way usually have to be read more than once to be understood — actually defeating the purpose of short sentences. The following instruction for cleaning a power punch press assembly (a machine that punches holes and other patterns into materials), for example, is not easily understood at first reading.

UNCLEAR	Pass brush through punch area for debris.

The meaning of the phrase *for debris* needs to be made clearer. Revised, the instruction is readily understandable.

CLEAR	Pass *a* brush through *the* punch area *to clear away* any debris.

In any operation, certain steps must be performed with more exactness than others. Anyone who has ever boiled a three-minute egg for four minutes understands this all too well. Alert your reader to the steps that require exact timing or measurement.

VAGUE	Let the liquid cool.
PRECISE	Let the liquid cool for two hours.

Learn to Perform the Operation Yourself

To write accurate and easily understood instructions, you must thoroughly understand the task you are describing. Otherwise, your instructions could prove embarrassing or even dangerous. For example, the container of a brand-name cleaner carries the following warning:

■ Use only as directed.

Then the instructions direct the user to

■ Fill sink with 1 to 2 inches of water, then close off drain opening.

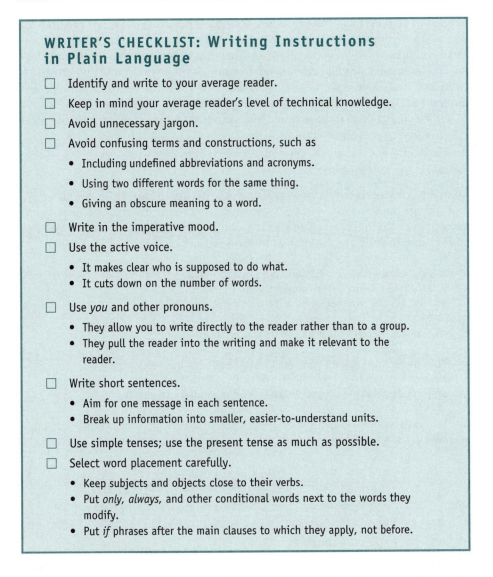

WRITER'S CHECKLIST: Writing Instructions in Plain Language

☐ Identify and write to your average reader.

☐ Keep in mind your average reader's level of technical knowledge.

☐ Avoid unnecessary jargon.

☐ Avoid confusing terms and constructions, such as

- Including undefined abbreviations and acronyms.
- Using two different words for the same thing.
- Giving an obscure meaning to a word.

☐ Write in the imperative mood.

☐ Use the active voice.

- It makes clear who is supposed to do what.
- It cuts down on the number of words.

☐ Use *you* and other pronouns.

- They allow you to write directly to the reader rather than to a group.
- They pull the reader into the writing and make it relevant to the reader.

☐ Write short sentences.

- Aim for one message in each sentence.
- Break up information into smaller, easier-to-understand units.

☐ Use simple tenses; use the present tense as much as possible.

☐ Select word placement carefully.

- Keep subjects and objects close to their verbs.
- Put *only, always,* and other conditional words next to the words they modify.
- Put *if* phrases after the main clauses to which they apply, not before.

Users would find it difficult to raise the water level in the sink *before* closing the drain! Because users simply ignored the instructions and performed the task according to common sense, no harm was done. Suppose such confusing instructions were given for administering intravenous fluid or assembling high-voltage electrical equipment. The results of such inaccurate advice could be both costly and dangerous.

The writer of the drain-cleaning instructions undoubtedly knew better and was just careless. Sometimes, though, a writer may attempt to write instructions for a procedure that he or she does not understand adequately. Don't let that happen to you. Perform the procedure yourself if possible; if it is not possible for you to do it yourself, have someone else perform the procedure while you observe and take notes. As you watch, ask questions about any step that is not clear to you. Direct observation should enable you to write instructions that are exact, complete, and clear. Also make certain that you know the reason for the procedure, the materials and tools required, and the end result of the task.

Once you understand the procedure yourself, you must determine the most effective way to present it to your reader.

Organize the Instructions

To make your instructions easy to follow, divide them into short, simple steps, and arrange the steps in the correct sequence (review the information on sequential sequence in Chapter 2). The steps can be given in either of two ways. You can label each step with a sequential number, as follows:

■ 1. Connect each black cable wire to a brass terminal. . . .
2. Attach one 4-inch green jumper wire to the back. . . .
3. Connect both jumper wires to the bare cable wires. . . .

or you can use words that indicate time or sequence, as follows:

■ *First,* determine what the problem is that the customer is reporting to you.
Next, observe and test the system in operation. *At that time,* question the operator until you believe that the problem has been explained completely.

When two operations must be performed at the same time, include both operations in the same step.

WRONG 4. Hold the CONTROL key down.
5. Press the BELL key before releasing the CONTROL key.

RIGHT 4. While holding the CONTROL key down, press the BELL key.

Include Warnings and Cautions

Warnings and cautions can be an extremely important part of instructions. You must warn readers of potentially hazardous steps or materials before the steps are taken or the materials are handled. The conditions that require such warnings are numerous: electrical, chemical, mechanical, biological, and radioactive work, for example, all require caution.

A *warning* tells readers that a step can endanger their safety if it is not performed correctly. A *caution* tells readers to measure weights or dosages exactly, check an instrument panel, use care in operating a machine, wear protective clothing, etc. Cautions and warnings should be highlighted graphically so that readers cannot miss them. Although the format for cautions and warnings vary, those shown in Figures 7–8 and 7–9 are typical. Place cautions and warnings

WARNING

- It is the responsibility of assembler/owner to assemble, install, and maintain gas grill.
- Use the grill outdoors only.
- Do not let children operate or play near your grill.
- Keep the grill area clear and free from materials that burn, gasoline, bottled gas in any form, and other flammable vapors and liquids.
- Do not block holes in bottom and back of grill.
- Visually check burner flames on a regular basis.
- Use the grill in a well-ventilated space. Never use in an enclosed space, carport, garage, porch, patio, or building made of combustible construction, or under overhead construction.
- Do not install your grill in or on recreational vehicles and/or boats.
- Keep grills a distance of 36″ or 3 ft. (approximately 1m) from buildings to ensure there is no fire or melting of materials on the building.

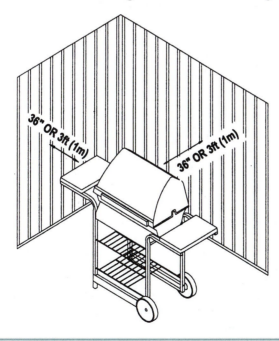

Figure 7–8   A Warning in a Set of Instructions   *Source:* "Char-Broil Use and Care Manual," Courtesy of W. C. Bradley Company, 1997, Columbus, GA.

⚠ CAUTION

Safety Precautions

- Installation of grill must conform with local codes, or in absence of local codes, with **National Fuel Gas Code, NFPA 54 / ANSI Z223.1**-latest edition or **CAN/CGA-B149.2,** propane installation code-latest edition. Handling of LP tanks must conform to **NFPA/ANSI 58**-latest edition.

- If external electrical source is utilized with accessories (such as rotisserie), they must be electrically grounded in accordance with local codes or, in the absence of local codes, with the **National Electrical Code, ANSI / NFPA 70**-latest edition or **Canadian Electrical Code, CSA C22.1**. Keep any electrical cords and/or fuel supply hoses away from any heated surfaces.

Figure 7–9   A Caution in a Set of Instructions   *Source:* "Char-Broil Use and Care Manual," Courtesy of W. C. Bradley Company, 1997, Columbus, GA.

immediately before the step to which they apply, and make them explicit so readers know exactly what to expect or what precautions to take.

Use cautions and warnings only when absolutely necessary, however, because too many will have the effect of causing readers to ignore them and actually defeat their very purpose.

Use Illustrations Where Needed

Not all instructions require illustrations, but you should always *consider* whether they would help your reader follow your instructions. Illustrations can simplify the process considerably for your reader by *showing* the steps in your instructions instead of telling them. Well-thought-out illustrations can make even the most complex instructions easier to understand. In addition to demonstrating the steps of your instructions, drawings, photographs, and diagrams can help your reader identify parts and the relationships between them. Whether illustrations will be useful depends on your reader's needs and on the nature of the project. Instructions for inexperienced readers should be more heavily illustrated than those for experienced readers. Do not rely on an illustration alone to do the entire job; it is important to explain what is shown in an illustration.

Sometimes it is necessary or advisable to illustrate each step in your instructions (Figure 7–10). Place an illustration next to the step it illustrates so the reader immediately perceives the connection between the two. Make certain that the illustration is an accurate representation (not, for example, of an older model of the same product). If you use six or more illustrations, assign figure numbers and figure titles to them. For a complete discussion of how to create and use effective illustrations, see Chapter 12.

Figure 7–11 shows instructions that guide a medical lab technician through the steps of streaking a saucer-sized disk of material (called *agar*) used to grow bacterial colonies for laboratory examination. The objective is to thin out the original specimen (the *inoculum*) so that the bacteria will grow in small, isolated colonies. The streaking process makes certain that part of the saucer is inoculated heavily, while its remaining portions are inoculated progressively more lightly. The streaking is done by hand with a thin wire, looped at one end for holding a sample of the inoculum.

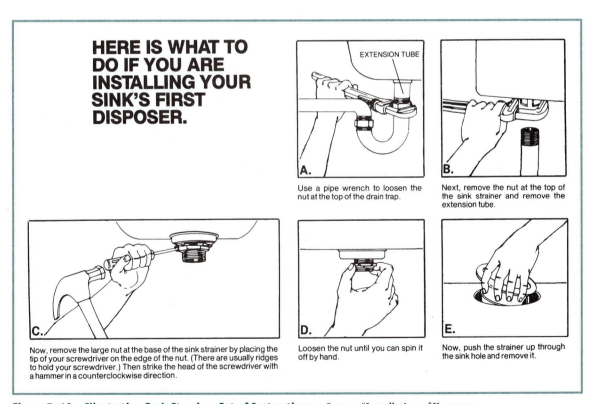

Figure 7–10   Illustrating Each Step in a Set of Instructions   *Source:* "Installation of Kenmore Waste Disposers," Courtesy of Sears, Roebuck and Company, 1997, Hoffman Estates, IL.

STREAKING AN AGAR PLATE

Distribute the inoculum over the surface of the agar in the following manner:

Step 1. Beginning at one edge of the saucer, thin the inoculum by streaking back and forth over the same area several times, sweeping across the agar surface until approximately one-quarter of the surface has been covered. *Sterilize the loop in an open flame.*

Step 2. Streak at right angles to the originally inoculated area, carrying the inoculum out from the streaked areas onto the sterile surface with only the first stroke of the wire. Cover half of the remaining sterile agar surface. *Sterilize the loop.*

Step 3. Repeat as described in Step 2, covering the remaining sterile agar surface.

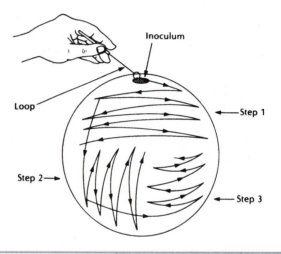

Figure 7–11   Step-by-Step Instructions with Illustration

Test Your Instructions

To test the accuracy and clarity of your instructions, ask someone who is not familiar with the operation to use the instructions you have written to perform the task or procedure. A first-time user of your instructions can spot missing steps or point out passages that should be worded more clearly. As you watch your tester follow your instructions, note any steps that seem especially puzzling or confusing.

DIGITAL SHORTCUTS: Organizing and Highlighting Instructions

When writing instructions, use the features of your word-processing software to organize and highlight information.

- font size and boldface
- outlining feature

- numbered-list feature
- bulleted-list feature
- clip art icons and symbols

WRITER'S CHECKLIST: Creating Effective Instructions

- ☐ Avoid technical terminology that your readers might not know.
- ☐ Verify that measurements, distances, times, and relationships are precise and accurate.
- ☐ Use effective illustrations, and place them properly.
- ☐ Include warnings and cautions wherever necessary.
- ☐ Use the imperative mood and the active voice as much as possible.
- ☐ Use short sentences as much as possible.
- ☐ Eliminate any ambiguity.
- ☐ Test your instructions by having someone else use them while you observe.

■ Explaining a Process

When you prepare instructions, your goal is to enable your reader to complete a specific task by following the step-by-step procedure you have outlined. You know that your reader will use your directions to become a *doer*. If, however, you are asked to write an explanation of a *process*, you will have a different purpose in mind: You will tell your reader how something works or how something is done — but your reader probably will not do the process himself or herself. The process you explain might be an event that occurs in nature (the tidal pull of the moon), a function that requires human effort (conducting a marketing survey), or an activity in which people operate machinery to produce goods or services (automobile assembly-line production).

Just as it is essential for you to be familiar with a task before you can write clear instructions for carrying it out, so you must thoroughly understand a process yourself before you can explain it to your reader. As in all on-the-job writing, you must aim your writing at a level appropriate to your reader's background. Beginners, you will find, require more basic information, and less technical vocabulary, than do experienced workers.

The explanation of a process has something else in common with written instructions: Both kinds of writing are composed of steps. The steps in a process explanation should be as clear, accurate, and complete as those in a set of instructions. Process explanations, like instructions, benefit from illustrations that show the steps of the process from beginning to end.

In your opening paragraph, tell your reader why it is important to become familiar with the process you are explaining. Before you explain the steps necessary to form a corporation, for example, you could cite the tax savings that incorporation would permit. To give your reader a framework for the details that will follow, you might present a brief overview of the process. Finally, you might describe how the process works in relation to a larger whole of which it is a part. In explaining the air-brake system of a large dump truck, for example, you might note that the braking system is one part of the vehicle's air system, which also controls the throttle and transmission-shifting mechanisms.

A process explanation can be long or short, depending on how much detail is necessary. The following elementary description of the way a camera controls light to expose photographic film, intended for beginning photographers, fits into one paragraph. Note the writer's choice of words and definitions that are designed to communicate the ideas to an audience unfamiliar with the subject. Simple language is used, and specialized terms are defined.

■   The camera is the basic tool for recording light images. It is simply a *box* from which all light is excluded except that which passes through a small opening at the front. Cameras are equipped with various devices for controlling the light rays as they enter this opening. At the press of a button, a mechanical blade or curtain, called a *shutter,* opens and closes automatically. During the fraction of a second that the shutter is open, the light reflected from the subject toward which the camera is aimed passes into the camera through a piece of optical glass called the *lens.* The lens focuses, or projects, the light rays onto the wall at the back of the camera. These light reflections are captured on a sheet of film attached to the back wall.

The passage in Figure 7–12 explains the process by which drinking water is purified. It provides essential background information in the context of a discussion of how drinking water may be contaminated as it is treated before distribution to homes. The information is intended for the average homeowner, but the vocabulary does assume an elementary familiarity with biological and chemical terms. The description is enhanced by a step-by-step illustration that complements the pattern of the writing by providing an overview image (first panel in Figure 7–13) and then three more-detailed drawings of the water-treatment process (remaining three panels in Figure 7–13). Note that the title (or heading) for the process accompanies the explanation and that a citation for the *source* follows.

The Treatment Process

After it has been transported from its source to a local water system, most surface water must be processed in a treatment plant before it can be used. Some groundwater, on the other hand, is considered chemically and biologically pure enough to pass directly from a well into the distribution system that carries it to the home.

Although there are innumerable variations, surface water is usually treated as follows: First, it enters a storage lagoon where a chemical, usually copper sulfate, is added to control algae growth. From there, water passes through one or more screens that remove large debris. Next, a coagulant, such as alum, is mixed into the water to encourage the settling of suspended particles. The water flows slowly through one or more sedimentation basins so that larger particles settle to the bottom and can be removed. Water then passes through a filtration basin partially filled with sand and gravel where yet more suspended particles are removed.

At that point in the process, the Safe Drinking Water Act has mandated an additional step for communities using surface water. . . . [W]ater is to be filtered through activated carbon to remove any microscopic organic material and chemicals that have escaped the other processes. Activated carbon is extremely porous—one pound of the material can have a surface area of one acre. This honeycomb of minute pores attracts and traps pollutants through a process called adsorption. . . .

The final stage of water treatment is disinfection, where an agent capable of killing most biological pathogens is added to the water. Until the chlorination process was developed, devastating epidemics—such as the outbreak of typhoid and cholera that took 90,000 lives in Chicago in 1885—once spread wildly through community water systems. By 1910, most large water utilities had begun to chlorinate their surface water, and chlorine gas remains the disinfectant most widely used among community water systems. . . . A further step in the treatment process, used by about 60 percent of the nation's water utilities, is the addition of fluoride to reduce tooth decay.

Figure 7–12   Sample of a Process Description (Excerpt)   *Source: Indoor Pollution* by S. Coffel and K. Feiden (New York: Fawcett Columbine, 1990), pp. 127–130. Reprinted by permission.

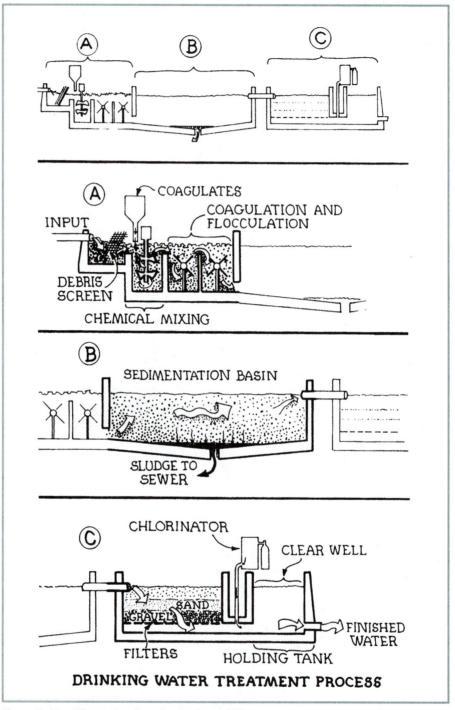

Figure 7–13 **Illustration for a Process Description** *Source: Indoor Pollution* by S. Coffel and K. Feiden. Copyright © 1990 by Steve Coffel and Karyn Feiden. Reprinted by permission of Ballantine Books, a division of Random House, Inc.

■ Describing Information

When you give your reader information about an object's size, shape, color, method of construction, or other features of its appearance, you are describing it. The kinds of description you will write on the job depend, of course, on where you work and on what you do. Office administrators describe office space and layouts. Equipment maintenance workers write parts and equipment descriptions. Engineers often must describe products they have designed to corporate specifications. Marketing professionals must describe the products they are marketing to potential customers. Software developers face the daunting task of describing something the reader cannot see. Police descriptions of accident scenes are routinely used in court cases. The key to effective descriptions is the accurate presentation of details. To select appropriate details, determine what use your reader will make of the description. Will your reader use it to identify something? Will your reader have to assemble or repair the object you are describing? Which details you include, then, will depend on the task the reader will perform.

Your description may be of something concrete, such as a machine, or of something abstract, such as computer software. Figure 7–14 is an example of

When the disk initializer prepares a disk for use, it sets the disk to a predefined format, which includes reserving those software areas required by the operating system. Of the available 8,192 sectors, approximately 1,154 sectors are reserved for disk information, system software, and system use. The remaining sectors are available to the user. Initialization of the disk reserves the areas as shown in this figure.

a.	Disk Volume Header	5 Sectors
b.	Monitor Boot	6 Sectors
c.	Skip Area	41 Sectors
d.	Disk Directory	20 Sectors
e.	System Storage	41 Sectors
f.	System-Software Overlays	801 Sectors
g.	Work Storage	240 Sectors

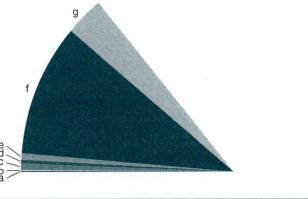

**Figure 7–14
An Abstract
Description:
Software Sectors
on a Computer
Disk**

something the reader will never actually see: how and where the different sectors of software are located on a computer disk—that is, its format.

When describing a physical object (a piece of equipment or a system made up of connected objects), give an overview of the object or system before describing its parts in detail. The level of detail you must provide will depend on the reader's familiarity with what is being described. You must, of course, become thoroughly familiar with the object before attempting to describe it.

Descriptions can be brief and simple, or they can be highly complex. Simple descriptions usually require only a simple listing of key features. A purchase order, shown in Figure 7–15, is a typical example of simple descriptive writing. Purchase-order descriptions should be clear and specific. An inaccurate or omitted detail may result in the delivery of the wrong item. Even an order for something as ordinary as trash-compactor bags needs, in addition to the part number, four specific descriptive details.

Complex descriptions, of course, require more detail than simple ones (see Figure 7–16). The details you select should accurately and vividly convey what you are describing. If it is useful for your readers to visualize an object, for instance, include details—such as color and shape—that appeal to the sense of sight. The example that follows is a description of the leaf abnormalities that occur when trees are planted in soil lacking the necessary minerals. The writer, a forester writing for other foresters, offers precise details of the changes in color that were observed.

■ Foliage of the black cherry trees showed striking and unusual discolorations in mid-August. Bright red margins extended one half the distance to the midrib and almost to the tip of the leaf. Nearly all leaves were similarly discolored and showed a well-defined line of demarcation between the pigmentation and the normal coloration. By late September, the pigmentation margins had widened and extended to the tips of the leaves. The red deepened in intensity and, in addition, blue and violet hues were apparent for the first time.

The description of leaf abnormalities concentrates on appearance—it tells the reader what the discolored leaves look like. Sometimes, however, you may want to describe the physical characteristics of an object and at the same time

Figure 7–15
A Simple Description: Purchase Order

	PURCHASE ORDER	
Part No.	Description	Quantity
GL/020	Trash-compactor bags, 31″ × 50″ tubular, nontransparent, 5-mil thickness, including 100 tie wraps per carton	5 cartons@ 100 per carton

The Die Block Assembly consists of two machined block sections, eight Code Pins, and a Feed Pin. The larger section, called the Die Block, is fashioned of a hard, noncorrosive beryllium-copper alloy. It houses the eight Code Pins and the smaller Feed Pin in nine finely machined guide holes.

Number of features and relative size differences noted

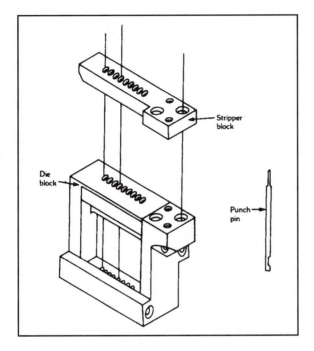

The guide holes in the upper part of the Die Block are made smaller to conform to the thinner tips of the Feed Pins. Extending over the top of the Die Block and secured to it at one end is a smaller, armlike block called the Stripper Block. The Stripper Block is made from hardened tool steel, and it also has been drilled through with nine finely machined guide holes. It is carefully fitted to the Die Block at the factory so that its holes will be precisely above those in the Die Block and so that the space left between the blocks will measure .015″ (± .003″). The residue from the operation, called chad, is pushed out through the top of the Stripper Block and guided out of the assembly by means of a plastic Residue Collector and Residue Collector Extender.

Use of analogy

Definition

Figure 7–16   A Complex Description: Die Block Assembly

itemize the parts that go into its makeup. If you intended to write a description of a piece of machinery, for example, you would probably find this approach, called the *whole-to-parts method,* the most useful for your purpose. You would first present a general description of the device, because an overall description would provide your reader with a frame of reference for the more specific details that follow—the physical description of the various parts and the location and function of each in relation to the whole. The description would conclude with an explanation of the way the parts work together to get their particular job done.

The text for Figure 7–17 describes a body harness tethered to a line that protects ironworkers from falls as they walk on beams high above the ground at building construction sites. The illustration is intended for occupational safety officials who must assess such devices as they seek ways to protect worker health and safety on the job.

Figure 7–17
Illustration to Aid
Description

Approximately 50 ironworkers fall to their deaths each year in the United States. The latest fall-protection system may change all this. The following illustration shows a system that protects ironworkers from falls without interfering with their work. This system complies with the Occupational Safety and Health Administration's strict fall-protection requirements.

Known as the Beamwalker, the system consists of two stanchions that clamp to a standard I-beam. A 40-foot line, to which workers can attach their lifelines, runs between the stanchions. The Beamwalker is installed while the beam is on the ground.

The Beamwalker

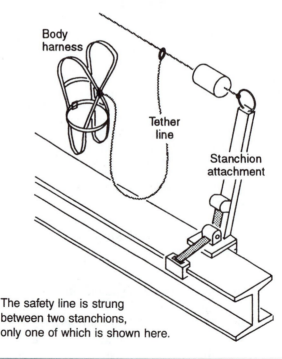

Body harness

Tether line

Stanchion attachment

The safety line is strung between two stanchions, only one of which is shown here.

Illustrations can be powerful aids in descriptive writing, especially when they show details too intricate to explain in words, as in Figure 7–18, which describes and illustrates the operation of a computer disk unit that uses multiple platters. Note that each illustration appears immediately after the text that discusses it. All illustrations should be positioned as close to the text they illustrate as possible.

Do not hesitate to use an illustration with a complex description if the illustration creates a clearer image. Detailed instructions on the use of illustrations appear in Chapter 12.

The disk pack contains six recording surfaces, each plated with cobalt-nickle to provide long disk life and a high-density magnetic recording surface. Each of the six surfaces is serviced by 12 read/write heads; therefore, each pack is serviced by 72 read/write heads. Of these 72 heads, 64 are available to the user and 8 are reserved for use by the hardware.

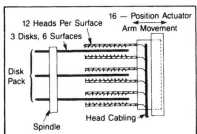

Tracks

A track is the area covered by one read/write head during one complete rotation of the disk. Since 64 read/write heads are available to the user, there are 64 tracks for reading or recording data in each of the 16 positions. Therefore, over the entire recording surface, there are 1,024 tracks available for data.

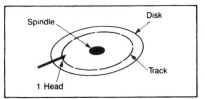

- The area of the disk covered by one read/write head during a revolution is called a track.
- A total of 64 tracks are available in any one of the 16-actuator positions.
- A total of 1,024 tracks are available over the entire 16 positions.

Sectors

Each track of the disk is divided into eight addressable units called sectors. Since there are 64 available tracks in an actuator position, 512 sectors are available in each of the 16 positions of the actuator. Therefore, over the entire 16 positions, 8,192 sectors are available for storage. Each sector may contain up to 512 characters.

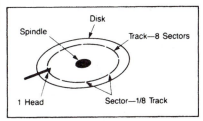

- Each track is divided into eight sectors.
- Each of 16 positions has 512 sectors.
- Each pack has 8,192 sectors.
- Each sector may contain 512 characters.
- Each pack may contain 4,194,304 characters.

Figure 7–18   Illustrations to Add Descriptive Details

■ Defining Terms and Concepts

Accurate definitions are crucial to many kinds of writing, especially for readers unfamiliar with your subject. Depending on your reader's needs, your definition can be formal, informal, or extended.

Formal Definitions

A formal definition is a form of classification. In it, you place a term in a class of related objects or ideas and show how it differs from other members of the same class.

Formal Definitions

Term	Class	Difference
spoon	eating utensil	that consists of a small, shallow bowl on the end of a handle
auction	public sale	in which property passes to the highest bidder through successive increased offers
annual	plant	that completes its life cycle, from seed to natural death, in one growing season

Informal Definitions

In an informal definition, a familiar word or phrase is used as a synonym for an unfamiliar word or phrase.

- An invoice is a *bill.*

- Many states have set aside wildlife habitats (or *living space*).

- Plants live in a symbiotic, or *mutually beneficial,* relationship with certain kinds of bacteria.

- The system is controlled by a photoelectric (*optical*) sensing device.

- Equipment functioning with transverse motion (*motion in a straight, continuous line*) can be hazardous.

The advantage of informal definitions is that they permit you to explain the meaning of a term with a minimum of interruption in the flow of your writing. Informal definitions should not be used, however, if the completeness of a formal definition is needed to make the term easier to understand.

Extended Definitions

An extended definition, used when more than a phrase or a sentence or two is needed to explain an idea, explores a number of qualities of what is being defined. Some extended definitions may take only a few sentences, while others may run for several paragraphs. How long an extended definition ought to be depends on your reader's needs and on the complexity of the subject. A reader familiar with a topic or an area might be able to handle a long, fairly technical definition, whereas a newcomer to a topic would require simpler language and more basic information.

Compare the language and detail provided in the following two definitions, which explain the chemical concept of *pH*. The first definition is intended for people in the graphic arts who need a general understanding of the concept but not a detailed explanation of the principles underlying the concept.

■ **pH.** A number used for expressing the acidity or alkalinity of solutions. A value of 7 is neutral in a scale ranging from 0 to 14. Solutions with values below 7 are acid, above 7 are alkalines.[1]

The second definition of pH, from an article about hydrogen ion activity in human blood, is intended for chemistry students and clinical laboratory technicians. The author assumes that readers are familiar with chemical symbols (H^+), abbreviations (*mol/liter*), and terms (*ions*).

■ About 70 years ago, the pH scale was devised to express hydrogen ion concentration in convenient numbers. The pH value, the exponent of the H^+ concentration in mol/liter with the sign changed from minus to plus, increases as hydrogen ion concentration increases. The normal pH of blood lies between 7.38 and 7.42 and a small change in pH can mean a big change in the H^+ concentration. For example, when pH changes from 7.4 to 7.0, the H^+ concentration increases 2½-fold, from 4×10^{-8} to 10×10^{-8} mol/liter.[2]

Clarifying Definitions

Perhaps the easiest way to define a term is to give specific examples of it. A landscape architect, for example, performed a land-use analysis of a regional park for officials of the Parks Department. Crucial to the analysis were a number of abstract concepts, such as *form, line,* and *color,* used in precise ways not necessarily corresponding to their everyday use. Without an understanding of these concepts, the officials would be unable to understand the analysis. Specific examples and easy-to-picture details bridge the gap between writer and reader, as in this definition of *form.*

■ Form, which is the shape of landscape features, can best be represented by both small-scale features, such as *trees* and *shrubs,* and by large-scale elements, such as *mountains* and *mountain ranges.*

[1]International Paper Company, *Pocket Pal—A Graphic /Arts Production Handbook,* 16th ed. (New York: International Paper Company, 1995), p. 200.

[2]John A. Lott, "Hydrogen Ions in Blood," *Chemistry* 51 (May 1978): 6.

Another way to define a difficult concept, especially when you are writing for nonspecialists, is to link the unfamiliar to the familiar by means of an analogy (comparison). Defining radio waves in terms of their length (long) and frequency (low), a writer develops an analogy to show why a low frequency is advantageous.

■   The low frequency makes it relatively easy to produce a wave having virtually all its power concentrated at one frequency. Think, for example, of a group of people lost in a forest. If they hear sounds of a search party in the distance, they all will begin to shout for help in different directions. Not a very efficient process, is it? But suppose that all the energy that went into the production of this noise could be concentrated into a single shout or whistle. Clearly the chances that the group will be found would be much greater.

Some terms are best defined by an explanation of their causes. Writing in a professional journal, a nurse describes an apparatus used to monitor blood pressure in severely ill patients. Called an indwelling catheter, the device displays blood-pressure readings on an oscilliscope and on a numbered scale. Users of the device, the writer explains, must understand what a *dampened wave form* is.

■   The *dampened wave form,* the smoothing out or flattening of the pressure wave form on the oscilliscope, is *usually caused by an obstruction* that prevents blood pressure from being freely transmitted to the monitor. The obstruction might be *a small clot or bit of fibrin* at the catheter tip. More likely, *the catheter tip has become positioned against the artery wall* and is preventing the blood from flowing freely.

The most significant point about the occurrence of a dampened wave form is that it is usually the result of a potentially dangerous obstruction. The definition therefore emphasizes cause and indicates what factors may, in turn, produce the obstruction in blood-pressure transmission.

Some writers make a formal definition easier to understand by breaking a concept into manageable parts.

FORMAL DEFINITION	Fire is the visible heat energy released from the rapid oxidation of a fuel. A substance is "on fire" when the release of heat energy from the oxidation process reaches visible light levels.
DIVISION INTO COMPONENT ELEMENTS	The classic fire triangle illustrates the elements necessary to create fire: *oxygen, heat,* and *burnable material* or *fuel.* Air provides sufficient oxygen for combustion; the intensity of the heat needed to start a fire depends on the characteristics of the burnable material or fuel. A burnable substance is one that will sustain combustion after an initial application of heat to start it.

The techniques for dividing the elements of a concept follow the guidelines discussed in Chapter 2.

Under certain circumstances, the meaning of a term can be clarified and made easier to remember by an exploration of its origin. Because they sometimes have unfamiliar Greek and Latin roots, scientific and medical terms benefit especially from an explanation of this type. Tracing the derivation of a word can also be useful when you want to explain why a word has favorable or unfavorable associations—particularly if your goal is to influence your reader's attitude toward an idea or an activity.

■ Efforts to influence legislation generally fall under the head of *lobbying,* a term that once referred to people who prowl the lobbies of houses of government, buttonholing lawmakers and trying to get them to take certain positions. Lobbying today is all of this, and much more, too. It is a respected—and necessary—activity. It tells legislators which way the winds of public opinion are blowing, and it helps inform them of the implications of certain bills, debates, and resolutions they must contend with.[3]

Sometimes it is useful to point out what something is *not* to clarify what it *is.* A what-it-is-not definition is effective only when the reader is familiar with the item with which the defined item is contrasted. If you say *x* is not *y,* your reader must understand the meaning of *y* for the explanation to make sense. In a crane operator's manual, for instance, a "negative definition" is used to show that, for safety reasons, a hydraulic crane cannot be operated in the same manner as a lattice boom crane.

■ A hydraulic crane is *not* like a lattice boom crane in one very important way. In most cases, the safe lifting capacity of a lattice boom crane is based on the *weight needed to tip the machine.* Therefore, operators of friction machines sometimes depend on signs that the machine might tip to warn them of impending danger.
 This is a very dangerous practice with a hydraulic crane. . . .[4]

Problems in Definitions

When you use a definition as a means of presenting your material, you should keep in mind a few pitfalls that may result in confusing, inaccurate, or incomplete definitions.

Avoid circular definitions, which merely restate the term to be defined and therefore fail to clarify it.

INCORRECT   *Spontaneous combustion* is fire that begins spontaneously.

      [Using the word *spontaneously* to define *spontaneous combustion* is circular and incorrect.]

CORRECT   Spontaneous combustion is the self-ignition of a flammable material through a chemical reaction such as oxidation and temperature buildup.

---

[3]Bill Vogt, *How to Build a Better Outdoors* (New York: McKay, 1978), p. 93.

[4]*Operator's Manual* (Model W-180), Harnischfeger Corporation.

Avoid "is when" and "is where" definitions; such definitions overlook what is essential to formal definition—they do not classify the term being defined.

INCORRECT   A *contract* is when two or more people agree to something.

CORRECT   A *contract* is a binding agreement between two or more people.

                 [*Binding agreement* is the class of which *contract* is a member.]

INCORRECT   A *day-care center* is where working parents can leave their preschool children during the day.

CORRECT   A *day-care center* is a facility at which working parents can leave their preschool children during the day.

                 [*Facility* is the class of which *day-care center* is a member.]

Do not use definitions made up of terms your reader won't understand. Even informally written material will occasionally require the use of a term in a special sense unfamiliar to your reader; such terms should be defined too.

■   In these specifications, the term *safety can* refers to an approved container of not more than five-gallon capacity having a spring-closing spout cover designed to relieve internal pressure when exposed to fire.

■ Explaining Cause and Effect

When your purpose is to explain why something happened, or why you think something will happen, cause-and-effect analysis is a useful writing strategy. For instance, if you were asked to report on why the accident rate for the company truck fleet rose by 30 percent this year over last year, you would use cause-and-effect analysis. In this case, you would be working from an effect (higher accident rate) to its cause (bad driving weather, inexperienced drivers, poor truck maintenance, and so on). However, if your purpose were to report on the possible effects that the switch to a four-day workweek (ten hours per day) would have on the office staff, you would also use cause-and-effect analysis—but this time you would start with cause (the new work schedule) and look for possible effects (changes in morale, in productivity, in absenteeism, and the like).

The goal of cause-and-effect analysis is to make the relationship between a situation and either its cause or its effect as plausible as possible. The conclusions you draw about the relationship will be based on the evidence you have gathered. *Evidence* is any pertinent fact or argument that helps explain the circumstances of an event. Because not all evidence will be of equal value to you as you draw conclusions, it's a good idea to keep some guidelines in mind for evaluating evidence.

Evidence Should Be Pertinent

The facts and arguments that you gather should be pertinent, or relevant, to your topic. That is, even if the evidence you collect is accurate, you should be careful not to draw a conclusion that your evidence does not lead to or support. You may have researched some statistics, for example, that show that an increasing number of Americans are licensed to fly small airplanes. However, you cannot use this information as evidence that there is a slowdown in interstate highway construction in the United States—the evidence does not lead to that conclusion. Other, more relevant evidence is available to explain the decline in interstate construction—greatly increased construction costs, opposition from environmental groups, new legislation that transfers highway construction funds to mass transportation, and so on. Statistics on the increase in small-plane licensing may be relevant to other conclusions, however. You could argue that the upswing has occurred because small planes save travel time, provide easy access to remote areas, and, once they are purchased, are economical to operate.

Evidence Should Be Sufficient

Incomplete evidence can lead to false conclusions.

FALSE CONCLUSION   Driver-training classes in the schools do not help prevent auto accidents. Two people I know who completed driver-training classes were involved in accidents.

Although the evidence cited to support the conclusion may be accurate, there is not enough of it here to even justify making a statement about the driver-training program at one school. A thorough investigation of the usefulness of driver-training classes in keeping the accident rate down would require many more than two examples. It would require a comparison of the driving records of those who had completed driver training with the records of those who had not.

Evidence Should Be Representative

If you conduct a survey to obtain your evidence, be sure that you do not solicit responses only from individuals or groups whose views are identical to yours—that is, be sure you obtain a representative sampling. A survey of backpackers in a national park on whether the park ought to be open to off-road vehicles would more than likely show them overwhelmingly against the idea. Such a survey should include opinions from more than one interested group.

Evidence Should Be Plausible

Two events that occur close to each other in time or place may or may not be causally related. Thunder and black clouds do not always signal rain, but they do so often enough that if we are outdoors when the sky darkens and we hear thunder, we seek shelter unless we're prepared to get wet. However, if you walk under a ladder and shortly afterward sprain your ankle on a curb, you cannot conclude that walking under a ladder brings bad luck—unless you are superstitious. Although the two events occurred close to each other in time, the first did not cause the second. Merely to say that *x* caused *y* (or will cause *y*) is inadequate. You must demonstrate the causal relationship with pertinent facts and arguments.

For example, a driver lost control of his car one summer day and crashed into a tavern. He told the police that the accident had occurred because his car had been in the sun so long and absorbed so much solar energy that he could no longer control it. The cause the driver gave for the accident cannot be taken as either plausible or objective. A careful examination of the event would probably reveal that the driver had been a patron of the tavern shortly before the crash took place, but even this explanation would have to be demonstrated with convincing facts. The police would have to interview other tavern patrons and test the driver to determine breath- and blood-alcohol levels. If the patrons identified the driver as a recent customer in the tavern, and if the breath and blood tests showed intoxicating levels of alcohol in his system, the evidence would be sufficient to explain why the car had hit the tavern.

Evidence Should Link Causes to Effects

To show a true relationship between a cause and an effect, you must demonstrate that the existence of the one *requires* the existence of the other. It is often difficult to establish beyond any doubt that one event was *the* cause of another event. More often, a result will have more than one cause. As you research your subject, your task is to determine which cause or causes are most plausible.

When several probable causes are equally valid, report your findings accordingly, as in the following excerpt from an article on the use of an energy-saving device called a furnace-vent damper. The damper is a metal plate fitted inside the flue or vent pipe of natural-gas or fuel-oil furnaces. When the furnace is on, the damper opens to allow the gases to escape up the flue. When the furnace shuts off, the damper closes, thus preventing warm air from escaping up the flue stack. The dampers are potentially dangerous, however. If the dampers fail to open at the proper time, they could allow poisonous furnace gases to back up into the house and asphyxiate anyone in a matter of minutes. Tests run on several dampers showed a number of probable causes for their malfunctioning.

■ One damper was sold without proper installation instructions, and another was wired incorrectly. Two of the units had slow-opening dampers (15 seconds) that prevented the [furnace] burner from firing. And one damper jammed when exposed to a simulated fuel temperature of more than 700 degrees.[5]

---

[5]Don DeBat, "Save Energy But Save Your Life, Too," *Family Safety,* Fall 1978, p. 27.

The investigator located more than one cause of damper malfunctions and reported on them. Without such a thorough account, recommendations to prevent similar malfunctions would be based on incomplete evidence.

■ Persuading Your Reader

Suppose you and a friend are arguing over whether the capital of Maine is Portland or Augusta. The issue is a simple question of fact that can be easily checked in an almanac or an atlas. (It's Augusta.) Now suppose you are trying to convince management at your company that it ought to adopt flexible working hours for its employees or that it ought to adopt a plain-language program to improve communications with its customers. A quick look in a reference book will not settle the issue. Like Christine Thomas in Chapter 1, you will have to *persuade* management that your idea is a good one. To achieve your goal—to convince your company to accept your suggestions and act on them—you will probably have to put your recommendations in writing.

In all on-the-job writing, it is important to keep your reader's needs, as well as your own, clearly in mind. This is especially true in persuasive writing, in which your purpose may often be to ask your reader to change his or her working procedures or habits. You may think, as Christine Thomas did, that most people would automatically accept a recommendation for an improvement in the workplace, but improvement means change, and people tend to resist change. What you see as an improvement others may see as change for the sake of change ("We've always done it this way. Why change?"). The idea you are proposing may be a threat to a staff member's pet project, or it may make the knowledge and experience that a veteran employee has accumulated seem out of date—so both will probably resist your suggestion. To overcome their resistance, you'll have to convince them that your suggestion has merit. You can do this most effectively by establishing the need for your recommendation and by supporting it with convincing, objective evidence.

Keep in mind, as you seek to persuade your reader, that the way you present your ideas is as important as the ideas themselves. Be thoughtful of your reader's needs and feelings by applying some basic manners in your writing. Avoid sarcasm or any other hostile tone that will offend your reader. If anger shows through in your writing, you will quickly turn the reader against your point of view. Also avoid exaggeration or being overly enthusiastic. Your reader may interpret such an attitude as insincere or presumptuous. Of course, you should not conceal genuine enthusiasm; just be careful not to overdo it.

The memo in Figure 7–19 was written by an MIS (management information systems) administrator to persuade her staff to accept and participate in a change to a new computer system. Notice that not everything in this memo is presented in a positive light. Change brings disruption, and the writer acknowledges that fact.

Figure 7–19
Persuasive
Memo

Memo

TO: Engineering Sales Staff
FROM: Bernadine Kovak, MIS Administrator   *BK*
DATE: April 8, 20--
SUBJECT: Plans for Changeover to NRT/R4 System

As you all know, our workload has jumped by 30 percent in the past month. It has increased because our customer base and resulting technical support services have grown dramatically. This growth is a result, in part, of our recent merger with Datacom.

This growth has meant that we have all experienced the difficulty of providing our customers with up-to-date technical information when they need it. In the next few months, we anticipate that the workload will increase another 20 percent. Even a staff as experienced as ours cannot handle such a workload without help.

To cope with that expansion, in the next month we will be installing the NRT/R4 mainframe and QCS enterprise software with Web-based applications and global sales and service network. The system will speed processing dramatically as well as give us access to all relevant company-wide databases. It should enable us to access the information both we and our customers need.

The new system, unfortunately, will cause some disruption at first. We will need to transfer many of our existing programs and software applications to the new format. And all of us need to learn to navigate in the R4 and QCS environments. However, once we have made those adjustments, I believe we will welcome the changes.

I would like to put your knowledge and experience to work in getting the new system into operation. Let's meet in my office to discuss the improvements on Friday, April 12, at 1:00 p.m. I will have details of the plan to discuss with you. I'm also eager to get your comments, suggestions, and—most of all—your cooperation.

For persuasive communications outside the company, you must take equal if not greater care in the way you present information. In the letter in Figure 7–20, the writer is disappointed because she did not expect the response she got, but attempts to further persuade her reader. (See also Persuasive Writing in Chapter 14.) Instead of responding with anger or sarcasm ("Your fee is highway robbery!"), the writer compliments the publisher on their prompt response and gets quickly to the point: her concern for the high fee and her attempt to have it reduced. She indicates that using the poem is certainly desirable, but as "nontechnical" or "ancillary" material it's not essential. She explains her project's budgetary constraints and completes her

**Figure 7–20
Persuasive
Letter**

Commuter Aircraft Corporation
7328 Wellington Drive
Partridge, Ohio 45424

March 7, 20--

Adele Chu, Permissions Editor
Poet's Press, Inc.
One Plaza Way, Suite 3
Bolton, Massachusetts 08193

Dear Ms. Chu:

Thank you for responding so quickly to my request for permission to reprint
the poem "Flight" in the pilot's manual for our new Aerosoar 100 Commuter.

I am writing to express concern about the fee you have requested for the use
of this selection. It is much higher than we expected. Because the manual is
an instructional booklet distributed to pilots free of charge, the budget for
this project is strictly limited, particularly for nontechnical, ancillary materials such as poetry. We continue to feel that the poem would add an element
of interest and even inspiration for our readers, however, and we would like
to ask you to consider lowering your fee to make this possible. To meet the
demands of our budget, we are able to pay no more than $300 for each selec-
tion in the manual—considerably less than the $900 you have requested.

I hope you understand our position and that you will consider reducing your
fee for the use of this material. Thank you for considering my request. I look
forward to hearing from you.

Sincerely,

J.T. Walters

J.T. Walters
Publications Manager

cc: Legal Department

**(890) 321-1231
Fax (890) 321-5116**

http://www.commair.com

explanation with a counter offer. Throughout, her tone and language are courteous and respectful. She ends her letter by leaving the door open for the publisher: "I look forward to hearing from you."

Finally, when writing to persuade your reader, do not overlook opposing points of view. Most issues have more than one side, and you should acknowledge them. For example, if you were writing a memo to your supervisor listing reasons why flexible working hours are a good idea, it would be a mistake to overlook the added paperwork that might be required to keep track of separate schedules for all employees. It would be most effective to admit that the paperwork will increase—and then go on to show that the added burden would be more than compensated for by improved employee morale and perhaps by greater productivity. By including differing points of view, you gain several advantages. First, you show your reader that you are honest enough to recognize opposite views when they exist. Second, you can demonstrate the advantage of your viewpoint over those of others. Finally, by bringing up opposing views *before* your coworkers do, you may be able to blunt some of their objections.

■ Writing for the Web

The Web is the most popular way to access the Internet, and it has become a powerful tool for disseminating information. As Web technology becomes more important for news, marketing, research, and shopping, you may be asked to write a paper, a report, or an article that will appear on a Web site.

Web sites can serve many purposes. In business, companies may use their sites to entice Web users to purchase their products or services online, to provide detailed information about products, or even to recruit new employees. Some companies offer sites that provide up-to-the-minute information on current events, entertainment, or sports, while other sites are oriented toward providing resources for research, and may include essays, historical documents, or statistical data.

This section contains advice for how to create and organize effective content for the Web. For a general introduction to the Internet and the World Wide Web, see The Electronic Office, on pages 728–736. For guidelines for designing clear, effective Web sites, see Web-Page Design, on pages 503–508.

Write for Rapid Consumption

When you write for the Web for your company or organization, your audience might consist of thousands of people with many different backgrounds and different reasons for looking at your Web site. Some of those people may never have heard of your product or organization before, and others may be longtime clients or investors looking for specific information. The people looking at your Web site have one important thing in common—they are all reading on a computer screen.

Most Web users scan a Web page very quickly, moving from heading to heading to find the author's main ideas. In a matter of seconds, Web users decide either to stay and read more or to try to find their information elsewhere. A poorly organized Web page, as shown in Figure 7–21, may deter a Web user from reading to the end of your document, while a well-organized Web page, as shown in Figure 7–22, can persuade a Web user to remain at your site and continue reading.

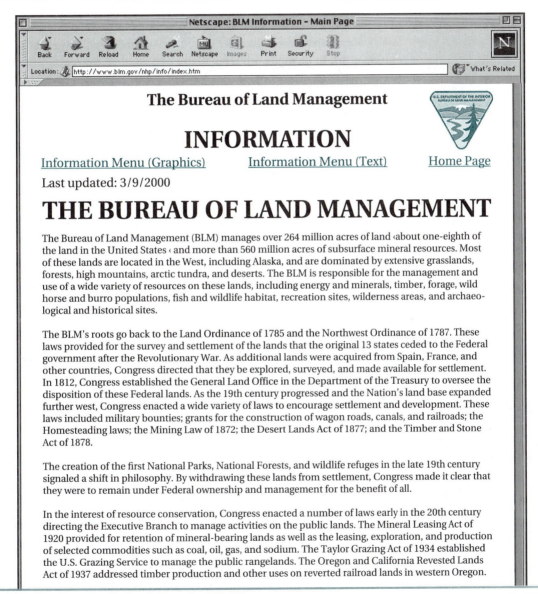

Figure 7–21   Example of a Poorly Organized Web Page

(continued)

The Grazing Service was merged with the General Land Office in 1946 to form the Bureau of Land Management within the Department of the Interior. At that time, there were more than 2,000 unrelated and often conflicting laws concerning management of the public lands. The BLM had no unified legislative mandate until Congress enacted the Federal Land Policy and Management Act of 1976 (FLPMA).

In FLPMA, Congress recognized the value of the remaining public lands to the American people and declared that these lands generally would remain in public ownership. Congress also codified the principle of "multiple use" management, defined as "management of the public lands and their various resource values so they are utilized in the combination that will best meet the present and future needs of the American people."

While adhering to this multiple use mandate, the BLM's management of the public lands has evolved over the last 20 years in response to new Congressional directives and court decisions, changing demand patterns, and a maturing understanding of what is required to use natural resources on a sustainable basis.

The BLM performs a wide variety of functions in managing the public lands, including, but not limited to, taking inventory of resources; preparing land use plans and assessing environmental impacts; conducting land surveys; issuing use authorizations; enforcing permit conditions; designing and constructing roads and improvements; restoring degraded fish and wildlife habitat; identifying and managing significant natural, cultural, and recreational resources; protecting public resources; and monitoring use. In addition, the BLM maintains the original property title and cadastral survey records of the United States. All of these activities are conducted with extensive public participation and in coordination with other Federal agencies; State, Tribal, and local governments; and other affected interests.

The BLM is headquartered in Washington, D.C., with field offices primarily in the western United States. It also operates six National Centers specializing in training, fire management support, resource sciences, human resources management, information resources management, and business and fiscal services.

Figure 7–21 (continued) *Source:* Courtesy of The Bureau of Land Management, an agency within the U.S. Department of the Interior.

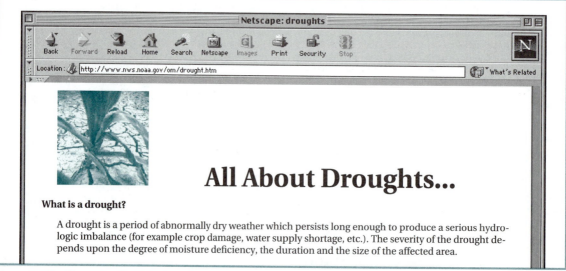

All About Droughts...

What is a drought?

A drought is a period of abnormally dry weather which persists long enough to produce a serious hydrologic imbalance (for example crop damage, water supply shortage, etc.). The severity of the drought depends upon the degree of moisture deficiency, the duration and the size of the affected area.

Figure 7–22   Example of a Well-Organized Web Page

There are four different ways that drought can be defined:

Meteorological - a measure of departure of precipitation from normal. Due to climatic differences what is considered a drought in one location may not be a drought in another location.
Agricultural - refers to a situation when the amount of moisture in the soil no longer meets the needs of a particular crop.
Hydrological - occurs when surface and subsurface water supplies are below normal.
Socioeconomic - refers to the situation that occurs when physical water shortage begins to affect people.

What are the impacts of a drought?

The impacts of a drought can be

economic,
social or
environmental

Lack of rainfall for an extended period of time can bring farmers and major metropolitan areas to their knees. It does not take very long; a few rain-free weeks spreads panic and shrivels crops. We are told to stop washing our cars, cease watering the grass and take other water conservation steps. Continued sunshine without sufficient rain can turn a rain forest into a desert; so maybe sunny weather is not always the best weather.

The Dust Bowl days of the 1930's affected 50,000,000 acres of land, rendering the farmers helpless. In the 1950's, the Great Plains suffered a severe water shortage when several years went by with rainfall well below normal. Crop yields failed, the water supply fell. California suffered a severe drought some years ago. Rainfall was below normal for 1 1/2 years, and by the time September, 1970, rolled around, the fire potential was extremely high and dangerous. Temperatures rose to near the century mark and fires began. Losses were in the tens of millions of dollars.

The worst drought in 50 years affected at least 35 states during the long hot summer of 1988. In some areas the lack of rainfall dated back to 1984. In 1988, rainfall totals over the mid-west, Northern Plains and the Rockies were 50% to 85% below normal. Crops and livestock died and some areas became a desert. Forest fires began over the Northwest and by autumn, 4,100,000 acres had been destroyed. A government policy called "Let Burn" was in effect for Yellowstone National Park. The result? Half of the Park— 2,100,000 acres were charred. On September 11th, three inches of snow fell over Yellowstone, helping to extinguish the fire. During the great drought of 1988, Governor Guy Hunt of Alabama led a statewide prayer for rain. It came the very next day, and the thunderstorms continued for weeks (taken from Newport, NC Homepage).

How do Meteorologists predict droughts?

Meteorologists determine the onset and the end of a drought by carefully monitoring meteorological and hydrological variables such as precipitation and stream flow. To do this Meteorologists make use of various indices.

Where can I find out more about droughts?

National Drought Mitigation Center
NCDC
FEMA
The Weekly Weather and Crop Bulletin is jointly prepared by the U.S. Department of Commerce, National Oceanic and Atmospheric Administration, and the U.S. Department of Agriculture.

Figure 7–22 (continued) *Source:* Courtesy of the National Oceanic and Atmospheric Administration, National Weather Service.

In many ways, writing for the Web is very much like writing for print. You need to understand your purpose and your reader, and you need to carefully research your subject, organize your thoughts, use straightforward language, and make sure your text is free of typographical or grammatical errors. However, what makes writing for the Web different from writing for other mediums—and perhaps even more challenging—is that Web users expect to get information quickly and efficiently. To keep the attention of your reader, you need to be clear, concise, and well organized.

Use a Clear Style and Tone

If you want your text to make an impact on the Web, your writing style must be simple, straightforward, and to the point. Web users are looking for information, not salesmanship. To this end, you should avoid empty promotional language or business jargon that says very little about your topic.

UNSUPPORTED CLAIM	Acme's Widget is the best product on the Internet! Buy one today!
IMPROVED, SUPPORTED CLAIM	Acme's Widget is a powerful, cost-effective tool. It has been proven 100% effective in industry tests, and was voted the #1 Widget for 20-- by Widgets Magazine.

Note that the improved version contains hyperlinks to the source of the evidence (industry tests and *Widgets Magazine*) that support the company's claims about the product. Web users are unlikely to start reading at the beginning of an online document and they rarely read it carefully all the way through. To help them, stay away from directional cues such as "as shown in the example below" or "in the graph at the top of this page." Directional phrases like these can be confusing when there is no real reference for "above" and "below," and no "top" or "bottom" of the document.

Like email, the Web often invites informality. Remember that regardless of the technology used to reach your reader, your words and tone represent your company or project. Of course, you should resist the temptation to insert unnecessary and inappropriate humor, offhand comments, or personal opinions in any document—Web or otherwise—intended for the public.

Keep Your Text Short

Generally, try to present your information in short paragraphs, and limit the amount of detail that you try to present on any one page. Web users will probably not scroll through large blocks of text on screen if they don't see the pertinent information right away.

Try to keep your text under 500 words per Web page. However, even if your document is shorter than 500 words, you should use lists, headings, graphics, and extra white space to break up the look of the page. Short, visually compact prose is likely to raise the chances of holding your reader's attention. (See also Page and Site Layout (pages 505–507) in the section on Web-Page Design in Chapter 12.)

Figure 7–23 is a good example of the use of white space, graphics, and short paragraphs to divide information into visually scannable portions.

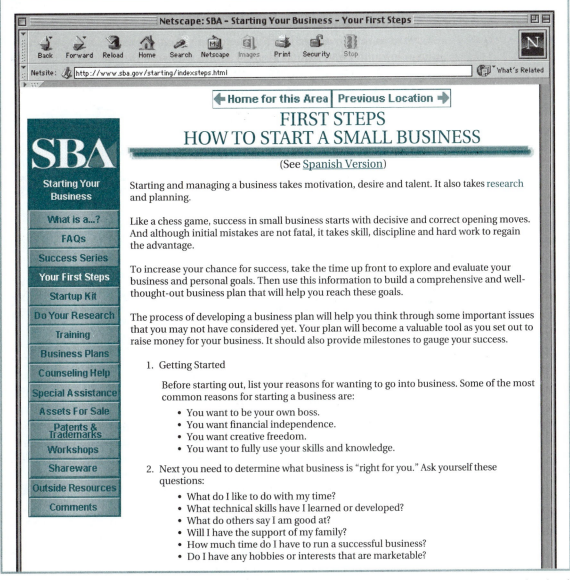

Figure 7–23   Example of a Visually Compact Web Page

(continued)

3. Then you should identify the niche your business will fill. Conduct the necessary research to answer these questions:

- What business am I interested in starting?
- What services or products will I sell?
- Is my idea practical, and will it fill a need?
- What is my competition?
- What is my business's advantage over existing firms?
- Can I deliver a better quality service?
- Can I create a demand for my business?

4. The final step before developing your plan is the pre-business checklist. You should answer these questions:

- What skills and experience do I bring to the business?
- What will be my legal structure?
- How will my company's business records be maintained?
- What insurance coverage will be needed?
- What equipment or supplies will I need?
- How will I compensate myself?
- What are my resources?
- What financing will I need?
- Where will my business be located?
- What will I name my business?

Your answers will help you create a focused, well-researched business plan that should serve as a blueprint. It should detail how the business will be operated, managed and capitalized.

One of the most important cornerstones of starting a business is the business plan. SBA offers you a tutorial on preparing a solid plan with all its essential ingredients. Be sure to review and peruse this section.

Once you have completed your business plan, review it with a friend or business associate. When you feel comfortable with the content and structure, make an appointment to review and discuss it with your banker. The business plan is a flexible document that should change as your business grows.

Figure 7–23   (continued)   *Source:* Courtesy of the U.S. Small Business Administration (SBA).

Use Hyperlinks to Expand Information

Hyperlinks—words or images that act as gateways to other Web pages—are the most popular way to navigate on the Web. A hyperlinked word usually appears in a different color from the text, so that the user's eye will be drawn to it. Keep in mind that while hyperlinks are a helpful way to offer expanded information, they can also be very distracting. If the link looks interesting, your users might even click on it before they read anything on your page!

Figure 7–24 shows a page from the White House Web site that contains dozens of links embedded into the text of the page. Not only do the numerous links make it difficult to scan the text for information (the links are underlined and appear in a second color), there are dozens of opportunities for the reader to leave the page before reaching the end of the document.

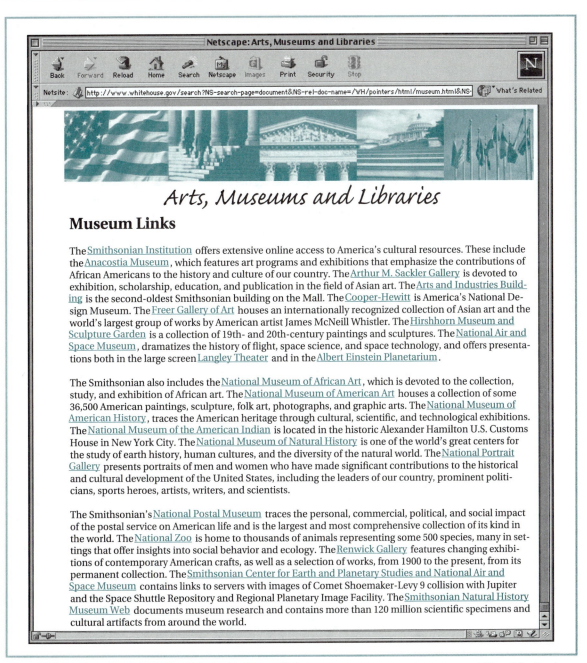

Figure 7–24 Example of Poor Use of Embedded Hyperlinks *Source:* Courtesy of the Executive Office of the President, the White House Web site.

Rather than embedding hyperlinks throughout your text, combine them into short, well-organized lists that are introduced with explanatory text. You can use these lists periodically throughout your document to break up the large blocks of text, or—even better—place a list of links at the end of your document, as you would with footnotes. In Figure 7–25, the hyperlinks at the end of the document are still available without being distracting.

Use Headings and Lists to Present Long Documents

You may find that you need lots of supporting detail and information to present your topic effectively. Give your readers a helpful outline to follow by dividing your document into small sections, each containing only one or two related paragraphs. Above each section, use subheads—in boldface—to set apart each new idea or topic, which will help the reader find each section quickly. You may also use boldface within the text to emphasize important pieces of information such as due dates, prices, or other essential details.

Subheads are also a good opportunity to grab the reader's attention, particularly if your subheads are provocative or controversial. Remember, subheads should always be informative as well as interesting.

Figure 7–26 shows a press release from the Library of Congress. Although it appeared on the Library's Web site, it was clearly formatted for a print mailing. The language is clear and concise, but the press release contains too much text in one block. This document would be much easier to read on the screen if it had a larger, more interesting headline, more white space, and boldface subheads to emphasize the location of important ideas or concepts, as in Figure 7–27.

Notice that the last paragraph of the original document (Figure 7–26) was moved into the section titled About the New Facility, where it is easier to find. Phone numbers were moved to the bottom of the page so that the reader sees the most important part of the document—the headline—first.

For documents longer than 500 words, provide a short summary and a table of contents at the beginning of the Web pages. The reader should be able to tell immediately if, and where, his or her questions will be answered within your document. It may be helpful to use hyperlinks to connect the headings in a table of contents to their locations in the document so that the reader can access a specific section quickly and easily. A good example of a hyperlinked table of contents is shown in Figure 7–28. Each topic is linked to several paragraphs of information, which appear further down the page under boldface subheadings. The reader can either scroll down to read the whole document or use the hyperlinks in the table of contents to access a piece of the information quickly and easily.

Use Keywords for Fast Retrieval

A particular challenge of writing for the Web is making sure that readers are able to find your page. To increase the odds that Web search engines will locate your

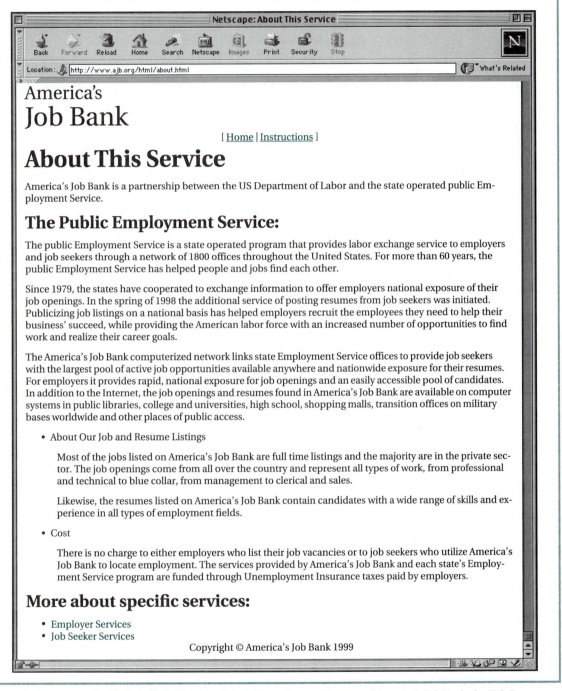

America's
Job Bank

[Home | Instructions]

About This Service

America's Job Bank is a partnership between the US Department of Labor and the state operated public Employment Service.

The Public Employment Service:

The public Employment Service is a state operated program that provides labor exchange service to employers and job seekers through a network of 1800 offices throughout the United States. For more than 60 years, the public Employment Service has helped people and jobs find each other.

Since 1979, the states have cooperated to exchange information to offer employers national exposure of their job openings. In the spring of 1998 the additional service of posting resumes from job seekers was initiated. Publicizing job listings on a national basis has helped employers recruit the employees they need to help their business' succeed, while providing the American labor force with an increased number of opportunities to find work and realize their career goals.

The America's Job Bank computerized network links state Employment Service offices to provide job seekers with the largest pool of active job opportunities available anywhere and nationwide exposure for their resumes. For employers it provides rapid, national exposure for job openings and an easily accessible pool of candidates. In addition to the Internet, the job openings and resumes found in America's Job Bank are available on computer systems in public libraries, college and universities, high school, shopping malls, transition offices on military bases worldwide and other places of public access.

- About Our Job and Resume Listings

  Most of the jobs listed on America's Job Bank are full time listings and the majority are in the private sector. The job openings come from all over the country and represent all types of work, from professional and technical to blue collar, from management to clerical and sales.

  Likewise, the resumes listed on America's Job Bank contain candidates with a wide range of skills and experience in all types of employment fields.

- Cost

  There is no charge to either employers who list their job vacancies or to job seekers who utilize America's Job Bank to locate employment. The services provided by America's Job Bank and each state's Employment Service program are funded through Unemployment Insurance taxes paid by employers.

More about specific services:

- Employer Services
- Job Seeker Services

Copyright © America's Job Bank 1999

Figure 7–25   Example of Hyperlinks Presented as a List   *Source:* Courtesy of America's Job Bank, the U.S. Department of Labor, and the public Employment Service.

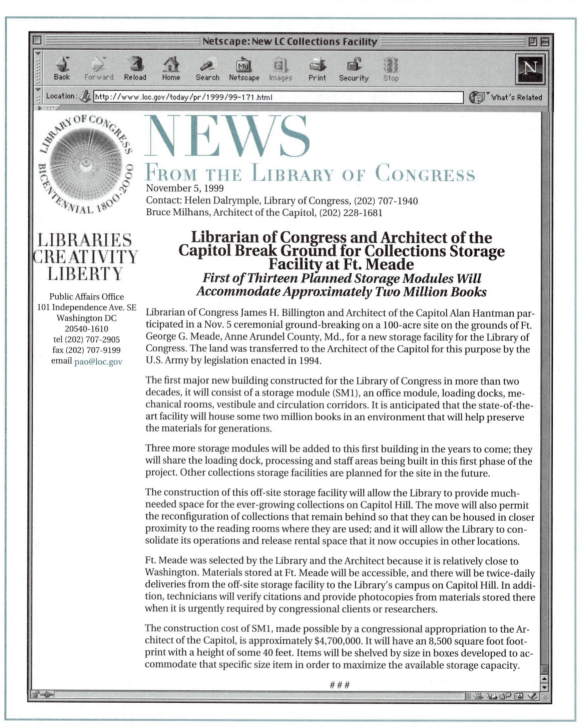

Figure 7–26   Example of a Poorly Formatted Web Document *Source:* Courtesy of the Library of Congress.

Library of Congress Collections Find New Home at Ft. Meade
Storage Modules Will Accommodate Approximately Two Million Books

November 5, 1999, Ground-breaking Ceremony
Librarian of Congress James H. Billington and Architect of the Capitol Alan Hantman participated in a Nov. 5 ceremonial ground-breaking on a 100-acre site on the grounds of Ft. George G. Meade, Anne Arundel County, Md., for a new storage facility for the Library of Congress. The land was transferred to the Architect of the Capitol for this purpose by the U.S. Army by legislation enacted in 1994.

About the New Facility
The first major new building constructed for the Library of Congress in more than two decades, the Fort Meade facility will consist of a storage module (SM1), an office module, loading docks, mechanical rooms, vestibule and circulation corridors. It is anticipated that the state-of-the-art facility will house some two million books in an environment that will help preserve the materials for generations.

Three more storage modules will be added to this first building in the years to come; they will share the loading dock, processing and staff areas being built in this first phase of the project. Other collections storage facilities are planned for the site in the future.

The construction cost of SM1, made possible by a congressional appropriation to the Architect of the Capitol, is approximately $4,700,000. It will have an 8,500 square foot footprint with a height of some 40 feet. Items will be shelved by size in boxes developed to accommodate that specific size item in order to maximize the available storage capacity.

Ft. Meade Site Addresses an Urgent Need for Space
The construction of this off-site storage facility will allow the Library to provide much needed space for the ever-growing collections on Capitol Hill. The move will also permit the reconfiguration of collections that remain behind so that they can be housed in closer proximity to the reading rooms where they are used; and it will allow the Library to consolidate its operations and release rental space that it now occupies in other locations.

Ft. Meade was selected by the Library and the Architect because it is relatively close to Washington. Materials stored at Ft. Meade will be accessible, and there will be twice-daily deliveries from the off-site storage facility to the Library's campus on Capitol Hill. In addition, technicians will verify citations and provide photocopies from materials stored there when it is urgently required by congressional clients or researchers.

For More Information

Contact: Helen Dalrymple, Library of Congress, (202) 707–1940
Bruce Milhans, Architect of the Capitol, (202) 228–1681

Date of Release: November 5, 1999.

Figure 7–27
Example of a Web Document (Figure 7–26) with Improved Format

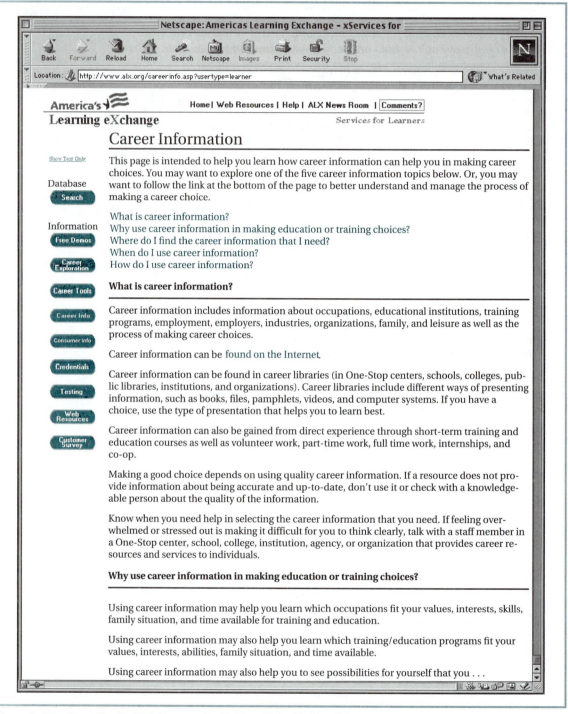

Figure 7–28   Example of a Web Document with Hyperlinked Table of Contents   *Source:* Courtesy of America's Learning Exchange (ALX), the U.S. Department of Labor, and America's Career Kit.

site, be specific in describing your important points. Using keywords and concepts throughout your text will help the search engine find your page.

WITH NO KEYWORDS	We are proud to introduce a new commemorative coin honoring our company's founder and president. The item will be available on this Web site after December 1, 20--, which is the 100th anniversary of our first sale.
IMPROVED, WITH KEYWORDS	The new Acme commemorative coin features a portrait of George G. Acme, the founder and president of Acme Corporation. The coin can be purchased on our Web site (http://www.acmewidgetscompany.com/) after December 1, 20--, in honor of the 100th anniversary of the sale of the first Acme widget.

By using words such as "Acme," "George G. Acme," and "the coin" instead of "our company's," "our founder," and "the item," you will give the search engines much more specific information that they, in turn, can give to users.

WRITER'S CHECKLIST: Writing Effectively for the Web

Write for rapid consumption.

☐ Present your information in short paragraphs.

☐ Use short, bulleted lists of hyperlinks to expand your information.

☐ Use informative subheads in boldface to introduce new or important points.

☐ Use lists, hyperlinks, and extra white space to present long documents and to break up dense passages of text.

☐ For documents of more then 500 words, provide a brief summary or table of contents that is hyperlinked to each section.

Use a clear, straightforward style and tone.

☐ Avoid promotional language or business jargon.

☐ Choose language and use a tone appropriate to the organization or product that you represent.

Use keywords so that Web search engines will find your page.
Check carefully for grammar and typographical errors.

CHAPTER 7 SUMMARY: Instructions and Other Writing Strategies

To give *instructions:*

☐ Make sure that you understand the task thoroughly (for technical instructions, learn to perform the operation yourself).

☐ Assess your reader's needs.

☐ Write directly to your reader, using the active, imperative voice.

☐ Write clearly and concisely—short sentences are best.

☐ Use plain language (avoid technical jargon).

☐ Present the information at a level appropriate to your reader's background.

☐ Organize the task into short, simple steps.

☐ Present each step in the correct sequence.

☐ Mention any necessary details, background information, and preparation; for technical instructions, list all essential equipment at the beginning.

☐ For technical instructions, include necessary warnings and cautions.

☐ Illustrate steps and procedures where needed.

☐ For technical instructions, verify that measurements, times, and relationships are precise and accurate; have someone test your instructions while you observe.

To write *process explanations:*

☐ Ensure that you understand the process thoroughly.

☐ Introduce the process with information about its purpose and significance.

☐ Divide the process into steps.

☐ Present each step in its proper sequence.

☐ Illustrate steps and procedures when this aids clarity.

☐ Present the information at a level appropriate to your reader's background.

☐ Write concisely.

To write *descriptions:*

☐ Select details carefully based on what use your reader will make of the description.

☐ Ensure that you are thoroughly familiar with what you are describing.

☐ Provide a brief explanation of the function of any physical objects you describe, such as equipment.

☐ Do not overwhelm your reader with unnecessary details.

☐ Add illustrations where they aid clarity.

To *define terms:*

☐ For formal definitions, state which grouping or class the term belongs to and show how it differs from all other members of that class.

☐ For informal definitions, substitute familiar words and phrases for the unfamiliar term.

☐ Avoid circular and "is when" and "is where" definitions.

To write *cause-and-effect explanations:*

☐ Establish a plausible relationship between an event and its cause.

☐ Evaluate evidence for the relationship carefully:

- Is it pertinent?
- Is it representative?
- Is it sufficient?
- Is it coincidental?

☐ Do not overstate conclusions.

To write *persuasively:*

☐ Take your reader's feelings into account.

☐ Avoid a hostile tone.

☐ Appeal to your reader's good sense.

☐ Acknowledge other points of view where an issue is controversial.

To write *for the Web:*

☐ Consider your audience — Web readers are geared toward rapid consumption.

- Present your information in short paragraphs.
- Use short, bulleted lists of hyperlinks to expand on information.
- Use informative subheads in boldface to introduce new or important points.
- Use hyperlinks and extra white space to present long documents and break up dense sections of text.
- For documents of more than 500 words, provide a brief summary or table of contents that is hyperlinked to each section.

☐ Use a clear, straightforward style and tone.

- Avoid promotional language or business jargon.
- Choose language and a tone appropriate to the organization or product you represent.

☐ Use keywords so that Web search engines will find your page.

☐ Check your document carefully for grammar and typographical errors.

■ Exercises

1. Write a set of instructions for one of the following topics. Assume that your reader has no knowledge of the subject. Use illustrations where they would be helpful to the reader.
   a. How to program your VCR to record a television show that will be broadcast in several hours from the time you programmed your machine
   b. How to clean an automobile battery's terminals
   c. How to build a bookshelf
   d. How to use a particular type of software to create a document
   e. How to introduce a new pet into the home
   f. How to prepare a room, apartment, or house for a tornado or other type of storm

2. Write directions for two of the following locations:
   a. From your hometown to the town or city where your university is located
   b. From your university address to your university student union
   c. From the building where your favorite course on campus is held to the campus sports arena
   d. From your hometown address to the nearest airport

3. Choose one of the following topics and explain the process involved. Assume that your reader has no knowledge of the subject. Use illustrations where they would help the reader.
   a. Operating a fax machine
   b. Measuring blood pressure
   c. Purchasing or selling ten shares of common stock online
   d. Evaluating a long-term maintenance agreement for a new vehicle
   e. Watering and feeding houseplants
   f. "Personalizing" a personal digital assistant
   g. Responding to a crisis such as a car accident
   h. Designing and creating a slide, transparency, or other visual for a presentation
   i. Finding an apartment to rent or a condominium or house to purchase
   j. Choosing a reputable lending institution

4. Write a description of one of the following items or an item of your choice. Specify who your reader will be, and write the description in sufficient detail to permit your reader either to visualize or to locate the item without further assistance. Do not illustrate this assignment.
   a. The prominent features of a close friend or relative to be used as a model in an advertising campaign for a soft drink company
   b. A small mechanical device with no more than five moving parts (pencil sharpener, can opener, etc.)
   c. A nonmechanical household or recreational device (spatula, tennis racquet, etc.)
   d. A piece of land. First give an overview, then establish its location relative to city streets or natural boundaries; complete the description with significant details of the land
   e. Your favorite childhood park or other recreational area, as you remember it
   f. Your favorite pair of shoes, coat, or other item of clothing

5. Locate two sets of instructions from products that you have recently purchased. They could be assembly instructions, how-to-use instructions, cleaning instructions, and so forth. Key the instructions on your word processor. Using the *insert comment* technique you learned in Chapter 6 (Digital Shortcuts, page 185), critique the instructions you have copied, and compare the two using the Writer's Checklist on page 221. Discuss ways that the instructions could have been improved and comment on what is well written.

6. Describe the functions of the following.
   a. The controls on the dashboard of your car
   b. The keys on the keyboard of your computer and the mouse
   c. All of the settings on the copy machine in your office
   Assume that your audience has never operated these items.

7. Write a detailed job description of either your current job or your most recent work experience. When describing your responsibilities, be specific and choose the work that best describes the action. When you have completed your job description, use it to develop a list of your own job-performance skills and abilities. Use as many action verbs as possible, such as *adapt, administer, calculate, code, define, estimate, identify, implement, monitor, persuade, program, relate, train, update,* and *write.* Could you update your résumé based on the words you generated for your list?

8. In recent years, many new words have entered our language that began as the practical vocabulary of high-tech lexicon. *Software, hardware, login,* and to *boot a computer* are examples. Make a list of other high-tech terms that are now found in the general-language dictionary. Make an additional list of high-tech slang that could possibly be included in future editions of the same dictionary. Can you invent any high-tech words that would be useful to the lexicon? List these words with your definitions. Your instructor may ask you to share your findings in class.

9. Writing descriptions intended for a diverse audience brings special challenges to the writer. Assume that your university is involved in an outreach program for international students. Assume that one of the following offices from your campus has asked you to write a description of the services, clubs, and organizations offered on campus in the categories specified. Keeping your audience in mind, describe as completely as you can the services, clubs, and organizations in a category that you select. Include details such as membership information, mission statement, activities, and so forth.
   a. Athletic office: sports offerings
   b. Recreation center: fitness offerings
   c. Office of diversity: international student support groups
   d. University Club Coordinator: special-interest activities
   e. Student Volunteer Coordinator: volunteer opportunities for students

10. Writing for people from a different culture, who may or may not speak the same language as you speak, presents a challenge to the writer. Assume your boss is expecting guests from your firm's sister company in Japan, Germany, France, or Mexico (select one). Your boss has asked you to prepare a description of your town's entertainment opportunities that will be given to them when they arrive. Choose a week six weeks in advance and list the entertainment that you think your firm's guests might enjoy. Keeping your readers in mind, describe the available

activities so that they will be able to make informed choices about what they would like to experience. Include details such as the nature of the entertainment, price, time, date, etc.

11. Write a summary (approximately 200 words) of the following information.

THE WRITING PROCESS: TECHNICAL WRITING

Writing a technical document is much like writing any document, though in some ways it is more demanding. The writing process can be divided into five major parts: (1) preparing for the writing job, (2) researching, (3) outlining, (4) writing the first draft, and (5) rewriting and polishing the draft.

Preparation. As you prepare to write, you must determine three things: (1) the objective of the writing task, (2) the audience, and (3) the extent to which the subject should be covered. Until you have made these determinations, you cannot proceed effectively.

What do you want your readers to know, or to be able to do, when they have finished reading your document? When you have answered this question, you have established your objective. To be useful, however, an objective must be specific. "Produce a document on the Model 'A' Ford" is too general to be of any help to the writer. "Explain how to operate a Model 'A' Ford" is a specific objective that will serve to keep the writer on the right track throughout the writing process. Without a specific objective, you will inevitably find yourself wandering from the subject.

A speaker explaining the theory of relativity would approach an audience of nuclear physicists quite differently from a high school class. As a writer, you must also adjust your approach to fit your audience. For instance, if your readers were novice programmers, the technical level of your document would be much simpler than if they were experienced systems analysts.

If you know your objective and the composition of your audience, you should have no difficulty determining the extent to which your subject should be covered. Determining the scope of your coverage should enable you to avoid the common mistake of including too much or too little information. It should also help you avoid being led down side paths that are not directly related to your subject—a time-consuming and wasteful mistake made frequently by beginning writers.

Research. The best and surest way to learn a complex technical subject well enough to write about it is to compile a complete set of notes during research and then to create a working outline from the notes. (In addition to gathering together the necessary information in one place, compiling notes achieves one other major objective—it gets you started on the project. Surely no one ever feels more helpless than the writer who doesn't know where to begin.) Three sources of research material are available: (1) printed material, (2) the personal interview, and (3) your own background and knowledge.

(continued)   Page 2

Your starting point in the research process is the available printed material. First read through the material rapidly to get a feel for both the material and the subject; then study the material slowly and deliberately, taking notes and jotting down questions as they arise. (The answers to many of the questions will appear later in the material; however, it is better to jot down questions now and mark them out later than not to jot them down and forget them later.) Take notes on all information that you *may* need; it is easier to delete information that is not needed than it is to go back and try to find information that is needed.

Before going to an interview with a technical expert, formulate a series of exact and to-the-point questions. (Never go to an interview without prepared questions, or with only general questions.) As the interview progresses, the answers to some questions will provoke additional questions. Ask these questions as they arise. If you do not, you will probably find yourself requesting an additional interview later.

The final source of information is your own knowledge and experience. If you are an experienced writer, you have a large reservoir of knowledge about related subjects that you draw on in researching every job. You must use discretion in drawing upon your own knowledge, however, making certain that it is directly applicable to the subject at hand.

Outlining. The creation of a good final outline is a three-step procedure: (1) organizing your random notes, (2) converting your organized notes into a rough outline, and (3) converting your rough outline into a detailed sentence outline.

After compiling a complete set of notes from the published material, from the personal interview, and from your own knowledge, evaluate your notes carefully and eliminate those that you now feel certain you will not need. If you are still in doubt about any note, include it—you can always eliminate it later if it isn't needed. You now have a body of material with which you are thoroughly familiar. You know the major subjects that you must cover, and you should be able to see how they move logically from one to another. First write down the major subjects on a notepad; they should become the major heads you use to tell your readers what they will learn in each section. Then skim through your notes again, jotting down beneath each major head any minor heads you consider necessary. Use the major heads and subheads not only to break your document into logical parts but to guide the readers through the publication as well.

Now you are ready to start creating the rough outline. By designating each major head with a Roman numeral (I, II, etc.) and each minor head, or subhead, with a capital letter (A, B, etc.), you can mark each individual note with its appropriate major head and subhead (II-C, V-A, I-D, etc.). When all the notes are so designated, type the title of your publication. Beneath the title, type the first major head; then, beneath that, type the first minor head. Then type all the notes marked "I-A." Do not attempt to put them in any order at this time (the notes are much too scattered for you to do this effectively at this stage). Then type the

(continued)

(continued) Page 3

second minor head, followed by all the notes marked "I-B," and so on until you have included all the notes under their appropriate major and minor heads. When you have completed this first pass, go over the outline again, concentrating exclusively on achieving the best sequence of your notes. For a long document, this may require several passes.

The major tasks involved in converting the rough outline into a final outline are to write a lead sentence to follow each major head, to provide transition between topics wherever necessary, and to determine where illustrations should be used.

Writing the first draft. Your primary objectives in converting your final outline to a first draft are (1) to bring the readers into your writing, (2) to convert notes to sentences and paragraphs, and (3) to simplify and clarify your subject. Do not underrate the professional writing skills required for technical writing. This type of writing makes greater demands on the basic writing skills than any other. To explain a complex technical subject simply and directly, so that the reader can grasp it quickly and easily, puts the basic writing skills of the best writers to the test.

Rewriting. If the writing process has been properly executed up to this point, rewriting should not be necessary—only polishing should be required. The process of polishing the draft is a matter of continuing, through successive passes, to smooth out awkward sentences, eliminate needless words and phrases, and ensure transition.

■ In-Class Activities

1. Divide into groups of four to six members each. For approximately 20 minutes, brainstorm as a group a list of short, common, yet specific action verbs that would be useful in writing directions for using everyday household or office items. Appoint a recorder to jot down your words. Samples include words like turn, screw, hammer, rinse, etc. Remember to include terms for electronic items. When you have finished, your recorder will read your list to the rest of the class. As a class, discuss why directions written for the consumer use short, common action verbs.

2. Your instructor (or a student volunteer) will bring three common measuring devices to class. The articles will be placed in a large brown paper bag. Using one hand, each of you will be allowed one minute to reach into the bag and examine the articles. However, you will not be allowed to see the articles. If the class is large, additional sets of measuring devices should be brought to class so that more than one student can examine the articles at the same time. During the next 30 minutes, describe the three articles in a written narrative, including as many specific features of each article as you can. If possible, include the name for the devices you've described.

3. In this exercise, you will have fun while discovering the importance of using correct, descriptive terminology. Use the first ten minutes of the class to draw a floor plan of a small, typical ranch-style house—with one story, two bathrooms, and three bedrooms. You may draw the rooms in any arrangement you wish, labeling each. Dimensions are not required. When you have finished with your drawings, pass your paper to the person to your left. During the next fifteen minutes, write a description of the floor plan that is in front of you. Describe the arrangement of the rooms. When you have finished, pass your written description to the person two students to your left and return the original floor plan to its author. Next, draw a floor plan based on the narrative description in front of you. When you have finished, compare your floor plan to the first floor plan drawn by the person two students to your right. They should match. Discuss why the floor plans do or do not match.

4. Assembly instructions are often confusing. Bring to class at least one example of confusing assembly (or other how-to) instructions. Divide into groups of five or fewer members. During the next ten minutes, as a group, read all of the samples and choose one sample to revise. In no more than twenty minutes revise the instructions, using Chapter 7 as your reference. When you are finished, your group may share the revisions with the rest of the class.

5. Select a place on campus. The place may not be a part of the campus where the building you are now in is located; however, it must be a place that is listed in the school's directory as a campus location. Write out the directions to the location you have selected, using your classroom as a starting point. You may use the names of streets and campus landmarks, but you may not use names of buildings. When you are finished, pass your paper to the person to your right and ask him or her to identify the place indicated in your directions. If your directions are successful, you may be asked to read them to the rest of the class. As a class, discuss what makes directions work—including the necessary components such as the use of common terms.

■ Research Projects

1. Research and write a paper, of assigned length, on one of the following topics by *comparing* the two items cited. Before you begin to write, specify who your reader will be. Make your comparison detailed enough to suit the needs of your reader.
   a. Two career choices
   b. Two job offers
   c. Two products or services with which you are familiar
   d. Two persons who are being considered for promotion to the same position
   e. A comparison of your choice, organized by either the whole-by-whole method or the part-by-part method (for example, a comparison of two products or appliances designed to do the same job)

2. Choose one of the following topics to research and write about. First, decide whether you will develop the topic through *division* (separation of a complex whole into several smaller units) or *classification* (grouping of a number of small units into larger, related categories). Then, using the approach you have selected,

write a paper, of assigned length, on the topic. Before you begin your research, be sure that you have determined who your reader will be and what your scope will be.

a. Road signs in your area
b. Home-heating methods
c. Hand-held personal digital assistant
d. Community service organizations in your city or town
e. Digital cameras
f. Recreational or athletic programs in your community
g. A college library or media center
h. Safety regulations where you work
i. Laptop computers
j. Fire extinguishers
k. The set-up of an office, hospital, or other organization with which you are familiar
l. The computer set-up for an organization or business

3. Write an *extended definition* of a key concept or term related to your area of study or occupational interest. Gather any information necessary and create an extended definition of the concept using some or all of the techniques discussed in the chapter. Assume that your reader is unfamiliar with the term.

4. Choose one of the following statements to research and write about. First, decide whether you will develop the topic through *cause and effect* or *persuasion.* Then, using the approach you have selected, write a paper of assigned length on the topic. Before you begin to research and draft your paper, be sure that you have determined who your reader will be and what your scope will be.

a. A dangerous practice or condition in your office or school is likely to cause an accident.
b. You ought to be promoted to a job with greater responsibility.
c. Businesses should be encouraged to locate in your community.
d. Setting up job-training programs in connection with a college will lead to higher employment in your community.
e. Some aspects of your present job (such as working conditions, equipment, availability of help, organization of your work area) should be changed.
f. Some aspect of your school (such as the grading system, the library facilities, media resources, work programs) should be changed.
g. Smoking should (or should not) be permitted in public places.
h. Computer facilities on campus should be updated or upgraded.
i. Your school should provide each student with a laptop computer.

5. You work for a day-care center that employs 20 full-time people. The center has a high turnover rate, even though the pay scale is comparable to that offered at other centers in the area. A high turnover rate is expensive. The center spends about $2,000 to advertise for, screen, and train each new employee. The center's profit margin is low, so that pay increases are not possible at present; however, you believe that one way to stem the turnover rate is to increase employee benefits. You propose allowing workers time off to take care of a newborn or to look after sick children or other family members without having to use their annual two weeks of paid vacation time. Workers currently receive one week of paid sick leave each year that can be accumulated in unlimited amounts if it's not used.

Write an eight- to ten-page (or whatever length is specified by your instructor) memo to Margaret Lomax, president of the Jefferson Child Care Center, requesting that a family leave policy be put in place. The policy would allow employees to use their sick leave for family purposes. Those workers in need of more time could take it without pay and be assured that their jobs would be held for them until they returned. As you write the memo, consider the potential benefits to the center (better morale, more careful use of sick leave by employees, emphasis on family-friendly workplace, etc.). Also consider the potential liabilities (possible abuse by some employees, possibility that the center will be understaffed at times, some increased record keeping, etc.).

■ Web Projects

1. Assume you are interested in becoming a sales representative for a product related to your area of study or occupational interest, or one of the following products: word-processing software, computers and related equipment, prestressed concrete, herbicides, recycled tires, nutrition supplements and vitamins, managed health-care insurance programs, health-care administration software, or payroll software. Using the Internet, look for information that describes the product, how to use it, advantages, disadvantages, costs, and so forth. Consider the descriptive writing styles you encounter as you complete the assignment. Analyze your findings in a brief descriptive summary.

2. Explore the Internet to find Web sites that offer tips and techniques related to business and technical writing strategies. Sample sites include the Business and Professional Writing page at the Purdue Online Writing Lab at http://owl .english.purdue.edu/Files/business-writing.html; the Business and Technical Communication page hosted by the English Department at Ohio State University at http://www.cohums.ohio-state.edu/english/areas/bizcom.htm; the Literacy Education Online page at St. Cloud State University, Minnesota (see Business Writing) at http://leo.stcloudstate.edu/catalogue.html#business; Resources for Business Writing at Inkspot.com at http://www.inkspot.com/ss/genres/biz.html; Resources for Tech/Scientific Writers at Inkspot at http://www.inkspot.com/ss/ genres/tech.html; the Business Writing page hosted by About.com at http:// techwriting.about.com/jobs/techwriting/msub13.htm; and the Technical Writing page at About.com at http://techwriting.about.com/jobs/techwriting/mbody .htm. At the sites that you target, find three pages that you think would be useful for business and technical writers and write a paragraph summarizing each site. (Be certain to include the URL of each site.) Your instructor will collect the summaries and assemble them in a notebook so the entire class may use them for reference during the remainder of the course.

3. Find at least three Web sites that describe a similar piece of office equipment, power tool, or wireless communication product. Prepare an outline listing the information you have found regarding the use of the product. Are the how-to instructions found online clear, concise, and easy to understand? Why or why not? In a brief narrative analyze, compare, and contrast the information at the site you explored. Note from your outline which sites included too much detail, not enough detail, etc.

4. Find at least three Web sites related to your chosen field of study that use persuasion to convince the viewer of their ideas. Notice the Web sites' content, organization, and use of visuals. Are the sites credible? Why or why not? In a brief narrative, analyze what makes the sites effective.

5. Explore the following two Web sites to discover how they use illustrations to help convey their message to the consumer: SafetyStore, an online catalog of safety and preparedness products, at http://www.safetystore.com/, and The United States Coast Guard, Office of Boating Safety, at http://www.uscgboating.org. Make a list of the variety of illustrations used and their individual purposes. Analyze the style of text that accompanies the illustrations. What are the goals of these sites? Do these sites accomplish their goals? Why or why not? Support your conclusions with examples.

8 Principles of Business Correspondence

Business correspondence, the communication between people within or among organizations through letters, memos, email, and other means, is essential to the success of individuals, businesses, and their customers or clients. Because of their importance, such communications should be well written; those that are not waste considerable time and money. For example, the poorly written letter shown in Figure 8–1 (page 267) was actually sent to a law firm. The staff at the law firm could not understand it, even though a number of attorneys, paralegal assistants, and secretaries were familiar with the case. Staff members exchanged emails and phone calls with Ralph Madison and others at his company without success, and finally the law firm had to send someone to the company to identify the specific services the company wanted its legal counsel to perform.

This letter wasted the time of a highly paid staff—and caused a delay in legal services to Ralph Madison's company. Further, carelessly written letters or emails, because they project such a poor image of the writer, can result in other kinds of losses. A reader's negative reaction to an unclear or unprofessional message, for example, can cost a firm its reputation and future business—and can even cost an employee his or her job.

■ Selecting the Appropriate Medium

Important as they are, letters and email are not the only means of communication available to businesspeople. The law firm, for example, eventually had to meet with Ralph Madison to accurately interpret his request to "review and advise." You can choose from a wide array of possibilities, from relatively recent technologies such as email, fax, voice mail, and videoconferencing to more traditional means of communication such as letters and memos, telephone calls, and face-to-face meetings. With so many means of communication available, how do organizations and individuals decide which is preferable in a given situation?

Basic considerations in selecting the appropriate medium are the audience and the objective of the communication. For example, when you need to contact someone immediately, a written message (even one by email) can take too long. A telephone call is then the more efficient choice. When you need precise wording and you and your reader need a permanent record of the information exchanged, a written message (letter, memo, or email) will be the best option.

Voices from the Workplace

Kate Bishop, *Smithsonian Magazine*

As a publishing assistant at *Smithsonian Magazine,* Kate Bishop manages all content and production for the *Smithsonian Magazine* Web site, which includes putting the magazine's text and images online every month as well as overseeing all special contests and promotions, photographers' portfolios, and more. Kate also sends out two email newsletters each month—to roughly 48,000 subscribers—that generate a lot of email in response. Whether emailing her coworkers or reading and responding to hundreds of Web users (her customers) every day, email is her primary mode of communication. Kate offers the following tips for using email:

"Although the ease of email invites informality, be careful. Sarcasm and humor are often misunderstood when they are used in emails, because there are no voice or facial cues to imply a humorous intent. As a rule of thumb, if you think the recipient could possibly misinterpret the tone of a statement, find another way to say it. In a business environment, it is also crucial that you maintain standard rules of capitalization, sentence structure, spelling, and punctuation. Stick to proper grammatical and editorial style. And always carefully reread your message at least twice before you hit 'send.' Check for the following common mistakes: typographical/spelling errors, incorrect or unnecessary recipient(s), remarks that could be misinterpreted based on tone, inappropriate or offhand comments."

Check out the latest issue of *Smithsonian Magazine* online at http://www.smithsonianmag.si.edu.

Entry-Level
Joanna Honig, Hill and Knowlton

As a public relations consultant at Hill and Knowlton, Joanna Honig does a lot of writing that often deals with highly sensitive situations. For a number of projects, she has been asked to create a memo or letter to company employees about a merger that could result in layoffs. She would then be asked to write a press release about the same situation, geared toward the media who will in turn report the information to the public.

Although the medium that she uses to communicate with the press is limited to the press release, Joanna carefully considers the medium that she uses to communicate with employees: "If a company uses email frequently, such changes . . . can be made to seem smaller in an email." For this reason, many companies prefer that the news be communicated in a formal letter: "Job losses and major restructurings affecting the recipient directly should always be addressed through a formal letter, even if it will eventually be sent as an attachment."

Joanna talks about the different purposes and audiences that she addresses in these documents. For example, when writing to the press about a possible merger, she understands that "the most important factor is to ensure that the language, style, and content are being communicated in the best interest of my client . . . poor communication to the press can be disastrous." However, when writing to employees about the merger, her strategy is to "try to think of how the news will affect the employees personally. Will they have a new boss? Will they have to let anyone go? What will their severance package include?" She is also careful not to omit important information: "If there is any information that cannot be given at the time, say so. . . . Anything that you do not include is open for speculation, which can derail any, if not all, of your key messages."

Find out more about Hill and Knowlton at http://www.hillandknowlton.com.

Figure 8–1
Sample of
a Poorly
Written
Letter

New Haven Credit and Collection Services, Inc.

3 Ashburton Place
New Haven, CT 06501
(860) 212-5577
http://www.nhcc.com

February 15, 20--

Mr. Stewart R. Cassidy
Fiorello and Cooke, Attorneys at Law
1212 Broadway
Hartford, CT 06119

Dear Mr. Cassidy:

In regard to claim on Account #5-861 see enclosed copy of letter received and
copy of delivery receipt regarding same. There had been a claim which was
disallowed and debtor withheld payment on the bill, and the one we referred
to your office for collection, as no pro was mentioned but the one the claim
was on was referred to the bill is still open and they still owe Universal, please
review and advise.

Sincerely,

Ralph Madison

Ralph Madison
Account Manager

When you wish to establish a close rapport with someone in the interest of a long-term working relationship, a face-to-face meeting is indispensable.

You also need to consider what is typical or expected in your organization. For example, in one organization, email is used almost exclusively because individuals are widely separated and are often meeting with clients. At another organization, email is seldom used because the staff works in very close proximity and meets often or exchanges paper copies of documents for review. Still other organizations may follow practices based on management philosophy, historical practice, or the customs of a certain profession. Be aware as well of the national business and cultural practices as you communicate internationally. (See pages 308–315 for a discussion of international correspondence.)

Following is a description of the primary methods of communicating and some of their salient characteristics. All are currently in use because each communicates certain kinds of information better than the others, even though the advantages overlap in some cases.

Letters on Organizational Stationery

Letters are most appropriate for first contacts with new business associates or customers as well as for other official business communications. Stationery with an organization's printed letterhead and the writer's handwritten signature communicates formality, respect, and authority.

- A letter represents a commitment on the part of the writer. A written promise, conveyed above the signature of an employee who has the authority to act on behalf of an organization, ensures that the information is accurate and that the sender will honor it. For example, a formal letter is often used to summarize the terms and conditions of a proposed business relationship.
- A carefully planned letter can create a favorable impression — and sometimes stimulate business — even when customers or clients are dissatisfied with a product or service.

If you use express or overnight deliveries for letters and other documents, phone or send an email or fax message ahead to alert the recipient that the material has been sent. In some cases, if you believe the reader will find it appropriate, you may be able to fax a letter (see page 269).

Memos: Printed and Electronic

Printed and electronic memos are one of the most frequently used forms of communication among members of the same organization, even when offices are geographically separated. These in-house communications have many of the same characteristics of letters, but memos are convenient for a wider variety of functions—from announcements of organizational policy to short reports.

Memo formats in most organizations are standardized. These formats eliminate the need for a letterhead, an inside address, a salutation, goodwill paragraphs, and formal closing elements. As discussed later in this chapter, memo writers must follow their organization's protocol and traditional forms. This includes whether to use a "MEMO" header; what order to use for "To:", "From:", "cc:", "Date:", and "Subject:"; and where to place your initials or signature, if required.

Email Messages

Email (electronic mail) is used to send information, maintain professional relationships, elicit discussions, collect opinions, and transmit many other kinds of messages. Email quickly reaches those inside organizations as well as customers and others outside the organization who have access to a conferencing system or the Internet. Email is important when speed counts. Email can be a less formal means of communication than either letters or memos; however, as discussed later in this chapter, it is rapidly becoming *the* medium through which text as well as data and graphic files are transmitted, even replacing printed letters and memos in organizations.

Email provides the advantage that the same information can be sent simultaneously to many recipients. For groups that may often exchange email, creation of a discussion group (or listserv) is a convenience. (See page 731 for an explanation of listserv communications.) Because email recipients can print copies of messages they receive or easily forward them to others, business messages should always be written with care and reviewed for accuracy before being sent. Note that email is a less private form of communication than the other types described here. For guidance about writing email messages and ensuring their confidentiality, see pages 300–308.

Faxes

A fax (facsimile transmission) is most useful when speed is essential and when the information—a drawing or contract, for example—must be viewed in its original form. Faxes are also useful when the recipient does not have access to email or the programs to view email attachments or when the material has not yet been converted into electronic form. Note that faxed correspondence may seem less official than a traditional letter, in part because the recipient does not receive the original stationery. However, faxes are growing in acceptance even in legal correspondence (some courts now allow filing of official documents by fax). Of course, if an original is also important, the paper copy can be sent separately by overnight or regular mail. Faxed letters should be sent with a fax cover sheet (available as a word-processing template) or a commercially prepared fax stick-on label.

Telephone Calls and Conferences

The range of information exchanged by telephone calls is virtually unlimited— everything from a call of less than a minute to confirm a meeting time to a call lasting an hour or more to negotiate or clarify the terms and conditions of a contract. One of the advantages of phone calls is that they enable participants to interpret tone of voice, so they are often helpful in resolving misunderstandings or clarifying information. Of course, a phone call does not provide the visual and other physical cues possible during face-to-face meetings.

Conference calls take place among three or more participants. They are a less expensive alternative to a face-to-face meeting that would require the participants to travel to a central meeting place. They also provide a setting for the immediate resolution of issues. Conference calls are more efficient if the person setting up the call works from an agenda shared by all the participants. That person must be prepared to direct the discussion as though he or she were leading a meeting. Of course, the call must be planned to ensure that everyone is available at the same time. Timing is especially important when participants are located in different time zones—especially for international calls. The participants should also take notes on any key points or decisions made during the call. (For further information on such conferences, see the discussion of meetings in Chapter 15, pages 662–675.)

Voice-Mail Messages

Because many organizations use voice-mail systems that allow callers to record messages when the person called is not available, you should plan a short message before you call. When leaving a voice-mail message, enunciate clearly and leave your name, phone number, and the date and time of the call. Leave a succinct message ("Call me about the deadline for the new project" or "I got the package from RTL, so you don't need to call the distributor"). Speak as if you were actually talking to the person rather than simply recording a message. If the message is complicated or contains numerous details, use another medium, such as an email message or a letter, to ensure that the information is communicated accurately. If you want to discuss a subject, let the recipient know the subject so he or she can prepare a response when returning your call.

Face-to-Face Meetings

Face-to-face meetings are most appropriate for initial or early contacts with business associates and customers with whom you intend to develop an important long-term relationship. Meetings are also the best medium for exchanges in which you need to solve a serious problem. The most productive meetings occur when all participants come prepared to contribute to a collective effort toward a well-defined objective. (See Taking Minutes of Meetings in Chapter 14 for how to record the meeting discussions and decisions and see Chapter 15 for a more detailed discussion of how to conduct effective meetings.)

Videoconferencing

Two-way or three-way videoconferencing is becoming an increasingly common medium for business communication. Videoconferences are particularly useful for meetings where travel is impractical or too expensive. Unlike telephone conference calls, videoconferences have the advantage of allowing participants to see as well as to hear one another. Videoconferences work best with participants who are at ease in front of a camera.

WRITER'S CHECKLIST: Selecting the Medium

Consider your audience, purpose, and what is typical or expected in your organization as you select the medium for communicating.

- ☐ Generally, use written forms and messages for precise wording; use voice, visual, and in-person communication when you need, for example, to resolve a misunderstanding.

- ☐ Use letters on organizational stationery for first contacts; printed letterhead on quality paper communicates formality, respect, and authority.

- ☐ Use memos (printed and electronic) for in-house business communications—from policy announcements to short reports.

- ☐ Use email to send messages and electronic documents, maintain professional relationships, elicit discussions, and collect opinions from distant as well as wide audiences.

- ☐ Use faxes when the exact image of nondigital documents must be viewed and when speed matters.

- ☐ Use telephone calls and conferences when give and take or tone of voice is important; conference calls, when carefully planned, are often a less expensive alternative to a face-to-face meeting for participants in distant locations.

- ☐ Use voice mail for short, uncomplicated messages.

- ☐ Use face-to-face meetings for early contacts with business associates and customers or solving problems.

- ☐ Use videoconferencing as a substitute for face-to-face meetings when travel is impractical; participants need to be at ease in front of a camera.

This chapter focuses on three of the most common forms of written correspondence: business letters, memos, and email messages. It also covers the increasingly important subject of international correspondence.

■ Writing Business Correspondence

Much of the advice given in this section applies to business letters, memos, and email. The process of writing business correspondence involves many of the steps that go into most other on-the-job writing, as described in Chapter 1, as well as some special considerations.

1. Establish your purpose, your reader's needs, and your scope.

2. Prepare an outline. For a short letter, memo, or email, the outline may involve little more than jotting down the points you wish to make and the order in which you wish to make them (see Chapter 2).

3. Write a rough draft from the outline.

4. Allow for a cooling period (see Chapter 4). The cooling period is especially important when a letter or email, for example, has been written in response to a problem. Business correspondence is not the place to vent emotions. A cooling period, even if it is only a lunch hour, gives the writer a chance to remove any hasty and inappropriate statements made in the heat of the situation. One chief executive of a large company always allows the rough draft of a crucial letter or message to cool overnight before revising and mailing it — regardless of the pressure to send it out right away. This executive believes that a slightly delayed — but appropriate — response is preferable to an immediate reply that may cause misunderstanding later.

5. Revise the rough draft. Go over your work carefully and critically, checking for sense as well as for grammar, spelling, and punctuation.

6. Check the design, especially the arrangement and spacing of letter parts. It is a good idea to print out a preliminary copy of the letter. Set the margins you will use and, as you type, insert the correct spacing between parts of the letter (see pages 285–286).

7. Assume final responsibility. Even if a secretary or an assistant does your word processing, be sure to check his or her work; when you sign a letter or a memo, you are responsible for its appearance and accuracy.

Tone: Goodwill and the "You" Viewpoint

As a writer of business correspondence addressing your reader directly, you have an opportunity that a report writer doesn't have: You are addressing the reader directly, and therefore you are in a very good position to take your reader's needs into account and build goodwill for yourself and for your company. If you ask yourself, "How might I feel if I were the recipient of such a letter?" you can gain some insight into the needs and feelings of your reader — and then tailor your message to fit those needs and feelings. Remember that you have a chance to build goodwill for your business or organization. Many companies spend millions of dollars to create a favorable public image. A letter to a client that sounds impersonal and unfriendly can quickly tarnish that image; a thoughtful letter that communicates sincerity can greatly enhance it.

Suppose, for example, you are a store manager who receives a request for a refund from a customer who forgot to enclose the receipt with the request. In a letter to the customer, you might write:

■ The sales receipt must be enclosed with the merchandise before we can process the refund.

However, if you consider how you might keep the goodwill of the customer, you might word that request this way:

■ Please enclose the sales receipt with the merchandise, so that we can send your refund promptly.

Notice that this version uses the word *please* and the active voice ("Please enclose the sales receipt"), while the first version uses only the passive voice ("The sales receipt must be enclosed"). In general, the active voice creates a friendlier, more courteous tone than the passive, which tends to sound impersonal and unfriendly. (For a discussion of the active and passive voices, see Chapter 5.) Polite wording, such as the use of *please,* also helps to create goodwill.

However, in business correspondence, you can go one step further. You can put the reader's needs and interests first by writing from the reader's point of view. Often, but not always, doing so means using the words *you* and *your* rather than the words *we, our, I,* and *mine.* That is why the technique has been referred to as using the "you" viewpoint or "you" attitude. For example, consider the point of view of the original sentence in the example just given:

■ The sales receipt must be enclosed with the merchandise before *we can process* the refund.

The italicized words suggest that the writer is focusing on his or her need to process the refund. Even the second version, although its tone is more polite and friendly, emphasizes the writer's need to get the receipt "so that we can send your refund promptly." (The writer, of course, may want to get rid of the problem quickly.)

What is the reader's interest? The reader is not interested in helping the business process its accounts. He or she simply wants the refund—and by emphasizing that need, the writer encourages the reader to act quickly. Consider the following revision, which is written from the "you" viewpoint:

■ So you can receive your refund promptly, please enclose the sales receipt with the merchandise.

This sentence stresses that it is to the reader's benefit to act on this matter. Consider another example:

■ So that we can complete our file records, please send your Form 1040-A by March 10.

Even though the recipient has little incentive to send the form, the "you" viewpoint can suggest that the recipient's interests are at stake:

■ So that your file is complete, please send your Form 1040-A by March 10.

Be aware, however, that both goodwill and the "you" viewpoint can be overdone. Used thoughtlessly, both techniques can produce a fawning, insincere tone—what might be called *plastic goodwill.* Avoid language full of false praise and sickeningly sweet phrases. Any attempt at goodwill that is insincere will be recognized by your reader and thus will be counterproductive. Consider the opening of the letter on page 275 from a writer who has corresponded only once with the recipient:

WRITER'S CHECKLIST: Using Tone to Build Goodwill

The following guidelines will help you achieve a tone that builds goodwill with recipients of your correspondence.

☐ *Be respectful,* not demanding.

DEMANDING	Submit your answer in one week.
RESPECTFUL	I would appreciate your answer within one week.

☐ *Be modest,* not arrogant.

ARROGANT	My report is thorough, and I'm sure that you won't be able to continue without it.
MODEST	This report contains a detailed description of the refinancing options, and I hope you find it useful.

☐ *Be polite,* not sarcastic.

SARCASTIC	I just received the shipment we ordered six months ago. I'm sending it back—we can't use it now. Thanks!
POLITE	I am returning the shipment we ordered on March 12, 20--. Unfortunately, it arrived too late for us to be able to use it.

☐ *Be positive and tactful,* not negative and condescending.

NEGATIVE	Your complaint about our prices is way off target. Our prices are definitely not any higher than those of our competitors.
TACTFUL	Thank you for your suggestion concerning our prices. We have found, however, that our prices are competitive with, and are in some cases below, those of our competitors.

EXCESSIVE GOODWILL You are just the kind of customer that deserves the finest service that anyone can offer—and you deserve our best deal. Knowing how careful you are at making decisions, I know you'll think about the advantages of using our consulting service.

In this example, the writer barely knows the customer, yet makes an assumption about what "kind of customer" the recipient may be. Further, the writer characterizes the customer as careful "at making decisions." The sentence sounds phony. A far better approach is to make goodwill reasonable for the circumstances and provide specifics that are appropriate to your knowledge of the reader.

APPROPRIATE GOODWILL From our earlier correspondence, I can understand your need for reliable service—we strive to give all our priority customers our full attention. After you have reviewed our proposal, I am confident you will appreciate our five-point emergency consulting service.

To organize correspondence that will achieve goodwill, it is best to present the main point or good news early—at the outset, if at all possible. The pattern for neutral or good news should be as follows:

1. Main point or good news
2. Explanation of details or facts
3. Goodwill

By presenting the main point or good news first, you increase the likelihood that the reader will pay careful attention to details, and you achieve goodwill from the start. Figure 8–2 shows an example of a good-news letter.

Negative Messages and the Indirect Pattern

Unfortunately, communicating bad news is sometimes necessary in the workplace. When you must do so, presenting bad news or refusals indirectly is often more effective than presenting them directly. Research has shown that people form their impressions and attitudes very early when reading letters. Here is an example. A college student who had applied for a scholarship received a letter explaining that he had not won it. The letter began: "I'm sorry, but you were not a recipient of this year's Smith Scholarship." In disappointment, the student threw the letter on his desk and left his apartment. Three days later, he picked up the letter and read further. It went on to say that the committee thought his record was so strong that he should call immediately if he were interested in another, but lesser-known, scholarship. The student called but was told that the other scholarship had been awarded to someone else. Because the student had not called immediately, he lost an important opportunity.

Southtown Dental Center
3221 Ryan Road   San Diego, CA 92217
Phone: (714) 321-1579   Fax: (714) 321-1222
sdc@exec3.com

November 11, 20--

Ms. Barbara L. Mauer
157 Beach Drive
San Diego, CA 92113

Dear Ms. Mauer:

Good news

Please accept our offer of the position of records administrator at Southtown Dental Center.

Explanation

If the terms we discussed in the interview are acceptable to you, please come in at 9:30 a.m. on November 15. At that time, we will ask you to complete our personnel form, in addition to . . .

Goodwill

I, as well as the others in the office, look forward to working with you. Everyone was favorably impressed with you during your interview.

Sincerely,

Mary Hernandez

Mary Hernandez
Office Manager

Figure 8–2   A Good-News Letter

Although the relative directness of correspondence may vary, it is generally more effective to present bad news indirectly, especially if the stakes are high for a reader.[1] This principle is based on two related facts: (1) as suggested earlier, readers form their impressions and attitudes very early in correspondence and (2) you as a writer may wish to subordinate the bad news to reasons that make the bad news understandable. Further, in international correspondence, far more cultures in the world are generally indirect in their business communication than they are direct.

Consider the thoughtlessness in the direct rejection shown in Figure 8–3. Although the letter is concise and uses the pronouns *you* and *your,* the writer has apparently not considered how the recipient will feel as she reads the letter. The letter is, in short, rude. The pattern of this letter is (1) bad news, (2) explanation, (3) close. A better general pattern for bad-news correspondence is the following:

1. Context
2. Explanation
3. Bad news
4. Goodwill

The context opening introduces the subject and establishes a professional tone. Then the body should provide an explanation by reviewing the details or facts that lead, for example, to a negative decision or refusal. Give the negative message simply, based on the facts, but do not belabor the bad news or apology. Neither the details nor an overdone apology can turn bad news into something positive. Your goal should be to establish for the reader that the writer or organization has been *reasonable* given the circumstances. To accomplish this goal, you need to organize the explanation carefully and logically, as discussed in Chapter 2.

The closing should establish or reestablish a positive relationship through goodwill or helpful information. Consider, for example, the revised rejection letter shown in Figure 8–4. This letter carries the same disappointing news as the first one, but the writer begins by not only introducing the subject but also thanking the reader for her time and effort. Then the writer explains why Ms. Mauer was not accepted for the job and offers her encouragement in finding a position in another office. Bad news is never pleasant; however, information that either puts the bad news in perspective or makes the bad news seem reasonable maintains respect between the writer and the reader. The goodwill closing is intended to reestablish an amicable business relationship. (See Sensitive and Negative Messages on pages 337–358 in Chapter 9 and Persuading Your Reader on pages 237–240 in Chapter 7 for more examples.)

---

[1]Gerald J. Alred, "'We Regret to Inform You': Toward a New Theory of Negative Messages." In *Studies in Technical Communication,* ed. Brenda R. Sims (Denton, TX: University of North Texas and NCTE, 1993), pp. 17–36.

Southtown Dental Center
3221 Ryan Road   San Diego, CA 92217
Phone: (714) 321-1579   Fax: (714) 321-1222
sdc@exec3.com

November 11, 20--

Ms. Barbara L. Mauer
157 Beach Drive
San Diego, CA 92113

Dear Ms. Mauer:

Your application for the position of records administrator at Southtown Dental Center has been rejected. We have found someone more qualified than you.

Sincerely,

Mary Hernandez

Mary Hernandez
Office Manager

Figure 8–3   A Poor Bad-News Letter

Southtown Dental Center
3221 Ryan Road   San Diego, CA 92217
Phone: (714) 321-1579   Fax: (714) 321-1222
sdc@exec3.com

November 11, 20--

Ms. Barbara L. Mauer
157 Beach Drive
San Diego, CA 92113

Dear Ms. Mauer:

Thank you for your time and effort in applying for the position of records ad- *Context*
ministrator at Southtown Dental Center.

Because we need someone who can assume the duties here with a minimum *Explanation*
of training, we have selected an applicant with over ten years of experience. *leading to*
bad news

I am sure that with your excellent college record you will find a position in *Goodwill*
another office.

Sincerely,

Mary Hernandez

Mary Hernandez
Office Manager

Figure 8–4   A Courteous Bad-News Letter

Openings and Closings

Most other correspondence should follow the patterns for openings and closings discussed in Chapter 3, pages 74–81. That is, they must identify the subject and catch the interest of your reader.

■ Our annual inventory revealed some interesting surprises that should help your order department.

Certainly, if the recipient is involved with ordering for an organization, this opening would both identify the subject and catch his or her attention.

Because business correspondence is often a more personal form of communication, an opening must also establish a tone that is appropriate and achieves your purpose.

■ I'm seeking advice about organizational communication, and several people have suggested that you are an authority on the subject.

The tone of respect in this opening is not only appropriate but also effective, because it appeals to the reader's pride. Other openings might appeal to the reader's curiosity or personal interests, as in the following:

■ I have a problem you may be willing to help solve.

■ Mr. Walter Jenkens has given us your name as a reference for his company's services. I hope you'll be willing to help us by answering some specific questions about his company.

Closings for correspondence, in addition to following the principles illustrated in Chapter 3, can also provide incentive for the reader to act, as in the following:

■ Please sign the forms today, mark the changes you want made, and return the material to me in the preaddressed envelope. If you can approve everything for me within two days, I should have the amended contract in your hands by the end of the week.

For more examples of openings and closings in specific circumstances, review the examples in Chapter 9.

Writing Style in Business Correspondence

Business correspondence may legitimately vary from informal, in an email to a close business associate, to formal (or restrained), in a letter to someone you do not know. (Even if you are writing to a close associate, you should always follow the rules of standard grammar, spelling, and punctuation.)

INFORMAL	It worked! The new process is better than we had dreamed.
RESTRAINED	You will be pleased to know that the new process is more effective than we had expected.

You probably will use the restrained style more frequently than the informal one. Remember that an overdone attempt to sound casual or friendly, like overdone goodwill, can sound insincere. However, do not adopt so formal a style that your letters or memos read like legal contracts; that type of writing appears wordy, pompous, and affected—and may well irritate your reader.

Consider the letter shown in Figure 8–5. The excessively formal writing style is full of largely out-of-date business jargon; expressions such as *query* (for request or question), *I wish to state, be advised that,* and *herewith* are old-fashioned and pretentious. Good business letters today have a more personal, down-to-earth style, as the revision of the letter in Figure 8–6 illustrates.

The improved version is not only less stuffy but also more concise. Being concise in writing is important, but don't be so concise that you become blunt. Responding to a written request that is vague with "Your request was unclear" or "I don't understand," could easily offend your reader. What you need to do is ask for more information and establish goodwill to encourage your reader to provide the information.

■ I will need more information before I can answer your request. Specifically, can you give me the title and the date of the report you are looking for?

Although this version is a bit longer, it promotes goodwill and will elicit a faster, more helpful response.

Accuracy in Business Correspondence

A letter, memo, or email (as described later) is a written record, so it must be accurate. Facts, figures, and dates that are incorrect or misleading can cost time, money, and goodwill. Remember that when you sign a letter or initial a memo, you are responsible for it. Therefore, allow yourself time to review any correspondence carefully before sending it. Whenever possible, ask someone who is familiar with the situation to review an important letter or other message. Listen with an open mind to any criticisms of what you have said. Make whatever changes you believe are necessary. Review Accuracy and Completeness on page 93 in Chapter 4.

Also review the mechanics of writing—punctuation, grammar, and spelling. In business as elsewhere, accuracy and attention to detail are equated with carefulness and reliability. The kindest conclusion a reader can come to about a letter containing mechanical errors is that the writer was careless. Do not give your reader cause to form such a conclusion.

Amex Laboratories

Fax: (205) 743-6221
Email: amex@aol.com

327 Wilson Avenue
Birmingham, AL 35211
(205) 743-6218

September 7, 20--

Mr. Roland E. Lacharité
3051 Chemin de Chambly
St. Hubert, PQ
J3Y 3M1 CANADA

Dear Mr. Lacharité:

In response to your query, I wish to state that we no longer have an original
copy of the brochure requested. Be advised that a photographic reproduction
is enclosed herewith.

Address further correspondence to this office for assistance as required.

Sincerely yours,

E. T. Hillman

E. T. Hillman

ETH/knt
Enclosure

Visit our Web site at http://www.amexlabs.com.

Figure 8–5   Overly Formal Letter-Writing Style

Amex Laboratories

Fax: (205) 743-6221
Email: amex@aol.com

327 Wilson Avenue
Birmingham, AL 35211
(205) 743-6218

September 7, 20--

Mr. Roland E. Lacharité
3051 Chemin de Chambly
St. Hubert, PQ
J3Y 3M1 CANADA

Dear Mr. Lacharité:

Thank you for your interest in our water-testing systems. We are currently out of original copies of our brochure. However, I am sending you a photocopy of it.

If I can be of further help, please let me know.

Sincerely yours,

E. T. Hillman

E. T. Hillman

ETH/knt
Enclosure

Visit our Web site at http://www.amexlabs.com.

Figure 8–6   Up-to-Date, Concise Letter-Writing Style

Appearance and Parts of Business Letters

As described earlier in this chapter, letters are often used to communicate formality, respect, and authority. So, just as the clothes you wear to job interviews play a part in the first impression you make on potential employers, the appearance of a business letter may be crucial in influencing a recipient who has never seen you. A neat appearance alone will not improve a poorly written letter, but a sloppy appearance will detract from a well-written one.

The rules for preparing a neat, attractive letter are not difficult to master, and they are important—particularly if you type your own letters. Use good-quality, white paper of standard size and use envelopes of the same quality. Center the letter on the page so that the top margin is about equal to the bottom margin. Doing so may mean you need to adjust the letter template or reset the margin settings in your word-processing program. The margins, or white space surrounding the text, serve as a frame, a function referred to as the picture-frame effect. When you use company letterhead, consider the bottom of the letterhead as the top edge of the frame. For precise spacing, see Figures 8–7 and 8–8.

Almost all business letters have at least five major parts: the heading, inside address, salutation, body, and complimentary close. According to variations in the alignment of the parts on the page, letters may be in one of several formats. If your employer recommends or requires a particular format and style, use it. Otherwise, follow the guidelines provided here and refer to Figures 8–7 and 8–8. You may also create macro commands in your word-processing program that will allow you to save and recall with a single keystroke often-repeated elements for many of the following sections.

Heading

The heading is the writer's full address—street or post-office box, city and state, postal code—or printed letterhead and the date. The writer's name is not included in the heading (unless it is part of a printed letterhead) because it appears at the end of the letter. In giving your address, do not use abbreviations for words such as Street, Avenue, First, or West (as part of a street or city name). You may either spell out the name of the state in full or use the standard Postal Service abbreviations. The date usually goes directly beneath the last line of the address. Do not abbreviate the name of the month.

HEADING   1638 Parkhill Drive East
               Great Falls, MT 59407
               April 8, 20--

If you are using company letterhead that gives the address, enter only the date three lines below the last line of printed copy or two inches from the top of the page.

520 Niagara Street
Braintree, MA 02184

Phone: (781) 787-1175
Fax: (781) 787-1213
Email: 92000.121@CompuServe.com

Letterhead

May 15, 20--

Date

Mr. George W. Nagel
Director of Operations
Boston Transit Authority
57 West City Avenue
Boston, MA 02210

Inside
address

Dear Mr. Nagel:

Salutation

Enclosed is our final report evaluating the safety measures for the Boston Intercity Transit System.

We believe that the report covers the issues you raised and that it is self-explanatory. However, if you have any further questions, we would be happy to meet with you at your convenience.

Body

We would also like to express our appreciation to Mr. L. K. Sullivan of your committee for his generous help during our trips to Boston.

Sincerely,

Complimentary
close

Carolyn Brown

Signature

Carolyn Brown, Ph.D.
Director of Research

Typed name

Title

CB/ls
bt515.doc
Enclosure: Final Safety Report
cc: ITS Safety Committee Members

Additional
information

Figure 8–7   Full-Block Style Letter (with Letterhead)

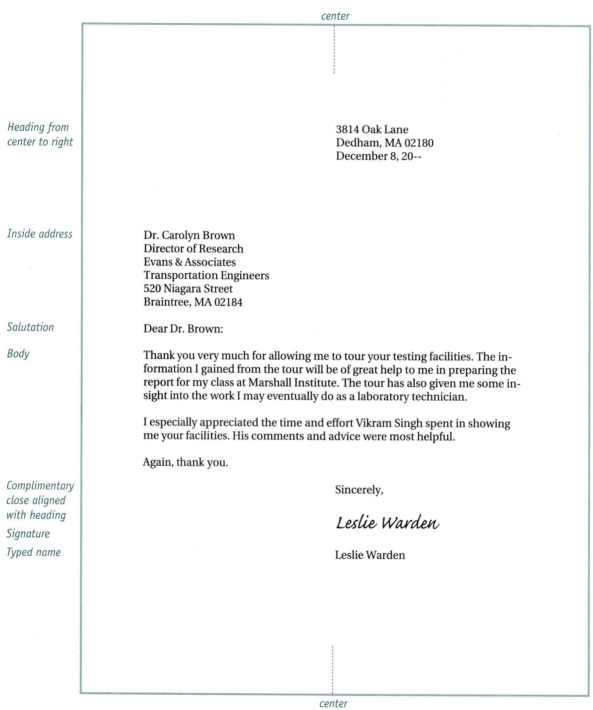

center

Heading from center to right

3814 Oak Lane
Dedham, MA 02180
December 8, 20--

Inside address

Dr. Carolyn Brown
Director of Research
Evans & Associates
Transportation Engineers
520 Niagara Street
Braintree, MA 02184

Salutation

Dear Dr. Brown:

Body

Thank you very much for allowing me to tour your testing facilities. The information I gained from the tour will be of great help to me in preparing the report for my class at Marshall Institute. The tour has also given me some insight into the work I may eventually do as a laboratory technician.

I especially appreciated the time and effort Vikram Singh spent in showing me your facilities. His comments and advice were most helpful.

Again, thank you.

Sincerely,

Leslie Warden

Complimentary close aligned with heading
Signature
Typed name

Leslie Warden

center

Figure 8–8   Modified-Block Style Letter (without Letterhead)

Inside Address

The inside address is the recipient's full name, title, and address.

INSIDE   Ms. Gail Smith
ADDRESS   Production Manager
                  Docuform Printing Company
                  14 President Street
                  Sarasota, FL 33546

Place the inside address two to six lines below the date, depending on the length of the letter. The inside address should be flush with (or aligned with) the left margin, which should be at least one-inch wide.

Salutation

Place the salutation (or greeting) two lines below the inside address, also flush with the left margin. In most business letters, the salutation contains the recipient's title (Mr., Ms., Dr., etc.) and last name, followed by a colon. If you are on a first-name basis with the recipient, you would include his or her title and full name in the inside address but use only the first name in the salutation.

- Dear Ms. Smith:

- Dear Mr. Smith:

- Dear Dr. Smith:

- Dear Captain Smith:

- Dear Professor Smith:

  [Note that titles such as Captain and Professor are not abbreviated.]

- Dear Gail:

  [if you are on a first-name basis]

For women who do not have a professional title, use Ms. (for either a married or an unmarried woman). If the woman has expressed a preference for Miss or Mrs., honor her preference. When you do not know whether the recipient is a man or a woman, you may use a title appropriate to the context of the letter. The following are examples of titles you may find suitable:

- Dear Customer:

  [letter from a retail store]

- Dear Homeowner:

  [letter from an insurance agent soliciting business]

- Dear Parts Manager:

  [letter to an auto-parts dealer]

When a person's name could be either feminine or masculine, one solution is to use both first and last names in the salutation.

■   Dear Pat Smith:

In the past, writers to large companies or organizations customarily addressed their letters to "Gentlemen." Today, however, this is inappropriate. Writers who do not know the name or the title of the recipient often address the letter to an appropriate department in the attention line or identify the subject in a subject line in place of a salutation (Figures 8–9 and 8–10).

Body

The body of the letter should begin two lines below the salutation (or below the inside address if no salutation appears). Single-space within paragraphs and double-space between paragraphs with the first line of each new paragraph at the left margin or indented five spaces from the left margin. The right margin should be approximately as wide as the left margin. (In very short letters you may increase both margins to about an inch and a half.)

Complimentary Close

Start the complimentary close or conventional "goodbye" a double-space below the body. Use a standard expression such as *Sincerely yours, Yours truly,* or *Respectfully yours.* (If the recipient is a friend as well as a business associate, you can use a friendly, less formal close: *Best wishes, Cordially, Sincerely, Best regards.*) Only the first word of the complimentary close is capitalized, and the expression is followed by a comma. Four lines below the complimentary close, and aligned

**Figure 8–9
Sample Attention
Line Used in Place
of Salutation**

National Business Systems
501 West National Avenue
Minneapolis, MN 55107-5011

Attention: Customer Relations Department

I am returning three pagers that failed to operate. . . .

**Figure 8–10
Sample Subject
Line Used in Place
of Salutation**

National Business Systems
501 West National Avenue
Minneapolis, MN 55107-5011

Subject: Defective Parts for SL-100 Pagers

I am returning three pagers that failed to operate. . . .

at the left with the close, type your full name. On the next line, place your business title if it is appropriate to do so. Then sign your name in the space between the complimentary close and your typed name. If you are writing to someone with whom you are on a first-name basis, it is acceptable to sign only your given name; otherwise, sign your full name.

■ Sincerely yours,

Gail Silver

Gail Silver
Production Manager

Second Page

If a letter requires a second page, carry at least two lines of the body over to page two. Do not use a continuation page to type only the complimentary close of the letter. The second page also should have a heading containing the recipient's name, the page number, and the date. (Never use letterhead for a second page.) The heading starts one inch from the top edge of the page and may go in the upper-left-hand corner or across the page, as shown in Figure 8–11.

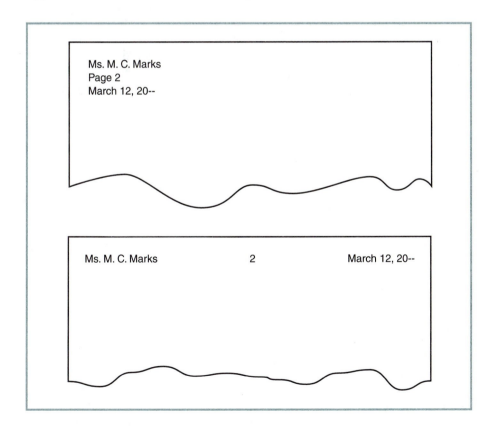

Ms. M. C. Marks
Page 2
March 12, 20--

Ms. M. C. Marks   2   March 12, 20--

**Figure 8–11
Sample Headers for
the Second Page
of a Letter**

Additional Information

Business letters sometimes require additional information—the initials of the typist (if other than the writer), an enclosure notation, or a notation that a copy of the letter is being sent to one or more named people. Place any such information flush left with the margin, a double-space below the last line of the complimentary close in a long letter, two double-spaces below in a short letter.

Initials are not used when the writer is also the person typing the letter, as is common. If an assistant has typed the letter, however, that person's initials should appear two lines below the last line of the complimentary-close block either by themselves or following the author's initials.

- pst or weo/pst or PST or WEO/PST

Filenames are helpful if you do a high volume of correspondence. If so, place the file name of the document in lowercase letters just below the typist's initials.

- silver.d15

Enclosure notations, which indicate that the letter writer is sending material along with the letter (an invoice, an article, and so on), may take several forms. Choose the form that seems most helpful to your reader. Be aware that no matter which form of enclosure notation you select, you should still make a reference in the body of the letter to the fact that material is enclosed. Enclosures are described briefly if the letter is long and formal, or if the nature of the enclosed items is not obvious. Enclosures are not described if the letter is short and the nature of the enclosures is obvious to the reader.

- Enclosure

  [a single item]

- Enclosures (2)

- Enclosures: Preliminary report invoice
  Draft contract

Copy notations (cc:) tell the reader that a copy of the letter is being sent to one or more named individuals.

- cc: Ms. Marlene Brier
  Mr. David Williams

  [Brier and Williams receive only the letter.]

- cc/enc: Mr. Tom Lee

  [Lee receives both the letter and the enclosure.]

A blind-copy notation is used when the sender does not want the addressee to know that a copy is being sent to one or more other recipients. That means the

**Figure 8–12
Sample Closing with
Initials, Filenames,
Enclosure
Notations, and
Copy Notations**

Sincerely yours,

Jane T. Rogers

Jane T. Rogers
Manager

pst
jrogers.n14
Enclosure: Preliminary proposal
cc: Ms. Marlene Brier
bcc: Dr. Brenda Shelton [appears only on letter to blind-copy
     recipient]

blind-copy notation must not appear on the original letter, only on the letter to the blind-copy recipient.

■   bcc: Dr. Brenda Shelton

A business letter may, of course, contain all the items of additional information described in this section (Figure 8–12).

Sample Letter Styles

The two most common styles of business letters are the full block and the modified block. The full-block style, which is easier to type in because every line begins at the left margin, is suitable only with letterhead stationery (see Figure 8–7). In the modified-block style, the heading (return address and date) and complimentary close are aligned just to the right of the center of the page (see Figure 8–8). The remaining elements are aligned at the left margin. All other letter styles are variations of these two basic styles. Again, if your employer recommends or requires a particular style, follow it carefully. Otherwise, choose the style you are most comfortable with and follow it consistently.[2]

Preparing the Envelope

The most widely used form for addressing envelopes is the block form. The U.S. Postal Service has established postal addressing standards, which ensure that automated equipment with optical character readers (OCRs) can process mail

---

[2]For more detailed guidance on business-letter format, see William A. Sabin, *The Green Reference Manual,* 9th ed. (New York: Glencoe, 2000).

Leslie Warden
3814 Oak Lane
Dedham, MA 02180

DR CAROLYN BROWN
EVANS & ASSOCIATES
TRANSPORTATION ENGINEERS
520 NIAGARA ST
BRAINTREE, MA 02184

Figure 8–13   A #10 Envelope, Addressed

quickly and accurately. Figure 8–13 shows a typical envelope using these standards. Publications that illustrate postal-addressing standards are available through your local U.S. Post Office.

Because they omit punctuation, abbreviate place names, and use all capital letters, such postal-address forms are usually not appropriate for inside addresses when you need a less mechanical, more personalized look.

■ Writing Memos: Printed and Electronic

Much of the general advice on business correspondence given earlier in this chapter applies to memos. However, the memo—printed or electronic—is routinely used for a wide range of internal communications—from short notes to one-page reports and internal proposals. Among many other uses, memos

Announce policies	Request information
Confirm conversations	Transmit documents
Exchange information	Instruct employees
Delegate responsibilities	Report results

As this partial list illustrates, memos provide a record of the decisions made and many actions taken in an organization. For this reason, clear and effective memos are essential to the success of any organization. A carelessly prepared memo sends a garbled message that could baffle readers, cause a loss of time, produce costly errors, or even offend.

Memo Protocol and Strategy

The decision to send memos on paper, attached to an email message, or delivered as an email depends on the organizational practice and the purpose of the communication, as discussed earlier in Selecting the Appropriate Medium (pages 265 and 268). Some organizations may prefer the printed memo for announcements and other official messages while reserving email for informal communications. Others may use email almost exclusively not only because of its speed but also because it fosters the easy exchange of information. Even when email substitutes for printed memos, some recipients print copies of important emails to highlight sections or to save a hard copy for their records.

Although such practices vary, it is important to be alert to the protocol of sending memos in your organization. For example, remember to observe the practice in an organization that acknowledges rank by dictating who receives a memo and in what order—senior managers, for example, take precedence over junior managers. Failure to observe rank in the "To" line is a strategic mistake that can undermine the effectiveness of any memo, no matter how well written. Observing rank reflects well on the writer because it demonstrates his or her understanding of the organizational structure of the department or company.

Memos play a strategic role in the management of organizations; that is, managers can use memos to (1) keep employees informed about company goals, (2) motivate employees to achieve these goals, and (3) build employee morale. Managers who write clear and accurate memos gain respect and credibility. Consider the unintended secondary messages the following notice conveys:

POOR   It has been decided that the office will be open the day after Thanksgiving.

The first part of the sentence ("It has been decided") not only sounds impersonal but also communicates an authoritarian, a management-versus-employee tone: Somebody "decides" you work. The passive voice also suggests that the decision-maker does not want to say "I have decided" and thus be identified (in any case, the office staff would undoubtedly know). One solution, of course, is to remove the first part of the sentence.

BETTER   The office will be open the day after Thanksgiving.

Even this statement sounds impersonal. The best solution would be to suggest both that the decision is good for the company and that employees should be privy to (if not a part of) the decision-making process.

BEST   Because we must meet the December 15 deadline to be eligible for the
          government contract, the office will be open the day after Thanksgiving.

By subordinating the bad news (the need to work on that day), the writer focuses on the reasoning behind the decision to work. Employees may not necessarily like the message, but they at least understand that the decision is not arbitrary because it is tied to an important deadline. As this example illustrates, much of the strategy for business letters discussed earlier in this chapter, such as in Negative Messages and the Indirect Pattern, applies to memos as well.

Memo Style and Tone

To produce a memo that is both effective and efficiently written, outline your memo, even if you simply jot down points to be covered and then order them logically. (To review this process, see Chapter 2.) With careful preparation, your memos will be both concise and adequately developed. Adequate development of your thoughts is crucial to the memo's clarity, as the following example indicates.

INCOMPLETE   Be more careful on the loading dock.

DEVELOPED   To prevent accidents on the loading dock, follow these procedures:
1. Check to make sure . . .
2. Load only items that are rated . . .
3. Replace any defective parts . . .

Although the original version is concise, it is not as clear and specific as the revision. Don't assume your reader will know what you mean. Readers may be pressed for time and misinterpret your memo if it is vague. State what you mean explicitly.

Each memo should address only one subject, as the memo in Figure 8–4 illustrates. If you need to cover two subjects, write two memos. Multisubject memos are not only difficult to file (thus easily lost) but also confusing to a hurried reader.

Whether your memo is formal or informal depends entirely on your reader and your objective. Is your reader a coworker, superior, or subordinate? A memo to a coworker who is also a friend is likely to be informal, while an internal proposal to several readers or to someone two or three levels higher in your organization is likely to be more formal. Consider the following versions of a statement:

TO AN EQUAL   I can't go along with the plan because I think it poses serious logistical problems. First, . . .

[informal, casual, and forceful response written to an equal]

TO A SUPERIOR   The logistics of moving the department may pose serious problems. First, . . .

[formal, impersonal, and cautious response to a superior]

A memo giving instructions to a subordinate should also be relatively formal and impersonal, but more direct—unless you are trying to reassure or praise. Using an overly chatty, casual style in memos to your subordinates may confuse them about the relationship and make you seem either insincere or ineffectual. However, if you become too formal, sprinkling your writing with fancy words, you may seem stuffy and pompous. You may also be regarded as rigid and incapable of moving the organization ahead. When writing to subordinates, remember that *managing* does not mean *dictating.* An imperious tone—like false informality—will not make a memo an effective management tool. When you write a memo to a subordinate, adopt a positive yet reasonable tone, as in the following example.

■ Because we must meet the December 15 deadline to be eligible for the government contract, the office will be open the day after Thanksgiving. I am also temporarily re-assigning several members of the office staff as shown below.

Memo Openings

Memo openings are crucial because readers in the workplace are busy. So, although methods of development vary, a memo should begin with a statement of the main idea. Even if your opening gives the background of a problem, the main point should appear early in the first paragraph.

MAIN IDEA	Because of our inability to serve our present and future clients efficiently, I recommend we hire an additional attorney.
BACKGROUND	Last year we did not hire new staff because of the freeze on hiring. As a result, we need to make two additional hires this year.
MAIN IDEA AND BACKGROUND	ACM Electronics has asked us to prepare a comprehensive brochure for its Milwaukee office by August 9, 20--. We have worked with electronics firms in the past, so this job should be relatively easy to prepare.

When the reader is not familiar with the subject or with the background of a problem, provide an introductory background paragraph before stating the main point of the memo. Doing so is especially important in memos that serve as records for crucial information months (or even years) later. Generally, longer memos or those dealing with complex subjects benefit most from more thorough introductions. However, even when writing a short memo about a familiar subject, remind readers of the context. Readers have so much crossing their desks that they need a quick orientation. In the following examples, words that provide context are shown in italics.

■ *As we discussed after yesterday's meeting,* we need to set new guidelines for . . .

■ *As Maria recommended,* I reviewed the office reorganization plan. I like most of the features; however, the location of the receptionist and administrative assistant . . .

However, do not state the main point first when (1) the reader is likely to be highly skeptical or (2) you are disagreeing with a person in a position of higher authority. In such cases, a more persuasive tactic is to state the problem first, then present the specific points supporting your final recommendation. For more information on openings and closings, see pages 74–81 in Chapter 3.

Memo Lists and Headings

Using lists is an effective strategy to give your points impact in a memo. Lists can be read and their meaning grasped more quickly than a paragraph that says the same thing. Be careful, however, not to overuse lists. A memo that consists almost entirely of lists is difficult for the reader to understand because he or she must mentally connect the separate and disjointed terms on the page. Further, lists lose their impact when they are overused. A particularly useful type of list is one for messages sent to numerous readers whose responses you need to tabulate.

■   I can meet at 1 p.m. ____
                      2 p.m. ____
                      3 p.m. ____

Another attention-getting device, particularly in long memos, is headings. Headings have a number of advantages:

1. They divide material into manageable segments.
2. They call attention to main topics.
3. They signal a shift in topic.

Especially for memos to several readers, headings allow each reader to scan them and read only the section or sections appropriate to his or her needs. Notice the use of both a list and headings in Figure 8–14.

Memo Formats and Parts

Memo formats vary from organization to organization. Some companies provide computerized formats and, less frequently, printed sheets or memo stationery. Although there is no single, standard form, Figure 8–14 shows a typical 8½" × 11" format with a company name.

Regardless of the parts of the memo included, the element requiring perhaps the most careful preparation is the subject-line title (such as "Schedule for ACM Electronics Brochure" in Figure 8–14). Subject-line titles in both memos and email messages function much like the titles of reports: They announce the topic. They are also an important aid to filing and later retrieval. Therefore, they must be accurate. The memo should deal only with the single subject announced in the subject line, and the title should be complete. However, the title in the subject line should not substitute for an opening that provides a context for the message.

VAGUE	Subject: Tuition Reimbursement
VAGUE	Subject: Time-Management Seminar
SPECIFIC	Subject: Tuition Reimbursement for Time-Management Seminar

PROFESSIONAL PUBLISHING SERVICES MEMO

TO: Barbara Smith, Publications Manager
FROM: Hannah Kaufman, Vice President   *HK*
DATE: April 14, 20--
SUBJECT: Schedule for ACM Electronics Brochure

ACM Electronics has asked us to prepare a comprehensive brochure for its Milwaukee office by August 9, 20--. We have worked with electronics firms in the past, so this job should be relatively easy to prepare. My guess is that the job will take nearly two months. Ted Harris has requested time and cost estimates for the project. Fred Moore in production will prepare the cost estimates, and I would like you to prepare a tentative schedule for the project.

Additional Personnel

In preparing the schedule, check the availability of the following:

1. Production schedule for all staff writers
2. Available freelance writers
3. Dependable graphics designers

Ordinarily, we would not need to depend on outside personnel; however, because our bid for the *Wall Street Journal* special project is still under consideration, we could be short of staff in June and July. Further, we have to consider vacations that have already been approved.

Time Estimates

Please give me the time estimates by April 19. A successful job done on time will give us a good chance to obtain the contract to do ACM Electronics' annual report for its stockholders' meeting this fall.

I know your staff can do the job.

cc: Ted Harris, President
      Fred Moore, Production Editor

Figure 8–14 Typical Memo Format

Capitalize the first letter of all major words in a title. Do not capitalize articles, prepositions, or conjunctions of fewer than four letters unless they are the first or last words of the title.

If you are sending a printed memo, the final step is signing or initialing a memo, a practice that lets readers know that you have approved its contents. Where you sign or initial the memo depends on the practice of your organization: Some writers sign their name at the end of a memo, others sign their initials next to their typed name. Follow the practice of your employer. Figure 8–14 shows a typical placement of initials.

■ MEETING THE DEADLINE: The Time-Sensitive Memo

Deadlines are a part of every job. More than once in your career you will be asked to do a seemingly impossible task—write an important one-page memo that requires some information gathering in less than an hour.

Assignments such as these are generally given to you by your supervisor, often at the last minute, to meet a time-sensitive deadline. These memos are often written for someone else's signature who is higher up in the organization. When you get such an assignment, do not panic. Instead, use the following straightforward principles drawn from this book to focus all your mental energies on the task at hand.

Understand the Assignment

Make sure that you understand the assignment. Nothing could be worse than to waste time under a short deadline by misunderstanding the purpose or intended reader of the memo. Ask the person giving you the assignment to be as explicit as possible about

- The topic
- The reader and the reader's background
- The purpose and intended outcome
- The key points that must be covered
- The person in the organization who will sign the memo

Gather Information

Gather the information that will help you write the memo. This essential background information can almost always be located within your company or organization. Sources include previous letters and memos, press releases, contracts, budget data, handbooks, speeches by senior officials, legal opinions, and the like. Be careful to gather *only* the information pertinent to the memo. The person asking for the memo will usually provide essential background information or tell you where to find it. If the information is not forthcoming, be sure to ask for it.

As long as the information originated in your organization, fits your context, and is accurate and well written, use as much of it as you need. If necessary, revise such material for consistency of content, style, and format as you draft the memo. For information from other sources, make sure you avoid plagiarism and any violation of copyright (see page 452). However, all works created by U.S. government agencies are in the public domain—that is, they are not copyrighted—and can be used without prior approval.

On the job, you will have another source of information that you may not always have in the classroom—your experience. In fact, one reason you may receive such an assignment is your knowledge of the subject, reader, organization, or professional area. Practicing the techniques of brainstorming, discussed on pages 8–9, will prepare you to draw the most benefit from your experience when you are under pressure.

Organize Your Thoughts

Do not overlook this important step. Your memo should have an opening, a middle, and a closing. Organizing the information into this structure does not have to be a formal process—you won't have time to create a full-blown outline, nor will one be necessary. Jot down the points you need to make in a sequence that makes sense. Keep it simple. In some cases, you will organize by classifying and dividing your subject matter, presenting the information on one subject before going on to another subject. Sometimes a problem-and-solution order makes sense. At other times, a chronological, sequential, or general-to-specific order will be appropriate.

Write the Draft

With the right information and a structure for organizing it, the writing will not be difficult. Stick to your plan—your rough outline—and begin. Make the structure easy for you and your reader to follow. Cover only one subject in each paragraph. After a topic sentence, provide essential supporting information—facts, examples, policy, procedures, guidelines.

Write a quick draft first; you can polish it later. Put your ideas down as quickly as you can. Write without worrying about grammar, sentence structure, or spelling. Given the limited time available, your main focus should be on getting your ideas down.

Polish the Draft

Turn to your written draft as a critic would to someone else's work. You will not have much time left, but discipline yourself to read the draft several times, concentrating on different elements each time.

First, concentrate on larger issues. Is the information accurate? Is it complete? Have you made all your points? Are they organized in the right sequence? Have you provided too much information? Revise accordingly.

Next, focus on polishing at the sentence and word level. Aim for simple sentences in the active voice. Don't use only short sentences, however. Longer sentences break the monotony of too many simple sentences strung together. Structure longer sentences so that subjects and verbs agree and primary ideas are distinct from subordinate ideas. Use parallel structure to convey matching ideas. Use lists where possible to ensure that each item is given equal weight and is expressed in the same grammatical form. Don't forget to review punctuation. A misplaced comma or semicolon can change the meaning of a sentence. Remember, in this situation you do not have time for a cooling period, so watch for any emotionally charged language.

As a final review, use your spell checker, but don't rely solely on the spell checker to catch all of your spelling errors. Make sure you read through a paper version of the memo at least once to catch any remaining errors. If you have time, ask a second reader to help you.

Take a Well-Deserved Break

After your draft is written, you may email it to a superior for review before you prepare the final form for signature and distribution.

Now sit back and enjoy the sense of professional pride you have earned from a job well done under pressure!

■ Sending Email: Protocol and Strategies

Email has changed business communication, enabling people in both small and large organizations to write and respond to messages more frequently and more rapidly. Correspondence, reports, meeting notices, questionnaires, and digital files of all kinds are routinely sent to colleagues throughout an organization and to others worldwide through email. As described in Selecting the Appropriate Medium (page 265), email is particularly useful for facilitating discussions and collecting opinions. Email enables a collaborative writing team, for example, to exchange multiple drafts of a document to produce the final document. (See Chapter 6, "Collaborative Writing.") When used for exchanging ideas rapidly, email is often conversational in tone and can become something between a telephone conversation and a memo. Even in these informal exchanges, you need to think carefully about your reader and the accuracy and appropriate level of detail of the information you send.

The writing advice given earlier in this chapter also applies to email messages, especially when they replace memos inside an organization or when they replace business letters for communications to those outside an organization. Be aware, however, that recipients outside an organization may consider email to be less appropriate than business letters on printed organizational stationery. Moreover, some customers, clients, and others may have limited access to email or may check their email infrequently.

Review and Confidentiality Implications

Email is a quick and easy way to communicate, but avoid the temptation to dash off a first draft and send it as is. Be careful to follow the rules of netiquette, discussed in the section that follows. As with other workplace correspondence, maintain a high level of professionalism when you send an email: The message should be grammatically and factually correct, with no ambiguities or unintended implications. It should include all crucial details. When you send an informal message to a colleague, you can correct misunderstandings relatively easily—but at the expense of wasted time. Take even more care when sending messages to superiors in your organization or to people outside the organization. Time spent reviewing your email can save a great deal of time and embarrassment sorting out misunderstandings resulting from sending a careless message.

Confidentiality is another issue to keep in mind when you are sending email. All messages sent by email, no matter how personal, sensitive, or proprietary, can be intercepted by someone other than the intended recipient. Remember, email messages are never truly deleted, even when you think you've removed them from your computer. Not only can the information be printed, circulated, and forwarded, but most companies back up and save all company email on computer tape. Employers can legally monitor email communications. Some companies make this policy known, but others do not. Companies can also be legally

Dilbert

compelled to provide email messages to a third party, like a court of law. Consider the content of all your messages given these possibilities. The potential for the unintended release of inappropriate information makes the need for a careful review of your text before you click "Send" all the more important.

Observing Netiquette

Because you need to maintain a high level of professionalism in email for business communication, it is important to observe some rules of etiquette, or netiquette (*Internet + etiquette*). Keep in mind the following conventions of netiquette:

- Check your incoming email regularly and respond as quickly as you can; in fact, some organizations have expectations of employees regarding the frequency for checking and responding to email.

- If you receive an assignment or question by email that will take a longer-than-expected time to complete, send an interim response saying so.

- Keep workplace email professional—do not send off-color jokes, use biased language, or discuss office gossip.

- Do not send *flames,* emails that contain abusive, obscene, or derogatory language, to attack someone. If you're tempted to dash off an angry message, wait until you're in a better frame of mind so your message focuses on the issues rather than on a personal attack.

- Do not send *spams,* mass distributed emails that often promote personal projects and interests or circulate jokes and humorous stories. Remember, *all* your recipients do not share your interests—or sense of humor.

- Be scrupulous about typing email addresses and otherwise ensuring that the intended recipient gets the message. It is easy to transpose letters and numbers when you type an address and have the message returned or sent to the wrong person, thereby wasting time and jeopardizing confidentiality. The workplace is filled with stories of unflattering or critical messages inadvertently sent to or intercepted by the person being criticized because the sender used the wrong address or clicked "Reply" rather than "Forward."

- Do not write in all-uppercase letters. Such text is difficult to read and is the electronic equivalent of shouting. Use uppercase and lowercase letters as you would for any other written document.

- Do not use emoticons for business and professional email messages, especially those going to superiors or to clients, customers, or suppliers outside the organization. Emoticons are sideways faces made with punctuation marks and letters used to represent the writer's mood. Use them only for personal emailing—casual messages with friends or in chat rooms. For advice on providing typographic emphasis in emails, see the following section, Design Considerations.

- Avoid email abbreviations used in personal email and chat rooms (BTW for *by the way*, IOW for *in other words*). Many such abbreviations will likely be incomprehensible to non-native speakers of English. Generally, use abbreviations only when you are sure your reader will understand them.

DIGITAL SHORTCUTS: Sending an Email Attachment

Sending long documents, spreadsheets, and graphics as attachments to your email messages is a quick, convenient alternative to sending paper copies or disks of your files through regular mail. The recipient can view the file when it arrives, save it to a hard drive, or print it. When you send email attachments, consider the email message itself as the transmittal for the attachment.

Depending on the email software you're using, the steps necessary to send an attachment will differ. The following guidelines are general enough that they will apply to most systems.

- Create, save, and name your file (document or spreadsheet).

- Draft the transmittal email message and insert the recipient's email address.

- Click on the File Attachment button (usually a button with a paper clip icon) to open the dialog box containing your files.

- Open the folder with your file and click on the file name to highlight it.

- Click on the Attach or Open button on your Attachment dialog box and the file will appear in the Attachment window of your email.

- Click the Send button and your message and file are on their way.

When your recipient opens the file directly from the email in-box (by clicking on the file name), the computer will start the program that corresponds to the type of file sent. For example, if the file was originally created in Microsoft Word, the recipient's computer will open Word to display the file. (The software of the file being sent must be available on the recipient's computer before it can be opened.)

The time needed to transmit email files grows in proportion to the size of the file sent. Files that contain graphics, for example, are very large compared with text-only files. Also, your recipient's software or Internet Service Provider may not be able to accept large files. If you need to send one large file or several files at once, consider compressing the file size with a compression software utility like WinZip. This software typically reduces the file size by 80 percent and more. The recipient must unzip the file after receiving it.

Be aware: Because viruses can be embedded with email attachments, make sure you regularly upgrade your virus-scanning software.

Design Considerations

The dynamics of a computer screen and the limitations of some Internet service providers require that you need to keep in mind some special design considerations when you are sending email. The following are especially important:

- Be sure to break the text into brief paragraphs. No one wants to read long, dense blocks of text on a computer screen.

- Do not overwhelm your reader with lengthy passages. If your message runs much longer than a screen of text, consider sending it as an attached file along with a brief email message that functions as a cover memo for the longer attachment.

- Tables and bulleted lists, like many formatting features, do not always transmit well. If you must send a document with such features, do so in an attachment to your message, after making sure that the recipient has compatible software to view and save the attachment.
- Be considerate of the technical capabilities of your recipient. Check before sending memory-hungry attachments that may not be accepted by your recipient's software or Internet service provider or that may download very slowly.
- Put your response to someone else's email message at the beginning (or top) of the email window. Don't make the recipient scroll down to the end of the original message to find your response.
- In quoting the message you're replying to, include only those parts relevant to your reply. To clearly indicate the difference between your response and the text quoted in the incoming email, mark the beginning of the quoted text with a greater-than symbol (>).
- Always fill in the subject line with a concise phrase that describes the topic of your message. The recipient can then decide at a glance when he or she needs to read it. Subject lines, as discussed earlier, also help your reader organize and file incoming messages.

Many email systems do not offer the array of typographical cues that most word-processing programs provide or may not be compatible with the system you are using. For that reason, avoid using boldface, italics, and a variety of fonts because your recipient's email system may not be able to read them. Instead, use a variety of alternative highlighting devices, but be consistent. For example, capital letters or asterisks, used sparingly, can substitute for boldface, italics, and underlines as emphasis:

■ Dr. Wilhoit's suggestions benefit doctors AND patients.

■ Although the proposal is sound in *theory,* it will never work in *practice.*

Intermittent underlining can replace solid underlining or italics when referring to published works in an email message:

■ My report follows the format outlined in _The Business Writer's Handbook_.

Salutations, Closings, and Signature Blocks

Email can function as a letter, memo, or personal note; therefore, finding a suitable salutation or greeting as well as a complimentary closing can be difficult. If your employer follows a certain form, adopt that practice. Otherwise, the following guidelines should be helpful:

- When an email functions as a personal note to a friend, many use very informal salutations and closings:
  - Hi Mike,
  - Hello Jenny,
  - Take care,
  - Cheers,
- When email goes outside an organization to someone with whom you have not yet corresponded, writers often use the standard letter salutation and a slightly informal closing:
  - Dear Ms. Schmidt:
  - Dear Professor Jucker:
  - Dear Docuform Customer:
  - Best wishes,
  - Sincerely,
- When email functions as a memo to numerous recipients, you may omit the salutation and closing because both your name and the names of the recipients appear in the "To" and "From" sections of the message. However, some email users adopt a slightly more personal greeting, especially if the distribution list is relatively small or the recipient is an individual:
  - Development team colleagues,
  - Best,
  - Andreas,
  - Kathryn,
    [only the writer's first name following the message]

Of course, you may wish to use some combination of these approaches, depending on your relationship with the recipients and the practice among those with whom you exchange email. Further, be aware that in some cultures, business correspondents do not use first names as quickly as in U.S. correspondence (page 309). See examples of inappropriate and appropriate email messages in Figures 8–15 and 8–16, respectively.

Because email does not provide letterhead with standard addresses and contact information, many companies and individual writers include *signature blocks* (called *signatures* for short) at the bottom of their messages. Signatures, which writers can usually preprogram to appear on every email they send, supply information that company letterhead usually provides in other correspondence. Some email signature blocks can include automated links that connect a Web site or blank email message already addressed. If your organization recommends a certain format or restricts the content of signatures, adhere to that standard. Otherwise, choose a signature that lets your reader know your full name, official title, department or division, and the organization for which you work. Other items often included in a signature are telephone and fax numbers, mailing addresses, and Internet addresses. Many email programs allow you to create multiple signature blocks, so you can have one for professional and one for personal use.

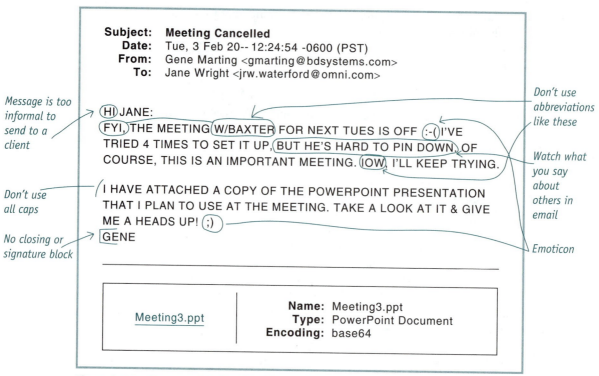

Figure 8–15 **Inappropriate Email (with Attachment)**

When you use a signature block at the bottom of an email message, use typographical highlighting cues to separate the signature from the message. Two or three spaces between the message and the signature can provide the necessary white or blank space to keep the parts distinct, but many other cues can highlight the signature: a line of hyphens (-), underlines (_), equals signs (=), tildes (~), or asterisks (*) can effectively separate a signature from the email message. Usually, typographical highlights begin at the left margin and continue until the end of the signature's longest line as shown in Figure 8–17.

Avoid using quotations, aphorisms, and other messages ("May the Force be with you") in professional signatures. As with all design features, signature blocks should be appropriate for both the tone of your usual correspondence and the professional image of both yourself and your organization.

Subject: **Baxter Meeting Cancelled**
Date: Tue, 3 Feb 20-- 12:24:54 -0600 (PST)
From: Gene Marting <gmarting@bdsystems.com>
To: Jane Wright <jrw.waterford@omni.com>

Jane:

I need to cancel the meeting with Thomas Baxter for next Tuesday (Feb 10). I will work to schedule another meeting because we need to meet with him.

I have attached a copy of the PowerPoint presentation that I'd like to use at the meeting. Let me know if you see possible improvements.

Thanks,

Gene

===============================
Gene Marting, Manager
Sales Division, Building Systems, Inc.
3555 South 47th Street, Boise, ID 83703
Off: 208-719-6620 Fax: 208-719-5500
http://www.building/sys/com
email: gmarting@bdsystems.com
===============================

Meeting3.ppt	**Name:** Meeting3.ppt **Type:** PowerPoint Document **Encoding:** base64

Figure 8–16 **Revised, Appropriate Email (with Attachment)**

===================================
Daniel J. Vasquez, Publications Manager
Medical Information Systems
TechCom Corporation
P.O. Box 5413 Salinas CA 93962
Office Phone 888.229.4511 (x 341)
General Office Fax 888.229.1132
http://www.tcc.org/
===================================

Figure 8–17 **Sample Email Signature Block**

WRITER'S CHECKLIST: Managing Email

With so many email messages coming into mailboxes, it is easy to be overwhelmed and for messages to be lost or difficult to find when they are needed. So, it is important to use good management principles in handling email. The following tips are useful in managing email:

☐ Respond to a message when you read it if at all possible; do not let messages pile up in your in-box.

☐ Set priorities for reading email by skimming sender names and topics; read your manager's emails, important topics, and time-sensitive messages first.

☐ Copy yourself on important emails and create your own subject-line titles with the care suggested earlier in this section and in the discussion of memos (see pages 268–269 and 292–300).

☐ For complex requests or issues, send a quick message that you'll respond to the question or problem after you gather more information.

☐ Print crucial messages that are complex or that you will need for meetings. (Keep them in file folders as you would paper correspondence.)

☐ Check your in-box several times a day; as suggested earlier, some organizations have expectations about the frequency with which you will need to check.

☐ Clear your in-box by the end of the day—or at least by the beginning of the next day.

☐ Create electronic folders for email, using personal names and key topics for folders.

☐ Learn the advanced features of your system so that you can use filters that organize messages as they arrive.

☐ Use the search command to find topics and individual names.

☐ Keep an up-to-date address book.

■ Writing International Correspondence

With organizations participating in the increasingly global marketplace, you may need to write letters, memos, or email messages to readers whose native language is not English. These readers may be outside your organization—as in the case of customers, suppliers, and distributors—or they may be inside your organization—for example, at branch offices outside the United States.

Because English is widely taught and used in international business, you will be able to send most international correspondence in English. If you must use a translator, however, be sure that the translator understands the purpose of your correspondence. It is also prudent to let your reader know (in the letter itself or in a postscript) that a translator helped write the letter. For first-time contacts, consider sending both the English version and a translation in the reader's native language.

Culture and Business Writing Style

Just as U.S. business writing style has changed over time, ideas about appropriate business writing style vary from culture to culture. You must be alert to the needs and expectations of readers from different cultural and linguistic backgrounds. For example, in the United States, direct, concise writing may demonstrate courtesy by not wasting another person's time; in other cultures (in countries such as Spain and India), such directness and brevity may suggest that the writer dislikes the reader so much that he or she wishes to make the communication as brief as possible. Whereas a U.S. business writer might consider one brief letter sufficient to communicate a request, a writer in another culture may expect an exchange of three or four longer letters to pave the way for action. The forms of courtesy and ideas about efficiency vary from culture to culture.

Japanese business writers, as another example, often use traditional openings that reflect on the season, compliment the reader's success, and offer hopes for the reader's continued prosperity. These traditional openings may strike some U.S. readers as being overly elaborate, literary, or even insincere. Likewise, Japanese business writers express negative messages and refusal letters indirectly to avoid embarrassing the recipient or causing a loss of face.

In U.S. business correspondence, traditional salutations such as *Dear* and complimentary closings such as *Yours truly* have, through custom and long use, acquired meanings quite distinct from their dictionary definitions. Understanding the unspoken meanings of these forms and using them naturally is routine for those who are a part of U.S. business culture. Likewise, people in many cultures are slower to use an individual's first name in communications than are most Americans. In fact, in some cultures, first names are never used in business settings—even if the individuals have worked together for years. Such customs vary from culture to culture and even within cultures. Therefore, when you read correspondence from business people in other cultures or countries, be alert to these differences and consider how you should address them and your own colleagues in correspondence.

As suggested earlier, the first step in avoiding misunderstandings is to be aware that differences exist and to learn how they affect communication. To learn more about this subject, use the term *intercultural communication* to search library and reliable Internet sources.

Language and Usage

Take special care in international correspondence to avoid American idioms ("it's a slam dunk," "give a heads up," and the like), unusual figures of speech, and allusions to events or attitudes particular to American life. Such expressions could easily confuse your reader. Avoid humor, irony, and sarcasm because they are easily misunderstood outside their cultural context.

Pretentious or overly ornate writing (as in affectation discussed in Chapter 4) will also impede the reader's understanding. Moreover, if you plan to use jargon or technical terminology, ask yourself whether the words you choose might be found in the abbreviated English-language dictionary that your reader would likely be using.

Write clear and complete sentences, as discussed in Chapters 4 and 5. Unusual word order or rambling sentences will frustrate and confuse a non-native reader of English. Read your writing aloud to identify overly long sentences and to eliminate any misplaced modifiers or awkwardness. Long sentences that contain more information than the reader can comfortably absorb should be divided into two or more sentences. Also avoid using an overly simplified storybook style. A reader who has studied English as a second language might be insulted by a condescending tone and childish language.

Finally, proofread your correspondence carefully; a misspelled word such as *there* for *their* or *discreet* for *discrete* will be particularly troublesome for a non-native reader of English—especially if that reader turns to a dictionary for help and cannot find the word because it is misspelled.

Dates, Time, and Measurement

Countries differ in their use of formats to represent dates, time, and other kinds of measurement. To represent dates, most countries typically write the day before the month and year. For example, 1/11/01 means 1 November 2001 in most parts of the world; in the United States, it means January 11, 2001. Write out the name of the month to make the entire date immediately clear to all international readers. Time poses similar problems, so you may need to specify time zones or refer to international standards, such as Greenwich Mean Time (GMT) or Universal Coordinated Time (UCT), for clarity.

Use of other international standards, such as commas for decimal points and the metric system (standard in most countries except the United States and the United Kingdom), will also help your reader. For up-to-date information about accepted conventions for numbers and symbols in chemical, electrical, data-processing, pharmaceutical, and other fields, consult guides and manuals specific to the subject matter.

Cross-Cultural Examples

Note the differences between the two versions of a letter written to a Japanese businessman, Mr. Ichiro Katsumi, Investment Director of Toshiba Investment Company, as shown in Figures 8–18 and 8–19. He is interested in investing in Sun West Corporation of Tucson, Arizona, and plans to visit Tucson for a week to meet with company officials, tour the company, and examine the company's products and financial records. Mr. Ty Smith of Sun West Corporation has been

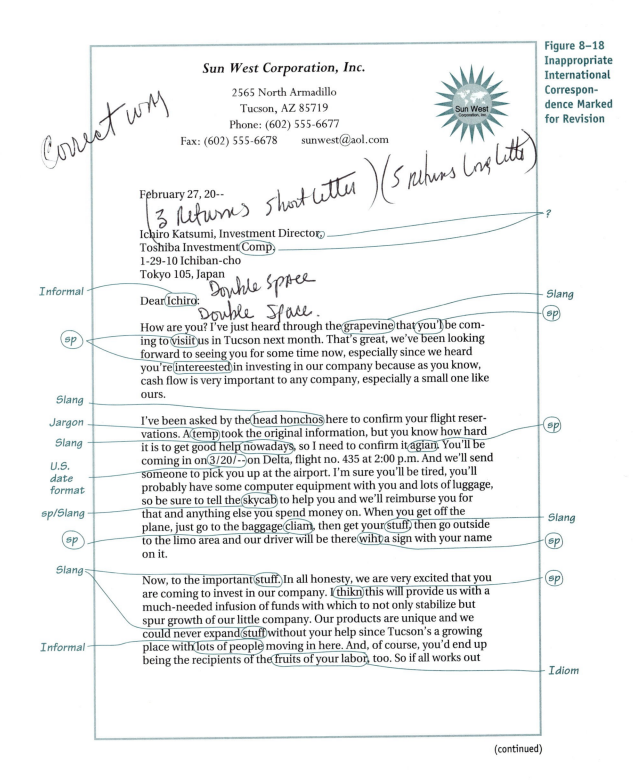

Figure 8–18
Inappropriate
International
Correspon-
dence Marked
for Revision

Correct wm

Sun West Corporation, Inc.

2565 North Armadillo
Tucson, AZ 85719
Phone: (602) 555-6677
Fax: (602) 555-6678   sunwest@aol.com

(3 Returns short letter)(5 returns long letter)

February 27, 20--

?

Ichiro Katsumi, Investment Director,
Toshiba Investment Comp,
1-29-10 Ichiban-cho
Tokyo 105, Japan

Informal

Double space
Double Space.

Slang

sp

Dear Ichiro:

sp

How are you? I've just heard through the grapevine that you'll be coming to visiit us in Tucson next month. That's great, we've been looking forward to seeing you for some time now, especially since we heard you're intereested in investing in our company because as you know, cash flow is very important to any company, especially a small one like ours.

Slang
Jargon
Slang

sp

U.S. date format

I've been asked by the head honchos here to confirm your flight reservations. A temp took the original information, but you know how hard it is to get good help nowadays, so I need to confirm it agian. You'll be coming in on 3/20/-- on Delta, flight no. 435 at 2:00 p.m. And we'll send someone to pick you up at the airport. I'm sure you'll be tired, you'll probably have some computer equipment with you and lots of luggage, so be sure to tell the skycab to help you and we'll reimburse you for that and anything else you spend money on. When you get off the plane, just go to the baggage cliam, then get your stuff, then go outside to the limo area and our driver will be there wiht a sign with your name on it.

sp/Slang

sp

Slang

sp

Slang

Now, to the important stuff. In all honesty, we are very excited that you are coming to invest in our company. I thikn this will provide us with a much-needed infusion of funds with which to not only stabilize but spur growth of our little company. Our products are unique and we could never expand stuff without your help since Tucson's a growing place with lots of people moving in here. And, of course, you'd end up being the recipients of the fruits of your labor, too. So if all works out

sp

Informal

Idiom

(continued)

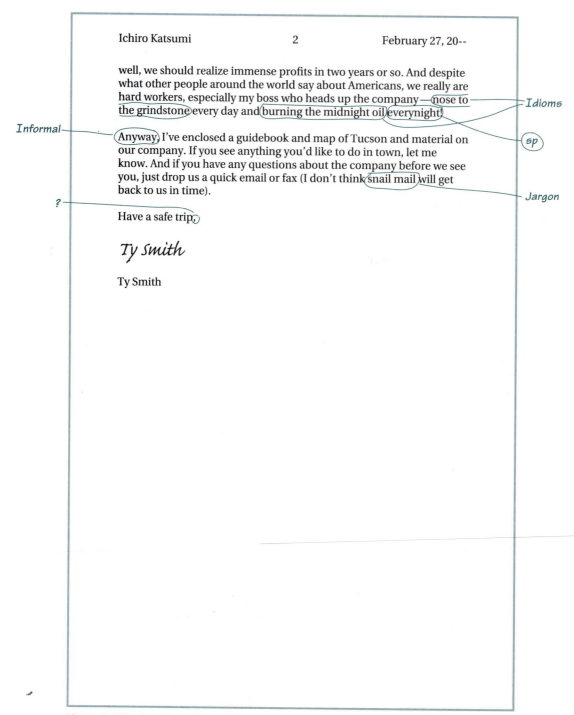

Ichiro Katsumi   2   February 27, 20--

well, we should realize immense profits in two years or so. And despite
what other people around the world say about Americans, we really are
hard workers, especially my boss who heads up the company—nose to
the grindstone every day and burning the midnight oil everynight!

Idioms

sp

Informal

Anyway, I've enclosed a guidebook and map of Tucson and material on
our company. If you see anything you'd like to do in town, let me
know. And if you have any questions about the company before we see
you, just drop us a quick email or fax (I don't think snail mail will get
back to us in time).

Jargon

?

Have a safe trip.

Ty Smith

Ty Smith

Figure 8–18   (continued)

312

Sun West Corporation, Inc.

2565 North Armadillo
Tucson, AZ 85719
Phone: (602) 555-6677
Fax: (602) 555-6678   sunwest@aol.com

March 1, 20--   ← NOT WIDE ENOUGH

Ichiro Katsumi
Investment Director
Toshiba Investment Company
1-29-10 Ichiban-cho
Tokyo 105, Japan

Dear Mr. Katsumi: NO GOOD?

I hope that you and your family are well and prospering in the new year. We
at Sun Corporation are very pleased that you will be coming to visit us in
Tucson this month. It will be a pleasure to meet you, and we are very gratified
and honored that you are interested in investing in our company.

So that we can ensure that your stay will be pleasurable, we have taken care
of all of your travel arrangements. You will

- Leave Narita-New Tokyo International Airport on Delta Airlines flight #75
  at 5:00 p.m. on March 20, 20--
- Arrive at Los Angeles International Airport at 10:50 a.m. local time and de-
  part for Tucson on Delta flight #186 at 12:05 p.m.
- Arrive at Tucson International Airport at 1:30 p.m. local time on March 20
- Depart Tucson International Airport on Delta flight #123 at 6:45 a.m. on
  March 27
- Arrive in Salt Lake City, Utah, at 10:40 a.m. and depart at 11:15 a.m. on
  Delta flight #34 and arrive in Portland, Oregon, at 12:10 p.m. local time
- Depart Portland, Oregon, on Delta flight #254 at 1:05 p.m. and arrive in
  Japan at 3:05 p.m. local time on March 28

If this information is not accurate or if you need additional information about
your travel plans or information on Sun West Corporation, please call, fax, or
email me directly. That way, we will receive your message in time to make the
appropriate changes or additions.

Figure 8–19   Appropriate International Correspondence   (continued)

313

After you arrive in Tucson, a chauffeur from Skyline Limousines will be waiting for you at Gate 12. He or she will be carrying a card with your name, will help you collect your luggage from the baggage claim area, and will then drive you to the Loews Ventana Canyon Resort. This is one of the most prestigious resorts in Tucson, with spectacular desert views, high-quality amenities, and one of the best golf courses in the city. The next day, the chauffeur will be back at the Ventana at 9:00 a.m. to drive you to Sun West Corporation.

We at Sun West Corporation are very excited to meet you and introduce you to all the members of our hard-working and growing company family. After you meet everyone, you will enjoy a catered breakfast in our conference room. At that time, you will receive a schedule of events planned for the remainder of your trip. Events include presentations from the president of the company and from departmental directors on

- The history of Sun West Corporation
- The uniqueness of our products and current success in the marketplace
- Demographic information and benefits of being located in Tucson
- The potential for considerable profits for both our companies with your company's investment

We encourage you to read through the enclosed guidebook and map of Tucson. In addition to events planned at Sun West Corporation, you will find many natural wonders and historical sites to see in Tucson and in Arizona in general. If you see any particular event or place that you would like to visit, please let us know. We will be happy to show you our city and all it has to offer.

Again, we are very honored that you will be visiting us, and we look forward to a successful business relationship between our two companies.

Sincerely,

Susan Roberts

Susan Roberts
Vice President

Encl. as stated

Figure 8–19   (continued)

asked to write a letter to Mr. Katsumi confirming his travel arrangements and mentioning the benefits that an investment in Sun West Corporation would bring.

The letter shown in Figure 8–18 would be very confusing to Mr. Katsumi or to any international or non-native recipient. Aside from the spelling errors, the letter is filled with slang (*grapevine, head honchos*), clichés (*fruits of your labor, nose to the grindstone, burning the midnight oil*), jargon (*snail mail*), and the inappropriate use of "stuff," an American expression that is not specific enough to communicate anything useful.

Compare this with the letter to Mr. Katsumi that was rewritten by a writer more sensitive to the needs of a multicultural audience, as shown in Figure 8–19. This version of the letter is written in language that is literal and specific. The slang, clichés, and jargon are gone. For easier comprehension and translation, the sentences are shorter, bulleted lists are used to break up the paragraphs, contractions are eliminated, and the expression of dates is made clearer.

Writing correspondence for readers in other cultures requires careful thought because we are all, to greater or lesser degrees, embedded in the language habits of our cultures. When you are writing for international readers, rethink the ingrained habits that define how you express yourself. Doing so will help you achieve clarity and mutual understanding.

CHAPTER 8 SUMMARY: Principles of Business Correspondence

Choose the medium that best suits your communication needs.

☐ Letters on your organization's stationery
- To represent a commitment to the recipient
- To formalize a business relationship

☐ Memos: printed and electronic
- To communicate and circulate information within your organization

☐ Email messages
- To communicate quickly within your organization and with customers and others outside of your organization
- To transmit text and graphics files electronically

☐ Faxes
- To transmit a document that is not available in electronic format
- To transmit a document that must be viewed in its original form (for instance, a letter with a signature or official seal)

(continued)

CHAPTER 8 SUMMARY (continued)

☐ Telephone calls and conferences
- To provide a setting for clarifying information and resolving issues
- To provide an alternative to a face-to-face meeting
- To enable participants to hear each other's voices

☐ Voice-mail messages
- To communicate brief messages

☐ Face-to-face meetings
- To make initial or early contacts with associates and customers with whom you wish to build a relationship
- To plan a project, to make group decisions around specific objectives, or to solve a serious problem

☐ Videoconferencing
- To provide an alternative to a face-to-face meeting
- To enable participants to hear and see one another

Writing Business Letters

☐ Follow the writing process.

☐ Use goodwill and the "you" viewpoint.

☐ Use the direct pattern for good news:
1. Good news or main point
2. Explanation of facts
3. Goodwill close

☐ Use the indirect pattern for some negative messages:
1. Context
2. Explanation
3. Bad news
4. Goodwill close

☐ Review letter opening and closing.

☐ Consider writing style and accuracy.

☐ Determine the appropriate format and parts.

Writing Memos: Printed and Electronic

☐ Follow memo protocol and strategy.

☐ Organize your ideas.

☐ Adjust the style and tone.

☐ Prepare an opening.

☐ Use lists and headings strategically.

☐ Use appropriate memo format.

☐ Prepare the subject-line title.

Meeting the Deadline: The Time-Sensitive Memo

☐ Make sure that you understand the assignment.

☐ Gather pertinent background information.

☐ Organize your major points into a sequence that makes sense.

☐ Write the draft quickly—one subject to a paragraph.

☐ Polish the draft, focusing on content and organization before revising at the sentence level.

Sending Email: Protocol and Strategies

☐ Consider appropriate use of email.

☐ Do not send a message without reviewing it for accuracy and readability.

☐ Recognize that all email messages are subject to interception by someone other than the person or persons for whom the message is intended; write them accordingly.

☐ Observe the rules of netiquette.

☐ Consider the design needs of email messages.

☐ Create an appropriate salutation, closing, and signature block.

Writing International Correspondence

☐ Use words likely to appear in your reader's English-language dictionary.

☐ Adjust for cultural preferences in the organization of ideas.

☐ Consider the decision-making style of your recipient's culture.

☐ Eliminate humor and slang.

☐ Read the letter aloud for ambiguity and confusing sentence structure.

☐ Check for appropriate forms of dates, times, and measurements.

■ Exercises

1. You are the manager of accounting for a company that sells computer-software packages throughout the United States. You have just received word from the comptroller that there has been a change in the expense allowances for employees using their own cars on business. Research done by your company's business office has revealed the need to set different allowance rates for two categories of drivers— *regular* and *nonregular*. (Previously, one rate was applied to all employees.)

Regular drivers are those who use their own cars frequently on the job. Typically, these would be employees who regularly drive to their sales territories. Nonregular drivers are those employees who only occasionally use their cars on business; most home-office personnel would be included in this category.

The revised allowance is effective immediately. It will be reimbursed according to formulas for each category. Regular drivers will receive 30¢ per mile for the first 650 miles driven per month, and 10¢ for each additional mile. Nonregular drivers will receive 30¢ per mile for the first 150 miles per month, and 10¢ for each additional mile.

To ensure that these categories are used properly, you want to set up a control procedure. The Accounts Payable supervisor has suggested that the manager of each department notify Accounts Payable, by letter, which employees in his or her department should be classified as regular drivers. You agree and decide that Accounts Payable will reimburse those employees not identified by the letter according to the nonregular-driver formula.

Prepare a memo or listserv message to communicate this information to all employees.

2. Explore the templates offered by your word-processing software. Most word-processing packages offer several styles of business-document templates, both contemporary and traditional. (This feature is included in Microsoft Word in the pull-down menu under Tools.) Select a template offered by your software and enter one of the sample business letters included in Chapter 8. Print out the letter when you have finished and add in pencil or pen the answers to the following questions:
   a. Why did you choose this particular template?
   b. Did the template make writing your letter easier? Why or why not?
   c. Why do businesses request that their employees use a template when formatting business letters?

3. To complete this assignment, perform *a* through *c* in Exercise 2 either on your own or as part of a collaborative team.
   a. You are director of corporate communications for a nationwide insurance company called The Provider Group. Management has asked you to design a letterhead that reflects a "modern, yet responsible image." For this project, collect as many samples of letterheads as you can. Then, using word-processing software with graphics capability, design a letterhead for The Provider Group (using a local address, phone number, and any other appropriate details).

   As you design, consider the image and personality your design will project as well as the amount of information you should provide.
   b. Survey six organizations in your area (including your college) to determine the letter formats they use (full block, modified block, etc.). Who makes the decisions (secretaries? word-processing staff? management?)? Is everyone required to use a standard form? Why do they use the forms they do? Prepare a report according to your instructor's directions.
   c. Using the results in parts *a* and *b*, determine the best format for letters to be sent to the clients of The Provider Group on the letterhead you have designed.

4. Write a brief narrative describing how you plan to use or have used email to collaborate on a writing assignment with fellow students or with colleagues at your job.

5. Write a brief narrative describing an on-the-job email message you have received that was inappropriate from the standpoint of netiquette or that communicated information so poorly that you had to ask for a clarification.

6. Prepare an email to a group of international customers whom your company wants to inform of the following changes:

   a. Your company's newsletter will now be mailed electronically instead of through the mail.

   b. The newsletter will now be updated every month instead of bi-monthly.

   c. It will be the customer's responsibility to inform the company if he or she does not want to receive the newsletter.

   d. If the customer wishes to receive the newsletter in printed format there will be a $30.00 (U.S. dollars) annual handling fee.

   e. New items listed in the newsletter can be ordered via the Internet with a 10 percent discount.

   > You will want to present these changes in a positive manner so that the customers will look forward to the change. You may want to refer to the sections titled Sending Email: Protocol and Strategies and Writing International Correspondence.

7. a. Rewrite the following statement to make it more positive and less blunt:

   - I will not pay you because you have not sent the final software upgrade. If you do not send the right one immediately, I will not pay you at all.

   b. Rewrite the following passage to make it less unfriendly:

   - I wrote for the Music Collection you advertised on TV, and not only did it take six weeks to get here, but it was the wrong set of CDs. Can't you get anything right? I'm canceling payment on my check and sending this set of CDs back!

   c. Revise the following passage to make it clearer and less pretentious:

   - With reference to your recent automobile accident, I have been unable to contact you due to the fact that I have been in Chicago working day and night on a proposal—a biggie. I should be back in the office in the neighborhood of the 15th or so. In the unforeseen and unlikely event that I should be delayed, you can utilize Mr. Strawman, of my office, who will also endeavor in your behalf.

   d. Revise the following statements so they reflect the "you" viewpoint:

   - I want you to buy this "Handy-Fone" so I can win the sales award for this month.
   - We must receive a copy of your W-4 form to complete our files.
   - Our business is built on our commitment to quality that we pass on to our customers.
   - I can't finish your income-tax calculations until I receive your December receipts. Then I'll be able to file for the expected refund.

   e. Improve the business-letter style or memo-writing strategy of the following statements:

   - As per your request, please find enclosed a copy of the report that was requested by your office.
   - Pursuant to V. B. Lanham's instructions, I have prepared a thorough analysis that your department should have prepared last year.

■ Records of all long-distance telephonic communications should be submitted prior to the penultimate day of the subsequent month.

■ You are hereby notified that your vacation schedule must be submitted to my office two months prior to the dates so that I may avoid disruptive interferences. It is hoped this practice will find the acceptance of all staff members. If you have any questions, please feel free to call me. Thanks.

8. Assume that you are writing an inquiry letter to Mr. José Espinosa of the Spanish Tourist Bureau in Madrid, Spain. You wish to obtain information about work opportunities in Madrid because you are interested in relocating to Spain after you graduate.

   You must determine a realistic street address in Madrid and gather information about both the proper protocol and the format of the letter. To do so, write a draft of the letter as you would if you were writing to a local tourist office. With the approval of your instructor, ask a faculty member at your college who teaches Spanish (and would understand the form and protocol of such a letter) to comment on the appropriateness of the letter you have drafted.

9. Write a memo on one of the following topics, based on your own experience as a student. Use no more than 30 minutes to produce your memo, which will be addressed to your instructor. Cover the points you feel must be included to support your conclusion. Refer to your text for correct memo format, or your instructor may advise you to use one of the memo templates offered in your word-processing software. Topics include the following:
   a. Should student tickets to athletic events on campus be included with the price of tuition?
   b. Should smoking be permitted in campus facilities?
   c. Should students be allowed to bring laptop computers to class for taking notes? Your instructor may substitute other current campus issues.

10. Your boss has asked you to draft a complaint letter to your software supply company because the level of service and technical support that your business, Smith Consultants, has received to date does not meet your boss' expectations. He or she has asked you to include the following points:
   a. Telephone calls from your employees to the software help department are often not returned in a timely fashion. Sometimes they are not returned at all.
   b. Software assistance personnel often blame your hardware for the problem; however, when consulted, the hardware representative reports that the problem is with the software.
   c. Promised monthly four-hour in-service training sessions have not been scheduled for the past three months.
   Your boss also suggests that you mention that your company is considering not paying the software provider the remaining 30 percent of the purchase amount. Your boss further reminds you that this is a very delicate matter because Smith Consultants has already invested thousands of dollars in the software system and would like to resolve the problem without losing the investment. Following the principles of business correspondence offered in Chapter 8, submit your draft in correct business-letter format to your instructor.

■ In-Class Activities

1. Divide into collaborative teams of four to six members to consider the following problem. A division of your company is a wholesale office-supply warehouse. For more than five years, your company has been able to charge mail-order customers a flat shipping rate of $5.95 for any order under $300.00. In fact, this has been a strong advertising point for the past five years. However, in the past two years, profits have fallen steadily. Recently, the president of your company has announced that shipping charges will increase in two months. At that time, shipping will be $5.95 for orders under $100.00 and will increase by $3.00 for each additional $1.00 to $100.00 worth of product. Your writing team is responsible for informing your existing customers of the change. This will be a difficult task because the customers have been conditioned by your marketing representatives to expect "the industry's most reasonable" shipping charges. After you have appointed a team leader, draft a letter as a group explaining the changes in shipping charges to the customer. The letter should provide the context and explanation of the charges, the bad news, and a goodwill close. Follow the guidelines in this chapter for reference.

2. Divide into two groups of equal numbers. One group will be consumers and the other group will be the local utility company's marketing representatives. For the next 30 minutes, the consumers will write a letter to their utility rate commissioner asking that the rate increase requested by their local electric company not be granted. The local utility company's marketing representatives will write a letter asking the utility commissioner to grant their rate-increase request. Both groups should address the following issues:
   a. Dependability of service of the utility
   b. Need for a rate increase
   c. Ability of customers to pay for the increase
   Then the groups will trade letters. During the next 30 minutes, each person will respond to the letter as if he or she were a representative of the utility commission. The replies to the letter are to be written to explain why the sender's request will not be granted—that is, the consumers will receive the bad news that a rate increase will probably be necessary, and the utility company's representatives will receive the bad news that a rate increase will not be granted. Remember to provide a context, an explanation, the bad news, and a goodwill close when drafting your replies.

3. Divide into small groups and appoint a group leader to facilitate a discussion of how email is used in the workplace. For 45 minutes, discuss the ways that email can save a company time and money. Also discuss how email can cause problems when misused. We have all received annoying unsolicited advertising, topical jokes, or other unprofessional email at work. Ask each member of the group how he or she has handled inappropriate emails at work in the past. Discuss how to discourage inappropriate email at work. During the last fifteen minutes of your session, create an outline with the following headings:
   a. Emails save time and money at work.
   b. Inappropriate email at work is a problem.
   c. What the future of email in the work environment will be.
   Your instructor may ask you to share your outlines with the rest of the class.

4. Divide into eight groups to explore the different media used for communicating on the job. Assign each group one of the following categories:
   a. Letter on organization's stationery
   b. Memo
   c. Email
   d. Fax
   e. Phone
   f. Voice mail
   g. Videoconference
   h. In-person meeting

   In your group, brainstorm to make a list of the different situations in the workplace for which you might use the medium assigned to your group. Group members should draw on their varied experiences to provide a wide range of situations. Each group can then share their lists with the rest of the class.

5. In 30 minutes or less, write a memo describing one of the following topics or one similar. You may use your textbook as a reference for memo style and format.
   a. Describe to a visiting professor your last three class assignments. Include what you learned.
   b. Describe to a visiting student the food services available on campus.
   c. Describe to an incoming freshman the campus policy on computer use by students. If possible, describe the location of computer labs and their availability to students.

■ Research Projects

1. Bring to class one business letter that you believe is well written and one that you believe is poorly written. Be prepared to explain your reasons for thinking that one is better than the other. If you are working full- or part-time, you may be able to find letters in your office. If not, obtain letters from friends or relatives, or find examples among the correspondence you receive in the mail.

2. Find a letter containing bad news that you believe is unnecessarily blunt. Rewrite the letter to protect the goodwill of the organization that sent it. Attach your revision to the original, and submit both to your instructor.

3. Find an example of overdone goodwill. (Mass-produced sales letters, for example, may be useful.) Rewrite the letter or message, retaining goodwill while eliminating poor style.

4. As directed by your instructor, interview a middle manager at a local corporation. Determine generally (a) how many different forms of communications media (letters, memos, email, etc.) that person uses, (b) which medium he or she uses most often, and (c) how that person determines which medium to use. Review the section Selecting the Appropriate Medium in this chapter before you begin. Report your results as your instructor directs.

5. Form a collaborative group to write an informal investigative report on cultural differences in the following areas of writing: punctuation marks; religious symbols; colors; people, body parts, and gestures; directional signals; technology

symbols; reading practices; cultural symbols; slang expressions and technical jargon; methods of addressing people; or other aspects of written communication.

You may choose one culture to compare to the United States in great detail or more than one culture to compare on differing points. Before beginning your research and writing, determine who your audience will be and what the purpose and scope of your report will be. For example, you may assume that your company is expanding to include several international branches.

Remember, this is written communication. You will likely find examples of verbal and nonverbal differences, but investigate until you can find a way to demonstrate how they can be used effectively in writing.

Document your sources as directed by your instructor.

■ Web Projects

1. The Internet is becoming widely used during the job-search process by both job seekers and companies looking to hire. Find three Web sites of companies advertising open positions in your field. Draft an email to respond to each of the open positions—consider how your email will compare to the more traditional, formal, written application letter. Your instructor will advise you to either send her or him your emails electronically or print your emails and bring them to class.

2. Search the Web for sites dedicated to the subject of email etiquette. Briefly scan the sites, and then choose one to review in detail. Some sample sites include: Frank's Friendly Guide to Email by a professor of engineering at North Carolina State University at http://www.ncsu.edu/provost/people/abrams (click on "Frank's Friendly Guide to Email"); A Beginner's Guide to Email at http://www.webfoot.com/advice/email.top.html; and Electronic Mail Etiquette, a page created by an instructor in the United Kingdom, at http://www.uel.ac.uk/pers/1412/pegasus/etiquette/html. In a brief narrative, analyze the site you have selected, discussing the content and writing style. Based on your own email experience and advice offered in this chapter, mention points made by the site's author that you agree or disagree with. Explain why you agree or disagree.

3. Conduct your own Internet search for online articles about email etiquette. Using two or three different search engines with the keywords "Email Etiquette" and "article," locate four articles dedicated to email etiquette. Write a brief analysis in which you compare and contrast the content of the articles. Be certain to include the URL address of each site (and any further documentation required by your instructor), and send your analysis to your instructor electronically. You may wish to include links to the articles in your email.

4. Search the Web to find three or more sites designed to help the Web user locate government sites available to the public. Sample sites include: FedWorld.gov., hosted by the Department of Commerce, at http://www.fedworld.gov/; FedStats, hosted by the Federal Interagency Council on Statistical Policy, at http://www.fedstats.gov; and Galaxy's directory of government sites, at http://galaxy.einet.net/galaxy/Government.html. Review three sites of your choice and submit an email to your instructor recommending one of the sites for classroom use. Be

certain to include your specific reasons for selecting this site, and be sure to include a link or URL to the site in your email.

5. Search online to find articles on appropriate style and tone for business correspondence. A good resource is the *Business Communication Quarterly* available online at http://bcq.theabc.org. Select one article to summarize in 150 to 250 words. Your instructor may also ask you to prepare an oral summary for class discussion.

9 Types of Business Correspondence

There are almost as many types of correspondence as there are reasons for writing. That is why it is important to study the principles discussed in Chapter 8 for letters, memos, and email, then apply them to both the situation and your reader's needs. This chapter, however, is devoted to a number of common types of correspondence: routine and positive messages that include acknowledgments, cover (or transmittal) messages, inquiries and responses, recommendations, and sales and promotions; and sensitive and negative messages that include refusals, complaints, adjustments, resignations, and collections. For each of these types, you must also determine what format—such as letter, memo, or email—is best. Although each of the following sections illustrate typical formats used, you should also review the section Selecting the Appropriate Medium on pages 265–271. Further, keep in mind that any company or organization follows a protocol for the form or medium used for specific types of messages.

Because of their importance to breaking into a profession as well as career advancement, job-application letters and résumés are discussed separately in Chapter 16, along with other job-seeking strategies.

■ Types of Routine and Positive Messages

The types of correspondence discussed in this section, many of which are written routinely in the workplace, provide the opportunity to build goodwill with readers and create a positive image of your organization.

Acknowledgments

One way to build goodwill with colleagues and clients is to let them know that something they sent arrived and to express thanks. A letter, email, or memo that serves this function is usually a short, polite note. The example shown in Figure 9–1 is typical and could be sent as a letter or an email.

Voices from the Workplace

Nancy Spain, Empire Blue Cross and Blue Shield

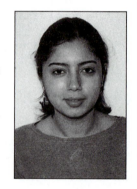

Nancy Spain is a team leader for the Financial Claims Department at Empire Blue Cross and Blue Shield. The Financial Claims Department is responsible for requesting money back for overpaid insurance claims. Each week, Nancy's team sends out from 300 to 500 collection letters to subscribers, providers, and hospitals.

Nancy describes the delicacy of the collection-letter series as follows:

"One of the biggest challenges in requesting money is the timeliness factor. The more time that passes, the less collectible the refund becomes. The goal of the department is to get the first letter out within five days of discovering that an error has occurred in the payment of the claim.

"Each letter that goes out to the debtor states that an error has been made and includes the reason why the refund is being requested. The letter also provides a phone number for the debtor to call if he or she has a question, disagrees with, or has already paid the refund, and states what will happen next if the payment is not received. Also included is a time frame for returning the payment and an envelope for the return.

"Thirty days is allowed from the time the first letter is sent out until the next step. The second letter, although still courteous, is more demanding and only allows ten days for a response. The letter informs the debtor that unless payment is received, the case will be turned over to a collection agency.

"An important aspect of our work is to stand by what we state in the letters and not make idle threats. If we have stated that the case will be turned over to a collection agency after ten days, then the case is indeed turned over and we require the agency to contact the debtor within a very short amount of time."

Empire Blue Cross and Blue Shield can be found on the Web at http:www.empirehealthcare.com

Entry-Level
Priya Ratneshwar, Bedford/St. Martin's

Priya Ratneshwar is an editorial assistant at Bedford/St. Martin's where she assists in the editorial development of rhetoric, composition, and literature textbooks. One of her main responsibilities — organizing review projects for textbooks in development — involves heavy correspondence with reviewers.

"I begin by sending invitations to review a text — this takes the form of a letter that is tailored to each review project, and for each potential reviewer. These letters describe the text and project, and detail my expectations of the reviewer. I also send letters of instruction to accompany review materials, and once I've received reviewer's responses I send a thank-you letter to each reviewer to acknowledge and express gratitude for his or her contribution.

"I usually draft, and save as a file, a generic version of these and other types of standardized letters. I then customize these letters to make them appropriate to each new project and person. This method is efficient, and, at the same time, allows me to write letters that are informative and friendly because I am able to personally address the subject and recipient at hand.

"Because I am often a person's first contact with Bedford/St. Martin's, I aim, in my letters, to be friendly, informative, and, above all, respectful. It is important that reviewers and customers know that their comments and their time are much valued by the company, its authors, and its employees."

Explore Bedford/St. Martin's books and resources at http://www.bedfordstmartins.com.

Figure 9–1
Acknowledg-
ment by
Email

Subject: Report Received
   Date: Mon, 2 Feb 20-- 12:24:54 -0600 (CST)
  From: Roger Hammersmith <hammer@eci2.com>
     To: James G. Evans <jge.waterford@omni.com>

Dear Mr. Evans:

I received your report today; it appears to be complete and well done.

When I finish studying it in detail, I'll send you our cost estimate for the installation of the Mark II Energy Saving System.

Again, thanks for your effort.

Regards,

Roger

==============================
Roger Hammersmith, Manager
Sales Division, Ecology Systems, Inc.
1015 Clarke Street, Chicago IL 60615
Off: 312-719-6620 Fax: 312-719-5500
http://www.ecology.sys/com
email: hammer@eci2.com
==============================

Covers (or Transmittals)

When you send a formal report, proposal, brochure, or similar material, you should include with it a short message, often called a cover (or transmittal) letter, which identifies what you are sending and why you are sending it. As discussed in Chapter 8, an email message that is used to send an electronic attachment also serves this purpose. A cover letter (or perhaps memo, if sent within a company or organization) that accompanies a report, for example, may contain the title of the report, a brief description of the report, an acknowledgment of any help received during its preparation, and the authorization or reason for the report. The cover message provides the writer with a record of when and to whom the material was sent.

    Keep your remarks brief. Your opening should explain what is being sent and why. In an optional second paragraph, you might include a summary of the information you're sending. A letter accompanying a proposal, for example, might point out any sections in the proposal of particular interest to the reader. The letter could then go on to present a key point or two as to why the writer's firm is the best one to do the job. This paragraph could also mention the conditions under which the material was prepared, such as limitations of time or budget. The closing paragraph should contain acknowledgments, offer additional assistance, or express the hope that the material will fulfill its purpose. (For an example of such a letter, see Figure 14–7.)

Figure 9–2 is an example of a cover letter that is brief and to the point. Figure 9–3 is a bit more detailed, touching on the manner in which the information was gathered.

Inquiries and Responses

An inquiry letter or email can be as simple as a request for a free brochure or as complex as asking a consultant to define the specific requirements for establishing a usability testing lab.

There are two broad categories of inquiries: those that benefit the recipient and those that benefit the writer. Inquiries of obvious benefit to the letter's recipient include letters asking for information about a product that a company has recently advertised. Inquiries that primarily benefit the writer include, for example, a request to a nonprofit professional association to send demographic information about its members in a geographic area. If the inquiry you are writing is of the second kind, it is particularly important to be considerate of your reader's needs. Your objective in writing will probably be to obtain, within a reasonable period of time, answers to specific questions. You will be more likely to receive a prompt, helpful reply if you follow the guidelines in Writer's Checklist: Writing Inquiries.

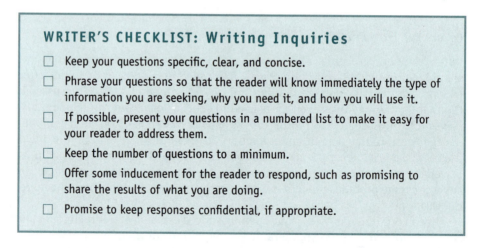

WRITER'S CHECKLIST: Writing Inquiries

☐ Keep your questions specific, clear, and concise.

☐ Phrase your questions so that the reader will know immediately the type of information you are seeking, why you need it, and how you will use it.

☐ If possible, present your questions in a numbered list to make it easy for your reader to address them.

☐ Keep the number of questions to a minimum.

☐ Offer some inducement for the reader to respond, such as promising to share the results of what you are doing.

☐ Promise to keep responses confidential, if appropriate.

In the closing, thank the reader for taking the time to respond. In addition, make it convenient for the recipient to respond by providing contact information, such as a phone number or an email address as shown in Figure 9–4.

ECOLOGY SYSTEMS AND SERVICES

39 Beacon Street
Boston, Massachusetts 02106
(617) 351-1223
Fax: (617) 351-2121

May 23, 20--

Mario Espinoza, Chief Engineer
Louisiana Chemical Products
3452 River View Road
Baton Rouge, LA 70893

Dear Mr. Espinoza:

Enclosed is the final report on our installation of pollution-control equipment at Eastern Chemical Company, which we send with Eastern's permission. Please call me collect (ext. 1206) or send me an email message at the address below if I can answer any questions.

Sincerely,

Susan Wong

Susan Wong, Ph.D.
Technical Services Manager
swong.ecology@omni.com

SW/ls
Enclosure: Report

Figure 9–2   Brief Cover Letter (for a Report)

WATERFORD PAPER PRODUCTS
P.O. Box 413
WATERFORD, WI 53474

Phone: (414) 738-2191
Fax: (414) 738-9122

January 16, 20--

Mr. Roger Hammersmith
Ecology Systems, Inc.
1015 Clarke Street
Chicago, IL 60615

Dear Mr. Hammersmith:

Enclosed is the report estimating our power consumption for the year as requested by John Brenan, Vice President, on September 4.

The report is a result of several meetings with the Manager of Plant Operations and her staff and an extensive survey of all our employees. The survey
was delayed by the transfer of key staff in Building "A." We believe, however,
that the report will provide the information you need in order to furnish us
with a cost estimate for the installation of your Mark II Energy Saving System.

We would like to thank Diana Biel of ESI for her assistance in preparing the
survey. If you need any more information, please let me know.

Sincerely,

James G. Evans

James G. Evans
New Projects Office
jge.waterford@omni.com

Enclosure

Figure 9–3   Long Cover Letter (for a Report)

University of Dayton
P.O. Box 113
Dayton, OH 45409
March 11, 20--

Jane E. Metcalf
Engineering Services
Miami Valley Power Company
P.O. Box 1444
Miamitown, OH 45733

Dear Ms. Metcalf:

Could you please send me some information on heating systems for a computerized, energy-efficient house that a team of engineering students at the University of Dayton is designing?

The house, which contains 2,000 square feet of living space (17,600 cubic feet), meets all the requirements stipulated in your brochure "Insulating for Efficiency." We need the following information:

1. The proper-size heat pump to use in this climate for such a home.
2. The wattage of the supplemental electrical heating units that would be required for this climate.
3. The estimated power consumption and current rates of those units for one year.

We will be happy to send you a copy of our preliminary design report and any further information about the project that may be of interest to you. If you have questions or suggestions, please contact me at kjp@fly.ud.edu or call 513-229-4598.

Thank you for your help.

Sincerely,

Kathryn J. Parsons

Kathryn J. Parsons
Engineering Student

Figure 9–4   Inquiry Letter

Responding to Inquiries

Sometimes, of course, you may be the recipient of an inquiry. When you do receive an inquiry, read it quickly to determine whether you have both the information and authority to respond. If you are the right person in your organization to respond, answer as promptly as you can, and be sure to answer every question asked. How long and detailed your response should be depends on the nature of the questions and the information provided in the letter by the writer. Even if the writer has asked a question that seems silly or one to which you feel the answer is obvious, answer it courteously and as completely as you can. You may tactfully point out that the writer has omitted or misunderstood something.

If you have received an inquiry that you feel you cannot answer, find out who can and forward the inquiry to that person. Notify the writer that you have forwarded the inquiry, as shown in Figure 9–5.

The person to whom an inquiry has been forwarded should state in the first paragraph of his or her response why someone else is answering the original inquiry, as shown in Figure 9–6.

Subject: Report Received
   Date: Mon, 19 March 20-- 11:42:25 -0500 (EDT)
   From: Jane E. Metcalf <metcalf@mvpc.org>
     To: Kathryn J. Parsons <kjp@fly.ud.edu>

Dear Kathryn Parsons:

Thank you for inquiring about the heating system we recommend for use in homes designed according to the specifications outlined in our brochure "Insulating for Efficiency."

Because I cannot answer your specific questions, I have forwarded your inquiry to Michael Wang, Engineering Assistant in our Development Group. He should be able to answer the questions you have raised. You should be hearing from him shortly.

Best wishes,

Jane E. Metcalf

====================================
Jane E. Metcalf, Director of Public Information
Miami Valley Power Company
P.O. Box 1444 ~ Miamitown, OH 45733
Office 513-264-4800 ~ Fax 513-264-4889
Web ~ http://www.enersaving.com
====================================

Figure 9–5   **Response Indicating That an Inquiry Has Been Forwarded (Email)**

MIAMI VALLEY POWER COMPANY
P.O. BOX 1444
MIAMITOWN, OH 45733
(513) 264-4800

March 24, 20--

Ms. Kathryn, J. Parsons
University of Dayton
P.O. Box 113
Dayton, OH 45409

Dear Ms. Parsons:

Jane Metcalf forwarded to me your inquiry of March 11 about the house that
your engineering team is designing. I can estimate the insulation requirements of a typical home of 17,600 cubic feet as follows:

1. For such a home, we would generally recommend a heat pump capable of
   delivering 40,000 Btus. Our model AL-42 (17 kilowatts) meets that requirement.
2. With the AL-42 efficiency, you don't need supplemental heating units.
3. Depending on usage, the AL-42 unit averages between 1,000 and 1,500
   kilowatt-hours from December through March. To determine the current
   rate for such usage, check with Dayton Power and Light Company.

I can give you an answer that would apply specifically to your house only
with information about its particular design (such as number of stories, windows, and entrances). If you send me more details, I will be happy to provide
more precise figures. Your project sounds interesting.

Sincerely,

Michael Wang

Michael Wang
Engineering Assistant
mwang@mvpc.org

http://www.enersaving.com

Figure 9–6   Response to an Inquiry (Letter)

Recommendations

A recommendation can range from completing a statement on a form provided by a prospective employer to composing a detailed reference letter evaluating the professional accomplishments and personal characteristics for someone seeking employment.

To write an effective recommendation or reference letter, you must be familiar enough with the applicant's abilities or actual performance to offer an evaluation. You must truthfully and without embellishment communicate that evaluation to the inquirer. For the reference letter to achieve its purpose, you must specifically address the applicant's skills, abilities, knowledge, and personal characteristics in relation to the requested objective.

In a recommendation or reference letter solicited by a prospective employer, always respond directly to the inquiry, being careful to address any specific questions asked. For the record, you must identify yourself: name, title or position, employer, and address. You could begin by stating the circumstances of your acquaintance and how long you have known the person about whom you are writing the letter. You should mention, with as much substantiation as possible, one or two outstanding characteristics of the applicant. Organize the details in your letter in decreasing order of importance. Conclude with a brief summary of the applicant's qualifications and with a clear statement of recommendation. Figure 9–7 is a typical reference letter.

When you are requested to serve as a reference or to supply a letter of reference, be aware that applicants have a legal right to examine the materials in an organization's files that concern them, unless they sign a waiver of their right to do so. Organizations may offer applicants the option of signing a waiver against reading letters of reference written about them.

Sales and Promotions

A sales letter or message that promotes a product, service, or business requires both a thorough knowledge of the product or service and an understanding of the potential customer's needs. For this reason, many businesses (such as major retail businesses) employ specialists to compose their sales letters and other promotional material. However, if you are employed in a small business or are self-employed, you may need to write sales letters yourself.

An effective sales message accomplishes four tasks:

1. It catches the reader's attention.
2. It arouses the reader's interest.
3. It convinces the reader that your product or service will fulfill a need or desire.
4. It confidently asks the reader to take the course of action you suggest.

Your first task is to determine your audience: those who should receive your letter or other material. One good source of names is a list of customers; people

IVY COLLEGE

DEPARTMENT OF BUSINESS
WEST LAFAYETTE, IN 47906
(691) 423-1719

(691) 423-2239 (FAX)
IVCO@IC.EDU (EMAIL)

January 14, 20--

Mr. Phillip Lester
Director of Human Resources
Thompson Enterprises
201 State Street
Springfield, IL 62705

Dear Mr. Lester:

As her employer and her former professor, I am happy to have the opportunity to recommend Kerry Hawkins. I've known Kerry for the last four years, first as a student in my class and for the last year as a research assistant.

Kerry is an excellent student, with above-average grades in our program. On the basis of a GPA of 3.6 (A = 4.0), Kerry was offered a research assistantship to work on a grant under my supervision. In every instance, Kerry completed her library search assignment within the time agreed upon. The material provided in the reports Kerry submitted met the requirements for my work and more. These reports were always well written. While working 15 hours a week on this project, Kerry has maintained a class load of 12 hours per semester.

I strongly recommend Kerry for her ability to work independently, to organize her time efficiently, and to write clearly and articulately. Please let me know if I can be of further service.

Sincerely yours,

Michael Paul

Michael Paul
Professor of Business

How long writer has known applicant and the circumstances

Outstanding characteristics of applicant

Recommendation and summary of qualifications

Figure 9–7 **Reference Letter**

WRITER'S CHECKLIST: Writing Effective Sales Letters

After you decide whom your mailing list will include, prepare your sales letter carefully, keeping the reader's interests and the following points in mind.

☐ Attract your reader's attention and arouse his or her interest in the opening. Start out, for example, by describing a feature of the product or service that you believe would appeal strongly to your reader's needs. A representative of a company that installs home insulation might use the following opening, in a letter addressed to "Dear Homeowner."

  ■ If you think that home insulation is a good idea but too expensive, think again. With the money you'll save from lower fuel bills, energy rebates, and increased comfort, you'll find our insulating package a real bargain.

☐ Be careful, of course, that any claim you make in a sales letter is valid. Mail fraud carries heavy legal penalties. Make no claims that are not true. Be careful of overstatement. If you say that a product is safe, you could be guaranteeing its absolute safety. Therefore, say that the product is safe *provided that normal safety precautions are taken.*

☐ Present evidence to convince your reader that your product or service is everything you claim it to be. You can offer a money-back guarantee, a free trial use of your product, testimonials, and case histories, among other things. Don't exaggerate; you will lose your reader's confidence if your claims sound unreasonable. Don't speak negatively of a competitor — you could be accused of using unfair tactics.

☐ Minimize the negative effect price can have on your reader. You might mention the price along with a reminder of the benefits; state the price in terms of a unit rather than a set ($5 per item instead of $60 per set); identify the daily, monthly, or even yearly cost based on the estimated life of the product; suggest a series of payments rather than the total; or compare the cost with that of something the reader accepts readily ("costs the same as a movie and a dinner out").

☐ Suggest ways that the reader can make immediate use of the product or service. A sales letter from a men's store might give instructions for tying neckties and measuring neck size for shirt purchases.

☐ Make it easy and worthwhile for the customer to respond. You might include a local street map showing how to get to your store, a discount coupon, instructions for convenient phone-in orders and free delivery, or a Web address where the customer can find more information, view special discounts, and order online.

who have at some time purchased a product or service from you may do so again. Other sources are lists of people who may be interested in certain products or services. Companies that specialize in marketing techniques compile such lists from the membership rolls of professional associations, fraternal and religious organizations, lists of trade-show attendees, and the like. Because outside lists tend to be expensive, select them with care.

Once you determine who is to receive your sales letter, learn as much as you can about your readers. Knowledge of their sex, age, vocation, geographical location, educational level, financial status, and interests will help determine your approach. You must be aware of your readers' needs so you can effectively tell them how your product or service will satisfy those needs.

Analyze your product or service carefully to determine your strongest psychological sales points. Psychological selling involves promoting a product's intangible benefits rather than its physical features. Select the most important psychological selling point about your product or service, and build your sales letter around it. Show how your product or service will make your reader's job easier, increase his or her status, make his or her personal life more pleasant, and so on. The body of the letter should show how your product or service can satisfy the need or desire identified in your opening. Then describe the physical features of your product in terms of their benefit to your reader. Help your reader imagine him- or herself using your product or service—and enjoying the benefits of doing so.

Figure 9–8 shows a typical sales letter. Notice that it is written in a light, friendly tone—sales letters from small, local businesses frequently adopt that tone because their purpose is to make the reader feel comfortable about coming to them. Note that such sales letters are sometimes signed not by an individual but by the shop itself, as is the case in this example.

Notice that the sales message in the email in Figure 9–9 uses an informal but professional tone to make the reader feel comfortable while instilling confidence in the company's ability to provide timely and useful information. The link at the bottom makes it easy for the reader to respond.

■ Sensitive and Negative Messages

Writing sensitive or negative messages requires careful thought. You must decide, for example, how direct or indirect your message should be and what words you need to choose to maintain a professional relationship with a correspondent under sometimes difficult circumstances. Although each of the following sections provide useful strategies, you should also review Negative Messages and the Indirect Pattern on pages 275–280 as well as Tone: Goodwill and the "You" Viewpoint on pages 272–275 in Chapter 8.

Janice's Cycle Shop
775 First Avenue
Ottumwa, IA 52501
(515) 273-5111

April 3, 20--

Mr. Raymond Sommers
350 College Place
Sharpsville, IA 52156

Dear Mr. Sommers:

Are you ready to go bike riding this spring—but your bike isn't?

Janice's Cycle Shop is ready to get your bike in shape for the beautiful days ahead. We will lubricate all moving parts; check the tires, brakes, chain, lights, horn, and all other accessories; and make any minor repairs—all for only $29.95 with the coupon enclosed with this letter.

Just stop in any day, Monday through Saturday, between 8:00 a.m. and 9:00 p.m. We are conveniently located at the corner of First and Walker. You can pay with cash, check, or credit card.

If you bring your bike in before 10:00 a.m., you can enjoy a spring bike ride that evening.

Happy riding!

Janice's Cycle Shop

Fax: (515) 273-5511   Janice@nc2.com

Figure 9–8   Sales Letter (from a Small Company)

From: WSJ.COM Editors [update@LISTSERV.DOWJONES.COM]
Sent: Monday, January 31, 20-- 2:41 PM
To: NEW_FEATURES@LISTSERV2.DOWJONES.COM
Subject: Now Available: Personalized E-mail Lets You Track Companies, Top News

---

NEW FEATURES
from The Wall Street Journal Interactive Edition.

Dear Subscriber:

I wanted to let you know that personalized e-mail, the new service we told you about last week, is now available.

It takes just a minute to sign up for your daily delivery, which gives you one-click access to all the WSJ.com articles behind the headlines. Each delivery includes top news as well as the most recent news on and quotes for companies you include in your own, personalized Watch List.

I believe you'll find that personalized e-mail is a great complement to your WSJ.com subscription, helping to ensure that you never miss a story that's important to you. To sign up, visit:

http://home.strategy.com/wsj/signup.asp

Sincerely,
Neil F. Budde
Editor and Publisher
WSJ.com

Figure 9–9 Sales Email (from a Large Company)   Reprinted by permission of Dow Jones & Company, Inc. All rights reserved.

Refusals

When you receive a request or any correspondence to which you must give a negative reply, you may need to write a refusal in the form of a letter, memo, or email message. As discussed in Chapter 8, such a message is difficult to write because it contains bad news that a reader does not want to receive.

Your writing should lead logically to the refusal. Unless the stakes for the reader are very low, stating the bad news in your opening can affect your reader negatively. The ideal refusal says *no* in such a way that you not only avoid antagonizing your reader but also manage to maintain goodwill. To do so, you must convince your reader that your reasons for refusing are logical or understandable *before* you present the bad news. The following pattern is an effective way to deal with this problem:

1. *Context.* In the opening, introduce the subject and establish a professional tone.
2. *Explanation.* Review the facts that lead logically to the bad news.
3. *Bad news.* Give the refusal, based on the facts, but do not belabor the bad news or apology.
4. *Goodwill.* In the closing, establish or reestablish a positive relationship.

Figure 9–10 shows a memo rejecting an internal proposal.

The primary purpose of the opening is to establish a professional tone and introduce the subject. In the case of a rejected proposal, you can express appreciation for your reader's time, effort, or interest, if appropriate and genuine, to lessen the disappointment.

Figure 9–10 Memo Rejecting an Internal Proposal (continues through page 341)

Memo

To: Darrell Munro
From: Amelia Jackson, Screening Procedures Committee   *AJ*
Date: May 15, 20--
Subject: Response to Proposed Security-Clearance Procedures

The Screening Procedures Committee appreciates very much the time and effort you spent on your proposal for a new security-clearance procedure.

Next, analyze the circumstances of the situation sympathetically. Place yourself in your reader's position and try to see things from his or her point of view. Clearly establish the reasons you cannot do what the reader wants—even though you have not yet said you cannot do it. A good explanation should so thoroughly detail the reasons for your refusal that the reader will accept your refusal as a logical conclusion.

Figure 9–10 (continued)

We reviewed the potential effects of implementing your proposed security-clearance procedure on a companywide basis. We asked the Systems and Procedures Department to review the data, survey industry practices, seek the views of senior management and department heads, and submit the idea to our legal staff. As a result of this process, we have reached the following conclusions:

- The cost savings you project are correct only if the procedure could be universally required.
- The components of your procedure are legal, but most are not widely accepted by our industry.
- Based on our survey, some components could alienate employees who would perceive them as violating an individual's rights.
- Enforcing companywide use would prove costly and impractical.

Don't belabor the bad news—state your refusal quickly, clearly, and as positively as possible.

Figure 9–10 (continued)

For these reasons, the committee recommends that divisions continue their current security screening procedures.

Close your message in a way that reestablishes goodwill. You might provide an option, offer a friendly remark, assure the reader of your high opinion of his or her product or service, or merely wish the reader success.

Figure 9–10 (continued)

Because some components of your procedure may apply in certain circumstances, we would like to feature your ideas in the next issue of *The Guardian.* I have asked the editor to contact you next week. On behalf of the committee, thank you for the thoughtful proposal.

Refusals often vary in what is at stake for the writer or reader because of specific circumstances. The refusal in Figure 9–11 declines an invitation to speak and the stakes for the writer are relatively low; however, the writer wishes to acknowledge the honor of being asked to speak. Figure 9–12 shows a letter refusing a job offer in which the stakes are slightly higher for both the writer and the reader. Figure 9–13 shows a letter rejecting a job applicant. Finally, Figure 9–14 shows a refusal letter sent to a supplier whose product was not selected, yet the writer wishes to maintain a harmonious business relationship.

WATASHAW ENGINEERING COMPANY

301 Industrial Lane
Decatur, IL 62525
Phone: (708) 222-3700
Fax: (708) 222-3707

March 28, 20--

Javier A. Lopez, President
TNCO Engineering Consultants
9001 Cummings Drive
St. Louis, MO 63129

Dear Mr. Lopez:

Positive context

I am honored to have been invited to address your regional meeting in St. Louis on May 17. That you would consider me as a potential contributor to such a gathering of experts is indeed flattering.

Review of facts and refusal

On checking my schedule, I find that I will be attending the annual meeting of our parent corporation's Board of Directors on that date. Therefore, as much as I would enjoy addressing your members, I must decline.

Goodwill close

I have been very favorably impressed over the years with your organization's contributions to the engineering profession, and I would welcome the opportunity to participate in a future meeting.

Sincerely,

Ralph P. Morgan

Ralph P. Morgan
Research Director

RPM/lcs

Figure 9–11   Letter Refusing a Speaking Invitation

127 Idlewild Rd.
Boston, MA 02173
October 17, 20--
(617) 276-1859

Ms. Juanita Perez, Director
Human Resources Department
National Insurance Company
P.O. Box 4133
Boston, MA 02101-4133

Dear Ms. Perez:

I am pleased to receive your offer of employment as an Administrative Assistant in the Executive office. I was favorably impressed with your company and with the position as you described it.

Positive context

Since interviewing with you, however, I have been offered another position that is even more in line with my long-range goals and have accepted that position.

Review of facts and refusal

Thank you for your time and consideration. I enjoyed meeting with you and your staff.

Goodwill close

Sincerely,

Jason L. Wytosh

Jason L. Wytosh
jwytosh@execpc.com

Figure 9–12 Letter Refusing a Job Offer

Liberty Associates
3553 West Marshall Road
San Diego, California 92101

Phone: (619) 555-1001
Fax: (619) 555-0110
Email: invest@exec.com

Ms. Sonja Yadgar
2289 South 63rd Street
Hartford, CT 06101

Dear Ms. Yadgar:

Positive context

Thank you for your interest in financial counseling at Liberty Associates. I respect your investment experience and professionalism, and I enjoyed our conversation.

Review of facts and refusal

Shortly after our meeting, a well-qualified internal candidate applied for the position, and we have decided to offer the job to that individual. I say in all honesty that the decision was very difficult. Both Nancy Linh and I were impressed with your qualifications and believe that you have a great deal to offer our profession.

Goodwill close

Please do stay in touch. Best wishes for the future.

Sincerely,

Meike Künkel

Meike Künkel
Vice President
Director of Development

MK:ls

Figure 9–13   Letter Rejecting a Job Applicant

MARTINI BANKING AND DATA SYSTEMS

251 West 57th Street
New York, New York 10019
Phone: (212) 555-1221   Fax: (212) 555-2112
email: martini@nynet.com

11 February 20--

Mr. Henry Coleman
Abbott Office Products, Inc.
P.O. Box 544
Detroit, MI 48206

Dear Mr. Coleman:

Thank you for your cooperation and your patience with us as we struggled to reach a decision. We believe our long involvement with your company indicates our confidence in your products.

Positive context

Based on our research, we found that the Winton Check Sorter has all the features that your sorter offers and, in fact, has two additional features that your sorter does not. The more important one is a back-up feature that retains totals in its memory, even if the power fails. The second additional feature is stacked pockets, which are less space-consuming than the linear pockets on your sorter. After much deliberation, therefore, we have decided to purchase the Winton Check Sorter.

Review of facts and refusal

Although we did not select your sorter, we were very favorably impressed with your system and your people. Perhaps we will be able to use other Abbott products in the future.

Goodwill close

Sincerely,

Muriel Johansen

Muriel Johansen
Business Manager

Visit our Web site at http://www.martini.com

Figure 9–14   Letter Rejecting an External Proposal

Complaints

The best complaint letters do not sound complaining. That statement may sound contradictory, but it's not. By the time it becomes necessary for you to write a complaint letter (sometimes called a "claim letter"), you may be irritated and angry. If you write a letter that reflects only your annoyance and anger, you may not be taken seriously—you may simply seem petty and irrational.

Remember, too, that the person who receives your complaint may not be the one who was directly responsible for the situation about which you are complaining. An effective letter should assume that the recipient will be conscientious in correcting the problem.

Although the circumstances and severity of the problem may vary, effective complaint letters generally follow this pattern.

1. They identify the faulty item or items and include relevant information such as invoice numbers, part names, and dates, as well as a copy of the bill or contract.

2. They explain logically, clearly, and specifically what went wrong—especially for a problem with a service. (Avoid expressing an opinion of why you *think* some problem occurred if you have no way of knowing.)

3. They state what you expect the reader to do to solve the problem to your satisfaction.

Large organizations often have special departments called Customer Service, Consumer Affairs, or Adjustments to handle complaints. If you address your correspondence to one of these departments, it should reach someone in the company who can help you. In smaller organizations, you might write to a vice president in charge of sales or service. For very small businesses, write directly to the owner. As a last resort, you may find that sending copies of a complaint letter to more than one person in the company will get fast results. Each employee who receives the letter will know (because of the notation at the bottom of the page) that others, possibly higher in the organization, have received the letter and will take note of whether the problem is solved. Figure 9–15 shows a typical complaint letter.

BAKER MEMORIAL HOSPITAL

Diagnostic Services Department
501 Main Street
Springfield, OH 45321
(513) 683-8100
Fax (513) 683-8000

September 23, 20--

Manager, Customer Relations
Computer Solutions, Inc.
521 West 23rd Street
New York, NY 10011

Subject: HV3 Monitors

On July 9, I ordered nine HV3 monitors for your model MX-15 scanner. The monitors were ordered from your Web site.

An August 2, I received from your Newark, New Jersey, parts warehouse seven HL monitors. I immediately returned these monitors with a note indicating the mistake that had been made. However, not only have I failed to receive the HV3 monitors I ordered, but I have also been billed repeatedly.

Would you please either send me the monitors I ordered or cancel my order. I have enclosed a copy of my original order letter and the most recent bill.

Sincerely,

Paul Denlinger

Paul Denlinger
Manager
pld@baker.org

Enclosures

www.baker.org

Figure 9–15   Complaint Letter

Adjustments

An adjustment letter is written in response to a complaint and tells the customer what your company intends to do about the complaint. You should settle such matters quickly and courteously, and always try to satisfy the customer at a reasonable cost to your company.

Although sent in response to a problem, an adjustment letter actually provides an excellent opportunity to build goodwill for your company. An effective adjustment letter both repairs the damage that has been done and restores the customer's confidence in your company.

Grant adjustments graciously; a settlement made grudgingly will do more harm than good. The tone of your correspondence is critical. No matter how unreasonable the complaint, your response should be positive and respectful. Avoid emphasizing the unfortunate situation; instead, focus on what you are doing to correct it. Not only must you be gracious, you must also acknowledge the error in such a way that the buyer will not lose confidence in your company.

Before granting an adjustment to a claim for which your company is at fault, you must determine what happened and what you can do to satisfy the customer. Be certain that you are familiar with your company's adjustment policy. In addition, be careful about your wording; for example, "we have just received your letter of May 7 about our *defective product*" could be ruled in a court of law as an admission that the product is, in fact, defective. Treat every claim individually, and lean toward giving the customer the benefit of the doubt. An adjustment letter in which the company acknowledges it is at fault is shown in Figure 9–16.

Sometimes you may decide to grant a partial adjustment, even though the claim is not really justified, as in Figure 9–17. You would do that only to regain the lost goodwill of the customer.

You may sometimes need to educate your reader about the use of your product or service. Customers sometimes submit claims that are not justified, even though the customers honestly believe them to be (for example, a problem resulting from a customer not following prescribed maintenance instructions properly). You would grant such a claim only to build goodwill. When you write a letter of adjustment in such a situation, it is wise to give the explanation before granting the claim—otherwise, your reader may never get to the explanation. If your explanation establishes customer responsibility, be sure to do so tactfully. Figure 9–18 is an example of such an educational adjustment letter.

AmericanAirlines®

EXECUTIVE OFFICE

September 26, 20--

Ms. Elizabeth Shapiro
2374 N. Kenwood Ave.
Fresno, CA 93650

Dear Ms. Shapiro:

We are sorry that your daughter's and granddaughter's travel with us did not go smoothly. Providing dependable service is what's expected of us—and when we don't operate flights on schedule, it's easy to understand our customers' disappointment. I truly wish we had performed better and that their plans had not been disrupted.

We are eager to restore your confidence in our ability to provide dependable, high-quality service. Please accept the enclosed transportation voucher which you may apply toward future tickets on American. I hope we will have the pleasure of welcoming your family aboard again soon.

Ms. Shapiro, in addition, we appreciate your taking the time to write. It helps to receive comments such as yours, and we conscientiously follow through to be sure proper procedures are met. I assure you your letter is being put to good use.

Yours truly,

Ms. M. J. Matthews

Ms. M. J. Matthews
Executive Office

P.O. Box 619612, MD 2400, Dallas/Fort Worth Airport, Texas 75261-9612
817-967-2000   http://www.amrcorp.com/corp_con.htm

Figure 9–16   Adjustment Letter When Company Is at Fault   *Source:* Reprinted by permission of American Airlines, AMR Corporation, Inc. All rights reserved.

Computer Solutions, Inc.
521 West 23rd Street
New York, NY 10011

Customer Relations
Phone: (212) 574-3894
Fax: (212) 574-3899
ssiegel@compsol.com

September 28, 20--

Mr. Fred J. Swesky
7811 Ranchero Drive
Tucson, AZ 85761

Dear Mr. Swesky:

Thank you for your letter regarding the replacement of your CS5 Portable PC.

You said in your letter that you used the unit on an open deck. As our service representative pointed out, this model is not designed to operate in extreme heat. As the instruction manual accompanying your new CS5 states, such exposure can produce irreparable damage. Because your unit was used in such extreme heat conditions, we cannot honor the warranty.

However, we are enclosing a certificate entitling you to a trade-in allowance equal to your local CSI dealer's markup for the unit. This means you can purchase a new unit at wholesale, provided you return your original unit to your local dealer.

Sincerely yours,

Susan Siegel

Susan Siegel
Assistant Director

SS/mr
Enclosure

Figure 9–17 Adjustment Letter When the Customer Is at Fault

SWELCO Coffeemaker, Inc.

9025 North Main Street   Phone: 800-233-5656
Butte, MT 59702   Fax: 800-233-3010

August 26, 20--

Mr. Carlos Ortiz
638 McSwaney Drive
Butte, MT 59702

Dear Mr. Ortiz:

Enclosed is your SWELCO Coffeemaker, which you sent to us on August 17.

In various parts of the country, tap water may contain a high mineral content. If you fill your SWELCO Coffeemaker with water for breakfast coffee before going to bed, a mineral scale will build up on the inner wall of the water tube—as explained on page 2 of your SWELCO Instruction Booklet.

We have removed the mineral scale from the water tube of your coffeemaker and thoroughly cleaned the entire unit. To ensure the best service from your coffeemaker in the future, clean it once a month by operating it with four ounces of white vinegar and eight cups of water. To rinse out the vinegar taste, operate the unit twice with clear water.

With proper care, your SWELCO Coffeemaker will serve you faithfully and well for many years to come.

Sincerely,

Helen Upham

Helen Upham
Customer Services

HU/mo
Enclosure

Email: swelco@janus.com   Web: http://www.swelco.com

Figure 9–18   Instructional Adjustment Letter (Accompanying a Product)

> ## WRITER'S CHECKLIST: Writing Tactful Adjustment Letters
>
> Use the following guidelines to help you write adjustment letters.
>
> ☐ Open with what the reader will consider good news:
>
> - Grant the adjustment, if appropriate, for uncomplicated situations ("Enclosed is a replacement for the damaged part").
> - Reveal that you intend to grant the adjustment by admitting that the customer was right ("Yes, you were incorrectly billed for the delivery"). Then explain the specific details of the adjustment. This method is good for adjustments that require detailed explanations.
> - Apologize for the error ("Please accept our apologies for not acting sooner to correct your account"). This method is effective when the customer's inconvenience is as much an issue as money.
> - Use a combination of these techniques. Often, situations that require an adjustment also require flexibility.
>
> ☐ If such an explanation will help restore your reader's confidence or goodwill, explain what caused the problem.
>
> ☐ Explain specifically how you intend to make the adjustment if it is not obvious in your opening.
>
> ☐ Express appreciation to the customer for calling your attention to the situation, explaining that this helps your firm keep the quality of its product or service high.
>
> ☐ Point out any steps you may be taking to prevent a recurrence of whatever went wrong, giving the customer as much credit as the facts allow.
>
> ☐ Avoid recalling the problem in your closing ("Again, we apologize . . ."). Close pleasantly, looking forward, not back.

Resignations

When leaving a job, for whatever reason, you usually write a resignation letter or memo to your supervisor or to an appropriate person in the Human Resources Department. Start a resignation letter on a positive note, regardless of the circumstances under which you are leaving. You might, for example, point out how you have benefitted from working for the company or say something complimentary about how well the company is run. Or you might say something positive about the people with whom you have been associated. For strategies concerning negative messages, see the previous section as well as Chapter 8.

Then explain why you are leaving. Make your explanation objective and factual, and avoid recriminations. Your resignation letter or memo will become part of your permanent file with that company, and if it is angry and accusing, it could haunt you in the future when you need references.

Your letter or memo should give enough notice to allow your employer time to find a replacement. It might be no more than two weeks, or it might be enough time to enable you to train your replacement. Some organizations may ask for a notice equivalent to the number of weeks of vacation you receive. Check the policy of your employer before you begin your letter.

The sample resignation memo in Figure 9–19 is from an employee who is leaving to take a job offering greater opportunities. The memo of resignation in Figure 9–20 is written by an employee who is leaving under unhappy circumstances. Notice that it opens and closes positively and that the reason for the resignation is stated without apparent anger or bitterness.

Memo

To: W. R. Johnson, Director of Purchasing
From: J. L. Washburn, Purchasing Agent *JLW*
Date: January 7, 20--
Subject: Resignation from Barnside Appliances, effective January 21, 20--

My three years at Barnside Appliances have been an invaluable period of learning and professional development. I arrived as a novice, and I believe that today I am a professional—primarily as a result of the personal attention and mentoring I have received from my superiors and the fine example set both by my superiors and my peers.

Positive opening

I believe, however, that the time has come for me to move on to a larger company that can give me an opportunity to continue my professional development. Therefore, I have accepted a position with General Electric, where I am scheduled to begin on January 26. Thus, my last day at Barnside will be January 21.

Reason for leaving

Many thanks for the experience I have gained and best wishes for the future.

Positive closing

Figure 9–19   Sample Resignation Memo (to Accept a Better Position)

Memo

To: T. W. Haney, Vice President, Administration
From: L. R. Rupp, Executive Assistant   *LRR*
Date: February 12, 20--
Subject: Resignation from Winterhaven, effective March 1, 20--

Positive opening

My five-year stay with the Winterhaven Company has been a very pleasant experience, and I believe that it has been mutually beneficial.

Reason for leaving

Because the recent restructuring of my job leaves no career path open to me, however, I have accepted a position with another company that I feel will offer me greater advancement opportunities. I am, therefore, submitting my resignation, to be effective on March 1, 20--.

Positive closing

I have enjoyed working with my coworkers at Winterhaven and wish the company success in the future.

Figure 9–20   Sample Resignation Memo (under Negative Conditions)

Collections

Collection letters are often prepared by attorneys in some states because certain language and requirements must be followed when they demand payment. However, even if you never need to write a collection letter, understanding the collection-letter series offers important insights into strategies for business correspondence. Collection letters serve two purposes: (1) to collect the overdue bill and (2) to preserve the customer relationship.

Most companies use a series of collection letters in which the letters become increasingly demanding and urgent. Even so, collection letters should always be polite; you can demonstrate insistence with the letters' frequency and tone.

A series of collection letters usually proceeds in three stages, each of which may include several letters as well as follow-up phone calls. All letters should be courteous and show a genuine interest in the customer as well as concern for whatever problems are preventing prompt payment.

The first stage consists of reminders stamped on the invoice, form letters, or brief personal notes. These early reminders should maintain a friendly tone that emphasizes the customer's good credit record until now. They should remind the customer of the debt and may even solicit additional business by including promotional material for new sales items. As in the example of a first-stage collection letter in Figure 9–21, you might suggest that nonpayment may be a result of a simple error or oversight.

ABBOTT OFFICE PRODUCTS, INC.

P.O. Box 544
Detroit, MI 48206
Phone: (313) 567-1221
Fax: (313) 567-2112

August 30, 20--

Mr. Thomas Holland
Walk Softly Shoes
1661 East Madison Boulevard
Garfield, AL 36613

Dear Mr. Holland:

With the new school year about to begin, your shoe store must be busier than ever as students purchase their back-to-school footwear. Perhaps in the rush of business you've overlooked paying your account of $742.00, which is now 60 days overdue.

Enclosed is our fall sales list. When you send in your check for your outstanding account, why not send in your next order and take advantage of these special prices.

Sincerely,

Henry Bliss

Henry Bliss
Sales Manager

http://www.abbott.com

Figure 9–21   First-Stage Collection Letter

In the second stage, the collection letters are more than just reminders. You now assume that some circumstances are preventing payment. Ask directly for payment, and inquire about possible problems, perhaps inviting the customer to discuss the matter with you. You might suggest an optional installment payment plan if you are able to offer one. Mention the importance of good credit, appealing to the customer's feeling of pride, self-esteem, and sense of fairness. Remind the customer that he or she has always received good value from you. Make it easy to respond by enclosing a return envelope or by offering a toll-free telephone or fax number or a Web address where the payment can be made. At this stage, your tone should be firmer and more direct than in the early stage, but never rude, sarcastic, or threatening. Notice how the second-stage letter shown in Figure 9–22 is more direct than the first-stage letter, but no less polite.

The third stage of collection letters reflects a sense of urgency, for the customer has not responded to your previous letters. Although your tone should remain courteous, make your demand for payment explicit. Point out how reasonable you have been, and urge the customer to pay at once to avoid legal action. Again, make it easy to respond by providing a return envelope, a toll-free telephone or fax number, or perhaps a Web address where the customer can pay with a credit card. An example of a third-stage letter is shown in Figure 9–23.

ABBOTT OFFICE PRODUCTS, INC.

P.O. Box 544
Detroit, MI 48206
Phone: (313) 567-1221
Fax: (313) 567-2112

December 1, 20--

Mr. Thomas Holland
Walk Softly Shoes
1661 East Madison Boulevard
Garfield, AL 36613

Dear Mr. Holland:

We are concerned that we have not heard from you about your overdue account of $742.00 even though we have written three times in the past 90 days. Because you have always been one of our best customers, we have to wonder if some special circumstances have caused the delay. If so, please feel free to discuss the matter with us.

By sending us a check today, you can preserve your excellent credit record. Because you have always paid your account promptly in the past, we are sure that you will want to settle this balance now. If your balance is more than you can pay at present, we will be happy to work out mutually satisfactory payment arrangements.

Please use the enclosed envelope to send in your check, or call (800) 526-1945, toll-free, to discuss your account.

Sincerely,

Henry Bliss

Henry Bliss
Sales Manager

http://www.abbott.com

Figure 9–22   Second-Stage Collection Letter

ABBOTT OFFICE PRODUCTS, INC.

P.O. Box 544
Detroit, MI 48206
Phone: (313) 567-1221
Fax: (313) 567-2112

March 1, 20--

Mr. Thomas Holland
Walk Softly Shoes
1661 East Madison Boulevard
Garfield, AL 36613

Dear Mr. Holland:

Your account in the amount of $742.00 is now 180 days overdue. You have already received a generous extension of time and, in fairness to our other customers, we cannot permit a further delay in payment.

Because you have not responded to any of our letters, we will be forced to turn your account over to our attorney for collection if we do not receive payment immediately. Such action, of course, will damage your previously fine credit rating.

Why not avoid this unpleasant situation by sending your check in the enclosed return envelope within 10 days or by calling (800) 526–1945 to discuss payment.

Sincerely,

Henry Bliss

Henry Bliss
Sales Manager

http://www.abbott.com

Figure 9–23   Third-Stage Collection Letter

CHAPTER 9 SUMMARY: Types of Business Correspondence

This chapter covers the typical reasons for writing business correspondence in two general categories: messages that are routine or positive and messages that are sensitive or negative. Evaluate correspondence that you send according to the principles of this chapter.

Routine and Positive Messages

☐ *Acknowledgments* build goodwill with colleagues and clients by confirming the arrival of something they sent and expressing thanks. (See page 325.)

☐ *Covers* (or *transmittals*) accompany material sent to a recipient with a message that identifies an item and why it is being sent. (See pages 327–328.)

☐ *Inquiries and responses* state clearly and concisely what information is wanted, who wants the information, and why the information is wanted. Answer inquiries by responding to all the sender's questions or forwarding the inquiry to someone who can. (See pages 328–333.)

☐ *Recommendations* evaluate the professional accomplishments and personal characteristics of someone seeking employment. (See page 334.)

☐ *Sales and promotions* attract the reader's attention to a product, service, or business by arousing the interest, emphasizing the benefits of a product or service, and inviting readers to respond. (See pages 334–337.)

Sensitive and Negative Messages

☐ *Refusals* deny requests or give negative replies while working to maintain goodwill. Use an indirect pattern in which facts lead to a clear refusal followed by some level of goodwill. (See pages 339–345.)

☐ *Complaints* use a professional tone and logical approach indicating that a situation must be corrected. (Avoid whining or sounding angry.) (See pages 346–347.)

☐ *Adjustments* tell customers how your company intends to redress a complaint and apologize if the company is at fault. (See pages 348–352.)

☐ *Resignations* maintain a positive tone, regardless of the reasons for leaving the job, acknowledging any benefits gained from the work experience. (See pages 352–354.)

☐ *Collections* work to preserve the customer relationship while soliciting payment on an overdue account through messages that become increasingly demanding. (See pages 354–358.)

■ Exercises

1. Write a cover letter for a report or a term paper that you are preparing for another course. Address the letter to the appropriate instructor.

2. The following exercises present situations in which you are asked to respond with different types of correspondence. For the events described, write the letters, memos, or emails assigned by your instructor. In all exercises, follow the proper format for business letters. Use the format shown in Figure 9–1 for email messages.

   a. Assume that you are writing a letter requesting a free booklet that explains how college students can apply for special scholarships to study abroad. You must write to an organization called the Global Initiative Center at 1012 Third Avenue, New York, NY 10021. You are writing to Nancy Reibold, who is the executive director. You learned about this booklet when you were surfing the Internet but do not recall the specific Web site. You've checked the Global Initiative Center Web site, but there's no mention of such a booklet.

   b. Assume that you are Nancy Reibold in Exercise *a*. You have received the inquiry letter asking for the booklet. You are out of copies at the moment, however, because you have received more requests for the booklet than you had anticipated. You expect to receive more copies of the booklet within two weeks. Your organization will include this information on its Web site next month. Write a response to the inquiry letter explaining the circumstances and telling the reader that you will send the booklet, titled "Study Abroad," as soon as you can—and offering the alternative of downloading a document that you will make available at your Web site.

   c. You are Nancy Reibold's assistant at the Global Initiative Center (see Exercises *a* and *b*). You have just received 10,000 copies of the booklet from the Jones Printing Company, 105 East Summit Street, New Brunswick, NJ 08910. Both you and Nancy Reibold are very angry. When you opened the box containing the booklets, you discovered that several pages of each booklet had been omitted. This is the second printing mistake made by Jones Printing, and the shipment is late as well. Robert Mason, the sales representative for Jones Printing, promised that you would have no problems this time. Nancy Reibold asks you to write a complaint letter to Robert Mason to "get this problem corrected immediately." Write the letter for Ms. Reibold to sign.

   d. Assume that you are Robert Mason (see Exercise *c*). You have received the complaint letter about the printing mistake. After checking, you discover that the booklets sent to the Global Initiative Center had been subcontracted to another printing firm (ILM Printing Company) because of the backlog of printing jobs at Jones. You know that Jones Printing will not be billed for the booklets if you return them to ILM Printing within five working days. You decide that you must write an adjustment letter to Ms. Reibold quickly. You will need to ask her to return the incorrectly printed booklets.

   e. Assume that you are Robert Mason (see Exercise *d*). Send a memo to J. R. Jones, your boss and president of Jones Printing, recommending that ILM Printing Company not be used for future subcontracting work. Use the details from Exercises *a* through *d* to make the memo convincing.

3. You are the manager of Sunny River Resort. Charles James, director of the Sunny River Business League, has written you requesting the use of your lodge for a two-day meeting of his staff. His letter is as follows:

Sunny River Business League

Charles James, Director

200 Federal Street, Suite 7-G
Buffalo, NY 14201
(716) 557-1081

(your name)
(your address)
(your town; state; zip code)

Dear _____:

The Sunny River Business League will hold its annual staff retreat on
June 15–16, 20--. We would like to use your lodge for this two-day
meeting, which will include about 50 staff members.

We would need to use your meeting room from 9 a.m. to 4 p.m. each
day. We would also need a presentation screen, Internet access, a video
player and monitor, a flip chart, and a podium for the various speakers
who will address our group.

Because some of the staff members will stay at the lodge for two days
or more and we will be paying for meals in your dining room, we would
like to use your meeting room free of charge. I'm sure the exposure
your lodge will receive during the two days will more than pay for the
facilities in your meeting room.

Please let me know by December 10 if we can use your lodge.

Sincerely,

Charles James

Charles James
Director

http://www.srbl.com

You will need to write to Mr. James, and you'd like his organization to use your
meeting room, but you have a problem: You charge $250 per day to any group
that uses the meeting room. The room has a number of fixed and variable costs—
you can't afford to give it away. (Hint: You may want to consider the costs required to clean the room, pay for lighting and air conditioning, supply and repair
equipment. Also, what might happen if others knew you had provided the room
at no cost?) Write a letter to Mr. James selling him on the idea of using your lodge

while holding to the position that the $250 fee would apply. Use tact, a positive tone, and persuasive details to write the letter.

4. You are the manager of a small store called Hamon's Fine Clothing. Dr. Klaus Müller, a busy cardiac surgeon, has purchased two suits (total $1,275) from you — and is six months overdue in paying for them. You've already sent several standard-form notices about the late payment. You'll now need to start a series of collection letters, but you want to make the pace slow. You understood, when you gave Dr. Müller a credit line, that he was a well-respected physician in the community. Write a series of collection letters, spacing them appropriately (date the first letter January 2).

5. You are the manager of BT Discount Auto Parts. Jeff Price, a 23-year-old friend of your nephew's, owes $325 for parts. You allowed him to charge his purchase because your nephew said Jeff was reliable and promised to cover Jeff's bill if he didn't pay. It's been two months since the purchase. Your nephew has offered to give you a check, but you prefer to collect the money from Jeff. Write a collection-letter series to Jeff Price starting on July 1.

6. You are Mr. Henry Coleman of Abbott Office Products, Inc., who received the refusal letter in Figure 9–14. After thinking over the situation, write a letter to R. P. McMurphy, Vice President of Engineering (with a copy to Pat Smith, Director of Marketing), recommending improvements in the check sorter (or another office system of your choice). Collect facts by visiting a local office-systems store or examining its catalog.

7. You have recently purchased a local high-end camera store and wish to build your business. You have a mailing list of the previous owner's customers. You understand that many of these customers were unhappy with the previous owner's products and service. You would like to get those customers back. You specialize in the highest quality digital and SLR cameras as well as accessories. When you purchased the shop, you also became an authorized repair service for Nikon and Sony cameras and lenses. You have a partner who is highly qualified both as a photographer and as an expert in digital imaging for commercial and Web applications.

   The community you serve is relatively affluent, but you understand that one of the complaints against the former owner is that he overcharged customers, and was not willing to service what he sold at the store. Your store is located on East Capitol Drive in a section with a wide variety of appliance stores, restaurants, and even a chain electronics retail store that sells cameras but is not known for quality service. You are ambitious and you believe that satisfied customers will improve your business.

   Write a sales letter, addressed to the previous owner's customers, effectively promoting your services. You want to use this letter as the basis for other promotional materials.

8. You are the owner and director of a successful daycare center. Tiny Tots Daycare started with six children and has grown to a capacity of 65 children. The reputation of your center is so high that there is a waiting list of 78 children. As the director and owner of the center, you are now faced with a problem that you have not encountered in your eight years of running the center. You must expel a child

from the center, and it is your responsibility to write a letter to the parents explaining the reasons and your position.

You need to write a letter to Mr. and Mrs. Brady telling them that their four-year-old son, Brett, is being expelled from Tiny Tots. Brett entered your center two months ago and things haven't been the same since. This child gives new meaning to the term "brat." The child is not able to get along with other children. In his two months at Tiny Tots, he has bitten six children (causing one child to require stitches); kicked a teacher; and scratched, hit, and pulled hair on a regular basis. Several parents have threatened to pull their children out of your center if Brett does not leave. You have had several conferences with Brett's parents, but have observed no changes in his behavior. Mr. and Mrs. Brady seemed reasonable and concerned about the future of their son. Write the letter to the Bradys using the pointers suggested for the refusal letter in this chapter. Remember that this is the Bradys' only child, and choose your words carefully.

9. As your instructor directs, write a 300- to 500-word analysis of one of the refusal letters shown as an example in this chapter. Evaluate the letter, describing how each sentence contributes to the refusal-letter strategy.

10. Format is an important component of business-letter writing. The word-processing program of your office software most likely offers templates to be used in formatting various styles of business letters. Common styles include classic, contemporary, or block. Click to open a new file in your word processor and then click on letters and faxes to explore the options available to you. Select a style to compose a brief letter to your instructor in which you evaluate the course. When you have completed your letter, choose an alternate style in which to prepare a second version of your letter. To copy the text of your letter, you may use digital shortcuts, such as cut and paste. Submit both copies of your letter to your instructor.

11. In a brief essay, discuss why you think email will or will not replace the traditional (paper) business letter (sent in hard copy). Relate your essay to your major field of study or occupational interest and give examples of areas that you think will change in the workplace of the future. Be sure to consider all areas relevant to your field, such as customers, clients, suppliers, competitors, technology, and so forth.

■ In-Class Activities

1. As a class, or in collaborative groups, create a made-up situation similar to the one in Exercise 2, *a* through *e*. From the events and details you have developed, assign various types of letters to be completed as your instructor requires.

2. Choose a partner in class. For the next 45 minutes, write a recommendation letter for your partner as part of an application package for an upcoming leadership conference. The conference is sponsored by an Industrial Consortium and is being facilitated by faculty from your university's Organizational Leadership Center. Include in your letter:
   a. How you know the applicant.
   b. Specific leadership skills you have noticed in class about this person.
   c. Why you think he or she would be a good applicant for the program.

    d. What you think the applicant will learn from the conference. Your letter should be no more than one page. To get started on this project, you and your partner should agree on the best system for exchanging information concerning each other's skills, abilities, knowledge, and personal characteristics in relation to leadership training. When you have completed the exercise, exchange your letters with another pair of students and, in the time allotted by your instructor, evaluate with your partner the two letters you receive. Review the letters as if you were part of the selection committee choosing applicants for the retreat. Decide if the recommendation is helpful and write any comments or questions on the letters before you return them to their owners. Your instructor may want to collect the letters.

3. Form groups of five or fewer members. Assume that your company, an office supply business, has just mistakenly sent a letter to all your customers stating that they are entitled to a 20 percent discount off the *total* of their next order. The letter was supposed to have stated that customers could take a 20 percent discount off the most expensive *item* in their next order. After receiving input from all appropriate departments, the company president has decided the business cannot afford to grant a 20 percent discount for customers' entire orders. You have been instructed to draft a letter to your customers explaining the mistake and clarifying that they will be allowed to take 20 percent off the most expensive item, but not 20 percent off of their entire order. Your company president asks that you appeal to your customers' vested interest in your company's ability to keep prices competitive in the long term and advises you to ask for their understanding of the error. Appoint a team leader and, as a group, take no more than 20 minutes to brainstorm the points you will want to include in the letter. During the following 20 minutes, draft your letters individually. As a group, select one letter that best represents your group's ideas.

4. Form a collaborative group of five or fewer members with classmates who are majoring in the same area of study that you are. Appoint a team leader. Assume that you are members of an academic or professional organization in need of funds for a particular project or trip. As a group, come up with a fund-raising event that your organization will sponsor and draft a letter to prospective contributors. Begin by brainstorming a list of services related to your area of study and expertise that your group could offer for the fund-raiser. Then take 20 minutes to draft a letter that does the following:
- Describes your group and its objectives
- Explains why your group is raising money (Perhaps you are raising money for a trip to observe a facility or to participate in a conference related to your area of study. Your group may need money for travel, accommodations, and registration fee.)
- Explains why your group has sent the letter to its recipient (For example, the recipient is likely an alumnus of your organization or supporter of your university.)
- Explains what your group hopes to learn or gain from the trip or project (For example, students of management may visit a successful company to observe its management methods and training system as part of a research project.)
- Makes clear to the reader the benefits of contributing to the fund-raiser—both in terms of the services they will receive and the good that they will do by supporting your trip or project

- Provides specific details of the particular fund-raising services available
- Inspires the reader to want to contribute to the fund-raiser and provides information for doing so

Overall, your letter should catch the attention of your readers, arouse their interest, and convince them that your fund-raiser provides a worthwhile service while raising money for a worthwhile cause.

5. Your class has been asked to organize a three-hour workshop on business writing for your university's continuing education department. As a class, you have discussed this with your instructor and have decided that because of your course loads, your jobs, and other outside responsibilities you are unable to volunteer to conduct a successful workshop at this time. Appoint a class leader or facilitator and a class recorder and, as a group, draft a letter to the Department of Continuing Education explaining why your class cannot help. Begin by brainstorming to develop a list of all points to include in your letter. Remember that the letter should open with an explanation of the context, introducing the subject and establishing the tone. The letter should then explain the facts, provide a refusal based on facts, and conclude with goodwill in order to establish a positive relationship with the department. (Keep in mind that your class's refusal creates a sensitive situation for your instructor and that your instructor will be working again with the Department of Continuing Education in the future.) After you have completed your letter, your instructor may want to give the class feedback.

■ Research Projects

1. Find an actual letter refusing a request or delivering bad news (job-application refusal, denial of credit, and so on) that you believe is unnecessarily blunt. Rewrite the letter using the refusal strategy discussed in this chapter. Submit to your instructor a copy of the original letter and your revision.

2. Write a 300- to 500-word report on how correspondence fosters positive customer relations in business and industry. Your research may include books, journals, and other printed material. You may even want to research one or more companies, in terms of their use of correspondence to attract and keep customers. Discuss styles or techniques that companies use when writing to customers. What factors do companies consider when replying to customers' complaints, for instance? Do companies try to answer every customer's letter? Why or why not? Conclude your report with your own observations.

3. Conduct a personal or telephone interview with someone in business who you know uses letter writing or email to contact customers. Realtors, self-employed service businesses, product representatives, politicians, medical caseworkers, and government employees are examples of possible candidates for an interview. Be sure to prepare a list of questions before the interview and plan on taking no more than 30 minutes of your interviewer's time. Possible questions include the following: Why do you write letters or email your customers or clients? What results do you expect from your letters or email? What writing styles do you find to be most successful? Can you describe a specific scenario in which a letter or email helped to solve a difficult problem? Develop similar questions of your own to ask. When you have completed your interview, write a brief narrative summarizing your findings.

4. Choose one of the following topics:
   a.   How to write effective sales letters. (Or, more generally, how to write persuasively.)
   b.   How to write recommendation letters.
   c.   How to respond to complaint letters.
   d.   How to write effective complaint letters.
   Research printed material to learn what experts have written about your chosen topic. First, write a brief critical analysis of at least three articles on your topic. Compare and contrast the articles and, in conclusion, give your opinion on the article that offers the most helpful advice. Support your analysis with examples from the articles.

5. You are an employee of a large company that is considering in-house daycare. As part of the research committee formed to explore this option, you have been asked to identify three companies that already offer this service to their employees. You are to write to each of the three companies and ask for a description of their service and daycare center. Include questions such as the following:
   a.   How many employees use the daycare service?
   b.   How many children on average use the center daily?
   c.   How many hours a day or night is the center open?
   d.   How many staff persons are employed at the center?
   e.   What is the salary of the director of the center?
   f.   How large is the center in square feet?
   g.   Is the center new construction, or is it a remodeled part of the company's facility?
   h.   Are the company and employees pleased with the daycare center?
   i.   How are the center's operating costs covered?
   You may include any additional relevant questions. Your instructor may ask you to submit the letters in class, or he or she may ask you to write a cover letter to each company stating that this is a class project, in which case you will then send the letters directly to the three companies. If the latter option is chosen, your instructor will advise you on how to compare and present your results. You may choose to substitute an alternative topic such as job-sharing, flextime, or a company menu of benefits that allows employees to select their own benefits.

■ Web Projects

1. a.   Write a brief report on how online companies use email to solicit business and maintain good customer relations. Research the Web, focusing on three or four specific companies that have a significant presence on the Web — perhaps companies with whom you have done business such as an online bookstore or newspaper, for example. Gather as many examples of email from these companies as possible and write a brief critical analysis of each. Include any information about styles or techniques used. Are these emails effective sales tools? Why or why not? Support your views with examples from the texts, and include printouts of the emails with your report.
   b.   Write a brief report on how online companies reply to emails that they receive from customers. Research the Web, focusing on three or four specific

companies that have a significant presence on the Web, and research any printed materials available on this subject. You may even wish to contact the department or individuals responsible for replying to customer correspondence. Include in your report any information you discover about styles or techniques that companies use when replying to customers' emails. What factors do companies consider when replying to customers' complaints, for instance? Do companies try to answer every customer's email? Why or why not? Be sure that your report includes any necessary documentation.

2. You work for a small, budget-conscious company of fewer than 50 employees. Your boss has asked you to investigate one of the items in the following list for possible purchase by your company. Your boss's primary consideration is cost. Using the Web, review information provided by at least three online vendors about the product or service you are interested in. Email the vendors to obtain any further specific information you may need. Which vendor offers the best value? Write a persuasive memo to your boss that explains your recommendation for the product or service. Include key points of your research and support your recommendation with specific details. Possible products and services to investigate include
   - A wireless communication system
   - A company vehicle (for purchase or lease)
   - A computer software package
   - A security system
   - An accounting or other business-related service

3. Think of an issue relevant to your area of study and professional interest that you feel requires new or different legislation. Search Web sites hosted by the federal government or by your state or local government for information on this topic. (A good resource for links to federal sites is hosted by the Federal Interagency Council on Statistical Policy at http://www.fedstats.gov/. Click on "agencies.") After evaluating the issue and possible solutions, based on the information you have gathered, write a persuasive letter to your state senator or representative (or other appropriate official) with your suggestions for changing existing legislation or creating new legislation concerning the issue. Remember to use good sales-letter techniques to persuade your reader. Your letter should include a brief summary of the problem, your solution, and the benefits and practical application of your solution. Be specific and concise when stating your ideas.

4. Search the Web to find sites offering examples of business letters from the past. One such collection is offered by the National Mail Order Association (NMOA). The NMOA site features a portfolio of "20 Winning Letters" that were circulated in 1942 by Prentice-Hall, Inc. These sales letters were originally chosen as winners of the "Better Letter Contest" sponsored by the Business Ideas Service and are presented in order (first-place letter, then second place, etc.) at http://www .nmoa.org/Museum/letters/index.htm. Although more than half a century old and dated in some respects, many of these letters continue to serve as examples of good sales letters.
   a. Print out three to five letters and write a brief analysis on the style, tone, language, and concerns of the letters. Do they follow the principles of good correspondence outlined in this chapter? Are they effective? Why or why not? How are they different from or similar to contemporary business sales correspondence in style, in tone, in language, and in regard to the audience they address? Be specific.

b. Print out three to five letters from the site that seem to you to be particularly dated, and rewrite them so that they are contemporary in style, tone, and language, and geared toward present-day readers. When you hand in your assignment, include printouts of the original letters with your revised letters.

c. Print out three to five letters from the site that you feel presents good examples of sales letters. Select the best example on which to model your own sales letter. When you hand in your assignment, include a printout of the letter that served as your model.

5. Marketing by email is big business on the Internet. Enter the key search terms "email marketing," "online marketing," "Internet marketing," or "Internet email marketing," using at least three different search engines, such as Infoseek, Lycos, Yahoo!, Alta Vista, Excite, or other browsing tools. Locate and review at least three online companies that specialize in Internet email marketing (one such site is Opt-In Email.com at http://opt-inemail.com/). In your review, address the following questions: What do these companies promise to provide the customer? What are the differences or similarities among these companies in terms of their goals and business styles? Why do these companies hire professional writers to develop their sales-oriented email correspondence? Compare and contrast the information offered by the email marketing companies with those offered in Chapter 9. Also, consider the ways in which the sales email is different from or similar to the traditional sales letter.

6. You are part of the management team of a small manufacturing firm. You have been appointed to find a replacement for your company's _____ (select a position from the following list) because the person currently holding this position has resigned:
   a. Human resources director
   b. Accountant
   c. Computer programmer or systems analyst
   d. Computer operator
   e. Quality control engineer
   f. Maintenance engineer
   g. Registered nurse
   h. Attorney
   i. Security supervisor

   You have been asked to search online to find a replacement; however, you are to use no more than thirty minutes each day for a week to conduct your search. Keep a journal of each day's search activities in which you record search engines and keywords you used, sites you found credible and why. Did you find Web pages of individuals searching for the positions? Did you find online employment services you would enlist to help? In your final entry, make a recommendation to the management team as to what the next step in the search process should be. Submit your seven daily journal entries to your instructor.

10 Informal Reports

Reports make up a large part of on-the-job communication. The successful operation of many firms depends on reports that either circulate within the company or are submitted to customers, clients, and others with whom a company does business. It would be difficult, in fact, to find a job in business or industry that did not require, at least on occasion, the writing of reports.

What is a report? Although the term is used to refer to hundreds of different types of written communication, it can be defined as an organized presentation of information, serving an immediate and practical purpose by furnishing requested or needed data.

Reports fall into two broad categories: *formal reports* and *informal reports.* Formal reports, which are explained in detail in Chapter 13, generally grow out of projects that require many months of work, large sums of money, and the collaboration of many people. Formal reports, which may run several hundred pages, are usually accompanied by a letter of transmittal to the recipient; frequently, such reports have a table of contents and other devices to aid the reader. Informal reports, however, normally run from a few paragraphs to a few pages and include only the essential elements of a report (introduction, body, conclusions, and recommendations on occasion). They are used to report on shorter projects that typically take only a few hours or days to complete. Informal reports (the subject of this chapter), because of their brevity, are customarily written as a letter (if the report is to be sent outside the company) or as a memo (if it is to be distributed within the firm). (See Chapters 8 and 9 for advice on how to write and format letters and memos.)

■ Writing the Report

If you must write a report on an activity in which you are participating (a special project, for example), collect information and keep notes as the activity progresses. You may have trouble obtaining all the information later on, when you prepare to write the report.

In determining what notes to take, include all the information that will meet the objective of your report (for example, whatever information will persuade your reader to adopt the plan of action you are proposing) and the needs of your

Voices from the Workplace

Macie Whittington, Amdahl Corporation

Macie Whittington is a director of sales for Amdahl Corporation, a high-technology company that provides computing, data management, and telecommunications hardware, software, and services. She spends much of her time traveling from one district office to another, maintaining a very busy schedule. She consolidates reports from her sales executives into a regional status report on a monthly basis.

"My sales executives do not normally give me an opening and a closing in their monthly reports because I just need the facts, but when I write my report for the Vice President of Sales, I summarize all the activity in an introduction and project what I anticipate happening next month in the closing. If I didn't understand the functions of introductions and closings and know how to use them, I'd spend a lot of time spinning my wheels."

Learn more about Amdahl Corporation at http://www.amdahl.com.

Entry-Level
Kevin Buckley, Office of Massachusetts State Senator Brian P. Lees

Kevin Buckley is a policy advisor for Massachusetts Senate Minority Leader Brian P. Lees. In this capacity, it is his duty to provide up-to-date information on economic, political, and social trends that affect the Commonwealth of Massachusetts.

Kevin says: "There is no such thing as a typical day; I may find myself meeting with a lobbyist, attending a committee hearing, drafting press releases, or helping a constituent. Due to the Senator's demanding schedule, there is not time necessarily to sit down and discuss with him every idea about future legislation, or brief him on a recently released study or an interesting meeting with a business group. Thus, informal reports are an essential component of the office's communication. Informal reports are not only beneficial in an informational capacity, but they can ensure that your voice is heard and can document your activities, letting your boss know how hard you are working. Most importantly, they allow your ideas to be conveyed and reviewed when it is convenient for a boss or coworker who has a hectic schedule.

"One of the lessons that I have learned about the actual drafting of informal reports is that 'less is more.' The key to successful informal reports is to be direct and concise. Make sure that the person reading the report does not have to try and determine what the purpose is; it should be evident. Informal report writing is not the way to demonstrate your creative side; just the particulars are necessary.

"Double-check all figures, statistics, polls, etc. These things are looked at as being infallible; in the event of a misquote or a typo, the rest of your report will be reviewed with a sense of caution. How can your conclusions be correct if you were working with the wrong numbers? The simple answer is that they cannot be; there is no room for error. I frequently ask a coworker to proofread my report before I submit it.

"The care and effort you put into your informal reports will be an indication of how seriously you take your job. Don't let the word 'informal' fool you into thinking that you shouldn't care enough to present a correct and conscientious informal report."

Visit the official home page of the Commonwealth of Massachusetts for information about the state's governmental offices, policies, and publications at http://www.state.ma.us/index.htm.

readers (exactly the information that will enable your reader to understand your proposal and to see its logic and benefits).

The purpose of taking notes is to record, in an abbreviated form, the information that will go into your report. The advantage of taking notes is that you don't have to rely on your memory to recollect every detail at exactly the moment when you need to include it in your report. Be careful, however, not to make a note so brief that you forget what you intended when you wrote it. The critical test of a note is whether, a week later, you are still able to recall all the information and significance that you had in mind when you made the note. (Notetaking is discussed in more detail in Chapter 11.)

Once you have prepared all your notes, organize your thoughts as explained in Chapter 2. If you need an outline, work your notes into the appropriate places. Review the section titled Determine Your Reader's Needs in Chapter 1, especially how to address multiple audiences.

An informal report is almost always intended for one specific reader or for a small group of readers. Because in most cases you will know how much technical background your reader has, you should be able to determine just how much specialized or technical language to use. You should also have a good idea of how much background information you will need to provide for your reader.

■ The Parts of the Report

Most reports that you will be called on to write have at least three, and sometimes four, main parts: the introduction, the body, conclusions, and recommendations.

The *introduction* serves several key functions: It announces the subject of the report, gives its purpose, and, when appropriate, provides essential background information. The introduction should also concisely summarize any conclusions, findings, or recommendations made in the report. Managers, supervisors, and clients find a concise summary useful because it gives them essential information at a glance and helps focus their thinking as they read the rest of the report.

The *body* of the report presents a clearly organized account of the report's subject—the results of a market survey, the results of a test carried out, the status of a construction project, and so on. The amount of detail you include in the body depends on the complexity of the subject and on your reader's familiarity with the subject.

The *conclusion* of the report presents a summary of your findings and tells the reader what you think the significance of those findings may be.

Some reports may contain a final section giving *recommendations*. (Sometimes the conclusions and recommendations may be combined.) In this section, you would make suggestions based on the information you have presented—suggestions, say, for instituting new work procedures, for developing new products or marketing campaigns, for setting up new departmental responsibilities, or for hiring new employees.

DIGITAL SHORTCUTS: Automating the Format of Standard Communication

Your word-processing software will permit you to create and save customized reports, memos, forms, envelopes, and even labels for your routine communications. When you click on **File** and **New**, an options menu of dozens of standard-format templates opens. When you select one, the software prompts you to enter customized personal or organizational information. This information includes names in headings, slogans and page numbers in headers and footers, subject headings throughout a report, addressees in the **To:** lines of memos, routine salutations and closings for correspondence, and the like. You can even enter clip-art images. After you customize the format, you can save it as a template for future use. (The template has its own icon for ease of location.) Each time you open the template, the identical format appears for you to enter new information, saving you the time of creating the same formatting commands over and over.

■ Types of Reports

Because there are so many different types of informal reports, and because the categories sometimes overlap (a trip report, for example, might also be a progress report), it would be unrealistic to attempt to study every type. However, it is possible to become familiar with report writing in general and to examine some of the most frequently written kinds of reports. In this chapter, we will examine the trouble report, the investigative report, the progress (and periodic) report, the trip report, and the test report. If you master the techniques of writing these kinds of informal reports, you should be able to prepare other kinds as well.

Trouble Report

In many kinds of work, accidents, equipment failures, and work stoppages (caused by equipment failures, worker illnesses, etc.) will occur. Every such incident must be reported so that its cause can be determined and any necessary steps taken to prevent a recurrence. The record of an accident or a breakdown, a *trouble report*—also called an *accident report* or an *incident report,* depending on the situation—may even be used by the police or by a court of law in establishing guilt or liability. Because it can be vital in preventing further injury or disruption in service and because it may become legal evidence, a trouble report should be prepared as accurately, objectively, and promptly as possible.

The trouble report should normally be in the form of a memo written by the person in charge of the site where the incident occurred and addressed to his or her superior. (Some companies have printed forms for specific types of trouble reports, but even form reports include a section in which the writer must explain in detail what happened.) On the subject-line title of the memo, briefly state the nature of the incident you are reporting.

SUBJECT   Personal-Injury Accident in Section A-40

Then, after a brief introductory summary, state exactly when and where the accident or breakdown took place. Describe any physical injury or any property damage—no matter how slight—that occurred. Itemize any expenses that resulted from the incident (for example, an injured employee may have missed a number of workdays, or an equipment failure may have caused a disruption in service to the company's customers). Because insurance claims, worker's compensation awards, and lawsuits may hinge on the information in a trouble report, be sure to include precise data on times, dates, location, treatment of injuries, the names of any witnesses, and any other crucial information. Include in the report a detailed analysis of what you believe caused the trouble. Avoid any tone of condemnation or blame. Be thorough, exact, and objective, and support any opinion you offer with facts. Mention what has been or will be done to correct the conditions that may have led to the incident. Finally, present your recommendations for the prevention of a recurrence of the trouble (such as increased safety precautions, improved equipment, or the establishment of training programs). If you are speculating on the cause of the accident, make sure that this is clear to the reader; your guess is no doubt an educated one, but it still should be labeled as a guess.

WRITER'S CHECKLIST: Writing a Trouble Report

- ☐ Who is the audience for the report?
- ☐ Do you need to interview workers or others about the accident or incident?
- ☐ Are your notes thorough enough to accurately summarize the accident or incident?
- ☐ Have you organized your thoughts into a concise outline to guide your writing?
- ☐ Does the introduction state the subject and purpose of the report?
- ☐ Does the body include sufficient detail to lead the reader to the same findings and conclusions that you present?
- ☐ Do the findings and conclusions logically follow from the details described in the body?
- ☐ Do the recommendations make sense based on your conclusions?

Figure 10–1 shows a trouble report written by a safety officer after interviewing all the people involved in an accident.

Consolidated Energy, Inc.

To: Marvin Lundquist, Vice President
          Administrative Services
From: Kalo Katarlan, Safety Officer   *KK*
          Field Service Operations
Date: August 19, 20--
Subject: Field Service Employee Accident on August 7, 20--

An Accident Review was conducted on Friday, August 16, 20--, at the Reed Service Center. The attendees were as follows:

John Markley, Injured Representative

Harry Hartsock, Union Representative

Carl Timmerinski, Employee's Supervisor

Kalo Katarlan, Safety Officer

Marie Sonora, Safety Officer, Field Service Operations

Date of Accident: August 7, 20--

Days of Lost Time: 2

Accident evaluation method

Accident Summary

John Markley stopped by a rewiring job on German Road. Chico Ruiz was working there, stringing new wire, and John was checking with Chico about the materials he wanted for framing a pole. Some tree trimming had been done in the area, and John offered to help remove some of the debris by loading it into the pickup truck he was driving. While John was loading branches into the bed of the truck, a piece broke off in his right hand and struck his right eye.

What happened, who was involved, resulting injury

Accident Details

1. John's right eye was struck by a piece of tree branch. John had just undergone laser surgery on his right eye on Monday, August 5, to reattach his cornea.
2. John immediately covered his right eye with his hand, and Chico Ruiz gave him a paper towel with ice to cover his eye and help ease the pain.
3. After the initial pain subsided, John began to back up his truck to return to the Service Center. Chico reminded John about the pole trailer parked behind his truck and then returned to the crews he was supervising. John continued backing up, without seeing the tree behind him because his visibility was blocked by the tree debris in his truck bed.
4. As John struck the tree, his head struck the back window of the truck, shattering the glass. He was not wearing a safety helmet because he was inside the truck cab.

Accident events in chronological order

Figure 10–1   Trouble Report (Memo with Corrective Actions)

Figure 10–1
(continued)

Lundquist   2   August 19, 20--

5. John returned to the Service Center to report the accident to his supervisor. However, because he had pieces of glass inside his clothes and on his neck, he decided to go home to shower and change clothes. He also used eye drops prescribed to him after his surgery to thoroughly wash his eye.
6. The next day, August 8, John went to Downtown Worker's Care because he was experiencing headaches. He was diagnosed with a bruised eyeball and eyelid. The headaches were caused by his head hitting the rear window of the pickup truck.
7. On Monday, August 12, John returned to his eye surgeon. Although bruised, his eye was not damaged, and the surgically implanted lens was still in place.

To prevent a recurrence of such an accident, the Safety Department will require the following actions in the future:

- When working around and moving debris, such as tree limbs or branches, all service-crew employees must wear safety eyewear with side shields.
- All service-crew employees must always consider the possibility of shock for an injured employee. If crew members cannot leave the job site to care for the injured employee, someone on the crew must call for assistance from the Service Center. The Service Center phone number is printed in each service-crew member's Handbook.
- All service-crew employees must conduct a "circle of safety" check around any vehicle before moving it.

Corrective actions

Investigative Report

Although an investigative report may be written for a variety of reasons, it is most often produced in response to a request for information. You might be asked, for instance, to check the range of prices that companies charge for a particular item, to conduct an opinion survey among customers, to study a number of different procedures for performing a specific operation, to review a recently published work, and so on. You would then present your findings in an investigative report.

An investigative report is usually prepared as a memo within an organization and as a letter if it is prepared by an outside consultant. The results of longer, complex investigations are usually submitted as formal reports. For memo and letter reports, open with a brief introductory summary that includes a statement of the information you were seeking. Then describe the extent of your investigation. Finally, state your findings and any recommendations you have based on the findings.

In the example shown in Figure 10–2, a store manager has investigated three alternative ways of reducing shoplifting in his store and recommended the one most suitable for the store's size and budget. In Figure 10–3, a consulting company reports to the New York Metropolitan Transit Authority on an immediate and inexpensive way to increase subway ridership. This report—sent in the form of a letter—is longer and more comprehensive than the report in Figure 10–2 because of the scope of information covered.

**Figure 10–2
Investigative
Report
(Memo with
Recommenda-
tions)**

Green Department Stores
Memo

To: William Bernardi, Regional Manager
From: Julius Chernoff, Department Manager
Date: September 23, 20--
Subject: Shoplifting Problems at Store E-5150

Introduction

As we have discussed over the last several months, shoplifting problems at Store E-5150 have increased since the store opened one year ago this month. Although we have budgeted $10,000 a year for shoplifting losses, our current losses have exceeded this amount. We have lost $11,800 in merchandise this year based on our monthly inventory check. The rate of loss is increasing and was especially evident during the summer months. It is time to take action to reverse this trend.

Proposed Solutions

My staff and I have researched several different options for preventing or at least minimizing shoplifting in our store. In investigating options available to us, we considered effectiveness, convenience, and price.

Security Guards
We first considered hiring security guards. I met with the president of Hall Security Services on July 25. They are a local security company and have been in business ten years. I also talked to other store managers in the area for which Hall Security provides security services. All of them stated that they are very pleased with the service and its effectiveness. They believe that the presence of uniformed security guards in their stores discourages theft. The managers surveyed report shoplifting reduction rates of from 50 to 70 percent. I can provide you with detailed data from these interviews at your convenience.

If we decide to have one security guard on duty during all store hours, we would pay a flat monthly rate of $1,900. One guard on duty from 4 p.m. until 10 p.m. daily, our busiest hours, would cost $500 a month. We are not considering the option of a night guard because we have not had any problems with break-in burglaries after hours.

*Options
investigated
and
findings*

Security Cameras
We next considered the use of security cameras placed strategically throughout the store. This technique is used in department stores nationwide. The cameras

**Figure 10–2
(continued)**

William Bernardi   2   September 23, 20--

provide a record of thefts in progress and will make prosecuting the shoplifters much easier when they're caught.

The technicians from TSC Inc., a camera service company, visited our store on August 5. They studied the floor plan to determine the most effective placement of cameras throughout the store. They recommend six cameras placed so that we have a view of the whole store at all times. We would need to purchase a single monitor that would display each camera's view on a rotational basis every ten seconds. The monitor would be located in the store manager's office where I or, in my absence, someone I designate, can observe activity throughout the store's retail space. The videotapes can be kept for a week and then reused.

TSC Inc. would install the system and train our employees to operate it. TSC Inc. also provides a five-year on-site service warranty for the cameras and monitor. They make service calls to the store during business hours within four hours of being called. Total cost, including installation, will be $3,000. We were impressed with the knowledge, experience, and professionalism of the TSC representatives. They provided data for stores comparable to ours that showed an average 60 to 75 percent drop in the incidence of shoplifting. I called several store managers where the cameras are in use and they verify these results.

Undercover Employees
The third option examined is the use of undercover employees. This option involves having regular store employees stroll throughout the store as regular shoppers while they monitor customers for shoplifting. We estimate that this option would require two employees each shift. They would alternate between their regular duties, such as stocking shelves, and performing inventory-control tasks. If we also have security guard services, these two units could work in conjunction to help discourage theft.

However, the option has some risks associated with it. It would require that our employees receive training in the legal rights of customers and could potentially put our employees at risk in encounters with criminals. Hall Security Services can provide training over a one-week period at a cost of $1,200 per employee.

Recommendations

After completing our research on these possibilities for theft prevention, my staff and I believe that the best option is the installation of security cameras. After comparing the cost for the system with the amount of merchandise we are losing, we believe that the expense is worth the investment. Once the system is installed, there will be negligible expense in its use and maintenance. Our research shows that theft has declined in more than 90 percent of the stores that have security cameras. Pending our approval, TSC Inc. can install the system in four days. Once installed, we will evaluate the effectiveness of the system on a monthly basis and I will provide you with a monthly status report. I look forward to your assessment of this recommendation.

Recommendations

Bensson and Associates

721 42nd Street
New York, NY 10010
www.banda.com

(212) 933-1212
Fax: (212) 933-5723

March 17, 20--

Mr. Aubrey Powaton, President
The Metropolitan Transit Authority
867 Fifth Avenue
New York, NY 10011

Dear Mr. Powaton:

At the request of the Metropolitan Transit Authority, Bensson and Associates conducted an investigation to determine whether there is a way to increase subway ridership that could be done immediately and inexpensively. This report gives the results of that investigation.

Introduction

Introduction

New York benefits when more people take the city's subways because more riders on public transportation mean fewer people in automobiles on the streets, resulting in less traffic congestion, cleaner air, and quieter neighborhoods; more ridership also generates more revenues and helps keep fare costs down. Unfortunately, the city's transit system has attracted too few riders in recent years because of fare increases, service cuts, the slow pace in rebuilding the system, competition from other forms of transportation, and a weak local economy. A recent study of automobile drivers to find out why they shunned the subway indicated that they wanted more reliable service, easier and cheaper connections, faster trips, less crime and crowding, and clear and useful announcements about system problems.

The "clear and useful announcements about system problems" is an improvement that could be made immediately because it is neither expensive nor time consuming. For the subway to compete with automobiles, the system needs to communicate with passengers in a more straightforward way about disruptions, delays, and improvements—and to recognize that doing so is not an extra or a low priority. Better subway-car announcements could be a simple, inexpensive, do-able part of a strategy of keeping and winning new subway riders.

Figure 10–3 Investigative Report (Letter with Recommendations)

Mr. Aubrey Powaton   2   March 17, 20--

To determine whether clear and useful announcements could be an important part of the campaign to increase ridership, Bensson and Associates recruited 57 volunteers to rate the quality of subway-car announcements during their normal daily commutes. They made 9,088 observations of announcements on 2,420 subway trips between August 1 and October 31, 20--. They rated whether announcements were made that gave the names of upcoming stations and transfer information, as well as whether announcements were made when trains were delayed or service was changed.

Delays and Changes in Service

Subway commuters dread delays and changes in service because they often cause the commuter to be late for work, miss an appointment, or end up in the wrong place. At a minimum, delays and re-routings are stressful—and when poor information or no information about them is forthcoming, they can be worrisome.

We asked our volunteers to rate the announcements made when they were delayed for two minutes or more or when they experienced a change in service. They noted whether any explanation was offered and whether it was clear, garbled, or inaudible. They also evaluated whether announcements were useful. Our commuters experienced delays (ranging from 2 minutes to 30 minutes) or re-routings 179 times, and they found that 67 percent of the time there was either no announcement or one that was garbled, inaudible, or of no value.

Station-Transfer Information

Transit Authority policy requires that station names be announced "as the train is entering the station" and that announcements be made of "connecting services and any and all out-of-the-ordinary transfers." Our commuters were able to evaluate a total of 8,927 station-name or transfer announcements. They were asked to rate (1) whether the conductor announced the name of the subway station at which they stopped at three specified points on their trip (the first stop, the second stop, and the last stop), and (2) whether the conductor announced transfer information at the first transfer point during their trip. In more than a third of the announcement opportunities, our commuters did not receive a clear station name or transfer announcement (announcements either were not made or were garbled and inaudible).

Line-by-Line Results

We analyzed and ranked the announcement practices of conductors on most subway lines in announcing station names and transfer information. We found a large and statistically significant difference between the best and worst practices. The F Train ranked best, and the Number 6 Line ranked worst. Conductors on the F Train performed two-and-a-half times better than those on the Number 6 Line. Of the announcements they were able to evaluate, our commuters received no announcement or a garbled or inaudible announcement 55 percent of the time on the Number 6 Line, compared to 19.5 percent of the time on the F Train.

Method of investigation

Method of investigation

Method of investigation

Findings

Figure 10–3   (continued)

Mr. Aubrey Powaton   3   March 17, 20--

Past Improvement

In 19--, Bensson and Associates conducted a similar survey of subway-car announcements. It did so then because that year the Transit Authority pledged to do a better job of making announcements. There has been both progress and disappointment since then. At that time, delays were announced only 54 percent of the time and changes in service were announced only 17 percent of the time. Nearly 74 percent of delays and changes are announced today, although 55.5 percent of them were garbled, inaudible, or useless. So there has been improvement since 19--, but a great deal more improvement is needed.

Recommendations

The Transit Authority's weak performance in making station-name, transfer, delay, and service-change announcements is costing the Transit Authority ridership. Getting helpful information to commuters does not receive the priority it should from the subway system's management. The experts we spoke to, both within and outside of the Transit Authority, believe the Transit Authority can increase ridership— if it devotes new attention to providing information to the commuter. Following are our recommendations:

Recommendations

1. Convene an internal task force to tackle the announcement problem. The task force should include the following representatives from the Transit Authority: the executive vice president, the chief transportation officer, select conductors, and select train operators. This task force should come up with imaginative ways of improving announcements by a specified date—such as improved training, better command-center coordination, and morning-crew checks—and consult with commuters and commuter groups before implementing its ideas.
2. Make sure that commuters get announcements about short delays. Such delays are often not announced by conductors at present. The task force should present an analysis of why riders do not learn what is going on when there are delays that are not considered "major" by the Transit Authority. These are the two-, three-, and five-minute delays that can mean lateness, missed connections, and general frustration for commuters. These delays often go unnoticed by busy command-center personnel. The task force should also review how information gets to conductors and consider adding personnel at the command center to solve this long-standing problem.
3. Require daily tests of each car's public-address system and repair broken speakers quickly. Nearly a quarter of the time (23 percent), our commuters did not even get a chance to hear announcements; they rated them as inadequate because they were either garbled or inaudible.
4. Urge commuters to inform conductors if speakers are not working. An ad campaign asking commuters to supply information to conductors or to report public-address-system problems by telephone might hasten repairs. The Transit Authority should consider instituting regular tests of the public-address systems,

Figure 10–3   (continued)

Mr. Aubrey Powaton   4   March 17, 20--

perhaps during less-crowded midday hours. At noon, for instance, conductors could make a "test announcement" asking commuters to report problem public-address speakers, along with the car number, to the conductor.

We believe that if the Transit Authority concentrates on solving the problem of clear and useful announcements, ridership will increase for that reason alone. This problem can be tackled immediately and inexpensively. Then the more expensive and time-consuming problems—more reliable service, easier and cheaper connections, faster trips, and less crime and crowding—can be addressed and resolved so that even more automobile drivers will abandon the hassle of driving in downtown New York City and leave the driving to the Transit Authority.

Sincerely,

Henry R. Paxton

Henry R. Paxton, Director
Field Research Group
hrpaxton@banda.com

Figure 10–3   **(continued)**

Progress and Periodic Reports

Progress and periodic reports are similar in that both are used to report on the status of work being performed over the course of a project. The chief difference between them is in how often they are written. The progress report is issued at certain stages or milestones during a project. The periodic report, sometimes called a status report, details the status of an ongoing project at regular intervals—weekly, monthly, quarterly. Both types of reports may be required for work being performed by an organization's own employees or by an outside consultant or contractor.

Progress Reports

The purpose of a progress report is to keep an individual or a group—usually management—informed of the status of a project. In answering various questions (Is the project on schedule? Is it staying within its budget? Is the staff running into any unexpected snags?), the report lets the reader know precisely what work has been completed and what work remains to be done. Often the report will include recommendations for changes in procedure or will propose new courses of action. Progress reports are generally prepared when a particular stage of a project is reached.

The projects most likely to generate progress reports are those that last for a considerable period of time and are fairly complex. The construction of a building, the development of a new product, and the opening of a branch office in another part of town are examples of such projects. Sometimes, too, a progress report is a specified requirement in the contract for a project that will take weeks or months to complete.

The chief value of a progress report is that it allows management not only to check on the status of a project but also to make any necessary adjustments in assignments, schedules, and budget allocations while the project is underway. Progress reports can make it easier for management to schedule the arrival of equipment and supplies so that they will be available when needed. Such reports can, on occasion, avert crises. If a hospital had planned to open a new wing in February, for instance, but a shortage of wallboard caused a two-month lag in construction, a progress report would alert hospital managers to the delay—in time for them to prepare alternative plans.

Many projects, of course, require more than one progress report. In general, the more complicated the project, the more frequently management will want to review it. All reports issued during the life of a project should be of the same format to make it easier for readers to absorb the information. Progress reports to be sent outside the company are normally prepared as letters (see Figure 10–4); otherwise, they can be written as memos. The first in a series of reports should identify the project in detail and specify what materials will be used and what procedures will be followed throughout the project. Later reports contain only a transitional introduction that briefly reviews the work discussed in the previous reports. The body of the reports should describe in detail the current status of the project. Every report should end with any conclusions or recommendations—for instance, alterations in schedule, materials, or procedures.

In the example shown in Figure 10–4, a contractor reports to the city manager on his progress in renovating the county courthouse. Notice that the emphasis is on meeting specified costs and schedules.

Periodic Reports

Periodic reports are issued at regular intervals—daily, weekly, monthly, quarterly, annually—rather than at particular stages in a project. Status reports, submitted by employees about their ongoing projects, are examples of periodic reports.

Quarterly and annual reports, because of their scope, are usually presented as formal reports (see Chapter 13). Most other kinds of periodic reports seldom run longer than a page or two. Like progress reports, these shorter reports are most often written as memos or emails within an organization and as letters when sent to clients and customers outside an organization.

Many kinds of routine information that must be reported periodically—and that do not require a narrative explanation—can be either recorded on forms or entered into computer databases or spreadsheets. Examples include personnel,

Hobard Construction Company
9032 Salem Avenue
Lubbock, TX 79409

www.hobardcc.com
(808) 769-0832
Fax: (808) 769-5327

August 17, 20--

Walter M. Wazuski
County Administrator
109 Grand Avenue
Manchester, NH 03103

Dear Mr. Wazuski:

The renovation of the County Courthouse is progressing on schedule and within budget. Although the cost of certain materials is higher than our original bid indicated, we expect to complete the project without exceeding the estimated costs because the speed with which the project is being completed will reduce overall labor expenses.

Costs

Materials used to date have cost $78,600, and labor costs have been $193,000 (including some subcontracted plumbing). Our estimate for the remainder of the materials is $59,000; remaining labor costs should not exceed $64,000.

Work Completed

As of August 15, we had finished the installation of the circuit-breaker panels and meters, of level-one service outlets, and of all subfloor wiring. The upgrading of the courtroom, the upgrading of the records-storage room, and the replacement of the air-conditioning units are in the preliminary stages.

Work Schedule

We have scheduled the upgrading of the courtroom to take place from August 25 to October 5, the upgrading of the record-storage room from October 6 to November 12, and the replacement of the air-conditioning units from November 15 to December 17. We see no difficulty in having the job finished by the scheduled date of December 23.

Sincerely yours,

Tran Nuguélen

Tran Nuguélen
ntran@hobardcc.com

Figure 10–4   Progress Report (Letter)

accounting, and inventory records; production and distribution figures; and travel and task logs.

Preprinted forms have established formats (see Chapter 12), as do formal reports (see Chapter 13). One- and two-page periodic reports, however, can be organized in a variety of ways. The standard format of introduction, body, and conclusions and recommendations may serve your needs. Otherwise, modify the organizational pattern to suit your reader's reporting requirements.

The sample periodic report shown in Figure 10–5 is sent monthly from a company's district sales manager to the regional sales manager. This periodic report would be sent to the regional sales manager either with a brief cover memo or as an attachment to a brief email. Notice that there is no traditional opening and closing, which are superfluous because the report is routine; that is, it goes to the same person every month and covers the same topics. For this reason, the format and headings do not change from month to month. It also goes to a high-level manager who receives many such reports each month so he does not have time to read unnecessary narrative. Because it is written to someone completely familiar with the background details of the projects discussed, the district sales manager can write a spare narrative with many shorthand references to equipment, customers, and project status. For example, he mentions a "best and final" presentation to Watsorg rather than writing that Rockport, his company, has presented its final sales proposal to Watsorg, Inc., for equipment and services. He need not spell out the details of the project because the regional sales manager is already familiar with them. Such an abbreviated narrative is appropriate for the intended audience.

**Figure 10–5
Periodic
Report**

Rockport
Customer Services
Monthly Report
June, 20--

Mid-Atlantic District

Current personnel: 13
Changes this month: none
Awards/relocations/promotions:
- Alonzo Berg attended the Field Business Conference.
- Dawon Washington was honored by his peers for superior customer satisfaction at Southwest Utility.

Personnel Issues: none

Figure 10–5
(continued)

Monthly Report, Mid-Atlantic District   2   June, 20--

Product Revenue

Customer	Equipment	Maint. $	Notes
Southwest Utility	6650–200	$ 6,200/mo	None
Demeter, Inc.	SVR	$ 800/mo	Installing a new SVR in February
Barg Aerospace	6650–900	$10,000	Installation charge
Barg Aerospace	6650–900	$ 9,000/mo	New monthly maintenance (2 years)

Top Prospects

Customer	Service	Revenue	Odds	Comments
Herndon Bank	PPR	$ 5,600	100%	LAR Services
Southwest Utility	PPR	$10,000	100%	Configuration
MacDonalds	PPR	$10,000	100%	Maintenance
MacDonalds	PPR	$ 6,900	100%	Conversion
Reece Corp.	PPR	$13,000	100%	Upgrades
Reece Corp.	PPR	$ 2,300	100%	Maintenance
Gabbard Mfg.	PPR	$25,000	80%	Cynergy Installation
Gabbard Mfg.	ERCAR	$95,000	50%	ERCAR Upgrades

Competitive Customer or Marketplace News

Charlestown Marketing is still waiting to hear from Bitnolds Metals on a CMOS decision. The odds of our getting this new business are about 25%, as they seem to be happy with Cynergy.

Charlestown Marketing is starting to go outside the greater Charlestown area. Meetings are scheduled with Sailco at the Norfolk Shipyard and BCC in Lynchburg, VA. We will explore potential CMOS or used 6650-2903 opportunities. Plans are to contact at least one new customer a week to try to expand our business.

Cynergy, Inc.'s new maintenance offering is not going over well with some customers. We should be able to take advantage of this.

Watsorg's announcement will be awarded on February 24–28. This is for $18 to $20 million, going either to us or to Cynergy. The problem is that we finished our "best and final" presentation in the first week of February, and Watsorg gave Cynergy an extension to the end of the month. Dragging this out increases Cynergy's odds of winning. However, the last word is that the negotiations are not going well with Cynergy, so we are keeping our fingers crossed.

AREDOT is installing the largest Saki tape library system in the world. The salesman said that Saki had been working with a company to develop a "virtual tape system" when Embry was sold to Jordan. This caused Jordan to not get the contract. We have a question as to why Rockport didn't pursue this business. Saki is supposed to be our partner and Customer Services could use the business.

(continued)

Figure 10–5 (continued)

Monthly Report, Mid-Atlantic District   3   June, 20--

Charlestown Marketing is bidding on some LIPSUM directors at AREDOT after some persuasion from Charlestown Marketing Services. This bid has no service attached and lowest price will most likely win.

Charlestown Customer Services met with a CARL Team Director from Columbus, Ohio, to discuss future services with CARL. He is considering Rockport as the prime contractor for all necessary services in Charlestown. He will base his decision on the cost analysis.

Significant Wins/Accomplishments

Hector Martinez convinced Barg Aerospace to acquire two additional 6650A-900s from us on a rental (loaner) basis with a two-year maintenance contract worth $9,000 per month per machine. The installation team has installed the second 900 and will install the third in coming weeks.

Charlestown Customer Services completed installation of a Cynergy 2063 and a Rockport 1006 at Ft. Lee, VA. We partnered with Rathbone Corporation to win the business.

Product Issues

Lareneg's shortlink dual copy was attempted again and failed, with catastrophic results. The software support center has spent a great deal of time on this problem with no support from the Lareneg customer. Their management is escalating this issue to Isotoru Nagabishi and Will Reynolds. The local Customer Services team is being unduly burdened with costs associated with what seems to be a product problem. The cost of mileage, conference calls, and expenses is significant.

Secard performance issues have continued from last month. We applied new code with high hopes, but no improvement was noted by the customer. Currently, ERT traces are running to gather more information. The customer is getting very concerned with this issue, and they are our only Secard customer in Charlestown.

Trip Report

Many companies require or encourage employees to prepare reports on their business trips. A trip report not only provides a permanent record of a business trip and its accomplishments but also enables many employees to benefit from the information that one employee has gained.

A trip report can be a memo or an email, addressed to your immediate superior. On the subject line, give the destination (or purpose) and dates of the trip. After a brief introductory summary, explain why you made the trip, whom you visited, and what you accomplished. The report should devote a brief section to each major event and may include a heading for each section (you needn't give

**Figure 10–6
Trip Report
(Email)**

Subject: Trip to Smith Electric Co., Huntington, West Virginia, January 20--
To: Roberto Camacho <rcamacho@smithelec.com>
From: James D. Kerson <jdkerson@smithelec.com>
cc:
Date: Tues, 13 Jan 2000 12:16:30

I visited the Smith Electric Company in Huntington, West Virginia, to determine the cause of a recurring failure in a Model 247 printer and to fix it.

Problem
The printer stopped printing periodically for no apparent reason. Repeated efforts to bring it back online eventually succeeded, but the problem recurred at irregular intervals. Neither customer personnel operating the printer nor the local maintenance specialist was able to solve the problem.

Action
On January 3, I met with Ms. Ruth Bernardi, the Office Manager, who explained the problem. My troubleshooting did not reveal the cause of the problem then or on January 4.

Only when I tested the logic cable did I find that it contained a broken wire. I replaced the logic cable and then ran all the normal printer test patterns to make sure no other problems existed. All patterns were positive, so I turned the printer over to the customer.

Conclusion
There are over 12,000 of these printers in the field and to my knowledge this is the first occurrence of a bad cable. Therefore, I do not believe the logic cable problem found at Smith Electric Company warrants further investigation.

==================================
James D. Kerson, Maintenance Specialist
Smith Electric Company
1366 Federal St., Allentown PA 18101
(610) 747-9955 Fax: (610) 747-9956
jdkerson@smithelec.com
http://www.smithelec.com
==================================

equal space to each event but instead, elaborate on the more important events). End the report with any appropriate conclusions and recommendations.

A sample trip report appears in Figure 10–6.

Test Report

The test report, also called the laboratory report when the test is performed in a laboratory, records the results of tests and experiments. Normally, those who write test reports do so as a routine part of their work. Tests that form the basis of reports are not limited to any particular occupation; they commonly occur in many fields, from chemistry to fire science, from metallurgy to medical technology, and include studies on cars, blood, mercury thermometers, pudding mixes, smoke detectors—the list is endless. Information collected in testing may be used to upgrade products or to streamline procedures.

Because the accuracy of a test report is essential, be sure to take careful notes while you are performing the test. When you prepare the report, state your findings in clear, straightforward language. If graphs or illustrations would be advantageous to your reader, use them (see Chapter 12 for guidance). Because a test report should be objective, it is one of the few writing formats in which the passive voice is usually more suitable than the active voice (see Chapter 5). A test report may be written as a letter for a customer or as a memo for work performed in-house.

On the subject line, identify the test you are reporting. If the purpose of the test is not obvious to your reader, explain it in the body of the report. Then, if it is helpful to your reader, outline the testing procedures. You needn't give a detailed explanation of how the test was performed; rather, provide just enough information for your reader to have a general idea of the testing methods. Next, present the data—the results of the test. If an interpretation of the results would be useful to your reader, furnish such an analysis in your conclusion. Close the report with any recommendations you are making as a result of the test.

Figure 10–7 shows a test report that does not explain how the test was conducted because such an explanation is unnecessary. Figure 10–8 shows a test report that does explain how the tests were performed.

**Figure 10–7
Test Report
(Letter)**

BIOSPHERICS Inc.

4928 Wyaconda Road
Rockville, MD 20852
(301) 492-3331
Fax: (301) 492-1832
www.biosphericsinc.com

March 14, 20—

Mr. Luigi Sebastiani, General Manager
Midtown Development Corporation
114 West Jefferson Street
Milwaukee, WI 53201

SUBJECT: Results of Analysis of Soil Samples for Arsenic

Dear Mr. Sebastiani:

The results of our analysis of your soil samples for arsenic showed considerable variation; a high iron content in some of the samples may account for these differences.

Following are the results of the analysis of 8 soil samples. The arsenic values listed are based on a wet-weight determination. The moisture content of the soil is also given to allow conversion of the results to a dry-weight basis if desired.

Hole	Depth	Moisture (%)	Arsenic Total (ppm)
1	12"	19.0	312.0
2	Surface	11.2	737.0
3	12"	12.7	9.5
4	12"	10.8	865.0
5	12"	17.1	4.1
6	12"	14.2	6.1
7	12"	24.2	2,540.0
8	Surface	13.6	460.0

I noticed that some of the samples contained large amounts of metallic iron coated with rust. Arsenic tends to be absorbed into soils high in iron, aluminum, and calcium oxides. The large amount of iron present in some of these soil samples is probably responsible for retaining high levels of arsenic. The soils highest in iron, aluminum, and calcium oxides should also show the highest levels of arsenic, provided the soils have had approximately equal levels of arsenic exposure.

If I can be of further assistance, please do not hesitate to contact me.

Yours truly,

Gunther Gottfried

Gunther Gottfried, Chemist
ggottfried@biosphericsinc.com

GG/jrm

389

BIOSPHERICS
Inc.

4928 Wyaconda Road
Rockville, MD 20852
(301) 492-3331
Fax: (301) 492-1832
www.biosphericsinc.com

April 4, 20--

Mr. Leon Hite, Administrator
The Angle Company, Inc.
1869 Slauson Boulevard
Waynesville, VA 23927

Dear Mr. Hite:

On August 30, Biospherics Inc. performed asbestos-in-air monitoring at your Route 66 construction site, near Front Royal, Virginia. Six persons and three construction areas were monitored.

All monitoring and analyses were performed in accordance with "Occupational Exposure to Asbestos," U.S. Department of Health and Human Services, Public Health Service, National Institute for Occupational Safety and Health, 1995. Each worker or area was fitted with a battery-powered personal sampler pump operating at a flow rate of approximately two liters per minute. The airborne asbestos was collected on a 37-mm Millipore-type AA filter mounted in an open-face filter holder. Samples were collected over an eight-hour period.

In all cases, the workers and areas monitored were exposed to levels of asbestos fibers well below the standard set by the Occupational Safety and Health Administration. The highest exposure found was that of a driller exposed to 0.21 fibers per cubic centimeter. The driller's samples were analyzed by scanning electron microscopy followed by energy-dispersive X-ray techniques that identify the chemical nature of each fiber, to identify the fibers as asbestos or other fiber types. Results from these analyses show that the fibers present are tremolite asbestos. No non-asbestos fibers were found.

Yours truly,

Allison Jones

Allison Jones, Chemist
AJ/jrm

Figure 10–8   Test Report with Methodology Explained (Letter)

CHAPTER 10 SUMMARY: Informal Reports

Much on-the-job writing consists of various kinds of reports. Informal reports, normally no longer than a few pages, may take the form of a memo that circulates within an organization or be prepared as a letter to be sent to someone outside the organization. Informal reports should generally adhere to the following format. Check your informal reports to make sure that:

☐ The *introduction* states the subject and purpose and summarizes your conclusions and recommendations.

☐ The *body* presents a detailed account of the work reported on.

☐ The *conclusion* summarizes findings and indicates their significance.

☐ The *recommendations* of actions you believe should be taken are based on the conclusions.

The following types of informal reports are typical:

☐ Trouble reports

- Identify the precise details, such as time and place of an accident or other trouble.
- Indicate any injuries or property damage.
- State a likely cause of the trouble or accident.
- Specify what's being done to prevent a recurrence, if that's possible.

☐ Investigative reports

- Open with a statement of the information the writer has sought.
- Define the extent of the investigation.
- Present the findings, interpretations, conclusions, and, when appropriate, recommendations.

☐ Progress and periodic reports

- Inform the reader of the status of an ongoing project.
- Alert readers to any necessary adjustments in scheduling, budgeting, and work assignments.

☐ Trip reports

- Include the destination and dates of the trip.
- Explain why the trip was made, who was visited, and what was accomplished.
- State any findings or recommendations based on the purpose of the trip.

☐ Test reports

- State the purpose of the test and indicate the procedures used to conduct the test.
- Indicate the results of the test or experiment and any interpretations helpful to the reader.

■ Exercises

1. Write one of the following trouble reports in the form of a memo.
   a. You are the traffic manager of a trucking company that has had four highway accidents within a one-week period. Using the following facts, write a trouble report to your company president, Millard Spangler.
      - Your company operates in your state.
      - The four accidents occurred in different parts of the state and on different dates (specify the date and location of each).
      - Each accident resulted in damage not only to the truck (specify the dollar amount of the damage) but to the cargo (specify the type of cargo and the dollar amount of the damage).
      - Only one of the accidents involved another vehicle (a company truck swerved into a parked car when a tire blew out). Give the make and year of the damaged car and its owner's name.
      - Only one of the accidents involved injury to a company driver (give the name).
      - Your maintenance division traced all four of the accidents to faulty tires, all the same brand (identify the brand), and all purchased at the same time and place (identify the place and date).
      - The tires have now been replaced and your insurance company, Acme Underwriters, has brought suit against the tire manufacturer to recover damages, including lost business while the four trucks are being repaired (specify the dollar amount of the lost business).
   b. You are the dietitian at a hospital. A fire has occurred in the cafeteria, which is under your supervision. Using the following information, write a trouble report to the hospital's administrator, Mildred Garnett.
      - The chief cook, Pincus Berkowitz, came to work at 5:30 a.m. (specify the date).
      - He turned on the gas jets under the grill. The pilot light had gone out, and the jets did not light.
      - The cook went to find a match, neglecting to turn off the gas jets.
      - He found matches, returned, and lit a match, thus igniting the accumulated gas under the grill.
      - The resulting explosion destroyed the grill (estimate the damage) and injured the cook.
      - The fire was put out by the security force, but the fire department was called as a precaution.
      - The cook was treated by the emergency-room physician, then admitted to the hospital's burn unit as a patient, with second degree burns on his hands, face, and neck.
      - He was hospitalized for three days and will be away from work for four weeks.

2. You are a human-resources specialist assigned to investigate why your company is not finding enough qualified candidates to fill its need for electronics technicians and to recommend a solution to the problem. You have conducted your investigation and determined the following:

- In the past, you recruited heavily from among military veterans, but the downsizing of the military has all but eliminated this source. Want ads are not producing adequate numbers of veterans.
- The in-house apprentice program, which recruits graduating high-school students, has produced a declining number of candidates in recent years because more students are going to college.
- Several regional technical schools are producing very well-trained and highly motivated graduates. Competition for them is keen, but you believe that an aggressive recruiting campaign will solve your problem.

Write an investigative report to your boss, Cynthia Mitchum, Director of Human Resources, explaining the causes of the problem and offering your recommended solution.

3. As the medical staff secretary at a hospital, you must write a progress report to the director of the hospital outlining the current status of the annual reappointment of committees. Using the following facts, write the report:
   - A total of ten committees must be staffed.
   - The chief of staff has telephoned each person selected to chair a committee, and you have sent each of them a follow-up letter of thanks from the chief.
   - You have written letters to all physicians who are currently on committees but are not being reappointed, informing them of the fact.
   - You have written letters to all physicians being asked to serve on committees.
   - You expect to receive replies from those physicians declining the appointment by the 15th of the following month.
   - Once committee assignments have been completed, you will type the membership lists of all committees and distribute them to the complete medical staff.

4. You are a field-service engineer for a company that markets diesel-powered emergency generators. You have just completed a five-day trip to five cities to inspect the installation of your company's auxiliary power units in hospitals. You visited the following hospitals and cities:

   May 26 — New Orleans General Hospital in New Orleans
   May 27 — Our Lady of Mercy Hospital in San Antonio
   May 28 — Dallas Presbyterian Hospital in Dallas
   May 29 — St. Elizabeth Hospital in Oklahoma City
   May 30 — Jefferson Davis Memorial Hospital in Atlanta

   You found each installation to have been properly done. With the cooperation of the administrators, you switched each hospital to auxiliary power for a one-hour trial run. All went well. You held a brief training session for the maintenance staff at each hospital, teaching them how to start the engine and how to regulate its speed to produce 220 volts of electricity from the generator at 60 hertz. You want to commend your company's sales staff and field personnel for creating a positive image of your company in the minds of all five customers you visited. Write a trip report to your boss, José Cruz, Manager of Customer Services.

5. a. Locate a test report that you wrote for a laboratory class that you are taking or have taken. Rewrite the report according to the guidelines in this chapter, and submit it in memo form to your instructor.

      b. Submit a project report explaining any processes or projects that you have re-
cently completed for school, for work, or for your home. Review this chapter
for guidelines for writing project reports.

6. Each of the following topics presents a situation in which a company plans a significance change that could potentially threaten its existing customer base. Select
one of the following topics (or create your own topic based on your area of study
and professional interest) and write a memo in which you offer your recommendations for assuring that the change that your company proposes will not jeopardize its existing customer base. With your customers in mind, make concrete
and specific suggestions for facilitating as smooth and positive a transition as
possible.

    a. Assume that you are part of the management team of a fast-food restaurant
with a "burgers only" identity—and a loyal customer base—that wants to
add distinctive and healthful menu items.

    b. Assume that you are part of the management team for an apparel manufac-
turing firm known for its conservative fashions. Your firm is about to introduce a new line of clothing with a distinctly contemporary appeal.

    c. Assume that you work for a catalog distributor that currently contracts out
their printing. To save money, your boss has decided to move the print operation in-house, where there is limited staff and equipment. However, to cover
the costs of the additional salaries and equipment needed, customers will
have to pay more to purchase the catalog.

    d. Assume that you work for a medical insurance company concerned with the
rising number of medical claims being submitted by your customer base. To
combat this, your company has initiated a campaign designed to entice your
customer base to adopt healthier lifestyles, and has begun sending brochures
and personalized letters to customers with particular medical histories. Many
customers have expressed concern that this is an indication that the company will become more reluctant to pay their claims.

7. Prepare an experiment at home that involves trying a new or better method to accomplish a task. For example, explore a new email option on your computer, try
balancing your checkbook using the computer, use a different method for paying
this month's bills, or try a different system for doing the week's laundry or the
week's grocery shopping. Once you have selected your topic and performed your
test or experiment, write a test report in the form of a memo to your instructor.
Include each step of the process or the procedures you used, and indicate the results of your test. If appropriate, compare the test process to your old way of ac-
complishing the task. Include in your memo any observations that would be
helpful in interpreting your test report.

8. Write a daily report of your study habits. For one week, write a brief summary of
your study time for each day. In your final entry, draw some conclusions about
your study habits—what habits were most successful and why?—and submit to
your instructor your seven brief reports, including your final analysis.

9. Based on your personal observations, write a trouble report on something that
you feel is not running smoothly, either on campus or at your workplace. Choose
a topic that in your opinion has a simple solution. Examples include a busy inter-

section that you think needs a traffic signal; an area of campus that needs better lighting, a sidewalk, or a bike path; or a parking problem that could be relieved by providing students with incentives to use the bus system. Other topics might address overly complicated procedures for dropping or adding a class, returning books, or using online resources at the library. When considering your workplace, think about issues such as the specified use of personal days, day-care guidelines, travel reimbursement procedures, parking guidelines, and so forth. Companies often reward their employees for suggestions to improve working conditions. Include in your trouble report an explanation of the current situation, the change you propose, and the expected results. Your report should be submitted to your instructor in memo form.

10. Reorganize a workspace or study area at home, or reorganize your files on your computer. Write a report on your progress in memo form to your instructor. Include all relevant steps involved in the process, your reasons for taking each step, and your observations of the effectiveness of your results. You may also include suggestions for maintaining your new system.

■ In-Class Activities

1. Write the following trip report during the next 45 minutes. All of the specifics you need to prepare the report are provided. Your instructor will collect your letters.

Write a two-page letter to Ms. Monica Jenkins, CEO, Jenkins, Johnson, and Jenkins, Marketing Specialists, Inc., 876 Fifth Avenue, Jackson, MS 38702, thanking her for supporting your request to attend the Business Etiquette Conference. The conference was sponsored by the Business Management Association and was held at Delta State University in Cleveland, Mississippi, at Broom Hall, College of Business. The six-day conference was held April 18–23, 20--. You stayed at a five-star DSU Conference Center on the campus.

Purpose of the Assignment: Organizations want to know their money was well spent in sending employees to conferences, seminars, conventions, and workshops. Thus, a trip, conference, or convention report is prepared to inform management about new procedures, equipment, or laws, or to supply information affecting products, operations, and services.

General Outline for the Assignment:
- *Introductory paragraph:* Identify the event (exact date, sponsor name, conference theme/name, and location) and preview the topics to be discussed in your report.
- *Body:* Summarize in the body three to five main points from one presentation you attended each day at the conference. State how you benefitted from the conference and how what you learned will also benefit the reader and Jenkins, Johnson, and Jenkins, Marketing Specialists, Inc.

Highlight—using typographical tools such as boldface, headings, and bullets—the facts that will most interest and help the reader.

Itemize your expenses on a separate page as an attachment to your letter.
- *Close:* Express appreciation, suggest action to be taken, or synthesize the value of the trip or conference.

2. Contact a friend or individual who works in a field related to your professional area of interest. (If you completed the interviewing exercise in Chapter 1, get in touch with the person you interviewed.) Ask if he or she would be able to provide you with a copy of one of the types of reports discussed in this chapter. (Remember that many reports in organizations are confidential, so you may wish to ask for a report that is several years old on an issue that is no longer current.) Bring the report to class and be prepared to discuss how it is similar to or different from the examples in this chapter. Discuss what specific circumstances (readers' needs, objectives, specific organizational or corporate practices) account for the differences.

3. Form groups of five members or fewer. Assume that everyone in your group is part of a company's management team. Your company is old and well-established—such as companies like Coca-Cola, Procter & Gamble, and Quaker Oats—and is well-known by an established logo. Your company, however, is not realizing its desired growth, and you have learned from your marketing department that your company's image is considered by the youngest generation of new consumers to be flat and uninspiring. In response, your company has contacted a savvy new public relations (PR) and design firm to develop a new upscale logo and promote a fresh company image. Assume that your group will be giving instructions to the PR firm. Or, if you prefer you may assume that your group *is* the PR firm. Your group will have approximately 30 minutes to brainstorm a strategy and then 15 minutes to develop an outline of your collective instructions or suggestions. Your instructor may ask you to share your outline with the rest of the class.

4. Assume that when class began today, one of your classmates walked into the room just as class was convening. The classmate, not realizing your instructor had already moved the overhead projector into place, tripped over the electrical cord just before reaching a seat. Unfortunately, it appears as though your classmate's arm was broken when he tried to catch himself during the fall. Your instructor sent another student to the main office to call an ambulance and the injured student has been taken to your campus health center for X-rays and treatment. Your assignment is to write an accident report. Use your own classroom as the setting as you supply the details of the accident, the nature of the injury, the cause of the accident and injury, and what could be done to prevent future accidents of this kind. You will have 30 minutes to prepare your report in the form of a memo addressed to your school's campus safety division.

5. As a class, plan to visit a lab or learning center on campus, preferably one outside your department. Determine as a group which lab you would like to visit, and the specific purposes of your visit. The lab may be a science lab, a finance computer lab, an engineering lab, or any relevant hands-on learning center. After an explanation of the lab's procedures and a tour of the lab or center, your class will reconvene in your own classroom. Your instructor may choose to substitute a video guided tour of a plant, business, or other relevant facility. If so, watch the video as though you were actually on a tour. When your tour is completed, write a trip report about the visit. Include the date of visit, your destination, the purpose of your trip, and an explanation of what you learned during the visit. Your instructor may want to use more than one class session to complete this assignment.

■ Research Projects

1. Gather information pertinent to one of the following topics and present the information in an investigative report. Your instructor will specify the length of the assignment.
   a. Your energy-consumption habits at home
   b. Your recommendations on the best hotel or motel in your area for out-of-town guests
   c. Which of two local garages that have serviced your car you would recommend to a friend
   d. Which Internet access provider you would recommend to a colleague and why

2. You want to volunteer 10 to 12 hours a week for a local community organization. Investigate at least three such organizations that accept volunteers, such as nursing homes, hospitals, day-care centers, political and civic groups, museums, and schools. Find out from each the type of volunteer help it needs, the hours when the help is needed (weekdays, weekends, evenings), whether any training is required, and whom you'll report to. Also be sure to find out whether their volunteers do hands-on work with people (walking, talking, or playing games with children or adults; bathing, lifting, or turning those who aren't mobile, etc.) or if volunteers work behind the scenes (making solicitation calls, addressing envelopes, typing, repairing equipment, stocking supplies, etc.).

   Write an eight- to ten-page investigative report in which you evaluate each of the three organizations in the light of the above criteria, as well as from the point of view of your own background, experience, and future vocational goals. Then select the one that is most suitable for you and explain the reasons for your selection.

3. Choose one of the types of informal reports discussed in this chapter—trouble, investigative, progress or periodic, trip, or test—and create a report based on an article that you find in the Business Day section of the *New York Times.* Turn in the article with your report. The report should be a minimum of 1,000 words (approximately four pages) and no longer than 1,500 words. Use any visual aids you think necessary for your reader to understand the report.

   Before you write the report, submit to your instructor a memo or an email message that discusses your informal report, and include a brief outline. Discuss the type of report you will write and provide the following details:
   • Who are you as the writer of the report? What is your title? What company do you work for?
   • Who is your reader? What is his or her title? What company does he or she work for?
   • What is the purpose of the report? Why are you writing it?
   • How do you expect the reader to use the information provided in this report? Or, what would you like to have happen as a result of your report?

4. Write an informal investigative report on one of the following topics. Read a minimum of three articles from newspapers, journals, books, or other printed material to gather information about your subject. Your instructor will advise you of the required length of the report.

- Electronic meetings
- Cultural differences in business
- Writing that gets the job done
- The effectiveness of sales letter or persuasion techniques
- How to talk to employees, employers, or customers effectively
- Body language in the business setting
- Whether computers create more work
- English-only policies in the workplace
- Ethics in hiring practices
- Checking references
- Writing recommendation letters
- Dealing with a difficult coworker

5. Choose an ongoing current issue that has been in the news for at least one month. Suggested topics include political campaigns, tax issues, unsolved crimes of major importance, international crises, finance issues (including the stock market or economic policy), and educational issues (such as safety in schools or the ability of schools to prepare students for the workplace). You may choose another topic with your instructor's approval. For the next six weeks, submit to your instructor a regular progress report. Include in each report any change in the status of the issue that you have chosen. Be certain to document your media sources. In your final report, suggest what you think could be done to solve the problem. Be as specific as possible.

6. For this project, you may be assigned to a collaborative writing team with three or four classmates. Although you may write to people in other countries using English, you must be aware of differences between cultures that make communicating with international colleagues different from communicating with English speakers native to North America.

   Write an informal investigative report (of 500 to 700 words, or of the length required by your instructor) on cultural differences in one or more of the following areas as they relate specifically to written communication: punctuation, religious symbols, colors, parts of the body, physical gestures, cultural symbols, slang expressions and technical jargon, methods of addressing people, or other topics of your choosing.

   Compare two different cultures within or outside of the United States in detail. Decide on the specific readers that you are writing to and your purpose(s) for writing the report. Document your sources carefully. Although you may find examples of verbal and nonverbal differences between these cultures, relevant examples must relate directly to writing. If you cannot clearly demonstrate how a difference might be used in writing, keep investigating.

■ Web Projects

1. You are responsible for the Web site at a professional organization. Write a progress report on the current status and future plans for your organization's new Web site. To help you write your report, search the Internet to find the site of a well-established organization or company. Assume that you are responsible for that site. In your report, discuss the elements that you plan to keep, those that

you will cut, and those that need to be refined. Explain why and how you plan to carry out these tasks.

2. Search the Internet to locate the Web site of a well-established company or organization. Review that site for examples of the reports included in this chapter — trouble, investigative, progress and periodic, trip, or test. Select one report from your chosen site and print it out. Write a one- or two-page critique of the report, comparing it against the advice and examples offered in this chapter. Is the report a good example of its type? Explain why or why not. *Note:* A good place to start a search for major corporations on the Web is at *CIO Magazine*'s Web Central site at http://www.cio.com/central/business.html.

3. Research online a business, organization, or governmental agency and write a 300- to 500-word investigative informal report. Your report should focus on one specific function or feature of the organization. Define the function or feature, investigate its effectiveness, evaluate its effectiveness, and conclude by making specific recommendations for improving the function or feature.

4. Assume that your boss, the president of a small business, has asked you to gather information from the Small Business Administration (SBA) concerning business expansion. Search the SBA Web site at http://www.sba.gov/ (click on "Expansion"). Your boss would like you to gather information about financing — specifically on special programs, opportunities for government contracts, marketing, net information, and training opportunities available through the SBA. Prepare an investigative report of 300 to 500 words and submit it to your instructor.

5. Search the Government Printing Office (GPO) official Web site to gather information needed for this assignment at http://www.access.gpo.gov/. The GPO produces and distributes federal government information products to the public in printed publications and on the Web. The information circulated by the GPO also supplies the information needed by the U.S. Congress, and U.S. federal agencies. Choose one of the following topic areas from the GPO's home page and prepare an informal report about its contents. Choices include but are not limited to the following:
   a. Acccess to Government Information Products
   b. Business and Contracting Opportunities
   c. Employment Opportunities
   d. Establishing Links to Documents in GPO WAIS Databases

   Your report should be in memo form and addressed to your class as a group (for example, to the Students of Business Writing, 200). Your instructor may request that you email your memo to your classmates.

11 Researching Your Subject

Tom Cabines, production manager of Nebel Desktop Publishers, received a memo from Alice Enklend, purchasing director, asking him how many copies of an employee manual a corporate customer had commissioned the firm to print. Tom probably had the answer at his fingertips or would be able to find it after a quick look at his computer's production-scheduling spreadsheet. Tom's *research*—or tracking down of information on the topic—would be minimal.

Suppose, instead, that Tom were asked to review current literature on the influence of gender on the development of technology and to prepare a presentation on that topic. How would he go about obtaining the necessary information? For these tasks he would have to do some extensive research, which could involve a search for information in his company library, in a public library, on the Internet, or through some combination of these sources.

Libraries offer organized paths to the world of scholarship and information and to the Internet. Access points might include an online catalog (few libraries have retained a traditional card catalog), indexes and bibliographies, databases of articles, and computer terminals with access to library materials, the Web, and specialized tools for using the Web. While you can access many of the library's resources online from your own computer, going to the library, enlisting the help of a research librarian, and searching the vastness of the Web through the subject guides of your library's home page can help you to take advantage of quality resources and save time.

This chapter discusses tools, strategies, and resources for researchers of various levels of expertise. You will find sections on Library Research, which takes you step-by-step through an online catalog search; Internet Research with coverage of online searching with subject directories, search engines, and meta-search engines; Evaluating Internet and Library Sources, with helpful checklists and guidelines, as well as sections on conducting research using interviews and questionnaires. Also featured is a section on Documenting Sources that offers guidelines and examples for the Modern Language Association (MLA) and American Psychological Association (APA) styles of documentation.

Voices from the Workplace

Susan U. Ladwig, Medical College of Wisconsin

Susan U. Ladwig is Associate Director of Development at the International Bone Marrow Transplant Registry of the Medical College of Wisconsin. Her responsibilities include research and grant writing, which often involve working with the National Institutes of Health (NIH) as well as with other government and private medical organizations. Most of Susan's work involves research on the Internet.

Susan describes the Internet as a valuable tool and resource in her business: "The Internet has become a basic research tool for proposal writers seeking grant funds from government and private sources. It is very useful for quickly accessing the most up-to-date information on funding opportunities and technical subjects. Learning how to efficiently gather key data from the Internet is an important skill for students."

A valuable source of information on federal grant programs is the GrantsNet page at the Department of Health and Human Services at http://www.hhs.gov/progorg/grantsnet/. For information about other grant sources, see the site hosted by the Medical Library Association (an affiliate of the American Library Association) at http://www.mlanet.org.

To learn about resources used by Susan Ladwig and medical researchers on the Internet, see http://www.mcw.edu.

Entry-Level
Molly Lawless, JuniorNet

Molly Lawless is an art and production staff member at a multimedia company called JuniorNet. JuniorNet produces an Internet software hybrid that aims to provide a commercial-free, educational, safe, and fun Internet environment for kids. Because Molly does much of her research on the Internet, she must know how to evaluate the resources that she finds there.

"When you're trying to educate, the last thing you want to do is mislead. The Internet is a seductive — and somewhat dangerous — resource in this respect. It takes no time at all to have an 'answer' from one of a countless number of search engines. What we must realize, and what I remind myself of constantly, is that it is not always the *right* answer.

"The rule that I follow when doing Web research is this: Facts must be supported by two to three Web sites, as opposed to the one print source (book, magazine, encyclopedia article) that typically supports a finding contained in published print sources. Beyond that, it just takes a critical, realistic eye and common sense to come to a conclusion about a Web site. 'Official' Web sites are generally a good resource as are sites that include a bibliography. Some search engines supply a list of the 'Top Ten' Web sites for the subject that you searched for. The 'Top Ten' lists can be a good way of determining which sites attract repeat visitors; it follows that they may be quality sites — and that is usually the case."

To find out more about JuniorNet, visit their Web site at http://www.juniornet.com.

■ Library Research

Get thee to the best library in your area and take advantage of it! Libraries are there for your use; they're funded by tax dollars, tuition fees, and the generosity of people who love books and ideas. Librarians are research professionals and, while they may not have a mastery of your topic, they can save you enormous amounts of time by pointing you toward the appropriate databases, collection areas, and subject listings, and by helping you locate what you may need through an interlibrary loan. Further, librarians can tell you where to begin and how to refine your search strategy, and they can help you connect with the research materials related to your project.

Two Web sites that might help you select a library in your area are LibWeb: Library Servers via WWW at http://sunsite.berkeley.edu/Libweb/. The site is hosted by Berkeley, Digital Library SunSITE and currently lists over 3,000 library home pages in more than 90 countries. Another good site for finding library cata-

---

ESL TIPS: Using Common Library Terms

When researching in the library, you will need to understand some common library terms that may not appear in all dictionaries.

- *Abstract:* a shortened version of a long document that gives the reader the important points
- *Bibliographic information:* the author and publication information needed to locate an item in a library
- *Bibliography:* (1) a listing of sources used in the writing of a document; (2) in the Modern Language Association (MLA) format, it is called a Works Cited page; in the American Psychological Association (APA) format, it is called the References page
- *Bound periodical:* several issues of a journal or magazine that are secured together in book form
- *Call number:* the number assigned to every item in the library to help locate the item
- *Circulation desk:* the desk where a patron can check out, return, and renew library materials
- *Interlibrary loan:* material requested from another library and sent to the patron's library for use
- *Journal:* a periodical containing scholarly articles written by experts in a particular subject area
- *Magazine:* a periodical meant for the general public
- *Microform:* books or articles on film that must be viewed on a particular machine
- *Periodical:* a publication issued regularly such as a newspaper, magazine, or journal

logs is WebCats: Library Web-based OPACs (online public access catalog) at http://www.lights.com/webcats/. You can search the catalogs of thousands of libraries from this site, but in most cases you must still have either a public library card or a student identification card to take materials with you or to participate in the interlibrary loan services.

Searching Online Catalogs

Online catalogs provide easy and broad access to the library's resources. Many online catalogs can be accessed through the Web. However, the format or organization of online catalogs can vary widely. This section offers guidance on how best to use the online catalogs currently available.

When using an online catalog, read the instructions included on the introductory or FAQ (Frequently Asked Questions) page or Help menu because each catalog has its own set of rules. Most permit searching through library collections of books, videos, musical scores, reports, government documents, and other materials by author, title, keyword, subject heading, or call number. Some provide search enhancements. For example, subject headings and author names can be linked to all of the materials available from that author or under that subject heading. The citation record usually includes a statement to indicate whether the material is available for circulation.

Methods for searching online catalogs vary. Catalog searches work by retrieving only records that fit an initial query that the searcher may gradually narrow the focus of by adding other search terms to these results. Automated searches now allow for search combinations and access that could not have been imagined in previous days. Ask a reference librarian to give you a brief tour of the online catalog. Information on a few basic steps and some directions about physical locations of materials on the catalog will prepare you to start your research.

Follow these basic steps to begin an online search:

- *Start with a question or a thesis statement.* If your topic is unfamiliar, it may be best to find a background article on your topic. Is there a specialized encyclopedia, reference book, or summary that brings some of the research and history of the topic together in one location? Talk to a reference librarian about good starting points.

- *Limit the scope of your search.* Do you need to describe why the topic is important? Will the chronology of changes in the topic strengthen your argument? The catalog may have a shortcut to the library's reference section built into the search process.

- *Look for the help screens.* They describe the various search strategies possible and help you locate the most appropriate records in a library. Most catalogs allow you to specify a date or date range for the materials.

The Library of Congress Online Catalog

The Library of Congress is the largest library in the world. Its collections are comprehensive and include research materials. The Library of Congress catalog is available at http://catalog.loc.gov/. The FAQ page at the Library of Congress Online, shown in Figure 11–1, describes search methods and services available for researchers.

Academic Online Catalogs

Academic libraries classify their collections according to the Library of Congress cataloging scheme. See the Library of Congress classification outline at http://www.tlcdelivers.com/tcl/crs/lcso0001.htm shown in Figure 11–2 for an online

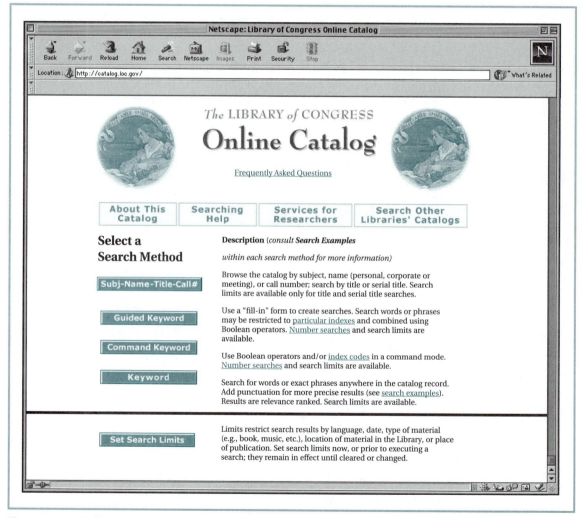

Figure 11–1 Online Catalog for the Library of Congress *Source:* Courtesy of the Library of Congress.

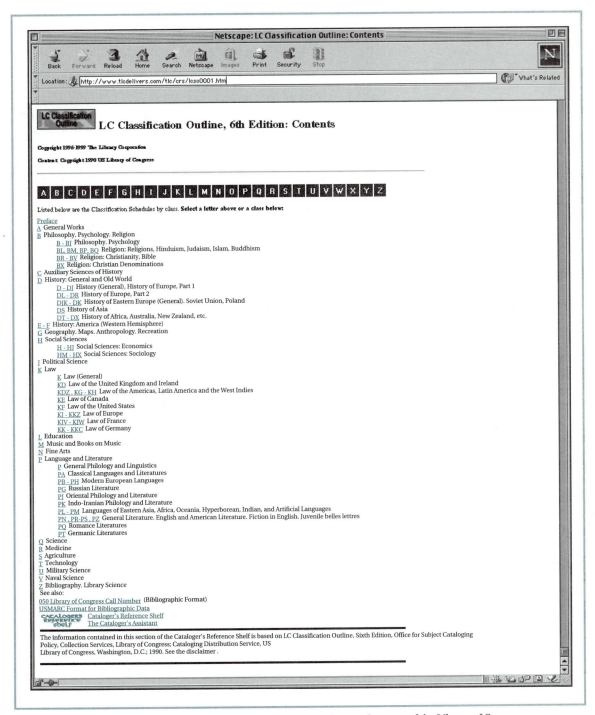

Figure 11–2 The Library of Congress Classification Outline   *Source:* Courtesy of the Library of Congress.

description of the categories. Each book is given a unique call number that determines its location on the shelves. By linking to that location number, the online catalog permits you to browse a listing of the call numbers and titles of all the books in that section from your computer.

The Advanced Search.   While books may have more than one author, it is usually only possible to search for one name at a time in the basic search mode. If a work has a corporate or organizational author, such as a volume produced by the American Medical Association, you can search for the book using "AMA" as the author's name. The Advanced Search option shown in Figure 11–3 permits you to search for two authors at a time.

A Step-by-Step Search.   Figures 11–4 through 11–9 show a step-by-step approach to an online catalog search for a book and a journal article. Although search methods vary among libraries, there are many common elements from system to system.

If you were asked to research a presentation on the topic of women and their influence on the Internet and technology, for example, your search might evolve in this manner. As shown in the Basic Search screen in Figure 11–4, you would begin by selecting from the basic categories the type of search that you want to conduct: Keyword; Title, keyword; Subject Heading, keyword; Author; Title, exact; or Subject Heading, exact. Most online catalogs also have an advanced search component that allows searching by a call number (the location descriptor of the item), or by a series title.

The simplest way to search an online catalog is to begin with broad, general terms, and then, in incremental steps, refine the results more and more specifically. The "Subject Heading, keyword" search shown in Figure 11–5 will retrieve records that contain either of the terms *Internet* or *Technology*—and will limit the search to records that include the term *Women*. Because your presentation will deal with the contemporary social effects or aspects of women and their influence on the Internet and Technology, you would limit your search by adding the word *Social*, and for the publication year, *After 1997*, as shown in Figure 11–6. Many online catalogs also permit you to limit your search by format, for example, to books, videotapes, or sound recordings.

Figure 11–7 displays a list of results and some options for printing out a list of citations—citations that are likely to be relevant to your presentation topic are selected with checkmarks. Figure 11–8 shows a bibliographic record for a possible source relevant to your topic. The record gives the book's title, author, location (call number), information on the book's availability, and publication information. Because the subject headings are all linked, another search of the subject *Computers and women* would likely yield other fruitful sources.

Expanding Your Search.   Despite the deluge of information that you may retrieve on an online catalog, it may be helpful to expand your search during the early stages of your research. Expanding your search can give you a quick overview of the possible scope of your topic and may be helpful in focusing your assignment.

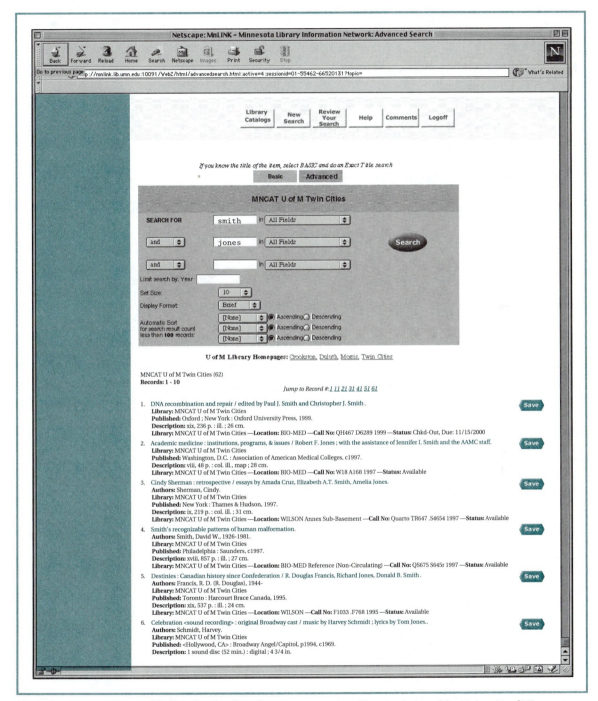

Figure 11–3 An Advanced Online Catalog Search *Source:* Reprinted by permission of the University of Minnesota, University Libraries.

Figure 11–4
Online Catalog
Search: Basic
Search Screen
Source: Reprinted
by permission of
the University of
Minnesota, Uni-
versity Libraries.

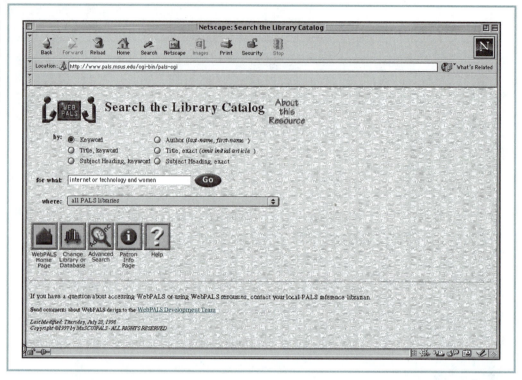

Figure 11–5
Online Catalog
Search: Subject
Keyword Search
Source: Reprinted
by permission of
the University of
Minnesota, Uni-
versity Libraries.

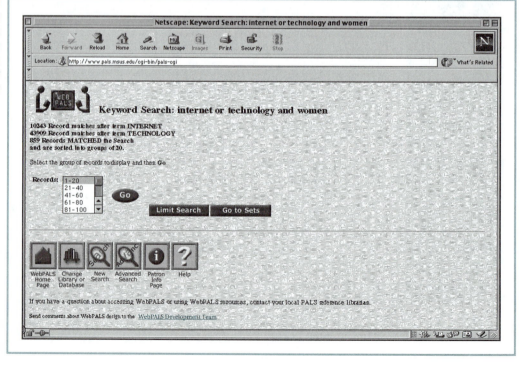

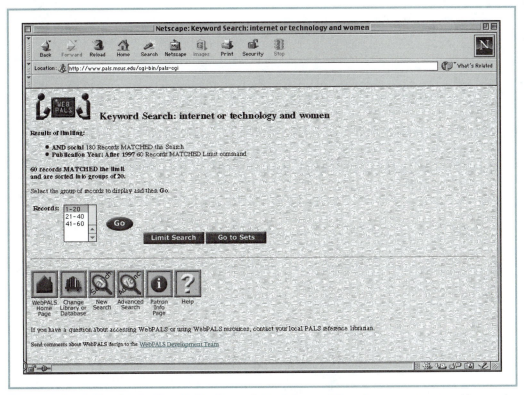

Figure 11–6   Online Catalog Search: Limiting a Subject Keyword Search   *Source:* Reprinted by permission of the University of Minnesota, University Libraries.

Truncation.   Truncation—a powerful expansion tool that was not available before the advent of online searching—allows you to take the root of a word, add a wild-card symbol, and retrieve many alternative endings. The term *sail#* retrieves the words *sailor, sailing,* and *sails.* Check any available Help screens to determine which symbol will work for the particular database or online catalog that you are accessing. Figure 11–9 describes how to use truncation in one system.

Reference Works

As a student or employee, you are likely to be asked to prepare presentations, papers, or reports on topics unfamiliar to you. In this case, it may be useful to do some reading to develop a sense of the possible approaches to the task. An encyclopedia such as the *Encarta Encyclopedia* at http://www.encarta.msn.com can provide you with an overview of your topic and may give you a framework for asking questions about it. In addition, most good encyclopedia articles are signed by the author and contain bibliographies that are useful during the beginning stages of your research.

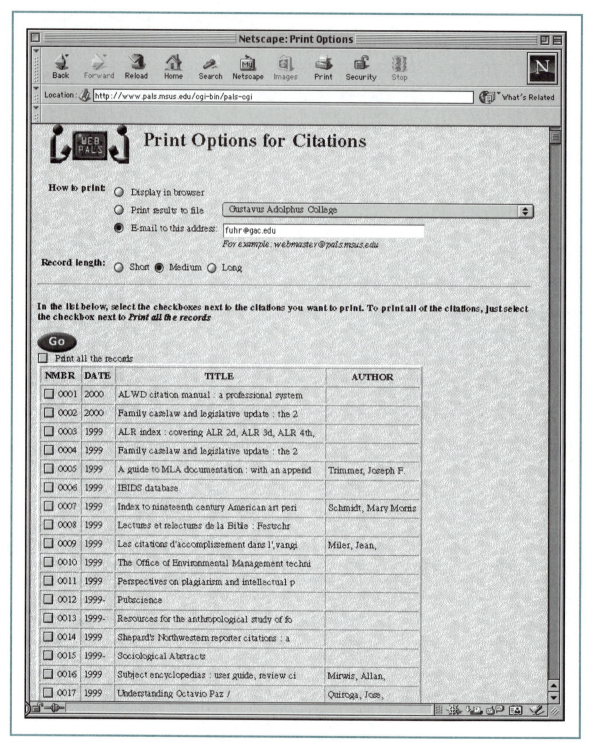

Figure 11–7 Online Catalog Search: Print Options for Citations *Source:* Reprinted by permission of the University of Minnesota, University Libraries.

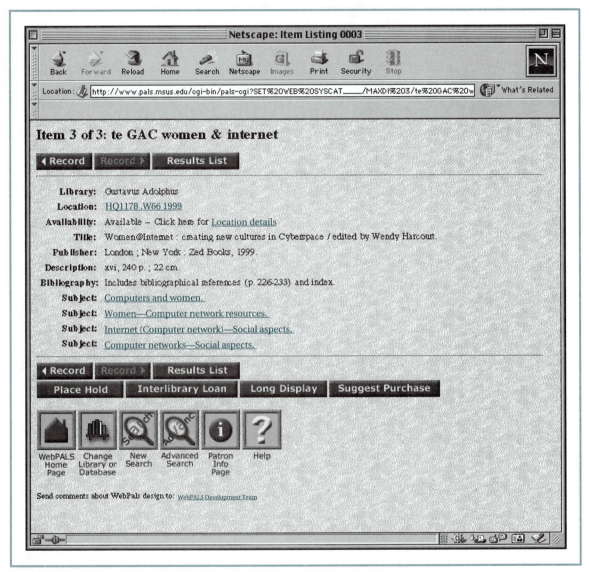

Figure 11–8 Online Catalog Search: A Relevant Bibliographic Record   *Source:* Reprinted by permission of the University of Minnesota, University Libraries.

An online search for an encyclopedia at the Colorado Alliance of Research Libraries (CARL), using a title and keyword search, yields more than three thousand hits. By limiting that search to materials published after 1990 in English, and by including a keyword, such as *Economics,* in the title, the search yields four likely resources, as shown in Figure 11–10.

Reference books are increasingly becoming available online. For example, Bartleby.com: Great Books Online at http://www.bartleby.com/ provides users

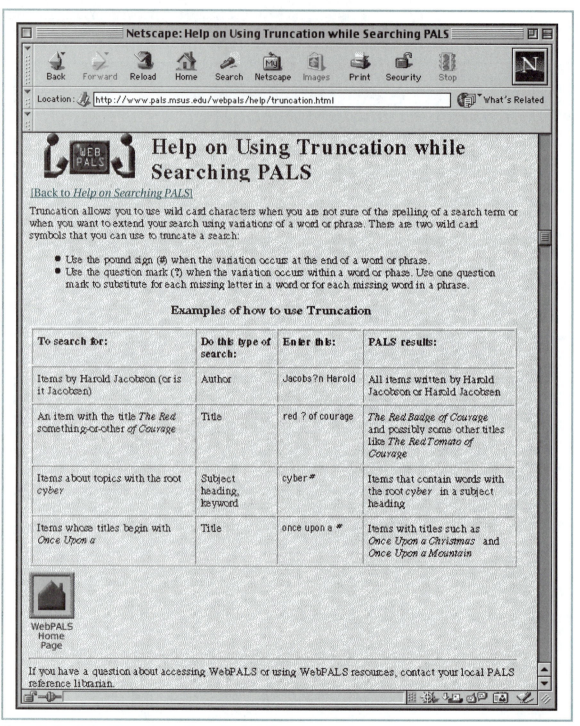

Figure 11–9   Online Catalog Search: Truncation Help Screen   *Source:* Reprinted by permission of the University of Minnesota, University Libraries.

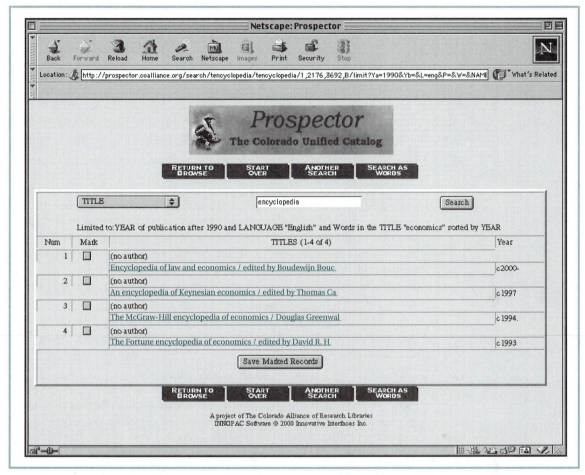

Figure 11–10   Online Catalog Search: Encyclopedia   *Source:* Reprinted by permission of The Colorado Alliance of Research Libraries and INNOPAC Software © 1998, Innovative Interfaces Inc.

with access to electronic versions of the *Columbia Encyclopedia,* Sixth Edition; *The American Heritage Dictionary of the English Language,* Third Edition; *Roget's II: The New Thesaurus,* Third Edition; *Simpson's Contemporary Quotations;* and *The American Heritage Book of English Usage.*

Encyclopedias

Encyclopedias are comprehensive, usually multivolume, collections of articles arranged alphabetically and often illustrated. Some encyclopedias cover a wide range of subjects, while others specialize in a particular subject. *General encyclopedias* provide the researcher with an overview of a particular subject that can be helpful to someone new to the topic. As a source of background information, the articles in general encyclopedias usually include the terminology essential to an understanding of the subject. Many articles contain bibliographies that can lead the researcher to additional information. Three of the best-known general encyclopedias are *Collier's Encyclopedia,* with 24 volumes; *Encyclopedia Americana,* 30 volumes; and *Encyclopedia Britannica,* 30 volumes.

Subject encyclopedias provide detailed information on all aspects of a particular field of knowledge. Their treatment of a subject is sufficiently thorough to make it desirable that the researcher have some background information on the subject in order to use the information to full advantage. There are many more specialized encyclopedias than there are general encyclopedias. The following list indicates the range available.

Subject Encyclopedias.

American Decades. Detroit: Gale, 1994. A set that chronicles American history by decade. Each volume includes a chronology of world events and chapters that explore significant developments in a variety of areas: the arts, business and the economy, government and politics, lifestyles and social trends, and so on.

The Arnold Encyclopedia of Real Estate. 2nd ed. Alvin Arnold. New York: Wiley, 1993. This encyclopedia defines and explains the economic, financial, and legal aspects of real estate, with coverage of acquisition, disposition and ownership, government regulations, leasing, and property descriptions and management.

CQ Researcher. Washington: Congressional Quarterly, 1991–. An excellent resource for coverage of controversial current events, including developments in science and technology. Each weekly update focuses on a topic of general interest and provides an overview, various viewpoints, statistics, and a bibliography for further research.

Encyclopedia of Applied Ethics. San Diego: Academic, 1998. This four-volume set provides lengthy, scholarly discussions of the ethical aspects of current issues in all areas, including affirmative action, animal rights, and genetic testing, as well as contemporary views on theories of ethics such as humanism, hedonism, and utilitarianism.

Encyclopedia of Associations. Detroit: Gale, annual. This directory lists all kinds of organizations, giving a little background for each as well as addresses, phone numbers, and Web sites where available. Also by online subscription at http://www.silverplatter.com/catalog/eass.htm.

Encyclopedia of Banking and Finance. 10th ed. Charles J. Woelfel. New York: McGraw-Hill, 1996. Considered a standard authority on banking in the United States with a comprehensive index. Also available on CD-ROM.

Encyclopedia of Bioethics. Revised edition. New York: Macmillan, 1995. Covers issues and controversies in bioethics in substantial, scholarly articles, each one accompanied by a current bibliography of key sources.

The Encyclopedia of Careers and Vocational Guidance. 11th ed. Holli Cosgrove. Chicago: Ferguson Publishing Company, 1999. Published in four volumes, this set features career guidance, including information on applying for a job, with quick reference articles on 91 career fields with job descriptions and advice on how to gain experience and advance in the workplace.

Encyclopedia of Computer Science. 4th ed. Ed. Anthony Ralston, Edwin D. Reilly, Jr., and David Hemmendinger. New York: Groves Dictionaries, Inc., 2000. Considered the leading authority in the field of computer science, this edition of the encyclopedia provides a range of information from the history of electronic computing to contemporary research in the field, with current data on computing systems, operating systems, and distributed environments.

The Encyclopedia of Economics. 2nd ed. Douglas Greenwald. New York: McGraw-Hill, 1994. This edition includes 306 articles covering economics, econometrics, statistics, and marketing written by experts from academic, business, and government sectors. It contains a subject index, extensive bibliographical references, topical cross-references within articles, and biographical sketches of the authors.

The Encyclopedia of Statistical Sciences. 9 vols. Samuel Kotz and Norman Joynson. New York: Wiley, 1983–89. Offers more than 4,000 entries by major figures in the field of statistical sciences, with coverage of format, theories, methods, applications, and historical background, with a comprehensive index.

McGraw-Hill Encyclopedia of Science and Technology. 8th ed. New York: McGraw-Hill, 1997. A 20-volume set covering topics in the sciences in detail, giving technical discussions fully illustrated with charts, diagrams, and photographs. Also published on CD-ROM.

Worldmark Encyclopedia of Cultures and Daily Life. Detroit: Gale, 1998. A multivolume set that offers lengthy articles on over 500 culture groups worldwide. Each article surveys the location and homeland of the people and covers a wealth of information on such topics as their language, folklore, religion, rites of passage, interpersonal relations, living conditions, family life, cultural heritage, work, and social issues.

Atlases

Atlases are classified into two broad categories based on the type of information they present—general maps, which represent physical and political boundaries; and thematic maps, which represent a special subject, such as climate, population, natural resources, or agricultural products. Following is a list of well-known general atlases.

Hammond Atlas of the World. 2nd ed. Ed. Hammond Staff. Maplewood, NY: Hammond, 1997.

Microsoft Encarta World Atlas 2000. CD-ROM for Windows. Microsoft Corporation, 2000.

National Geographic Atlas of the World. 7th ed. Washington, D.C.: National Geographic Society, 1999.

The New York Times Atlas of the World. 2nd ed. Ed. The *New York Times* Staff. New York: Random House, 1997.

The Times Atlas of the World. 10th ed. Ed. *London Times, Times Books* Staff. London: Crown Publishing Group, 1999.

Following is a list of thematic atlases:

The Atlas of American Society. Alice C. Andrews and James W. Fonseca; cartography and graphic design by Daniel F. Van Dorn. New York: New York U.P., 1995. This book offers graphical depictions of various aspects of society today.

CyberAtlas. http://cyberatlas.internet.com/. The site provides readers with valuable statistics and Web marketing information, enabling them to understand their business environment and make more informed business decisions. CyberAtlas gathers online research from the best data resources to provide a complete review of the latest surveys and technologies available.

Growing Up in America: An Atlas of Youth in the USA. Rickie Sanders and Mark T. Mattson. New York: Macmillan Library Reference USA; London: Prentice Hall International, 1998. Demographic profile of American children.

The Rand-McNally Commercial Atlas and Marketing Guide, 1999. 130th ed. Ed. Rand-McNally Staff. Skokie, IL: Rand McNally, 2000.

The State of the World Atlas: A Unique Visual Survey of Global Political, Economic, and Social Trends. 5th ed. Ed. Michael Kidron et al. New York: Penguin U.S.A., 1995.

The World Bank Atlas 2000. Ed. The World Bank Staff. Washington, D.C.: The World Bank, 2000.

Dictionaries

The vocabulary section of the Writer's Guide at the end of this book lists a selection of desk-size English-language dictionaries. *Unabridged dictionaries,* which are larger and more comprehensive in their coverage, often contain basic terms from many specialized subjects.

Unabridged Dictionaries.

The Oxford English Dictionary. 2nd ed. Ed. Edmund S. Weiner, Oxford, U.K.: Oxford U.P., 1989. The standard historical dictionary of the English language from the Middle Ages to the present, emphasizing British English. Its 20 volumes contain over 600,000 words and give the chronological developments of over 240,000 words, providing numerous examples of uses and sources. It is also available on CD-ROM for Windows and can be accessed by subscribers at http://www.oed.com.

The Random House Dictionary of the English Language. 2nd ed. Eds. Stuart Berg Flexner and Leonore Crary Hauck. New York: Random House, 1987. Provides about 315,000 up-to-date entries and copious examples. It lists a word's most current meaning first and includes biographical and geographical names.

Webster's Third New International Dictionary of the English Language, Unabridged. Ed. Philip Babcock Gove. Springfield, MA: G & C Merriam Co., 1961. The largest dictionary of modern English, and considered to be the most authoritative of its type, with an emphasis on American usage. Over 450,000 entries list a word's meaning in historical order, with the current meaning given last.

Desk and Multimedia Dictionaries.   Desk and multimedia dictionaries are often abridged versions of larger dictionaries. When choosing a dictionary, select one that contains upward of 125,000 entries, and make sure you have its most recent edition. If you are interested in hearing the pronunciation of words, you may want to choose a dictionary on CD-ROM, as many of these have a human-voice pronunciation feature. Also, research the Internet for general and specialized dictionaries. For example, one site that is able to translate words from one language to another is Research It! at http://www.itools.com/research-it. Another site that suggests alternative spellings for misspelled words is Dictionary.com at http://www.dictionary.com.

The American Heritage College Dictionary. 3rd ed. Eds. Robert B. Costello et al. Boston: Houghton Mifflin, 1993. Based on *The American Heritage Dictionary of the English Language,* the third *College* edition offers 200,000 definitions and 15,000 new words, with usage and regional notes and synonyms. Includes biographical and geographic entries.

The American Heritage College Dictionary. 3rd ed. with CD-ROM. Ed. Houghton Mifflin Staff. Boston: Houghton Mifflin, 1997. This package offers the hardcover of the dictionary with a searchable CD-ROM of the book's contents.

Encarta World English Dictionary. Ed. Anne H. Soukhanov. New York: St. Martin's, 1999. Based on the work of 250 lexicographers in 10 countries, the *Encarta* traces the written, spoken, and electronic forms of English, emphasizing it as a global language, with 400,000 entries and 20,000 new words and definitions. Web users can access parts of the *Encarta* at http://dictionary.msn.com.

Microsoft® Encarta® World English Dictionary, CD-ROM. Microsoft Corporation, 1999. The software version of the *Encarta World English Dictionary* includes Roget's *Thesaurus of English Words and Phrases,* a style and usage manual, an almanac, and a computer and Internet dictionary.

Merriam Webster's Collegiate Dictionary. 10th ed. Ed. Merriam-Webster Staff. Springfield, MA: Merriam-Webster Inc., 1996. With 211,000 definitions, this dictionary includes verbal illustrations, quotations, etymologies, usage guidance, drawings, biographical and geographic information, and a handbook of style. Web users can link to Merriam-Webster's browser at the Merriam Webster's Online Language Center at http://www.m-w.com.

Merriam Webster's Collegiate Dictionary and Thesaurus, electronic edition (CD-ROM). Ed. Merriam-Webster Staff. Springfield, MA: Merriam-Webster Inc., 1999. Windows or Macintosh compatible, Merriam Webster's CD-ROM provides 21 search options for finding information in the complete dictionary and the thesaurus.

Random House Webster's College Dictionary. 2nd ed. Ed. Random House Staff. New York: Random House, 1999. Based on the *Random House Webster's Unabridged Dictionary,* this comprehensive *College* edition contains 180,000 entries, with 800 drawings, maps, and diagrams.

Subject Dictionaries.   For the meanings of words too specialized for a general dictionary, a subject dictionary is useful. Subject dictionaries define the terms used in a particular field, such as business, geography, architecture, or consumer affairs. Definitions in subject dictionaries are generally more current and complete than those found in general dictionaries.

The American Heritage Stedman's Medical Dictionary. Boston: Houghton Mifflin Co., 1995.

Dictionary of Computer and Internet Terms. 6th ed. Douglas A. Dowling, Michael A. Covington, and Melody M. Covington. Hauppauge, NY: Barron's, 1998.

Dictionary of Architecture. James Curl. Oxford: Oxford University Press, 2000.

Dictionary of Architecture and Construction. 2nd ed. Ed. Cyril M. Harris. New York: McGraw-Hill, 1992.

Dictionary of Business and Management. 3rd ed. Jerry M. Rosenberg. New York: Wiley, 1993.

Dictionary of Earth Sciences. English-French; French-English. New York: Wiley, 1992.

Dictionary of Environmental Science and Technology. Rev. ed. Andrew Porteous. New York: Wiley, 2nd ed. 1996.

Dictionary of Geological Terms. 3rd ed. rev. American Geological Institute Staff. New York: Doubleday, 1984.

Dictionary of Nutrition and Food Technology. 6th ed. Arnold E. Bender. Stoneham, MA: Butterworth-Heinemann, 1990.

Dictionary of Retailing and Merchandising. Jerry Martin Rosenberg. New York: Wiley, 1995.

Fairchild's Dictionary of Retailing. New York: Fairchild, 1984.

FOLDOC: Free Online Dictionary of Computing. http://wombat.doc.ic.ac.uk/foldoc/. A helpful resource for defining computer terms.

The IEBM Dictionary of Business and Management. London; Boston: International Thomson Publishing Services Ltd., 1998.

Longman Dictionary of Geography: Human and Physical. Audrey M. Clark. White Plains, NY: Longman, 1986.

Mosby's Medical, Nursing, and Allied Health Dictionary. 5th ed. St. Louis, MO: Mosby, 1998.

Professional Secretary's Encyclopedic Dictionary. 5th ed. Prentice-Hall Editorial Staff and Mary A. DeVries. Englewood Cliffs, NJ: Prentice-Hall, 1995.

Although all of these dictionaries are specialized and offer detailed definitions of field-specific terms, they are written in language straightforward enough to be understood by nonspecialists.

Handbooks and Manuals

Handbooks and manuals are typically one-volume compilations of frequently used information in a particular field of knowledge. The information they offer can include brief definitions of terms or concepts; explanations of how certain organizations function; and graphs and tables that display basic numerical data, maps, and the like. Handbooks and manuals offer a ready source of fundamental information about a subject, although, unlike dictionaries, they are usually intended for the researcher who has some basic knowledge, particularly in scientific or technical fields. Every field has its own handbook or manual; the following list shows some typical examples.

American Electrician's Handbook. 13th ed. Croft Terrell and Wilford Summers. New York: McGraw-Hill, 1996.

The Business Writer's Handbook. 6th ed. Gerald Alred, Charles Brusaw, and Walter Oliu. Boston: Bedford/St. Martin's, 2000.

CRC Handbook of Chemistry and Physics, 1999–2000. 80th ed. Ed. David R. Lide. Boca Raton, FL: CRC, 1996. Also available by subscription online at http://www.crcpress.com. (The *Handbook* is listed in the Web Products menu.)

Fire Protection Handbook. 18th ed. Ed. Arthur E. Cok and Jim L. Linville. Quincy, MA: National Fire Protection Association, 1997.

The Gregg Reference Manual. 9th ed. Ed. William A. Sabin, Gregg Division. New York: McGraw-Hill, 2000.

Handbook of Applied Mathematics: Selected Results and Methods. 2nd ed. Ed. Carl E. Pearson. New York: Van Nostrand Reinhold, 1990; Thomson Business Press, 1999.

The Handbook of International Direct Marketing. 3rd ed. Ed. Adam Baines and Sheila Lloyd. London: Kogan Page, Limited, 1997.

Occupational Outlook Handbook, 1998–99. Washington, D.C.: U.S. Department of Labor, Bureau of Labor Statistics, 1998. http://stats.bls.gov/ocohome.htm. Descriptions of the work in various occupations, plus projections regarding growth and employment in the field.

Standard Handbook for Civil Engineers. 4th ed. Ed. Frederick S. Merritt, M. Kent Loftin, and Jonathan T. Ricketts. New York: McGraw-Hill, 1996.

The United States Government Manual, 1999/2000. Office of the Federal Register, National Archives and Records Administration. Rev. June 1, 1999. Washington, D.C. The Federal Register, U.S. Government Printing Office, 1999. http://www.access.gpo.gov/nara/nara001.html.

Statistical Sources

Statistical sources are collections of numerical data. They are the best source for such information as the height of the Washington Monument; the population of Boise, Idaho; the cost of living in Aspen, Colorado; and the annual number of motorcycle fatalities in the United States. You can find answers to many statistical reference questions in almanacs and encyclopedias. You can also find statistical information at federal government Web sites, including those for the U.S. Department of Commerce at http://www.dor.gov and the U.S. Census Bureau at http://www.census.gov/, and at the FedStats Web site, hosted by the Federal Interagency Council on Statistical Policy at http://www.fedstats.gov/. However, for answers to more difficult or comprehensive questions, you may need to consult specific works devoted exclusively to statistical data, a selection of which follows:

American Statistics Index. Washington, D.C.: Congressional Information Service, 1978 to date. Monthly, quarterly, and annual supplements.

The *American Statistics Index* lists and summarizes all statistical publications issued by agencies of the U.S. government. The publications cited include periodicals, reports, special surveys, and pamphlets.

U.S. Bureau of the Census. *County and City Data Book.* Washington, D.C.: U.S. Government Printing Office, 1952 to date. Issued approximately every five years.

The *Data Book* includes a variety of data from cities, counties, congressional districts, metropolitan areas, and the like. The information, arranged by geographic and political area, covers such topics as climate, dwellings, population characteristics, school districts, employment, and city finances.

U.S. Bureau of the Census. *Statistical Abstract of the United States.* Washington, D.C.: U.S. Government Printing Office, 1879 to date. Annual.

The *Statistical Abstract* includes statistics on social, political, and economic conditions in the United States. Compiled by the U.S. Bureau of the Census, the data include vital statistics and cover broad topics such as population, education, and public land. Some state and regional data are given, as are selected international statistics.

Periodical Indexes, Bibliographies, and Abstracting Services

Periodical indexes and bibliographies are lists of journal articles and books. *Periodical indexes* are devoted specifically to journal, magazine, and newspaper articles (the term *periodical* is applied to publications that are issued at regular intervals—daily, weekly, monthly, and so on). *Bibliographies* list books, periodicals, and other research materials published in a particular subject area, such as business, engineering, the humanities, medicine, or the social sciences. (To find a bibliography on your subject using your library's online catalog, type in the proper term for your topic, then add the word *bibliography*). Finally, *abstracting services* provide brief summaries of the source cited, giving an idea of its content so that you can judge whether it is relevant to your research.

One way to begin your search for relevant indexes, bibliographies, and abstracts is to consult an appropriate reference guide. The following guides list thousands of reference books, indexes, and other items useful to researchers, annotated and arranged so that you can find your subject quickly.

> *Guide to Reference Books.* 11th ed. Robert Balay, Gualala, CA: American Library Association, 1996.
>
> *Walford's Guide to Reference Material.* Vol. 1: Science and Technology, 1999. Vol. 2: Social and Historical Sciences, Philosophy, and Religion, 1993. Vol. 3: Generalities, Languages, the Arts and Literature, 1993. A. J. Walford. Lanham, MD: UNIPUB.

However, a more efficient way to begin your research is to consult with a librarian about reference sources available online at your library. Libraries purchase subscriptions to various databases that support the needs of their users and, in the case of academic libraries, the curriculum of their users. Although most libraries provide indexes and other reference sources in print and electronic format, some are beginning to drop the print in favor of the electronic resources. Electronic resources make it easy to search across multiple years and databases, dramatically reducing the time-consuming task of wading through decades of print volumes.

Hundreds of options for databases are available to libraries, and each database has its own set of rules, searching procedures, Help screens, and license restrictions. Some databases may require passwords and some are restricted to use on a single workstation or campus network. Although there are a few databases that are limited to use by professional researchers or librarians, most are available to all library users.

Before doing an online search for books or journal articles, consult with a reference librarian for suggestions on the databases most relevant to your topic. When searching an online index for journal articles, follow the process similar to that used for searching for books, as described earlier in this chapter. However, because journal articles focus on more specific topics than do books, search terms for journal articles can be more specific. Index databases for journals provide citations that include an abstract or summary of an article; some also provide the full text of an article. Lists of citations or the text of an article, when available, can often be printed out or sent to your email account.

After you have selected and located the indexes, bibliographies, or abstracts that deal with your subject, consult the instructions in the front of each work, or in the first volume of the works that are a series. There you will find a key to the abbreviations and symbols used; an explanation of the way information is arranged; a listing of the specific subjects covered; and, for periodical indexes, a listing of the newspapers, magazines, and journals that are included.

Some of the indexes and abstracts that you are likely to find useful are included in the following list. As indicated here, many of these are available in electronic format. Check with a reference librarian to find out if the index or abstracting service you're interested in is available online at your library.

Applied Science & Technology Index, 1958–. Online coverage available from 1983. This resource provides information on all areas of engineering, technology, and science with coverage of important trade and industrial publications, journals, and a range of other specialized-subject periodicals. The database also includes product reviews and references to conferences and seminars.

Bibliography and Index of Geology, 1969–. Bibliography of world literature dealing with the earth sciences; entries are arranged within 29 subject areas; issued monthly.

Bibliography of Agriculture, 1942–. Listing of literature covering agriculture and allied subjects; issued monthly.

Biological & Agricultural Index, 1964–. Online coverage available from 1983. Index provides wide-ranging coverage of agriculture and related topics from agriculture to zoology.

Business Periodicals Index, v. 1–Jan. 1958–June 1959–. Covers finance, management, business technology, and economics. Many online formats are available.

Cumulative Index of the National Industrial Conference Board Publications, 1962–. Subject index of publications of interest to commerce and industrial managers; issued annually.

Cumulative Index to Nursing and Allied Health Literature, 1977–. Subject and author index to nursing journals, also available online: CINAHL. Figure 11–11 shows an online search form for this index.

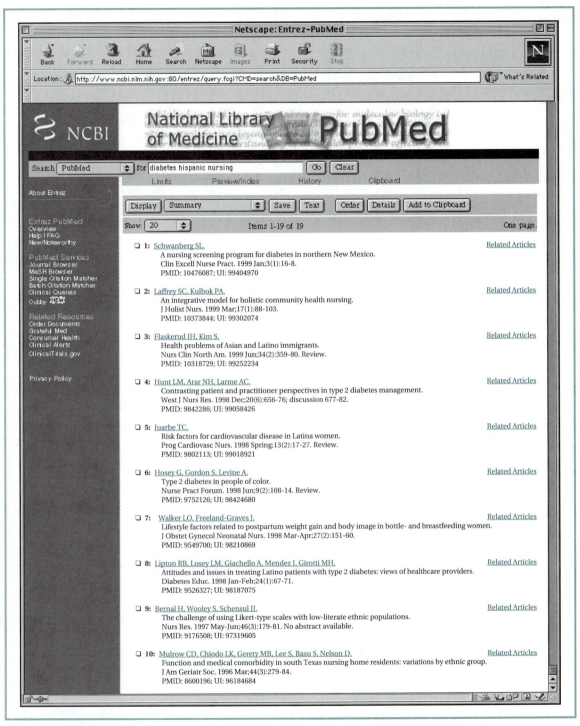

Figure 11–11 Online Search Form for the *Cumulative Index to Nursing and Allied Health Literature*

Source: Reprinted by permission of the Regents of the University of Minnesota, Copyright © 1999, and Ovid Technologies, Inc., Copyright © 1998.

Economics Literature, 1969–. Also available through online services, ECONLIT. Subject indexing and abstracts of economic journals and over 500 collective volumes per year, plus books, dissertations, and working papers.

Employment Relations Abstracts, 1958–. (Issued monthly)

The Engineering Index Monthly, 1984–. This alphabetical subject listing contains brief abstracts covering periodical materials in the field of engineering. COMPENDEX is the online version.

Essay and General Literature Index, 1900–. Semiannual index to information on all subjects in collections of articles in books; generally organized by subject, but sometimes by title.

Government Printing Office (GPO) Access http://www.access.gpo.gov/su_docs/dpos/adpos400.html. The GPO catalog is a search-and-retrieval service that provides bibliographic records of U.S. government information resources, as shown in Figure 11–12. Coverage begins with January 1994 and new records are added daily. Use this source to link to federal agency online resources or to identify materials distributed to Federal Depository Libraries. To locate the nearest depository library in your area, visit the Federal Depository page at http://www.access.gpo.gov/su_docs/dpos/adpos003.html.

Government Reports Announcements and Index, 1965–. Semimonthly index of reports arranged by subject, author, and report number.

Index to The Times (London), 1790–. (Issued monthly)

Monthly Catalog of U.S. Government Publications, 1895–. Unclassified publications of all federal agencies listed by subject, author, and report number; issued monthly.

The New York Times *Index,* 1913–. Subject and author index to *New York Times* articles. This index can also be located in various online vendors and the full text of articles is available from 1980 on LexisNexis.

PAIS International in print, 1991–. Also available through various online subscription services. Coverage is primarily in political science, government, legislation, international relations, and sociology.

Psychological Abstracts, 1927–. v. 1–Jan. 1927–. Contains citations and abstracts of articles dealing with all aspects of psychology and related fields, such as industrial psychology; issued monthly.

PsycINFO [computer file], 1996–. Also available through various online subscription services. Contains citations and summaries of journal articles, book chapters, books, and technical reports in the field of psychology and psychological aspects of related disciplines, including medicine, psychiatry, nursing, sociology, education, pharmacology, physiology, linguistics, anthropology, business, and law.

PubMed: National Library of Medicine Access http://www.ncbi.nlm.nih.gov/PubMed/. This site provides access to more than nine million citations.

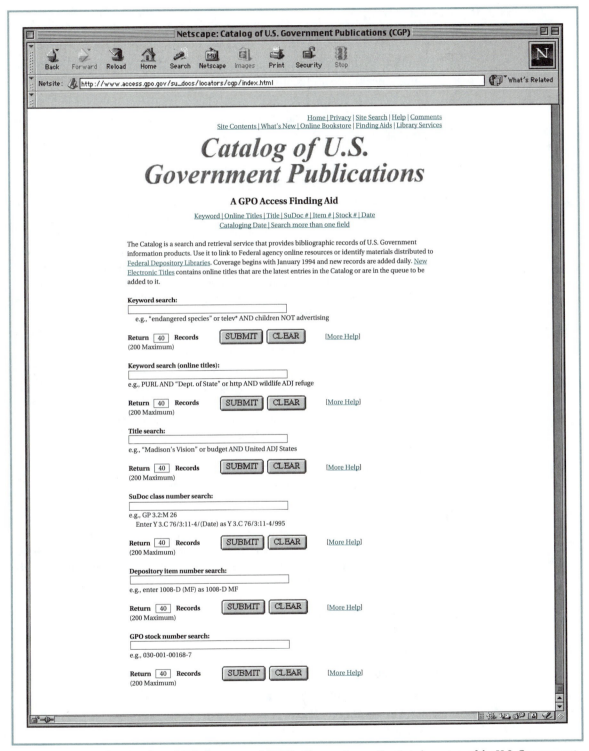

Figure 11–12 **Online Catalog of U.S. Government Publications** *Source:* Reprinted courtesy of the U.S. Government Printing Office.

Readers' Guide to Periodical Literature, 1901–. Provides citations for journal and magazine articles published since the beginning of the twentieth century. Invaluable for locating older materials.

Safety Sciences Abstracts Journal, 1974–. Listing of literature on industrial and occupational safety, transportation, environmental and medical safety; issued quarterly.

Social Sciences Index, 1974–. Indexes periodicals in anthropology, area studies, psychology, public administration, sociology, environmental science, economics, and related areas. The Institute for Scientific Information publishes the Social Sciences Citation Index (SSCI), which provides online access to current bibliographic information and cited references, covering more than 1,700 of the world's leading social sciences journals in a broad range of disciplines. It also covers individually selected, relevant articles from more than 3,400 of the world's leading natural and physical science journals. A powerful capability is *cited reference searching,* a process in which one tracks the number of times a specific work has been cited or referenced in other works.

Sociological Abstracts, 1952–. Monthly abstracting service covering all subjects related to social behavior.

U.S. Supreme Court, *United States Reports,* 1754–. The text of Supreme Court decisions are published in this series in chronological order. As decisions are made, they are published in pamphlet form, called *slip decisions,* before being cumulated into volumes. A searchable database of decisions from 1893 to the present can be found at http://www.findlaw.com/casecode/supreme.html.

Wall Street Journal Index, 1957–. This monthly index of business and financial news is available in print and online.

This list is selective. Many more indexes and abstracting services are published and made available online for different fields of research than are described here.

Typical of specialized indexes is the *Applied Science & Technology Index,* which is available both in printed and electronic formats. This index lists, by subject, articles in the following fields:

aeronautics and space science	food and the food industry
atmospheric sciences	geology
chemistry	machinery
computer technology and applications	mathematics
the construction industry	metallurgy
energy resources and research	mineralogy
engineering	oceanography
fire and fire prevention	petroleum and gas research

physics　　　　　　　　　　　　　the textile industry

plastics technology　　　　　　　transportation

The index also lists articles in other industrial and mechanical arts. In addition, the index covers several branches of engineering—chemical, civil, electrical and telecommunications, environmental, industrial, mechanical, mining, and nuclear. Figure 11–13 shows the explanation that appears at the front of the index. Figure 11–14 shows part of a column in the index proper. In the first entry under *Engineering colleges*, for example, the index refers to an article about design automation information on the Internet that appears on page 421 in volume 47 of the journal *Electronic Design*. The article was published in December 1999.

Computerized Information Retrieval for Bibliographies

In addition to offering a computer service for the compilation of indexes, most libraries offer the same service for bibliographies. With the help of a research librarian, you can draw on hundreds of available bibliographic databases. You may wish to do so for the following reasons:

1. Your topic brings together several different concepts and would require you to search in a printed or online index or catalog under several different terms to filter out much irrelevant material.

2. You want the most up-to-date information. (Printed and online indexes and catalogs typically are from six weeks to one year behind the literature they cite.)

3. You are doing research on a very new concept, perhaps described by a newly coined word that has not yet appeared as a subject heading in indexes or catalogs.

4. You are in a hurry. A computer search can find in under an hour what a manual search could take weeks to locate.

5. Finally, you are searching for a work by a specific author, but the printed and online indexes provide only subject access.

The search is conducted by entering keywords and key phrases on the terminal to establish the boundaries of the search. Libraries that provide this service employ a librarian skilled in the strategies that selecting keywords involves: The researcher goes to the librarian and explains his or her problem, the librarian typically determines the keywords that best represent the researcher's area of study and enters them on the terminal, and the screen indicates how many items are available. If the researcher wishes to expand or limit the number of available items, a different arrangement of keywords is entered. Once a satisfactory number of items is obtained, the librarian can print out a bibliography. Figure 11–15 shows a sample citation from such a search.

PREFATORY NOTE

The *APPLIED SCIENCE & TECHNOLOGY INDEX* is a cumulative index to English language periodicals. The main body of the Index consists of subject entries to periodical articles arranged in one alphabet. In addition there are separate listings of citations to book reviews and product reviews following the main body of the Index.

Subject fields indexed include acoustics, aeronautics and space science, automatic control, ceramics and glass, chemistry, computers and data processing, construction industry, energy resources and research, food and food industry, geology, machinery, mathematics, meteorology, metallurgy, oceanography, optical and neural computing, petroleum and gas, physics, plastics and rubber, robotics, safety and fire prevention, telecommunication, textile industry and transportation.

The following engineering disciplines are covered: aeronautic, automotive, chemical, civil, electrical and electronic, environmental, industrial, mechanical, mining, nuclear and water supply.

The Committee on Wilson Indexes of the American Library Association's Reference and User Services Association advises the publisher on indexing and editorial policy by means of in-depth contents studies conducted at intervals of several years. The Committee as part of its study prepares a list of periodicals, representative of all subject areas included in the Index, for consideration by the subscribers.

Selection of periodicals for indexing from this list is accomplished by subscriber vote. In voting their preferences subscribers are asked to place primary emphasis on the reference value of the periodicals under consideration. They are also asked to give particular consideration to subject balance in order to insure that no important field be overlooked in proportion to overall Index coverage.

While the responsibility for all indexing and editorial decisions rests with The H.W. Wilson Company, every effort is made by the Company to follow the recommendations of the Committee and the subscribers to a given periodical index.

Suggestions for addition or deletion of titles should be brought to the attention of The H.W. Wilson Company, 950 University Avenue, Bronx, N.Y. 10452.

June 2000. Vol. 88. No. 6.

APPLIED SCIENCE & TECHNOLOGY INDEX (ISSN 0003-6986) is published monthly except July, with a bound cumulation each year. This publication is priced on a service basis; the subscriber's periodical holdings determine its annual subscription rate. The minimum annual subscription price is $345. For a specific price quotation, the subscriber should apply to the Publisher. Copyright © 2000 by The H. W. Wilson Company, 950 University Avenue, Bronx, N.Y. 10452. All rights reserved. No part of this work may be reproduced or copied in any form or by any means, including but not restricted to graphic, electronic, or mechanical—for example, photocopying, recording, taping, or information storage and retrieval systems—without the express written permission of the Publisher. Periodical postage paid at Bronx, N.Y. Printed in U.S.A. POSTMASTER: Send address changes to APPLIED SCIENCE & TECHNOLOGY INDEX, c/o The H. W. Wilson Company, 950 University Avenue, Bronx, N.Y. 10452.

Figure 11–13   Prefatory Note to the *Applied Science & Technology Index*

Figure 11–14   Sample Column from the *Applied Science & Technology Index*

Engineering—*cont.*
Political aspects
Eight ways to build strength. B. T. Pallasch. *Civ Eng (Am Soc Civ Eng)* v70 no2 p8 F 2000
Study and teaching
See Engineering education
Great Britain
Voice in the valleys [interview with head of Professional Engineering Institutions] H. Beasley. por *Engineer* v289 no7495 p14 Mr 17 2000
Engineering, Genetic *See* Genetic engineering
Engineering and Physical Sciences Research Council (Great Britain)
New blood to take analytical chairs. D. Bradley. *Anal Chem* v72 no5 p190A Mr 1 2000
Engineering colleges
Curriculum
Bone up on design automation via the Internet. *Electron Des* v47 no26 p42 D 17 1999
Failure of constructed facilities in civil engineering curricula. K. L. Rens and others. bibl *J Perform Constr Facil* v14 no1 p27-37 F 2000
A professionals guidebook: how to start and properly support a four-year geomatics engineering program. J. K. Crossfield. bibl il *Surv Land Inf Syst* v60 no1 p13-18 Mr 2000
The Tuskegee academic experiment. W. D. Jones. *IEEE Spectr* v37 no2 p64R2-64R9 F 2000
Finance
NACME: funds will help retain minority engineering students. *IIE Solut* v31 no12 p8 D 1999
Graduate work
See also
Graduate students
Articulation planning in geographic information science: new opportunities. G. A. Jeffress and others. il *Surv Land Inf Syst* v60 no1 p47-9 Mr 2000
Education: a neverending quest. D. Bursky. *Electron Des* v47 no26 p18 D 17 1999
Laboratories
Integration of technology into a surveying engineering curriculum. H. Turner and F. A. Neto. il *Surv Land Inf Syst* v60 no1 p37-46 Mr 2000
Relations with industry
See also
Engineering education—Industry cooperation
Learning curve. G. Taylor. il *Engineering* v240 no11 p E8-E9 D 1999
The Tuskegee academic experiment. W. D. Jones. *IEEE Spectr* v37 no2 p64R2-64R9 F 2000
Teaching methods
BLM and NMSU—a cooperation in teaching. S. Frank. il *Surv Land Inf Syst* v60 no1 p51-4 Mr 2000
Engineering contracts
See also
Roads—Contracts
Turnkey contracts
Engineering databases
See also
Engineering—Internet resources
Industrial engineering—Internet resources
Manufacturing execution systems
Municipal engineering databases
Petroleum databases
See also Engineering databases in Product Reviews section
Enabling allied concurrent engineering through distributed engineering information management. Y.-M. Chen and Y.-D. Jan. bibl il *Rob Comput-Integr Manuf* v16 no1 p9-27 F 2000
Engineering departments
See also
Industrial engineering
Engineering design
See also
Computer aided design
Design expert systems
Earthquake resistant design

```
AU – Gausche M
AU – Henderson DP
AU – Seidel JS
TI – Vital signs as part of the prehospital assessment of the
     pediatric patient: a survey of paramedics.
AB – Vital signs are an integral part of the field assessment
     of patients. A two-part study was undertaken to determine
     which vital signs are taken in the field assessment of
     pediatric patients and to determine whether the frequency
     of vital signs taken is influenced by base station
     contact, patient's severity of illness or injury, or
     paramedic demographic factors such as parenting and field
     experience. An initial pilot study of prehospital care
     records (run sheets) from two base hospitals in Los
     Angeles County revealed that there were significant
     differences between field vital sign assessment in
     pediatric and adult patients (P less than .0001). A
     retrospective review of 6,756 pediatric run sheets from
     Los Angeles County showed that the frequency of vital sign
     assessment varied with the age of the pediatric patient
     (P less than .05) (ie, the frequency of vital sign
     assessment increased correspondingly with the age of the
     patient). Base hospital contact occurred in 26% of the
     runs; when contact was made, vital signs were more likely
     to be taken in all age groups studied. Vital signs often
     were not assessed in children less than 2 years old, even
     if the patient's chief complaint suggested the
     possibility of a major illness or trauma. The second part
     of the study was a field assessment survey that was
     distributed to 1,253 active paramedics in Los Angeles
     County; the results showed that paramedics were less
     confident in their ability to assess vital signs in
     children less than 2 years old. Confidence increased with
     age of the patient. (ABSTRACT TRUNCATED AT 250 WORDS)
LA – Eng
AD – Department of Emergency Medicine, Harbor–UCLA Medical
     Center, Torrance.
SO – Ann Emerg Med 1990 Feb; 19(2):173-8
```

Suppose, for example, that you were researching the role of supertankers in the U.S. merchant fleet. Your librarian might begin the search with the key phrase *cargo ships,* and read on the terminal screen that 874 articles pertain to that broad subject. You do not wish to wade through this many articles, so the librarian limits the search by entering the keywords *American* and *oil.* The revised number is pared down to 211 articles—still too many for your purposes. You decide that you are really only interested in articles published during the past year. When this limitation is entered, the number of pertinent articles is reduced to a manageable 14. You then request a printout of a bibliography of the 14 items.

The printout of a bibliographic citation and abstract shown in Figure 11–15 was retrieved after a search of MEDLARS (Medical Analysis and Retrieval System). The citation shows the title, abstract, and other pertinent information for a survey study of the factors affecting the type and frequency of vital signs taken by paramedics for pediatric patients before they arrive at a hospital. The printout abbreviates key features of the citation as follows:

AU = author(s)

TI = title

AB = abstract

LA = language

AD = corporate affiliation of author(s)

SO = source or location of the journal article

To find the full text, a researcher would look in the February 1990 issue of *Annals of Emergency Medicine*, pages 173–178. Note the message at the end of the abstract indicating that although the article's abstract runs longer than 250 words, the printout will print only 250 words.

Usually the library will charge a fee based on the database used, the results achieved, and the time spent online. Discuss the policy and anticipated charges with the librarian before proceeding.

Following are some examples of computerized databases. The frequency with which they are updated depends on the vendor through which your library acquires rights to access the database. As always, ask a librarian about sources available for your research needs.

ABI/INFORM, Dialog, 1971–. Weekly updating. Citations and abstracts from more than 1,000 business and management publications, including over 350 English-language titles outside the United States, such as *Financial Times, Business Week, Fortune, Forbes,* and *Chemical Week,* with an emphasis on business concepts rather than on specific industries or companies.

Agricola, Dialog, 1970–. Monthly updating. Indexes of more than 600 publications worldwide in food and food research.

Bibliographic Retrieval Service, 1975–. Accesses indexes from more than 160 databases from government agencies, professional organizations, and publishers, including AIDS articles, *Books in Print,* Computer and Mathematics Search, Family Resources, Magazine Index, MEDLINE, National Technical Information Service, Resources in Vocational Education, and Robotics Information Database.

Biobusiness, Nexis, 1985–. Monthly updating. Abstracts from more than 1,000 journals on business applications of biological and biomedical research.

Computer Data Base, Nexis, 1983–. Biweekly updating. Abstracts from about 500 periodicals on computers, telecommunications, and electronics.

Dow Jones News/Retrieval, 1985–. Access to articles found in the *Wall Street Journal* and *Barron's.*

ERIC (Educational Resources Information Center) 1966–. Indexes for more than 70 journals and magazines in education and related areas.

Ethnic NewsWatch. Softline, 1991–. CD-ROM or online. Full text of many ethnic publications from North America, including ones from African American, Asian/Pacific Islander, Hispanic, Jewish, European, Middle Eastern, and Native American communities.

General Reference Center (Magazine Index), 1980–. Bibliographic citations, abstracts, and selective full text. Indexes 415 general-interest magazines, including full text for more than 315 of these titles. Full text of newspaper articles from the current two years of the Knight-Ridder/Tribune News Service. Indexes the most recent two months of the *New York Times* and *Wall Street Journal.*

Governments on the WWW: http://www.gksoft.com/govt/en/. A clear organized directory of government sites from around the world, as well as links to political parties and general information on countries of the world.

Lexis Nexis Academic Universe, 1995–. Online vendor. Indexes nearly 5,000 publications covering news and financial, medical, and legal information. This compilation of databases provides more than a billion documents. It is updated daily and most titles are full text.

Management Contents, Dialog, 1974–. Monthly updating. Abstracts of about 90 periodicals on management.

National Technical Information Service, Nexis, 1980–. Biweekly updating. Abstracts of technical reports and other materials in science and technology.

PTS F&S Indexes, Dialog, 1972–. Weekly updating. Indexes of about 2,500 periodicals, with brief summaries, emphasizing a particular company or industry.

Scisearch, Dialog, 1974–. Biweekly updating. Indexes of about 4,500 journals in science, technology, and related fields.

Statistical Universe, Subset of LexisNexis Academic Universe. Indexing and selected full text for articles, reports, and other materials containing or relating to statistics. Covers international, national, state, local, and association resources.

■ Internet Research

Anyone with Internet access can search through the staggering amount of information that it offers. Although the Internet contains a wealth of information, the lack of an overall organization makes it a daunting resource. Unlike a library, the Internet has no one indexing scheme, no single catalog that brings the information together for browsing or easy access. In addition, the servers of many Internet databases change or move, making it sometimes difficult to relocate information used before. Nevertheless, the information on the Internet can be located using what is currently the fastest and most comprehensive access to Internet resources: the World Wide Web.

Located on the Internet, the World Wide Web is a system that simplifies navigation on the Internet through *hyperlinks,* which are links embedded in Web pages when they are created that allow you to move from page to page and site to site at the click of your mouse. You can access the Web using software instructions called a *browser* (or *client*), such as Netscape Navigator®[1] or Microsoft Internet Explorer®.[2]

Clifford Lynch, executive director of the Coalition for Networked Information, described the Web as "a library whose books, periodicals, and newspapers have been strewn all over the floor." This huge virtual warehouse stores books, journal and newspaper articles, business reports, scientific data, recipes, meeting minutes, videos, homework assignments, advertisements, speeches, photographs, maps, government reports and laws, proposed legislation and court decisions, business and health-care material, the lyrics of popular songs, audio recordings, public access to library collections, transcripts of conversations, and catalogs for purchasing everything from stocks to pizzas. The Internet also contains some objectionable materials that are jumbled together with everything else in an immense, electronic warehouse. With the Web estimated to be in excess of 320 million pages, searching through the digital haystack can lead to numerous insignificant results that can stymie your research process.

If your research question has to do with current events, pop-culture trends, commercial products, government information, health care, or technology, the Web can be an excellent resource. However, if you are looking for scholarly information or research, scholarly databases are likely a better resource.

Locating Information

To locate specific subjects, you can use two types of search tools: a *subject directory* and a *search engine*. A subject directory (also known as an index) organizes information by broad subject categories (business, entertainment, health, sports) and related subtopics (marketing, finance, investing). A subject-directory search eventually produces a list of specific sites that contain information about the topics you request. On the Web, the list is hyperlinked to each site. Once you locate a site of interest that you want to revisit, you can bookmark it. (A bookmark is a browser feature that saves Uniform Resource Locators, URLs, or the online addresses of these sites in a special file. To revisit the site, you open the bookmark list, which is displayed as a dropdown menu, and click on it.)

---

[1]Netscape Navigator® is a registered trademark of Netscape Communications Corporation in the United States and other countries.

[2]Microsoft Internet Explorer® is either a registered trademark or trademark of Microsoft Corporation in the United States and other countries.

One popular subject-directory program is Yahoo! at http://www.yahoo.com. It offers 14 broad topic categories, shown in Figure 11–16. When you click on *Business & Economy*, you retrieve a search screen (Figure 11–17) that lists a broad range of related topics. A click on *Electronic Commerce* retrieves a third screen (Figure 11–18) listing 17 separate subtopics (e.g., Barcodes, Digital Money, Electronic Data Interchange). This and the next screen (not shown) list several dozen specific sites in alphabetical order that can be accessed at the click of your mouse. If you were interested in the topic *Digital Money*, you could locate a site called *Network Payment Mechanisms and Digital Cash*, which is described as "A collection of papers, articles, reports, press releases, discussions, implementation tools, links to related sites, and more to do with Network Payment Mechanisms and Digital Cash." A click on this site would yield the list shown in Figure 11–19. You could continue your search until you located a specific article, press release, or report that covered your topic.

A *search engine* locates information based on words or combinations of words that you specify. The software "engine" then lists for you the documents or files that contain one or more of these words in their titles, descriptions, or text. Also available are *meta-search engines*—tools that do not maintain an internal database but instead launch your query to multiple databases of various Web-based resources (other search engines or subject directories). Some meta-tools search these resources one at a time and others launch simultaneous queries to many engines or directories at once. The following subject directories, search engines, and meta-search engines are among the most widely used on the Web.

Subject Directories

The Clearinghouse. http://www.clearinghouse.net. The Argus Clearinghouse is a subject directory maintained by research librarians who identify, describe, and evaluate Web resources.

Galaxy. http://www.einet.net/galaxy.html. The Internet's oldest searchable directory, Galaxy categorizes Web resources by type, such as commercial organization, collection, article, or directory.

Infomine. http://lib-www.ucr.edu/. Infomine is a Web directory specializing in Web resources of interest to academics and scholars.

Librarians' Index to the Internet. http://lii.org. Geared toward librarians and nonlibrarians, the Librarians' Index to the Internet is a searchable, annotated directory of more than 6,500 Internet resources that are evaluated and described by research librarians.

Signpost. http://www.signpost.org/signpost/. Signpost searches and classifies by Library of Congress headings and aims to direct students and scholars to only high-quality Web resources.

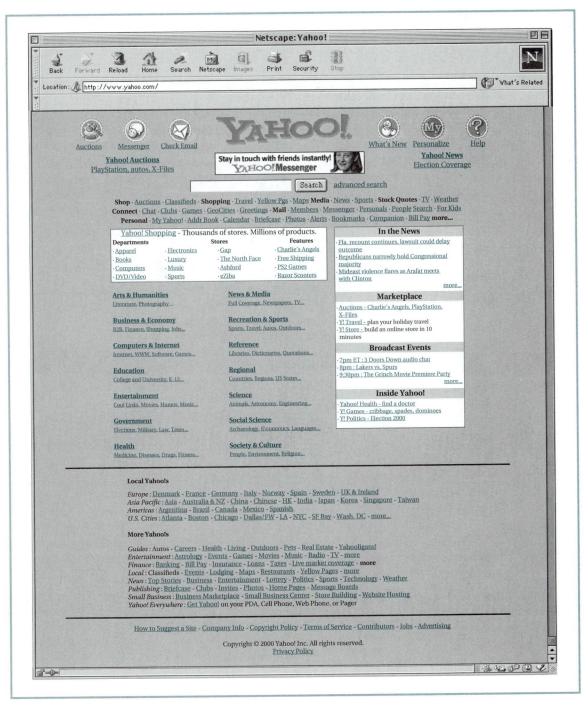

Figure 11–16 Initial Yahoo! Search Screen *Source:* Text and artwork copyright © 2000 by Yahoo!, Inc. All rights reserved. Yahoo! and the Yahoo! logo are trademarks of Yahoo!, Inc.

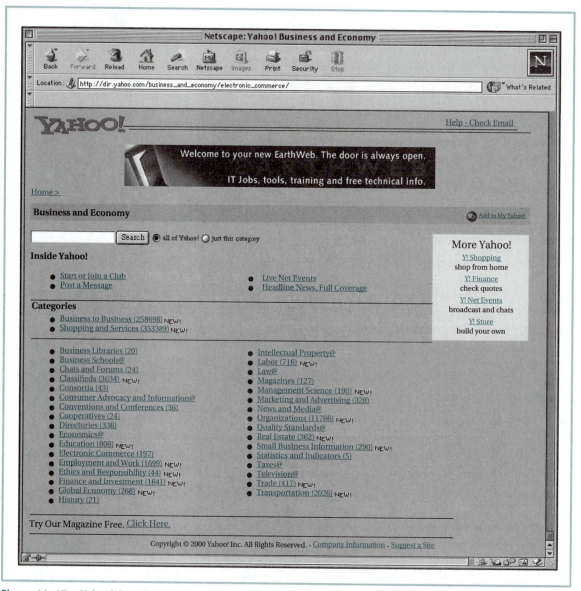

Figure 11–17   Yahoo! Search Screen Showing Scope of Business Information Available   *Source:* Text and artwork
copyright © 2000 by Yahoo!, Inc. All rights reserved. Yahoo! and the Yahoo! logo are trademarks of Yahoo!, Inc.

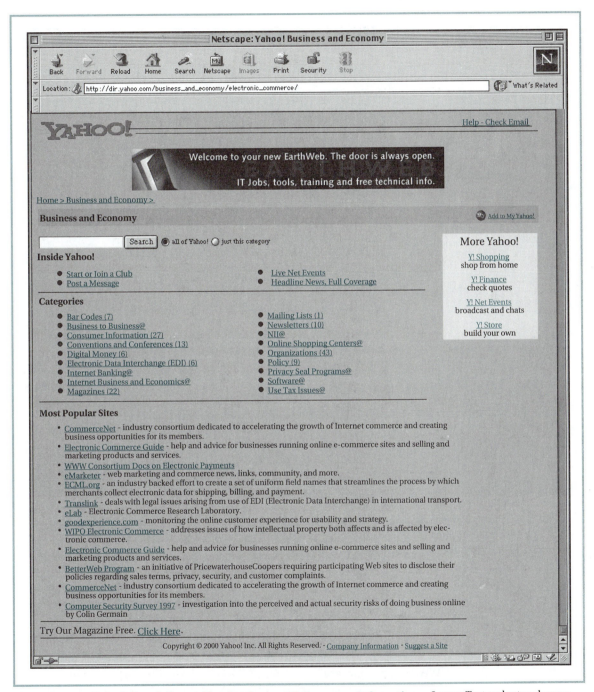

Figure 11–18 Yahoo! Search Screen Showing Scope of E-Commerce Information *Source:* Text and artwork copyright © 2000 by Yahoo!, Inc. All rights reserved. Yahoo! and the Yahoo! logo are trademarks of Yahoo!, Inc.

Figure 11–19 **Screen Showing Scope of Information Available about Mechanisms for Conducting Cash Transactions Online (Accessed through the Yahoo! Electronic Commerce Directory)** *Source:* Reprinted by permission of the Networks and Telecommunications Research Group (NTRG) and Michael Peirce.

Yahoo! http://www.yahoo.com. The popular Yahoo! Directory is the most detailed subject directory available.

WWW Virtual Library. http://www.vlib.org/Home.html. The Virtual Library is a noncommercial catalog of the Web started by the creator of HTML and the World Wide Web itself.

Search Engines

AltaVista. http://altavista.com. AltaVista is one of the largest, most comprehensive search engines, with a strong advanced query option. This engine also allows you to search for sites by their modification dates.

FastSearch. http://www.alltheweb.com. FastSearch may be the biggest and fastest search engine, searching 300 million Web pages in under half a second.

Google. http://google.com. Google is a fast, easy-to-use, and advertisement-free search engine that provides a relevancy ranking for all sites. You can opt to use the "I'm Feeling Lucky™" button, that takes you directly to the Web site of the first search result.

InfoSeek. http://www.infoseek.go.com. Though smaller than other search engines, Infoseek offers excellent content and allows you to conduct a search based on the results of a previous search.

WRITER'S CHECKLIST: Learning Web Jargon

Before beginning your search, become familiar with the following Web terminology:

☐ *Clients* (also called *browsers*): computers that users use to access resources on the Web; clients request pages from *servers* and display them on the monitor (see *servers* below)

☐ *Host:* the address of a server

☐ *HTTP:* Hypertext Transfer Protocol; a standard resource that supports the transfer of information between clients and servers

☐ *Path and File name:* the location of a resource on a server

☐ *Protocol:* a type of resource used by a server that will provide the file (by http, mailto, ftp, telnet, or other transfer resources)

☐ *Servers:* computers that store the information and resources that make up the Web; servers store and send documents requested by *clients* (see *clients* above)

☐ *URL:* Uniform Resource Locator; a standard locator of Internet resources and serves as an address for a given resource. The URL makes links possible from one item to another and specifies the type of process being accessed, the address of the server, and where the page is located on the server. URLs are case sensitive.

Note: The *Encarta* online dictionary and encyclopedia are also good resources for terms related to the Web and are available at http://encarta.msn.com/.

Northern Light. http://www.northernlight.com. Northern Light is a large site that helps you narrow your search by organizing the results into separate folders; it also includes a *for-a-fee* section.

Search-engines World Wide. http://www.twics.com/~takakuwa/search/. This engine enables you to select a search engine for a particular country.

Meta-Search Engines

Dogpile. http://www.dogpile.com. Dogpile searches other search engines for responses to your query and reports what each one found.

Inference Find. http://www.infind.com. Infind searches a select group of search engines for responses to your query, merges the results, removes redundancies, and presents the results in concise clusters.

Metacrawler. http://www.metacrawler.com. Also accessible at http://www.metafind.com. Metacrawler searches other engines for your query, lists the search engines where relevant sites were found, and allows you to email the results.

Table 11–1 provides a quick reference for choosing among the Web search tools available: subject directories, search engines, and meta-search engines. Another valuable resource is the University of California Library at Berkeley's *Recommended Search Engines and Subject Directories* page. This site at http://www.lib.berkeley.edu/TeachingLib/Guides/Internet/ToolsTables.html offers a clear overview of Web search tools, tips, and detailed advice for using them.

Business, Media, and Government Resources on the Web

In addition to general-topic indexes and search engines, the Web also includes numerous sites devoted to specific subject areas. To get started with research on a business-related topic, you could begin at one of the following sites.

Business Resources on the Web

@brint.com. http://www.brint.com/interest.html. This is a popular site hosted by the BizTech Network™ with portals for e-business and e-commerce, Internet business technology, knowledge management, and general business and technology.

Annual Reports Service. http://www.annualreportservice.com/. Provides the full text of company annual reports.

Argus Clearinghouse. http://www.clearinghouse.net/. This directory reviews, ranks, and categorizes Web sites to help in locating useful Web sites.

Center for the Study of American Business (CSAB). http://csab.wustl.edu/home.asp. CSAB is a public-policy research institute analyzing critical issues facing American business.

Table 11–1
Tools for
Searching
the Web

	Subject directories (indexes)	Search engines	Meta-search engines
Functions and organization	List links to other sites by topic and function like the *Yellow Pages* Are organized from general to specific; may contain cross-references Are maintained by trained indexers	Allow keyword(s) searches and functions like the index of a book Create a database index of URLs, extracts, and full-text information Offer a search interface for searching the contents of the index with little human intervention	Launch user's query to multiple databases of various and numerous Web resources (other search engines and directories) May sort results into a ranked system
How to use	User selects and navigates links User may be able to perform keyword searches of some directories	User types query into Web form and may refine query using Boolean logic, proximity, among others User can see a list of results with links to sources	User types in a couple of keywords or a phrase
Advantages	List information on broad topics Are logically organized and easy to use Offer a high degree of accuracy because of selectivity of human indexers May include abstracts and reviews	Contain large document collections Allow a user to refine a search and to search only relevant portions of documents New sites can be added rapidly by automation	Are convenient when few results are anticipated Can find plentiful information at many locations on the Web
Disadvantages	May lack controlled vocabulary, reducing the relevancy of a search May result in a slow search because of the depth of searches Human involvement may delay inclusion of new sites and the removal of outdated sites	No two work exactly the same way May be a lack of precision and quality because of the number of results and lack of human involvement in selection process Abstracts and reviews not included	May not offer a full range of tools, so searches can be less refined May result in a slower response time than a search of an individual directory or index

Edgar Database of Corporate Information. http://www.sec.gov/edgarhp.htm. This is the government's database of corporate reports; full texts available online.

Hoover's Online: The Business Network. http://www.hoovers.com/. This is a subscription service that may be available in some libraries; some company information is available online.

Intellifact.com Business Information Central. http://www.intellifact.com. Intellifact provides research information regarding industries, regions, and company resources.

The New York Public Library: Research Libraries: Science, Industry and Business Library. http://www.nypl.org/research/sibl/. This well-organized site is ideal for business and industry researchers.

Small Business Administration: SBA Technology. http://www.sba.gov/SBIR/. The Office of Technology at the SBA provides information on its programs for strengthening and expanding small, high-tech business in the U.S.— especially those doing research and development.

Small Business Innovation Research: U.S. Department of Education. http://www.ed.gov/offices/OERI/SBIR/. Find out what is new in small business endeavors in the area of education.

Thomas: Legislative Information on the Internet. http://thomas.loc.gov/. This government site offers current U.S. federal legislative information regarding bills, laws, and other information. It includes House and Senate bills, public laws, the *Congressional Record,* and committee reports.

United States Tax Code On-Line. http://www.fourmilab.to/uscode/26usc/ustax.html. This site, maintained by software developer John Walker (coauthor of AutoCAD), offers a searchable and cross-referenced version of the U.S. Internal Revenue Code, Title 26. The document is an HTML version of the U.S. House of Representatives Gopher file, and allows you to quickly locate sections of the code by content. (For additional tax information, visit the Internal Revenue Service at http://www.irs.gov.)

WWW Virtual Library: Ecology and Biodiversity. http://conbio.rice.edu/vl/. The Virtual Library of Ecology and Biodiversity division of The Virtual Library Project specializes in reviewing Internet information sources pertaining to ecology and biodiversity based on their educational value.

Media and Government Resources on the Web

AJR Newslink. http://ajr.newslink.org/. Primarily aimed at working journalists, this site offers links to newspapers, magazines, and radio and television sites on the Web as well as provides coverage of news and information about the news professions.

Kidon Media Link. http://www.kidon.com/media-link/index.shtml. An excellent source of links to international media sources, clearly organized and frequently updated. Created by a Dutch political-science student, the site is well maintained and thorough.

U.S. Federal Statistics. http://www.fedstats.gov/. More than 70 agencies in the federal government produce statistics of interest to the public. The Federal Interagency Council on Statistical Policy maintains this site to provide easy access to the full range of statistics and information produced by the following agencies for public use:

> *Bureau of Justice Statistics.* http://www.ojp.usdoj.gov/bjs/
>
> *Bureau of Labor Statistics.* http://www.bls.gov/
>
> *Energy Information Administration.* http://www.eia.doe.gov/
>
> *Environmental Protection Agency.* http://www.epa.gov/
>
> *National Cancer Institute.* http://www.nci.nih.gov/
>
> *National Center for Education Statistics.* http://nces.ed.gov/
>
> *National Institutes of Health.* http://www.nih.gov/
>
> *National Science Foundation.* http://www.nsf.gov/
>
> *Plants Database.* http://plants.usda.gov/
>
> *U.S. Census Bureau.* http://www.census.gov/

DIGITAL SHORTCUTS: Searching the Web

- Use your browser's features to assist your search.
  - Read the available help screens and use advanced search modes.
  - Use the Find command (under Edit or ctrl + f) to find a word or a phrase within a given page.
  - Review the sites you have visited by scrolling from the arrow at the end of the URL address line.
- Use common protocols.
  - Put a phrase in quotes: "Applied business ethics."
  - Combine concepts with AND (when you want to include both terms), OR (when you want to include either term), and NOT (when you want to exclude a term).
  - End a word root with a wildcard (usually *) to find any word starting with that root (e.g., "run*" retrieves runners, running).

- Shorten a URL to get to a root page by deleting everything after the first slash (/).
- Look for links that indicate a page's author or sponsoring organization.
- Use clues in the unique address of each document to access the source:
  - *.com*   a company or personal site
  - *.edu*   higher education site
  - *.gov*   federal government site
  - *.k12*   primary or secondary school site
  - *.net*   a network
  - *.org*   an organization's site
- Note any abbreviations within the URL that indicate the country where the site is based; for example, ca (Canada), au (Australia), uk (United Kingdom), jp (Japan).

■ Evaluating Internet and Library Sources and Creating a Working Bibliography

Evaluating Internet Sources

Access to the vast amount of information available on the Internet is not only useful but irresistible for casual browsers and researchers alike. Yet, a word of caution is in order. Evaluate the usefulness of information on the Internet with the same standards that you use to evaluate information from other sources. Is it accurate? Is it up to date? Is the author qualified and reputable? Is the sponsor of the site or journal reputable? These standards apply for printed material, for people you interview, or for any other source. (For detailed criteria for evaluating authors, see page 445.) One of the best ways to access the Internet is through your library's home page. Many libraries—in addition to offering online catalogs and indexes of their own holdings as well as databases of articles—offer excellent tools for searching the Web. These tools can include Web subject guides and links to select sites that have already been evaluated by research librarians. Such features are designed to focus your research on quality sources and save time. In fact, you may want to begin your search on the Web by first consulting with a research librarian who can point you toward tools and select reputable sources on the Web, making your search more efficient.

The easiest way to ensure that information is valid is to obtain it from a reputable source. For example, data from the Bureau of Labor Statistics, the Securities and Exchange Commission, and the Bureau of the Census is widely used by

---

WRITER'S CHECKLIST: Evaluating Internet Resources

Because there are few (if any) barriers determining who can publish—or what can be published—on the Internet, the value and accuracy of information varies widely. It's up to you to critically evaluate the sources that you find on the Internet. Ask the following questions of each site that you encounter:

- ☐ *Who* is the author? Why should that author be trusted?
- ☐ *What* is the main focus of the page? Does it make sense?
- ☐ *Where* does the site originate? Is it put out by an organization, an individual, or an institution?
- ☐ *When* was it put online? Is it updated regularly?
- ☐ *Why* does that page exist? Can you find a purpose statement? Is there a particular bias?
- ☐ *Does* the information available compare favorably with at least two other reputable online sources?

U.S. businesses. Likewise, online versions of established, reputable journals in medicine, engineering, computer software, and other fields merit the same level of trust as the printed versions. However, as you move away from established, reputable sites, exercise more caution. Be especially wary of unmoderated discussion groups on Usenet and other public bulletin-board systems. Remember that anyone with access can place information on the Internet, so for many sources there are no editorial checks and balances in place. Treat information obtained from these sources cautiously.

Evaluating Library Sources

After completing your catalog search, locate the necessary books and articles. Many articles will be available online, but older material may not be. You may find that periodicals are arranged alphabetically by title and located in a separate section of the library. If the periodicals you need are not in your library, submit an interlibrary loan request. This service permits you to borrow books and photocopied periodical articles from other libraries.

After you have located a number of books and articles, you need to make decisions about whether to continue to use particular sources in your research. A factor to consider is the author's reputation: Is the writer considered an authority in the field? Has he or she written other, highly regarded books or articles in the field or in a related field? You might ask a librarian, an instructor, or an expert in the field who is familiar with the subject area, whether the author has an established reputation in the field.

WRITER'S CHECKLIST: Evaluating Library Resources

When you obtain a copy of a book or article, you can examine it in the library before deciding whether to use it. As you scan a work, ask yourself the following questions:

☐ Does the book have an index? Indexes are indispensable in tracking down specific topics within a book.

☐ Does the book contain a comprehensive bibliography that you can use in locating additional material for your research?

☐ Does the article contain a comprehensive list of references or explanatory footnotes that you can use in locating additional material?

☐ Does the book or article have informative diagrams, charts, tables, lists, and graphs?

☐ Is the book or article reasonably up to date? Timeliness is especially important in any fast-changing field such as computer technology.

Document the following information about any book that you decide to include in your research: call number, author (if the author is an organization, indicate that fact), title, city of publication, publisher's name, and year of publication. For an article, record the author, the title of the article, the name of the journal in which it appears, the journal volume and issue numbers, the date of publication, and the page numbers of the article. When you are ready to prepare a bibliography for your research report, you can do so easily using this information. To document sources, you can use the PRINT SCREEN key to print out the search screen containing the full bibliographic citation. You can even download the bibliographic citation for all pertinent information from a full-text database from the library terminal to your own disk for fuller evaluation after you leave the library.

If you make a habit of sending the results of your electronic searches to your email address, you will have a record of your research that will be valuable when you write your paper or presentation. You can also save the email file and use the citations for preparing the works-cited page.

■ Taking Notes

The purpose of taking notes is to condense and record information from the books, articles, Web sites, and other sources used for your research. The notes you take will furnish much of the material for your outline and final written work.

When working with paper sources (books and journals), you can photocopy material and highlight important passages with a highlighter, jot notes on three-by-five-inch or four-by-six-inch index cards, or keyboard them with your laptop or desktop computer. If you are using Internet sources, you can highlight passages and cut and paste them into a word-processing file, in addition to taking notes. When you cut and paste information from the Internet, always include the source to provide proper credit in your final work. Otherwise, you will be plagiarizing from the source. If the source is copyrighted, you may also be guilty of copyright infringement. (See Plagiarism on page 452.)

Whichever method you use, identify the source of the information and include the author's last name (include first name or initials if you have two authors with the same last name) and the page number or numbers on which the material appears in the original source. If you have consulted more than one book or article by an author, include the title as well; for long titles, you may use a shortened form.

As you take notes, make a list of the topics you will cover in your research (as Christine Thomas did in Chapter 1). Identify your notes as appropriate with these topics (sometimes called *slugs*). When you arrange the cards or word-processing notes by topic in preparation for preparing an outline, you can use the slugs as a guide in organizing your material.

For the sake of accuracy and correctness, be careful to distinguish whether you are writing down a *direct quotation* from your source, whether you are *paraphrasing* (restating the text you're using in your own words), or *summarizing* (writing down a highly condensed version of the text). If you are a beginning researcher, you should probably stick to writing down direct quotations. Then, when you turn to actually writing your research paper, you can decide whether you want to quote directly, paraphrase, or summarize.

Quoting Directly

A direct quotation is an exact, word-for-word copy of an original source. Such quotations, which can be of a word, a phrase, a sentence, or, occasionally, a paragraph, should be used sparingly and chosen carefully. A direct quotation is appropriate when the wording of an original source will support a point you are making, or when you feel that your reader will gain some insight from a particularly well-expressed passage. In both instances, the quoted material should be fairly brief. In addition, material such as policy statements, laws, and mathematical and scientific formulas ordinarily should be quoted exactly.

There are two ways of presenting direct quotations within a paper or report. If the quotation you have chosen occupies more than four lines of typed copy, it should be set off from your text. Set-off quotations are usually separated from the text by a double space; every line of the quotation is indented five spaces or one tab stop from the left margin; the quotation is single-spaced; and quotation marks are not needed. It is a good idea to introduce the quotation smoothly— that is, to tell the reader, in your own words, what significance the quotation has for your report.

```
    In a study of design principles as they apply to the develop-
ment of corporate intranet sites, the researcher notes the impor-
tance of hierarchy to user needs.

        The hierarchy of a well-organized intranet is inherently
        macro/micro. Pages should be made accessible to users based
        on audience needs: pages relevant to everyone are considered
        macro and are given the most prominent place on the in-
        tranet; next are pages relevant to many; and then pages rel-
        evant to few. For example, the home page links users to var-
        ious department pages, which in turn link users to topical
        pages, which in turn link users to increasingly specialized
        pages.[1]
```

The following note, which appears either at the bottom of the page or at the end of the paper, would identify the source of the quotation (see the discussion of documentation):

[1]Jackson, Lisa Ann. "The Rhetoric of Design: Implications for Corporate Intranets." *Technical Communication* 47:2 (May 2000): 212–219.

The second way to present a direct quotation, one that takes up four or fewer lines of printed copy, is run in with the text, not set off, and enclosed in quotation marks.

```
The size of corporate intranets and the variety of organizations
contributing to them can mean that "consistency and standardi-
zation can be difficult to manage and may be disregarded"
(Jackson 217).
```

Again, a footnote, endnote, or parenthetical citation identifies the source. The above example uses parenthetical documentation (see the discussion on documenting sources).

There may be times when you want to quote directly from only part of a passage. Suppose, for example, you saw the following sentence in a company newsletter.

> SpeedMail, Incorporated, just hired two entry-level copywriters, who will report to the advertising manager, and a direct-mail assistant, who will be working closely with the director of promotion.

If you wanted to quote only the portion of the sentence that pertains to the direct-mail assistant, you would omit the text relating to the copywriters. When you omit material that falls *within a quoted passage,* you insert *ellipses,* or *three spaced dots,* to indicate where the omission occurs.

> SpeedMail, Incorporated, just hired . . . a direct-mail assistant, who will be working closely with the director of promotion.

However, if you intended to quote the portion of the sentence that deals with the copywriters, you would delete the reference to the direct-mail assistant. To indicate the omission of material that comes *at the end of a quoted passage,* you place *a period followed by ellipses* after the last quoted word.

> SpeedMail, Incorporated, just hired two entry-level copywriters, who will report to the advertising manager. . . .

Paraphrasing

A *paraphrase* of a written passage is a restatement of the essential ideas of the passage in the researcher's own words. Because a paraphrase does not quote the source word for word, quotation marks are not necessary. When you use paraphrased material in your own work, however, you must credit the source in a footnote or a parenthetical note.

As you are getting ready to write a paraphrase, you may find it helpful, after you've read the passage, to put it aside for a moment while you decide how to word the paraphrase; this brief period of reflection will give you a chance both to make sure that you understand the writer's message and to prepare your own version of it. When you start to write, pick up the original and refer to it. Check to be certain that you include every important point in the original that is relevant to your topic.

The passage should be paraphrased, according to your topic and the scope of your written work; if the source contains more information than is pertinent to your subject, paraphrase only the material that relates to your purpose in writing. As an example, consider the following passage and two paraphrases of it. The passage discusses the standardization of production in the book-publishing industry and how it permitted long-term contracts between book publishers and printers.

> About 15 years ago, the book industry came up with an innovative way to create standards-based long-term contract purchasing where it did not exist naturally. The technique can be applied to many other publishing areas, especially manuals of various kinds in the corporate electronic publishing world.
>
> Books, unlike magazines, are one-time productions, each a little different from the next. Traditionally, each book was put out to several printers for competitive bids. With more than 40,000 new books being published each year, the processing of bids required a small army of purchasing managers in publishing houses, and job planners and estimators in printing firms. In addition, lack of standardization required each book to be produced individually at highest cost.
>
> A number of major publishers and printers analyzed the products they were producing and created standards on which to base long-term contracts. They discovered, for example, that they could reduce more than 100 common page sizes to less than a dozen if they grouped the sizes in clusters and then chose one size for each cluster. This enabled printers to establish standard press settings for faster setup and to purchase paper in standard sizes at minimum cost. They also standardized paper grades and binding styles and materials by types of book.
>
> Unlike with magazines, a book publisher could not assign specific books to production slots at the beginning of a contract. However, publishers found that they could predict average monthly production levels by class of book even though they did not know the exact titles to be printed each month. So they started writing contracts with printers for blocks of production time to handle specified volumes of work to be produced to predefined standards. Contracts contain unit-pricing structures similar to those in the magazine business. During the contract term, titles are simply assigned production slots. The savings on both sides have been substantial, and costs during the contract life have become predictable.[3]

---

[3]Paul D. Doebler, "Standard Practices Play a Role in Cost Management," *EP&P*, December/January 1987: 32–33.

If your purpose were to gather information to write about how book production was standardized, your paraphrase might read as follows.

STANDARDIZED BOOK PRODUCTION

More than 40,000 books are published annually in the United
States. Until about 15 years ago, each book was produced individually, thus keeping unit printing costs high. At that time, the
book industry standardized its products to save on production
costs. Publishers and printers agreed to reduce the number of
common page sizes from over 100 to fewer than a dozen. This
arrangement permitted printers to save time by reducing the number of press settings for faster job startups and to save money
by bulk purchasing of paper of standard sizes and grades. They
made similar savings by reducing binding styles and, as a result,
the types of binding materials needed.

If your purpose were to write about how standardization affected the contract arrangements between publishers and printers, your paraphrase might read this way.

STREAMLINED BOOK CONTRACTING

About 15 years ago, book publishers and printers standardized
book-production requirements as a basis for establishing long-
term contracts. Prior to standardization, each of the 40,000
books published annually in the United States was bid on competi-
tively by several printers. This process not only made each book
expensive to produce, but required publishers to employ many purchasing managers and printers to hire numerous job planners and
estimators. In a mutual agreement, publishers and printers standardized book sizes from over 100 to fewer than a dozen. Standardization allowed for standard press settings for faster job
setups and permitted savings for bulk purchases of paper of standard sizes and grades and of binding materials. Fewer book sizes
also made previously unpredictable contract schedules more predictable, because whole classes of books rather than separate
titles could be estimated. Hence, contracts with printers could
be written for blocks of production time, permitting printers to
contain unit costs, assign each book a production slot, and make
costs over the duration of the contract predictable.

Summarizing

A *summary* is a highly condensed version, in the researcher's own words, of an original passage. Summary notes present only the essential ideas or conclusions of the original. As such, they are considerably shorter than paraphrases of the same passage. As with directly quoted and paraphrased material, the source of summarized information must be credited in a footnote.

Figure 11–20 shows a summary of the following passage.

> Now that we have learned something about the nature of elements and molecules, what are fuels? Fuels are those substances that will burn when heat is applied to them. Some elements, in themselves, are fuels. Carbon, hydrogen, sulfur, magnesium, titanium and some other metals are examples of elements that can burn. Coal, charcoal, and coke, for example, are almost pure carbon; hydrogen, another element, is a highly flammable gas. But the most familiar combustible materials are not pure elements; they are compounds and mixtures.
>
> Wood, paper and grass are principally composed of molecules of cellulose, a flammable substance. If we examine the chemical makeup of this compound, we will discover what elements form the basic fuels in most solid materials. The cellulose molecule contains twenty-one atoms: six carbons, ten hydrogens and five oxygen atoms: $C_6H_{10}O_5$. Since oxygen is not flammable (see Oxygen, below), it follows that the carbon and hydrogen found in most common combustible solids are the elements that burn. This conclusion becomes even stronger when we look at common flammable liquids. Gasoline, kerosene, fuel oils and other petroleum compounds are composed of only carbon and hydrogen atoms, in varying amounts. These compounds, called hydrocarbons (hydrogen + carbon), will all burn.
>
> Other flammable compounds are composed of carbon, hydrogen, and oxygen atoms in a fixed ratio, making it appear as if there is a water molecule attached to each carbon atom. A good example is glucose, a common sugar, which has the formula $C_6H_{12}O_6$. Chemists call this type of molecule a "hydrated (watered) carbon," or carbohydrate. Carbohydrates also burn, but are not to be confused with hydrocarbons.
>
> Carbon and hydrogen are only two of the elements which will burn. But, since most common flammable materials contain a combination of carbon and hydrogen fuels, we will limit our discussion of combustion to them at this point.

Why fuels burn

   The chemical makeup of a substance determines whether it's flammable. Carbon and hydrogen are highly flammable elements, so material made up largely of these elements, called hydrocarbons, are good fuels. Substances made up of carbon, hydrogen, and oxygen, with hydrogen and oxygen in the same proportion as they are in water, are also flammable; they're called carbohydrates. Heat is required before any fuel will burn.

                    Meidl, pp. 8–9.

**Figure 11–20
Summary of a
Passage**

> Fuel, as we have seen, is only one side of the fire triangle. Before it will burn, any fuel requires the addition of heat, another side of the triangle.[4]

Take summary notes to remind yourself of the substance of a research source. Summarized information can also be useful to your reader because it condenses passages that give more details than the reader needs.

■ Plagiarism

Using someone else's exact words or original ideas or data acquired from their research in your writing without giving credit in a reference is known as *plagiarism*. Plagiarism is not only unethical, but illegal; in class or on the job it may be grounds for dismissal. Whether the words and ideas come from a published source or from a fellow student's work, plagiarism is a form of theft for which you can be held accountable.

You may present the words and ideas of another person as long as you give appropriate credit by documenting the passage. Reproducing text and images from the Internet that are cut and pasted elsewhere without credit is also plagiarism and may be copyright infringement, if the source is copyrighted. Treat information on the Internet as you would published information, whether quoted, paraphrased, or summarized. Ideas and facts considered common knowledge need not be documented. The dates and names of historical events, as well as many kinds of scientific and statistical information, are common knowledge. Specific examples of common knowledge include the temperature at which water boils, the year the Constitution was ratified, the number of passengers a 747 jetliner can hold, and the area in square miles that Dallas, Texas, occupies. Likewise, text, data, and graphics that originated in your company or organization generally can be used in other job-related work without documentation.

■ Interviewing for Information

If you need information that is not readily available in print, you may be able to do some of your research by *interviewing* someone who is an expert on the subject. If, for instance, your subject is nursing-home care in your community, the logical experts to interview would be the directors of several local nursing homes. Sources that can help you decide whom to interview—and how to get in touch with them—include membership lists of professional societies (the membership rolls of large professional organizations are available in many libraries), the Yellow Pages of the local telephone book, and a firm or organization in your area whose staff includes experts on your subject.

---

[4]James H. Meidl, *Flammable Hazardous Materials* (Beverly Hills, CA: Glencoe Press, 1970), pp. 8–9.

Once you have selected the person or persons you would like to interview, use the following guidelines to help you to obtain the information you need with a minimum of time and trouble for your interviewee and for yourself.

Before the Interview

Always request an interview in advance and make an appointment. You can do so by telephone, by email, or by letter, although a letter may sometimes take too long to permit you to meet a deadline. When you request the interview, explain who you are, what kind of information you are seeking, and why you have chosen to interview this particular expert. Also state that you will schedule the interview at the convenience of the interviewee. Gather some background information about the person and his or her occupation before the interview. You need not exhaust all information sources, of course; let common sense be your guide. How much time will you have before the interview? Is the information difficult to obtain? Be aware, however, that the more preparation you put into an interview, the more you will get out of it.

Your first contact with the interviewee is important because it gives you the opportunity to tell the expert exactly what kind of information you are seeking and allows the interviewee time to prepare for the interview. Some people are made nervous by a tape recorder, so if you would like to use one during the interview, request permission at this point. If the interviewee refuses permission, bring a notepad instead. If you intend to bring a tape recorder, check to see that it's in good working order. However, even a tape recorder that works well can malfunction unexpectedly. Prepare for the worst; bring a writing pad and several pens or pencils to the interview as a backup.

After you have made the appointment, prepare a list of specific questions that you will ask based on your writing purpose. Avoid the tendency of the beginning interviewer to ask general rather than specific questions. Analyze your questions to be certain that they are direct and to the point. "Tell me about the kinds of people admitted to Hillcrest Nursing Home" is too broad a request. You will probably get a rambling, general answer in reply. Productive questions would be "What is the average age of persons who come to Hillcrest?" "Are the majority from this vicinity?" "What's the ratio of men to women?" Such queries are much easier to answer than are general questions.

Conducting the Interview

Because an interview represents an imposition on someone's time—usually someone who is busy—arrive promptly at the appointed time.

After you arrive and introduce yourself, a few minutes of informal conversation will help both you and the interviewee to relax. But don't drag this period out; an interview is largely straightforward question and response.

During the interview, use the following guidelines:

1. Be pleasant but purposeful. The interviewee knows you are there to get information, so don't be timid about asking your questions. Don't confuse an elementary question on a subject with an ignorant question. If you are too timid, you will go away empty-handed.

2. Refer to the list of questions you prepared in advance, and follow them — don't let yourself become sidetracked. Avoid being rigid, however; if you realize that a prepared question is no longer suitable, go on to the next question.

3. Let the interviewee do most of the talking. Don't try to impress the interviewee with your knowledge of the subject on which he or she is the expert. Don't rebut every point the interviewee makes; after all, you are there to get information, not to debate.

4. Some answers prompt follow-up questions; ask them. "Mr. Bolchalk, has the automated mail-handling system been as efficient as originally planned?" If the answer is no, you can follow up with "Why?" or "In what specific areas has the system failed?" If the answer is yes, ask for details about the differences between the old and the new systems.

5. If the interviewee gets off the subject, be ready with a specific question to direct the conversation back on track. Your prepared list of questions will help.

6. Take only the notes you really need. Obviously, you cannot write down every word of the interview, so concentrate on the important ideas and the key facts and figures. You will be the best judge of how pertinent an idea or a statistic is. If the interviewee is talking too fast, ask him or her to speak more slowly. Anyone who wants to be quoted accurately will be glad to slow down. If you need a clarification of the facts, politely ask the speaker to explain a point.

7. As the interview is reaching a close, take a few minutes to skim your notes. If you feel there is time, ask for a clarification of anything that is still ambiguous. But be careful not to overstay your welcome.

8. If you use a tape recorder, do not be lulled into a feeling that all your work is being done for you and thereby neglect to ask crucial questions.

9. Thank the interviewee for his or her time and ask if you may call back if you need to clarify a point or two as you write up your interview notes.

After the Interview

As soon as possible after the interview, go over your notes again and fill in any material that is obviously missing. This is the time to summarize the speaker's remarks. Then key in or write out the notes using complete sentences. After writing out your notes, select the important information you need and transfer it to your notecards. Observe the same guidelines for creating interview notecards that you used for creating library-research cards. Provide a topic slug for each card.

■ Using a Questionnaire

A *questionnaire*—a series of questions on a particular topic, sent out to a number of people—is an interview on paper. It has several advantages over the personal interview, and several disadvantages. A questionnaire allows you to test the thinking of many more people than personal interviews would. It enables you to obtain responses from people in different parts of the country. Even people who live near you may be easier to reach by mail than in person. Those responding to a questionnaire do not face the constant pressure posed by someone jotting down their every word—a fact that could result in more thoughtful answers from questionnaire respondents. The questionnaire reduces the possibility that the interviewer might influence an answer by tone of voice of facial expression. Finally, the cost of a questionnaire is lower than the cost of numerous personal interviews.

Questionnaires have drawbacks too. People who have strong opinions on a subject are more likely to respond to a questionnaire than those who do not. This factor could slant the results. An interviewer can follow up on an answer with a pertinent question; at best, a questionnaire can be designed to let one question lead logically to another. Furthermore, mailing a batch of questionnaires and waiting for replies take considerably longer than conducting a personal interview does.

The advantages of a questionnaire will work in your favor only if the questionnaire is properly designed. Your goal should be to obtain as much information as possible from your recipients with as little effort on their part as possible. The first rule to follow is to keep the questionnaire brief. The longer the questionnaire is, the less likely the recipient will be to complete and return it. Next, the questions should be easy to understand. A confusing question will yield confusing results, whereas a carefully worded question will be easy to answer. Ideally, questions should be answerable with a "yes" or "no."

■   Would you be willing to work a four-day workweek, ten hours a day, with every Friday off?

    Yes _____
    No _____
    No opinion _____

When it is not possible to phrase questions in such a straightforward style, provide an appropriate range of answers.

■   How many hours of overtime would you be willing to work each week?

    4 hours _____   10 hours _____
    6 hours _____   More than 10 hours _____
    8 hours _____   No overtime _____

Questions should be neutral; they shouldn't be worded in such a way as to lead the respondent to give a particular answer.

When preparing your questions, remember that you must eventually tabulate the answers; therefore, try to formulate questions whose answers can be readily computed. The easiest questions to tabulate are those for which the recipient does not have to compose an answer. Questions that require a comment for an answer take time to think about and write. As a result, they lessen your chances of obtaining a response. They are also difficult to interpret. Questionnaires should include a section for additional comments, though, where recipients may clarify their overall attitude toward the subject. If the information will be of value in interpreting the answers, include questions about the recipient's age, education, occupation, and so on. Include your name, your address, the purpose of the questionnaire, and the date by which an answer is needed.

A questionnaire sent by mail must be accompanied by a letter explaining who you are, what purpose the questionnaire will serve, how the questionnaire will be used, and the date by which you would like to receive a reply. (Also include a stamped, self-addressed envelope.) If the information provided will be kept confidential, say so in the letter. If the recipient's identity will not be disclosed, state this in the letter too. Questionnaires can also be posted at Web sites. See Preparing Forms for the Web in Chapter 12, pages 511–516.

Selecting the proper recipients for your questionnaire may be easy or difficult, depending on your needs. If you want to survey the opinions of all the employees in a small shop or a laboratory, you simply send each worker a questionnaire. To survey the members of a club or a professional society, you would mail questionnaires to those who are on a membership list. But to survey the opinions of large groups in the general population—for example, all medical technologists working in private laboratories, or all independent garage owners—is not so easy. Because you cannot include everybody in your survey, you would have to choose a representative cross-section. Methods of large-scale sampling are beyond the scope of this text. The best sources of information on sampling techniques are research and statistics texts.

The sample questionnaire in Figure 11–21 was sent to employees in a large organization who had participated in a six-month program of flexible working hours. Under the program, employees worked a 40-hour, five-day week, with flexible starting and quitting times. Employees could start the work day between 7:00 and 9:00 a.m. and leave between 3:30 and 6:30 p.m., provided that they worked a total of eight hours each day and took a one-half-hour lunch period midway through the day.

**Figure 11–21
Sample
Questionnaire**

October 18, 20--

To: All Company Employees

From: Nelson Barrett, Director *NB*
             Human Resources Department

Subject: Review of Flexible Working Hours Program

Please complete and return the questionnaire below regarding Luxwear Corporation's trial program of flexible working hours. Your answers will help my staff and me to decide whether the program is worthwhile enough to continue permanently.

Return the completed questionnaire to Ken Rose, Mail Code 12B, by October 28. Your signature on the questionnaire is not necessary. Feel free to raise additional issues pertaining to the program. All responses will be given consideration.

If you want to discuss any item in the questionnaire, call Pam Peters in the Human Resources Department at extension 8812.

1. What kind of position do you occupy?

   Supervisory _____

   Nonsupervisory _____

2. Indicate to the nearest quarter of an hour your starting time under flextime.

   7:00 a.m. _____   8:15 a.m. _____

   7:15 a.m. _____   8:30 a.m. _____

   7:30 a.m. _____   8:45 a.m. _____

   7:45 a.m. _____   9:00 a.m. _____

   8:00 a.m. _____   Other, specify _____

3. Where do you live?

   Talbot County _____   Greene County_____

   Montgomery County _____   Other, specify _____

4. How do you usually travel to work?

   Drive alone _____   Walk _____

   Taxi _____   Bus _____

   Train _____   Motorcycle _____

   Car pool _____   Other, specify _____

   Bicycle _____

(continued)

Figure 11–21
(continued)

5. Has flextime affected your commuting time?

   Increase: Approx. number of minutes _____

   Decrease: Approx. number of minutes _____

   No change _____

6. If you drive alone or in a car pool, has flextime increased or decreased the amount of time it takes you to find a parking space?

   Increased _____   Decreased _____   No change _____

7. Has flextime had an effect on your productivity?

   a. Quality of work

      Increase _____   Decrease _____   No change _____

   b. Accuracy of work

      Increase _____   Decrease _____   No change _____

   c. Quiet time for uninterrupted work

      Increase _____   Decrease _____   No change _____

8. Have you had difficulty getting in touch with employees who are on different work schedules from yours?

   Yes _____   No _____

9. Have you had trouble scheduling meetings within flexible starting and quitting times?

   Yes _____   No _____

10. Has flextime affected the way you feel about your job?

    Feel better about job   Feel worse about job

    Slightly _____   Slightly _____

    Considerably _____   Considerably _____

                No change _____

11. How important is it for you to have flexibility in your working hours?

    Very _____   Not very _____

    Somewhat _____   Not at all _____

12. Has flextime allowed you more time to be with your family?

    Yes _____   No _____

Figure 11–21
(continued)

13. If you are responsible for the care of a young child or children, has flextime made it easier or more difficult for you to obtain babysitting or day-care services?

    Easier _____   More difficult _____

    No change _____

14. Do you recommend that the flextime program be made permanent?

    Yes _____   No _____

15. Do you have suggestions for major changes in the program?

    Yes (please specify)   No _____

THANK YOU FOR YOUR ASSISTANCE

■ Other Sources of Information

Two additional sources of information may provide you with materials for your research: first-hand observation and experience, and free or inexpensive materials from private and governmental agencies and organizations.

First-Hand Observation and Experience

Why not interview yourself? If your topic deals with something you know well (a hobby or an area of interest, for example) or relates to an occupation you are in or hope to be in, you may already have enough information to get started. Check your home or office for any materials you have acquired on the subject. From your knowledge of the topic, make a rough outline—it will tell you how much you know about the topic, which areas you are strong in, and which areas you are weak in. When your flow of ideas turns to a trickle and then stops, you can expand your knowledge from the other sources discussed in this chapter. For topics that involve a great deal of factual data, you should, in addition, check the accuracy of any facts and figures that you aren't certain about.

Free or Inexpensive Materials from Private and Governmental Agencies and Organizations

In your search for materials on your topic, do not overlook the field of private and governmental agencies and organizations. These include corporations, business and professional associations, nonprofit organizations, and the numerous bureaus and offices of the federal, state, and local governments. Most of these sources distribute free or inexpensive material on virtually any subject. A reference librarian can show you how to go about obtaining material from the agencies and organizations.

When you request information from governmental or private organizations, you must be specific in describing the material or materials you are seeking. If you know the title of a pamphlet or a booklet you want, refer to the title, and to any other information that will serve to identify the pamphlet, in your letter requesting the item. If you are aware that there is a charge for the material, send a check or money order with the request. Doing so will save time for both you and the recipient because it won't be necessary for the organization to write to you asking for payment before it can send you the materials. One final note: requests for information from private and governmental agencies are usually handled by mail, and postal deliveries can be slow. Therefore, do not rely too heavily on such materials for your research because the deadline for your written work may arrive before the requested material does.

■ Documenting Sources

By documenting their sources, writers identify where they obtained the facts, ideas, quotations, and paraphrases they have used in preparing a written report. This information can come from books; newspaper, magazine, or trade journal articles; manuals; proposals; investigative reports; interviews; email; the Internet; and other sources. Documenting sources achieves three important purposes. First, full, accurate, and consistent documentation allows readers to locate the source of the information given and to find further information on the subject. Second, documenting sources enables writers to support their work with evidence from existing research, which establishes credibility and makes a written work more persuasive. Finally, it gives proper credit to the authors cited so that the writer avoids plagiarism. As mentioned earlier in this chapter, the sources of all paraphrased facts, ideas, and opinions should be documented, as should the sources of all direct quotations and any graphic material from an electronic or written source.

Following are three principal methods of documenting sources:

1. *Parenthetical documentation*—putting brief citations in parentheses in the text and providing full information in a list of Works Cited

2. *Numbered references*—referring to sources with numbers in parentheses or by superscripts in the text and providing full information in a References section, where the entries are listed numerically in the order of their first citation in the text

3. *Notes*—using superscript numbers in the text to refer to notes either at the bottom of the page (footnotes) or at the end of the paper, article, chapter, or book (endnotes)

Whatever format you choose, be sure to follow it consistently in every detail of order, punctuation, and capitalization.

ESL TIPS: Documenting Sources

Writers must document all quotations, paraphrases, or summaries of another person's words or ideas for three principal reasons.

- Documentation credits the authors of the original source.
- Documentation enables the reader to locate the original source.
- Documentation supports the writer's assertions with evidence and makes a document more persuasive.

Sometimes a *bibliography* is included at the end of a work. A bibliography is a list of books, articles, or other sources arranged alphabetically at the end of a report or research paper. A bibliography differs from Works Cited, References, or endnotes in that it includes works consulted for background information, in addition to those actually cited in text. For that reason, a bibliography is appropriate only as a supplement to works included in the references.

Parenthetical Documentation

This section describes two principal systems for documenting sources, one developed by the Modern Language Association (MLA) and the other by the American Psychological Association (APA), and is based on their respective style manuals:

> *MLA Handbook for Writers of Research Papers,* 5th ed. (New York: MLA, 1999). The MLA style is used in the humanities. See the MLA Web site for updates to MLA style guidelines and information on citing Internet sources: http://www.mla.org.

> *Publication Manual of the American Psychological Association,* 4th ed. (Washington, DC: APA, 1994). The APA style is used in the social sciences. See the APA Web site for updates to APA style guidelines and information on citing Internet sources: http://www.apa.org.

The MLA documentation style consists of two parts: a brief citation of the author and page number that appears in parentheses in the text; and a works-cited list that appears at the end of the document. The APA documentation style consists of two parts: a brief citation of the author, year of publication, and page number (for direct quotations only) that appears in parentheses in the text; and a reference list that appears at the end of the document. Samples of both MLA and APA formats appear at the end of each discussion below. Many professional organizations and journals publish style manuals that describe their own formats for documenting sources. If you are writing for publication in a professional field, consult the manual for that particular field or the style sheet for the journal to which you are submitting your article. A list of some of those manuals appears at the end of this section.

MLA Style

Parenthetical Documentation

The parenthetical method recommended by the MLA is detailed in the *MLA Handbook for Writers of Research Papers* (5th ed.) and the *MLA Style Manual and Guide to Scholarly Publishing* (2nd ed.). This method gives an abbreviated reference to a source parenthetically in the text and lists full information about the source in a separate alphabetical section titled "Works Cited."

When you cite a source in text, give only the author's last name and the page number or numbers in parentheses: (Garcia 127). If the author's name is mentioned in the text, give only the page number of the source in parentheses: (38–39, 144–48, 2436–37). If two or more sources have authors with the same last name, include their initials or first names to avoid confusion. The parenthetical citation should include no more information than is necessary to enable readers to find the corresponding entry in the list of works cited. When you are referring to an entire work, rather than to a particular page in a work, mention the author's name in the text and omit the parenthetical citation. The following passages contain sample parenthetical citations in MLA style.

- ■ Preparing a videotape of measurement methods is cost-effective and can expedite training (Peterson 151).

- ■ Peterson summarized the results of these measurements in a series of tables (183–91).

- ■ These results were summarized forty years ago (Ralph Peterson 183–91). Sonia Peterson has recently suggested the reevaluation of these findings (29).

Place a parenthetical citation in text between the closing quotation mark or the last word of the sentence (or clause) and the end punctuation mark (usually a period). Use the spacing shown in the examples. If the parenthetical citation refers to an indented quotation, however, place it outside the last sentence of the quotation, as shown.

- ■ . . . a close collaboration with the physics and technology staff is essential. (Minsky 42)

If you are citing a page or pages of a multivolume work, give the volume number, followed by a colon, a space, and the page number(s): (Jones 2: 53–56). If the entire volume is being cited, identify the author and the volume: (Smith, vol. 3).

If your list of works cited includes more than one work by the same author, give the title of the work (or a shortened version if the title is long) in the parenthetical citation, unless you mention it in the text. If, for example, your list of works cited includes more than one work by Thomas J. Peters, a proper parenthetical citation for his book *The Pursuit of Wow: Every Person's Guide to Topsy-Turvy Times* would appear as (Peters, *Pursuit* 93). Use only one space between the title and the page number.

If you are citing a source written by two or three authors, include all of the names in your parenthetical citation: (Rotherson and Peters 467–75); for a source written by four or more authors, include the first author's name followed by the Latin phrase *et al.* (and others): (Kooper et al. 732). If you are citing a source in which a separate work is quoted, provide the name of the person being quoted.

- According to Billings, there is a greater potential for a small business to succeed in an urban area (qtd. in Kooper et al. 421).

If you are quoting a source written by a corporation or organization, use that name as the author.

- However, many declining industries that fueled the economy of the 1950s are now being faced with a government mandate to clean up and preserve the environment (Environmental Protection Agency 16–17).

If you are quoting a source by an unknown author, use a brief version of the title in your citation.

- The benefits of this treatment have been known since the early 1980s ("Audio Therapy" 56).

For a sentence that refers to two separate sources, include both in your parenthetical citation, separating them with a semicolon.

- Some analysts believe that the impact of electronic commerce caused the extreme market fluctuations of the late 1990s (Jones 174; Dragonetti 267).

When referring to electronic sources in your parenthetical citations, follow the same rules that you would for print sources, including as much identifying information as available (names and page numbers).

- As pointed out in a recent Slate.com article, America's poor are more numerous, but less visible than ever (Connors).

If no names are indicated in the document, use the title (full or shortened) in your citation; if no page numbers are indicated, do not cite any numbers, unless there are paragraph or section numbers. In this case, use the abbreviation *par.* or *sec.* in your citation. Do not include URLs in your parenthetical citations, but do include them in your Works Cited list.

- According to one online article, the organization's stated mission is to connect North American exporters with appropriate markets in Eastern Europe ("Business to Go" par. 18).

Citation Format for Works Cited

The list of Works Cited should begin on the first new page following the end of the text. Each new entry should begin at the left margin, with the second and subsequent lines within an entry indented five spaces or one-half inch. Double-space within and between entries.

Arranging Entries by Author.   List entries in alphabetical order by the author's last name (by the last name of the first listed author if the work has more than one author). For multiple works by the same author, alphabetize the entries by the first major word of the title (following *a, an,* or *the*) and put three hyphens and a period in place of the author's name for the second and subsequent entries.

```
Peters, Thomas J. The Circle of Innovation: You Can't Shrink Your
     Way to Greatness. New York: Knopf, 1997.

---. The Pursuit of Wow: Every Person's Guide to Topsy-Turvy
     Times. New York: Vintage, 1994.
```

If the author is a corporation, alphabetize the entry by the name of the corporation. If the author is a government agency, alphabetize the entry by the government entity, followed by the agency (for example, "United States. Dept. of Health and Human Services."). Some sources require more than one agency name (for example, "United States. Dept. of Labor. Bureau of Labor Statistics."). If no author is given, begin the entry with the title, alphabetized by the first significant word in the title. An editor's name is followed by the abbreviation *ed.* (or *eds.* for more than one editor).

```
Rogerson, Philip, ed. Essays on Management Culture. New Orleans:
     Leghorn, 1998.
```

Titles.   The second element of the entry is the title of the work. Capitalize the first word of the title and each significant word thereafter. Underline the title of a book (or pamphlet). Place quotation marks around the title of an article in a periodical, an essay in a collection, or a paper in proceedings. The title should be followed by a period.

Periodicals.   For an article in a journal, list the volume number, the date, and the page numbers immediately after the title of the periodical. For an article in a magazine or newspaper, omit the volume number. For a newspaper, give the edition and the section, if the newspaper has them.

Series or Multivolume Works.   For works in a series, give the name of the series and the series or volume number of the work after the title. If the edition used is not the first, specify the edition.

Publication Information.   The final elements of the entry for a book, pamphlet, or conference proceedings are the place of publication, publisher's name, and date of publication. Use a shortened form of the publisher's name (for example, *St. Martin's* for St. Martin's Press, Inc.; *Random* for Random House; *Oxford UP* for Oxford University Press), and include the publisher's city. If publication information cannot be found in the work, use the abbreviations *n.p.* (no publication place), *n.p.* (no publisher), and *n.d.* (no date). For familiar reference works, list only the edition and year of publication.

Online Sources.   Citations for online sources are similar to citations for printed sources. To cite an online source, begin with the author, title, and, if the information is included in a printed version, publication information. Indicate the date the information was retrieved and include in angle brackets the Web address (the URL) or enough address information to allow the reader to retrieve the source. Titles of entire Web sites should be either underlined or italicized consistently. Treat any articles or graphics included at the site as you would those from print sources. Personal communications, such as email messages and bulletin-board postings, follow the format for letters and interviews, with the URL provided for archived material.

Standards continue to evolve for citations of online and electronic sources. When citing online information, the two primary goals are to give credit to the author and, whenever possible, to enable readers to retrieve the source.

Indenting.   Use a hanging indent, with second and additional lines indenting five spaces or one-half inch from the left margin.

Spacing.   Double-space within and between the entries of the Works Cited list.

Dates.   The correct format for dates is as follows: day, month, year, with no commas (19 Jan. 2000). Abbreviate all months except May, June, and July.

Sample Entries (MLA Style)

The following models for entries in the list of Works Cited include a range of sources. For additional examples, refer to the *MLA Handbook for Writers of Research Papers* (5th ed.), or the MLA Web site at http://www.mla.org.

Book by One Author

Hassab, Joseph C. Systems Management: People, Computers, Machines, Materials. New York: CRC, 1997.

Book by Two or More Authors

Testerman, Joshua O., Thomas J. Kuegler, Jr., and Paul J. Dowling, Jr. Web Advertising and Marketing. 2nd ed. Rocklin: Prima, 1998.

Book by a Corporate or Organizational Author

Ernst and Young. Ernst and Young's Retirement Planning Guide. New York: Wiley, 1997.

Work in a Book Compiled by an Editor

Gueron, Judith M. "Welfare and Poverty: Strategies to Increase Work." <u>Reducing Poverty in America: Views and Approaches</u>. Ed. Michael R. Darby. Thousand Oaks: Sage, 1996. 237-55.

Book Edition Other Than First

Estes, Jack C., and Dennis R. Kelley. <u>McGraw-Hill's Interest Amortization Tables</u>. 3rd ed. New York: McGraw, 1998.

Journal Article

Rossouw, G. J. "Business Ethics in South Africa." <u>Journal of Business Ethics</u> 16 (1997): 1539-47.

Unsigned Article (in Weekly Periodical)

"American City Adds Nashville, Memphis." <u>Business Journal</u> 26 Sept. 1997: 16.

Magazine Article

Coley, Don. "Compliance for the Right Reasons." <u>Business Geographics</u> June 1997: 30-32.

Newspaper Article

Mathews, Anna Wilde. "The Internet Generation Taps into Morse Code." <u>Wall Street Journal</u> 1 Oct. 1997, natl. ed.: B1+.

Encyclopedia Article

Gibbard, Bruce G. "Particle Detector." <u>World Book Encyclopedia</u>. 1997 ed.

Article Included in a Book

May, Bruce, and James Deacon. "Amplification Systems." <u>Advances in Electronics</u>. Ed. Alvin Kooper. Miami: Valley, 1995.

Article from a Volume of Proceedings

Carlson, Carl T. "Advanced Organizers in Manuals." <u>Proceedings of the 45th International Business Communication Conference</u>. Ed. Ken Rainey. Fairfax: Soc. for Business Communication, 1995. RT56-58.

Government Document

United States. Dept. of Energy. <u>The Energy Situation in the Next
Decade</u>. Technical Pub. 11346-53. Washington: GPO, 1998.

Map or Chart

<u>Central Orange County</u>. Map. Mill Creek: King of the Road, 1999.

Lecture

Robbins, Bruce. "Trends in Secondary Education." Boise State U. 2
May 1999.

Translated Work

Bergner, Andreas. <u>Training and International Business</u>. Trans.
Edgar James. New York: Random, 1999.

Multivolume Work

Standard & Poor. <u>Standard & Poor's Register of Corporations,
Directors and Executives</u>. 3 vols. New York: McGraw, 1996.

Work in a Series

Pabrai, Uday O. <u>UNIX Internetworking</u>. 2nd ed. Artech House
Telecommunications Lib. Ser. 5. Norwood: Artech, 1996.

Report

Bertot, John Carlo, Charles R. McClure, and Douglas L. Zweizig.
<u>The 1996 National Survey of Public Libraries and the
Internet: Progress and Issues: Final Report</u>. Washington:
GPO, 1996.

Thesis or Dissertation

Thelen, Erik A. "The Evolution of the Application Letter in
America: 1880-1960." Diss. U of Wisconsin-Milwaukee, 1998.

Proceedings

Johnson, Peggy, and Bonnie MacEwan, eds. <u>Collection Management
and Development: Issues in an Electronic Era</u>. Proc. of the
Advanced Collection Management and Dev. Inst., 26-28 Mar.
1999, Chicago. Chicago: Amer. Lib. Assn., 1999.

Paper in Proceedings

Cline, Nancy M. "Staffing: The Art of Managing Change."
    <u>Collection Management and Development: Issues in an</u>
    <u>Electronic Era</u>. Proc. of the Advanced Collection Management
    and Dev. Inst., 26–28 Mar. 1999, Chicago. Ed. Peggy Johnson
    and Bonnie MacEwan. Chicago: Amer. Lib. Assn., 1999. 13–28.

Paper Presented at a Conference

Kim, R. "Management of Information." Intl. Conf. on MIS. U of
    Lima, Peru. 2 May 1999.

Letter to Author

Paluch, Dustin. Letter to the author. 20 Sept. 2000.

Letter to Other Person(s)

Viets, Hermann. Letter to all MSOE students, fac., and staff.
    1 Sept. 2000.

Interview You Conducted

Sariolgholam, Mahmood. Personal interview. 29 Nov. 2000.

Email Message

Kahl, Jonathan D. "Re: Web page." E-mail to the author. 2 Oct.
    2000.

Web Site

Hendl, Kevin B. <u>The Nursing Page</u>. 1 Jan. 2000. Northwest
    Consortium of Medical Professionals. 10 May 2000 <http://www
    .carney.edu/nursing/Index.html>.

Online Book

Rawlins, Gregory J. E. <u>Moths to the Flame</u>. Cambridge: MIT P,
    1997. 10 Feb. 2000 <http://mitpress.mit.edu/e-books/Moths/>.

Online Government Publication

United States. Federal Communications Commission. <u>FCC Consumer</u>
    <u>Alert on Telephone Slamming</u>. Jan. 1999. 8 Feb. 2000
    <http://www.fcc.gov/Bureaus/Common_Carrier/Factsheets/
    slamming.html>.

Document from an Online Subscription Service

Siegfried, Tom. "A Way to Get the Message without Using Up
    Energy." Dallas Morning News 1 July 1996: 7D. Electric Lib.
    O'Neill Lib., Boston Coll., Chestnut Hill. 8 Feb. 2000
    <http://www.elibrary.com>.

Synchronous Communication

Prisley, Lauren. "Seminar Discussion on FTP." 5 Oct. 1997. Tech
    MOOspace. 19 Nov. 1997 <telnet://moo.ku.ed/port=9999>.

Online Article

Shevlin, Diana. "Treasury Proposes EFT Regulation: New EFT 99 Web
    Site. Launches Rule's Release." Financial Connection 6.2
    (1997). 5 Oct. 1997 <http://www.fms.treas.gov/finconn/fcsep97
    .html>.

Listserv or Newsgroup Message

Armitage, Phillip. "AutoCAD Memory Requirements." Online posting.
    25 June 1997. 2 Oct. 1997 <news:comp.cad.autocad>.

Conference Proceedings at a Web Site (Electronic Version)

Mehringer, D. M., R. L. Plante, and P. A. Roberts, eds.
    Astronomical Data Analysis Software and Systems VIII. Proc.
    of the Eighth Annual Conf. on Astronomical Data Analysis
    Software and Systems, 1–4 Nov. 1998, Urbana. Astronomical
    Soc. of the Pacific Conf. Ser. 172. 1999. Astronomical Soc.
    of the Pacific. 2 Sept. 2000 <http://monet.astro.uicuc.edu/
    adass98/>.

Publication on CD-ROM

Money 99. CD-ROM. Redmond: Microsoft, 1998.

APA Style

Parenthetical Documentation

The parenthetical style recommended by the APA is described in the *Publication Manual of the American Psychological Association* (4th ed.). This method gives abbreviated references to sources parenthetically in the text and lists full information about the sources in a separate Reference list.

When you are documenting direct quotations in text, give the author's last name, the year of publication, and the page number in parentheses. The page number is optional for paraphrased information and ideas. If the author's name is mentioned in the text, give only the year of publication and the page number in parentheses. The parenthetical citation should include no more information than is necessary to enable readers to find the corresponding entry in the Reference list. In the rare case that the author's name and the year of publication are mentioned in the text, give only the page number for direct quotations and omit parenthetical information for paraphrased material. The following passages contain sample APA parenthetical citations.

■ The "first electronic war" (Butrica, 1996, p. 2) was fought as much in the research laboratory as on the battlefield.

■ World War II was the occasion of radar's first application in warfare, and Great Britain led the way in radar research (Butrica, 1996).

■ According to Butrica (1996), the use of radar as an offensive and defensive warfare agent made World War II "The first electronic war" (p. 2).

■ As Butrica pointed out in his 1996 research, "technology forever changed the way we make war" (p. 196).

■ In his 1996 research, Butrica pointed out the impact of technology on warfare.

When APA parenthetical citations are added in midsentence, place them after the closing quotation marks and continue with the rest of the sentence. If the APA parenthetical citation follows a block quotation, place the citation after the final punctuation mark. Use the spacing shown in the examples. Within the citation itself, separate the name, date, and page number with commas. Allow one space after each comma. Use the abbreviation *p.* or *pp.* before page numbers.

If your Reference list includes more than one work by the same author published in the same year, add the lowercase letters *a, b, c,* and so forth, to the year in both the Reference list entries and the text citations: (Ostro, 1993b, p. 347). When a work has two authors, cite both names joined by an ampersand: (Hey & Walters, 1997). For the first citation of a work with three, four, or five authors, include all names.

■ As Burns, Brooks, and MacNeil (1999) argued . . .

For subsequent citations, include only the name of the first author followed by *et al.*

■ Burns et al. (1999) put forth the alternate theory . . .

For a work with six or more authors, use the name of the first author followed by *et al.* in all citations.

■ Their findings lead to a radical change in the way the metals were processed (Hargrove et al., 2000, p. 21).

When two or more works by different authors are cited in the same parentheses, list the citations alphabetically and use semicolons to separate the citations: (Hey & Walters, 1997; Knapp, 1996; Ostro, 1993a). The works cited in the examples would be listed alphabetically, as follows, in a Reference list.

Burns, S., Brooks, J., & MacNeil, W. (1999). Science in the mirror: A retrospective look at physics. Cambridge, MA: Harvard University Press.

Butrica, A. J. (1996). To see the unseen: A history of planetary radar astronomy. The NASA History Series. Washington, DC: U.S. Government Printing Office.

Hey, T., & Walters, P. (1997). Einstein's mirror. Cambridge, England: Cambridge University Press.

Knapp, B. (1996). Grolier educational elements series: Vol. 6 Silicon. Danbury, CT: Grolier Educational.

Ostro, S. J. (1993a). Planetary radar astronomy. Reviews of Modern Physics, 65, 1235–1279.

Ostro, S. J. (1993b). Radar astronomy. In S. P. Parker & J. M. Pasachoff (Eds.), McGraw-Hill encyclopedia of astronomy (pp. 347–348). New York: McGraw-Hill.

If you are citing a source created by a corporation or organization, use its name as the author.

■ However, high employment rates in the Midwest affected this trend considerably (U.S. Department of Labor, 1999).

If you are quoting a source by an unknown author, use a brief version of the title in your citation.

■ Textile manufacture had replaced the local maritime trade well before the mid-nineteenth century ("A Short History," p. 19).

If two or more sources have authors with the same last name, use first initials in your citation (J. Kellogg, p. 414). When citing email, phone calls, or personal interviews, use the words *personal communication* in your parenthetical citation.

■ Linda Waters (personal communication, November 28, 2000), an executive at CorTex, stated the case succinctly. . . .

To refer to an entire Web site (not just to a particular article or document at that site), include the URL in your parenthetical citation.

■ The U.S. Department of Commerce provides current statistics on international trade at the Bureau of Economic Analysis Web site <http://www.bea.doc.gov/bea/rels.htm>.

However, you should not include the Web site in your Reference list, if you are citing the entire site. If you are citing a specific document from a Web site, you should follow the format that you would for a print document (citing the author, year, and page or paragraph number). If there are no page or paragraph numbers in the online document, include just the author and the year in your parenthetical citation (you will provide further details in the Reference list).

■   In his previous address to the group, he expressed his belief in
    the value of using technology in the classroom (Gore, 1999).

Citation Format for Reference List

The Reference list should begin on the first new page following the end of the text. Each new entry should begin at the left margin, with the second and subsequent lines indented five spaces or one-half inch from the left margin. (Your instructor may require you to use a paragraph indent instead. If so, begin at a paragraph indent, with subsequent lines continuing at the left margin.)[5] Double-space within and between entries.

Be sure to include full page numbers when citing a range of pages for articles (119–124, not 119–24) and to indicate with a comma if the page flow of an article is interrupted (119–124, 128–132). Use the abbreviation *p.* or *pp.* only with articles in newspapers (not in magazines or other sources), chapters in edited books, or proceedings.

In your reference list, include only sources that were essential to the preparation of your document; do not include background reading. Do not include forms of personal communication, such as letters, email, messages from electronic bulletin boards, and telephone conversations. Those information sources should be cited only in the text. (Also, see the footnote on page 477.)

Arranging Entries by Author.   Entries appear in alphabetical order by the author's last name (by the last name of the first author if the work has more than one author). Give the author's surname and initials only. Works by the same author should be listed chronologically according to the year of publication, from earlier to later dates. If the author is a corporation, alphabetize the entry by the name of the corporation; if the author is a government agency, alphabetize the entry by the government entity that published the work (for example, "U.S. Department of Health and Human Services"). Some sources require more than one agency name (for example, "U.S. Department of Health and Human Services, Indian Health Service"). However, if an agency that is part of a higher department is well known, it is not necessary to include the higher department (for example,

---

[5]At the printing of this book, the APA accepts the use of either a hanging indent (as shown here) or a regular paragraph indent for references, as long as the chosen format is used consistently throughout. (See the electronic reference formats recommended by the APA at http://www.apa .org/journals/webref.html for more information.) Check with your instructor for the method preferred in your course.

"Food and Drug Administration"). If no author is given, begin the entry with the title, alphabetized by the first significant word. For edited works, place the editor's name at the beginning of the entry, followed by *Ed.* (or *Eds.*) in parentheses.

Publication Date.   The second element of the entry is the work's date of publication. Place the copyright date or the date of production in parentheses. For periodicals other than journals, include the year, a comma, and the month, or day. Place a period after the parentheses. For journals and books, give only the year.

Titles.   Give the title of the work after the date of publication. For titles of articles, chapters, or books, capitalize only the first word of the title and the subtitle; all other words (except proper nouns) should be lowercase. Underline titles of books, but do not underline or use quotation marks for titles of articles or chapters. Follow the title with a period.

Periodicals.   For an article in a periodical (journal, magazine, or newspaper), give the title of the periodical in upper- and lowercase letters. The volume number and the page numbers should immediately follow the periodical title. Underline the periodical title and volume number. Separate the elements by commas and end with a period.

Series or Multivolume Works.   For works in a series, the series number of the work follows the title. For multivolume works, the number of volumes follows the title. If the edition is not the first, specify the edition.

Publishing Information.   The final elements of the entry for a book, a pamphlet, or conference proceedings are the place of publication and the publisher. Use a shortened form of the publisher's name when possible, and include both the publisher's city and state, unless the city is well known (for example, New York). Omit terms such as *Publisher, Co.,* and *Inc.,* but do not omit or abbreviate the words *Books* and *Press.*

Online Sources.   When citing online sources, begin with the author, the date of publication, and the title, just as for printed sources. At the end of the reference, indicate that the work was "retrieved [date of retrieval] from [source]." (The source may be the World Wide Web or a database such as EBSCO.) Include enough of the URL to allow interested readers to retrieve the source. Again, cite personal communications, such as email messages and bulletin-board postings, in the text only. Include the communicator's initials and surname and the date: (J. D. Kahl, personal communication, October 2, 2000).

Standards continue to evolve for citations of online and electronic sources. When citing online information, the two primary goals are to give credit to the author and, whenever possible, to allow the reader to find the source.

Sample Entries (APA Style)

The following models for entries in the reference list include a range of sources. For additional examples, refer to the *Publication Manual of the American Psychological Association* (4th ed.) or the APA Web site at http://www.apa.org.

Book by One Author

Hassab, J. J. C. (1997). <u>Systems management: People, computers, machines, materials.</u> New York: CRC Press.

Book by Two or More Authors

Testerman, J. J. O., Kuegler, T. J., Jr., & Dowling, P. J., Jr. (1998). <u>Web advertising and marketing</u> (2nd ed.). Rocklin, CA: Prima.

Book by a Corporate or Organizational Author

Ernst and Young. (1997). <u>Ernst and Young's retirement planning guide.</u> New York: Wiley.

Work in a Book Compiled by an Editor

Thorne, K. S. (1997). Do the laws of physics permit wormholes for interstellar travel and machines for time travel? In Y. Terzian & E. Bilson (Eds.), <u>Carl Sagan's universe</u> (pp. 121-134). Cambridge, England: Cambridge University Press.

Book Edition Other Than First

Estes, J. C., & Kelley, D. R. (1998). <u>McGraw-Hill's interest amortization tables</u> (3rd ed.). New York: McGraw-Hill.

Journal Article

Rossouw, G. J. (1997). Business ethics in South Africa. <u>Journal of Business Ethics, 16,</u> 1539-1547.

Magazine Article

Coley, D. (1997, June). Compliance for the right reasons. <u>Business Geographics, 13,</u> 30-32.

Unsigned Article (in Weekly Periodical)

American City adds Nashville, Memphis. (1997, September 26). <u>The Business Journal, 16,</u> 55-56.

Newspaper Article

Mathews, A. W. (1997, October 1). The Internet generation taps into Morse code. <u>Wall Street Journal,</u> pp. B1, B7.

Encyclopedia Article

Gibbard, B. G. (1997). Particle detector. In World Book
    encyclopedia. (Vol. 15, pp. 186–187). Chicago: World Book.

Article Included in a Book

May, B., & Deacon, J. (1995). Amplification systems. In A. Kooper
    (Ed.), Advances in electronics (pp. 101–114). Miami, FL:
    Valley Press.

Article from a Volume of Proceedings

Carlson, C. T. (1995). Advanced organizers in manuals. In K.
    Rainey (Ed.), Proceedings of the 45th International Business
    Communication Conference (pp. RT56–58). Fairfax, VA: Society
    for Business Communication.

Government Document

U.S. Department of Energy. (1998). The energy situation in the
    next decade (Technical Publication No. 11346–53).
    Washington, DC: U.S. Government Printing Office.

Translated Work

Daudel, R. (1999). The realm of molecules (N. Hartmann, Trans.).
    New York: McGraw-Hill.

Multivolume Work

Standard & Poor. (1998). Standard & Poor's register of
    corporations, directors and executives. (Vols. 1–3). New
    York: McGraw-Hill.

Work in a Series

Knapp, B. (1996). Grolier educational elements series: Vol. 6.
    Silicon. Danbury, CT: Grolier Educational.

Report

Bertot, J. C., McClure, C. R., & Zweizig, D. L. (1996). The 1996
    national survey of public libraries and the Internet:
    Progress and issues: Final report. Washington, DC: U.S.
    Government Printing Office.

Thesis or Dissertation

Thelen, E. A. (1998). The evolution of the application letter in
     America: 1880-1960. Unpublished doctoral dissertation,
     University of Wisconsin-Milwaukee.

Proceedings

Johnson, P., & MacEwan, B. (Eds.) (1999). Collection management
     and development: Issues in an electronic era. Chicago:
     American Library Association.

Paper in Proceedings

Cline, N. M. (1999). Staffing: The art of managing change. In P.
     Johnson & B. MacEwan (Eds.), Collection management and
     development: Issues in an electronic era. (pp. 13-28).
     Chicago: American Library Association.

Paper Presented at a Conference

Kim, R. (1999, May). Management of information. Paper presented at
     the International Conference on MIS, University of Lima, Peru.

Document from a Web Site[a]

Speech

Clinton, B. (1993, January 21). First inaugural address.
     Inaugural addresses of the presidents of the United States.
     Retrieved February 5, 2000, from the World Wide Web:
     http://www.bartleby.com/124/pres64.html

Abstract

Fisher, J. (1999). The value of the technical communicator's role
     in the development of information systems [Abstract]. IEEE
     Transactions on Professional Communication, 42, 145-155.
     Retrieved February 9, 2000, from the World Wide Web:
     http://www.leepcs.org/transactions/42-3_fisher.htm

Article

Carnevale, D. (2000, February 11). University uses new format to
     send televised courses by computer. The Chronicle of Higher
     Education, 32, A45. Retrieved February 8, 2000, from the
     World Wide Web: http://chronicle.com/weekly/v46/i23/
     23a04502.htm

---

[a]When using APA style, you can cite the use of an entire Web site parenthetically in your paper. However, you would not include the site in your reference list if your citation refers to the entire site. Only specific documents from a site are included in your reference list.

Document by an Organization or Corporation

Federal Communications Commission. (1999, January). FCC consumer
    alert on telephone slamming [Announcement]. Washington, DC:
    Author. Retrieved February 8, 2000, from the World Wide Web:
    http://www.fcc.gov/Bureaus/Common_Carrier/Factsheets/
    slamming.html

Conference Proceedings

Mehringer, D. M., Plante, R. L. & Roberts, P. A. (Eds.). (1999).
    Astronomical data analysis software and systems VIII.
    Proceedings of the Eighth Annual Conference on Astronomical
    Data Analysis Software and Systems. Retrieved December 1,
    2000, from the World Wide Web: http://monet.astro.uicuc
    .edu/adass98/

Document from an Electronic Database

Kohl, J. R. (1999, May). Improving translatability and
    readability with syntactic cues. Technical Communication,
    46(2), 149+. Retrieved February 14, 2000, from Info Trac
    on-line database (Boston Public Library General Business
    file ASAP A56065282)

Email Message

Email messages are cited in the text (as personal communications) but are not included in the Reference list.

Listserv or Newsgroup Message

Rajiv, C. V. (1998, May 25). Portable document formats.
    Retrieved June 10, 1998, from the TECHWR-L listserv
    at techwrl@listserv.okstate.edu

Synchronous Communication

Prisley, L. V. (1997, October 5). [Group discussion]. Retrieved
    November 19, 1997, from moo.ku.org/port=9999

Style Manuals

Many professionals societies, publishing companies, and other organizations publish manuals that prescribe bibliographic reference formats for their publications or publications in their fields. In addition, several general style manuals are well known and widely used.

Specific Areas

American Chemical Society. *ACS Style Guide: A Manual for Authors and Editors.* 2nd ed. Washington: Amer. Chemical Soc., 1998. Some content from the guide is available at http://www.aup=usa.org/j778/isbn/0841234620.html.

American Mathematical Society. *A Manual for Authors of Mathematical Papers.* Providence: Amer. Mathematical Soc., 1990. For AMS submission guidelines, see the AMS Authors and Reviewers page at http://www.ams.org/authors.

American Psychological Association. *Publication Manual of the American Psychological Association.* 4th ed. Washington: Amer. Psychological Assn., 1994. The APA Web site provides the most current documentation information at http://www.apa.org/journals/webref.html.

Council of Science Editors (formerly the Council of Biology Editors). *Scientific Style and Format: The CBE Manual for Authors, Editors, and Publishers.* 6th ed. New York: Cambridge UP, 1994. Although the council's Web site does not include content or updates to the *CBE Manual,* users can search for articles and access references and job bank pages at http://www.councilscienceeditors.org/.

U.S. Geological Survey. *Suggestions to Authors of the Reports of the United States Geological Survey.* 7th ed. Washington: GPO, 1991. The U.S.G.S. Web site provides submission guidelines to U.S.G.S. publications, a searchable database of articles, and an impressive online library at http://www.usgs.gov/.

General

The Chicago Manual of Style. 14th ed. Chicago: U of Chicago P, 1993. The University of Chicago Press Web site provides a handy FAQ page with *Chicago Manual of Style* documentation information at http://www.press.uchicago.edu/Misc/Chicago/comosfaq.html.

Gibaldi, Joseph. *MLA Handbook for Writers of Research Papers.* 5th ed. New York: Mod. Lang. Assn. of Amer., 1999.

Gibaldi, Joseph. *MLA Style Manual and Guide to Scholarly Publishing.* 2nd ed. New York: Mod. Lang. Assn. of Amer., 1998. The MLA Web site provides documentation information relevant to both the *MLA Handbook* and the *MLA Style Manual* at http://www.mla.org.

National Information Standards Organization. *Scientific and Technical Reports — Elements, Organization, and Design.* Bethesda: Natl. Information Standards Organization, 1995. ANSI Z39. 18–1995. The National Information Standards Organization (NISO) Web site provides resources related to NISO standards and a searchable database of publications at http://www.niso.org/.

Skillin, M. E., and R. M. Gay. *Words into Type.* 3rd ed. Englewood Cliffs: Prentice, 1974.

Turabian, K. L. *A Manual for Writers of Term Papers, Theses, and Dissertations.* 6th ed. Chicago: U of Chicago P, 1996. The University of Chicago Press (UCP) Web site, although it does not provide additional information on Turabian's manual, does provide a searchable database of online articles published by the UCP Journals Division at http://www.journals .uchicago.edu.

Additional Guidelines for Scientific and Technical Writing

Numbered References

In much scientific and technical writing, the form used to give credit to your information sources differs from the form used in other fields. Information sources are listed in a separate section called "References." The entries in the reference section frequently are arranged according to the order in which they are first referred to in the text. In this system, the number 1 in parentheses (1) after a quotation or a reference to a book or an article refers the reader to the information in the first entry in the reference section, the number 2 in parentheses (2) refers the reader to the second entry in the reference section, and so on. A second number in parentheses, separated from the first by a colon, indicates the page number in the report or book from which the information was taken—for example, the notation "(3:27)" in the text indicates that the material is found on page 27 of entry 3 in the reference section.

The reference section for relatively short reports appears at the end of the report. For reports with a number of major sections or chapters, the reference section appears at the end of the section or the chapter. (See Chapter 13 for information on the placement of a reference section in a formal report.)

The details of reference systems in the sciences vary widely from field to field. Although the following examples are common in scientific and technical publications, consult publications in your field for precise details.

Book

```
1. Roebuck, J. A., Jr. Anthropometric methods: designing to fit
     the human body. Santa Monica, CA: Human Factors and Ergonomic
     Society: 1995.
```

Note that the last name appears first, followed by one or two initials. In the title of the work, only the first word and proper nouns are capitalized, and underlining is not used.

Journal Article

```
2. Thornton, W. A. A rational approach to design of tee shear
     connections. Engineering Journal, 1996, 33: 34-37.
```

Only the first word and proper nouns in the article title are capitalized, and no quotation marks are used. The journal name is not underlined.

Notes

Notes in publications have two uses: (1) to provide background information or explanations that would interrupt the flow of thought in the text and (2) to provide documentation references.

Explanatory Footnotes.   Explanatory or content notes are useful when the basis for an assumption should be made explicit but spelling it out in the text might make readers lose the flow of an argument. Because explanatory or content notes can be distracting, they should be kept to a minimum. If you cannot work the explanatory or background material into your text, it may not belong there. Lengthy explanations should be placed in an appendix.

Documentation Notes.   Notes that document sources can appear as either endnotes or footnotes. Endnotes are placed in a separate section at the end of a report, article, chapter, or book; footnotes (including explanatory notes) are placed at the bottom of a text page. The only drawback to using endnotes is that readers may find them inconvenient to locate and difficult to correlate with the text. Footnotes are easier for readers to locate.

Use superscript numbers in the text to refer readers to notes, and number them consecutively from the beginning of the report, article, or chapter to the end. Place each superscript number at the end of a sentence, clause, or phrase, at a natural pause point such as this,[1] right after the period, comma, or other punctuation mark (except a dash, which the number should precede[2]—as here).

Footnote Format.   To key in footnotes, leave four line spaces beneath the last line of text on a page, and indent the first line of each footnote five spaces. If the footnote runs longer than one line, the subsequent lines should begin at the left margin. Single space within each footnote, and double space between footnotes. Assume that this is the last line of text on a page.

```
    ¹Begin the first footnote at this position. When it runs
longer than one line, begin the second and all following lines at
the left margin.


    ²The second footnote follows the same spacing as the first.
Single-space within footnotes and double-space between them.
```

Endnote Format.   Endnotes should begin on a separate page titled "Notes" after the end of the text. The individual notes should be typed as for footnotes, single-spaced within notes and double-spaced between notes.

CHAPTER 11 SUMMARY: Researching Your Subject

Many information sources are available to you as you research job-related topics.

☐ Libraries provide organized access to a wealth of information in their print, audiovisual, and digitized collections. Researchers can access the information through

- Online catalogs
- Reference books
- Indexes and bibliographies
- Journal and government document collections
- Interlibrary loans
- Staffed reference services for assistance with searches and search strategies
- Public-access computer terminals

☐ The Internet provides online access to immense amounts of information, although its lack of a coherent organization makes locating salient information a challenge. To increase the odds of locating what you need, you can use

- Search engines
- Topical directories of sites
- Meta-search engines

☐ Personal interviews with subject-matter experts can provide up-to-date information not readily available elsewhere, but they require thoughtful preparation.

- Select the subject-matter expert most likely to be most helpful.
- Prepare specific questions before the interview.
- Take careful notes during the interview.
- Review and summarize your notes after the interview.

☐ Questionnaires permit you to obtain the views of groups of people without the time and expense necessary for numerous personal interviews.

- Design the questionnaire to gather as much information as you need with as little effort as possible on those answering your questions.
- Formulate questions in such a way that the answers can be readily tabulated.
- Carefully select recipients to ensure that their responses sufficiently represent a cross-section of those questioned.

☐ Interview yourself. Your own knowledge and experience may provide essential information.

☐ Many companies, professional and trade associations, public-interest groups, and various governmental agencies provide pamphlets and booklets, reports, and other materials that may be of value to your research.

☐ Give complete and accurate credit to all your information sources, which will

- Allow readers to locate the source of the information given.
- Establish your credibility by supporting your work with information from existing sources.
- Give proper credit to your sources to ensure that the work is not plagiarized.

☐ Document the information that you quote, paraphrase, or summarize in your text.

- In brief *parenthetical citations* in text, with full information in an alphabetical list of Works Cited or References.
- In *numbered references* in text that refer to full information in a References section, where citations are listed numerically in the order of their first citation in text.
- In *notes* that appear either at the bottoms of text pages (footnotes) or in a separate section at the end of a chapter or section (endnotes).

■ Exercises

1. Using word-processing software, correctly prepare an MLA-style Works Cited page using the following list of sources:

John O'Connor, <u>Exploring American History</u>. Globe Book Company, New York, 1994

Randy Roberts, <u>American Experiences: Readings in American History</u>, third edition. HarperCollins, New York, 1994

Paul Rubenstein, <u>Writing for the Media</u>. Prentice Hall, Englewood Cliffs, NJ, 1988

<u>Highsmith's Complete School & Library Catalog</u>. Highsmith Inc., Fort Atkinson, WI, 1998

Lee Hopkins, <u>Do You Know What Day Tomorrow Is?</u> Scholastic Inc., New York, 1989

Anthony Burgess, <u>Ernest Hemingway and His World</u>. Charles Scribner and Sons, New York, 1985

Charles Elster, Tooth and Nail: a Novel Approach to the New SAT. Harcourt Brace & Company, San Diego, 1994

Donald Bolander, Instant Synonyms and Antonyms. Career Institute, Mundelein, IL, 1970

Andrew Hurley, Against All Hope: The Prison Memoirs of Armand Valladores. Alfred A. Knopf Inc, New York, 1987

James Miller, Jr., Russian and Eastern European Literature. Scott, Foresman and Company, Glenview, IL, 1976

James Mountford, The Revised Latin Primer. Longman's, London, 1966

Helen Jackson. A Century of Dishonor: A Sketch of the United States Government's Dealings with Some of the Indian Tribes. Corner House, Williamstown, MA, 1973

2. Using word-processing software, correctly prepare an APA-style Reference page using the following list of sources:

Donald Bolander, Instant Synonyms and Antonyms. Career Institute, Mundelein, IL, 1970

Anthony Burgess, Ernest Hemingway and His World. Charles Scribner and Sons, New York, 1985

George Clare, Last Waltz in Vienna: The Rise and Destruction of a Family, 1842–1942. Henry Holt and Company, New York, 1989

Genia Dunwich, Wiccan Love Spells. Citadel Press, Secaucus, NJ, 1998

Charles Elster, Tooth and Nail: a Novel Approach to the New SAT. Harcourt Brace & Company, San Diego, 1994

Andrew Roberts, The Concise Columbia Dictionary of Quotations. Avon Books, New York, 1990

Julien Hawthorne, Editor. The Masterpieces and the History of Literature. Hamilton Book Company, New York, 1966

Highsmith's Complete School and Library Catalog. Highsmith Inc, Fort Atkinson, WI, 1998

Lee Hopkins, Do You Know What Day Tomorrow Is? Scholastic Inc, New York, 1989

Andrew Hurley, Against All Hope: The Prison Memoirs of Armand Valladores. Alfred A. Knopf Inc., New York, 1987

John O'Connor, Exploring American History. Globe Book Company, New York, 1994

Helen Jackson. A Century of Dishonor: A Sketch of the United States Government's Dealings with Some of the Indian Tribes. Corner House, Williamstown, MA, 1973

Arthur Miller, Timebends: A Life. Grove Press, New York, 1987

James Mountford, The Revised Latin Primer. Longman's, London, 1966

Kenneth Koch, Sleeping on the Wing; An Anthology of Modern Essays on Reading and Writing. Random House, New York, 1973

David Lempert, Escape from the Ivory Tower: Student Adventures in Democratic Experience, Jossey-Bass, San Francisco, 1966

Paul Mussen, Child Development and Personality, third edition. Harper and Row, New York, 1969

Rand Roberts, American Experiences: Readings in American History, 3rd Edition. HarperCollins New York, 1994

Paul Rubenstein, Writing for the Media. Prentice Hall, Englewood Cliffs, NJ, 1988

Harry Shanker, The Stage and the School, seventh edition. Glencoe; McGraw Hill, New York, 1997

Janet Smith, Editor, Mark Twain on the Damned Human Race. Hill and Wang, New York, 1977

Graene Tytler, Physiognomy in the European Novel: Faces and Fortunes. Princeton University Press, Princeton, New Jersey, 1982

Herbert York, Readings from Scientific American. W. H. Freeman and Company, San Francisco, 1977

3. Using word-processing software, correctly prepare an MLA-style Works Cited page using the following list of online sources. (Annotations are provided in parentheses for the Web sites so that you can use these sources as research resources.)

   a. The SBA Web site at http://www.sba.gov. (The official SBA site includes information about financing and expanding a small business and links to related sites and government offices. The page also has a site-specific search engine.)

   b. The Pro-Net page at the SBA Web site at http://pro-net.sba.gov. (Pro-Net is a government resource that offers information on procurement and subcontracting opportunities. The resources at Pro-Net are geared toward small businesses, and include access to the *Commerce Business Daily*. You can register at the site to search the database.)

   c. A conference report prepared by the Office of Economic Research of the SBA's Office of Advocacy, titled "The Impact of Bank Mergers and Acquisitions on Small Business Lending." The report was published October 6, 1997, and can be retrieved online at the SBA Web site at http://www.sba.gov/advo/stats/marpt.html. (No individual author is provided.)

   d. The Microsoft Network's Business (MSN) Central Web site at http://www.bcentral.com/. (MSN offers articles, local business news, directories, and useful business links.)

   e. The Bloomberg.com Web site at http://www.bloomberg.com. (The Bloomberg company's site features articles, business tips, and stock-market information—with educational tools for current and aspiring entrepreneurs.)

   f. An online article by Caroline Baum, titled "Contradictory Explanations for Oil-Price Effect." The article was published at the Bloomsburg.com Web site on June 30, 2000, and can be found in the archive of articles by Baum at http://www.bloomberg.com/. The full address is: http://quote.bloomberg

.com/fgcgi.cgi?ptitle=Caroline%20Baum&touch=1&s1=blk&tp=ad_topright_b bco&T=markets_fgcgi_content99.ht&s2=blk&bt=blk&s=AOVzcYBVgSG931E9p.

g. The Edward Lowe Foundation's *Entrepreneurial Edge* Web site at http:// www.lowe.org. (The Edward Lowe Foundation, a not-for-profit organization, provides information, research, education, and other services for entrepreneurs. The Foundation's Web site offers resources for financing, franchising, marketing, and international trade, as well as research reports, books, business links, and the browsable Edward Lowe Digital Library.)

h. Quicken.com's Small Business Web site at http://www.quicken.com/ small_business/. (Quicken's resources for the small-business sector cover areas such as taxes and accounting, starting a business, office technology, and legal issues.)

i. An online document titled "Owner's Checklist for Starting a New Business," posted at the Quicken.com site, can be retrieved at http://www.quicken .com/small_business/cchtools/?article=strtch_mhttp://www.quicken.com/ small_business/cch/tools/?article=strtch_m. (No author or date is provided.)

j. The Research Engine page at the SmallBizPlanet.com Web site at http:// www.smallbizplanet.com/product/features.html. (SmallBizPlanet.com's search engine scans a catalog of prescreened, indexed sites for small-business owners, and offers select business articles organized into categories.)

k. An online government document titled "Publication 538: Accounting Periods and Methods," dated November 1997, and posted on November 19, 1998, by the Department of the Treasury, Internal Revenue Service (IRS). The document can be retrieved at the IRS Web site at http://www.irs.ustreas.gov/ forms_pubs/pubs/p538toc.htm.

l. The *CCH Business Owner's Toolkit* Web site at http://www.toolkit.cch.com/. (Resources at this site hosted by CCH Incorporated, a provider of business, legal, and tax information and software, include a guide to the Internet for small businesses, news articles, and information on how to start and maintain your own business.)

m. An online document titled "Telecommuting Checklist and Agreement: Help Evaluating and Setting Up a Work-at-Home Plan for Your Employees," posted November 16, 2000, at the *CCH Business Owner's Toolkit* Web site. The document can be retrieved at http://www.toolkit.cch.com/tools/telecm_m .asp. (No individual author provided.)

4. Using word-processing software, correctly prepare an APA-style Reference page using the following list of sources. (Note: When using APA style, you can cite the use of an entire Web site parenthetically, in your paper; however, you would not include the site in your *Reference list* if your citation refers to the *entire* site. Only specific documents from a Web site would be included in your Reference list. For this exercise, use the Web to find documents at the following sites. Annotations are provided in parentheses so that you can use them as research resources.)

a. An email or other document retrieved from the Northwest Educational Technology Consortium (NETC) Web site at http://www.netc.org/. (NETC's site provides technology-related resources for educators, including an Electronic Library, distance-learning and videoconferencing information, and tips on grant writing and seeking funding for technology projects.)

b. An article accessed through the Purdue University Libraries' Virtual Refer-

ence Desk page at the Purdue Libraries' Web site at http://thorplus.lib
.purdue.edu/reference. Purdue Libraries offer selected links to English, international, acronym, and technical dictionaries and thesauri, news databases,
government documents, and more.)

c. A tutorial or other document retrieved from the Mid-Continent Research for
Education and Learning Web site at http://www.mcrel.org/. (This site offers
resources geared toward educators, including online curriculum materials,
reports, and articles that can be retrieved from a searchable database.)

d. An article retrieved from the *Writer's Write* "Links and Resources for Writers"
page at http://www.writerswrite.com/writinglinks. (This page at the Writer's
Write Web site provides information for writers, divided into categories that
include business writing. Here you will find links to online articles, tutorials,
business plans, and electronic libraries.)

e. An article retrieved from the business area of the ABCNews Web site about
writing effective business letters at http://abcnews.go.com/sections/business/.
(See the business area of the ABCNews Web site at http://abcnews.go.com/
sections/business for other online business articles; the site includes a searchable archive.)

f. An article retrieved from the "Online Technical Writer Resources" page at the
Web site of the Society for Technical Communication (STC), San Francisco
Chapter at http://stc.org/region8/sfc/www/writer.html. (This page at the site
hosted by the San Francisco branch of the STC—an organization of technical
communicators including writers, editors, graphic designers, videographers,
multimedia artists, and Web-page designers—offers online technical-writing
resources, including links to information on a variety of software applications
and on writing user-friendly manuals and Help menus.)

g. A report titled "Charting the Impacts of Information Technology," by Eileen
Collins of the Division of Science Resources Studies, National Science Foundation (NSF) retrieved at http://www.nsf.gov. (See the NSF Web site for reports and studies in areas including biology, education, engineering, geo-
sciences, math, physical sciences, and more.)

h. An article entitled "Help Authoring Tools: A Round-Up" by Mike Hendry
retrieved from the Web site of the Society for Technical Communication at
http://stc.org/region2/phi/n&v/soft0598nf.html. (See the STC Web site at
http://stc.org for other online articles and educational resources and job information.)

i. An article retrieved from the Online Documentation page at the Professional
Writing at Purdue University site at http://addison.English.purdue.edu/pw/
doc/. (This page, edited by Professor Johndan Johnson-Eiola, provides documentation and tutorials to help business- and technical-writing students with
programs such as Excel, PageMaker, PowerPoint, and Netscape that are used
in professional writing courses.)

5. This exercise will give you some practice in creating MLA- and APA-style parenthetical citations—citations that are included within the text of your research
paper—and will help you provide the reader with information on the source(s)
that you are drawing from, either through direct quotations or by paraphrasing.
Using word-processing software, follow these steps.

a. Imagine that you are writing a paper that includes a discussion about the importance of organizing space. Here is an excerpt from that paper:

Organizing your home and work space can be one of life's greatest problems for some people. Having your spaces organized can make the difference between a peaceful existence and misery! To conquer this problem, you must first analyze your own organizational level. We each have a different way of organizing and also a different concept of what organized means in terms of our own homes and work spaces. Do you consider yourself "organized"? Are your drawers and closets as neat as you would like them? Or, are your rooms a mess, but you know exactly where to find any item that is missing? The first step to becoming organized is to define what the term means to you and to decide what degree of organization would bring peace to your life.

b. Incorporate into the above paragraph three direct quotations or three sentences of paraphrased content from the following excerpts from a book titled *A New Way of Looking at Organizing,* by Judy Morgenstern. The material is all from page 1 of the text, published in 1999 by Anchor Books in New York. You may insert the three sentences (quotations or paraphrased text) anywhere you wish in the paragraph as long as the context makes sense and as long as Morgenstern's three excerpts are not included consecutively within your paragraph. Also, create parenthetical documentation for this material—first in MLA style, and then in APA style. Refer to the text of this chapter for guidelines and examples for both styles of parenthetical citation. Following is the text from Judy Morgenstern's book to be incorporated into and cited in your paper:

If I asked you to describe an organized space, what would you say? From most people, I hear things like "neat and tidy," "spare," "minimalist," and "boring." But an organized space has nothing to do with these traits. There are people whose homes and offices appear neat as a pin on the surface. Yet, inside their desk drawers and kitchen cabinets, there is no real system, and things are terribly out of control. By contrast, there are many people who live or work in a physical mess, yet feel very comfortable in this environment and can always put their hands on whatever they need in a second. Could they be considered organized? Absolutely.

Being organized has less to do with the way an environment <u>looks</u> than how effectively it <u>functions</u>. If a person can find what she needs when she needs it, feels unencumbered in achieving her goals, and is happy in her space, then that person is well organized.

I'd like to propose a new definition of organization: Organizing is the process by which we create environments that enable us to live, work, and relax exactly as we want to. When we are organized, our homes, offices, and sched-

ules reflect and encourage who we are, what we want, and
where we are going.

Misconceptions affect the way you think about any
process, poisoning your attitude toward it and eroding
even your best efforts to succeed by convincing you before
you start that you're bound to fail.

Here are some of the most common beliefs about organizing, and the debunking facts that will change your
thinking.

Misconception: Organizing is a mysterious talent.
Some lucky people are born with it, while others, like
you, are left to suffer.

Fact: Organizing is a skill. In fact, it's a remark-
ably simple skill that anyone can learn.

▇ In-Class Activities

1. Choose a topic relevant to your area of study and create a ten-item sample questionnaire that you could use to gather information on the subject. Also, draft a
   letter to accompany your questionnaire.
2. *Paraphrase* each of the two following passages. Then, *summarize* the information
   from each. In each case, identify your notes by stating the topic of the passage.
   a. To keep pipes from freezing, wrap the pipes in insulation made especially for
      water pipes, or in layers of old newspaper, lapping the ends and tying them
      around the pipes. Cover the newspapers with plastic to keep out moisture.
      When it is extremely cold and there is real danger of freezing, let the faucets
      drip a little. Although this wastes water, it may prevent freezing damage.
      Know where the valve for shutting off the water coming into the house or
      apartment is located. You may as a last resort have to shut off this main valve
      and drain all the pipes to keep them from freezing and bursting.
   b. American energy production has leveled off in recent years. After peaking at
      almost 66 quadrillion British thermal units (Btu) in 1984, production in crude
      oil has dropped significantly over the last few years. (One "quad" Btu equals
      approximately 170 million barrels of crude oil.) Sometimes it has become too
      expensive to remove the oil from the ground as declining oil prices per barrel
      led to a situation where drilling costs could be higher than potential profits.
      In fact, the drop in oil prices contributed to a decline in the prices of other
      fossil fuels, particularly natural gas, which fell about 35 percent, and coal and
      lignite, which dropped around 14 percent over the 1986–87 period.
      Generally, since 1972, production of petroleum and natural gas has de-
      creased while coal and nuclear power production has increased. In 1972,
      nuclear-based and coal production of energy accounted for 23.5 percent of
      the total U.S. production; by 1987, it was 39 percent. In 1972, petroleum and
      natural gas produced 71.8 percent of total U.S. production; by 1987, it was 53
      percent. Reduced natural gas output accounted for most of the decline. Sta-
      tistically, these changes indicate major changes in energy usage in only a

decade and a half. Energy production leveled off during the 1980s with the total amount of production in 1987 equal to that of 1980. A drop in natural gas and crude oil production has been balanced by an increase in coal and nuclear production.

3. Prepare a brief parenthetical citation in MLA style and in APA style for each of the following reference items and then create an MLA-style list of Works Cited and an APA-style Reference list containing full information about each citation.

   a. A magazine article beginning on page 24 and ending on page 32 of the June 2000 issue of *Electronic Publishing,* by Sterling Ledet, titled "Reaching Customers on the Web." Your reference is on page 26.

   b. An unsigned article, "Power Play: Will Electricity Deregulation Jolt Consumers," in the June 2000 issue of *Consumer Reports,* volume 62, number 6. The article appears in its entirety on page 60.

   c. Roger M. Schwarz' book *The Skilled Facilitator: Practical Wisdom for Developing Effective Groups,* published by Jossey-Bass Publishers of San Francisco in 1994. Your reference is on page 149.

   d. An article in the *Washington Post* titled "Pension Errors May Be Rising, But Finding Them Is Up to You," by Albert Crenshaw. The article begins on page 1 and ends on page 4 of Section H of the June 22, 2000, issue. Your citation is on page H4.

   e. A Web site titled "The Trade Development Homepage" at http://www.ita.doc .gov/td/td_home/tdhome.html, hosted by the International Trade Administration and the U.S. Department of Commerce. The site has no copyright date, but you accessed it on September 13, 2000.

   f. An online article from the *New York Times Magazine,* "The Way We Live Now: Competitive States of America," by Mark Kingwell. The article was published on June 25, 2000, and you accessed it on July 10, 2000, at http://www .nytimes.com/library/magazine/home/20000625mag-waywelivenow.html.

   g. An online book titled *Hal's Legacy: 2001's Computer as Dream and Reality,* edited by David G. Stork. The book was published by the MIT Press in Cambridge, Massachusetts, in January 1997, and you accessed it online on August 1, 2000, at http://mitpress.mit.edu/e-books/Hal/.

   h. An online government publication titled *The United States Government Manual,* published by the National Archives and Records Administration and found at http://www.access.gpo.gov/nara/nara001.html. The page is dated January 7, 2000, and you accessed it on August 19, 2000.

   i. A booklet titled "Security in the Workplace: Improving the Safety of Federal Employees," by the Department of Justice, U.S. Marshal's Service and published in Washington, D.C., by the Government Printing Office in 1999. Your reference is on page 12.

   j. Your interview of the City Manager of Plainview, Texas, on March 1, 2000. Her name is Annette Diggs.

   k. An article titled "Creating electronic documents that interact with diagnostic software for onsite service," by Mark Harmison that appears on pages 92 through 101 of the journal *IEEE Transactions on Professional Communication.* It appears in the June 1997 issue of the journal, volume 40, number 21. You cite information on pages 95 and 99.

   l. Computer software called *Microsoft Money 2000: Business and Personal* issued by Microsoft Press in 2000. Available in disk or on CD-ROM, it requires MS Windows 95, 98, or NT.

m. The sixth edition of the *Dictionary of Computer and Internet Terms* by Douglas Downing, Michael Covington, and Melody M. Covington. The dictionary was published in Hauppauge, New York, in 1998. You cite material from the section, To the Reader, on page ix.

n. An article from the 1998 (4th) edition of the *McGraw-Hill Concise Encyclopedia of Science and Technology* titled "Virology."

4. Bring to class information from three Web sites related to your area of study. Print out relevant pages from each site and draft a brief synopsis of the resources provided there. Form groups with three to five students who share your major. Review the guidelines in this chapter for evaluating a Web site and draft a list of questions to consider when evaluating a Web site as a research resource specific to your field. Evaluate and compare each of the sites that your group members have found and decide which sites would be the most valuable for your research. Write a brief group summary of your findings to share with the class.

5. Using the online sources that you brought to class for In-Class Activity 4, work in a group of three to five students to create an MLA-style Works Cited list and an APA-style Reference list from your collective online sources. (Refer to the Documenting Sources section of this chapter as needed.)

6. Bring to class at least three printed sources of information related to your major field of study (including bibliographic information about each source) and break into groups of seven or eight members. Work together to compile an MLA-style works-cited list and an APA-style reference list for the sources in your group. (Refer to the Documenting Sources section of this chapter as needed.) The first group to complete this exercise may ask the instructor to check the lists and share the results with the class.

7. Bring to class either a general dictionary or one that is specific to your major field of study. Divide into groups of three or four students who share a major area of study. Appoint a group leader and a group recorder and for 20 or 30 minutes trace the origin of six or more words pertaining to your chosen field. Be prepared to share your group's results with the class.

■ Research Projects

Note: The Research Projects in this chapter may be used as the basis for the preparation of a formal report according to the guidelines presented in Chapter 13.

1. Select a topic from your career field or other area of interest. Using the online catalog in your library, locate five books on your topic. Document your sources according to the MLA or APA guidelines in this chapter.

2. Using the periodical index or indexes in your library, locate five articles, from magazines, newspapers, or journals, on the topic you chose for Exercise 1. Document your sources according to the MLA or APA guidelines in this chapter.

3. List five databases to which your college library has access that are pertinent to your field of study. Note how many periodicals or other sources of information each database contains, and indicate how frequently each database is updated. List three periodicals from each database that publish articles in your field of study.

4. Choose a topic related to your area of study. Interview someone knowledgeable about your subject and submit your organized notes of the interview to your instructor. Also submit the letter or email that you sent to request the interview. Incorporate the information that you gathered at your interview in a research paper and document the interview according to MLA or APA style.

5. Your campus has recently been in the news because of its lack of international students. You have been asked to serve on a student committee charged with the task of finding out why your campus does not attract more international students. Your committee has decided to develop a questionnaire to distribute to the international students on campus asking for their feedback concerning this issue. In preparing your questionnaire you will want to keep in mind the guidelines in this chapter for preparing a questionnaire, and also the guidelines for working with an international audience in Chapter 12. Submit your questionnaire to your instructor.

6. Your corporation employs several entry-level workers who do not speak fluent English. As part of the training committee you have been asked to prepare an interview for them to give feedback on the best way their employer can help them learn English to better learn their job and advance in the company. A specialist will translate the interviews into the languages needed for the employees and will also administer the interviews. Your assignment is to develop an interview for the specialist to use. Refer to the guidelines for developing a questionnaire and conducting interviews in this chapter. Keep in mind that your audience is from a variety of cultures, but that they all work for your company with limited English skills. Submit the interview to your instructor with a brief narrative summarizing how the cultural and language barriers makes this assignment challenging.

■ Web Projects

1. Locate three to five Web sites that feature information relevant to a topic that you would like to research—the topic should be related to your field of study. Evaluate these sites according to the guidelines in this chapter and write a brief explanation of what makes these sites credible and why they are potentially valuable to your research. Document these sites (either the whole site or specific pages or documents within the site) according to MLA or APA documentation guidelines. Incorporate these sites into your research project.

2. Locate five sources of information on the Internet about a topic related to your major area of study. The sources may include journals, Usenet and listserv discussion groups, books, reports, laws, graphics, and other special-interest sites. Bookmark your sources and document them in writing for use in a research paper following the documentation guidelines of this chapter.

3. Review the online catalog search in this chapter (illustrated in Figures 11–3 through 11–8). Choose a topic related to your area of study and conduct a step-by-step online catalog search, exploring each of the three basic categories for a simple search: Keyword; Title, keyword; Subject Heading, keyword; Author; Title, exact; or Subject Heading, exact. If you were to write a formal report on this topic based on your online searches, which of the three basic methods would you use?

Why? Summarize the steps of your search and your recommendation in a brief written narrative.

4. Prepare notes on information relevant to a topic of your choice from the Library of Congress at http://catalog.loc.gov, focusing on the following areas: "the FAQ page," "Services for Researchers," and "Search Other Libraries' Catalogs." Include in your notes how to use the site and specific resources that you find. Refer to this chapter for guidelines on paraphrasing and note-taking. Your instructor may ask you to submit your notes electronically.

5. Using at least three credible online reference works, find definitions for terms related to your area of study. You may begin by accessing the online reference works at Bartleby.com: Great Books Online at http://bartleby.com, and the Encarta online dictionary at http://www.encarta.com.

6. Assume you are a manager at a small manufacturing corporation (you choose the product that your company produces). Because of a rising national concern about the environment and land use, the board of directors has asked your department to develop a policy statement outlining your corporation's views on the conservation of natural resources. Your boss has asked you to research online and prepare a list of Web sites outlining the government's current policy on the use of natural resources. Develop a list of Web sites that contain information about how government policy on land use and other environmental issues affect businesses. Investigate government agencies such as the Environmental Protection Agency (EPA) at http://www.epa.gov, the Bureau of Land Management at http://www.blm.gov, the Department of Agriculture at http://www.usda.gov/, the U.S. Food and Drug Administration's Food Safety page at http://www.foodsafety.gov, and the National Forest Service home page at http://www.fs.fed.us/. (To locate additional government organizations, search FirstGov at http://www.firstgov.gov/index.html, a site that links to all federal agencies and that is organized by topic areas—Agriculture and Food, Business and Economy, Consumer Services and Safety, Environmental Energy, and more. You can also search the directory sponsored by the Libraries at Louisiana State University in conjunction with the federal government at http://www.access.gpo.gov/su_docs/dpos/agencies.html. Submit your list of at least six sites with your notes describing the information contained at each site and why you included these sites on your list. Include with your notes a Works Cited page using MLA style.

7. Research online to discover what occupations might be found in your field in the government. Although the administrators of a given governmental agency might include elected officials and also political appointees, there are also numerous positions of information gatherers working for the government—including biologists, educators (of various specialties), social scientists, economists—who provide data and other information to administrators. Prepare a list of online Web sites that contain government occupation possibilities for your field. Include with your list an MLA-style Works Cited page and an APA-style Reference list.

12 Designing Effective Documents and Visuals

This chapter is divided into two main parts: Creating Documents and Creating Visuals. The chapter begins with Creating Documents, a section that offers detailed information for document layout and design, Web-page design, and the creation of forms—both for print and the Web. The Creating Visuals section provides guidelines and models for designing illustrations—tables, graphs, drawings, charts, photographs, and maps—and integrating them with text as well as advice for using graphics to communicate with an increasingly international business audience.

Clarity and consistency are qualities that apply not only to good writing but also to the design and layout of any document, especially one in which visuals appear. Effectively designed documents—whether intended for print or for the Web—are those that are uncluttered and that highlight structure, hierarchy, and order. They help readers locate the information they need and grasp how the parts fit together. The Creating Documents section describes how to achieve these goals by providing your readers with carefully selected visual cues. Everything from your choice of type size and style to the arrangement of text and visuals on each page contributes to your reader's experience of your document.

Web-page design, though an extension of document design, differs from it in several important ways. Instead of designing your information for its appearance on a printed page, you design it for how it will appear on a computer screen. The size of the computer screen, the range of colors and images available, and the ability to link information, all make designing for the Web different from designing printed documents. Despite these obvious differences, Web designers must plan their pages and overall site from the perspective of their visitors' needs, just as document designers must plan the layout and design of the printed page from the perspective of their readers' needs. For the Web, these needs include establishing a uniform, consistent design so that visitors can navigate the site with confidence that they can locate the information they seek. Web-site designers must also consider a myriad of other concerns unique to Web pages, including the use of graphics and typography, the most appropriate links to sources of information within and outside the site, the viewing capabilities of site visitors, and the need to break up dense passages of text for ease of reading on a computer screen.

Another kind of communication, the form—whether created for print or for the Web—frequently requires a minimum amount of writing and yet can, in

Voices from the Workplace

Diane Schumacher, Co-owner of Eskie Adventures

Eskie Adventures is a mail-order business specializing in products for American Eskimo dogs, basset hounds, chow chows, samoyeds, shetland sheepdogs, and their owners. In a typical day, Diane's tasks range from taking, filling, and shipping orders, to tracking inventory, locating new suppliers, and maintaining the mailing database. However, her main responsibility is to create and produce the company's catalog. Diane describes the importance of planning in creating effective graphics.

"The key to setting up a good catalog and working with the various graphics elements is to have a clear concept that you can communicate to the customer. No matter how basic or complex the graphics elements are, their main purpose is to communicate, whether they are providing information about the look and texture of a particular product or statistical information in a pie chart.

"With that concept in mind, I begin each new catalog with a brainstorming session to flesh out the main theme I want to communicate. From there, I organize the catalog into pages, break down the graphics elements, and decide where each will go based on how they can best communicate the theme of the catalog. This all occurs before I ever touch the computer. Once I get to the computer and the graphics programs, most of the truly hard work is already done. From that point on, it is a question of remaining focused on and true to the theme."

For more information about Eskie Adventures or for a copy of their latest catalog, visit their Web site at http://www.eskieadventures.com.

Entry-Level
Christopher Smith, SquashBusters

As director of SquashBusters—an innovative community-service organization that provides mentoring, academic tutoring, life-skills training, and squash instruction for urban students in Boston and Cambridge, Massachusetts—Christopher Smith relies on the power of visuals for a variety of tasks. On the job, Christopher organizes the group's daily activities, manages the staff, schedules volunteers, tutors and coaches youth, and acquires organizational sponsors. The visuals he creates are integrated into magazine advertisements, spreadsheets, brochures, handouts, presentations, and other communications that benefit from the use of visuals to convey a message. Christopher points out the value of using visuals in day-to-day operations.

"The most important visual aid that I make every day is not for foundations or sponsors but for the participants in the program. It is a daily sheet called the 'Briefing' that includes important meeting times and locations, assignments, announcements, volunteer match-ups, inspirational quotes, community stories, and even squash diagrams. The success of the message in the Briefing depends on one thing—that the participants *read* it. Our program would not run smoothly if no one paid attention to the Briefing. To get my readers to pay attention to the information, I present the text in a way that makes the Briefing more fun and less technical looking. With this goal in mind, I try to incorporate effective visuals that will attract and hold the attention of my audience.

"To get the most out of your visuals, put yourself in your reader's place. Ask yourself how visual aids would attract your attention to the information at hand. To get the most out of your publications, ask yourself what the person viewing the document will want to see and how it will best be presented."

Learn more about SquashBusters and view the use of visuals on their Web site at http://www.squashbusters.org or http://www.fas.harvard.edu/~athletic/community/squash.html.

some circumstances, be the most effective and efficient way to communicate. Forms created for the Web perform most of the same functions as those created for print, only they do so interactively on a Web page. The advantage of Web forms is that they collect data online in an electronic format that can be transmitted to a database for compilation or sent directly to an email address for analysis and response.

The Creating Visuals section of this chapter focuses on how to use visual aids in your writing in order to increase your reader's understanding of your topic. Tables, graphs, drawings, charts, maps, and photographs—often collectively called visuals or visual aids—can frequently express ideas or convey information that words alone cannot. Tables allow the easy comparison of large numbers of statistics that would be difficult to understand if they appeared in sentence form. Graphs make trends and mathematical relationships immediately evident. Drawings, photographs, charts, and maps render shapes and spatial relationships more concisely and efficiently than text can. By allowing the reader to interpret data at a glance, visuals not only encourage faster decision-making but may add to the persuasiveness of your document or Web site.

When using tables and illustrations, consider your purpose and your reader carefully. For example, a drawing of the major regions of the brain for a high-school science class would be different from an illustration provided for research scientists studying brain abnormalities.

Many of the qualities of good writing—simplicity, clarity, conciseness, directness—are just as important in the creation and use of visuals. Presented with clarity and consistency, visuals can help your reader focus on key portions of your document. Be aware, though, that even the best visual enhances, or supports, the text. It is your writing that must carry the burden of providing context for the visual and pointing out its significance.

■ Creating Documents

Document Layout and Design

The layout and design of a document make even the most complex information look accessible and give readers a favorable impression of the writer and the organization. To accomplish those goals, a design should offer a simple and uncluttered presentation of the topic; highlight structure, hierarchy, and order; help readers find information easily; and reinforce an organization's image.

Effective design is based on visual simplicity and harmony, such as using compatible fonts and the same highlighting device for similar items. Design should reveal hierarchy by signaling the difference between topics and subtopics, between primary and secondary information, and between general points and examples. Writers can achieve effective layout and design through their selection of fonts, their choice of devices to highlight information, and their arrangement of text and visual components on a page. Such visual cues make information easy to find. Finally, the design of a document should project the appropriate image of an organization. For example, if clients are paying a high price for consulting services, they may expect a sophisticated, polished design; if employees inside an organization expect management to be frugal, they may accept—even expect—economical and standard company design.

Typography

Typography refers to the style and arrangement of type on a printed page. A complete set of all the letters, numbers, and symbols available in one typeface (or style) is called a *font*. The letters in a typeface have a number of distinctive characteristics, some of which are shown in Figure 12–1.

Typeface and Type Size.   For most on-the-job writing, select a typeface primarily for its legibility. Avoid typefaces that may distract readers with contrasts in thickness or with odd-looking features, as is often the case with script and cursive typefaces. In addition, avoid typefaces that fade when printed or copied. Choose popular typefaces with which readers are familiar, such as Times Roman or the following typefaces:

- Baskerville
- **Bodoni**
- Century
- Garamond
- Gill Sans
- Helvetica
- Palatino
- Univers

Do not use more than two typefaces in a document. With so many fonts available on most computers, a common mistake is to pepper the document with many odd-looking typefaces, thereby creating disharmony. To create a dramatic contrast between headlines and text, as in a newsletter, use a typeface that is distinctively different. You can also use a noticeably different typeface *within* a graphic element. In any case, experiment before making final decisions. (Keep in mind that not all fonts have the same assortment of symbols and other characters.)

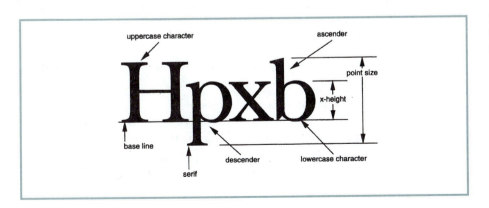

**Figure 12–1
Primary Features of
Letter Characters**

One way typefaces are characterized is by the presence or absence of *serifs*. Serifs, shown in Figure 12–1, are the small projections at the end of each stroke in a letter. Serif typefaces have projections; sans serif styles do not. (*Sans* is French for "without.") The text of this book is set in Utopia, a serif typeface. Although sans serif type has a modern look, serif type is easier to read, especially in the smaller sizes. Sans serif, however, works well for headings.

A font size that is too small will cause eye strain and make the text look crammed and intimidating. Six-point type is too small for almost any application other than footnotes and classified ads. However, type that is too large uses more space than necessary, makes reading difficult and inefficient, and makes readers perceive words in parts rather than as a whole. Figure 12–2 illustrates various type sizes.

Ideal point sizes for text on paper documents range from 8 to 13 points; 10- or 11-point type is most commonly used. For Web documents, you need to look carefully at both typeface and type size. Monitors display fonts in dramatically different sizes on the screen, even when the same typefaces are involved. There-fore, you should print out samples of a document to test your choice of sizes and typefaces and view your Web site on a variety of monitors, if possible.

The distance from which a document will be read should help determine type size. For example, instructions that will rest on a table at which the reader stands require a larger typeface than normal. Consider the age of your readers, too. Visually impaired readers and some older adults may need larger type sizes.

Left- or Full-Justified Margins.   Left-justified margins are generally easier to read than full-justified margins because the uneven contour of the right margin (or "ragged" right) provides the eyes with more landmarks to identify. Left justifi-cation also is better if lines are short and full justification causes your word-processing software to insert irregular-sized spaces between words, producing unwanted white space or unevenness in blocks of text.

However, because ragged-right margins look informal, full-justified text is more appropriate for publications aimed at a broad readership that expects a more formal, polished appearance. Further, full justification is often useful with multiple-column formats because the spaces between the columns (called *alleys*) need the definition that full justification provides.

**Figure 12–2
Samples of 6- to
14-Point Type**

6 pt.   This size might be used for dating a source.
8 pt.   This size might be used for footnotes.
10 pt.   This size might be used for figure captions.
12 pt.   This size might be used for main text.
14 pt.   This size might be used for headings.

Highlighting Devices

Writers use a number of methods to emphasize important words, passages, and sections within documents:

- Typographical devices
- Headings and captions
- Headers and footers
- Rules, icons, and color

When used thoughtfully, highlighting devices give a document a visual logic and organization. For example, rules and boxes can set off steps and illustrations from surrounding explanations. Consistency is important: Use the same technique to highlight a particular feature throughout your document.

Use typographical devices and special graphic effects in moderation; too many design devices clutter a page and interfere with comprehension.

Typographical Devices. One method of achieving emphasis through typography is to use **capital letters**. HOWEVER, LONG STRETCHES OF ALL UPPERCASE LETTERS ARE DIFFICULT TO READ BECAUSE THEIR UNIFORM SIZE AND SHAPE DEPRIVE READERS OF IMPORTANT VISUAL CUES AND THUS SLOW READING. Ascenders and descenders (see Figure 12–1) make lowercase letters distinctive and easy to identify; therefore, a mixture of uppercase and lowercase letters is most readable. Use all uppercase letters only in short passages or in headings.

Also use **italics** sparingly. *Continuous italic type reduces legibility and thus slows readers.* Of course, italics are useful if your aim is to slow readers, as in cautions and warnings. Boldface may be the best cuing device because it is visually different yet retains the customary shapes of letters and numbers. Of course, overuse of boldface type can be jarring to the eye.

Headings and Captions. *Headings* (or heads) reveal the organization of a document and indicate the hierarchy within it. Headings help readers decide which sections they need to read. Captions are titles that highlight or describe illustrations or blocks of text. Captions often appear below or above figures and tables and in the left or right margins next to blocks of text.

Headings appear in many typeface variations (boldface being most common) and often use sans serif typefaces. The most common positions for headings and subheadings are centered, flush left, indented, or by themselves in a wide left margin. Insert an additional line of space above a heading to emphasize the logical division. Major section or chapter headings normally appear at the top of a new page. Never leave a heading as the final line on a page—the heading is disconnected from its text and thus ineffective. Instead, move the heading to the start of the next page.

Headers and Footers. A *header* is identifying information carried at the top of each page; a *footer* contains similar information at the bottom of each page. Document pages may have headers or footers or both. Headers and footers carry such information as the topic or subtopic of a section, identifying numbers, the date the document was written, page numbers, the document name, or the section title. Although headers and footers are important reference devices, too much information in them can create visual clutter.

Rules, Icons, and Color. *Rules* are vertical or horizontal lines used to divide one area of the page from another or to create boxes. Avoid the temptation to overuse rules; too many rules and boxed elements create a cluttered look that counteracts their initial purpose, which is simplicity and ease of reading.

An *icon* is a pictorial representation of an idea; it can be used to identify specific actions, objects, or sections of a document. Commonly used icons include the small envelopes on Web pages to symbolize email links and national flags to symbolize different language versions of a document. To be effective, icons must be simple and intuitively recognizable or at least easy to define.

Color and *screening* can distinguish one part of a document from another or unify a series of documents. (*Screening* refers to shaded areas on a page.) Color and screening can set off sections within a document, highlight examples, or emphasize warnings. In tables, you can use screening to highlight column titles or sets of data to which you want to draw the reader's attention.

Page Design

Page design is the process of combining the various design elements on a page to make a coherent whole. The flexibility of your design is based on the capabilities of your word-processing software, how the document will be reproduced, and your budget. (High-quality offset color printing, for example, is far more expensive than black-and-white printing.)

Thumbnail Sketches. Before you spend time positioning actual text and visuals on a page, you may want to create a *thumbnail sketch,* in which blocks indicate the placement of elements. The thumbnails are usually sketched by hand on lined tablet or graph paper. They need not be formal or even neat. They are simply a way to brainstorm design options before you begin the actual layout of the report, newsletter, brochure, or other document. Figure 12–3 shows thumbnail sketches of designs for an 8½-by-11-inch report with two columns per page and for an 8½-by-11-inch newsletter with three columns per page. You can go further by roughly assembling all the thumbnail pages, showing size, shape, form, and general style of a large document. Such a mock-up, called a *dummy,* allows you to see how a finished document will look. As you work with elements on the page, experiment with different layouts. Often what seems like a good layout in principle turns out to be unworkable in practice.

Figure 12–3   Thumbnail Sketches for a Report (top) and a Newsletter (bottom)

Columns. As you design pages, consider the size and number of columns. A single-column format works well with larger typefaces, double-spacing, and left-justified margins. For smaller typefaces and single-spaced lines, the two-column structure enhances legibility by keeping text columns narrow enough so readers need not scan back and forth across the width of the entire page for every line.

A word or part of a word that falls on a line by itself on the last line of a paragraph is called a *widow.* The first line of a paragraph that begins on the last line of a page or a column is called an *orphan.* Avoid both widows and orphans.

White Space. White space visually frames information and breaks it into manageable chunks. For example, white space between paragraphs helps readers see the information in the paragraphs as units. Use extra white space between sections as a visual cue to signal that one section is ending and another is beginning. You need not have access to sophisticated equipment to make good use of white space. You can easily indent and skip lines for paragraphs, lists, and other blocks of material.

Lists. Lists are an effective way to highlight words, phrases, and short sentences. Further, they are easy to read. Lists are particularly useful for certain types of information:

- Steps in sequence
- Materials or parts needed
- Items to remember
- Criteria for evaluation
- Concluding points
- Recommendations

Avoid both too many lists and too many items in lists. See Chapter 5, pages 159–160, for more information about using lists.

Illustrations. Readers notice illustrations before they notice text, and they notice larger illustrations before they notice smaller ones. Thus, the size of an illustration suggests its relative importance. For newsletter articles and publications aimed at wide audiences, consider especially the proportion of the illustration to the text. Magazine designers often use the three-fifths rule of thumb: Page layout is more dramatic and appealing when the major element (photographs, drawings, illustrations, and so on) occupies three-fifths rather than half the available space. The same principle can be used to enhance the visual appeal of a report.

Remember that clarity and usefulness take precedence over aesthetics in many business and technical documents. Illustrations can be gathered in one place (for example, at the end of a report), but placing them in the text closer to their accompanying explanations makes them more effective. Using illustrations in the text also provides visual relief. (Creating visuals and integrating them with text are discussed later in this chapter, beginning on page 517.)

Web-Page Design

You can apply many of the business-writing principles covered throughout *Writing That Works* to designing Web pages. As you do when creating other documents, carefully consider your purpose and your readers' needs as you prepare your Web pages. Although some commercial and personal Web sites are intended for visitors with no specific purpose, most organizational sites have well-defined goals, such as reference, training, education, publicity, advocacy, or marketing. Before you begin building your site, create a clear statement of purpose that identifies your target audience.

EXTERNAL
SITE

The purpose of this site is to enable our customers to locate product information, place online orders, and contract our customer-service department with questions or comments.

INTERNAL
SITE

The purpose of this site is to provide SN Security Corporation employees with a single, consistent, and up-to-date resource for materials about SN Security's Employee Benefits Package.

As these examples of purpose statements suggest, there are two general kinds of sites: external sites and internal sites. External sites target an audience from the entire Internet; internal sites are designed for an audience on intranets. An *intranet* is a computer network within an educational institution or company that is not accessible to audiences outside that institution or company.

Web-Page Navigation and Links

Your foremost goal when you are designing a Web page is to establish a predictable environment in which users feel comfortable navigating your site and confident that they can easily find the information they need and move on. The information should be logically accessible to the user in the fewest possible steps (or clicks). To design an efficient navigation plan, it is especially helpful to draft a navigation chart of your site early in the process. Figure 12–4 shows an initial navigation plan for a company Web site. In Figure 12–4, each higher-level page (for example, Departments and Divisions) is linked to increasingly specific pages about the company's internal organization (Marketing, Accounting, Customer Relations, and so on). Human Resources, although logically a department in the company's organization, is given higher visibility on the home page because recruitment of new employees is important to the company.

The hypertext links that connect pages within a site as well as to pages at other sites make the Web site easy for visitors to navigate and to locate information. To make the Web site most useful, create links to sites related to your visitors' organizational or professional needs and interests. Links to customer service and online order forms are especially useful for cultivating potential customers.

**Figure 12–4
Initial Navigation
Plan for a Web Site**

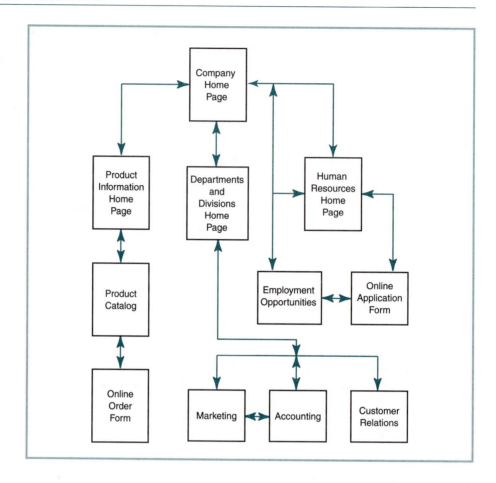

When you identify links, do not write out "click here for more information." Instead, write the sentence as you normally would and anchor the link on the most relevant word in the sentence, as illustrated in the following example.

■ For information about employment opportunities, visit <u>Human Resources</u>.

[Hypertext links for text anchors are underlined and appear in a different color than the surrounding text.]

Avoid writing paragraphs that are dense with links. Instead, list links alphabetically in groups of about four to seven to make them easier for the viewer to see at a glance.

➡ <u>Accounting</u>
➡ <u>Customer Relations</u>
➡ <u>Marketing</u>

➡ Product Help

➡ Related Links

In addition to identifying links with words, you can use icons and graphics, as shown in the preceding list; they are not only easy to use but also provide the visual cues Web users expect. Figure 12–5 shows some icons that can be used for links.

Include a link that allows visitors to send you email messages. Identify the email code with either text or a graphic like the mailbox icon shown in Figure 12–5. When visitors click on the icon, an email dialog box opens in which they can type their message.

Because Web sites change constantly, you must review your site periodically and check that your links are still appropriate and working properly. Your Web pages should include the date they were created or last updated so users can determine whether the information is current. You might also put an icon (like the fourth one in Figure 12–5) next to each new or updated item to alert users to changes.

Graphics and Typography

Your audience and your purpose should determine the graphic style and theme of your Web site. Graphic elements provide visual relief from dense text, which is difficult to read on a computer screen. However, do not overdo graphics, especially those with animation. Complex graphics and motion can backfire if they seem gratuitous or if they slow access to your site, especially if users depend on the site for accessible and visually clear information. Although it may seem like fun to use many different colors, avoid overly bold colors; opt instead for lighter colors, especially for backgrounds. Keep in mind that large or high-resolution graphics, like color photographs, can cause long delays as they download to the user's system. You might also consider giving visitors a graphics-free option for quicker access.

When you have decided on fonts, interparagraph spacing, heading sizes, and so on, consider creating a style sheet that lists the specifications. A style sheet is especially helpful for large sites with numerous pages. In general, aim for consistency to establish a visual sense of unity and to provide visual cues that help visitors find information. Consistency also encourages visitors to browse further and return to your site.

Page and Site Layout

Take into account the viewing capabilities of visitors to your site. Many computer monitors cannot display more than about half of the typical Web page at any one time; on many screen settings, only the top four or five inches may be visible. For

**Figure 12–5
Icons That Can Be
Used for Links**

WRITER'S CHECKLIST: Using Typography on a Web Page

Many of the guidelines on typography in Document Layout and Design earlier in this chapter are applicable to Web pages; however, not all apply, so keep the following in mind:

☐ Limit the number of typeface colors as well as styles.

☐ Make sure the typeface colors contrast sharply (but do not clash) with background colors for better readability.

☐ Do not use capital letters or boldface letters for all the text or large portions of it.

☐ Use generous blank space (the equivalent of white space) to separate text and graphics.

☐ Use only a few heading and subheading styles and use them consistently.

☐ Block-indent text sections that you expect viewers to read in detail.

---

that reason, you should place important graphic elements and information in the upper half of the page. Then use short narrative passages or lists so viewers can scan and access information quickly. Organize material in a logical, predictable pattern; use general-to-specific, sequential, chronological, or other traditional methods of development. When no such pattern is appropriate, use an alphabetical or numerical sequence.

Because most users do not like scrolling down long pages, many Web designers recommend that Web pages (home pages in particular) contain no more than roughly one or two screens of information. If a larger amount of information is covered, include a concise table of contents at the top of the page linked to specific sections elsewhere on the page. Viewers can then click on the section they want without having to scroll through the entire page. You can also provide a link that returns to the top of the page.

When viewers access Web pages randomly, they often have no context for where they are. Therefore, incorporate the name of your company or organization on each page. You can do that with page footers—sections in smaller typesize that contain basic information about the origin of each page and when it was last updated—which are especially useful when they also provide links to other pages. Another way to orient users is to provide a set of links in graphics or words called a *tool bar* or *button bar,* as shown here.

| Home | Search | Order | What's New | Reference |

A tool bar at the top, bottom, or sides of each page serves as a table of contents and shows visitors the structure of your site. Tool bars on each page help you avoid sending users to a dead-end page (one with no link); in fact, every page should, if nothing else, link back to your home page.

Home Pages

A home page is the point of entry for all pages in your Web site. Many organizational home pages include an image map, with links to other pages at the site. Figure 12–6 shows an image map for a federal agency, with icons that lead to content areas at the site. By clicking on a specific area, such as News & Information, viewers are linked to the relevant page or site. The image map also introduces visitors to the overall site design, identifies the purpose of the site, and provides an

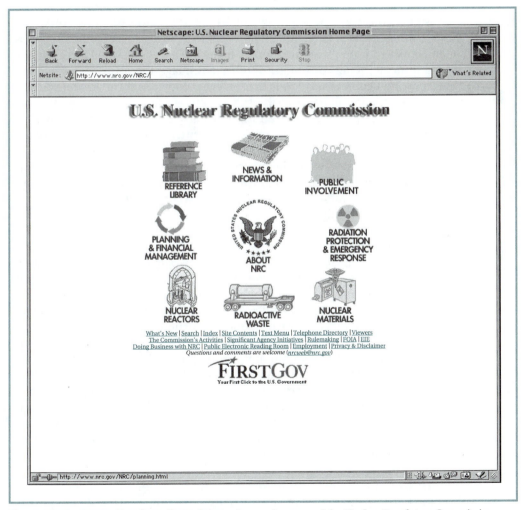

Figure 12–6   Image Map for a Home Page   *Source:* Courtesy of the Nuclear Regulatory Commission.

overview of major content areas. If you do not use an image map, at least display a small graphic banner, tool bar, or menu across the top of the home page.

An overly complex home-page graphic can take a minute or longer to download. If large graphics are important to your site, consider using relatively small ones on your home page, gradually increasing the size of the graphics for pages deeper into your site. Users who go beyond a page or two into a site are more committed and therefore more willing to tolerate longer delays, especially if you offer them warnings that particular pages contain graphics that take a while to download. View your pages on a variety of browsers, systems, and monitors—colors, sizes, and other features can vary dramatically from one environment to another.

Creating Forms for Print and the Web

Because they provide a time-saving, efficient, and uniform way to record data, *business forms* are used for countless purposes in almost all occupations. It is easier and quicker to supply information by filling out a well-designed form than by writing a memo, letter, or report. Another advantage the form has over other types of written communication is that on every copy of a form, each particular piece of information appears in the same place—a fact that is especially important when many people are furnishing similar information. If each person providing information sent in an individually written letter, every sheet of paper submitted would be different and would require time-consuming reading and interpretation. In contrast, when the information is supplied on a form, the person filling out the form will have spent less time and effort in furnishing the data, and the person using the information from the form will have a much easier task retrieving and evaluating the data.

Preparing Forms for Print

To be effective, a form should make it easy for one person to supply information and for another person to retrieve and interpret the information. Ideally, a form should be self-explanatory, even to a person who has never seen it before. If you are preparing a form, plan it carefully. Determine what kind of information you will be seeking and arrange the requests for information in a logical order—logical from the point of view of the person supplying the data and the person receiving it.

Make a pencil-and-paper draft of the form, putting in all the fields for information you've decided to include and arranging them in the order you consider the most logical. If any coworkers will be using the form, show the draft to them— you'll be rewarded for the extra time this step takes by the helpful criticism and suggestions you are likely to receive. Once you're satisfied with the draft, you can then prepare a final copy of the form using a forms-design software package for producing a paper form or for creating a Web-based form.

Instructions and Captions. To make certain that entering information on your form will be easy, give the proper instructions in the proper place. You've probably had the experience, at some time or another, of starting to fill out a form only to realize too late that you've put your name on the line intended for your street address. When the instructions are clear and properly placed, the person filling out the form will not be confused about which information goes where.

Instructions, which are used primarily for long, complicated forms, should go at the beginning of the form; they are often preceded by a heading designed to attract the reader's attention.

INSTRUCTIONS FOR COMPLETING THIS FORM

1. Complete the applicable blue-shaded portions on the front of pages 1, 2, and 3.
2. Mail page 1 to the Securi-Med Insurance Company at the address shown above.
3. Give page 2 to your doctor.
4. If services were rendered in a hospital, give page 3 to the hospital.
5. Use the back of page 1 to itemize bills that are to go toward your major medical deduction.

Instructions for distributing the various copies of multiple-copy paper forms are normally placed at the bottom of the form. These instructions are repeated on every copy of the form.

On the form itself, requests for information are normally worded as captions, such as the words "Make" and "Model" in the following example. Keep captions brief and to the point; avoid unnecessary repetition by combining requests for related pieces of information under an explanatory heading, such as the "Vehicle Information" heading in this example.

CHANGE

What make of car do you drive? _____
What year was it manufactured? _____
What model is it? _____
What is the body style? _____

TO

Vehicle Information

Make _____   Year _____
Model _____   Body style _____

Planning for Responses.   When preparing a form, it is important to provide questions that can be answered simply and briefly. The best responses are those that permit the user to make check marks, circles, or underlining; next best are numbers, single words, or brief phrases. Sentence responses, although necessary at times, are the least effective because they take the most time to write and to read.

Make captions as specific as possible. For example, if a requested date is a date other than that on which the form is being filled out, make the caption read "Effective date," "Date issued," or whatever it may be, rather than simply "Date." As in all job-related writing, put yourself in your reader's place and try to imagine what sorts of requests would be clear to you.

Sequencing of Data.   When designing a form, try to arrange your requests for information in an order that will be most helpful to the person filling out the form. At the top of the form, include *preliminary information,* such as the name of the organization, the title of your form, and any file number or reference number. In the *main portion* of the form, include the entries you need to obtain the necessary data. At the *end* of the form, include space for the signature of the person filling out the form and the date.

Within the main portion of your form, the arrangement of the entries will depend on several factors. First, the subject matter of the entries will frequently determine the most logical order. A form requesting reimbursement for travel expenses, for instance, would logically begin with the first day of the week (or month) and end with the last day of the appropriate period. Second, if the response to one item is based on the response to another item, be sure that the items appear in the correct order. Third, whenever possible, group requests for related information together. Fourth, if a form is to move from one individual or one department to another, to be partly filled out by each in turn, put the data to be supplied by the first individual or department at the top of the form, the data to be supplied by the second next, and so on; and arrange each section of the form, in general, from left to right and from top to bottom because that is the way we are accustomed to reading.

The title of the form should describe its use and application. A title should be no more than a few words long and should normally be positioned at the top center of your form. If space is critical, the title can be placed at the top left-hand corner of the form.

Entry Lines

When you prepare a form to be filled out manually in pen or pencil, pay particular attention to the arrangement of the entry lines (where the responses will be filled in). The form can be laid out so that the person completing it supplies information on a writing line, in a writing block, or in square boxes.

The *writing line* is simply a rule with a caption.

(Name)	(Telephone)

(Street Address)

(City)	(State)	(ZIP Code)

(Age)	(Weight)	(Height)	(Sex)

The *writing block* is essentially the same except that each entry is enclosed in a ruled block, making it easy for the person filling out the form to associate a caption with the right line.

Name			Telephone	
Street Address				
City		State		ZIP Code
Age	Weight	Height		Sex

When all the possible responses to any question can be anticipated, you can save the person filling out the form time and effort by writing the question on the form, supplying a labeled *square box* for each possible answer, and instructing the person filling out the form to put an *X* in the box that corresponds to the correct answer. Such a plan will also save you time and effort in retrieving the data. Be sure that your questions are both simple and specific.

EXAMPLE   Would you buy another Matrix computer?   ☐ Yes   ☐ No

The boxes may either precede or follow the question. Be sure, however, that the boxes and their labels are spaced so that they will not be mistakenly associated.

REVISE   red ☐ blue ☐ green ☐ yellow ☐

TO   red ☐   blue ☐   green ☐   yellow ☐

Spacing.   Be sure to provide enough space for the person filling out the form to enter the data. Everyone has filled out a form on which the address, signature, or other information could not possibly fit in the space allowed for it. Insufficient writing space or uneven lines are guaranteed to confuse the person filling out the form and make the information supplied hard to read. In a long form that is poorly designed, errors occur with increasing frequency as the person filling out the form becomes more and more frustrated. If you have trouble reading responses that are too tightly spaced or that snake around the side of the form, you may introduce additional errors as you retrieve the data.

Although forms increasingly are designed to be filled out and printed by computer, many forms continue to be filled out in longhand. Accordingly, design forms to allow sufficient space to accommodate both printed and handwritten responses. If you think that at least some people filling it out will use longhand, provide adequate space for relatively large handwriting.

Preparing Forms for the Web

Forms on Web pages are similar to paper forms in that they are used to collect information for job applications, class registration, customer and employee surveys, visitor logs, and the like. They are also used to initiate Web-site queries and searches. Unlike paper forms, Web forms are interactive—that is, users fill them out on a Web page and the information (or data) is sent elsewhere electronically at the Web site, to an email address or a database, where it is collected for response or analysis.

As with paper forms, think through the kinds of information you want to gather, and arrange the fields requesting the information in a logical order for the person filling out the form. (A *field* is a place where information can be entered on the screen.) However, before you plan the form, review this section for an overview of the options available for creating Web forms. Then make a draft of the form on paper and circulate it for comment. After review and revision, you're ready to create the form in a Web page.

The software for designing Web forms offers various options to display the form's entry fields. The objects used to create entry fields may include check boxes, option (radio) buttons, and text boxes. As with paper forms, the objects you use must be appropriate for the kind of information being requested.

Check Boxes.   Use a check box to allow the user to choose one or more or all of several options. Clicking on the square activates each choice selected.

> 9. Have you ever experienced any of the following forms of discrimination or harassment at this company?
>
> ❑ Racial discrimination
> ❑ Sexual harassment
> ❑ Age discrimination
> ❑ Gender discrimination
> ❑ Sexual orientation discrimination
> ❑ Other
> ❑ No

Radio Buttons.   Use radio (or option) buttons to make a single choice from a group of items.

> 8. Would you refer a friend to apply for a job at this company?
>
> ○ Yes
> ○ No
> ○ Maybe
> ○ Not sure

Text and Password Boxes.   Use text boxes to type a single line of text into a form. You can specify the number of characters a user can enter.

Name

A password box is a security feature to control access to the form. It displays a row of asterisks when users type in their password to prevent others from reading the password as it is being typed.

*Enter Your
Password*

Text Area.   Use a text-area box to type multiple lines of text into a window. You can control the size of the text area by setting the number of characters in each row and the length of the column.

*Enter Your Reasons for
Not Attending*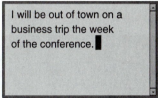

Selection List.   Use a selection list to display a window of choices. The list can be created to enable multiple choices.

*Job
Function*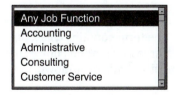

Combination Box.   Use a combination box to display a drop-down menu of choices.

Search for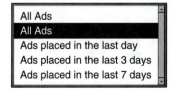

Command Buttons.   Add command buttons to make something happen at the site.

Search activates a search of the site.

Search

Submit permits you to submit information in the filled-in-form.

Submit

Clear or *Reset* clears out all data in the form fields should you decide to correct information in one field or opt to not submit the information at all.

Reset

Submit and *Clear* buttons at the end of a survey form could be arranged on the screen as follows:

Thank you for taking the time to complete this survey.

Please select Submit Survey now to send your
responses to us.

Submit Survey   Clear All Answers

The customer satisfaction survey form in Figure 12–7 appears at the Web site for the National Center for Health Statistics. The form contains check boxes for multiple choices (survey question 3, 7), a text-area box for one choice (the last question on the form), and several selection lists with drop-down menus (survey questions 1–2, 4, 5–6, 8–11).

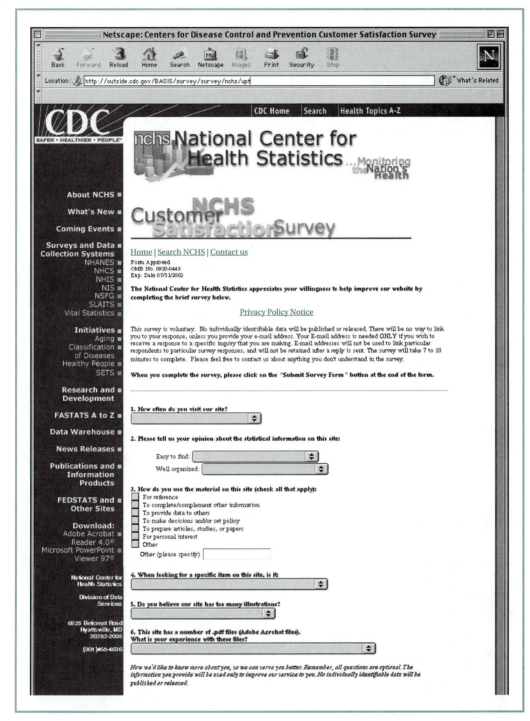

**Figure 12–7
Sample Web
Form for
Customer
Satisfaction
Survey**
Source: Courtesy of the U.S. Department of Health and Human Services, National Center for Health Statistics.

(continued)

Figure 12–7 (continued)

7. From where do you access the Internet? (check all that apply)

- [ ] home
- [ ] school/university classroom or computer lab
- [ ] public library
- [ ] work/office
- [ ] other

Other (please specify)

8. What is your occupation?

Other (specify)

9. What is your highest level of education completed?

10. For what type of organization do you work?

Other (specify)

11. If you have connected to our site from outside the U.S., please let us know where from:

Other (please specify):

Finally, please make specific suggestions anything you think we should change about our site. If you need a reply, please be sure to provide your e-mail address, or another way of contacting you in your message. Your contact information will be used only for the purposes of this reply.

[Submit Survey Form]   [Clear ALL Fields]

Takes a few seconds to be submitted...   Clear...

End of Customer Satisfaction Survey - Thank you for your time.
Form Approved
OMB No. 0920-0449
Exp. Date: 07/31/2002

This page last reviewed May 30, 2000

Home | Search NCHS | Contact us

CDC Home | Search | Health Topics A-Z

U.S. DEPARTMENT OF HEALTH AND HUMAN SERVICES
Centers for Disease Control and Prevention
National Center for Health Statistics
Division of Data Services
Hyattsville, MD
20782-2003

(301) 458-4636

■ Creating Visuals

Designing and Integrating Visuals with Text

To make the most effective use of visuals and to integrate them smoothly with the text of your document, consider your graphics requirements even before you begin to write. Plan your visuals—tables, graphs, drawings, charts, maps, or photographs—when you're planning the scope and organization of your final work, whether it's a report, newsletter, brochure, or Web site. Make graphics an integral part of your outline, noting approximately where each should appear throughout the text. At each place where you plan to include a visual, either make a rough sketch of the visual or write "illustration of . . ." and enclose each suggestion in a box in your outline. You can indicate the placement of visuals in your outline by hand or on the computer. You can also copy and paste graphics directly into your outline at the appropriate places using your computer's clipboard feature. As noted in Chapter 2, outlines are a means to an end, not an end in themselves, so like other information in an outline, these boxes and sketches can be moved, revised, or deleted as required. Planning your graphics requirements from the beginning stages of your outline preparation ensures their appropriate integration throughout all versions of the draft to the finished work. The following guidelines apply to most visual materials you might use to supplement or clarify the information in your text. (If your readers are international, be sure to read Using Graphics to Communicate Internationally, beginning on page 542, as well as the Writer's Checklist: Using International Graphics on pages 545–546.) These tips will help you create and present your visual materials effectively.

1. Make clear in the text why the illustration is included. The amount of description each illustration requires will vary with its complexity. An illustration showing an important feature or system may be central to an entire discussion. The complexity of the illustration will also affect the discussion, as will the background your readers bring to the information. Nonexperts require lengthier explanations than experts do, as a rule.

2. Keep the illustration to the point and uncluttered by including only information necessary to the discussion in the text and by eliminating unnecessary labels, arrows, boxes, and lines.

3. Keep terminology consistent. Do not refer to something as a "proportion" in the text and as a "percentage" in the illustration. Define all acronyms in the text, figure, or table. If any symbols are not self-explanatory, include a key that defines them.

4. Specify the units of measurement used or include a scale of relative distances, when appropriate. Ensure that relative sizes are clear or indicate distance by a scale, as on a map.

5. Position the lettering of any explanatory text or labels horizontally for ease of reading, if possible.

6. Give each illustration a concise title that clearly describes its contents.

7. Assign a figure or table number, if your final product is a document containing five or more illustrations. The figure or table number precedes the title:

   ■ Figure 1. Projected sales for 1998–2001

   Note that graphics (photographs, drawings, maps, etc.) are generically labeled "figures," while tables are labeled "tables."

8. In documents with more than five illustrations, list the illustrations by title, together with figure and page numbers, or table and page numbers, following the table of contents. The figures so listed should be titled "List of Figures." The tables so listed should be titled "List of Tables."

9. Refer to illustrations in the text of documents by their figure or table number.

10. If an illustration is central to a discussion, illuminating or strongly reinforcing it, place it as close as possible to the text where it is discussed. However, no illustration should precede its first text mention. Its appearance without an introduction in the text will confuse readers. If the illustration is lengthy and detailed, place it in an appendix and be sure to refer to the illustration in the text of your document.

11. Allow adequate white space on the page around and within the illustration. This principle is true for Web sites as well as for documents.

12. If you wish to use an illustration that is copyrighted, first obtain written permission from the copyright holder. Acknowledge such borrowings in a source or credit line below the caption for a figure and below any footnotes at the bottom of a table. Information that is in the public domain can be used without obtaining written permission to reproduce it. Publications of the federal government, for example, are not copyrighted, but you should acknowledge their source in a credit line. (Such a credit line appears in Figure 12–8.)

A discussion of visuals commonly used in on-the-job writing follows. Your topic will ordinarily determine the best type of visual to use.

Tables

A table is useful for showing large numbers of specific, related data in a brief space. Because a table displays its information in rows and columns, the reader can easily compare data in one column with data in another. If such data were presented in the text, the reader would read through groups of numbers and possibly not recognize their significance. Tables typically include the following elements (Figure 12–8):

- *Table number.* Table numbers are usually Arabic and should be assigned sequentially to the tables throughout the text.
- *Table title.* The title, which is placed just above the table, should describe concisely what the table represents.

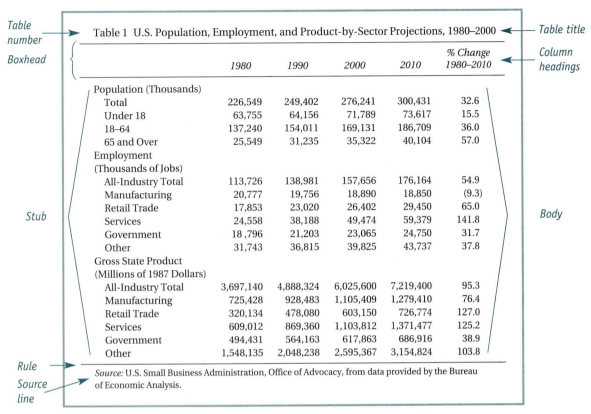

Figure 12–8 Sample Table

- *Boxhead.* The boxhead contains the column headings, which should be brief but descriptive. Units of measurement, where necessary, should be either specified as part of the heading or enclosed in parentheses beneath the heading. Standard abbreviations and symbols are acceptable. Avoid vertical lettering whenever possible.

- *Stub.* The left-hand vertical column of a table, called the stub, lists the items about which information is given in the body of the table.

- *Body.* The body comprises the data below the column headings and to the right of the stub. Within the body, columns should be arranged so that the terms to be compared appear in adjacent rows and columns. Where no information exists for a specific item, substitute a row of dots or a dash to acknowledge the gap.

- *Rules.* Rules are the lines that separate the table into its various parts. Horizontal rules are placed below the title, below the body of the table, and between the column headings and the body of the table. Tables should not be closed at the sides. The columns within the table may be separated by vertical rules if such lines aid clarity.

- *Source line.* The source line, which identifies where the data were obtained, appears below the table (when a source line is appropriate). Many organizations place the source line below the footnotes.

- *Footnotes.* Footnotes are used for explanations of individual items in the table. Symbols (*, †) or lowercase letters (sometimes in parentheses) rather than numbers are ordinarily used to key table footnotes because numbers might be mistaken for numerical data within the table and they could confuse the numbering system for text footnotes.

- *Continuing tables.* When a table must be divided so that it can be continued on another page, repeat the column headings and give the table number at the head of each new page with a "continued" label ("Table 3, continued").

To list relatively few items that would be easier for the reader to grasp in tabular form, use an informal table.

■ The sound-intensity levels (decibels) for the three frequency bands (in hertz) were determined to be

Frequency Band (Hz)	Decibels
600–1200	68
1200–2400	62
2400–4800	53

Although informal tables do not need titles or table numbers to identify them, they do require column headings that accurately describe the information listed.

Graphs

Graphs, like tables, present numerical data in visual form. Graphs (also called charts) have several advantages over tables. Trends, movements, distributions, and cycles are more readily apparent in graphs than they are in tables. Further, by providing a means for ready comparisons, a graph often shows a significance in the data not otherwise immediately evident. Be aware, however, that although graphs present statistics in a more interesting and comprehensible form than tables do, they are less accurate. For this reason, they are often accompanied by tables that give exact numbers. (Note the difference between the graph and table showing the same data in Figure 12–9.) If the graph remains uncluttered, the exact data can be added to each column, thereby giving the reader both a quick overview of the data and accurate numbers. (See Figures 12–15 and 12–16 on pages 526 and 527.) There are many different kinds of graphs, most notably line graphs, bar graphs, pie graphs, and picture graphs. All kinds of graphs can be easily rendered on a computer after the data has been entered into a spreadsheet or database application.

Line Graphs. The line graph, which is the most widely used of all graphs, shows the relationship between two or more sets of figures. The graph is composed of a

Table 3: U.S. Goods Imports

Imports	1997	1998	1999	98–99	94–99	92–99
	Billions of Dollars			Percent Change		
Total (BOP Basis)*	$876.4	$917.2	$1,030.2	12.3%	54.1%	92.0%
Food, feeds, and beverages	$39.7	$41.2	$43.6	5.7%	40.6%	57.9%
Industrial supplies and materials	$213.8	$200.1	$222.6	10.7%	36.7%	59.9%
Capital goods, except autos	$253.3	$269.6	$296.9	10.1%	61.0%	121.0%
Autos and auto parts	$139.8	$149.1	$179.5	20.4%	51.7%	95.6%
Consumer goods	$193.8	$216.5	$239.6	10.7%	63.8%	95.3%
Other	$29.3	$35.4	$43.9	24.1%	106.1%	148.0%

Source: U.S. Department of Commerce, Balance of Payment Basis for Total.
*Census Basis for Sectors.

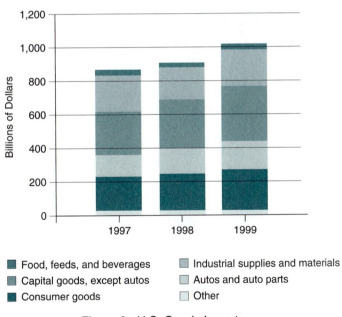

Figure 3: U.S. Goods Imports

Source: U.S. Department of Commerce, Census Basis.

Figure 12–9   Figure and Table Showing the Same Data

vertical axis and a horizontal axis that intersect at right angles. Each axis represents one set of data. The relationship between the two sets is indicated by points plotted along appropriate intersections of the two axes. Once plotted, the points are connected to form a continuous line, and the relationship between the two sets of data becomes readily apparent.

The line graph's vertical axis usually represent amounts (the vertical axis in Figure 12–10 represents the percentage of change for a 50-year period) and its horizontal axis usually represents increments of time (the horizontal axis in Figure 12–10 represents 10-year periods).

Line graphs with more than one plotted line allow for comparisons between two sets of statistics. In creating such graphs, be certain to identify each plotted line with a label or a legend, as shown in Figure 12–11. You can emphasize the difference between the two lines by shading the space that separates them. Line graphs can also be shaded to emphasize the quantity or magnitude of the data depicted, as in Figures 12–11 and 12–12. The following guidelines apply to most line graphs:

1. Give the graph a title that describes the data clearly and concisely.

2. Indicate the zero point of the graph (the point where the two axes meet). If the range of data shown makes it inconvenient to begin at zero, insert a break in the scale, as in Figure 12–13; otherwise, the graph would show a large area with no data.

3. Divide the vertical axis into equal portions, from the least amount at the bottom to the greatest amount at the top. The caption for this scale may be

Figure 12–10
Single-Line Graph

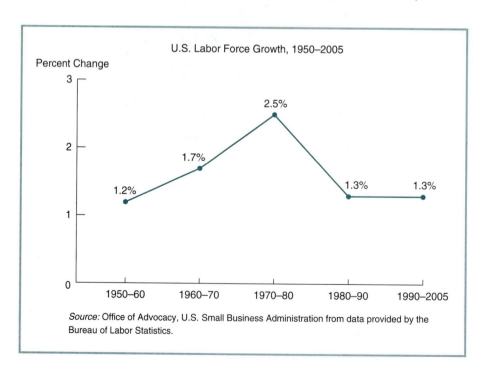

U.S. Labor Force Growth, 1950–2005

Source: Office of Advocacy, U.S. Small Business Administration from data provided by the Bureau of Labor Statistics.

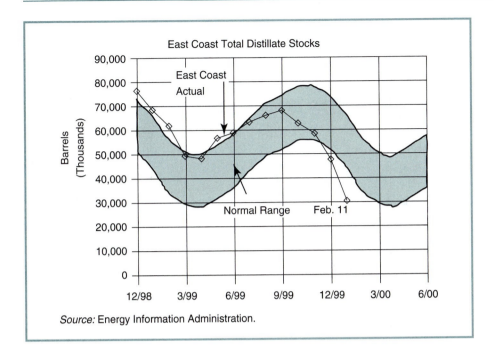

Figure 12–11
Double-Line Graph
with Shading

placed at the upper left (as in Figure 12–10), or, as is more often the case, vertically along the vertical axis (as in Figure 12–11).

4. Divide the horizontal axis into equal units from left to right, and label them to show what values each represents.

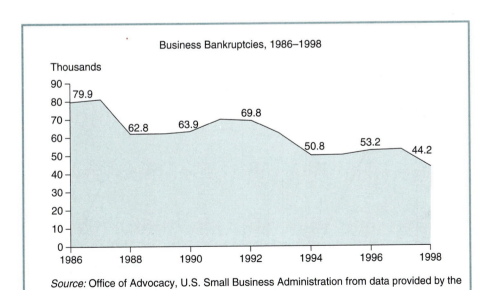

Figure 12–12
Single-Line Graph
with Shading

**Figure 12–13
Line Graph with
Vertical Axis
Broken**

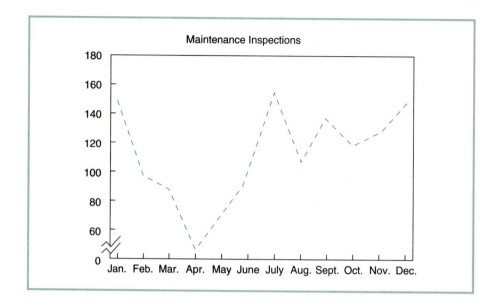

5. The angle at which the curved line rises and falls is determined by the number of points plotted. Attempting to show trends with too few data points will distort the depiction of the trends. (See Figure 12–14.)

6. Keep grid lines to a minimum so that the curved lines stand out. Because precise values are usually shown in a table of data accompanying a graph, detailed grid lines are unnecessary.

**Figure 12–14
Two Graphs: Distorted Expression of Data (left) and Distortion-Free Expression of Data**

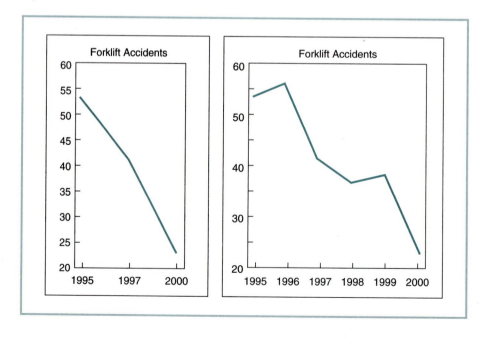

7. Include a label or a key when necessary.

8. If the information comes from another source, include a source line under the graph at the lower left, as in Figures 12–8 through 12–12.

9. Place explanatory footnotes directly below the figure caption. (See Figure 12–18.)

10. Make all lettering read horizontally if possible, except the caption for the vertical axis, which is usually positioned vertically.

Bar Graphs. Bar graphs consist of horizontal or vertical bars of equal width but scaled in length or height to represent some quantity. They are commonly used to show the following proportional relations:

- Different types of information during different periods of time (Figure 12–15).
- Quantities of the same kind of information at different points in time (Figure 12–16).
- Quantities of different information during a fixed period of time (Figure 12–17).
- Quantities of the different parts that make up a whole (Figure 12–18).

Note that in Figure 12–21, showing Christmas tree sales, the exact sales quantities appear at the end of each bar. This eliminates the need to have an accompanying table giving the sales data. If the bars are not labeled, as in Figures 12–16 and 12–19, the different portions must be clearly indicated by shading, crosshatching, or other devices. Include a key that represents the various subdivisions.

Bar graphs can also indicate what proportion of a whole the various component parts represent. In such a graph, the bar, which is theoretically equivalent to 100 percent, is divided according to the proportion of the whole that each item sampled represents. (Compare the displays of the same data in Figures 12–18 and 12–20.) In some bar graphs, the completed bar does not represent 100 percent because not all the parts of the whole have been included in the sample. (See Figure 12–19.)

Pie Graphs. A pie graph presents data as wedge-shaped sections of a circle. The circle equals 100 percent, or the whole, of some quantity (a tax dollar, a bus fare, the hours of a working day), with the wedges representing the various parts into which the whole is divided. In Figure 12–20, for example, the circle stands for a city tax dollar and is divided into units equivalent to the percentages of the tax dollar spent on various city services. Note that the slice representing salaries is slightly offset (exploded) from the others to emphasize that data. This feature is commonly available on computer software that produces pie graphs.

The relationships among the various statistics presented in a pie graph are easy to grasp, but the information is often general. For this reason, a pie graph is often accompanied by a table that presents the actual figures on which the percentages in the graph are based.

**Figure 12–15
Bar Graph Showing
Different Types of
Information during
Different Periods
of Time**

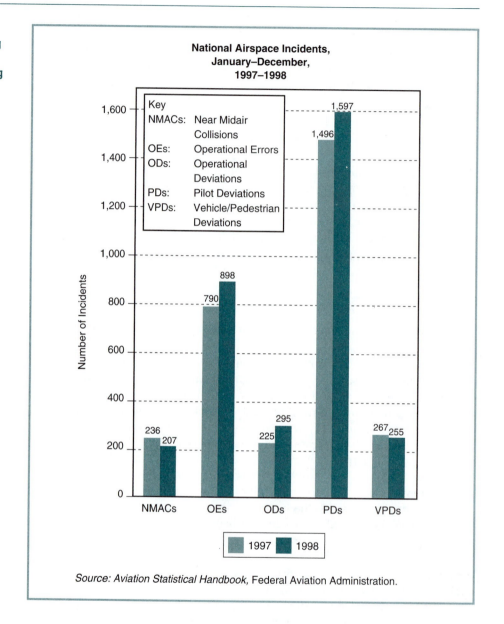

**National Airspace Incidents,
January–December,
1997–1998**

Key
NMACs: Near Midair Collisions
OEs: Operational Errors
ODs: Operational Deviations
PDs: Pilot Deviations
VPDs: Vehicle/Pedestrian Deviations

Number of Incidents

	1997	1998
NMACs	236	207
OEs	790	898
ODs	225	295
PDs	1,496	1,597
VPDs	267	255

1997   1998

Source: Aviation Statistical Handbook, Federal Aviation Administration.

When you construct a pie graph, keep the following points in mind:

1. The complete 360° circle is equivalent to 100 percent.
2. When possible, begin at the 12 o'clock position and sequence the wedges clockwise, from largest to smallest. (This is not always possible because the default setting for some charting software sequences the data counterclockwise.)

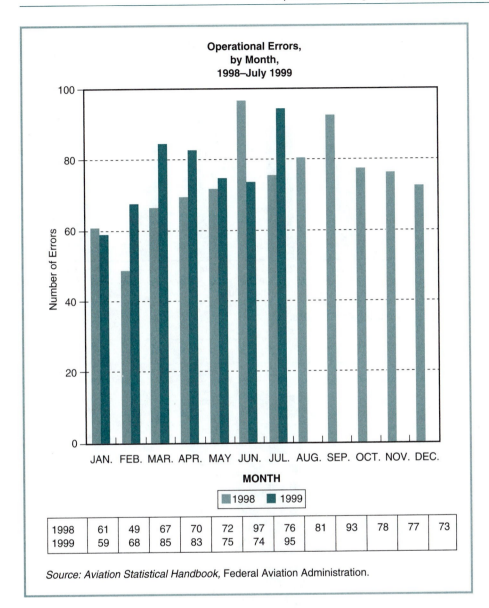

Figure 12–16
Bar Graph Showing
Quantities of the
Same Kind of Infor-
mation at Different
Periods of Time

Operational Errors,
by Month,
1998–July 1999

	JAN.	FEB.	MAR.	APR.	MAY	JUN.	JUL.	AUG.	SEP.	OCT.	NOV.	DEC.
1998	61	49	67	70	72	97	76	81	93	78	77	73
1999	59	68	85	83	75	74	95					

Source: Aviation Statistical Handbook, Federal Aviation Administration.

3. Each wedge appears with a distinctive pattern or is shown in various shades of gray.
4. Keep all labels horizontal and, most important, give the percentage value of each wedge.
5. Check to see that all wedges, as well as the percentage values given for them, add up to 100 percent.

Figure 12–17
Bar Graph Showing
Quantities of Dif-
ferent Information
during a Fixed
Period of Time

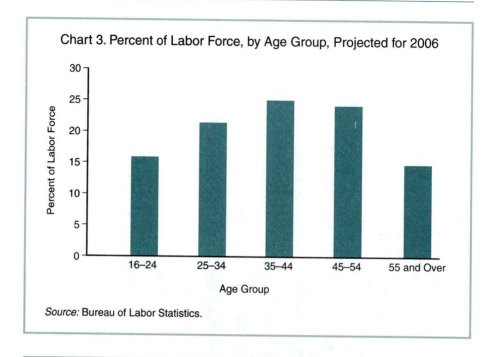

Chart 3. Percent of Labor Force, by Age Group, Projected for 2006

Source: Bureau of Labor Statistics.

Figure 12–18
Bar Graph Showing
Different Quantities
of Different Parts
of a Whole

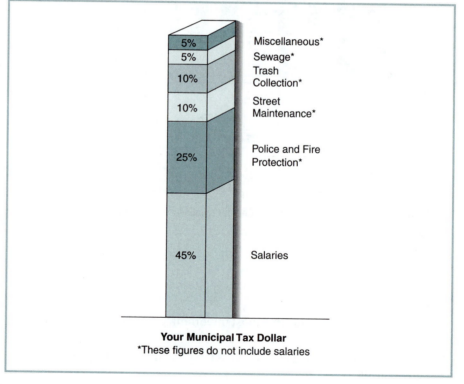

Your Municipal Tax Dollar
*These figures do not include salaries

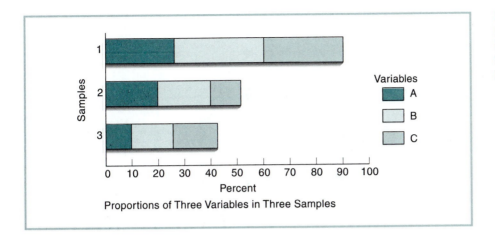

Figure 12–19
Bar Graph in Which
Not All Parts of a
Whole Have Been
Included

Although pie graphs have a strong visual impact, they also have drawbacks. If more than five or six items of information are presented, the graph looks cluttered, and, unless percentages are labeled on each section, the reader cannot compare the values of the sections as accurately as on a bar graph.

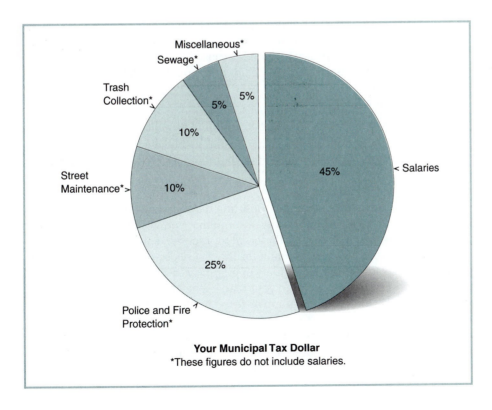

Figure 12–20
Exploded Pie Graph
(with Same Data as
in Figure 12–18)

Figure 12–21
Picture Graph

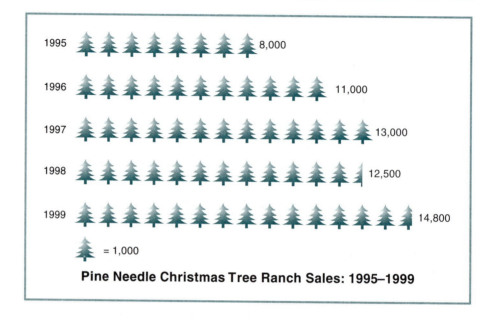

Pine Needle Christmas Tree Ranch Sales: 1995–1999

Picture and Dimensional-Column Graphs.   Picture graphs are modified bar graphs that use picture symbols to represent the item for which data are presented. Each symbol corresponds to a specified quantity of the item, as shown in Figure 12–21. Note that precise figures are also included because the picture symbol can indicate only approximate figures. Here are some tips on preparing picture graphs:

1. Make the symbol self-explanatory.
2. Have each symbol represent a specific number of units.
3. Show larger quantities by increasing the number of symbols rather than by creating a larger symbol because if the latter is done it is difficult to judge relative size accurately.

Consider a common on-the-job reporting requirement—tracking a series of expenses over a given period of time. Assume that you wish to show your company's expenses over a three-month period for security, courier, mail, and custodial services. Once you enter the data for these services into a spreadsheet program, you can display them in a variety of graph styles. As you select from among the options available, keep in mind your reader's need to interpret the data accurately and quickly and keep the graph style as simple as possible for the information shown.

Graphs that depict columns as three-dimensional pillars are popular—they give the data a solid, almost building-block appearance. They can, however, obscure rather than clarify the information, depending on how they are displayed. Consider the graph in Figure 12–22. Although the data are accurate, they cannot

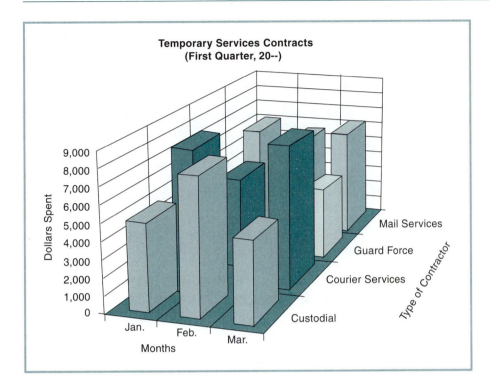

**Figure 12–22
Three-Dimensional
Column Graph**

be interpreted as shown. The axis showing expenditures cannot be correlated with most columns representing the various services. The graph also obscures the columns for courier and guard-force services. Finally, this graph style does not allow readers to spot trends for expenditures over the three-month period, which is key information to decision-makers.

The graph in Figure 12–23 presents more clearly the same data as that shown in Figure 12–22. The trends of expenditures are easy to spot and all the data are at least visible. Yet this graph is not ideal. To interpret the information, the reader would need to put a ruler on the page and align the tops of the columns with the axis showing expenditures.

The three-dimensional appearance can also cause confusion: Is the front or back of each column the correct data point? Also somewhat confusing is that, at first glance, the reader is tricked into interpreting the spaces between the column clusters as columns.

The graphs in Figures 12–24 and 12–25 would best represent the data, depending on your intent. Figure 12–24 avoids the ambiguity of the graph in Figure 12–23 by showing the data in two dimensions. It also displays the horizontal lines for expenditures on the vertical axis, thus making the data for each column easier to interpret. If you wished to show relative expenses among the four variables for a given quarter, this graph would be ideal. However, if you wished to show trends

Figure 12–23
Three-Dimensional
Column Graph
(Showing Same
Data as in Figure
12–22)

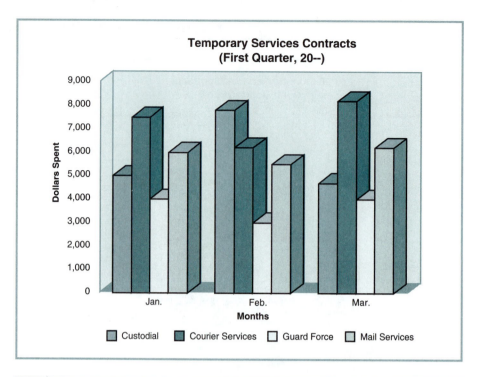

Figure 12–24
Two-Dimensional
Column Graph
(Showing Same
Data as in Figures
12–22 and 12–23)

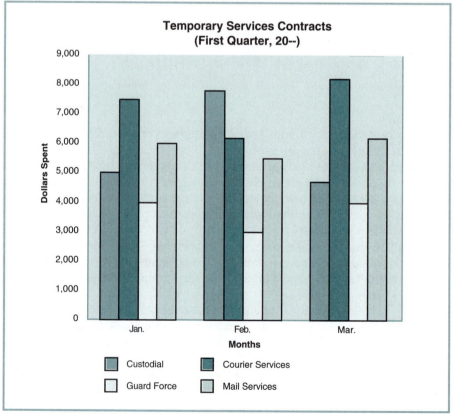

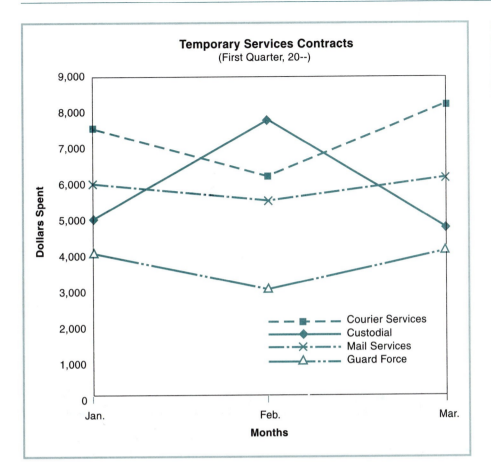

for the entire three-month period in contract expenditures at a glance, the graph in Figure 12–25 is preferable.

When precise dollar amounts for each service are equally important, you can provide a table showing that information.

As Figures 12–22 through 12–25 show, the more complicated a graph looks, the harder it is to interpret. On balance, simple is better for the reader. Use this principle when you review your computer graphics on screen in several styles and consider your reader's needs before deciding which style to use.

Drawings

A drawing is useful when your reader needs an impression of an object's general appearance or an overview of a series of steps or directions. Note, for example, the sequence of drawings in Chapter 7 that show the steps used to install a waste disposal (Figure 7–10). Drawings are the graphic of choice when it is necessary to focus on details or relationships that a photograph cannot capture. A drawing can emphasize the significant piece of a mechanism, or its function, and omit

**Figure 12–26
Cutaway Drawing of
a Hard Disk Drive**

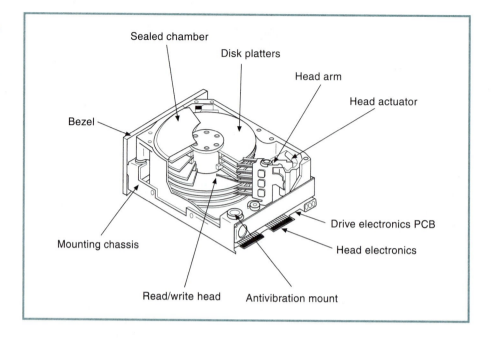

Sealed chamber

Disk platters

Head arm

Head actuator

Bezel

Drive electronics PCB

Head electronics

Mounting chassis

Read/write head   Antivibration mount

**Figure 12–27
Drawing of Stretch-
ing Exercises to
Prevent Repetitive-
Stress Injuries**

Exercises You Can Do

Before beginning keying and during breaks throughout the day, take time
to do the following stretching exercises:

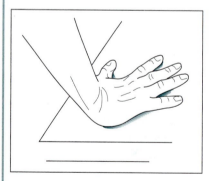

*Gently press the hand against a
firm flat surface, stretching the
fingers and wrist. Hold for
five seconds.*

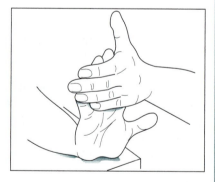

*Rest the forearm on the edge of a
table. Grasp the fingers of one hand
and gently bend back the wrist,
stretching the hands and wrist.
Hold for five seconds.*

what is not significant. A cutaway drawing can show the internal parts of a piece of equipment in such a way that their relationship to the overall equipment is clear (Figure 12–26).

Drawings are also an ideal option when you must illustrate something but find it either impractical or too expensive to reproduce a photograph (Figure 12–27). However, if the actual appearance of an object (a dented fender) or a phenomenon (a wind-tunnel experiment) is necessary to your document, a photograph is essential. An exploded-view drawing can show the proper sequence in which parts fit together or the details of each individual part (Figure 12–28).

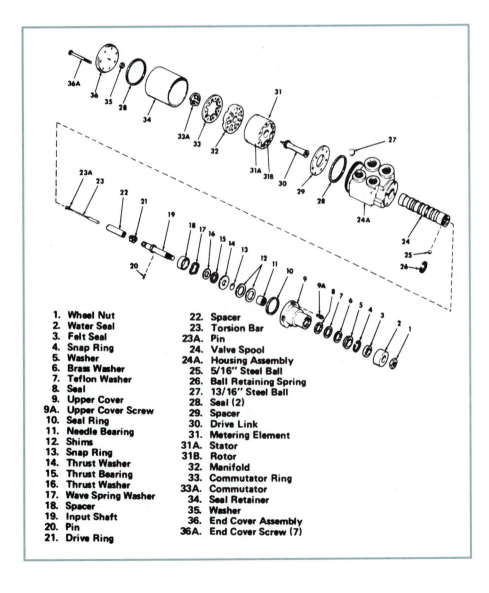

Figure 12–28 Exploded-View Drawing of a Power-Steering Valve
Source: Courtesy of the Harnischfeger Corporation.

1. Wheel Nut
2. Water Seal
3. Felt Seal
4. Snap Ring
5. Washer
6. Brass Washer
7. Teflon Washer
8. Seal
9. Upper Cover
9A. Upper Cover Screw
10. Seal Ring
11. Needle Bearing
12. Shims
13. Snap Ring
14. Thrust Washer
15. Thrust Bearing
16. Thrust Washer
17. Wave Spring Washer
18. Spacer
19. Input Shaft
20. Pin
21. Drive Ring
22. Spacer
23. Torsion Bar
23A. Pin
24. Valve Spool
24A. Housing Assembly
25. 5/16" Steel Ball
26. Ball Retaining Spring
27. 13/16" Steel Ball
28. Seal (2)
29. Spacer
30. Drive Link
31. Metering Element
31A. Stator
31B. Rotor
32. Manifold
33. Commutator Ring
33A. Commutator
34. Seal Retainer
35. Washer
36. End Cover Assembly
36A. End Cover Screw (7)

Figure 12–29
Clip-Art Images

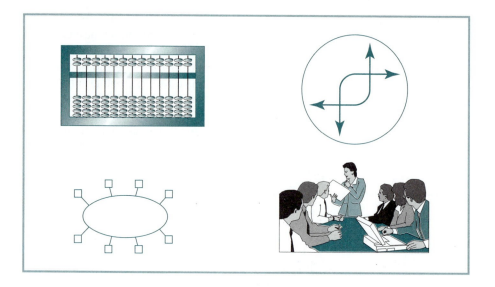

Drawings requiring a high degree of accuracy and precision are generally rendered by graphics specialists. General-interest images needed to illustrate newsletters and brochures can be found in the clip-art libraries that come with desktop computer-graphics programs and even with word-processing programs. They contain thousands of noncopyrighted symbols, shapes, and images of people, equipment, furniture, buildings, and the like. Figure 12–29 shows several examples of clip-art icons and images.

Many organizations have their own format specifications for drawings. In the absence of such specifications, the following tips should be helpful:

1. Show the equipment from the point of view of the person who will use it.
2. When illustrating a subsystem, show its relationship to the larger system of which it is a part.
3. Draw the different parts of an object in proportion to one another, unless you indicate that certain parts are enlarged.
4. Where a sequence of drawings is used to illustrate a process, arrange them from left to right and from top to bottom.
5. Label parts in the drawing so that text references to them are clear and consistent.
6. Depending on the complexity of what is shown, label the parts themselves, or use a letter or number key. (See Figure 12–31.)

Flowcharts

A flowchart is a diagram of a process that involves stages, with the sequence of stages shown from beginning to end. The flowchart presents an overview of the process that allows the reader to grasp the essential steps quickly and easily. The

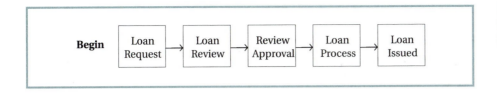

**Figure 12–30
Flowchart Using
Labeled Blocks**

process being illustrated could range from the stages by which bauxite ore is refined into aluminum ingots for fabrication to the steps involved in preparing a manuscript for publication.

Flowcharts can take several forms to represent the steps in a process. They can consist of labeled blocks (Figure 12–30), pictorial representations (Figure 12–31), or standardized symbols (Figure 12–32). The items in any flowchart are always connected according to the sequence in which the steps occur. The normal direction of flow in a chart is left to right or top to bottom. When the flow is otherwise, be sure to indicate it with arrows.

Flowcharts that document computer programs and other information-processing procedures use standardized symbols. The standards are set forth in U.S.A. Standard Flowchart Symbols and Their Usage in Information Processing, published by the American National Standards Institute, publication X3.5. When creating a flowchart, follow the guidelines at the top of page 539.

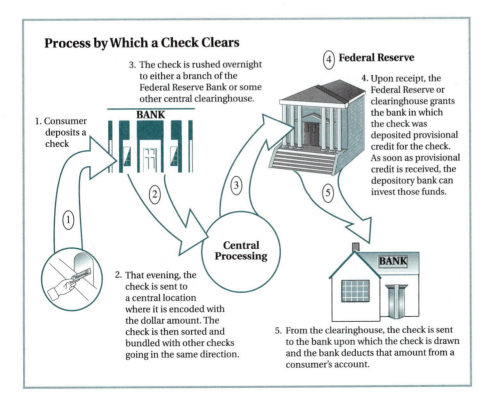

**Figure 12–31
Flowchart Using
Pictorial Symbols**

**Figure 12–32
Flowchart Using
Standardized
Symbols**

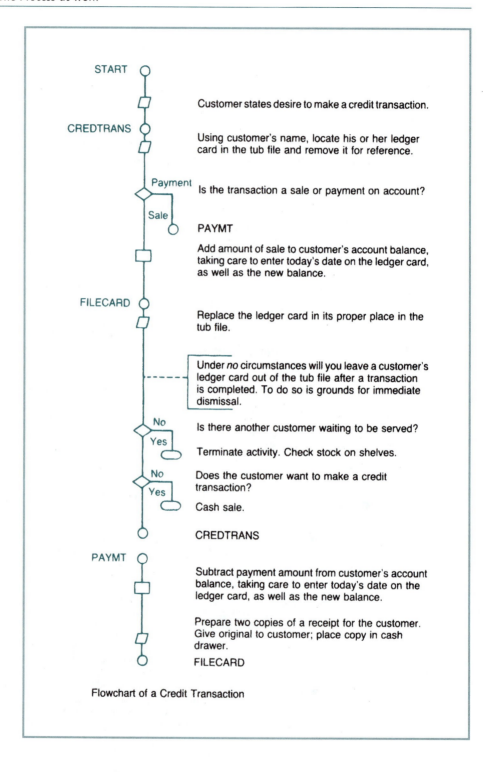

START

Customer states desire to make a credit transaction.

CREDTRANS

Using customer's name, locate his or her ledger card in the tub file and remove it for reference.

Payment

Is the transaction a sale or payment on account?

Sale

PAYMT

Add amount of sale to customer's account balance, taking care to enter today's date on the ledger card, as well as the new balance.

FILECARD

Replace the ledger card in its proper place in the tub file.

Under *no* circumstances will you leave a customer's ledger card out of the tub file after a transaction is completed. To do so is grounds for immediate dismissal.

No

Is there another customer waiting to be served?

Yes

Terminate activity. Check stock on shelves.

No

Does the customer want to make a credit transaction?

Yes

Cash sale.

CREDTRANS

PAYMT

Subtract payment amount from customer's account balance, taking care to enter today's date on the ledger card, as well as the new balance.

Prepare two copies of a receipt for the customer. Give original to customer; place copy in cash drawer.

FILECARD

Flowchart of a Credit Transaction

1. With labeled blocks and standardized symbols, use arrows to show the direction of flow, especially if the flow is opposite to the normal direction. With pictorial representations, use arrows to show the direction of all flow.
2. Label each step in the process, or identify it with a conventional symbol. Steps can also be represented pictorially or by captioned blocks.
3. Include a key if the flowchart contains symbols that your reader may not understand.
4. Leave adequate white space on the page. Do not crowd your steps and directional arrows too close together.

Organizational Charts

An organizational chart shows how the various components of an organization are related to one another. Such an illustration is useful when you want to give readers an overview of an organization or indicate the lines of authority within the organization (Figure 12–33).

The title of each organizational component (office, section, division) is placed in a separate box. These boxes are then linked to a central authority. If your readers need the information, include the name of the person occupying the position identified in each box. As with all illustrations, place the organizational chart as close as possible to the text that refers to it.

Maps

Maps can be used to show the specific geographic features of an area (roads, mountains, rivers) or to show information according to geographic distribution (population, housing, manufacturing centers, and so forth).

Bear these points in mind as you create maps for use with your text (see Figure 12–34):

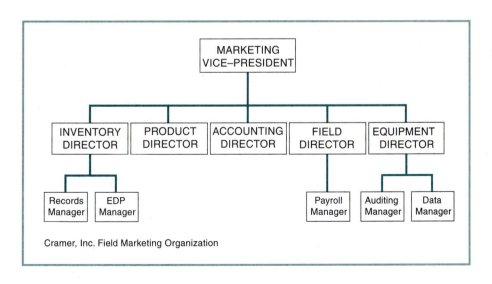

Cramer, Inc. Field Marketing Organization

**Figure 12–33
Organizational
Chart**

Figure 12–34
Sample Map

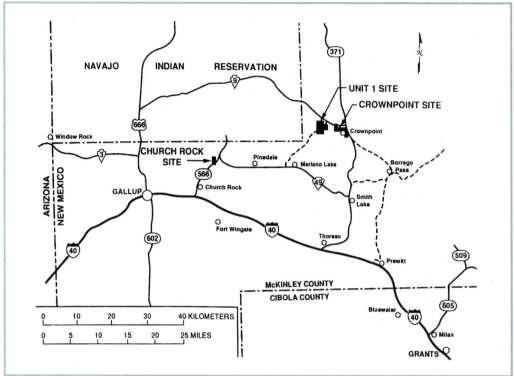

1. Make sure all boundaries within the map are clearly identified. Eliminate unnecessary boundaries.

2. Eliminate unnecessary information from your map. For example, if population is the focal point, do not include mountains, roads, rivers, and so on.

3. Include a scale of miles or feet, or kilometers or meters, to give your reader an indication of the map's proportions.

4. Indicate which direction is north.

5. Emphasize key features by using shading, dots, crosshatching, or appropriate symbols, and include a key telling what the different colors, shadings, or symbols represent (see Figure 12–35).

Photographs

Photographs are vital to many publications. They are often the best way to show the surface appearance of an object or to record an event or the development of a phenomenon over a period of time. Not all representations, however, call for photographs. They cannot depict the internal workings of a mechanism or below-the-surface details of objects or structures. Such details are better shown in drawings or diagrams.

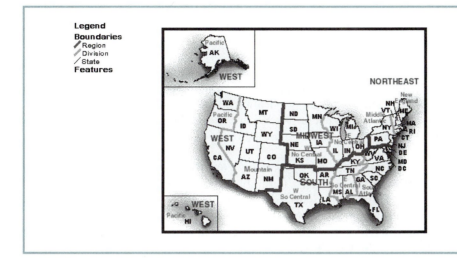

Figure 12–35
Sample Map Show-
ing Legend and
Shading to Depict
Data *Source:*
Courtesy of the U.S.
Census Bureau.

Highlighting Photographic Objects. If you are taking the photo, stand close enough to the object so that it fills your picture frame. To get precise and clear photographs, choose camera angles carefully. A camera will photograph only what it is aimed at; accordingly, select important details and the camera angles that will record these details. To show the relative size of an unfamiliar object, place a familiar object—such as a ruler, a book, a tool, or a person—near the object that is to be photographed. The photograph in Figure 12–36 shows a control device being held by a human hand to illustrate its relative size.

Ask the printer reproducing your publication for special handling requirements if you use glossy photographs. If you use digitized photos, ask about the preferred resolution of the images. The higher the resolution, the better the

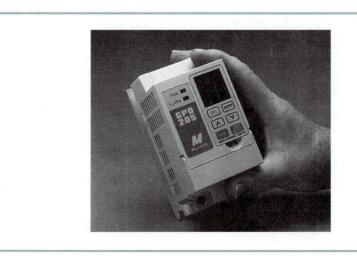

Figure 12–36
Photo of Control
Device *Source:*
Photo courtesy
of Ken Cook
Company.

quality. You can create digitized photos using scanners and digital cameras, so ensure that the equipment has the necessary memory for the resolution required by the printer.

Using Color.   The advantages of using color photographs are obvious: Color is in many cases the only way to communicate crucial information. In medical, chemical, geological, and botanical publications, for example, readers often need to know exactly what an object or phenomenon looks like to accurately interpret it. In these circumstances, color reproduction is the only legitimate option available.

Posting color images at a Web site is no more complicated or expensive than posting black-and-white images. For publications, however, the preparation and printing of color photographs are complex technical tasks performed by graphics and printing professionals. If you are planning to use color photographs in your publication, discuss with these professionals the type, quality, and number of photographs required. Generally, they prefer that you provide color transparencies (slides) and color negatives (negatives of color prints) for reproduction.

Be mindful, too, that color reproduction is significantly more expensive than black-and-white reproduction. Color can also be tricky to reproduce accurately without losing contrast and vividness. For this reason, the original photographs must be sharply focused and rich in contrast.

DIGITAL SHORTCUTS: Creating Computer Graphics

Computer software permits you to create a large variety of visual images, to access and modify clip-art images, and to display numerical information in graphs and charts. The computer visuals you create afford numerous advantages over pen-and-paper renderings in that they can be

- Saved for future use and updated as necessary
- Printed as is on paper or used in reports, other documents, and Web sites
- Sent to presentation software programs to produce transparencies and 35-mm slides for meetings
- Communicated to others electronically via email

Your computer may also allow you to share data among documents created in different applications. Data sharing automates redundant tasks. For example, the data entered into spreadsheet software can be reproduced in graphical form (usually as pie charts and bar graphs), which can be embedded into documents (in word-processing software) and presentations (in presentation software). When the spreadsheet data are updated, the corresponding graphic in the document or presentation is automatically redrawn to reflect the changes, thus saving you the time and effort of manually revising the graphic.

Using Graphics to Communicate Internationally

Business and technical communicators increasingly will use graphics in the years to come to communicate with international audiences. This trend will grow because of the globalization of markets: Companies want to expand their markets in Saudi Arabia, China, South America, the countries of the former Soviet Union, and dozens of other places. Global markets mean increased global trade because of the prevalence of multinational corporations, the international subsidiaries of many companies, multination trade agreements, the increasing diversity of the U.S. workforce, and even increases in immigration. The audiences for these communications will include clients, business partners, colleagues, and current and potential employees and customers. Even though English is rapidly becoming the global language of business and science, many people speak it as a second or third language. For this reason, graphics offer distinct advantages for communicating in a global business climate.

- Graphics can communicate a message more effectively than text, particularly in the context of safety warnings or cautions.
- Graphics can sometimes replace technical terms that are difficult to translate.

Despite their unquestionable value in communicating with international audiences, symbols, images, and even colors are not free from cultural associations: They are context dependent, and context is culturally determined. Thus, there are no universally accepted graphics standards, with the exception of the symbols used in mathematics and certain scientific and engineering disciplines (e.g., the voltage symbol used in electrical engineering).

Writers who create documents for international readers can avoid confusing and possibly offending a global audience by understanding the following cultural differences in connotation.

Punctuation Marks

Punctuation marks, like words, are language specific. For example, in North America the question mark generally represents the need for information or the Help function in a computer manual or program. In many countries, this symbol is not understood at all.

Religious Symbols

Religious symbols that carry simultaneous religious and nonreligious meanings have long been used in North America, where it is common to use the cross as a symbol for first aid or hospital. In Muslim countries, a cross represents Christianity; a crescent (usually green) is a symbol for first aid.

Colors

The use of a particular color can distort or even change the meaning of graphics symbols. Red commonly indicates warning or danger in North America, Europe, and Japan. In China, however, red symbolizes joy. In Europe and North America, blue generally has a positive connotation; in Japan, the color represents villainy. In Europe and North America, yellow represents caution or cowardice; in Arab countries, yellow generally means fertility or strength.

People, Parts of the Body, and Gestures

Depicting people and parts of the body in graphics can be problematic (see Table 12–1). If your graphics will reach an international audience, it is better to avoid depictions of people eating or representations of bare arms and feet. Nudity in advertising, for example, generally is acceptable in Europe but not in North America. Even showing isolated body parts could lead to communications difficulties. For example, some Middle Eastern cultures regard the display of the soles of one's shoes to be disrespectful and offensive. Therefore, a technical manual that attempts to demonstrate the ease of running a software program by showing a user with his feet up on a desk would be considered offensive in the Middle East.

Communicators producing instructions often use hand gestures such as the victory sign (☝) or the "OK" sign (🖐) as positive motivators. However, the meaning of each of these gestures varies by culture. In Australia, for example, the victory sign conveys the same meaning as holding up the middle finger in North America. Similarly, the gesture that means "OK" in North America can mean "worthless" in France, can mean "money" in Japan, and is a sexual insult in many other parts of the world. Even a smile may have different connotations. In Japan, smiling can be a sign of joy or can be used to hide displeasure; in some Asian cultures, smiling may be considered a sign of weakness.

Further, a manual that contains a pointed finger to indicate "turn the page" might offend someone in Venezuela. A writer preparing a manual for export to Honduras could indicate "caution" by using a picture of a person touching a finger below the eye.

Cultural Symbols

Signs and symbols are so culturally rooted that we often lose sight of the fact that they may be understood only in our culture. A Michigan manufacturer of fans wanted to use easily understood symbols to represent the two speeds of its product: fast and slow. The technical communicators selected a rabbit and a turtle.

Table 12–1
International Implications of Gestures and Body Language

Body part	Gesture	Country	Interpretation
Head nodding	Up and down	Bulgaria	No
Left hand	Showing palm	Muslim countries	Dirty, unclean
Index finger	Pointing to others	Venezuela, Sri Lanka	Rude
Index-to-thumb circle	Circular "OK"	Germany, Netherlands	Rude
Ankle and leg	Crossing over knee	Indonesia, Syria	Rude
Eye	Touching finger below eye	Honduras	Caution

However, recognition of these animals as symbols of speed and slowness requires familiarity with Aesop's fables—a Western tradition.

Technology Symbols

The symbols or icons we create to represent technology are laden with cultural assumptions. If users do not have regular contact with fax machines, photocopiers, computers, or cellular phones, technical and business communicators cannot predict how users will interpret representations of these devices.

Reading Practices

Whether text is read right to left or left to right influences how graphics are sequenced. In Israel, for example, text is read from right to left. For this audience, you will need to alter the design and sequencing of text and graphics.

Directional Signs

The signs we use to represent direction or time are open to misinterpretation. For example, the arrow sign on shipping cartons can be interpreted to mean either that the carton should be placed with the arrow pointing up to the top of the carton, or pointing down to the carton's most stable position. Western cultures tend to indicate the future (or something positive) by pointing to the right ($\rightarrow$) and the past (or something negative) by pointing to the left ($\leftarrow$); in the Chinese culture, left represents honor and right self-destruction.

Careful attention to the different connotations visual elements may have for an international audience makes translations easier, saves a company from potential embarrassment, and, over time, earns respect for the company and its products and services.

WRITER'S CHECKLIST: Using International Graphics

The complex cultural connotations of visuals challenge communicators to think beyond their own experience. The following general guidelines will help you meet the needs of international and multicultural audiences:

- ☐ Consult with someone from your intended audience's country who is very familiar with the culture and who will be able to recognize and explain the effects of subtle visual elements on your intended readers.

- ☐ Acknowledge diversity within your company and recognize that not everyone interprets visual information in the same way.

- ☐ Learn about the use of gestures in other cultures as a first step to learning about cultural context, because the interpretation of gestures differs widely.

(continued)

WRITER'S CHECKLIST (continued)

☐ Invite international and intercultural communication experts to speak to your employees and contact companies in your area that may have employees who could be resources for cultural discussions.

☐ Be sure that the graphics you use have no unintended religious or symbolic implications. Be aware, for example, that using a cross to represent first aid can be misinterpreted in Middle Eastern societies, where the cross solely represents Christianity.

☐ Use few colors in your graphics. Generally, black-and-white or gray-and-white illustrations are less problematic.

☐ Be consistent in labeling elements. Use simple, consistent signs for all visual items.

☐ Create simple visuals. Simple shapes with few elements are easier to read in most cultures.

☐ Use outlines or neutral abstractions to represent human beings. For example, use stick figures for bodies or a circle for a head.

☐ Explain the meaning of icons or symbols. Include a glossary to explain technical symbols that cannot be changed (e.g., company logos).

☐ Test icons and symbols in context with members of your target audience. Usability testing with cultural experts is critical.

☐ Organize visual information for intended audiences. North American readers tend to read visuals from left to right in clockwise rotation. Middle Eastern cultures read visuals from left to right in counterclockwise rotation.

CHAPTER 12 SUMMARY: Designing Effective Documents and Visuals

Use the following revision checklist to ensure that the graphics, design elements, and forms in your documents and Web pages effectively convey the information you intend.

Integrating Visuals and Text

☐ Have you noted in your document or Web-site planning outline the approximate location of your graphics?

☐ Does the text preceding a table or figure make clear why the visual is there and what it shows?

☐ Is the language in the text describing the graphic consistent with the language in the graphic?

☐ Do all graphics have clear, concise captions?

☐ Is the graphic located as close as possible to the text describing it?

☐ Have you allowed adequate white space around and within the graphics in your documents and Web pages?

☐ Have you obtained permission to reproduce copyrighted graphics in your document or Web site?

☐ Do the layout and design of your finished document highlight the organization and hierarchy of your information?

Planning a Web Site

☐ Have you written and had reviewed a clear statement of purpose *before* you begin work on your Web site?

☐ Have you outlined the structure of your Web site to get users to the information they want in the fewest number of clicks?

☐ Are the pages throughout your Web site uniform and consistent in design and color?

☐ Does your Web site have one or more email links so that site visitors can submit comments and questions?

☐ Do pages and information collections at your Web site include the dates for when the information was last revised or replaced?

Designing Forms

☐ Are your paper and Web-based forms organized in a logical order for those filling them out and for those interpreting the information they contain?

☐ Did your coworkers review the draft form before you printed it or posted it to a Web site?

☐ Have you designed questions that can be answered simply and briefly and that provide the information that you need?

■ Exercises

1. Create a table that shows the features of a task, such as a seasonal maintenance, that you perform over the period of a year. (Lawn and automobile care are among the kinds of seasonal tasks you may perform on a routine schedule.)

2. Prepare a pie graph showing the distribution of 100 companies by type of industry in a survey. Distribution percentages by type of industry are as follows: computer-related, 32 percent; industrial equipment, 7 percent; business services, 8 percent; telecommunications, 10 percent; media and publications, 10 percent; consumer goods, 10 percent; medical and pharmaceutical, 14 percent; other, 9 percent.

3. Create a line or bar graph that compares sales in thousands of dollars among the various truck-parts divisions of the ABC Corporation for 1997, 1998, and 1999. Sales for each division are as follows:

   axles: 1997 ($225), 1998 ($200), 1999 ($75)

   universal joints: 1997 ($125), 1998 ($100), 1999 ($35)

   frames: 1997 ($125), 1998 ($100), 1999 ($50)

   transmissions: 1997 ($75), 1998 ($65), 1999 ($50)

   clutches: 1997 ($35), 1998 ($30), 1999 ($15)

   gaskets and seals: 1997 ($28), 1998 ($25), 1999 ($20)

4. Briefly explain whether a photograph or a line drawing would better illustrate features of the following subjects: a dry-cell battery (for an article in a general encyclopedia), a flower arrangement (in a florist's brochure), an electrical-outlet box (in a wiring instructions booklet), an automobile accident (for an insurance claims adjuster), the procedure for wrapping a sprained ankle (for a first-aid handbook), and a deer tick (in a backpacker's handbook).

5. Create a flowchart for a process or procedure important to your field of study or to the topic of your current writing project. Introduce and explain the flowchart, relating it to your topic and explaining discrete actions, decisions, or repetitions of specific procedures that occur in the process that the flowchart depicts.

6. Beginning at the main entrance and ending at the checkout desk, draw a flowchart that traces the path you follow in the process of locating and obtaining books from your library (as outlined in Chapter 11).

7. Create an organizational chart for a club or group to which you belong or for the department in your area of study.

8. Design a weekly time card for factory employees at United Agricultural Products. Employees work Mondays through Fridays, 8:00 a.m. to noon, 12:30 p.m. to 3:30 p.m., and have a half-hour for lunch. Include on the time card a column listing the days of the week (vertical column) and columns labeled "Time In," "Time Out" (morning), "Lunch," "Time In," "Time Out" (afternoon), and "Overtime" (horizontal columns). Supervisors are to fill in the times that employees actually arrive at work and leave for the day and the times of their lunch breaks. They are also to fill in the number of hours of overtime (if any) that employees work each day. Include columns for the total hours worked each day and a final box or space for total hours worked for the week. Be sure to leave spaces for the dates that the time card covers and for the signatures of both the employee and the supervisor.

9. Design a print or electronic form to be used by the medical staff secretary of a hospital. The form is for the reappointment of staff physicians for the coming year. It should be designed to obtain the following information: the physician's name, office address, and office telephone number; the physician's status on the hospital's staff (temporary or permanent); the hospital department in which he or she wishes to admit patients (medicine or surgery); the number of the physician's state license; and the physician's birthdate. It should also provide for "yes" and "no" answers about whether the physician in question has attended a satisfactory number of committee meetings, whether the physician has satisfactorily completed all of his or her medical records, and whether the hospital has taken

any disciplinary action against the physician during the past year. Finally, the form should provide for the signature of the hospital's chief of staff and the date of that signature.

10. Design a print or electronic form for recording the amount of money you spend each month for the following typical items: housing, food, utilities, transportation (car, bus, subway), insurance (car, life, property, medical), school, clothing, entertainment, and the like. Include columns that show the amount you budgeted for each item, the amount actually spent, and the difference. Finally, include space for totaling expenses for each column.

■ In-Class Activities

1. Divide into groups of three to create an outline for a major class writing project. As you create the outline, indicate each place in which you plan to include a graphic. For each location marked, provide the following information:
   - The type of graphic and why that type was chosen
   - How it will benefit your document (be as specific as possible)
   - How it will be helpful to readers
   - A description of the data it will present
   - How you plan to prepare it or otherwise obtain it

2. Divide into teams with classmates who share a similar major area of study. If you have more than seven students in your group, you may divide into two smaller groups. Design a form that would be commonly used in your field. Refer to this chapter for examples of print and Web forms.

3. Bring to class a print form or electronic form that you found on the Web that you believe could be designed more effectively (for example, a college student form, a government registration form). As your instructor directs, do any of the following:
   a. Critique the form and create a list of what could be improved.
   b. Recommend specific steps for improving the form.
   c. Create a new form either yourself or in a group.

4. Divide into teams with classmates who share a similar major area of study. During the next hour, using thumbnail sketches, create a dummy for a brochure advertising a new student association for students majoring in your field. It should include the following information: the date, time, and place of your call-out meeting; your new association's purpose on campus; and a description of who is eligible to belong. Your brochure plan must include columns and visuals and be at least two 8½-by-11-inch pages.

5. Bring to class an example of a recent newsletter. Your sample newsletter may be from a campus group, organization, or department or from a source outside campus such as a community-service group, a business, or a government organization. Divide into groups of five or fewer. For the next forty-five minutes, rank your samples by order of their effectiveness. Which samples best accomplish their purpose? Why? Refer to this chapter for guidelines on page design. Be prepared to defend your choices to your classmates.

■ Research Projects

1. Interview someone from another country or culture and report (500 to 700 words) on any cultural differences between ideas held in that country or culture and ideas broadly held in the United States about any two of the following areas: punctuation marks; religious symbols; colors; people, body parts, and gestures; directional signals; technology symbols; reading practices; or cultural symbols. Do not use any specific examples already discussed in this chapter.

2. Select five drawings from reports, articles, or textbooks. Explain whether you think each illustration makes the text more meaningful or easier to follow. Take into consideration how well each illustration supports the ideas presented in the text and whether the illustration has been correctly placed in relation to the text.

3. Using magazines, journal articles, and other printed sources, gather information about how visuals are used in your field. In a brief narrative, show examples of visuals used in marketing, continuing education, job recruitment, and other areas relevant to your field. Document all sources correctly. Refer to this chapter for guidelines on the placement of visuals.

4. Graphics are such a vital part of doing business today that many places hire professionals to assist with their graphic and visual advertising. With graphics and visual design in mind, visit an advertising agency or marketing firm in your area. Review the kinds of work that they do for other businesses. Ask to see a copy of their price list and samples of their work, and ask what kinds of businesses use their services. Write a brief narrative summarizing the information you gathered on your visit and include your opinion of how a business in your field would use the services of an advertising agency or marketing firm.

■ Web Projects

1. Create a bar graph showing the median sales price of new single-family homes in the United States for 1975 and at five-year intervals through the most current data available at the Web site of the U.S. Census Bureau at http://www.census.gov/.

2. Create a line graph that plots home-mortgage interest rates (or population in any U.S. metropolitan area currently over 1 million, or employment in the U.S. auto industry of both men and women) over the past 20 years. Present the same information in a table. Use the Web to gather your data. You can access a list of federal agency Internet sites at http://www.access.gpo.gov/su_docs/dpos/agencies.html.

3. Design a brief online survey directed at high school seniors interested in your major field of study. In your survey, ask approximately six "yes" or "no" questions targeting why they are planning to choose this particular field of study. For example, if your field is nursing you might ask:
   Are you interested in nursing because of
   • your interest in helping people?
   • the predicted ease in securing jobs in the field?

- the pay scale?
- the chances for advancement?
- the flexibility of the job?
- your interest in medicine?

Include in your survey your name, the name of your institution, and a brief statement explaining that you are gathering information for your institution. Refer to this chapter for guidelines on creating online forms.

4. Design a Web home page for a group or organization to which you belong. Refer to this chapter for guidelines to creating online documents. Your instructor may ask you to email your final version to your classmates.

5. Design a Web page advertising your class to other students. Include a list of the practical applications you have learned in class. Remember that this is a marketing tool targeted for university students. Your instructor may give you specific information to include. Follow the guidelines presented in this text both for persuasive writing (Chapter 7) and for effective Web-page design, in this chapter.

13 Formal Reports

Formal reports are the written accounts of major projects. Projects that are likely to generate a formal report include research into new developments in a field, explorations of the feasibility of a new product or a new service, or an end-of-year review of developments within an organization. The scope and complexity of the project will determine how long and how complex the report will be. Most formal reports—certainly those that are long and complex—require a carefully planned structure and signposts that provide the readers with an easy-to-recognize guide to the material in the report. Such aids to the reader as a table of contents, a list of figures, and an abstract (brief summary of the report) make the information in the report more accessible. Making a formal topic outline, which lists the report's major facts and ideas and indicates their relationship to one another, should help you to write a well-organized report.

This chapter discusses the components of formal reports and explains how best to organize those components into an effective final product. As you read the chapter, keep in mind all that you've learned about the process of drafting and revising on-the-job writing tasks, because careful planning, drafting, and revising, as much as using the organizational frameworks covered in this chapter, form the base for a successful formal report. As you begin to plan for your own project, you will find that formal-report preparation involves researching and generating a substantial amount of information, which you will need to evaluate, select, and organize even before you begin the drafting process. Because the research required for a formal report can be extensive, you will want to do a great deal of brainstorming and topic-refining before you begin your actual research. See Chapter 1 to review information-gathering and brainstorming strategies.

In addition, you should plan to write several outlines for your report. One outline, as already mentioned, can serve as an overview of the project, and you can also create smaller, more specific outlines for individual sections. Breaking up your organizational work into parts can make the daunting task of pulling together a long report seem more manageable. Chapter 2 discusses a variety of outlining strategies.

Finally, you will need to write multiple drafts of the report. The drafts will need to be evaluated and revised for coherence, clarity, and correctness within separate sections of your report. You will also need to review drafts to see whether the sections of the report connect smoothly and logically, whether sources are used correctly and consistently, and whether figures—all drawings,

Voices from the Workplace

Mary Warren, Argonne National Laboratory

Mary Warren is a manager of Technical Communications Services at Argonne National Laboratory. She manages a staff of writers and editors who team up with researchers and administrators to prepare technical- and business-information products for print and electronic media.

"Preparing reports consumes lots of resources. Why spend the time and money on a report unless there's a real need for it? At a large R&D [research and development] institution like Argonne National Laboratory, reports are one of the best ways to communicate the work and results of projects paid for by federal income taxes. Readers use the report information for their individual needs. Fellow researchers use the information in their own projects. Federal agency staff and legislators use it to set funding priorities. Journalists need the latest information to keep their readers abreast of developments in science and technology. Citizens need current and accurate information for their roles as workers, voters, and parents. Reports—dowdy though they may seem—feed into the planning and decision-making taking place everyday in every corner of the globe."

Visit the Argonne National Laboratory Web site at http://www.anl.gov

Entry-Level
Chris Meeker, AMT Capital Management

Chris Meeker is a second-year analyst at AMT Capital Management, a financial-services organization specializing in mergers and acquisitions for financial-service companies, and in investment management for high net-worth clients. Chris's primary role at AMT Capital is to analyze economic and company-specific data that relates to equity and fixed-income markets. "One of the most important and difficult ways I transform analysis into an end product is through the writing of a formal research report."

Chris organizes his formal reports into three major topics. He begins with a section aimed at educating his readers. "In the case of securities research, this section is usually used to update the reader about a specific event or change in the company." Once the reader is updated, he explains the factors that caused the event or change. "This is where you want to enter supportive facts that are important to understanding the issue at hand." Finally, he gives his opinion on the matter. "This portion of the document should incorporate your analysis of the issue and how it will affect the company in the future."

Chris also conducts research and documents his sources in his formal reports carefully. "Just as in college, where no professor expects you to be an expert on the subject, you need to make sure you can support your ideas and your work. If the work is entirely your own, you do not need to cite a reference, but you do have to be able to explain and defend it. If your report requires research that you have gathered from sources, you must include a footnote for the source of the information. You want to make sure to use reliable and industry-accepted sources."

tables, graphs, charts, photographs, and maps—are well designed and positioned. Because of the extensive revisions required for a long report, collaborative reviews of your work will help you immensely; colleagues, fellow students, or instructors can offer revision suggestions to supplement your own evaluations of the report. For a review of revising strategies, see Chapters 4 and 5. Chapter 6 describes the collaborative reviewing process.

■ Order of Elements in a Formal Report

Most formal reports are divided into three major parts—front matter, body, and back matter—each of which, in turn, contains a number of elements. Just how many elements are needed and in what order they are presented for a particular report depends on the subject, the length of the report, the kinds of material covered, and the standard practice of the organization. Many companies and governmental and other institutions have a preferred style for formal reports and furnish guidelines that staff members must follow. If your employer has prepared a set of style guidelines, follow it; if not, use the format recommended in this chapter. Most formal reports are delivered with a transmittal letter or memo that presents the document to readers. The following list includes most of the elements a formal report might contain:

- Transmittal letter or memo (precedes front matter)
- Front matter
  - Title page
  - Abstract
  - Table of contents
  - List of figures
  - List of tables
  - Foreword
  - Preface
  - List of abbreviations and symbols
- Body
  - Executive Summary
  - Introduction
  - Text (including headings)
  - Conclusions
  - Recommendations
  - Explanatory footnotes
  - Works Cited (or References)
- Back matter
  - Appendixes
  - Bibliography
  - Glossary
  - Index

DIGITAL SHORTCUTS: Automating Report Formatting

You can use your word-processing software to create style sheets that permit you to develop automated formatting for your report. Once the format guidelines are specified, they can be saved as a file and used over and over to ensure consistency each time you create a formal report. You can automate a variety of formatting elements:

- Fonts and font sizes for text, headings, titles, footnotes, headers, and footers

- Paragraphs, including indentation and margins
- Lists, including indentation from the margin and spacing
- Number of columns on a page

Your software will also permit you to create an automated table of contents for your report based on the main headings and subheadings in the report.

■ Transmittal Letter or Memo

When you submit a formal report, you should include with it a brief transmittal (or cover) letter or memo that identifies the topic the formal report addresses and why the report was prepared. Written in the form of a standard business letter or memo, this transmittal material most often opens with a brief paragraph (one or two sentences) explaining what is being sent and why. The next paragraph contains a brief summary of the report's contents or stresses some feature that would be important to the reader. This section may also mention any special conditions under which the material was prepared (limitations of time or money, for instance). The closing paragraph may acknowledge any help received in preparing the report, or express the hope that the information fulfills its purpose.

Typically, most transmittal letters and memos are composed of these elements. In any case, they should be brief—usually one page. The report that the letter or memo accompanies should speak for itself. Figure 13–1 shows a sample transmittal memo. Examples of short and long transmittal letters are also shown in Figures 9–2 and 9–3.

■ Front Matter

The front matter, which includes all the elements that precede the body of the report, serves several purposes: It gives the reader a general idea of the author's purpose in writing the report; it indicates whether the report contains the kind of information that the reader is looking for; and it lists where in the report the reader can find specific chapters, headings, illustrations, and tables. Not all formal reports require every one of these elements. A title page and table of contents are usually mandatory, but whether an abstract, a list of figures, a list of tables, a foreword, a list of abbreviations and symbols are included will depend on the scope of the report and its intended audience. Scientific and technical reports, for example, often include a separate listing of abbreviations and symbols, while in most business reports, such lists are unnecessary. The front-matter pages are

BOEING AIRCRAFT CORPORATION
MEMO

To: Members of the Ethics and Business Conduct Committee
From: Merlin Mendez, Director of Ethics and Business Conduct   *MM*
Date: March 1, 20--
Subject: Reported Ethics Cases 20--

Enclosed is the annual Ethics and Business Conduct Report, as required by Boeing Policy NB-AAG-200, for your evaluation, covering the first year of our Ethics Program. This report contains a review of the ethics cases handled by Boeing Ethics officers and managers during 20--.

The ethics cases reported are analyzed according to two categories: (1) major ethics cases, or those potentially involving serious violations of company policy and/or illegal conduct, and (2) minor ethics cases, or those that do not involve serious policy violations and/or illegal conduct. The report also examines the mode of contact in all of the reported cases and the disposition of the substantiated major ethics cases.

It is my hope that this report will provide the Committee with the information needed to assess the effectiveness of the first year of Boeing's Ethics Program and to plan for the coming year. Please let me know if you have any questions about this report or if you need any further information. I may be reached at (111) 211-2121 and at email address <mm@boeing.com>.

Figure 13–1   Transmittal Memo for a Formal Report   *Source:* The report in this chapter is reprinted by permission of Susan Litzinger, a student at Pennsylvania State University. Sources and visuals by courtesy of the Boeing Aircraft Corporation.

numbered with lowercase Roman numerals. Throughout the report, page numbers are often centered either near the bottom or near the top of each page.

Title Page

Although the formats of title pages for formal reports may vary, the page should normally include the following information: the full title of the report; the name(s) of the writer, group, or department; the date of the report; the name of the organization for which the writer(s) works; and the name of the organization or person to which the report is submitted.

1. *Full title of the report.* The title should reflect the topic as well as the scope and objective of the report. Titles often provide the only basis on which readers decide whether to read a report. Titles too vague or too long not only hinder readers but can prevent efficient filing and information retrieval by librarians and other information specialists. Follow these guidelines when creating the title:
   - Avoid titles that begin "Notes on . . . ," "Studies on . . . ," "A Report on . . . ," or "Observations on . . . ," These phrases are often redundant and state the obvious. However, phrases such as "Annual Report . . ." or "Feasibility Study . . ." should be used in a title or subtitle because they help define the purpose and scope.
   - Do not use abbreviations in the title. Use acronyms only when the report is intended for an audience familiar enough with the topic that the acronym will be understood.
   - Do not include the period covered by a report in the title; include that information in a subtitle:

   EFFECTS OF PROPOSED HIGHWAY CONSTRUCTION
   ON PROPERTY VALUES
   Annual Report, 20--

2. *Name of the writer, principal investigator, or compiler.* Frequently, contributors simply list their names. Sometimes they identify themselves by their job title in the organization (Jane R. Lihn, Cost Analyst; Rodrigo Sánchez, Head, Research and Development). Sometimes contributors identify themselves by their tasks in contributing to the report (Antoine Baume, Compiler; Wanda Landowska, Principal Investigator).

3. *Date or dates of the report.* For one-time reports, list the date when the report is to be distributed. For periodic reports, which may be issued monthly or quarterly, list the period that the present report covers in a subtitle, as well as the date when the report is to be distributed.

4. *Name of the organization for which the writer works.*

5. *Name of the organization or individual to which the report is being submitted,* if the work is being done for a customer or client.

REPORTED ETHICS CASES
Annual Report 20--

Prepared by Susan Litzinger
Director of Ethics and Business Conduct

Report Distributed March 1, 20--

Prepared for
The Ethics and Business Conduct Committee
Boeing Aircraft Corporation

Figure 13–2   Title Page of a Formal Report

These categories are standard on most title pages. Some organizations may require additional information. A sample title page appears in Figure 13–2.

The title page, although unnumbered, is considered page i (small Roman numeral 1). The back of the title page, which is blank and unnumbered, is page ii, and the abstract then falls on page iii so that it appears on a right-hand (i.e., odd-numbered) page. For reports with printing on both sides of each sheet of paper, it is a long-standing printer's convention that right-hand pages are always odd-numbered and left-hand pages are always even-numbered. (Note the pagination in this book.) New sections and chapters of reports typically begin on a new right-hand page. Reports with printing on only one side of each sheet can be numbered consecutively regardless of where new sections begin.

Abstracts

An abstract is a condensed version of a longer work that summarizes and highlights the major points, enabling the prospective reader to decide whether to read the whole work. Usually 200 to 250 words long, an abstract must make sense independently of the work it summarizes. Depending on the kind of information they contain, abstracts are usually classified as either descriptive or informative.

A descriptive abstract includes information about the purpose, scope, and methods used to arrive at the findings contained in the report. It is thus a slightly expanded table of contents in paragraph form. Provided that it adequately summarizes the information, a descriptive abstract need not be longer than several sentences. (See Figure 13–3.)

An informative abstract is an expanded version of the descriptive abstract. In addition to information about the purpose, scope, and methods of the original report, the informative abstract includes the results, conclusions, and recommendations, if any. The informative abstract thus retains the tone and essential scope of the report while omitting its details.

Which of the two types of abstract should you write? The answer depends on the organization for which you are working. If it has a policy, comply with it. Otherwise, aim to satisfy the needs of the principal readers of your report. Informative abstracts satisfy the needs of the widest possible readership, but descriptive abstracts are preferable for information surveys, progress reports that combine information from more than one project, and any report that compiles a variety of information. For these types of reports, conclusions and recommendations either do not exist in the original or are too numerous to include in an abstract. Typically, an abstract follows the title page and is numbered page iii. Figure 13–4 shows an informative abstract, which is an expanded version of the descriptive abstract shown in Figure 13–3.

ABSTRACT

Purpose and scope

Methodology

This report examines the nature and disposition of 3,458 ethics cases handled companywide by Boeing Aircraft Corporation's ethics officers and managers during 20--. The purpose of this annual report is to provide the Ethics and Business Conduct Committee with the information necessary for assessing the effectiveness of the Ethics Program's first year of operation. Records maintained by ethics officers and managers of all contacts were compiled and categorized into two main types: (1) major ethics cases, or cases involving serious violations of company policies and/or illegal conduct, and (2) minor ethics cases, or cases not involving serious policy violations and/or illegal conduct. This report provides examples of the types of cases handled in each category and analyzes the disposition of 30 substantiated major ethics cases. All cases are analyzed according to the mode of contact used in reporting. Recommendations are offered for planning for the second year of the Ethics Program.

iii

Figure 13–3   Descriptive Abstract of a Formal Report

ABSTRACT

This report examines the nature and disposition of 3,458 ethics cases handled companywide by Boeing Aircraft Corporation's ethics officers and managers during 20--. The purpose of this annual report is to provide the Ethics and Business Conduct Committee with the information necessary for assessing the effectiveness of the Ethics Program's first year of operation. Records maintained by ethics officers and managers of all contacts were compiled and categorized into two main types: (1) major ethics cases, or cases involving serious violations of company policies and/or illegal conduct, and (2) minor ethics cases, or cases not involving serious policy violations and/or illegal conduct. This report provides examples of the types of cases handled in each category and analyzes the disposition of 30 substantiated major ethics cases. All cases are analyzed according to the mode of contact used in reporting. The effectiveness of Boeing's Ethics Program during the first year of implementation is most evidenced by (1) the active participation of employees in the program and the 3,458 contacts employees made regarding ethics concerns through the various channels available to them, and (2) the action taken in the cases reported by employees, particularly the disposition of the 30 substantiated major ethics cases. Disseminating information about the disposition of ethics cases, particularly information about the severe disciplinary actions taken in major ethics violations, sends a message to employees that unethical and/or illegal conduct will not be tolerated. Recommendations for planning for the second year of the Ethics Program are (1) continuing the channels of communication now available in the Ethics Program, (2) increasing financial and technical support for the Ethics Hotline, (3) disseminating the annual ethics report in some form to employees to ensure employees' awareness of Boeing's commitment to uphold its Ethics Policies and Procedures, and (4) implementing some measure of recognition for ethical behavior to promote and reward ethical conduct.

Purpose and scope

Methodology

Conclusions

Recommendations

iii

Figure 13–4   Informative Abstract of a Formal Report

Scope

Keeping in mind that at this point your readers know nothing except what your title announces about your report, you should include the following kinds of information in an abstract:

- The subject of the study
- The scope of the study
- The purpose of the study
- The methods used
- The results obtained (informative abstract only)
- The recommendations made, if any (informative abstract only)

Do not include the following kinds of information:

- A detailed discussion or explanation of the methods used
- Administrative details about how the study was undertaken, who funded it, who worked on it, and the like, unless such details have a bearing on the purpose of the report
- Illustrations, tables, charts, maps, and bibliographic references

Because abstracts may be published independently of the main document, it would make no sense if they referred to any visual material found in the report; therefore, the abstract must make no reference to such material.

WRITER'S CHECKLIST: Writing Abstracts

Because readers of abstracts do not yet know anything about your document, except what its title announces, you should include the following information:

- ☐ The subject
- ☐ The scope
- ☐ The purpose
- ☐ The methods used
- ☐ The results obtained [informative abstract only]
- ☐ The recommendations made, if any [informative abstract only]

Do not include the following kinds of information:

- ☐ A detailed discussion or explanation of the methods used
- ☐ Administrative details about how the research was undertaken, who funded it, who worked on it, and the like, unless such details have a bearing on the document's purpose
- ☐ Illustrations, tables, charts, maps, and bibliographic references
- ☐ Any information that does not appear in the original document

Writing Style

Write the abstract after finishing the report. Otherwise, the abstract may not accurately reflect the final report. Begin with a topic sentence that announces at least the subject and scope of the report. Then, using the major and minor heads of your table of contents to distinguish primary from secondary ideas, decide what material is relevant to your abstract. Write clearly and concisely, eliminating unnecessary words and ideas, but do not become so terse that you omit articles (*a, an, the*) and important transitional words and phrases (*however, therefore, but, in summary*). Write complete sentences, but avoid stringing a group of short sentences end to end; instead, combine ideas by using subordination and parallel structure. As a rule, spell out most acronyms and all but the most common abbreviations (°C, °F, mph). Finally, as you summarize, keep the tone and emphasis consistent with the original report. For additional advice, review Summarizing in Chapter 11 on page 451.

Table of Contents

A table of contents lists all the headings of the report in their order of appearance, along with their page numbers. It includes a listing of all front matter and back matter except the title page and the table of contents itself. The table of contents begins on a new right-hand page. Note that in Figure 13–5 the table of contents is numbered page v because it follows the abstract (page iii), and because page iv is blank.

Along with the abstract, a table of contents permits the reader to preview a report and to assess its interest to him or her. It also aids a reader who may want to look only at certain sections of the report. For this reason, the wording of chapter and section titles in the table of contents should always be identical to those in the text.

Sometimes, the table of contents is followed by lists of figures and tables contained in the report. These lists should always be presented separately, and a page number should be given for each item listed.

List of Figures

When a report contains more than five figures, list them, along with their page numbers, in a separate section beginning on a new page and immediately following the table of contents. Number figures consecutively with Arabic numbers. Figures include all illustrations — drawings, photographs, maps, charts, and graphs — contained in the report.

List of Tables

When a report contains more than five tables, list them, along with their titles and page numbers, in a separate section immediately following the list of figures (if there is one). Number tables consecutively with Arabic numbers.

TABLE OF CONTENTS

v

Figure 13–5   Table of Contents of a Formal Report

Foreword

A foreword is an optional introductory statement written by someone other than the author. The foreword author is usually an authority in the field or an executive of the company. The foreword author's name and affiliation and the date the foreword was written appear at the end of it. The foreword generally provides background information about the publication's significance and places it in the context of other works in the field.

Preface

A preface is an optional introductory statement that announces the purpose, background, or scope of the report. Sometimes a preface specifies the audience for whom the report is intended, and it may also highlight the relationship of the report to a given project or program. A preface may contain acknowledgments of help received during the course of the project or in the preparation of the report, and, finally, it may cite permission obtained for the use of copyrighted works. If a preface is not included, place this type of information, if it is essential, in the introduction (discussed later in this chapter).

The preface follows the table of contents (and the lists of figures or tables and foreword, if these are present). It begins on a separate page and is titled "Preface."

List of Abbreviations and Symbols

When the abbreviations and symbols used in a report are numerous, and when there is a chance that the reader will not be able to interpret them, the front matter should include a list of all abbreviations and symbols and what they stand for in the report. Such a list, which follows the preface, is particularly appropriate for technical reports whose audience is not restricted to technical specialists.

Figure 13–6 shows an example of a list of symbols that appear in a report as part of equations that calculate the transfer of heat and water vapor from the surface of cooling ponds. The list is made up of special symbols used in this report. The author assumes that the report readers have a technical education, however, because Btu (British thermal unit), Hg (chemical symbol for mercury), and similar terms are not identified.

■ Body

The body of a formal report includes the text and any accompanying headings, tables, illustrations, and references. In it the author introduces the subject, describes in detail the methods and procedures used, demonstrates how results

SYMBOLS

A	Pond surface area, ft² or acres
A_0	One-half the daily insulation, Btu/ft²
A_n	Surface area of nth segment of the plugflow model, ft²
C	Cloud cover in tenths of the total sky obscured
C_1	Bowen's ratio, 0.26 mmHg/°F
C_P	Heat capacity of water, Btu/lb/°F
E_1, E_2	Estimation of equilibrium temperatures using data from offsite and onsite records, respectively, °F
E(x)	Estimation of equilibrium temperature using monthly average meteorologic data, °F
e_a	Saturation pressure of air above pond surface, mmHg
e_s	Saturation pressure of air at surface temperature, T_s, mmHg
g	Skew coefficient
H	Heat content, Btu

vii

Figure 13–6   List of Abbreviations and Symbols

were obtained, and draws conclusions upon which any recommendations are based. The first page of the body is numbered page 1 in Arabic rather than Roman numerals.

Executive Summary

The body of the report begins with an executive summary that provides a more complete overview of a report than does either a descriptive or an informative abstract. The summary states the purpose of the investigation and gives major findings, conclusions, and recommendations, if any are to be made. It also provides an account of the procedures used to conduct the study. Although more complete than an abstract, the summary should not contain a detailed description of the work on which the findings, conclusions, and recommendations were based. The length of the summary is proportional to the length of the report; typically, the summary should be approximately 10 percent of the length of the report.

Some executive summaries are written to follow the organization of the report. Others highlight the findings, conclusions, and recommendations by summarizing them first, before going on to discuss procedures or methodology.

An executive summary enables people who may not have time to read a lengthy report to scan its primary points quickly and then decide whether they need to read the report in full or just certain sections of it.

The executive summary should be written so that it can be read independently of the report. It must not refer by number to figures, tables, or references contained elsewhere in the report. Because executive summaries are frequently read in place of the full report, all uncommon symbols, abbreviations, and acronyms must be spelled out.

Additional guidelines to keep in mind when writing an executive summary include the following:

- Write the executive summary last, after completing the report.
- Omit (or define) technical terminology if your readers include people unfamiliar with the topic of your report.
- Make the summary concise but not brusque. Be especially careful not to omit transitional words and phrases (*however, moreover, therefore, for example, in summary*).
- Do not include information that is not discussed in the report.

Figure 13–7 shows an executive summary of the report on the Ethics Program at Boeing Aircraft Corporation.

Introduction

The purpose of an introduction is to provide your readers with any general information they must have to understand the detailed information in the rest of the report. An introduction sets the stage for the report. In writing the introduction,

Figure 13–7
Executive
Summary of
a Formal
Report

Purpose

Background

Scope

Scope

Conclusions

EXECUTIVE SUMMARY

This report examines the nature and disposition of the 3,458 ethics cases handled by the Boeing Aircraft Corporation's ethics officers and managers during 20--. The purpose of this report is to provide Boeing's Ethics and Business Conduct Committee with the information necessary for assessing the effectiveness of the first year of the company's Ethics Program.

Effective January 1, 20--, the Ethics and Business Conduct Committee (the Committee) implemented a policy and procedures for the administration of Boeing's new Ethics Program. The purpose of the Ethics Program, established by the Committee, is to "promote a positive work environment that encourages open communication regarding ethics and compliance issues and concerns." The Office of Ethics and Business Conduct was created to administer the Ethics Program. The director of the Office of Ethics and Business Conduct, along with seven ethics officers throughout the corporation, was given the responsibility for the following objectives:

- Communicate the values and standards for Boeing's Ethics Program to employees.
- Inform employees about company policies regarding ethical business conduct.
- Establish companywide channels for employees to obtain information and guidance in resolving ethics concerns.
- Implement companywide ethics-awareness and education programs.

Employee accessibility to ethics information and guidance was available through managers, ethics officers, and an ethics hotline.

Major ethics cases were defined as those situations potentially involving serious violations of company policies and/or illegal conduct. Examples of major ethics cases included cover-up or defective workmanship or use of defective parts in products; discrimination in hiring and promotion; involvement in monetary or other kickbacks; sexual harassment; disclosure of proprietary or company information; theft; and use of corporate Internet resources for inappropriate purposes, such as conducting personal business, gambling, or access to pornography.

Minor ethics cases were defined as including all reported concerns not classified as major ethics cases. Minor ethics cases were classified as informational queries from employees, situations involving coworkers, and situations involving management.

The effectiveness of Boeing's Ethics Program during the first year of implementation is most evidenced by (1) the active participation of employees in the program and the 3,458 contacts employees made regarding ethics concerns through the various channels available to them, and (2) the action taken in the cases reported by employees, particularly the disposition of the 30 substantiated major ethics cases. Disseminating information about the disposition of ethics cases, particularly information about the severe disciplinary actions taken in major ethics violations, sends a message to employees that unethical and/or illegal conduct will not be tolerated.

1

Figure 13–7
(continued)

Based on these conclusions, recommendations for planning the second year of the Ethics Program are (1) continuing the channels of communication now available in the Ethics Program, (2) increasing financial and technical support for the Ethics Hotline, the most highly utilized mode of contact in the ethics cases reported in 20--, (3) disseminating this report in some form to employees to ensure their awareness of Boeing's commitment to uphold its Ethics Policy and Procedures, and (4) implementing some measure of recognition for ethical behavior, such as an "Ethics Employee of the Month" award to promote and reward ethical conduct.

*Recommen-
dations*

2

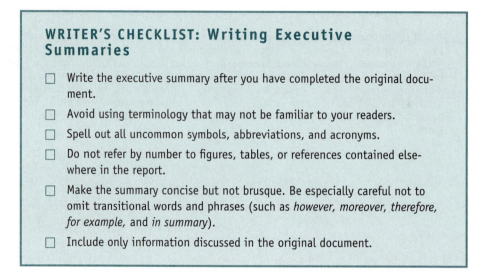

you need to state the subject, the purpose, the scope, and the way you plan to develop the topic. You may also describe how the report will be organized, but, as with the descriptive abstract, exclude the findings, conclusions, and recommendations. Figure 13–8 shows the introduction to the report on the Boeing Ethics Program. Note that the contents of the introduction and the contents of the preface may overlap in some cases.

Introducing the Subject

The introduction should state the subject of the report. However, it should also include necessary background information on the definition, history, or theory of the subject that provides context for the reader.

Stating the Purpose

The statement of purpose in your introduction should function as a topic sentence does in a paragraph. It should make your readers aware of your goal as they read your supporting statements and examples. It should also tell them why you are writing about the subject and whether your material provides a new perspective or clarifies an existing perspective.

Stating the Scope

This information tells the reader how much or how little detail to expect. Does your report present a broad survey of the topic, or does it concentrate on one part of the topic? Once you state your scope, stop. Save the details for the main body of the report.

**Figure 13–8
Introduction
to a Formal
Report**

INTRODUCTION

This report examines the nature and disposition of the 3,458 ethics cases handled company-wide by Boeing's ethics officers and managers during 20--. The purpose of this report is to provide the Ethics and Business Conduct Committee with the information necessary for assessing the effectiveness of the first year of Boeing's Ethics Program. Recommendations are given for the Committee's consideration in planning for the second year of the Ethics Program.

Purpose

Ethics and Business Conduct Policy and Procedures

Effective January 1, 20--, the Ethics and Business Conduct Committee (the Committee) implemented Policy NB-AAG-200 and Procedure NB-ACG-202 for the administration of Boeing's new Ethics Program. The purpose of the Ethics Program, established by the Committee, is to "promote a positive work environment that encourages open communication regarding ethics and compliance issues and concerns" (Boeing's "Ethical Business Conduct").

Background

The Office of Ethics and Business Conduct was created to administer the Ethics Program. The director of the Office of Ethics and Business Conduct, along with seven ethics officers throughout Boeing, was given the responsibility for the following objectives:

- Communicate the values and standards of Boeing's Ethics Program to employees.
- Inform employees about company policies regarding ethical business conduct.
- Establish companywide channels for employees to obtain information and guidance in resolving ethics concerns.
- Implement companywide ethics-awareness and education programs.

Employee accessibility to ethics information and guidance became the immediate and key goal of the Office of Ethics and Business Conduct in its first year of operation. The following channels for contact were set in motion during 20--:

Background

- Managers throughout Boeing received intensive ethics training; in all ethics situations employees were encouraged to go to their managers as the first point of contact.
- Ethics officers were available directly to employees through face-to-face or telephone contact, to managers, to callers using the ethics hotline, and by email.
- The Ethics Hotline was available to all employees, 24 hours a day, 7 days a week, to anonymously report ethics concerns.

Confidentiality Issues

Boeing's Ethics Policy ensures confidentiality and anonymity for employees who raise genuine ethics concerns. Procedure NB-ACG-202 guarantees appropriate discipline, up to and including dismissal, for retaliation or retribution against any employee who properly reports any genuine ethics concern.

(continued)

Figure 13–8
(continued)

Documentation of Ethics Cases

The following requirements were established by the director of the Office of Ethics and Business Conduct as uniform guidelines for the documentation by managers and ethics officers of all reported ethics cases:

Methodology

- Name, position, and department of individual initiating contact, if available
- Date and time of contact
- Name, position, and department of contact person
- Category of ethics case
- Mode of contact
- Resolution

Managers and ethics officers entered the required information in each reported ethics case into an ACCESS database file, enabling efficient retrieval and analysis of the data.

Major/Minor Category Definition and Examples

Major ethics cases were defined as those situations potentially involving serious violations of company policies and/or illegal conduct. Procedure NB-ACG-202 requires notification of the Internal Audit and the Law Departments in serious ethics cases. The staffs of the Internal Audit and the Law Departments assume primary responsibility for managing major ethics cases and for working with the employees, ethics officers, and managers involved in each case.

Methodology

Examples of situations categorized as major ethics cases:

- Cover-up of defective workmanship or use of defective parts in products
- Discrimination in hiring and promotion
- Involvement in monetary or other kickbacks from customers for preferred orders
- Sexual harassment
- Disclosure of proprietary customer or company information
- Theft
- Use of corporate Internet resources for inappropriate purposes, such as conducting private business, gambling, or access to pornography

Minor ethics cases were defined as including all reported concerns not classified as major ethics cases. Minor ethics cases were classified as follows:

- Informational queries from employees
- Situations involving coworkers
- Situations involving management

4

Previewing How the Topic Will Be Developed

In a long report, you need to state how you plan to develop or organize your topic. Is the report an analysis of the component parts of some whole? Is it an analysis of selected parts (or samples) of a whole? Is the material presented in chronological order? Does it move from details to general conclusions, or from a general statement to the details that verify the statement? Does it set out to show whether a hypothesis is correct or incorrect? Stating your topic allows your readers to anticipate how the subject will be presented and gives them a basis for evaluating how you arrived at your conclusions or recommendations.

Text (Body)

Generally the longest section of the report, the text (or body) presents the details of how the topic was investigated, how the problem was solved, how the best choice from among alternatives was selected, or whatever else the report covers. This information is often clarified and further developed by the use of illustrations and tables and may be supported by references to other studies.

Most formal reports have no single best organization. How the text is organized will depend on the topic and on how you have investigated it. The text is ordinarily divided into several major sections, comparable to the chapters in a book. These sections are then subdivided to reflect logical divisions in your main sections. See the sample table of contents (Figure 13–5) for an example of how the text for the report on the Ethics Program at the Boeing Aircraft Corporation was organized. Figure 13–9 shows the body of the same report.

Headings

In the body of formal reports, the use of headings (or heads) is important. Dividing the text with headings makes the report much more accessible to the readers by (1) dividing the body into manageable segments, (2) calling attention to the main topics, and (3) signaling changes of topics. Especially for long and complicated reports, you may need several levels of headings to indicate major divisions and subdivisions of the topic. Make headings most effective by following these guidelines:

1. Use a new heading to signal a shift to a new topic. Use lower-level headings to signal shifts to new subtopics within a major topic.

2. Within a topic, keep all headings at one level parallel in their relationship to the topic. Note in the sample table of contents (Figure 13–5) that "ANALYSIS OF REPORTED ETHICS CASES" is followed by four parallel and lower-level headings, all bearing the same relation to the higher-level heading; they all pertain to the cases analyzed and to the type of analysis.

3. Avoid the use of too many headings or too many levels of headings. They can make the report look cluttered, subdividing the topic too often for your reader to be able to sort out major from subordinate ideas.

**Figure 13–9
Body of
a Formal
Report**

ANALYSIS OF REPORTED ETHICS CASES

Reported Ethics Cases by Major/Minor Category

Boeing ethics officers and managers companywide handled a total of 3,458 ethics situations during 20--. Of these cases, only 172, or 5 percent, involved reported concerns of a serious enough nature to be classified as major ethics cases (see Figure 1). Major ethics cases were defined as those situations potentially involving serious violations of company policy and/or illegal conduct.

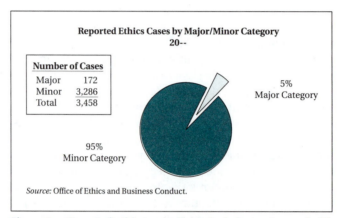

Figure 1.   Reported ethics cases by major/minor category in 20--.

Major Ethics Cases

Of the 172 major ethics cases reported during 20--, 57 percent, upon investigation, were found to involve unsubstantiated concerns. Incomplete information or misinformation most frequently was discovered to be the cause of the unfounded concerns of misconduct in 98 cases. Forty-four cases, or 26 percent of the total cases reported, involved incidents partly substantiated by ethics officers as serious misconduct; however, these cases were discovered to also involve inaccurate information or unfounded issues of misconduct. Only 17 percent of the total number of major ethics cases, or 30 cases, were substantiated as major ethics situations involving serious ethical misconduct and/or illegal conduct (Boeing "20-- Ethics Hotline Results") (see Figure 2).

5

**Figure 13–9
(continued)**

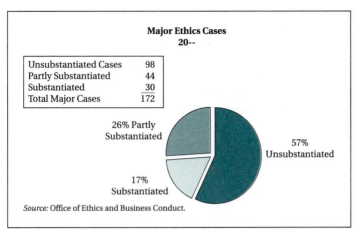

Figure 2.　Major ethics cases in 20--.

Of the 30 substantiated major ethics cases, seven remain under investigation at this time, and two cases are currently in litigation. Disposition of the remainder of the 30 substantiated reported ethics cases included severe disciplinary action in five cases: the dismissal of two employees and the demotion of three employees. Seven employees were given written warnings, and nine employees received verbal warnings (see Figure 3).

Figure 3.　Disposition of substantiated major ethics cases in 20--.

6

Figure 13–9
(continued)

Minor Ethics Cases

Minor ethics cases included those that did not involve serious violations of company policy and/or illegal conduct. During 20--, ethics officers and company managers handled 3,268 such cases. Minor ethics cases were further classified as follows:

- Informational queries from employees
- Situations involving coworkers
- Situations involving management

As might be expected during the initial year of the Ethics Program implementation, the majority of contacts made by employees were informational, involving questions about the new policies and procedures. These informational contacts comprised 55 percent of all contacts of a minor nature and numbered 2,148. Employees made 989 contacts regarding ethics concerns involving coworkers and 149 contacts regarding ethics concerns involving management (see Figure 4).

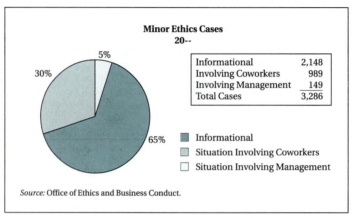

Figure 4.   Minor ethics cases in 20--.

Mode of Contact

The effectiveness of the Ethics Program rested on the dissemination of information to employees and the provision of accessible channels through which employees could gain information, report concerns, and obtain guidance. Employees were encouraged to first go to their managers with any ethical concerns, because those managers would have the most direct knowledge of the immediate circumstances and individuals involved.

Figure 13–9
(continued)

Other channels were put into operation, however, for any instance in which an employee did not feel able to go to his or her manager. The ethics officers companywide were available to employees through telephone conversations, face-to-face meetings, and email contact. Ethics officers also served as contact points for managers in need of support and assistance in handling the ethics concerns reported to them by their subordinates.

The Ethics Hotline became operational in mid-January 20-- and offered employees assurance of anonymity and confidentiality. The Ethics Hotline was accessible to all employees on a 24-hour, 7-day basis. Ethics officers companywide took responsibility on a rotational basis for handling calls reported through the hotline.

In summary, ethics information and guidance was available to all employees during 20-- through the following channels:

- Employee to manager
- Employee telephone, face-to-face, and email contact with ethics officer
- Manager to ethics officer
- Employee Hotline

The mode of contact in the 3,458 reported ethics cases was as follows (see Figure 5):

- In 19 percent of the reported cases, or 657, employees went to managers with concerns.
- In 9 percent of the reported cases, or 311, employees contacted an ethics officer.
- In 5 percent of the reported cases, or 173, managers sought assistance from ethics officers.
- In 67 percent of the reported cases, or 2,317, contacts were made through the ethics hotline.

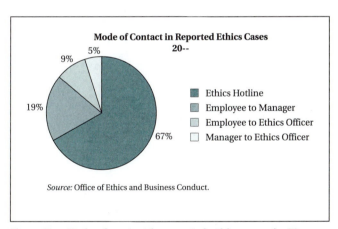

Figure 5.   Mode of contact in reported ethics cases in 20--.

Although various systems exist, the following guidelines for up to five levels of headings are common:

1. The first-level heading is in all-capital letters, centered, and underlined (or in 18-point boldface). There are two lines of space above and an extra line of space below the heading.

2. The second-level heading is in all-capital letters (or in 14-point boldface capital letters) and flush with the left margin on a line by itself. There is an extra line of space above and below the heading.

3. The third-level heading is in capital and lowercase letters (that is, the first letter of the first word and of every important word is capitalized as are prepositions and conjunctions of five letters or more). Like the first-level heading, this heading is underlined (or in boldface), but it is flush with the left margin on a line by itself and has one extra line of space above and below it.

4. The fourth-level heading is also in capital and lowercase letters as is the third-level heading, but it is neither underlined nor in boldface.

5. The fifth-level heading is indented as a paragraph, underlined (or in italic typeface). The first letter of the first word of the heading is capitalized; the remaining words are not (unless they are proper nouns). The heading is placed on the same line as the first sentence of the material it introduces. Therefore, a period generally appears after the heading to set it apart from the text that follows. There should be an extra line of space above the heading.

The following demonstrates two versions based on these guidelines:

<u>FIRST-LEVEL HEADING</u>

The text of the document begins here.

SECOND-LEVEL HEADING

The text of the document begins here.

<u>Third-Level Heading</u>

The text of the document begins here.

Fourth-Level Heading

The text of the document begins here.

    <u>Fifth-level heading.</u> The text of the document begins here.

FIRST-LEVEL HEADING

The text of the document begins here.

SECOND-LEVEL HEADING

The text of the document begins here.

Third-Level Heading

The text of the document begins here.

Fourth-Level Heading

The text of the document begins here.

Fifth-level heading. The text of the document begins here and continues normally to the next line of the page.

The *decimal numbering system* uses a combination of numbers and decimal points to subordinate levels of headings in a report. The system is used primarily for scientific and technical reports. The following outline shows the correspondence between different levels of headings and the decimal numbers used:

```
      1 FIRST-LEVEL HEADING
    1.1 Second-Level Heading
    1.2 Second-Level Heading
  1.2.1 Third-Level Heading
  1.2.2 Third-Level Heading
1.2.2.1 Fourth-Level Heading
1.2.2.2 Fourth-Level Heading
    1.3 Second-Level Heading
  1.3.1 Third-Level Heading
  1.3.2 Third-Level Heading
      2 FIRST-LEVEL HEADING
```

Although the second-, third-, and fourth-level headings are indented in an outline or table of contents, as headings they are flush with the left margin in the body of the report. For an example of how the headings help organize a portion of text, see the Writer's Guide at the end of this book.

Conclusions

The conclusions section of a report pulls together the results or findings presented in the report and interprets them in the light of its purpose and methods. Consequently, this section is the focal point of the work, the reason for the report in the first place. The conclusions must grow out of the findings discussed in the body of the report; moreover, they must be consistent with what the introduction stated as the purpose of the report and the report's methodology. For instance, if the introduction stated that the report's objective was to assess the market for a new product, then the conclusion should focus on the appropriateness or lack of appropriateness for the product in the market examined; it should not discuss whether the company producing the product may need to be reorganized.

Recommendations

Recommendations, which are sometimes combined with the conclusions, state what course of action should be taken based on the results of the study. What consulting group should the firm hire for a special project? Which Web-page-design service should the company sign a contract with? What new and emerging markets should the firm target? Which make of delivery van should the company purchase to replace the existing fleet? The recommendations section says, in effect, "I think we should purchase this, or do that, or hire them."

The emphasis here is on the verb *should*. Recommendations advise the reader on the best course of action based on the researcher's findings. Generally, a decision-maker in the organization, or a customer or client, makes the final decision about whether to accept the recommendations.

Figure 13–10 shows the conclusions and recommendations from the report on the Boeing Ethics Program.

Explanatory Footnotes

Occasionally, you will need to offer an explanatory comment on an idea mentioned in the main body of the text. This type of footnote is generally placed at the foot of the page on which the comment occurs. See Chapter 11, page 481, for additional guidance on the purpose of these notes.

A description of the 76 variables identified for inclusion in the regression equations, together with their method of construction, data, source, means, and ranges, is given in Appendix A. The following discussion elaborates on those variables that proved most important in explaining housing-price variations.[1]

[1]The number in parentheses refers to the variable number as used in regression equations.

CONCLUSIONS AND RECOMMENDATIONS

The effectiveness of Boeing's Ethics Program during the first year of implementation is most evidenced by (1) the active participation of employees in the program and the 3,458 contacts employees made regarding ethics concerns through the various channels available to them, and (2) the action taken in the cases reported by employees, particularly the disposition of the 30 substantiated major ethics cases.

One of the 12 steps to building a successful Ethics Program identified by Frank Navran in *Workforce* magazine is an ethics communication strategy. Navran explains that such a strategy is crucial in ensuring

> that employees have the information they need in a timely and usable fashion and that the organization is encouraging employee communication regarding the values, standards and the conduct of the organization and its members (Navran 119).

The 3,458 contacts by employees during 20-- attest to the accessibility and effectiveness of the communication channels that exist in Boeing's Ethics Program.

An equally important step in building a successful ethics program is listed by Navran as "Measurements and Rewards," which he explains as follows:

> In most organizations, employees know what's important by virtue of what the organization measures and rewards. If ethical conduct is assessed and rewarded, and if unethical conduct is identified and dissuaded, employees will believe that the organization's principals mean it when they say the values and code of ethics are important (Navran 121).

Disseminating information about the disposition of ethics cases, particularly information about the severe disciplinary actions taken in major ethics violations, sends a message to employees that unethical and/or illegal conduct will not be tolerated. Making public the tough-minded actions taken in cases of ethical misconduct provides "a golden opportunity to make other employees aware that the behavior is unacceptable and why" (Ferrell and Gardiner 129).

With these two points in mind, I offer the following recommendations for consideration for plans for the Ethics Program's second year:

- Continuation of the channels of communication now available in the Ethics Program
- Increased financial and technical support for the Ethics Hotline, the most highly utiltized mode of contact in the reported ethics cases in 20--
- Dissemination of this report in some form to employees to ensure employees' awareness of Boeing's commitment to uphold its Ethics Policy and Procedures
- Implementation of some measure of recognition for ethical behavior, such as an "Ethics Employee of the Month," to promote and reward ethical conduct

9

Figure 13–10
Conclusions and Recommendations of a Formal Report

(continued)

To ensure that employees see the value of their continued participation in the Ethics Program, feedback is essential. The information in this annual review, in some form, should be provided to employees. Knowing that the concerns they reported were taken seriously and resulted in appropriate action by Ethics Program administrators would reinforce employee involvement in the program. While the negative consequences of ethical misconduct contained in this report send a powerful message, a means of communicating the *positive* rewards of ethical conduct at Boeing should be implemented. Various options for recognition of employees exemplifying ethical conduct should be considered and approved.

Continuation of the Ethics Program's successful 20-- operations, with the implementation of the above recommendations, should ensure the continued pursuit of the Ethics Program's purpose: "to promote a positive work environment that encourages open communication regarding ethics and compliance issues and concerns."

10

Figure 13–10   (continued)

Works Cited (or References)

If, in your report, you refer to material in or quote directly from a published work or other research source, you must provide a list of references in a separate section called Works Cited. If your employer has a preferred reference style, follow it; otherwise, use the MLA or APA documentation guidelines provided in Chapter 11. (Note: If you use the APA style, your list of works cited is titled "References.")

For a relatively short report, the Works Cited section should appear at the end of the report. See Figure 13–11 for the Works Cited section of the Boeing Ethics Program report. For a report with a number of sections or chapters, the Works Cited section should fall at the end of each major section or chapter. In either case, every Works Cited section should be labeled as such and should start on a new page. If a particular reference appears in more than one section or chapter, it should be repeated in full in each appropriate Works Cited section. One important reason for using footnotes and citing works in reports is that they help you avoid plagiarism. Plagiarism in a college course may result in formal academic misconduct charges; plagiarism on the job can get you fired. Plagiarism in some cases is illegal; at the very least, it is unethical. For detailed information about documenting sources, as well as plagiarism, see Chapter 11, pages 452 and 461–481.

■ Back Matter

The back matter of a formal report contains supplemental information, such as the location of additional information about the topic (bibliography), clarification of information contained in the report, and a more detailed explanation (appendix).

Appendixes

An appendix contains information that clarifies or supplements the text. Material typically placed in an appendix includes long charts and supplementary graphs or tables, copies of questionnaires and other material used in gathering information, texts of interviews, pertinent correspondence, and explanations too long for explanatory footnotes but helpful to the reader who is seeking further assistance or clarification.

The report may have one or more appendixes; generally, each appendix contains one type of material. For example, a report may have one appendix presenting a questionnaire and a second appendix presenting a detailed computer printout tabulating questionnaire results.

Place the first appendix on a new page directly after the bibliography. Each additional appendix also begins on a new page. Identify each appendix with a title and a heading. Appendixes are ordinarily labeled Appendix A, Appendix B, and so on. If your report has only one appendix, simply label it "Appendix," followed by the title. To call it Appendix A implies that an Appendix B will follow.

If there is only one appendix, the pages are generally numbered 1, 2, 3, and so

WORKS CITED

Boeing. "Ethical Business Conduct Program." 5 April 1998. <http://www.boeing.com/company offices/aboutus/ethics/nbacg2.htm>.

Boeing. "1995 Ethics Hotline Investigation Results." 5 April 1998. <http://www.boeing.com/ companyoffices/aboutus/funfacts/html/ethics.html>.

Ferrell, O. C., and Gareth Gardiner. In Pursuit of Ethics: Tough Choices in the World of Work. Springfield: Smith Collins, 1991.

Kelley, Tina. "Corporate Prophets, Charting a Course to Ethical Profits." The New York Times 8 Feb. 1998: BU12.

Navran, Frank. "12 Steps to Building a Best-Practices Ethics Program." Workforce Sept. 1997: 117–122.

11

Figure 13–11 Works-Cited Section of a Formal Report

forth. If there is more than one appendix, the pages are double-numbered according to the letter of each appendix (for example, the first page of Appendix B would be numbered B-1).

Bibliography

The bibliography is the alphabetical listing of all the information sources you consulted to prepare the report. Accordingly, the bibliography may be longer than the Works Cited section. Further, because it is arranged alphabetically, it enables a reader interested in seeing whether you consulted a particular source to locate it quickly. Like other elements in the front and back matter, the bibliography starts on a new page and is labeled by name.

Glossary

A glossary lists and defines selected terms found in the report. You should include a glossary in your report only if it contains many words and expressions that will be unfamiliar to your intended audience. Arrange the terms alphabetically, with each entry beginning on a new line. Then give the definitions after each term. The glossary, labeled as such, appears directly after the appendix and begins on a new page.

Even though the report may contain a glossary, the terms that appear in it should be defined when they are first mentioned in the text.

Index

An index is an optional alphabetical list of all the major topics and their subcategories discussed in the report. It cites the page numbers where discussion of each topic can be found and allows readers to find information on topics quickly and easily. The index is always the final section of a report.

■ Graphic and Tabular Matter

Formal reports often contain illustrations and tables that clarify and support the text. These materials may be numbered and sequenced in varying ways. The following guidelines show one conventional system for numbering and smoothly integrating such materials into the text. For a full discussion of the creation and use of illustrations, see Chapter 12.

Figures and Tables

Identify each figure with a title and a number, in Arabic numerals, above or below the figure. For fairly short reports, number figures sequentially throughout the report (Figure 1, Figure 2, and so forth). For long reports, number figures by chapter or by section. According to this system, the first figure in Chapter 1 would be Figure 1.1 (or Figure 1–1), and the second figure would be Figure 1.2 (or Figure 1–2). In Chapter 2, the first figure would be Figure 2.1 (or Figure 2–1), and so on.

In the text, refer to figures by number rather than by location ("Figure 2.1" rather than "the figure below"). When the report is typed, the figures may not fall exactly where you originally expected.

Identify each table with a title and a number, centering both of these lines above the table. For fairly short reports, number the tables sequentially throughout the report (Table 1, Table 2, and so on). For long reports, number tables by chapter or by section according to the system described for figure numbering. As with figures, refer to tables in the text by number rather than by location ("Table 4.1" [or "Table 4–1"] rather than "the above table").

CHAPTER 13 SUMMARY: Formal Reports

Formal reports are written accounts of major projects. Following a transmittal letter or memo, they ordinarily contain three parts: front matter, body, and back matter. Although all reports do not contain every possible component, the following are typical.

The front matter consists of

- ☐ Abstract
- ☐ Table of contents
- ☐ List of figures and tables
- ☐ Foreword
- ☐ Preface
- ☐ List of abbreviations or symbols

The body includes

- ☐ The text of the report divided into sections or chapters, including figures, tables, and explanatory footnotes
- ☐ Executive summary
- ☐ Introduction
- ☐ Conclusions
- ☐ Recommendations
- ☐ Explanatory footnotes
- ☐ Works Cited (or References)

The back matter consists of

- ☐ Appendixes
- ☐ Bibliography
- ☐ Glossary
- ☐ Index

■ Exercises

1. Complete the following audience-profile questionnaire for a (hypothetical) formal report that you have been asked to prepare. Briefly explain the topic of your formal report and then answer the following questions:
   - Who are your readers? Try to write a 75- to 100-word description.
   - What do your readers already know about the subject?
   - What do you want them to know?
   - What might be their attitude toward the topic? Explore several alternatives.
   - Why will they be reading the report?
   - How will their perception of the report affect the project?
   - Are you able to think like the readers to anticipate their questions?

2. Prepare a definition of the scope for a formal report that would explain the benefits, risks, and costs of establishing an onsite fitness center at a local business with more than 200 employees.

3. Prepare an outline for a formal report that will compare two locations in the country in which to locate an actual business. The final report would be a comparative analysis of at least two locations; however, you are only being asked to prepare the outline for the project.

4. Using the most recent formal report you have written, prepare a transmittal letter addressed to your instructor explaining what the report concerns. Include as an attachment to the letter the title page and table of contents for the report.

5. Write a brief narrative explaining why you think either the executive summary or the abstract is the most important single piece of a formal report.

6. Keeping in mind that presentation is an important part of a formal report, prepare a title page and bring it to class. Assume that the title page is for a hypothetical formal report that you are developing. Refer to page 557 in your text for guidelines as you design your title page.

7. Write a brief narrative identifying different types of formal reports. For each type, list different situations where it might be used.

8. Assume you are starting a business of your own. Write a formal report that explains what your business will be, and what city would be the best location for your business and why. Assume that you are preparing this report to attach to your request for funding from the Small Business Administration.

9. Write a formal report based on information you know about a business, an organization, a sports team, or a government agency that suggests ways to cut costs or improve its financial earnings.

■ In-Class Activities

1. In groups of three or four members, consider the following questions before the next class session:
   a. Why should a formal report contain a table of contents?
   b. What is the function of a preface in a formal report?

    c. When is a descriptive abstract more appropriate than an informative abstract?

    d. What types of information should not appear in an abstract?

    e. What function do heads perform in a formal report?

    f.   What is the difference between conclusions and recommendations?

    g. What is the difference between a Works Cited section and a bibliography section?

    h. What types of material should appear in an appendix?

    i.   What is the function of a glossary in a formal report?

    Choose a group recorder to submit your answers to your instructor.

2. For this exercise, bring to class a sample of a journal abstract concerning your major field of study—the abstract can be obtained at your library. Divide into teams with classmates who share a similar major area of study. (For example, business majors would form one group, health sciences majors another, agricultural interests another, engineering students another, and so forth.) If you have more than seven students in your group, you may divide into two smaller groups. Appoint a group leader and a group recorder. Review each abstract and then make the following observations about each:

    a. How many words are in the abstract?

    b. Identify whether the abstract is descriptive or informative. How do you know?

    c. Identify and summarize the purpose, scope, and methods of each topic.

    d. Is the abstract clear and concise?

    e. Does the abstract encourage you to read the rest of the report?

    f.   How would you improve the abstract?

3. Divide into groups of five or six members each. Assume that your campus is considering purchasing a laptop computer for each student and plans to require students to use them for class and for homework assignments. For the next 45 minutes (or time prescribed by your instructor), develop a formal-report outline for an extensive investigative report to be written on the topic. Brainstorm as a group to include all areas of research that your report will need to cover, including areas such as sources for funding, fees for students, computerized class and testing procedures, the future of existing campus computer labs, and so forth. Your instructor may ask you to share your group's outline with your classmates when completed.

4. As a class, discuss the executive summary shown in Figure 13–12. Assume that the audience is, for example, the board of directors of Amalgamated Life Insurance. Consider these questions:

    a. What is the introduction? Is the correct information included?

    b. Is the background information sufficient?

    c. What is the purpose of the report?

    d. What is the scope of the report?

    e. Are costs an important concern of this report?

    f.   Are the conclusions effective?

    g. How long would you expect the report to be?

5. Bring to class an example of a formal report that you find at a government, nonprofit, or corporate organization. (*Note:* You may find these on the Web.) Cut the report into its separate sections—headings, subheadings, tables, graphs, text, scope, topic sentences, paragraphs, etc.—and place the pieces in an envelope.

Figure 13–12
Executive Summary
(for Analysis)

EXECUTIVE SUMMARY

In recent years, insurance companies have been under increasing economic pressure to find better ways to minimize losses. Thus, Amalgamated Life Insurance Company, like others, has shown increased interest in the link between exercise and the health of those it insures. Despite the reported advantages to overall health of long-distance running, questions have been raised about the long-term physical impact on bones and joints resulting from this form of exercise. Could long-time runners develop osteoarthritis and degenerative joint disease? When Amalgamated considered underwriting life insurance for the U.S. Senior Olympic Marathon Team, it sought this information because although the athletes are in good physical condition now, the possibility exists that the strain on bones and joints from long-distance running could lead to bone and joint disease later.

This study, based on research done at Stanford University and the University of Florida, was undertaken to examine existing information on these effects so that Amalgamated could assess the insurance risk factors for insuring the U.S. Senior Olympic Marathon Team. The Stanford study investigated the connection between long-distance running and bone density and osteoarthritis (including cysts, bone spurs, joint-space narrowing, and sclerosis). The Florida study sought a possible link between running and degenerative joint disease. Based on the findings of these studies. Amalgamated might also prepare a booklet for its agents and clients about some of the effects of long-distance running on health.

The researchers at Stanford located 539 runners and 422 control subjects and evaluated them by questionnaires according to their exercise and dietary habits and their medical histories. This initial pool was screened and divided into two study groups of 41 each (18 women and 23 men) matched by age, race, sex, education, and occupation. The prevalence of sclerosis and bone-spur formation in the population at large made the inclusion of women in this study mandatory. Then all finalists were combined into an "all subjects" study group. All were weighed and given a physical examination. The impact of their weight on weight-bearing joints was calculated. The disability rate for runners and non-runners was also established. All participants also had their weight-bearing (ankles, knees, hips) and non-weight-bearing joints (hands) X-rayed. Finally, all were given bone-density tests. All medical and X-ray examinations were performed "blind," with the examiners unaware of the group to which those examined belonged.

In the Florida study, which focused on degenerative joint disease, all participants were located and evaluated by questionnaire according to whether or not they were runners. They also reported their medical, musculoskeletal, and injury histories. Only men were chosen because there is no difference in the occurrence of joint disease between men and women in the population at large. They were divided into two groups of 23 long-distance runners and 11 nonrunners. Each participant then had an extensive medical history taken and was given

1

(continued)

Figure 13–12
(continued)

both medical and X-ray examinations of hips, knees, ankles, and feet. As at Stanford, these were blind tests.

The test results from both studies showed that control subjects were more prone to increased spur formation, sclerosis, and joint-space narrowing than runners. They also had somewhat more bone degeneration than runners. Runners showed increased joint space and bone density. Female long-distance runners, however, had somewhat more sclerosis in knee joints and the lumbar spine area than did matched control subjects.

In general, the researchers concluded that long-distance running is associated with increased bone mineral and not with clinical osteoarthritis or degenerative joint disease, regardless of the mileage or number of years spent running. The data also support the role of exercise in retarding bone loss with aging and the value of exercise programs. The Stanford study recommends estrogen and calcium therapy for women after menopause to retard bone loss.

Based on the data from these studies, we can conclude that the life-insurance risk factors for bone and joint diseases in long-distance runners between age 50 and 72 are smaller than for nonrunners in this age group. Therefore, the Amalgamated Life Insurance Company should underwrite life insurance for the U.S. Senior Olympic Marathon Team. Amalgamated should also inform its agents and clients that an exercise program that includes long-distance running can be beneficial to their health.

2

Form groups of three or four members and exchange envelopes. Your task is to reassemble the report as quickly as possible. (Be sure to photocopy the report before you begin so that you can compare the original with the reassembled version.)

■ Research Projects

1. Write a formal report on a topic from your career field or other area of interest. You may want to use the topic you selected and the information you gathered in doing the exercises for Chapter 11. Prepare a topic outline for the report, and submit it for your instructor's review. Include at least the following elements in the report (plus any additional elements your report may require): title page, descriptive abstract, table of contents, preface, executive summary, heads, conclusions and/or recommendations, references, and bibliography. Create a transmittal letter for the report addressed to your instructor.

2. Use the following topics for brainstorming a subject for your own formal report. The suggestions listed here illustrate the types of report topics you may wish to select; choose or (preferably) develop a topic that interests you. For any of these topics, you must determine a hypothetical audience and organizational setting.
   - A comparative analysis of the most desirable place in the country to relocate an actual business (compare at least two locations).
   - A site analysis to show why a specific location would be appropriate to locate a particular type of business.
   - An analysis of the value of establishing a day-care facility for working parents at a local company.
   - The feasibility of establishing a new professional sports team in the area.
   - An analysis of campus cultural and entertainment activities, showing that some should be eliminated, added, or both.
   - An analysis of the job opportunities in a specific field (for example, law, finance, accounting). Use at least six authoritative (government, academic, etc.) sources in your analysis.
   - A report recommending the most useful personal computer or network for an actual local small business.
   - An analysis of technical training facilities (colleges, trade schools, private agencies, etc.) in the area that would support a high-tech company planning to relocate here.

3. Conduct research to prepare an analytical formal report that compares two possible courses of action. Make sure that you compare the options using methodology that you clearly define, justify, and explain.
   - Define your hypothetical company and case.
   - Define the criteria on which you base your research, given your company and its needs.
   - Compare and contrast available options.
   - Explain your conclusion and recommendations.

   Possible scenario: You work for a small company that has revenues of about $100 million in sales (and profits of about $4 million a year). Your company's sales force

numbers 20 members who collectively travel approximately 1,000 miles a week. Your company now needs a new fleet of cars, all the same make and model for the sales force. The cars should be economical, but large enough to accommodate the samples (of equipment, books, etc.). You have been asked to determine whether the fleet should be purchased or leased. Begin by selecting three or four makes and models of cars and, given a clearly defined basis of comparison, determine which car is the most cost effective and the most suitable choice for your company. Address your report to the president of the company and include your recommendation(s). Develop a profile of your company that will be full enough to incorporate into the background section of your report and in your cover memo to the president. Be sure to inform your reader(s) how and where you found the information that supports your recommendation—include this information in appropriate sections of your report.

4. For this research project, select your own topic. If you are currently preparing an investigative report or feasibility study at work (or elsewhere), you may use it for this project. You may also choose to work on a personal issue, such as your research into graduate school, or housing arrangements, or on a governmental issue in your community. You may not submit a document you have already prepared. Explain to your instructor in a cover memo whether this document is part of a longer document, whether its format or organization was predetermined, and whether it incorporates sections prepared by others. Explain how and where you gathered your information. Refer to this chapter to make certain that you include front matter, body, and back matter and all appropriate optional sections in your formal report. Your instructor may advise you on specific sections to include.

■ Web Projects

1. Using the *Occupational Outlook Handbook* at the Bureau of Labor Statistics at http://stats.bls.gov/ocohome.htm, write a formal report in which you analyze two different job positions in your major area of study. Include in your report the required background, working conditions, pay scale, geographic expectations, and job outlook. Prepare your report as if you are trying to decide objectively between two occupations and include a conclusion and recommendations section.

2. Using the Bureau of Economic Analysis at http://bea.doc.gov, select the "Overview of the Economy" section and write a report explaining the last three years of economic data for the United States covering production, purchases, prices, and personal income. Assume the report is for your area's "Business and Industry Council" conference that you will be attending in the future.

3. Find the Web sites of car makers. Choose three similar vehicles, each from a different manufacturer. Prepare a comprehensive outline of what you would include in a report for your boss if you had been asked to recommend one of the vehicles for the company to purchase for employee use. You may assume the company will be purchasing a dozen vehicles and your boss is requesting a mid-sized car with good trunk space.

4. You are a company manager in a small manufacturing firm (100 employees) and are part of your company's team assigned to gather information about retirement funding programs. Using the Web, find at least three different programs to compare. After reviewing the three different sites, make a list of all components that should be considered when your team makes a recommendation to your company president. For this report, you will be concerned more with programs available than with individual companies.

5. Write a brief narrative describing how you think the Internet has changed formal-report writing. Search the Web to discover formal reports available on the Web. List examples and provide a brief comparative analysis of each. Are Web sites referenced in formal reports? Include any aspects of the Internet that you think have changed formal-report writing in business and industry today.

14 Proposals

A proposal is a document written to persuade a reader to follow a plan or course of action. Your reader may be a colleague within your organization or a potential client outside the organization. If your objective is to persuade your organization's management to make a change or improvement or perhaps to fund a project you would like to launch, you would write an *internal proposal*. If your objective is to persuade a potential customer to purchase your products or services, you would write a *sales* or *external proposal*. A sales (external) proposal may be either unsolicited or solicited.

Because a proposal offers a plan to fill a need, readers will evaluate your plan based on how well you answer the following questions: *What* do you propose to do? *How* do you plan to do it? *When* do you plan to do it? *How much* will it cost?

To answer these questions effectively, make certain that your proposal is written at your readers' level of knowledge. If you have more than one reader — and proposals often require more than one level of approval — take all of them into account. For example, if your primary reader is an expert on your subject, but his or her supervisor is not, you would provide an executive summary. The executive summary precedes the proposal's introduction and offers a consolidated version of the proposal's main points in nontechnical language. For guidance in writing executive summaries, see Chapter 13, pages 567–570. You might also include a glossary of terms used in the body of the proposal, or an appendix that explains highly detailed information in nontechnical language. If your primary reader is not an expert but his or her supervisor is, write the proposal with the nonexpert in mind and include an appendix that contains the technical details.

Any proposal — whether it is an internal proposal or an external (sales) proposal, or whether it is short and uncomplicated or long and complex — should be carefully planned. A short or medium-length proposal typically consists of an introduction, a body, and a conclusion. A long proposal, as will be discussed, generally contains more parts to accommodate the increased variety of information it represents.

The *introduction* of a proposal should state your purpose and scope; it should state the problem you propose to solve and your solution to it. The introduction should indicate the dates on which you propose to begin and complete work on the project, any special benefits of your proposed approach, and the total cost of the project. If you are writing a sales proposal, the introduction could

Voices from the Workplace

Susan McLaughlin, The Seldi Group

As a partner in The Seldi Group, Susan McLaughlin teaches seminars on communication to people in business and industry and supervises a marketing-research operation. Susan spends a typical nonteaching day meeting with clients and writing sales proposals. Her objective in writing a proposal is to persuade potential clients to do business with The Seldi Group.

"At first, I really sweated blood writing proposals," she says, "but I learned that simple logic is the answer. In the opening, I state the problem the client needs help with, as I understand it. Then, in the body of the proposal, I explain how I propose to solve the client's problem and what it will cost. Finally, in the closing, I offer to provide anything else that might be needed and thank the client for the opportunity to bid for the job."

She adds, "The really important thing about a proposal is its tone. Both the content and the tone must be persuasive, convincing the client that you not only have the solution to the problem but that you are capable of doing the job. The way you present your ideas is as important as the ideas themselves. You must support your appeal with logic, facts, statistics, and examples wherever possible."

Entry-Level
Terry Kalna, ISL United States, Inc.

As a senior account executive, Terry Kalna represents the country's leading open wheel racing series, CART, for the Swiss sports marketing company, ISL Marketing AG. He is responsible for generating millions of dollars in sponsorship revenue, which requires that he spend a lot of time working with current and prospective clients, on the phone and face-to-face. Another major part of his job is to write persuasive sales proposals.

"Proposals are one of the most important facets of the sales process. When soliciting companies that receive between 20 and 30 proposals per day, a proposal that is concise, unique, and exciting may be your only ticket in their door. The marketing or advertising executives reading your proposal have little time, so you must condense your thoughts into short and easily readable pieces. It is imperative that the client understand your message quickly and thoroughly.

"Typically, I try to draw on my audience's emotions by highlighting the glamour and passion of our sport. It is also essential that I establish a connection between my reader's products and services and what our company has to offer." Terry advises: "It is important to understand the needs of the company you are approaching — and here you function as a consultant — working with your client to understand your client's goals while highlighting what your company can offer to help meet those goals. This helps you to build a solid trust with your client, enabling you to take your proposal to the next level: the face-to-face meeting. I always request a meeting at the closing of my proposal and am certain to be proactive, letting the client know that I will follow up."

Learn about ISL at http://www.isl/world.com/homepage.html (select the marketing area for information about CART). Explore the CART open wheel racing site at http://www.cart.com.

also refer to any previous positive association your company may have had with the potential customer.

The *body* of a proposal should explain in detail (1) what products and services you are offering (if you are writing a sales proposal), (2) how the job will be done, (3) the procedures you will use to perform the work and the materials that you will use (if applicable), (4) a schedule indicating when each stage of the project would be completed, and (5) a breakdown of the costs of the project.

The *conclusion* should emphasize the benefits of your solution, products, or services, and should persuade the reader to take action. The conclusion should have an encouraging and confident tone. If you are concluding a sales proposal, express your appreciation for the opportunity to submit the proposal and your confidence in your company's ability to do the job. You might add that you look forward to establishing good working relations with the customer and that you would be glad to provide any additional information that might be needed. Your conclusion could also review any advantages your company may have over its competitors. It should specify the time period during which your proposal can be considered a valid offer. If any supplemental material (such as blueprints or price sheets) accompany the proposal, include a list of them at the end of the proposal.

WRITER'S CHECKLIST: Writing Proposals

A proposal is a plan to fill a need. Whether it is written to someone within or outside of your organization, your proposal should address the following questions:

☐ what you propose to do

☐ how you plan to do it

☐ when you plan to do it

☐ how much it will cost

■ Persuasive Writing

A proposal, by definition, is persuasive writing because you are attempting to convince your readers to do something. Your goal is to prove to your readers that they need what you are proposing to do, and that it is practical and appropriate. For an unsolicited proposal, you may even need to convince your readers that they have a problem serious enough to require a solution. You would then offer your solution by first building a persuasive case demonstrating the logic of your approach.

In persuasive writing, the way you present your ideas is as important as the ideas themselves. You must support your appeal with logic and a sound presentation of facts, statistics, and examples. Your supporting evidence must lead logically, even inevitably, to your conclusions and your solutions. Give your evidence in descending order of importance; that is, begin with the most important evidence and end with the least. Avoid ambiguity; do not wander from your main point; and, above all, never make trivial, irrelevant, or false claims. You should also acknowledge any real or potentially conflicting opinions; doing so allows you to anticipate and overcome objections to your proposal. By acknowledging negative details or opposing views, you not only gain credibility but also demonstrate good ethics.

The tone of your proposal should be positive, confident, and tactful. The following example demonstrates a tone that is arrogant and therefore inappropriate in a proposal:

■ The Qualtron Corporation has obviously not considered the potential problem of not having backup equipment available when a commercial power failure occurs. The corporation would also be wise indeed to give a great deal more consideration to the volume of output expected per machine.

The following version of the same passage is lacking in conviction and therefore equally inappropriate:

■ There could perhaps be a possibility of a problem with not having backup equipment available when commercial power fails. Also, it might be advisable to perhaps reconsider the volume of output expected per machine.

The following version of the same passage is positive, confident, and tactful:

■ The system should be redesigned so that it can provide backup equipment in the event of a commercial power failure. The system should also be based on realistic expectations of the output of each machine.

■ Internal Proposals

The purpose of an internal proposal is to suggest a change or an improvement within an organization. For example, an internal proposal can recommend one of the following:

1. A change in the way something is being done
2. That something new be done
3. That funding be authorized for a large purchase

An example of the first kind of proposal might recommend that the management of multiple manufacturing operations be decentralized. An example of the second kind might be a proposal to initiate telecommuting. The third kind might be a proposal to upgrade a computer system.

An internal proposal, often in memo format, is sent to a superior within the organization who has the authority to accept or reject the proposal.

Writing the Introduction

In the introduction of an internal proposal, you must establish that a problem exists that needs a solution. This section is sometimes called a "Problem Statement." (Internal proposals are also referred to as problem-solution memos.) If the readers who will judge your proposal are not convinced that there is a problem, your proposal will be unsuccessful.

After you identify the problem, summarize your proposed solution and indicate its benefits and total cost. Notice how the introduction in Figure 14–1 states the problem directly and then summarizes the writer's proposed solution.

Acme, Inc.
InterOffice Memo

To: Joan Marlow, Director, Human Resources Division
From: Leslie Galusha, Chief, Employee Benefits Department   *LG*
Date: June 12, 20--
Subject: Employee Fitness and Health-Care Costs

Introduction clearly states problem

Health-care and worker-compensation insurance costs at Acme, Inc., have risen 200 percent over the last five years. In 1995, costs were $600 per employee per year; in 2000, they have reached $1,200 per employee per year. This doubling of costs mirrors a national trend, with health-care costs anticipated to continue to rise at the same rate for the next 10 years. Controlling these escalating expenses will be essential. They are eating into Acme's profit margin because the company currently pays 80 percent of the costs for employee coverage.

Introduction summarizes proposal solution

Healthy employees bring direct financial benefits to companies in the form of lower employee insurance costs, lower absenteeism rates, and reduced turnover. Regular physical exercise promotes fit, healthy people by reducing the risk of coronary heart disease, diabetes, osteoporosis, hypertension, and stress-related problems. I propose that to promote regular, vigorous physical exercise for our employees, Acme implement a health-care program that focuses on employee fitness.

Figure 14–1   Introduction of an Internal Proposal

Writing the Body

The body of an internal proposal should offer a practical solution to the problem and provide as much detail as required to inform and persuade your readers. Try to put yourself in your readers' position—ask yourself what information *you* would need if you had to make the decision you are asking your readers to make. Then be sure to be as specific as possible. When applicable, include the following information:

1. Any background information needed to explain the extent of the problem
2. An explanation of the methods to be used in achieving the proposed solution
3. Information about equipment, material, and staff requirements
4. A breakdown of costs
5. A schedule for completing the project, possibly broken down into separate tasks

The sample body shown in Figure 14–2 is a continuation of the introduction in Figure 14–1.

<table>
<tr><td>

Background

The U.S. Department of Health and Human Services recently estimated that health-care costs in the United States will triple by the year 2013. Corporate expenses for health care are rising at such a fast rate that, if unchecked, in eight years they will significantly erode corporate profits.

Researchers have found that people who do not participate in a regular and vigorous exercise program incur double the health-care costs and are hospitalized 30 percent more days than people who exercise regularly. Nonexercisers are also 41 percent more likely to submit medical claims over $5,000 at some point during their careers than are those who exercise regularly.

U.S. companies are recognizing this trend. Tenneco, Inc., for example, found that the average health-care claim for unfit men was $1,003 per illness compared with an average claim of $562 for those who exercised regularly. For women, the average claim for those who were unfit was $1,535, more than double the average claim of $639 for women who exercised. Additionally, Control Data Corporation found that nonexercisers cost the company an extra $115 a year in health-care expenses.

These figures are further supported by data from independent studies. A model created by the National Institutes of Health (NIH) estimates that the average white-

</td></tr>
</table>

**Figure 14–2
Body of an Internal Proposal**

Information explaining extent of problem

(continued)

**Figure 14–2
(continued)**

collar company could save $466,000 annually in medical costs (per 1,000 employees) just by promoting wellness. NIH researchers estimated that for every $1 a firm invests in a health-care program, it saves up to $3.75 in health-care costs. Another NIH study of 667 insurance-company employees showed savings of $1.65 million over a five-year period. The same study also showed a 400-percent drop in absentee rates after the company implemented a companywide fitness program.

Solution

The benefits of regular, vigorous physical activity for employees and companies are compelling. To achieve these benefits at Acme, I propose that we choose from one of two possible options: build in-house fitness centers at our warehouse facilities, or offer employees several options for membership at a national fitness club.

In-House Fitness Center

*Explanation
of proposed
solution*

Building in-house fitness centers would require that Acme modify existing space in its warehouses and designate an area outside for walking and running. To accommodate the weight lifting and cardiovascular equipment and an aerobics area would require a minimum of 4,000 square feet. Lockers and shower stalls would also have to be built adjacent to the men's and women's bathrooms.

*Required
equipment
and material*

The costs to equip each facility are as follows:

1	Challenger 3.0 Treadmill	$4,395
3	Ross Futura exercise bicycles @ $750 each	$2,250
1	CalGym S-370 inner thigh machine	$1,750
1	CalGym S-260 lat pull-down machine	$1,750
1	CalGym S-360 leg-extension, combo-curl	$1,650
1	CalGym S-390 arm-curl machine	$1,950
1	CalGym S-410 side-lat machine	$1,850
1	CalGym S-430 pullover machine	$1,950
1	CalGym S-440 abdominal machine	$2,000
1	CalGym S-460 back machine	$2,000
1	CalGym S-290 chest press	$1,600
1	CalGym S-310 pectoral developer	$1,700
10	5710321 3-wide lockers @ $81 each	$810
4	5714000 benches and pedestals @ $81 each	$324
	Carpeting for workout area	$3,000
3	showers each, men's/women's locker room	$10,000
	Men's and women's locker-room expansion	$10,000
	Remodeling expenses	$350,000
	Total per Acme site	$398,979
	Grand Total	**$1,994,895**

*Breakdown
of costs*

Required staff

At headquarters and at the regional offices, our current Employee Assistance Program staff would need to be available several hours each workday to provide instructions for the use of exercise equipment. Aerobics instructors can be hired locally on a monthly basis for classes. The Buildings and Maintenance Department staff would clean and maintain the facilities.

**Figure 14–2
(continued)**

Fitness-Club Membership

Offering a complimentary membership to a national fitness club for all employees can also help reduce company health-care costs. AeroFitness Clubs, Inc., offer the best option for Acme's needs. They operate in over 45 major markets, with over 300 clubs nationwide. Most importantly, AeroFitness Clubs are located here in Bartlesville and in all four cities where our regional warehouses are located.

*Explanation
of proposed
solution*

AeroFitness staff are trained and certified in exercise physiology and will design individualized fitness programs for our employees. They offer aerobics classes for all levels, taught by certified instructors. Each club also features the latest in resistance exercise equipment from Nautilus, Universal, Paramount, and Life Fitness. Most AeroFitness facilities provide competition-size swimming pools, cushioned indoor running tracks, saunas, whirlpools, steam rooms, and racquetball courts.

Aerofitness offers a full range of membership programs that include corporate discounts. The basic membership of $400 per year includes:

- Unlimited use of exercise equipment
- Unlimited aerobic classes
- Unlimited use of racquetball, sauna, and whirlpool facilities
- Free initial consultation with an exercise physiologist for exercise and nutrition programs
- Free child care during daytime working hours

The club offers a full range of membership programs for companies. Acme may choose to pay all or part of employee membership costs. Three membership program options are available with AeroFitness:

- *Corporate purchase.* Acme buys and owns the memberships. With 10 or more memberships, Acme receives a 35-percent discount.

   Acme costs: $400 per employee × 1200 employees – 35% discount = $312,000 per year.*

- *Corporate subsidy.* Employees purchase memberships at a discount and own them. With 10 or more memberships, employees and the company each pay one-half of annual membership dues and receive a 30-percent discount off annual dues. The corporation also pays a one-time $50 enrollment fee for employees.

   Acme costs: $200 per employee × 1200 employees – 30% discount = $168,000 per year. The one-time enrollment fee of $50 per employee adds $60,000 to first-year costs.*

*Breakdown
of costs*

- *Employee purchase.* Employees purchase memberships on their own. With five or more memberships, employees receive 25 percent off regular rates. Club sales representatives conduct an onsite open enrollment meeting. Employees own memberships.

   Acme costs: None.

*Assumes that all employees will enroll.

Writing the Conclusion

The function of the conclusion in an internal proposal is to tie everything together, restate your recommendation, and close with a spirit of cooperation (offering to set up a meeting, supply additional information, or provide any other assistance that might be needed). Your conclusion should be brief, as in Figure 14–3.

Figure 14–4 shows a typical internal proposal. The proposal was written as a memo by a plant safety officer to the plant superintendent and recommends changes in the safety practices at the company.

Conclusion restates recommendation

Conclusion closes with spirit of cooperation

Conclusion and Recommendation

I recommend that Acme, Inc., participate in the corporate membership program at AeroFitness Clubs, Inc., by subsidizing employee memberships. By subsidizing memberships, Acme shows its commitment to the importance of a fit workforce. Club membership allows employees at all five Acme warehouses to participate in the program. The more employees who participate, the greater the long-term savings in Acme's health-care costs. Building and equipping fitness centers at all five warehouse sites would require an initial investment of nearly $2 million. These facilities would also occupy valuable floor space—on average, 4,000 square feet at each warehouse. Therefore, this option would be very costly.

Enrolling employees in the corporate program at AeroFitness would allow them to attend on a trial basis. Those interested in continuing could then join the club and pay half of the membership cost, less a 30-percent discount on $400 a year. The other half of the membership ($140) would be paid for by Acme. If an employee leaves the company, he or she would have the option of purchasing Acme's share of the membership. Employees not wishing to keep their membership could buy the membership back from Acme and sell it to another employee.

Implementing this program will help Acme, Inc., reduce its health-care costs while building stronger employee relations by offering employees a desirable benefit. If this proposal is adopted, I have some additional thoughts about publicizing the program to encourage employee participation. I look forward to discussing the details of this proposal with you and answering any questions you may have.

Figure 14–3   Conclusion of an Internal Proposal

**Figure 14–4
Internal
Proposal**

Memo

To: Harold Clurman, Plant Superintendent
From: Fred Nelson, Safety Officer   *FN*
Date: August 4, 20--
Subject: Safety Practices for Group 333

Many accidents and near-accidents have occurred in Group 333 because of the hazardous working conditions in this area. This memo identifies those hazardous conditions and makes recommendations for their elimination.

Hazardous Conditions

Employees inside the factory must operate the walk-along crane through aisles that are frequently congested with scrap metal, discarded lumber, and other refuse from the shearing area. Many surfaces in the area are oil-coated.

The containers for holding raw stock and scrap metal are also unsafe. On many of the racks, the hooks are bent inward so far that the crane cannot fit into them properly unless it is banged and jiggled in a dangerous manner. To add to the hazard, employees in the press group do not always balance the load in the racks. As a result, the danger of falling metal is great as the unbalanced racks swing practically out of control overhead. These hazards endanger employees in Group 333 and also employees in the raw-stock and shearing areas because the crane passes over these areas.

Hazards also exist in the yard and in the chemical building. The present method of dumping strip metal into the scrap bins is the most dangerous practice of all. To dump this metal, the tow-motor operator picks up a rack, with the rack straddling the tow-motor forks, and raises it over the edge of the scrap-metal bin. The operator then rotates the forks to permit the scrap metal to fall from one end of the rack. As the weight shifts, the upright frame at the other end of the rack slams into one of the tow-motor forks (now raised 12 feet above the ground, inside the scrap tub). This method of operation has resulted in two tow-motor tip-overs in the past month. In neither incident was the driver injured, but the odds are great that someone will be seriously harmed if the practice continues. Group 333 employees must also dump tubs full of scrap metal from the tow motor into the 10-foot-high scrap bins. In order to dump the metal on the tow-motor forks, the operator must raise the tubs high above his head. Because of the unpredictable way in which the metal falls from the tubs, employees have received many facial cuts and body bruises. Employees who work in the yard are also subject to danger in winter weather: All employees have been cut and bruised in falls that occurred as they were climbing up on scrap bins covered with snow and ice to dump scrap from pallets that had not been banded.

Introduction

*Explanation of
the problem*

(continued)

**Figure 14–4
(continued)**

Finally, nearly all Group 333 employees who must handle the caustic chemicals in the chemical building report damaged clothing and ruined shoes. Poor lighting in the building (the lights are nearly 20 feet above the floor), storage racks positioned less than two feet apart, and container caps incorrectly fastened have made these accidents impossible to prevent.

Recommendations

*Recommended
solution*

To eliminate these hazards as quickly as possible, I recommend that the following actions be taken:

1. That Group 333 supervisors rigorously initiate and enforce a policy to free aisles of obstructions
2. That all dangerous racks be repaired and replaced
3. That the Engineering Group develop a safe rack dumper
4. That heavy wire-mesh screens be mounted on the front of all tow motors
5. That Group 333 employees not accept scrap in containers that have not been properly banded
6. That illumination be increased in the chemical building and that a compulsory training program for the safe handling of caustic chemicals be scheduled

Conclusion

I would like to meet with you and the supervisor of Group 333 before the end of the month, as your schedule permits. You will have my complete cooperation in working out all of the details of the proposed recommendations.

Copy: Jim Hanchett, Supervisor, Group 333

WRITER'S CHECKLIST: Creating Internal Proposals

☐ Prepare your proposal for someone in the organization in a position to act on it

☐ Describe the problem clearly and unambiguously, providing any essential technical or historical background to clarify why the problem exists

☐ Offer your solution to the problem in sufficient detail that a decision-maker can evaluate your approach
  • Note any resource requirements necessary for a solution (personnel, equipment, materials)
  • Provide a schedule for completing the solution

☐ Specify the benefits expected to result from your solution

■ Sales Proposals

The *sales proposal* (or *external proposal*), one of the major marketing tools in use in business and industry, is a company's offer to provide specific goods or services to a potential buyer within a specified period of time and for a specified price. The primary purpose of a sales proposal is to demonstrate that the prospective customer's purchase of the seller's products or services will solve a problem, improve operations, or offer benefits.

Sales proposals vary greatly in length and sophistication. Some are a page or two written by one person; others are many pages written collaboratively by several people; still others are hundreds of pages written by a team of professional proposal writers. A short sales proposal might bid for the construction of a single home; a sales proposal of moderate length might bid for the installation of a network of computer systems; and a very long sales proposal might be used to bid for the construction of a multimillion-dollar shopping center.

Your first task in writing a sales proposal is to find out exactly what your prospective customer needs. To do that, survey your potential customer's business and needs. You must then determine whether your organization can satisfy the customer's needs. Your second task before preparing a sales proposal is to find out who your main competitors are. Then compare your company's strengths with those of competing firms, determine your advantages over them, and emphasize those advantages in your proposal. For example, say a small biotechnology company is bidding for the contract to supply several types of medical test kits to a regional hospital. The proposal writer who believes that the company has better-qualified personnel than its competitors might include the résumés of the key people who would be involved in the project, as a way of emphasizing that advantage.

Unsolicited and Solicited Sales Proposals

Sales proposals may be either unsolicited or solicited. Unsolicited proposals are not as unusual as they may sound: Companies often operate for years with a problem they have never recognized (unnecessarily high maintenance costs, for example, or poor inventory-control methods). You might prepare an unsolicited proposal for such a company if you were convinced that the potential customer could realize substantial benefits by adopting your solution to the problem. Of course, you would need to persuade the customer that a problem exists and that your proposal offers the best solution.

Many unsolicited proposals are preceded by a letter of inquiry to determine whether there is any potential interest. Once you have received a positive response, you would conduct a detailed study of the prospective customer's needs to determine whether you can be of help, and, if so, exactly how. You would then prepare your proposal on the basis of your study.

An unsolicited proposal should clearly identify the potential customer's problem. After stating the problem, the proposal must convince the customer that the problem needs to be solved. One way to do that is to emphasize the benefits that the customer will realize from the solution being proposed.

The other type of sales proposal—the solicited sales proposal—is a response to a request for bids on goods or services. To find the best method of doing a job and the most qualified company to do it, procuring organizations commonly ask competing companies to bid for a job by issuing a Request for Proposal (RFP). An RFP may be rigid in its specifications governing how the proposal should be organized and what it should contain, but it is normally quite flexible about the approaches that bidding firms may propose. Normally, the RFP simply defines the basic work that the procuring organization needs.

The procuring organization generally publishes its RFP in one or more journals, in addition to sending it to certain companies that have good reputations for doing the kind of work needed. Some companies and government agencies even hold a conference for the competing firms at which they provide all pertinent information about the job being bid for.

Managers interested in responding to RFPs regularly scan the appropriate publications and the Web. Upon finding a project of interest, an executive in the sales department obtains all available information from the procuring company or agency. The data are then presented to management for a decision on whether they are interested in the project. If the decision is positive, the technical staff is assigned to develop an approach to the work described in the RFP. The technical staff normally considers several alternatives, selecting the one that combines feasibility and a price that offers a profit for the bidder. The staff's concept is then presented to higher management for a decision on whether the company wishes to present a proposal to the requesting organization. If the decision is to proceed, preparing the proposal is the next step.

When you respond to an RFP, pay close attention to any specifications in the request governing the preparation of the proposal and follow them carefully.

Writing a Short Sales Proposal

Even a short and uncomplicated sales proposal should be carefully planned. The *introduction* should indicate the purpose and scope of the proposal. It should give the dates on which you propose to begin and complete work on the project, any special benefits of your proposed approach, and the total cost of the project. The introduction could also refer to any previous association your company may have had with the potential customer.

The *body* of a short sales proposal should itemize the products and services you are offering. It should include, if applicable, a discussion of the procedures you would use to perform the work and any materials to be used. It may also present a schedule indicating when each stage of the project would be completed. Finally, the body should include a precise breakdown of the costs of the project.

The *conclusion* should express your appreciation for the opportunity to submit the proposal and your confidence in your company's ability to do the job. You might add that you look forward to establishing good working relations with the customer and that you would be glad to provide any additional information that might be needed. Your conclusion could also review any advantages your company may have over its competitors. It should specify the time period during which your proposal can be considered a valid offer. If any supplemental materials, such as blueprints or price sheets, accompany the proposal, include a list of them at the end of the proposal. Figures 14–5 and 14–6 show two examples of short sales proposals.

Writing a Long Sales Proposal

While the simple sales proposal is typically divided into an introduction, body, and conclusion, the long sales proposal contains more parts to accommodate the increased variety of information that it must present. The long sales proposal may include some or all of the following sections:

- Cover letter or transmitted letter (Figure 14–7)
- Title page
- Executive summary or project summary (Figure 14–8)
- General description of products (Figure 14–9)
- Detailed solution or rationale (Figure 14–10)
- Cost analysis and budget (Figure 14–11)
- Delivery schedule or work plan (Figure 14–11)
- Site-preparation description (Figure 14–12)
- Training requirements (Figure 14–13)
- Statement of responsibilities (Figure 14–14)
- Description of vendor (Figure 14–15)
- Organizational sales pitch (optional) (Figure 14–15)
- Conclusion (optional)
- Appendixes (optional)

Optional sections may be included at the discretion of the proposal-writing team. A conclusion, for example, may be added to a very long proposal as a convenience to the reader, but it is not mandatory. A site-preparation section, however, is essential if the work proposed requires construction, remodeling, or such preparatory work as building rewiring before equipment can be installed.

A long sales proposal begins with a *cover letter*—sometimes called a *transmittal letter*—which expresses your appreciation for the opportunity to submit your proposal and for any assistance you may have received in studying the

Proposal
to Landscape the New Corporate Headquarters of the Watford Valve Corporation

Submitted to: Ms. Tricia Olivera, Vice President
Submitted by: Jerwalted Nursery, Inc.
Date Submitted: February 1, 20--

Introduction states purpose and scope of proposal, indicates when project can be started and completed

Jerwalted Nursery, Inc., proposes to landscape the new corporate headquarters of the Watford Valve Corporation, on 1600 Swanson Avenue, at a total cost of $14,871. The lot to be landscaped is approximately 600 feet wide and 700 feet deep. Landscaping will begin no later than April 30, 20--, and will be completed by May 31.

The following trees and plants will be planted, in the quantities and sizes given and at the prices specified.

Body lists products to be provided, cost per item

```
  4 maple trees (not less than 7 ft.) @ $110 each — $440
 41 birch trees (not less than 7 ft.) @ $135 each — $5,535
  2 spruce trees (not less than 7 ft.) @ $175 each — $350
 20 juniper plants (not less than 18 in.) @ $15 each — $300
 60 hedges (not less than 18 in.) @ $12 each — $720
200 potted plants (various kinds) @ $12 each — $2,400
```

Total Cost of Plants = $ 9,745
Labor = $ 5,126
Total Cost = $14,871

All trees and plants will be guaranteed against defect or disease for a period of 90 days, the warranty period to begin June 1, 20--.

The prices quoted in this proposal will be valid until June 30, 20--.

Conclusion specifies time limit of proposal, expresses confidence, and looks forward to working with prospective customer

Thank you for the opportunity to submit this proposal. Jerwalted Nursery has been in the landscaping and nursery business in the St. Louis area for 30 years, and our landscaping has won several awards and commendations, including a citation from the National Association of Architects. We are eager to put our skills and knowledge to work for you, and we are confident that you will be pleased with our work. If we can provide any additional information or assistance please call us at (809) 977-7271.

Figure 14–5   Short Sales Proposal

**Figure 14–6
Short Sales
Proposal
(Letter)**

Aerolite Bicycle Supply

1536 Bicycle Road
Bedford, Pennsylvania 16802

www.aerolitecycle.com
Phone 1-800-331-1221

November 22, 20--

Mr. Eric Shoop
Shoop Bicycle Shop
Squall Valley, Utah 19542

Dear Mr. Shoop:

Aerolite would like to congratulate you on the grand opening of your bicycle shop in Squall Valley, Utah. As you know, Aerolite makes quality equipment for bicycling. We carry bicycles, shorts, jerseys, helmets, gloves, shoes, and a variety of bicycle parts. We are confident that you will choose to carry our line of merchandise because it is quality equipment at an affordable price. *Introduction*

Bicycles

Our high-end bicycle frames are made of titanium, which makes them the strongest and the lightest frames on the market today. All of our other bicycle frames are made of butted aluminum, a very strong, anticorrosive, patented material that is very durable for all kinds of riding.

Our dual-suspended mountain bikes are unique because we developed the only Y frame used in such bikes. This frame eliminates the "pogoing" that compresses the rear shock in normal dual-suspended bikes instead of putting the power to the ground and to forward momentum. Our design puts the power the rider puts into the pedals straight to the ground, which pushes the rider forward instead of up and down.

Body

As you know, the components make a bike ride and function efficiently. All of our bikes have Natsuya components, ranging from the ALUMA at the low end to the XRT at the high end. Each component has a groupo, which includes derailleurs (front and back), shifters, gears, brakes, brake levers, crank, pedals, headset, handlebars, and wheel hubs. Every bike has a groupo for its specific level. The low-end bikes have an ALUMA groupo with aluminum frames. As the level of bike increases, the prices increase—but the quality goes right along with the price.

(continued)

**Figure 14–6
(continued)**

Mr. Eric Shoop   2   November 22, 20--

Most other bicycle manufacturers use chromoly steel frames, which are a lot heavier and not as strong as our butted aluminum frames. They use the same group, but the quality of the frames and the quality of the workmanship is not as evident as they are in Aerolite's bicycles.

Shorts

Our shorts, which are made from spandex material, are a great piece of merchandise for your store. They have fleece padding in the seat, which provides a softer ride. The shorts are of high quality, and your customers will be very pleased with the comfort they will receive from the shorts by Aerolite.

Jerseys

There is a huge market for jerseys in the mountains of Squall Valley because jerseys are worn by 75 percent of all mountain bikers and 93 percent of all road bikers. Our jerseys are made of an acrylic material that keeps the rider warm in the winter and cool in the summer. They pull the sweat away from the rider's body in summer and block the wind in winter.

Helmets

We sell the most ventral, the strongest, and the most comfortable helmets on the market. Our helmets can withstand a 300-foot vertical drop onto a pile of rocks without even getting scratched. Utah gets very hot in the summer, so your customers will really appreciate the availability of the coolest, strongest, most comfortable helmets on the market.

Gloves

All serious riders wear gloves to keep the sweat from running onto the handlebars and making them wet and slippery. Gloves also help protect the rider's hands if he or she should have an accident. The practicality of gloves makes them a very marketable product in a bicycle store, and Aerolite gloves are made with unique cotton-weave material coated with neoprene to keep the sweat in the gloves but off the hands.

Shoes

As you know, serious bikers have clipless pedals on their bikes. That means that serious bikers have to buy special shoes to ride with the clipless pedals. Our shoes have detachable soles so that riders need to replace only the sole of the shoe at the appropriate time. These shoes reduce the rider's costs by 25 percent, attracting them to your store.

**Figure 14–6
(continued)**

Mr. Eric Shoop   3   November 22, 20--

Please Consider Our Line of Merchandise

Utah is a rough and rugged state, with some awesome mountain-biking
trails. The riders there know what they want, and they are willing to pay for
equipment they know will stand up to the rough terrain of Squall Valley. You
can't go wrong by carrying our Aerolite line of bicycles and related merchandise; there is a huge market for our merchandise in your area. If you choose
to carry our line, you will be the exclusive Aerolite dealer between Awesome
View, California, and Boulder, Colorado. We offer higher quality equipment
than our competitors, and we are known around the world for the quality and
performance of our equipment.

I have enclosed a brochure that contains our entire line of merchandise. The
brochure includes prices and the recommended quantity of each piece of
merchandise a new shop should carry. I will send one of Aerolite's representatives to your store in three weeks to see if you are interested in carrying the
Aerolite line of merchandise and to answer any questions you may have.

Conclusion

Sincerely,

James Eugene

James Eugene
Sales Manager

customer's requirements. The letter should acknowledge any previous positive association with the customer. Then it should summarize the recommendations offered in the proposal and express your confidence that they will satisfy the customer's needs. Figure 14–7 shows the cover letter for the proposal illustrated in Figures 14–8 through 14–15—a proposal that the Waters Corporation of Tampa provide a computer system for the Cookson's chain of retail stores.

A title page and an *executive summary*—sometimes called a *project summary*—follow the cover letter. The title page contains the title of the proposal, the date, the company to which it is being submitted, your company's name, and any symbol or logo that identifies your company. The executive summary is written to the executive who will ultimately accept or reject the proposal. It should summarize in nontechnical language how you plan to approach the work. Figure 14–8 shows the executive summary of the Waters Corporation proposal.

If your proposal offers products as well as services, it should include a *general description* of the products, as in Figure 14–9. Following the executive summary and the general description, explain exactly how you plan to do what you are proposing. This detailed section, called the *detailed solution* or *rationale,* will be read by specialists who can understand and evaluate your plan, so you can feel free to use technical language and discuss complicated concepts. Figure 14–10 shows one part of the detailed solution appearing in the Waters Corporation proposal, which included several other applications in addition to the payroll application. Notice that the detailed solution, like the discussion in an unsolicited sales proposal, begins with a statement of the customer's problem, follows with a statement of the solution, and concludes with a statement of the benefits to the customer. In some proposals, the headings "Problem" and "Solution" are used for this section.

A *cost analysis* and a *delivery schedule* are essential to any sales proposal. The cost analysis—also called a *budget*—itemizes the estimated cost of all the products and services that you are offering; the delivery schedule—also called a *work plan*—commits you to a specific timetable for providing those products and services. Figure 14–11 shows the cost analysis and delivery schedule of the Waters Corporation proposal.

If your recommendations include modifying your customer's physical facilities, you would include a *site-preparation description* that details the modifications required. In some proposals, the headings "Facilities" and "Equipment" are used for this section.

If the products and services you are proposing require training the customer's employees, your proposals should specify the *required training* and its cost. Figure 14–12 shows the site-preparation section and Figure 14–13 the training-requirements section of the Waters' proposal.

To prevent misunderstandings about what you and your customer's responsibilities will be, you should draw up a *statement of responsibilities* (Figure 14–14), which usually appears toward the end of the proposal. Also toward the end of the proposal is a *description of the vendor,* which gives a description of your company, its history, and its present position in the industry. The description-of-the-

**Figure 14–7
Cover Letter
for a Long
Sales
Proposal**

The Waters Corporation

17 North Waterloo Blvd.
Tampa, Florida 33607
Phone: (813) 919-1213 Fax: (813) 919-4411
www.waters.corp.com

September 1, 20--

Mr. John Yeung, General Manager
Cookson's Retail Stores, Inc.
101 Longuer Street
Savannah, Georgia 31499

Dear Mr. Yeung:

The Waters Corporation appreciates the opportunity to respond to Cookson's Request for Proposal dated July 26, 20--. We would like to thank Mr. Becklight, Director of your Management Information Systems Department, for his invaluable contributions to the study of your operations that we conducted before preparing our proposal.

It has been Waters' privilege to provide Cookson's with retail systems and equipment since your first store opened many years ago. Therefore, we have become very familiar with your requirements as they have evolved during the expansion you have experienced since that time. Waters's close working relationship with Cookson's has resulted in a clear understanding of Cookson's philosophy and needs.

Our proposal describes a Waters' Interactive Terminal/Retail Processor System designed to meet Cookson's network and processing needs. It will provide all of your required capabilities, from the point-of-sale operational requirements at the store terminals to the host processor. The system uses the proven Retail III modular software, with its point-of-sale applications, and the superior Interactive Terminal, with its advanced capabilities and design. This system is easily installed without extensive customer reprogramming.

The Waters' Interactive Terminal/Retail Processor System, which is compatible with much of Cookson's present equipment, not only will answer your present requirements but will provide the flexibility to add new

(continued)

**Figure 14–7
(continued)**

Mr. J. Yeung
Page 2
September 1, 20--

features and products in the future. The system's unique hardware modularity, efficient microprocessor design, and flexible programming capability greatly reduce the risk of obsolescence.

Thank you for the opportunity to present this proposal. You may be sure that we will use all the resources available to the Waters Corporation to ensure the successful implementation of the new system.

Sincerely yours,

Janet A. Curtain

Janet A. Curtain
Executive Account Manager
General Merchandise Systems
JCurtain@netcom.TF.com

**Figure 14–8
Executive
Summary of
a Long Sales
Proposal**

EXECUTIVE SUMMARY

The Waters' 319 Interactive Terminal/615 Retail Processor System will provide your management with the tools necessary to manage people and equipment more profitably with procedures that will yield more cost-effective business controls for Cookson's.

The equipment and applications proposed for Cookson's were selected through the combined effort of Waters' and Cookson's Management Information Systems Director, Mr. Becklight. The architecture of the system will respond to your current requirements and allow for future expansion.

The features and hardware in the system were determined from data acquired through the comprehensive survey we conducted at your stores in February of this year. The total of 71 Interactive Terminals proposed to service your four store locations is based on the number of terminals currently in use and on the average number of transactions processed during normal and peak periods. The planned remodeling of all four stores was also considered, and the suggested terminal placement has been incorporated into the working floor plan. The proposed equipment configuration and software applications have been simulated to determine system performance based on the volumes and anticipated growth rates of the Cookson's stores.

The information from the survey was also used in the cost justification, which was checked and verified by your controller, Mr. Deitering. The cost effectiveness of the Waters Interactive Terminal/Retail Processor System is apparent. Expected savings, such as the projected 45-percent reduction in sales audit expenses, are realistic projections based on Waters' experience with other installations of this type.

Figure 14–9
General-
Description-
of-Products
Section of a
Long Sales
Proposal

GENERAL SYSTEM DESCRIPTION

The point-of-sale system that Waters is proposing for Cookson's includes two primary Waters' products. These are the 319 Interactive Terminal and the 615 Retail Processor.

Waters' 319 Interactive Terminal

The primary component in the proposed retail system is the Interactive Terminal. It contains a full microprocessor, which gives it the flexibility that Cookson's has been looking for.

The 319 Interactive Terminal provides you with freedom in sequencing a transaction. You are not limited to a preset list of available steps or transactions. The terminal program can be adapted to provide unique transaction sets, each designed with a logical sequence of entry and processing to accomplish required tasks. In addition to sales transactions recorded on the selling floor, specialized transactions such as theater-ticket sales and payments can be designed for your customer-service area.

The 319 Interactive Terminal also functions as a credit authorization device, either by using its own floor limits or by transmitting a credit inquiry to the 615 Retail Processor for authorization.

Data-collection formats have been simplified so that transaction editing and formatting are much more easily accomplished. Mr. Sier has already been provided with documentation on these formats and has outlined all data-processing efforts that will be necessary to transmit the data to your current systems. These projections have been considered in the cost justification.

Waters' 615 Retail Processor

The Waters' 615 Retail Processor is a minicomputer system designed to support the Waters' family of retail terminals. The processor will reside in the computer room in your data center in Buffalo. Operators already on your staff will be trained to initiate and monitor its activities.

The 615 will collect data transmitted from the retail terminals, process credit and check authorization inquiries, maintain files to be accessed by the retail terminals, accumulate totals, maintain a message-routing network, and control the printing of various reports. The functions and level of control performed at the processor depend on the peripherals and software selected.

Figure 14–9
(continued)

Software

The Retail III software used with the system has been thoroughly tested and is operational in many Waters customer installations.

The software provides the complete processing of the transaction, from the interaction with the operator on the sales floor through the data capture on cassette or disk in stores and in your data center.

Retail III provides a menu of modular applications for your selection. Parameters condition each of them to your hardware environment and operating requirements. The selection of hardware will be closely related to the selection of the software applications.

PAYROLL APPLICATION

Current Procedure

Your current system of reporting time requires each hourly employee to sign a time sheet; the time sheet is reviewed by the department manager and sent to the Payroll Department on Friday evening. Because the week ends on Saturday, the employee must show the scheduled hours for Saturday and not the actual hours; therefore, the department manager must adjust the reported hours on the time sheet for employees who do not report on the scheduled Saturday or who do not work the number of hours scheduled.

The Payroll Department employs a supervisor and three full-time clerks. To meet deadlines caused by an unbalanced work flow, an additional part-time clerk is used for 20 to 30 hours per week. The average wage for this clerk is $8.00 per hour.

Advantage of Waters' System

The 319 Interactive Terminal can be programmed for entry of payroll data for each employee on Monday mornings by department managers, with the data reflecting actual hours worked. This system would eliminate the need for manual batching, controlling, and data input. The Payroll Department estimates conservatively that this work consumes 30 hours per week.

Hours per week	30
Average wage (part-time clerk)	×8.00
Weekly payroll cost	$240.00
Annual Savings	$12,480

Elimination of the manual tasks of tabulating, batching, and controlling can save 0.25 hourly units. Improved work flow resulting from timely data in the system without data-input processing will allow more efficient use of clerical hours. This would reduce payroll by the 0.50 hourly units currently required to meet weekly check disbursement.

Eliminate manual tasks	0.25
Improve work flow	0.75
40-hour unit reduction	1.00
Hours per week	40
Average wage (full-time clerk)	9.00
Savings per week	$360.00
Annual Savings	$18,720

TOTAL SAVINGS: $31,200

**Figure 14–11
Cost Analysis
and Delivery
Schedule of a
Long Sales
Proposal**

COST ANALYSIS

This section of our proposal provides detailed cost information for the Waters 319 Interactive Terminal and the Waters' 615 Retail Processor. It then multiples these major elements by the quantities required at each of your four locations.

319 Interactive Terminal

	Price	Maint. (1 yr.)
Terminal	$2,895	$167
Journal Printer	425	38
Receipt Printer	425	38
Forms Printer	525	38
Software	220	—
TOTALS	$4,490	$281

615 Retail Processor

	Price	Maint. (1 yr.)
Processor	$57,115	$5,787
CRT I/O Writer	2,000	324
Laser Printer	4,245	568
Software	12,480	—
TOTALS	$75,840	$6,679

The following breakdown itemizes the cost per store:

Store No. 1

Description	Qty.	Price	Maint. (1 yr.)
Terminals	16	$68,400	$4,496
Digital Cassette	1	1,300	147
Laser Printer	1	2,490	332
Software	16	3,520	—
TOTALS		$75,710	$4,975

Store No. 2

Description	Qty.	Price	Maint. (1 yr.)
Terminals	20	$85,400	$5,620
Digital Cassette	1	1,300	147
Laser Printer	1	2,490	332
Software	20	4,400	—
TOTALS		$93,590	$6,099

(continued)

Figure 14–11
(continued)

Store No. 3

Description	Qty.	Price	Maint. (1 yr.)
Terminals	17	$72,590	$4,777
Digital Cassette	1	1,300	147
Laser Printer	1	2,490	332
Software	17	3,740	—
TOTALS		$80,120	$5,256

Store No. 4

Description	Qty.	Price	Maint. (1 yr.)
Terminals	18	$76,860	$5,058
Digital Cassette	1	1,300	147
Laser Printer	1	2,490	332
Software	18	3,960	—
TOTALS		$84,610	$5,537

Data Center at Buffalo

Description	Qty.	Price	Maint. (1 yr.)
Processor	1	$57,115	$5,787
CRT I/O Writer	1	2,000	324
Laser Printer	1	4,245	568
Software	1	12,480	—
TOTALS		$75,840	$6,679

The following summarizes all costs:

Location	Hardware	Maint. (1 yr.)	Software
Store No. 1	$72,190	$4,975	$3,520
Store No. 2	89,190	6,099	4,400
Store No. 3	76,380	5,256	3,740
Store No. 4	80,650	5,537	3,960
Data Center	63,360	6,679	12,480
Subtotals	$381,360	$28,546	$28,100
TOTAL	$438,416		

DELIVERY SCHEDULE

Waters is normally able to deliver 319 Interactive Terminals and 615 Retail Processors within 90 days of the date of the contract. This can vary depending on the rate and size of incoming orders.

All the software recommended in this proposal is available for immediate delivery. We do not anticipate any difficulty in meeting your tentative delivery schedule.

Figure 14–12 Site-Preparation Section of a Long Sales Proposal

SITE PREPARATION

Waters will work closely with Cookson's to ensure that each site is properly prepared prior to system installation. You will receive a copy of Waters' installation and wiring procedures manual, which lists the physical dimensions, service clearance, and weight of the system components in addition to the power, logic, and environmental requirements. Cookson's is responsible for all building alterations and electrical facility changes, including the purchase and installation of communication cables, connecting blocks, and receptacles.

Wiring

For the purpose of future site considerations, Waters' in-house wiring specifications for the system call for two twisted-pair wires and 22 shielded gauges. The length of communications wires must not exceed 2,500 feet.

As a guide for the power supply, we suggest that Cookson's consider the following:

1. The branch circuit (limited to 20 amps) should service no equipment other than 319 Interactive Terminals.
2. Each 20-amp branch circuit should support a maximum of three 319 Interactive Terminals.
3. Each branch circuit must have three equal-size conductors—one hot leg, one neutral, and one insulated isolated ground.
4. Hubbell IG 5362 duplex outlets or the equivalent should be used to supply power to each terminal.
5. Computer-room wiring will have to be upgraded to support the 615 Retail Processor.

TRAINING

To ensure a successful installation, Waters offers the following training course for your operators.

Interactive Terminal/Retail Processor Operations

Course number: 8256
Length: three days
Tuition: $500.00

This course provides the student with the skills, knowledge, and practice required to operate an Interactive Terminal/Retail Processor System. Online, clustered, and stand-alone environments are covered.

We recommend that students have department-store background and that they have some knowledge of the system configuration with which they will be working.

Figure 14–13   Training-Requirements Section of a Long Proposal

RESPONSIBILITIES

Based on its years of experience in installing information-processing systems, Waters believes that a successful installation requires a clear understanding of certain responsibilities.

Generally, it is Waters' responsibility to provide its users with needed assistance during the installation so that live processing can begin as soon thereafter as is practical.

Waters' Responsibilities

- Provide operations documentation for each application that you acquire from Waters.
- Provide forms and other supplies as ordered.
- Provide specifications and technical guidance for proper site planning and installation.
- Provide advisor assistance in the conversion from your present system to the new system.

Customer's Responsibilities

- Identify an installation coordinator and system operator.
- Provide supervisors and clerical personnel to perform conversion to the system.
- Establish reasonable time schedules for implementation.
- Ensure that the physical site requirements are met.
- Provide competent personnel to be trained as operators and ensure that other employees are trained as necessary.
- Assume the responsibility for implementing and operating the system.

Figure 14–14 **Statement-of-Responsibilities Section of a Long Proposal**

DESCRIPTION OF VENDOR

The Waters Corporation develops, manufactures, markets, installs, and services total business information-processing systems for selected markets. These markets are primarily in the retail, financial, commercial, industrial, health-care, education, and government sectors.

The Waters' total system concept encompasses one of the broadest hardware and software product lines in the industry. Waters' computers range from small business systems to powerful general-purpose processors. Waters' computers are supported by a complete spectrum of terminals, peripherals, data-communication networks, and an extensive library of software products. Supplemental services and products include data centers, field service, systems engineering, and educational centers.

The Waters Corporation was founded in 1934 and presently has approximately 26,500 employees. The Waters' headquarters is located at 17 North Waterloo Boulevard, Tampa, Florida, with district offices throughout the United States and Canada. For a comprehensive listing of Waters' products and services, visit our Web site at www.waters.corp.com.

WHY WATERS?

Corporate Commitment to the Retail Industry

Waters' commitment to the retail industry is stronger than ever. We are continually striving to provide leadership in the design and implementation of new retail systems and applications that will ensure our users of a logical growth pattern.

Research and Development

Over the years, Waters has spent increasingly large sums on research-and-development efforts to assure the availability of products and systems for the future. In 20--, our research-and-development expenditure for advanced systems design and technological innovations reached the $70 million level.

Leading Point-of-Sale Vendor

Waters is a leading point-of-sale vendor, having installed over 150,000 units. The knowledge and experience that Waters has gained over the years from these installations ensure well-coordinated and effective systems implementations.

Figure 14–15   Description of Vendor and Organizational Sales Pitch of a Long Sales Proposal

vendor section typically includes a list of people or subcontractors and the duties they will be responsible for. The résumés of key personnel may also be placed here or in an appendix. Following this description, many proposals add what is known as an *organizational sales pitch.* Up to this point, the proposal has attempted to sell specific goods and services. The sales pitch, striking a somewhat different chord, is designed to sell the company and its general capability in the field. The sales pitch promotes the company and concludes the proposal on an upbeat note. Figure 14–15 shows the vendor description and sales-pitch sections of the Waters' proposal.

Some long proposals include a *conclusion* section that summarizes the proposal's salient points, stresses your company's strong points, and includes information about whom the potential client can contact for further information. It may also end with a request for the date work will begin should the proposal be accepted. Figure 14–16 shows the conclusion of the Waters' proposal.

Depending on length and technical complexity, some proposals include *appendixes* made up of statistical analyses, maps, charts, tables, and personnel résumés. As with reports, appendixes to proposals should contain only supplemental information; the primary information should appear in the body of the proposal.

■ MEETING THE DEADLINE: The Time-Sensitive Proposal

Proposal writers must give top priority to meeting the procuring organization's deadline, while also producing a high-quality, persuasive proposal likely to receive favorable evaluations. The following time-management strategies can help toward meeting these goals.

1. *Assign coordinators.* The project manager should immediately choose a writing coordinator (for example, a writing specialist) to organize the generation and production of text and graphics, and a compiler (often an administrative assistant) to integrate all sections and elements of the final proposal draft and to make sure that they adhere to the potential customer's requirements (such as those in a request for proposal or RFP).

2. *Hold an initial planning session.* The project manager should start the writing process by meeting with the coordinator, the compiler, the budget specialist, and the key contributors to introduce the project team members and set priorities, determine and delegate tasks, and set milestone deadlines for each task.

3. *Set priorities.* The proposal sections or features likely to weigh most heavily during the evaluation of the proposal should receive the most attention from the writers and the most space in the final product. At the beginning of the project, proposal writers need to decide which sections of the proposal will be of the greatest importance to reviewers. These are the sections that will require the most time to write. These sections also tend to be longer than

CONCLUSION

Waters welcomes the opportunity to submit this proposal to Cookson's. The Waters Corporation is confident that we have offered the right solution at a competitive price. Based on the hands-on analysis we conducted, our proposal takes into account your current and projected workloads and your plans to expand your facilities and operations. Our proposal will also, we believe, afford Cookson's with future cost-avoidance measures in employee time and in enhanced accounting features.

Waters has a proven track record of success in the manufacture, installation, and servicing of retail business information systems stretching over many decades. We also have a demonstrated record of success in our past business associations with Cookson's. We believe that the system we propose will extend and strengthen this partnership.

Should you require additional information about any facet of this proposal, please contact Janet A. Curtain, who will personally arrange to meet with you or arrange for Waters' technical staff to meet with or send you the information you need.

We look forward to your decision and to continued success in our working relationship with Cookson's.

Figure 14–16   Conclusion of a Long Sales Proposal

sections of lesser importance. For example, for a ten-page proposal including four sections, the two most important sections might be four pages each, while the two least important sections might be one page each.

4. *Delegate tasks.* To expedite research and writing, assign more than one person to work on each section, and allow them to work out a way to collaborate efficiently to meet their section deadline. This strategy is especially useful when proposal contributors have diverse schedules and areas of specialization. Often, two or three subject experts coauthor parts of a single section, with the writing coordinator ensuring that those parts result in a clear and coherent draft.

5. *Work out a schedule and sequence.* During the initial planning session, determine how much time each task is likely to require. Start work immediately on tasks likely to take a longer time to complete, but also begin to collect other important pieces, such as résumés, biographies, and project descriptions. Decide which tasks can be done simultaneously and which tasks must precede others. When establishing a schedule, work backwards from the proposal deadline, leaving at least a day for the proposal to reach its destination by express delivery, half a day before that for collecting company signatures and making multiple copies of the proposal, and a half a day before that for last-minute edits and proofreading.

6. *Use boilerplate material.* When possible, import into the proposal standard pieces of information from previous proposals, such as biographies and descriptions of past projects, and company goals and accomplishments. This is known as boilerplate material.

7. *Select the best media for interpersonal communication.* While collecting information and section drafts for the proposal, choose media according to how fast you need information or drafts. For example, if you need written material immediately, use email attachments or faxes; if you need written material within a day or two, interoffice mail or express mail or delivery services might suffice. If you need information immediately that is not yet in writing, rely on phone calls or in-person meetings.

8. *Track progress and deadlines.* Use email or phone messages periodically to send out reminders about deadlines, or as needed to prompt someone to deliver material that you need soon or right away. Hold interim meetings if doing so will speed up your work. If interim task deadlines are missed and you need information, materials, or finished products immediately, ask everyone on the project team to abandon other projects to devote full time and extra hours to the proposal effort, so that you can meet the final deadline.

Even when these strategies are used, problems can arise that jeopardize the quality of your proposal or your ability to meet the final deadline. After sending out the proposal, hold a debriefing session in which you identify those problems and plan strategies for avoiding them when planning and writing future proposals.

WRITER'S CHECKLIST: Meeting the Deadline

To create effective proposals under the pressure of a deadline, use the following guidelines:

☐ Assign project coordinators to ensure that all sections and elements are complete, consistent, and comply with the requirements of the request for proposal.

☐ Hold a planning meeting with the proposal team to assign work and establish due dates for all tasks.

☐ Set priorities so that the most important sections of the proposal receive adequate attention.

☐ Delegate work to ensure that subject-area experts are available within the schedule established to meet the deadline.

☐ Schedule the project so that work begins on the sections that will take the longest, doing as many sections as possible simultaneously.

☐ Use boilerplate as extensively as possible, being careful to adapt it to the prospective customer.

☐ Select the best media for proposal team communications.

☐ Track the status of each part of the proposal carefully, sending periodic reminders about upcoming deadlines.

CHAPTER 14 SUMMARY: Proposals

A proposal

☐ Is written to persuade a reader to follow a plan or course of action.

☐ Consists of the following parts (and may include additional parts, based on the needs of your topic):
- An **introduction** that states
  ☐ The problem you propose to solve and your solution to it.
  ☐ The dates on which you propose to begin and complete work.
  ☐ Any special benefits of your proposed approach.
  ☐ Total cost of the project.
  ☐ (If a sales proposal) any previous positive association between your company and the potential customer.

- A **body** that explains
  - ☐ (If a sales proposal) what products and services you are offering.
  - ☐ How the job will be done.
  - ☐ The procedures you propose to use to perform the work.
  - ☐ The materials that you will use (if applicable).
  - ☐ The schedule, breaking down each stage.
  - ☐ Detailed costs.
- A **conclusion** that emphasizes
  - ☐ The benefits of your solution, products, or services that persuades the reader to take action.
  - ☐ The advantages of your company over its competitors.
  - ☐ Your confidence in your ability—or, if a sales proposal, of your company's ability—to carry out the project.
  - ☐ Your appreciation for the opportunity to submit the proposal.
  - ☐ Your willingness to provide further information.

  and includes
  - ☐ The time period during which the proposal is valid.
  - ☐ Any supplemental materials.

An internal proposal

☐ Is written to a colleague within your organization.

☐ Is usually written to persuade management to make a change or improvement, or to fund a project that you would like to launch.

A sales (or external) proposal

☐ Is written to a potential client outside of your organization.

☐ Is written to persuade a potential customer to purchase your company's products or services.

☐ May be solicited or unsolicited.

☐ May be short or long, depending on the complexity of the topic.

■ Exercises

1. Write a proposal in which you recommend a change in a procedure. The procedure should be one with which you are familiar, either at school or at work. The proposal should state the nature of the problem and explain how the new procedure would be put into effect. Give at least three reasons for the change, and support your reasons with facts that show the advantages of your proposal. Address the proposal to a dean or other school official (if the proposal is school-related) or to your immediate supervisor (if the proposal is work-related).

2. Address an internal proposal to your boss recommending that your company begin a tuition-refund plan or technology-training program. Propose at least three major advantages to having either of these educational programs, and present them in decreasing order of importance.

3. Assume that you are a landscaping contractor and would like to respond to the following RFP, which appears in your local newspaper:

> Lawn-mowing agreement for the Town of Augusta, Oregon. Weekly mowing of 5 miles of Route 24 median and sidings, 10 acres in Willoughby Park, and 23 acres at Augusta Memorial Golf Course, May 30 through September 30. Proposals are due April 30.

Indicate in your proposal the number of labor-hours that you estimate the contract would require, what you would charge, the ability of your personnel and equipment to do the job, your firm's experience and qualifications, and the weekly schedule that you propose to follow.

4. Write a proposal in which you recommend a change in a government process— for example, in the way we pay our taxes, the way the census is completed, the way we vote, the way we become citizens. Be specific when listing the advantages of your idea. Address your short, informal proposal to a local, state, or federal legislator, as appropriate.

5. Write a specific proposal to change a rule or regulation of an organization to which you belong. This could be your school, your religious organization, a professional association, a fitness club, an athletic group, or any organization in which you are registered as a member. List the current rule or regulation, then present your proposed changes and explain why your new rule or regulation will be more effective. Address your short proposal to the president or head of the organization.

6. By definition, proposals are persuasive writing. In persuasive writing, the way that you present your ideas is as important as the ideas themselves. You must support your appeal with logic and a sound presentation of facts, statistics, and examples. Your supporting evidence must lead logically to your conclusions. Prepare a short, internal proposal written in memo form to your instructor. You must convince your instructor that your idea is valid based on facts and not emotion. Present as many logical reasons as possible in selling your idea. Choose one of the following issues, or develop a topic of your own:
   a. No class sessions should be held the last day before Christmas vacation.
   b. Students should automatically be excused from class on Mondays immediately following school vacations.
   c. Students should be allowed to bring snacks or soft drinks to class.
   d. There should be no penalty for missing class.
   e. Students should be allowed up to three days to submit papers late without penalty.
   f. If students have more than three tests in one week, permission should be granted to make up one exam the following week.
   g. If students are within three percentage points of reaching the next highest grade, extra-credit opportunities should be granted for the purpose of raising the grade.

h. Computer problems are a valid excuse for submitting homework late.

7. With attention to format, prepare three different versions of a title page as if you were submitting a proposal. All three versions should be visually appealing to the reader. The first version should include text only. The second version should include text and one graphic in black and white. The third version should include text and a different graphic than that used in the second version and should be prepared in color. Include in each of the versions:

   a. Title of proposal
   b. Your name
   c. Name of company you represent
   d. Date of submission
   e. Name of recipient
   f. Name of recipient's company

   You may develop your title using one of the following proposal ideas or provide one of your own.

   - Employee Health Care
   - Employee Financial Investment
   - Employee Day Care
   - Employee Food Vendor
   - Employee Fitness Center
   - Computer System
   - Wireless Communication System
   - Fleet of Vehicles
   - Environmental Clean Up or Pollution Control
   - Remodeling Existing Facility
   - New Facility Design
   - New Facility Construction

8. Your company recently discovered that July and January have the highest monthly rates of ambulance calls for employees. Two recurring problems have been identified, one for each month. In July of the last five years, an average of four ambulance calls were made because employees were dehydrated. It has been determined that the high temperatures in July are a contributing factor. In January of the last five years, an average of three ambulance calls were made because employees slipped on water-covered floors. It has been determined that employees entering the building with ice on their shoes are responsible for the water on the floors. Ambulance runs cost the company an average of $600 per occurrence.

   Your supervisor feels these accidents can be prevented by employees; however, the employees do not share this opinion. Your boss has asked you to provide a solution that would lower the number of ambulance calls in both July and January, and that would be affordable to the company and beneficial to the employees. Prepare your solution in the form of a memo directed to your supervisor.

9. One of the pieces of boilerplate information often included in a proposal is a chart showing the organizational format of the employees of the company. Using word-processing, presentations, or graphics software, develop an organizational chart based on the following information.

The Wesson Consulting firm consists of 29 employees.
- The principal employees are
  Joyce Maggle, President
  John Wanber, Vice President
  Sally Janes, C.P.A., Comptroller
  Sandra Mitchell, Chief Engineer
- The senior consultants are
  John Smit, Engineer
  Debbie Williams, Ph.D.
  Mary Rober, Ph.D.
  Samuel Ebbs, 20 years of experience with the company
  Tom Jewell, 20 years of experience with the company
- The associate consultants are
  Becky Crow, B.A.
  James Johns, B.Sc.
  Cris Widdel, M.S.
  Mark Mann, M.S.
  Fran Blackwell, M.S.

The remaining 15 employees are support staff: 2 accounting personnel, 2 computer specialists, 1 office manager, 9 clerical workers, and 1 mail clerk/maintenance chief.

Your organizational chart, which will be included in your company's upcoming proposals, should be well-designed and submitted on 8½-by-11 paper or in an electronic file. It may be in portrait or landscape orientation.

10. The purpose of this assignment is to give you practice in formatting lists of numbers. Using your word-processing or spreadsheet software, prepare a one-page cost analysis for a proposal. Your cost analysis should be well-formatted and include the following breakdown of costs for the project:
    - Cost of personnel or labor
    - Cost of new equipment
    - Cost of overhead
    - Total cost of project

    You may submit any amounts you wish in these categories and you may change the title of a category with the approval of your instructor. Each category except the "Total Cost" must contain at least four different line items. For example, cost of personnel or labor might include the hourly rate of the time the company president will spend on this project along with the cost of other staff specialists required on the project. The cost of overhead might include the cost of support staff used for this project, use of company vehicles, company computer time, cost of supplies, and so forth. The cost of new equipment would include the cost of anything purchased solely for the client or the cost of equipment to be used by your company specifically for this project. In preparing your cost analysis, keep in mind the importance of clarity for the client. Although you may use any numbers you wish in the line items, all subtotals should equal the total cost when added together.

■ In-Class Activities

1. In teams of five to seven members, develop an internal proposal asking the Dean's office to improve or upgrade a facility, technology, course offering, or other area. Your proposal is due in three weeks. Spend 45 minutes developing a plan for completing your group's proposal. Refer to Meeting the Deadline: The Time-Sensitive Proposal in this chapter, pages 625 and 627.
   a. Your team will need to assign a project manager, a writing coordinator, a compiler, and a budget specialist.
   b. Once chosen, the project manager will begin the session by introducing team members, setting priorities, and determining and delegating tasks.
   c. In a collective effort, make a list of the tasks that will need to be completed.
   d. Decide what sections will be included in the proposal.
   e. Develop a timeline including scheduling and sequencing of the tasks. Include any other details you feel are relevant as you develop your plan.
   As directed by your instructor, present your plan for how your team will meet the deadline orally to the class or submit the plan to your instructor. Submit the finished proposal to your instructor.

2. In teams of three to five members, review the Description of Vendor included in Figure 14–15, and develop and design an organizational sales pitch. Referring back to this chapter, develop a rough draft including an original layout and design created by your team. Set priorities for the information to be included and be creative in the manner you choose to present the information. Take 45 minutes to one hour to complete this assignment.

3. Often the appendix of a sales proposal will include a brief résumé of all of the key project personnel. During the next 30 minutes, assume that you are the project coordinator of a sales proposal related to your major area of study. Using no more than six to eight lines, list your name, current educational status, relevant job experience, and a personal mission statement as if it were to be included in the personnel page of an appendix to a proposal.

4. Divide into teams with classmates who share a similar major area of study (business majors would form one group, health sciences another, agricultural interests another, engineering students another, and so forth). If you have more than seven students in your group, divide into two smaller groups. During the next hour, your team assignment is to write a short proposal in the form of a persuasive letter directed to your instructor. In your letter, propose an overnight educational field trip to a place of interest. Include the following in your proposal:
   - Why this place is of educational value to your team
   - What you expect to learn from the trip
   - Suggested mode of travel, accommodations, and arrangements for meals
   - A breakdown of costs
   - Suggested sources for funding
   - Any other relevant points

5. In teams of five members or fewer, begin work on a proposal for a new cafeteria, health club, day-care center, or other amenity for your company, which has

approximately 200 employees. Appoint a project manager and a recorder and in the next 60 minutes, develop a detailed outline for your proposal. Assume that your proposal is an unsolicited, internal proposal. Include areas that will require further research for your team to complete this assignment during future class meetings.

■ Research Projects

1. Prepare a short proposal on one of the following topics (or on a topic of your choice):
   - A new human-resource policy manual for your company
   - A new vendor for your company's phone system, office supplies, or computer equipment
   - A new health-insurance provider for your company

   Your proposal should include a transmittal letter, an introduction, body, and conclusion. Assume that your proposal is a solicited internal proposal. Refer to this chapter for guidelines.

2. Divide into teams of six or fewer members with classmates who share a similar major area of study. As a group, investigate the continuing-education program available for your major area of study and submit to a professional association in your field a proposal detailing a specific, beneficial change.
   a. Your team will need to assign a project manager, a writing coordinator, one or more compilers, and a budget specialist.
   b. Once chosen, the project manager will begin the session by introducing team members, setting priorities, and determining and delegating tasks.
   c. As a group, make a list of the tasks that will need to be completed.
   d. Decide what sections will be included in the proposal.
   e. Develop a timeline including scheduling and sequencing of the tasks.
   f. Include any other details you feel relevant as you develop your plan.

   Your instructor will advise you whether your group should meet weekly or twice monthly, your proposal due date, and the components that are required in your proposal.

3. Within your major area of study, identify a problem that you feel needs to be solved. For example, in health care, the problem might be rising consumer costs; in agriculture, the problem might be the use of pesticides; in engineering, the problem might concern uniform measurement standards (metric and English units); in business, the problem might be how to best use Web technology; in human-service administration, perhaps the problem will be finding the best method to hire new employees for your company. Your assignment is to write a proposal offering a solution to the problem—so be sure to select a topic that is relevant to your interests and also challenging. Your instructor may want to approve your topic selection. Depending on the topic you select, assume that your proposal is internal, written to an outside vendor, or in response to a Request for Proposals from a government agency. Include the following in your proposal:
   - Transmittal letter
   - Executive summary

- Introduction, body, conclusion
- Cost analysis
- Timeline or schedule of delivery
- Description of vendor

Your completed proposal will be seven to ten pages long, with the executive summary less than one page single-spaced. Your introduction, body, and conclusion will be approximately three pages of text, 1½ spaced. Insert at least two visuals within the text.

4. Locate a professional in your major area of study who is involved with proposal writing. Schedule a 20-minute interview with that person, remembering to offer a telephone-interview option. Make a list of questions regarding the proposal-writing process, such as the following:
   - How does your interviewee's company use proposals?
   - What is the procedure for assigning proposals? Who writes them? Are all departments involved? Are specialists hired for writing proposals? What portions of proposals are boilerplate?
   - What advice would your interviewee offer about writing effective proposals?
   - What advice would your interviewee offer about writing effective proposals to meet a challenging deadline?

   Write a brief narrative summarizing the interview.

5. Numerous institutions and firms must dispose of hazardous wastes. Physicians' and dentists' offices; hospitals; service stations; medical, photographic, and testing laboratories; trucking firms; manufacturers; military bases; and your own college or university are all likely generators of hazardous wastes. For this assignment, write an unsolicited proposal to a local or national environmental group offering to identify the location of active hazardous-waste sites within a five- or ten-mile radius of your campus if the group will fund you. Also offer to determine the types of wastes that are routinely disposed of at each site. (Enlarge the search area if the suggested radius is too small.) You do not actually have to conduct the survey, but you must research the topic in sufficient detail to make the proposal credible enough to prompt an environmental organization to seriously consider funding your search. Include an estimated timetable for the survey, the methodology you plan to use (some or even all sites will be identified in various but scattered public records), the form in which you will submit the survey to the organization (for example, a written report with maps, photographs, or other visual aids), and an estimate for the cost of the survey based on the time and materials required.

■ Web Projects

1. The Small Business Administration (SBA) offers a brochure prepared to assist businesses who wish to participate in the Small Business Innovative Research, found online at http://www.sba.gov/SBIR/section03f06.html. Write a brief analysis of this Web site, with an emphasis on Section III, which includes general information on effective proposal writing.

2. The online Writer's Center at Colorado State University offers tips for business writing. Two areas particularly useful to proposal writing are executive summaries at http://www.colostate.edu/Depts/WritingCenter/references/documents.htm and tables and graphics at http://www.colostate.edu/Depts/WritingCenter/references/graphics.htm. After reviewing these Web pages, create a list of reminders for both writing executive summaries and creating tables and graphics. When you have completed your lists, write a brief narrative combining the information you gathered from this source with that from this chapter, that focuses on executive summaries and graphics in proposal writing.

3. Your company depends on government contracts for much of its business. Because competition in your field is becoming tougher and tougher, your boss has asked you to investigate the possibility of hiring professional government proposal writers to help secure future government contracts. Using the search words *government requests for proposals,* select at least three firms online who offer these services. Prepare a letter of inquiry for each in the form of emails detailing what your company would need to know before hiring a professional proposal writer.

4. Your small business is interested in changing its check-writing procedures from paper-based to electronic. You have been asked to investigate at least three online banking services and write a proposal letter to your boss recommending that your company use one of the banks you investigated. Include salient details such as how the process operates, its security guarantee, the cost of the service, and advantages over traditional banking methods.

5. An important part of writing government proposals is making certain that your company complies with the regulations of the U.S. Equal Employment Opportunity Commission (EEOC), the agency that enforces the federal laws that prohibit employment discrimination on the basis of an individual's race, color, religion, sex, national origin, age, or disability.

   Review the EEOC Web site at http://www.eeoc.gov. In a brief narrative, summarize the following issues presented by the EEOC in their Small Business Information section:

   - What laws does the EEOC enforce and do they apply to my business?
   - How does the EEOC count employees?
   - What employment records must I keep?
   - What documents must I file with the EEOC?
   - What are some kinds of employment discrimination?
     - What is age discrimination?
     - What is disability discrimination?
     - What is pregnancy discrimination?
     - What are racial and ethnic harassment?
     - What religious accommodations do I have to give my employees?
     - What is sexual harassment?
   - What is the Immigration Reform and Control Act and must my business comply with it?
   - How do I comply with the Americans with Disabilities Act?
   - If I've violated the law, what could happen?

- What is the Small Business Regulatory Enforcement Fairness Act?
- Do other federal agencies dealing with small businesses have Web sites that can help me?

6. Search the Web to find dependable information on writing sales proposals. Evaluate the sites that you encounter and share those that you find useful with your class in a brief presentation or by sending a group email. You may want to begin your search at the online Science, Industry, and Business Library at The New York Public Library at http://www.nypl.org/research/sibl or at the sales proposals page at Minnesota's Management Assistance Program for Nonprofits' "Free Management Library" at http://www.mapnp.org/library/sales/proposals.htm.

15 Presentations and Meetings

Although most of this book covers the principles of writing that work in business and industry, writing is not the sole means of communication in the workplace. Much information is presented orally as well, and what may seem like simple, everyday components of such communications—listening and responding effectively—are both critically important and not simple at all.

Writing and speaking have much in common. Both written and oral communications must be logically organized and are most effective when delivered clearly and succinctly. The principles of writing discussed throughout this text are also applicable to presentations in the workplace: Know your audience, organize your information, and determine the amount of information necessary to convey your message. However, there is also much that is different about presentations, and this chapter explores those elements unique to this form of communication. Oral communication is most widely used in the workplace for presentations and in leading meetings. Central to the success of both is effective listening.

■ Presentations

The steps required to prepare an effective presentation parallel the steps you follow to write a document. As with writing a document, first determine your purpose and analyze your audience when preparing for a presentation. Next find and gather the facts to support your point of view and proposal. Then logically organize your information. However, presentations differ from written documents in a number of important ways. They are intended for listeners, not readers. Because you're giving a talk rather than writing a memo or report, your manner of delivery, the way you organize the material, and your supporting visual aids require as much attention as your content.

Determining Your Purpose

Every presentation is given for a purpose—even if it is only to share information. To determine the purpose of your presentation, use the following questions on page 640 as a guide.

Voices from the Workplace

Paul B. Greenspan, TIS Worldwide

Paul B. Greenspan is vice president of sales with TIS Worldwide, an architect of Internet systems. Paul spends much of his time meeting with prospective and established customers, and with the staff of sales representatives that report to him. Strong oral communication and presentation skills are important to Paul's role at TIS. He has developed these skills through study and practice.

"I learned a lot of dos and don'ts in a course I once took on presentation skills. One important point I learned is that a good presenter uses techniques to minimize the amount of work the audience has to do. For example, I learned to use arresting visuals and to avoid long, bulleted lists that basically duplicate my notes. I have also learned that where a speaker stands in relation to his or her visual aids can either help or hinder the presentation. Body language is also important—how you use your arms, how you gesture. The 'big' gesture that may seem exaggerated to the presenter looks natural to the audience. Finally, you have to demand interactivity from your audience. The day of the 'droning, talking head' with an inch-thick stack of transparencies is gone forever."

To find out more about TIS Worldwide, visit their Web site at http://www.tisworldwide.com.

Entry-Level
Corey Ann Eaton, First Union Brokerage Services, Inc.

Corey Ann Eaton is a training analyst and technical writer for First Union Brokerage Services, Inc. Presentation software plays a crucial role in her development of course work when she trains operations personnel and stockbrokers. As a trainer, Corey spends time gathering information, developing the course, and delivering presentations to groups of 15 to 20 employees. The topics she addresses vary from systems and software, to operations, to "soft" topics, such as phone etiquette. Corey offers the following tips for using presentation software.

"Presentation software can assist you by prompting each new topic, leading the discussion, and ensuring no point is forgotten. If the audience leads the discussion away from the intended route, the presentation slides can move the discussion back on track.

"As a presenter, you should remember that the software is there to *assist* with your message, not deliver it for you. The easiest way to ensure this is to keep it simple. Use the software to make the most important messages clear, and don't allow yourself to put every point you need to make in the slide presentation; include only enough to prompt the information or discussion you are delivering.

"When writing the presentation, keep in mind the importance of concise and easily understood language. The audience will be attentive to the slide for only a few seconds and will shift its focus to your verbal message thereafter. The font (typeface) and background color you choose are important and should be associated with the message you are relaying, and the font should be simple, clean, and crisp. Imagine that you are sitting in the last row at the back of the room. Is the font still easy to read? If not, change it to a large, bold, and/or sans serif font. Regardless of how formal or creative you want to make the presentation, the slides should never distract from the message you are trying to convey."

To learn more about First Union Brokerage Services, Inc., visit their Web site at http://www.firstunion.com.

1. What do I want the audience to *know* when I've finished this presentation?
2. What do I want the audience to *believe* when I've finished this presentation?
3. What do I want the audience to *do* when I've finished this presentation?

Then, based on the answers to these questions, write a purpose statement that answers the questions *what* and *why.*

■ The purpose of my presentation is to explain to my classmates the various tasks I performed last semester as a part-time volunteer at the Maplewood Adult Day Care Center [*what*] so that other members of the class will want to become volunteers at Maplewood [*why*].

■ The purpose of my presentation is to convince my company's Chief Information Officer of the need to improve the appearance, content, and customer use of our company's Web site [*what*] so that she will be persuaded to include additional funds in the budget for site-development work next fiscal year [*why*].

Analyzing Your Audience

Once you determine the desired end result of the presentation, you need to analyze your audience so that you can tailor your presentation to your audience's needs. Ask yourself the following five questions about your audience:

1. What is your audience's level of experience or knowledge about your topic?
2. What is the general educational level and age of your audience?
3. What is the audience's attitude toward the topic you are speaking about, and—based on that attitude—what concerns, fears, or objections might your audience have?
4. Are there subgroups in the audience that might have different concerns or needs?
5. What questions could your audience ask about this topic?

Gathering Information

Now that you've focused the presentation, you need to find the facts that will support your point of view or the action you propose. While you gather information, keep in mind that you should give the audience only the facts necessary to accomplish your goals; too much information will overwhelm the audience, and too little information will leave the audience either with a sketchy understanding of your topic or with the feeling that you have not provided enough information to support the course of action you wish the audience to take. (For detailed guidance about gathering information, see Chapter 11, "Researching Your Subject.")

Structuring the Presentation

When structuring the presentation, keep the focus on your audience. As listeners, they remember openings and closings best because they are freshest at the outset and refocus their attention as you wrap up your remarks. Take advantage of this pattern. Give the audience a brief overview of your presentation at the beginning, use the body to develop your ideas, and end with a summary of what you covered and, if appropriate, a call to action.

Introduction

The introduction may include an opening—something designed to catch and focus the audience's attention. The following opening defines a problem:

■ You have to write an important report, but you'd like to incorporate the bulk of an old report into your new one. The problem is that you don't have an electronic version of the old report. You'll have to re-key many pages. You groan because that seems an incredible waste of time. Have I got a solution for you!

You could also have used any of the following types of openings:

- An *attention-getting statement:* As many as 50 million Americans have high blood pressure.
- A *rhetorical question:* Would you be interested in a full-sized computer keyboard that is waterproof, is noiseless, and can be rolled up like a rubber mat?
- A *personal experience:* As I sat at my computer one day last month deleting my eighth unwanted email (or spam) message of the day, I decided that it was time to find a solution to eliminate this time-waster that will work for you and me.
- An *appropriate quotation:* According to researchers at the Massachusetts Institute of Technology, "Garlic and its cousin the onion confer

---

ESL TIPS: Organizing a Presentation

- ■ When preparing for a presentation, follow the same guidelines that you follow for writing.
- ■ Use a logical structure based on that of the written essay: Include an introduction, a body, and a conclusion.
- ■ Be clear and direct, and use precise nouns.
- ■ Support your presentation with specific examples.
- ■ Between subtopics, use transitions to help your listeners understand how the parts are related.

major health benefits — including fighting cancer, infections, and heart disease."

(For additional examples, see Writing an Opening in Chapter 3.)

Following your opening, use the introduction to set the stage for your audience by giving an overview of the presentation. The overview may include general or background information that your audience will need to understand the more detailed information in the body of your presentation. It may also be an overview of how you've organized the material.

■ This presentation explains the options available to you, the employees of Acme Corporation, for making contributions through payroll deductions to a long-term retirement plan that will enhance the retirement income you will receive from Social Security and pension benefits.

■ This presentation will answer your questions:
  • How much can you save?
  • How much does Acme contribute to the plan?
  • What are your investment options?

Body

The body is the place to convince the audience to arrive at your conclusion. If there's a problem, demonstrate that it exists and offer a solution or range of possible solutions. If your introduction stated that the problem was low profits, high costs, outdated technology, or high employee absenteeism, use the following approach:

• Offer a solution.
  – Increase profits by lowering production costs.
  – Cut overhead to reduce costs or abolish specific programs or product lines.
  – Replace outdated technology or upgrade existing technology.
  – Offer employees more flexibility in their work schedules or other incentives.
• Prove your point.
  – Marshal the facts and data you need.
  – Present the facts and data using easy-to-understand visual aids.
• Call for action.
  – Do you want the audience to agree, to change their minds, to do something?
• Anticipate questions ("How much will it cost?") and objections ("We're too busy now. When will we have time to learn the new software?") and be ready for them.

Closing

The closing should achieve the goals of your presentation. If your purpose is to motivate the audience to take action, ask the audience to do what you want them to do; if your purpose is to get your audience to think about something, summarize what you want them to think about. Many presenters make the mistake of not actually closing—they simply quit talking, shuffle papers around, and then walk away.

Because your closing is what your audience is most likely to remember, it is the time to be strong and persuasive. Returning to the retirement savings plan example, consider the following possible closing:

- The next step to your future security . . .
  - Decide how much you can save each month.
  - Remember Acme's contribution.
  - Choose the investment options that best fit your needs.
  - ENROLL NEXT WEEK!

This closing brings the presentation full cycle and asks the audience to act on the information provided in the presentation—exactly what a closing should do.

Transitions

Planned transitions should appear between the introduction and the body, between the points in the body, and between the body and the closing. Transitions, simply a sentence or two, let the audience know that you're moving from one topic to the next. They also prevent a choppy presentation and provide you, the speaker, with assurance that you know where you're going and how to get there.

- Before getting into the specifics of the fund families available to you, I'd like to describe the investment goals and strategies of each. That information will provide you with the background you'll need to compare the differences among them to make an informed decision about what works best for you.

It is also a good idea to pause for a moment after you've delivered a transitional line between topics to let the audience shift gears with you. Remember, they don't know your plan.

The typical presentation follows a pattern made up of the components shown in Figure 15–1, although the number of slides and their content will vary depending on the speaker's topic. The complete presentation for the savings and investment program is shown in Figure 15–2.

Using Visual Aids

Well-planned visual aids add interest and emphasis to your presentation, and you can clarify and simplify your message because they communicate clearly, quickly, and vividly. Charts, graphs, and illustrations greatly increase audience

**Figure 15–1
Pattern for
a Typical
Presentation**

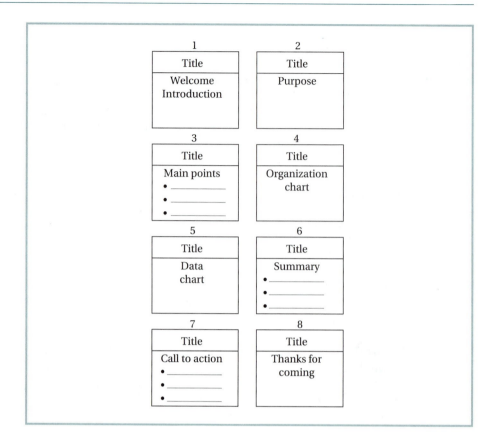

understanding and retention of the information, especially for complex issues and technical information that could otherwise be misunderstood or glossed over by your audience. A bar graph, pie chart, diagram, or concise summary of key points can eliminate misunderstanding and save many words.

You can create and present your visual aids in a variety of media, including flip charts, whiteboards and chalkboards, overhead transparencies, 35mm slides, and computer-presentation software.

Flip Charts

Flip charts are large sheets of white paper bound like a tablet and fastened to the top of an easel (see Figure 15–3). The presenter writes on the sheets with colored felt-tip pens, usually during the presentation. The charts are ideal for smaller groups in a conference room or a classroom. To avoid the distraction of writing as you speak, you can prepare text and sketches ahead of time on a series of sheets and flip through them during your presentation. Flip charts are also an ideal medium for brainstorming with your audience. You can fill sheet after sheet with

**Figure 15–2
Sample
Presentation**

EMPLOYEE BENEFITS

Acme Corporation

Presented by Laura Phelps

Office of Human Resources

Savings and Investment Program

Saving for Your Future

This slide show will explain our options for contributing to the employee savings plan through payroll deductions.

Acme Corporation considers this program a long-term retirement-oriented plan. It is intended to enhance your retirement security above the level of your pension and Social Security benefits.

(continued)

Figure 15–2
(continued)

Acme Corporation
Savings and Investment Program

Questions to Ask Yourself

- How much can I save?
- How much does Acme Corporation contribute?
- What are my investment options?

Acme Corporation
Savings and Investment Program

How Much Can I Save?

- Save from 2% to 20% of your gross earnings
- Elect to save on the following basis:
  - Pre-tax basis
  - After-tax basis
  - Combination of both

**Figure 15–2
(continued)**

Acme Corporation
Savings and Investment Program

How Much Does Acme Corporation Contribute?

- Acme Corporation matches 25¢ of every dollar you save each month!
- Example based on earning $2,000 per month.

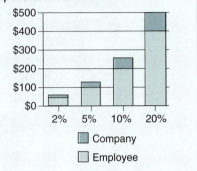

Acme Corporation
Savings and Investment Program

What Are My Investment Options?

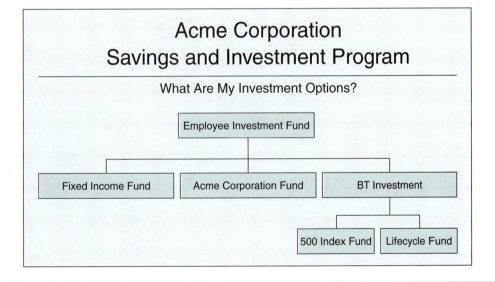

(continued)

Figure 15–2
(continued)

Acme Corporation
Savings and Investment Program

The Next Step to Your Future Security

- Decide how much you can save each month.
- Remember the company contribution.
- Choose the investment options that best fit your needs.
- ENROLL NEXT WEEK!

Acme Corporation
Thank You for Coming

Your Future Is Important to Us. . . .

- Consider your options.
- Enroll next week.
- Questions? Call or email the Benefits Office
  - 990-1200, extension 03
  - Email: benefits@acme.com

Figure 15–3
Flip Chart

ideas, tape them around the walls for everyone to see, and use a clean sheet or sheets to organize the ideas into an outline for follow-up work.

Whiteboard or Chalkboard

The whiteboard or chalkboard common to classrooms is convenient for creating impromptu sketches and for jotting notes during your presentation (see Figure 15–4). If your presentation requires extensive notes or complex drawings, create them before the presentation to minimize audience restlessness. Ensure before the presentation that you have ample chalk or marking pens.

Overhead Transparencies

Transparencies are page-size sheets of clear plastic on which the text and graphics for your presentation are copied using a computer printer or copy machine. During the presentation, you place the transparencies on an overhead projector (Figure 15–5) and the images are projected onto a screen or blank wall. The images can be black text on clear film to multicolored computer images.

Overheads are always prepared ahead of time so you could, depending on the complexity of the information you're discussing, create a series of overlays to explain a complex device or system as you add (or remove) one at a time. You can

Figure 15–4
Chalkboard

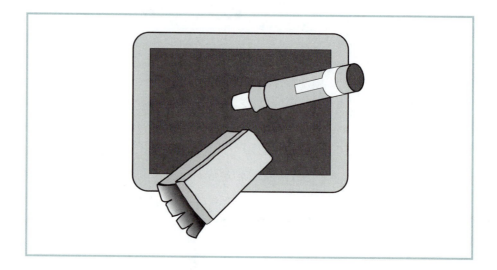

also lay a sheet of paper over a list of bulleted items on a transparency, uncovering one at a time as you discuss it, to focus audience attention on each point in the sequence.

Overhead transparencies are best seen in a darkened room, unlike flip charts and chalk- or whiteboards, which are best seen in a fully lighted room.

Slides

Slides refer to 2-inch by 2-inch 35mm film color transparencies inserted into a slide carousel on a slide projector and projected onto a screen or a blank wall. Color transparencies are especially useful if you need to include photographs in

Figure 15–5
Overhead-
Transparency
Projector

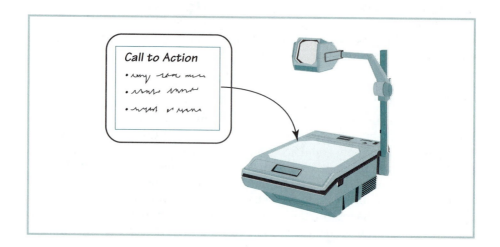

your presentation. As with overhead transparencies, they are best viewed in a darkened room. Slides also refer to the individual screens produced using presentation software, discussed in the next section.

Presentation Software

Visual information in workplace presentations is frequently displayed on computer monitors, for a small audience, or by projectors connected to a laptop computer that display the computer screen, for larger audiences (Figure 15–6). The software used to create computer presentations, such as PowerPoint, Corel Presentations, Freelance Graphics, and other packages, permits you to write most of a presentation with your word-processing program and create charts and graphs with data from spreadsheet software. These files can be imported into one of the presentation packages and formatted with standard templates and other aids that help you design effective visuals. These enhancements include a selection of typefaces, background textures and colors, and clip-art images. These images can also be printed out for use as overhead transparencies or on paper for use as handouts. (Figure 15–7 presents an example of a slide showing a bulleted list and

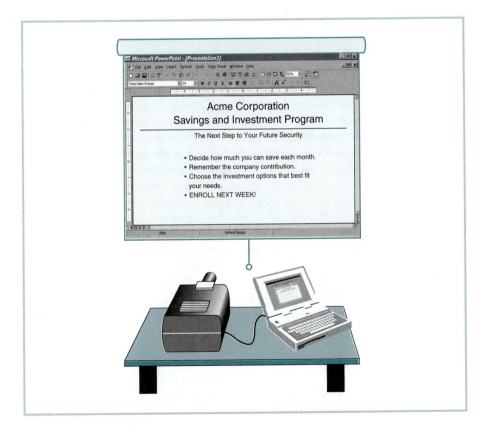

Figure 15–6 Computer Presentation Set-Up

**Figure 15–7
Presentation Slide
with Bulleted List
and Clip Art**

> ### Plain Language Award of the Month
>
> What Are the Criteria for the Award?
>
> Use "Plain Language Principles," such as--
>
> - Common, Everyday Words
> - Short Sentences
> - Active Voice
> - "You" and Other Pronouns (as appropriate)
> - Logical Organization
> - Easy-to-Read Design Features (lists and tables)
>
>

clip-art image.) In addition to helping with the layout, design, and format for your electronic slides, presentation software also permits you to add clip art, sound (including music), and video (such as animation). You can also convert the presentation to Web format and post it to an intranet site, a feature that makes your presentation accessible to a wide audience inside a company for viewing during the presentation or later. Avoid using too many enhancements because they could distract viewers from your message.

Be sure to integrate your visuals with your presentation when you rehearse. Practice loading the presentation and anticipate any technical difficulties that might arise. Should you encounter a technical snag during the presentation, stay calm and give yourself time to solve the problem. If you can't, say so and move on. As a backup, carry a copy of your electronic presentation printed out as transparencies in case there's a problem with the computer projection system. Also carry an extra copy of your presentation on a disk for backup.

Handouts

Handouts typically are paper copies of your presentation slides, although they may be a summary of key points, supporting data in tables, charts, and graphs, or other supplementary information. They benefit you and your audience by reinforcing what's said and by permitting your listeners to take notes and retain the material for future reference. They are usually distributed before the presentation, although some presenters distribute them afterward to avoid having the handouts distract their audience.

Delivering a Presentation

Once you've outlined and drafted your presentation and prepared your visuals, you are ready to think about practice and delivery techniques.

WRITER'S CHECKLIST: Creating Visuals for Presentations

☐ Use text sparingly. Instead of blocks of text, use bulleted or numbered lists and keep them parallel in content and grammatical form. Use numbers if sequence is important and bullets if not.

☐ Limit the number of bulleted or numbered items to five or six per slide. The slide should contain no more than 40 to 45 words. Any more will clutter the slide and force you to use a smaller type size that could impair the audience's ability to read it. (See Figure 15–7.)

☐ Make your slides consistent in type style, size, and spacing.

☐ Use a type size visible to members of the audience in the back of the room. Type should be no smaller than 30 point bold. For headings, 45 or 50 point is even better.

☐ Use graphs and charts rather than tables to show data trends. Use only one or two graphs or charts per slide; otherwise, the data will look cluttered and may be hard to see.

☐ Ensure that the contrast between your text and background is sharp. Use light backgrounds with dark lettering and avoid textured or fancy "wallpaper" backgrounds. (See Figure 15–6.)

☐ Aim for about 20 slides per presentation. More than that will tax any audience's concentration.

☐ Speak about the visual on the screen during your presentation. Don't put one set of words or images on the screen and talk about the previous slide or (worse) the next one.

☐ Don't read the text on your slides word for word. The audience can read and they look to you to summarize and cover salient points in detail.

Practicing the Presentation

Begin by familiarizing yourself with the sequence of the material—major topics, notes, and visuals—in your outline. Once you feel comfortable with the content, you're ready to practice the presentation itself.

Practice on Your Feet and Out Loud. Try to practice in the room where you'll give the presentation. Practicing here will help you learn the idiosyncrasies of the room: acoustics, lighting, how the chairs will most likely be arranged, where the electrical outlets and switches are located, and so forth. Practicing out loud is more effective than just rehearsing mentally because you process the information in your mind many times faster than you can possibly speak it. Rehearsing out loud will make clear exactly how long your presentation will take and will highlight any problems, such as awkward transitions. You can also rehearse eliminating or reducing verbal tics, such as "um," "you know," and "like."

Practice with Your Visuals. Integrating your visuals into your practice sessions will help your presentation go more smoothly. Operate the equipment (computer, slide projector, or overhead projector) until you're comfortable with it. Even if things go wrong, being prepared and having practiced will give you the confidence and poise to go on. You can also use your visuals as cues to the next point you wish to make.

Videotape Your Practice Session. Videotape is a very effective and sometimes painful way to catch what you are doing wrong. The tape will reveal how you present your material from the audience's perspective. If you do not have access to a videotape recorder, at the very least use an audiotape recorder to evaluate your vocal presentation. Another effective technique is to ask a friend or colleague to watch you and comment on your delivery.

Using Delivery Techniques That Work

Your delivery is both audible and visual. In addition to your words and message, your nonverbal communication affects your audience. To make an impression on your audience and keep their attention, you must be animated. Your words will have more staying power when they are delivered with physical and vocal animation. If you want the audience to share your point of view, show them your enthusiasm for your topic. The most common delivery techniques include making eye contact; using movement and gestures; and varying voice inflection, pace, and projection.

Make Eye Contact. The best way to establish rapport with your audience is with eye contact. For smaller audiences, make eye contact with as many people as possible. In a large audience, directly address those people who seem most responsive to you in different parts of the audience. Address each person sepa-

---

ESL TIPS: Making Eye Contact

When giving a presentation, keep the following needs of your audience in mind:

- Establish rapport and trust by looking in the eyes of as many audience members as possible. In North America, to "look someone in the eye" is to show honesty and credibility.
- Hold the interest of your audience by looking at your notes as little as possible. (Never read directly from your notes.)

ESL TIPS: Delivering a Presentation

For many international students, memorizing a speech may be easy, but to the audience a word-for-word memorized speech is boring because it does not sound natural. When a speaker memorizes a speech, the audience usually sees a speaker who stares blankly because he or she is concentrating on the memorized material and hears a speaker who uses a monotone voice because he or she is no longer actively talking about the subject. The lack of a natural-sounding presentation makes the listeners lose interest in the speaker, thereby missing the importance of the topic. It is a better speech if the speaker knows the subject well and is able to talk to the audience from an outline.

rately, and focus your attention on him or her for several seconds before moving on. Doing so helps you establish rapport with the audience by holding their attention. It also gives you important visual cues as to how you're doing. Are people engaged and actively listening? Are they looking around or staring at the floor? These cues may tell you that you need to speed up or slow down the pace of your presentation.

Use Movement.   Animate the presentation with physical movement. Simply take a step or two to one side or to the other after you have been talking for a minute or so. This type of movement is most effective at transitional points in your presentation, between major topics or after pauses for emphasis. Too much movement, however, can be distracting—so try not to pace.

Another way to integrate movement into your presentation is to walk to the screen and point to the visual as you're discussing it. Touch the screen with the pointer and then turn back to the audience before beginning to speak (touch, turn, and talk). If you are using an overhead projector, you can place the pointer directly on the overhead so that it casts a shadow that points to the appropriate item on the screen.

Use Gestures.   Gestures both animate your presentation and help communicate your message. Most people gesture naturally when they talk; however, nervousness can inhibit gesturing during a presentation. Keep one hand free and above your waist and use that hand to gesture. Try not to lock your hands into rigid positions; it looks unnatural and inhibits gesturing. Gestures will come more naturally during your presentation if you include them in your practice sessions.

Adjust Your Vocal Inflection.   Your voice can be an effective tool in communicating your sincerity, enthusiasm, and command of your topic. Use it to your advantage to project your credibility. Vocal inflection is the rise and fall of your voice at different times, such as the way your voice naturally rises at the end of a question ("You want it *when?*"). Keep your audience's attention by using this pattern as

ESL TIPS: Using Gestures and Space

Gestures

- Because gestures differ greatly from culture to culture, carefully choose those that you use when speaking.
- Practice your presentation in front of colleagues or friends and have them watch for any gestures that could be misinterpreted by your audience.

Space

- In North America, a comfortable distance between two people engaged in a conversation is generally 15 to 18 inches (38.1 to 45.72 centimeters).
- Because people have different requirements in terms of personal space, take note of any cues that indicate the requirements of those with whom you interact. Some people are more comfortable with less distance and move toward the other person; others need greater personal space.
- Cultural norms on touching vary greatly. Generally, in North America, any touching in the workplace—beyond the handshake—is unacceptable.

you would in a conversation. Do not fall into a monotone speech pattern that can hypnotize your audience and make them drowsy. Vocal variety also allows you to highlight differences between key and subordinate points in your presentation. Using conversational delivery and making eye contact also promote the feeling among members of the audience that you're addressing each one directly.

Adjust Your Vocal Pace. Pace is the speed at which you deliver your presentation. If you speak too fast, your words will run together, making it difficult for your audience to follow your presentation. If you speak too slowly, the audience will get impatient and their minds may wander.

Project Your Voice. Most speakers think they are projecting more loudly than they are. Remember that if anyone in the audience cannot hear you, your presentation has been ineffective for that person. If the audience has to strain to hear you, they may not hear what you're saying and give up trying to listen. You can correct for these problems by practicing out loud with someone listening from the back of the room.

Dealing with Presentation Anxiety

Everyone experiences nervousness before a presentation. Survey after survey reveals that dread of speaking before others ranks among the top five fears for most people. Typical reactions to this stress include shortness of breath, a racing heartbeat, trembling, perspiration, and even nausea. Some people react by clearing their throats repeatedly, tugging at their clothing or ear lobes, or moving continuously during the presentation. Instead of letting this stress inhibit you, focus on

---

WRITER'S CHECKLIST: Delivering a Presentation

- ☐ Practice out loud and, if possible, in the room where you'll deliver the presentation.

- ☐ Incorporate your visuals as you practice, using the computer, slide projector, or overhead transparencies.

- ☐ Videotape or audiotape your practice session and evaluate it critically, or have a colleague or classmate observe and comment.

- ☐ During the presentation, use eye contact to establish rapport with your audience.

- ☐ Be animated, moving to the screen to emphasize points and gesturing naturally.

- ☐ Use your voice to communicate sincerity and enthusiasm, and, above all, do not speak in a monotone. Project your voice so that you're heard by everyone and pace your delivery so that your words don't run together.

---

channeling this nervous energy into a helpful stimulant. That is, if you can't eliminate your stress entirely, manage it. The best way to master this feeling is to know your topic thoroughly. If you know what you are going to say and how you are going to say it, you will gain confidence and reduce anxiety as you become immersed in your subject.

Rehearsing your presentation will help. Do so alone or, if possible, in front of one or more listeners. You may find it helpful to write out the presentation in full, put it aside, and rehearse using only brief notes. If you falter, refer to your written version. After a practice session, imagine yourself in front of your audience delivering your material point by point. Begin by saying to yourself, "My subject is important. I am ready. My listeners are here to listen to what I have to say." If you cannot remember every point you wish to make during the practice presentation, review your notes or visuals. These will trigger your memory both as you imagine the presentation and when you're actually giving it.

You can use several techniques to quell the butterflies immediately before the presentation. Fill your lungs with a deep breath and hold it for a count of ten. (When your lungs are filled entirely, you should feel the lower part of your rib cage move inward and upward. Your breathing will be too shallow and ineffective if only the upper part of your chest moves as you inhale.) Then exhale and repeat, doing so several times or until you feel your body begin to relax. You can also clench your fists tightly. Tensing and relaxing muscles is another effective stress reducer. Clench both fists tightly and count to ten while inhaling and then exhale. Repeat several times until you feel the stress begin to diminish.

Reaching Global Audiences

The prevalence of multinational corporations, the international subsidiaries of many companies, multinational trade agreements, the increasing diversity of the U.S. workforce, and even increases in immigration mean that the ability to reach audiences with varied cultural backgrounds will be essential in the years to come. The cross-cultural audiences for your future presentations may include clients, business partners, colleagues, and current and potential employees and customers of varied backgrounds.

Presentations to global audiences involve special challenges. As with all materials intended for global readers and listeners, keep your language simple and consistent. Don't call something a "ratio" in one place and a "rate" in another. Puns and wordplay may entertain an American audience, but will likely confuse foreign listeners. State the main points of your presentation often and in the identical language each time. Follow this guidance whether you're addressing an audience for whom English is a second language or speaking through an interpreter. As you deliver your presentation, speak slowly and deliberately, enunciating clearly and pausing often. Avoid raising your voice. Doing so makes you seem condescending to your listeners. Keep in mind the following additional points about delivering presentations:

- Bland is better than colorful. Avoid idioms ("dog and pony show," "barking up the wrong tree"), jargon (emoticons, debugging), and acronyms. They will put an unnecessary impediment between you and your audience.

- Avoid U.S.-centered examples of business, political, or sports figures unless they are essential to your discussion. They will not be understood and, worse, they will suggest to your audience that your perspective about the world is narrowly focused on the United States.

- Do not use the trite sports metaphors that are all too common in U.S. speech (slam dunk, touchdown, home run). They will puzzle your audience and suggest to them that you're insensitive about their culture and customs.

- Jokes can backfire even with U.S. audiences, so they are especially tricky with foreign audiences. If you think that humor is important to your message, try it out on someone familiar with the country's language and culture beforehand and revise accordingly.

- With U.S. audiences, maintaining eye contact enhances the speaker's credibility and connectedness with the audience. In some Asian cultures, however, making direct eye contact is seen as an invasion of privacy. Try instead to sweep your gaze across the audience rather than looking at anyone too long.

(For additional information and tips on communicating with cross-cultural audiences, see Writing International Correspondence in Chapter 8 and Using Graphics to Communicate Internationally in Chapter 12.)

■ Listening

Active listening enables the listener to understand and then implement the instructions of a teacher, the goals of a manager, and the needs and wants of customers. It also lays the foundation for good interpersonal communication and cooperation between colleagues and members of work teams.

For communication to occur, there must be a message, a sender of the message, and a receiver of the message. At the most basic level, this model of how communication takes place works best when the sender (the speaker) and the receiver (the listener) each focus on and clearly understand the content of the message.

Because the speaker's background or cultural frame of reference may differ from the listener's, the listener needs to make sure he or she understands the message. The message may also be blocked by noise, lack of attention on the part of the listener, or impaired hearing. To the extent possible, the listener should block out distractions to focus on the message.

The listener then evaluates the message by separating fact from opinion and gauging the quality of the information in the message. The listener must be careful, however, not to dismiss the message because he or she doesn't like the speaker or because the speaker is wearing distracting clothing or has an unusual hairstyle. Nor must the listener let preconceptions or personal biases get in the way of effective evaluation of the message.

Finally, the listener may need to respond to the message. Doing so helps satisfy the speaker that the listener has understood what was said. Accurately interpreting the speaker's words requires conscious effort, as well as a willingness to become a responder rather than a reactor. A *responder* is a listener who can slow the communication down, if necessary, to be certain that he or she is accurately receiving the message sent by the speaker. To slow the communication down, the listener could clarify his or her understanding by asking for more information or by paraphrasing the message before offering his or her thoughts, opinions, or recommendations. A *reactor* simply says the first thing that comes to mind based on limited information and might easily leave the conversation with an inaccurate version of the message.

If you are the speaker, you must organize and present the message logically and succinctly. All the knowledge you have gained about writing will help you convey an oral message that is free of confusion and easy for the listener to understand. Everything you have learned about organizing information effectively and composing clear and succinct sentences will also help you communicate oral messages effectively. What you have learned about understanding your reader will help you determine the same things about your listener.

Fallacies about Listening

Listening is our most-used skill. Yet it is the skill we concentrate on least in our education and training, know the least about, and take most for granted. This is probably why most of us accept two fallacies about listening: (1) that hearing and listening are the same, and (2) that words mean the same to everyone.

Are Hearing and Listening the Same?

Most people assume that because they can hear, they know how to listen. In fact, listening is a skill that deserves development, just as reading, writing, and speaking do. The most basic distinction between hearing and listening is that hearing is passive and listening is active. Voices in a crowd, a ringing telephone, or a door being slammed are sounds that require no analysis, no active involvement of any kind. We hear such sounds without choosing to listen to them—we have no choice but to hear them. This kind of hearing is completely passive. Listening, however, requires effort and skill and involves related activities: interpreting the message and evaluating its value to the listener.

Do Words Mean the Same to Everyone?

Many people believe that words have absolute meanings, but words can have multiple meanings that are determined by the context in which they are used. Meaning may be affected by the speaker's occupation, education, culture, or other factors, such as idioms. The context is especially important when communicating with an international audience. Idiomatic expressions in American English cause confusion because their literal meaning is not understandable. Expressions such as "run for office" or "put up with" may not be at all clear to a non-native speaker of English. (For tips on idioms commonly used in business, see pages 884–886 in Writer's Guide Section D: English as a Second Language.) Jargon, which abounds in all occupations, also creates ambiguities. A "hot key" and a "home page" make as little sense outside of a computer context as "blue chip" and "bear market" do outside of discussions about financial markets. Homo-nyms—words that sound alike but differ in meaning—can also confuse non-native speakers. Such an audience will likely struggle to make distinctions between such spoken word pairs as *brake/break, bear/bare,* and *scent/sent.* (See pages 738–741 for a more complete listing of homonyms.)

Steps to More Effective Listening

To listen more effectively on the job, you should (1) consciously decide to listen effectively, (2) take specific actions to listen more efficiently, (3) define your purpose for listening, and (4) understand that different levels of listening efficiency are appropriate to different business situations.

Make a Conscious Decision

A major part of the battle to listen effectively can be won by simply making up your mind that you are going to do it. Effective listening requires conscious effort, something that does not come naturally. One way of thinking that can help you learn to listen effectively is to *seek first to understand and then to be understood.* If you follow this rule, you may find it easier to take the steps or the time required to ensure that you are indeed exerting a conscious effort to listen effectively.

Take Specific Actions

Three actions you can take as a listener will empower the speaker, and one of those will help you retain information: check your understanding of the speaker's intended message, demonstrate verbal and nonverbal empathy for the speaker, and take notes to help you remember the message.

One way to check your understanding of the speaker's intended message is to paraphrase in your own words what you believe the speaker has said. Your paraphrase should be concise and should try to capture the essence of the speaker's message. Paraphrasing is an effective tool to let the speaker know that you are listening, to give the speaker an opportunity to clear up any misunderstanding you may have about what was said, to keep yourself focused, and to remember the discussion.

Empathy is listening in a way that enables you to put yourself in the speaker's position or to look at things from the speaker's perspective. It means trying to understand the speaker's feelings, wants, and needs—trying to appreciate his or her point of view. The value of empathy is that it makes the speaker feel you are really trying to understand. When people feel they are being listened to, they tend to respond with appreciation and cooperation. Empathy by the listener can begin a mutually beneficial chain reaction—empathetic listening encourages better communication.

Taking notes while you are listening provides you with several benefits. It helps you stay focused on what the speaker is saying, especially during a presentation or lecture. Note-taking can help you remember what you've heard because you reinforce the message by writing it. You can also check these notes at a later date, when you need to recall what was said. Finally, taking notes communicates to the speaker that you are listening and that you are interested in what he or she is saying.

Define Your Purpose

To listen effectively, you must know your purpose for listening. Knowing why you are listening can go a long way toward managing the most common problems people have with listening: drifting attention, formulating your response while the speaker is still talking, and interrupting the speaker. When you know you are going to be involved in a situation that will require you to listen actively, take the time to focus on listening. Following are some possible questions you may want to answer for yourself:

- What kind of information do I hope to get from this conversation or meeting?
- How will this information benefit me?
- What kind of message do I want to send while I'm listening? (Do I want to portray understanding, determination, flexibility, competence, patience?)
- What kind of listening problems do I foresee during the interaction — boredom, mind wandering, anger, impatience? How can I keep these problems from preventing me from listening effectively?

WRITER'S CHECKLIST: Listening Effectively

☐ Make a conscious decision to become a better listener.

☐ Define your purpose for listening in a given situation:
- What kind of information do I want from this exchange?
- How can I use this information?

☐ Block out background distractions to focus on the message.

☐ Screen out personal biases or preconceptions that may hinder an impartial evaluation of the message.

☐ Slow down the speaker by asking for more information or by paraphrasing the message before responding to the speaker.

☐ Take notes to help stay focused on what the speaker is saying.

☐ Adapt to the situation.

Adapt to the Situation

It is not necessary to listen at peak efficiency at all times. For example, when you are listening to a lecture, you may be listening for specific information only. When someone stops you in the hall for an idle conversation when you are late for a meeting, you may legitimately listen without giving the conversation your full attention. However, if you are on a team project where the success of the project depends on everyone's contribution, your listening efficiency needs to be at its highest to enable you not only to gather information but also to pick up on other nuances the speakers may be communicating.

■ Conducting Productive Meetings

A meeting is a face-to-face interchange among a group of people who have come together to make a contribution to a collective effort that will produce better results than any one of the participants could have produced alone. A meeting requires planning and preparation, just as writing and oral presentations do.

Planning a Meeting

Any meeting must be carefully planned if it is to be effective. Planning consists of determining the focus of the meeting, who should attend, and the best time and place to hold the meeting. You also need to prepare an agenda for the meeting and determine who should take the meeting minutes.

What Is the Purpose of the Meeting?

The first step in planning a meeting is to focus on your desired outcome. To do so, ask yourself the following questions:

- What do you want people to know as a result of the meeting?
- What do you want people to believe as a result of attending the meeting?
- What do you want people to do or be able to do as a result of attending the meeting?

Let's take a hypothetical example. You need to design a sales campaign for a new scanner that will result in a successful launching of the new product. You call a meeting of the sales staff to get their ideas for a successful sales campaign. The answers to the questions just listed might be as follows:

- As a result of this meeting, I want the sales people to know that this is an outstanding scanner that can increase their sales considerably.
- As a result of this meeting, I want the sales people to believe that this is the best scanner on the market and that their customers want it.
- As a result of this meeting, I want the sales people to offer their ideas for the sales campaign.

ESL TIPS: Conducting and Attending Meetings

- Be punctual. When chairing a meeting, always begin and end on time. When attending a meeting, always arrive several minutes early. Being aware of time shows that a person acknowledges the value of another person's time.
- Be interactive. If you are new to the organization, spend time listening and observing, but do speak.
- Meetings are considered an opportunity for everyone to share ideas; share yours even if they differ from those expressed by other attendees.
- You may notice that in the United States, the speaking style is to wait only about three to six seconds before responding to a speaker. In many countries, there is a much longer wait time. Feel comfortable responding as your ideas come to you, without pausing for an extended length of time. Also, because meetings are considered a place for brainstorming, ideas are not expected to be expressed in perfect form.

Once you're focused, use the information to write a purpose statement for the meeting that answers the questions *what* and *why*.

■ The purpose of this meeting is to gather ideas from the sales staff that will create an effective sales campaign for our new scanner.

Who Should Attend?

Who must be at the meeting to enable you to achieve your purpose? There is really no sense in having the meeting if all the right people can't be present. However, sometimes you must have the meeting anyway. Should this happen, talk with the people who can't be there beforehand; this way, their contributions will be available for the meeting participants, and progress won't be stalled because of their absence.

Many times, meetings go off course because people bring in interests that are unrelated to the topic of the meeting. If you believe that is likely to happen, call the people you are thinking of inviting to the meeting and inform them of the purpose of the meeting. Ask for their thoughts on the topic, then spend some time discussing the topic. You will have a much better idea of what to expect from people during the meeting, as well as a sense of where they stand on certain issues. You may hear things you don't want to hear, but at least you'll know what issues are likely to come up in the meeting, and you will have a chance to think about the best way to handle them.

When Should It Be Held?

What is the best time to have the meeting? The time of day and how long the meeting lasts can have a negative or positive impact on the outcome of the meeting. Consider the following when planning your meeting:

- People need Monday morning to get focused on work after being off for two days.
- People need Friday afternoon to wrap up the week and take care of anything that must be finished before the week ends.
- During the hour following lunch, most people fall victim to a condition called postprandial letdown, which is the body's natural need to regroup after a meal.
- During the last fifteen minutes of the day, you can be assured of a quick meeting — but it is likely that no one will remember what went on.

Group productivity tapers off considerably after an hour and a half, and after two hours it drops drastically. Therefore, any single session should be less than an hour and a half. Several short meetings that are quick, sharp, and well planned are far more productive than fewer longer ones.

Breaks are critical in longer meetings, and the length of the break is equally critical. If a break is too long, participants can detach and it will take longer to get the group back to the point where they were before the break. If a break is too short, it will not be refreshing enough. Be sure to announce how long the break is. If you don't, you are leaving it up to participants to decide how long to break.

Where Should It Be Held?

When you're thinking of having a meeting (even a short one), think of those coming to the meeting as your guests—guests from whom you need something important: ideas and cooperation. It's important to recognize this because people's comfort can be paramount to a meeting's success.

Home-turf advantage means that when you're playing in your own field (or office) you stand a greater chance of winning (or getting your way) partly because your comfort level is higher and partly because other people feel somewhat awkward in surroundings other than their own. The home-turf advantage can put people on the defensive immediately. Having the meeting on the other person's turf, however, can send a signal that your intentions are cooperative.

Having a meeting off site neutralizes everyone's home-turf advantage because it equalizes everyone's comfort level. People often feel freer to speak when they're away from familiar surroundings.

What's on the Agenda?

The agenda is a road map of your meeting. Never begin a meeting without an agenda, even if it is only a handwritten list of topics you want to cover. It gives you a tool for focusing the group. Ideally, the agenda should be distributed a day or two before the meeting, so those attending have time to prepare or gather the necessary materials. For an elaborate meeting requiring that a participant make a presentation or be prepared to discuss an issue in detail, try to distribute the agenda a week or more in advance. If there is no time to distribute the agenda early, however, be sure to distribute it at the beginning of the meeting.

The agenda should focus on just a few major items. It should list the attendees, the time of the meeting, the place of the meeting, and the topics to be discussed. If there are people presenting material, the agenda should indicate the time allotted for each speaker. Finally, the agenda should indicate an approximate length for the meeting so that participants can plan the rest of their day. Figure 15–8 shows a sample agenda.

If distributed in advance of the meeting, the agenda should be accompanied by a memo that invites people to the meeting. The memo should include the following:

- The purpose of the meeting, so that everyone knows not only exactly why this meeting is going to happen, but also what you hope to accomplish.
- The meeting start and stop time, so people know how to budget their time. A word of warning: When you advertise an ending time for the meeting, be sure to end it on time unless everyone agrees to extend the meeting beyond the promised stop time.

**Figure 15–8
Sample
Meeting
Agenda**

Sales-Meeting Agenda

Purpose: To get input for a sales campaign for the new scanner

Date: January 27, 20--

Place: Conference Room 15-C

Time: 8:00–9:30

Attendees: Entire Sales Force

Topic	Presenter	Time
The Scanner	Bob Arbuckle	Presentation, 8:00–8:15
The Sales Strategy	Mary Winifred	Presentation, 8:15–8:30
The Campaign	Maria Lopez	Presentation, 8:30–8:45
Discussion	Led by Dave Grimes	Presentation, 8:45–9:30

- The date and place. Be sure that everyone knows how to get to the meeting location. If someone might get confused, be careful to give clear directions.

- The names of the people invited. Knowing the names of everyone who will be attending often has an effect on how people prepare for the meeting.

- Instructions on how to prepare for the meeting, so everything functions smoothly when the meeting begins. Because different people may need to prepare different things, tell them how to collectively and individually get ready for the meeting.

Figure 15–9 is an example of a cover memo to accompany an agenda.

Who Should Take Minutes?

It is difficult for the person chairing a meeting to steer the meeting, coach participants, and take minutes at the same time. If you try, something will suffer—the steering, the coaching, or the recording. Delegate the minute-taking to another participant. Avoid asking someone who is quiet and nonparticipative because taking minutes will only make it harder for that person to take part in the meeting. However, taking the meeting notes will help a talkative or dominating participant concentrate on what's going on.

Memo

To: Carolyn Lichener
From: Susan McLaughlin
Date: May 7, 20--
Subject: Planning Meeting

PURPOSE OF THE MEETING

The purpose of this meeting is to get your input for creating an effective sales campaign for our new scanner.

TIME, DATE, AND LOCATION

Date: May 11, 20--
Time: 8:00 a.m.–9:30 a.m.
Place: Conference Room E (go to the ground floor, take a right off the elevator, third door on the left)

WHO WILL BE ATTENDING

The sales force

MEETING PREPARATION

Everyone should be able to offer input on the following items:

• Sales features of the new scanner
• Techniques for selling scanners

Figures 15–9   Sample Memo to Accompany a Meeting Agenda

Conducting a Meeting

To conduct a successful meeting, follow your agenda—the topics that must be covered and the outcomes that you wish—and ensure that you have invited the right people with the necessary information. Equally important, keep in mind how the personalities of those attending a meeting may affect its success. Members of any group are likely to vary greatly in their personalities and attitudes. Most of the time, you need only be tactful and diplomatic in your dealings with everyone in attendance and the meeting will go well. Begin by setting an example for the group by listening carefully and by encouraging participants to listen to each other. (Review the section about listening earlier in this chapter.) To create an environment in which people listen to each other, adopt a "you" attitude by being considerate of other people's points of view.

1. Seek first to understand and then to be understood. Consider the feelings, thoughts, ideas, and needs of others; don't let your own agenda deafen you to other points of view.

2. Make others feel valued and respected by listening to them and commenting on their statements.

3. Respond positively to the comments of others as best you can.

4. Widen your acceptance level of new thoughts, different ways of doing things, and the differences between you and other people (particularly people from other cultures).

Occasionally, however, you will encounter one or more persons in a meeting who are interruptive, negative, rambling, too quiet, or territorial.

The Interruptive Person

An interruptive person rarely lets anyone finish a sentence and can intimidate the group's quieter members, undermining the effectiveness of the group. When such a person begins to be detrimental to the group, tell him or her in a firm but nonhostile tone to let the others finish what they are saying in the interest of getting everyone's best thinking. By addressing the issue directly, you signal to the group the importance of putting its common goals first.

The Negative Person

A negative person generally has difficulty accepting change and will often choose to take a negative point of view about a new idea or project. Such negativity, if left unchecked, can demoralize the group as a whole. If this person's points are invalid, say so and move the meeting to the next item on the agenda. Of course, not all negative views are invalid. As long as the negative person is making valid points, ask the group for its suggestions as to how to remedy the issues being raised. When these issues are outside the agenda of the meeting in progress, announce that you will schedule a separate meeting to see that the issues are addressed.

The Rambling Person

The rambling person cannot collect his or her thoughts quickly enough to verbalize them succinctly. It's easy for the group to become impatient with such people and try to finish their sentences for them. Although a rambling person has trouble saying what he or she means, this doesn't mean that his or her thoughts are of no value. You can actively help by restating or clarifying the ideas. Quite often, the person will nod in agreement and you can move on. However, don't preface your clarification with "What you mean is . . ." and then paraphrase your best interpretation of what that person said. That's condescending and even insulting. Try to strike a balance between providing your own interpretation and drawing out the person's intended meaning.

The Quiet Person

A quiet person may be timid or may be deep in thought. To draw such a person into a discussion, ask for his or her thoughts, being careful not to embarrass the person by putting him or her on the spot. Try indirect prompting instead. Your job is to get everyone's best thinking, regardless of how shy or disinclined a person is to share it. If all else fails, have such a person jot down his or her thoughts and give them to you later.

The Territorial Person

The territorial person fiercely defends his or her group against all threats—real and perceived. This narrow focus can polarize a meeting by driving others to protect their own territories at the cost of pursuing the organization's goals. To deal with this situation, point out that although the individual's territorial concerns may be valid, everyone is working for the same organization and its overall goals take precedence.

Dealing with Conflict

Conflict is as common as it is inevitable in meetings, whether because of personality differences or for other reasons. However, it is also potentially valuable. When viewed positively, conflict can stimulate creative thinking, as when a person or an organization is challenged out of its complacency to achieve its goals in ways that are more efficient or economical than formerly.

Conflict in organizations can be caused by some or all of the following conditions:

- Competition for scarce resources, such as money, personnel, space, and equipment
- Different goals or priorities, such as when the engineering staff emphasizes the quality and reliability of a product and is relatively indifferent to the costs and delivery dates—factors that are of prime interest to marketing, purchasing, and sales people

- Ambiguous authority, when questions arise about who's in charge and who makes decisions when responsibilities are unclear or overlap
- Communication barriers, such as those created by semantic or cultural differences, which can cause misconceptions and mistrust
- Personality traits, such as those that occur when some people are dogmatic, are authoritarian, or have a strong need to win
- Status problems that can occur because of perceived inequalities in rewards or working conditions

Try to deal with conflict so that its benefits are retained, and its negative effects are minimized. First, be sure that those involved in the conflict are aware of any areas of agreement, and emphasize these areas to establish a positive environment. Then identify any differences and ask why they exist. If the facts being discussed are different, determine which are correct. If the goals differ, encourage each party to try to look at the problem from the other person's point of view. You can take any of a number of approaches to resolve a conflict.

- You could take a negative win-or-lose approach. This means going all out to win at the other person's expense, usually a very bad idea. Most conflicts don't start out this way, but they can become win-or-lose conflicts if making concessions is regarded as defeat. When each side believes that it is completely right and the other side is completely wrong, no path to compromise is open.
- You could use noncombative tactics by avoiding accusations, threats, or disparaging comments and by emphasizing common interests and mutual goals. You reward conciliatory acts by praising them and reciprocating, and you express a desire for harmonious relations. This can have a very disarming effect on an aggressive person.
- You could try to use persuasion to convince the other party to accept your point of view. How successful this is likely to be will depend on your credibility with the other person and his or her willingness to consider your views. Provide facts to support your position. Point out how your position benefits the other person (if true). Show how your position is consistent with precedent, prevailing norms, or accepted standards. Tactfully point out any overlooked costs, any disadvantages, or any errors in logic in the other party's point of view.
- You could use bargaining—an exchange of concessions that continues until a compromise is reached. Compromising means settling for half a victory rather than risking an all-out win-or-lose struggle. A compromise must provide each side with enough benefits to satisfy minimal needs.
- Collaborating means that each side accepts the other's goal as well as his or her own, and works to achieve the best outcome for both sides. This could be called a win-win approach. Each side must understand the

other's point of view and discover the needs that must be satisfied. A flexible, exploratory attitude is a prerequisite for collaboration. Trust must be high, but collaborating to resolve conflict often leads to very creative results. Define the problem, then define alternative solutions, and then select the one that provides both sides with the most benefits.

Making a Record of Decisions and Assignments

When the meeting is under way, it will be important to record major decisions that the group makes as well as any assignments for follow-up work. Each assignment is usually given a due date—the date by which the assignment must be completed. Be sure that each assignment, the person responsible for it, and the date on which it is due are also recorded to avoid future misunderstandings.

If you are leading a meeting, assign someone else the task of recording this kind of information, preferably in a way that everyone present can see what's

---

WRITER'S CHECKLIST: Planning and Conducting Meetings

☐ Decide why you need to hold the meeting; develop a purpose statement to focus your thoughts.

☐ Determine who should attend; invite only those essential to fulfilling the purpose of the meeting.

☐ Select a meeting time and place convenient to all attendees.

☐ Create an agenda and distribute it a day or two before the meeting.

☐ Assign someone to take meeting minutes and make clear what the minutes should include.

☐ Follow the agenda to keep everyone focused on the purpose of the meeting and the time available.

☐ Be respectful of the views of others and their ways of expressing those views.

☐ Review the strategies in this chapter for dealing with attendees whose style of expression in some way prevents your getting everyone's best thinking.

☐ Deal with conflict to maximize its benefits and minimize its negative effects.

☐ Ensure that the meeting minutes record major decisions, assignments, and other due dates, and, if necessary, the date, time, and location of a follow-up meeting.

☐ Close the meeting by reviewing all decisions and assignments so that attendees collectively agree to them.

written. Flip charts are commonly used for this purpose. Information on the charts can be rewritten later and distributed to those who attended. A more efficient way to gather information during a meeting is to have it recorded on a laptop computer. The portability of a laptop allows you to take it wherever the meeting is held. You can also arrange to have the computer screen projected on a wall or other surface so that it can be seen by everyone as easily as a flip chart can. The electronic record of decisions and assignments can be revised for clarity, saved, and distributed to all attendees electronically or on paper.

Closing the Meeting

Just before closing the meeting, review all decisions and assignments. You can paraphrase each to help the group focus on what they have collectively agreed to do. This process also allows for any questions to be raised or misunderstandings to be clarified. It also promotes everyone's agreement about their decisions. Be sure to set a date by which everyone at the meeting can expect to receive copies of this information. Finally, thank everyone for their participation and close the meeting on a positive note.

Taking Minutes of a Meeting

Organizations and committees keep official records of their meetings; such records are known as *minutes* and are taken by a *recording secretary*. The duties of the secretary are to write down and distribute the minutes before the next meeting. At the beginning of each meeting, those attending vote to accept the minutes from the previous meeting as prepared or to revise or clarify specific items.

Because minutes are often used to settle disputes, they must be accurate, complete, and clear. When approved, minutes of meetings are official and can be used as evidence in legal proceedings.

Keep your minutes brief and to the point. Give complete information on each topic, but do not ramble—conclude the topic and go on to the next one. Following a set format will help you to keep the minutes concise. You might, for example, use the heading TOPIC, followed by the subheadings *Discussion* and *Action Taken*, for each major point that is discussed, as in Figure 15–10 on page 674.

Keep abstractions and generalities to a minimum and, most important, be specific. If you are referring to a nursing station on the second floor of a hospital, say "the nursing station on the second floor" or "the second-floor nursing station," not simply "the second floor."

Remember that the minutes you are preparing may be used, at some time in the future, by a lawyer, a judge, or jury members who probably won't be familiar with the situation you are describing—and that you may not be reachable to explain what you wrote. (Even if you are available, you may not remember any of the details of the situation.) After all, the reason for taking minutes is to create a permanent record that will be available if it should be needed—at any time and for any reason.

> **WRITER'S CHECKLIST: Recording the Minutes of a Meeting**
>
> In general, meeting minutes should include the following:
>
> ☐ The name of the group or committee holding the meeting
>
> ☐ The place, time, and date of the meeting
>
> ☐ The kind of meeting (a regular meeting or a special meeting called to discuss a specific subject or problem)
>
> ☐ The number of members present and, for committees or boards of ten or fewer members, their names
>
> ☐ A statement that the chairperson and the secretary were present or the names of any substitutes
>
> ☐ A statement that the minutes of the previous meeting were approved or revised
>
> ☐ A list of any reports that were read and approved
>
> ☐ All the main motions that were made, with statements as to whether they were carried, defeated, or tabled (vote postponed) and the names of those who made and seconded the motions (motions that were withdrawn are not mentioned)
>
> ☐ A full description of resolutions that were adopted and a simple statement of any that were rejected
>
> ☐ A record of all ballots with the number of votes cast for and against resolutions
>
> ☐ The time the meeting was adjourned (officially ended) and the place, time, and date of the next meeting
>
> ☐ The recording secretary's signature and typed name and, if desired, the signature of the chairperson

Be specific, too, when you refer to people. Instead of using titles ("the chief of the Marketing Division") use names and titles ("Ms. Florence Johnson, director of the Marketing Division"). Be consistent in the way you refer to people. Do not call one person *Mr.* Jarrell and another *Janet* Wilson. It may be unintentional, but a lack of consistency in titles or names may reveal a deference to one person at the expense of another. Avoid adjectives and adverbs that suggest either good or bad qualities, as in "Mr. Sturgess's *capable* assistant read the *extremely comprehensive* report of the subcommittee." Minutes should always be objective and impartial.

If a member of the committee is to follow up on something and report back to the committee at its next meeting, state clearly the member's name and the responsibility he or she has accepted. There should be no uncertainty as to what task the member will be performing.

Figure 15–10
Sample
Meeting
Minutes
(Formal)

NORTH TAMPA MEDICAL CENTER

Minutes of the Regular Meeting of the
Medical Audit Committee

DATE: July 26, 20--

PRESENT: G. Miller (Chair), C. Bloom, J. Dades, K. Gilley, D. Ingoglia (Secretary),
          S. Ramirez, D. Rowan, C. Tsien, C. Voronski

ABSENT: R. Fautier, R. Wolf

Dr. Gail Miller called the meeting to order at 12:45 p.m. Dr. David Ingoglia made a motion that the June 1, 20--, minutes be approved as distributed. The motion was seconded and passed.

The committee discussed and took action on the following topics.

(1) TOPIC: Meeting Time

Discussion: The most convenient time for the committee to meet.
Action taken: The committee decided to meet on the fourth Tuesday of every month, at 12:30 p.m.

When you have been assigned to take the minutes at a meeting, go adequately prepared. A laptop computer is an ideal tool for this task. If you write the minutes, bring more than one pen and plenty of paper. If it is convenient, you may bring a tape recorder as backup to your notes. Have ready the minutes of the previous meeting and any other material that you may need. Take memory-jogging notes during the meeting and then expand them with the appropriate details immediately after the meeting. Remember that minutes are primarily a record of specific actions taken, although you may sometimes need to summarize what was said or state the essential ideas in your own words. Figure 15–11 shows a sample set of minutes that uses a less-rigid format than that used in Figure 15–10.

WARETON MEDICAL CENTER
DEPARTMENT OF MEDICINE

Minutes of the Regular Meeting of the Credentials Committee

DATE: April 18, 20--

PRESENT: M. Valden (Chairperson), R. Baron, M. Frank, J. Guern, L. Kingston,
          L. Kinslow (Secretary), S. Perry, B. Roman, J. Sorder, F. Sugihana

Dr. Mary Valden called the meeting to order at 8:40 p.m. The minutes of the previous meeting were unanimously approved, with the following correction: the secretary of the Department of Medicine is to be changed from Dr. Juanita Alvarez to Dr. Barbara Golden.

Old Business

None.

New Business

The request by Dr. Henry Russell for staff privileges in the Department of Medicine was discussed. Dr. James Guern made a motion that Dr. Russell be granted staff privileges. Dr. Martin Frank seconded the motion, which passed unanimously.

Similar requests by Dr. Ernest Hiram and Dr. Helen Redlands were discussed. Dr. Fred Sugihana made a motion that both physicians be granted all staff privileges except respiratory-care privileges because the two physicians had not had a sufficient number of respiratory cases. Dr. Steven Perry seconded the motion, which passed unanimously.

Dr. John Sorder and Dr. Barry Roman asked for a clarification of general duties for active staff members with respiratory-care privileges. Dr. Richard Baron stated that he would present a clarification at the next scheduled staff meeting, on May 15.

Dr. Baron asked for a volunteer to fill the existing vacancy for Emergency Room duty. Dr. Guern volunteered. He and Dr. Baron will arrange a duty schedule.

There being no further business, the meeting was adjourned at 9:15 p.m. The next regular meeting is scheduled for May 15, at 8:40 p.m.

Respectfully submitted,

Leslie Kinslow   *Mary Valden*

Leslie Kinslow   Mary Valden, M.D.
Medical Staff Secretary   Chairperson

Figure 15–11   Sample Meeting Minutes (Less Formal)

CHAPTER 15 SUMMARY: Presentations and Meetings

In planning an oral presentation, ask the following questions:

☐ What is your purpose?

☐ Who is the audience?

☐ What amount of information should you prepare to adequately cover the topic for the audience and in the time available?

Gather the needed information, decide how to organize it, structure the presentation around this organization, and decide on the types of visuals you will need. In rehearsing your presentation:

☐ Become familiar with your presentation.

☐ Practice on your feet, out loud, and with your visuals.

☐ Videotape your practice sessions, if possible, and review the video for posture, gestures, and voice, as well as for content.

☐ Try to rehearse in the room where the presentation will take place to familiarize yourself with its layout.

In delivering the presentation:

☐ Remember that nervousness before a presentation is normal.

☐ Show enthusiasm for your topic through the use of effective movement, eye contact, gestures, and your voice.

In conducting effective meetings:

☐ Focus on the purpose of the meeting.

☐ Determine who should be invited.

☐ Determine the best time for the meeting.

☐ Determine the best place for the meeting.

☐ Create and distribute an agenda before the meeting.

☐ Select someone to take minutes.

☐ Manage different types of people effectively to achieve the best outcome for the group.

☐ Deal with conflict positively by adopting noncombative tactics, persuasion, bargaining, or collaborating.

☐ Review all decisions made and assignments to participants at the close of the meeting.

To maximize your effectiveness as a listener:

☐ Adapt your level of concentration to the situation.

☐ Take the time to understand what the speaker is saying before speaking yourself.

☐ Acknowledge the speaker through questions and gestures.

☐ Define what you need or hope to take away from listening to someone else.

☐ Consciously work to control yourself from letting boredom, distractions, anger, or other impediments affect you.

To record the minutes of a meeting:

☐ Be prepared. Bring the necessary tools for recording the proceedings—a laptop computer is ideal. Also bring minutes from the previous meeting and any other necessary materials.

☐ Be accurate, complete, and clear because minutes of a meeting may be used to settle disputes or as evidence in legal proceedings. Following a set format for taking notes is helpful.

☐ Be concise and avoid generalities.

☐ Be specific and consistent when referring to people, places, and events.

☐ Be objective and impartial, avoiding adjectives and adverbs that suggest either good or bad qualities.

☐ Record tasks and names of attendees who have agreed to perform these tasks.

☐ Expand your notes immediately after the meeting, adding appropriate details, if necessary.

■ Exercises

1. Select a topic for a presentation and write a purpose statement that is based on your answers to the following three questions.
   a. What do I want my audience to know when I've finished this presentation?
   b. What do I want my audience to believe when I've finished this presentation?
   c. What action do I want my audience to take when I've finished this presentation?
   Possible topics include the following:
   • Is war obsolete?
   • Should the Congress censor the Internet?
   • Are many heads better than one?
   • Are books a thing of the past?

2. Complete the following statements about the audience for your presentation:
   a. The experience or level of knowledge that my audience currently has about my subject is _____. So, based on their existing knowledge, I should _____
   _____.

   b. The general educational level of my audience is _____.
   So, based on their general educational level, I'll need to _____
   _____.

   c. The type of information I should provide this audience to achieve my objective is _____.

   d. Some of the questions that the audience may have throughout the presentation include _____, _____,
   _____, and _____.

3. Prepare an introduction for your presentation that includes the following:
   - An interesting opening
   - A statement of purpose
   - An explanation of how you are going to present the topic (method of development)

4. Create a closing for your presentation that asks the audience to do what you want them to do or that summarizes the main points and restates the purpose of your presentation.

5. Create an outline for your whole presentation.

6. Write a brief narrative describing the impact that the audience has on any presentation that you prepare. Consider the following:
   - How does the education or reading level of the audience guide your choices in what information to include and how you will convey it?
   - If the audience shares your field or major, how will that affect your choices in what information to include and how you will convey it?
   - How might your understanding of your audience affect the purpose of your presentation? How do your purpose and understanding of your audience affect the way that you organize your presentation? (It may be helpful to review Influence of Audience and Purpose in Chapter 2.)

7. Choose a presentation topic of interest to you and compose the following types of opening statements:
   - An attention-getting statement
   - A rhetorical question
   - A personal experience
   - An appropriate quotation
   - Another example of your own (see Chapter 3, "Writing an Opening," for suggestions)

8. Assume that you are preparing a presentation that solves a problem either in your major field of study or on your campus. Decide who your audience will be, then prepare a written outline of the body that does the following:
   - Offers a solution
   - Proves your point
   - Calls for action
   Make certain that you include at least two subheadings under each heading. (Refer to this chapter for additional suggestions.)

9. Sales representatives are taught that the close is the most important part of a presentation. Considering the audience and purpose, introduction, and body, why is the close regarded as critical in sales presentations? Is it always the most important piece of a presentation? Why or why not? Write a brief narrative explaining and defending your conclusions. List at least two examples of effective closings and explain why you think they accomplish their purposes.

10. Choose an educational, work-related, or motivational presentation topic. Using an 8½-by-11 spiral notebook, draft a flip chart of sketches to accompany your presentation. Submit an outline of your presentation with your flip-chart sketches to your instructor.

11. Prepare an outline of a presentation, with at least four headings and three subheadings under each heading. Include an opening, introduction, body, and close. Next, prepare at least six transparencies using bullet statements and keywords that will help keep the audience focused during your presentation. For this assignment, concentrate on using effective text and clip art, if desired, when preparing each transparency. You will discover that your finished product serves not only as an aid to your presentation, but as an outline for you to follow during the presentation, possibly eliminating the need for notes.

12. Add two of the following to the set of visuals you prepared for Exercise 11.
    - Table
    - Chart
    - Graph
    - Map
    - Pictorial other than clip art

■ In-Class Activities

1. Choose a presentation topic related to your area of study (or one approved by your instructor) and design an introductory transparency that includes the following:
    - Title of presentation
    - Title of company you represent
    - Your name
    - The name of the person or company you are addressing
    - Date
    - Artwork in the form of clip art, a water mark, an original computer design or logo

    Then, as a class, discuss the introductory visual in terms of the following:
    - Overall design: Does the artwork fit your subject matter?
    - Effectiveness of content: Does the visual *benefit* your subject?
    - Clarity and simplicity: Is the visual easy for your audience to read or understand?
    - Unity and balance: Does the visual show an effective use of color, fonts, and so on?

2. Bring to class a sample of a flowchart related to your major field of study or area of professional interest. Divide into groups with classmates who share a similar area of study. Appoint a group leader and a group recorder and review each

flowchart and analyze each sample. For what audience and purpose was the flowchart intended? Is the flowchart as simple and comprehensible as it can be? Although flowcharts are excellent tools for demonstrating a process, explaining a detail, or showing a sequential order of events, they are often difficult to produce in a manner simple enough to attract and sustain an audience's attention. Choose the flowchart that achieves its purpose in the simplest, most effective manner and share it with the class. Be prepared to explain why the flowchart is a good example.

3. During a presentation, verbal, visual, and nonverbal communications affect your audience. To make an impression on your audience and to keep their attention, you must convey your genuine enthusiasm for your topic. With this in mind, take turns in front of the class introducing yourselves and explaining what you plan to accomplish in your career. Speak for no more than three minutes, and pay attention to the nonverbal communication signals that you and your classmates use. Do some students seem more excited about their future careers than others? Do some seem bored? Think about which gestures and expressions work well and which should be avoided while speaking.

4. Prepare a presentation slide or transparency that you will share with the class that makes an announcement of a future event such as a meeting, a sports event, a club activity, or a public discussion. Include the following in your visual:
   • Title of event
   • Title of sponsoring organization
   • Date
   • Time
   • Name of the contact person
   • Any other pertinent information
   • Artwork in the form of clip art, a water mark, an original computer design or logo

   As you prepare your visual, consider the following:
   • Overall design: Does the artwork fit your subject matter?
   • Effectiveness of content: Does the visual *benefit* your subject?
   • Clarity and simplicity: Is the visual easy for your audience to read or to understand?
   • Unity and balance: Does the visual show an effective use of color, fonts, and so on?

   Present your information and visual to the class.

5. Plan a meeting, to take place outside of class, to organize a particular class activity or trip; to decide on a specific policy; or to vote on a specific campus, national, or international issue. The meeting will require the participation of everyone in your class. As a group, know what you expect to achieve at the meeting and prepare a short agenda. Appoint a meeting facilitator to keep the meeting focused and a meeting secretary to record the minutes. At the meeting, maintain an atmosphere in which students listen to each other and practice adopting the "you" attitude as discussed in the Conducting a Meeting section of this chapter. When the meeting is concluded and decisions made or actions decided upon, write a brief analysis of the interaction that occurred during the session. What, if anything, could have been improved? Did the environment encourage participation?

■ Research Projects

1. Gather good and poor examples of the following types of visuals used in presentations:
   - Flip chart
   - PowerPoint (or other computer software presentation aids)
   - Transparencies
   - Slides

   Write a brief analysis in which you compare and contrast these types of visuals, indicating the benefits and drawbacks of each style. Which is the best for your topics and audience? Why?

2. Prepare a three-minute historical perspective on a problem that affects your field of study. For example, business majors might choose financing issues; health sciences majors would choose rising health costs or medical personnel shortages; agricultural interests the problem of failing family farms or the government-subsidy issue; engineering students could explore the question of ethics or environmental problems. You must include at least five visuals in your presentation that further your analysis. Try not to refer to notes and be aware of your nonverbal communications. Your visuals should include the following:
   - An introduction
   - At least one map, graph, or table
   - Documentation listing resources for all visuals, if necessary

3. Prepare a six-minute presentation in which you offer a well-supported solution to the problem you researched in Research Project 2 or to another problem that historically affects your field of study. You must include at least ten visuals in your presentation and use a pointer when presenting. Do not use notes, and remember the importance of your nonverbal communication. Dress appropriately for your presentation. Your visuals should include the following:
   - An introductory visual
   - An original computer-generated graphic
   - At least two of the following: map, graph, table, or flowchart
   - A closing visual clearly defining your solution

4. Divide into teams of four to six members each, choose a facilitator, and work on the following scenario. Your boss has asked your group to purchase new audiovisual presentation equipment for your large company. Your building has a presentation room that seats 75. You need equipment for management to use in training, for the sales force to use in demonstrations, and for guest speakers. You have been asked to investigate available types of equipment and make a purchase recommendation to your boss. To begin, brainstorm as a team to develop a working outline. Assign team members areas to research. Include what is available, the costs, and the advantages and disadvantages of each system. Decide when you meet again to assemble the information. One or two members will need to prepare a draft to be approved by the team. Your instructor will let you know when the final equipment proposal is due; you may also be asked to prepare a presentation for your class.

5. Divide into presentation teams of three members each. Choose a current business-related problem for which you can offer a solution that you will convey in a group

presentation. Decide the organization of your presentation and who will be responsible for each portion of the presentation. Each team member will be required to use at least two visuals. Your instructor will give you the time limit for your presentations.

6. Learn how to use a particular type of presentation software (such as PowerPoint) and give a presentation on how to use it effectively. Your presentation should be conducted using the software.

7. Attend a meeting of an organization. Go to the meeting prepared to take careful, complete notes of the proceedings (make sure to obtain permission to do so). From the notes you have taken, write up the minutes of the meeting.

8. Attend a business meeting of a local service club (Kiwanis, Toastmasters, Jaycees, etc.). Write the minutes for the meeting. (You must first, of course, obtain permission to attend the meeting and to take its minutes.)

9. Attend a faculty committee meeting, with guidance from and permission of your instructor, and write the minutes of the meeting.

■ Web Projects

1. Using the U.S. Census Bureau Web site at http://www.census.gov/ locate a set of statistics of interest to you and prepare a table, graph, or chart on a transparency, listing the U.S. Census Bureau as your source. The transparency should be simple with a font large enough for an audience to read from a distance. Your instructor may choose to share the visuals with the class.

2. Search the Web to find two training programs offered in your field. The programs may be part of continuing education in your field, or they may be entry level, intermediate, or advanced—credit or noncredit programs. Prepare a table on a transparency comparing the programs. Include information on your sources.

3. Using the *Occupational Outlook Handbook* at the Bureau of Labor Statistics at http://www.access.gpo.gov/su_docs/dpos/agencies.html, prepare a pie chart showing the employee opportunities in your major area of study for the next five years. Use color to depict different categories. Print your finished product on a transparency and make certain that an audience would be able to read your labels. Include source information.

4. Using the *Occupational Outlook Handbook* at the Bureau of Labor Statistics at http://www.access.gpo.gov/su_docs/dpos/agencies.html, prepare a map on a transparency showing the geographic region that offers the highest rate of employment and the brightest outlook for careers related to your field of study. Include a scale for your map and indicate North, South, East, and West. To make your map easy to read, include only the necessary components and use clear labels. Include source information.

5. Locate on the Web an example of an educational site that uses good design principles such as unity, balance, simplicity, color, or text combined with artwork. Write a brief narrative comparing and contrasting the elements of good design that are inherent to both Web-page design and transparency visual design. How does purpose relate to both? What are the similarities of the needs of the users or audience?

16 Finding a Job

Before you begin your search for a job, do some serious thinking about your future. Decide first what you would most like to be doing in the immediate future. Then think about the kind of work you'd like to be doing two years from now and five years from now. Once you have established your goals, you can begin your job hunt with greater confidence because you'll have a better idea of what kind of position you are looking for and in what companies or other organizations you are most likely to find that position.

The search for a job can be logically divided into five steps, each of which is covered in this chapter:

1. Determining the best job for you
2. Preparing an effective résumé
3. Writing an effective letter of application
4. Doing well in the interview
5. Sending follow-up correspondence

For additional step-by-step advice and resources, visit our companion Web site and click on Finding a Job or Internship at www.bedfordstmartins.com/writing thatworks.

■ Determining the Best Job for You

Whether you are trying to land your first job or you want to change careers entirely, begin by assessing your skills, interests, and abilities, perhaps through brainstorming, as discussed in Chapter 1 on page 8. Next, ask yourself what your career goals and values are. For instance, does helping others interest you? How important are career stability and a certain standard of living? Do you prefer working independently or collaboratively?

Once you've reflected and brainstormed about the job that's right for you, a number of sources can help you locate the job you want:

- School placement services
- Internet resources
- Networking
- Letters of inquiry
- Advertisements in newspapers

Voices from the Workplace

Sherri Pfennig, University of Wisconsin–Milwaukee

Sherri Pfennig is Senior Career Counselor at the University of Wisconsin–Milwaukee's Career Development Center. Sherri stresses the importance of audience and purpose for effective résumé writing: "Your résumé is a commercial. Just like the commercials you see on TV or anywhere else. For a commercial to be successful, the creator has to know the product and the audience inside out. Creators of commercials might change the language or the 'packaging' to reach different audiences. Likewise, you need to know what you are trying to sell with your résumé, what your audience is buying, and how this audience 'talks' about those qualities and skills."

After advising hundreds of students seeking jobs, Sherri gives this advice for preparing for the successful interview: "There are five topics for which you need to be 'blue book' ready. This means you have sat down and thought about your strengths and weaknesses in these areas and you are ready to discuss them in depth. They are your education, work experience, career goals, personal qualities, and your knowledge of the field or the specific organization. Your ultimate goal is to help your interviewer 'see' how what you have to say about these five topics qualifies you for the job. If you aren't ready to do this, you aren't ready to interview."

To find out more about the University of Wisconsin–Milwaukee's Career Development Center, visit their Web site at http://www.uwm.edu/Dept/CDC/index.html.

Entry-Level
Samuel Rosenbaum, Adams, Harkness, & Hill

As a Research Assistant at the investment-banking firm Adams, Harkness, & Hill, Sam Rosenbaum provides up-to-date stock information for analysts and for the company's internal sales force.

During his recent job search—the search that led him ultimately to Adams, Harkness, & Hill—Sam discovered the value of using the Internet. "When looking for a job, it's important to use all resources available to you, including the Internet. Many companies post available jobs at their Web sites, and provide information on the qualifications that a prospective candidate should have. To find company sites, use any of the popular search engines or job sites to look for positions, or surf the employment opportunities posted at individual company Web sites."

Using the Web helped Sam learn about prospective employers and prepare for interviewing. "Information available at a company's Web site can help you to prepare for an interview and to write a persuasive cover letter. This background research enhances your knowledge of the company and your visible enthusiasm for the position. When you meet with a potential employer, always be sure that you have taken the time to familiarize yourself both with the position you are applying for and with the objectives of the company. The mission statement at the company's Web site is a valuable resource for learning what the company does and what your role there might be."

Find out more about investment banking at Adams, Harkness, & Hill by visiting http://www.ahh.com.

- Trade and professional journals
- Private and temporary employment agencies
- Other sources

College Career Services

Your school's career center is a great place to begin a job search. Government, business, and industry recruiters often visit job-placement offices to interview prospective employees; recruiters also keep career counselors aware of their company's current employment needs and submit job descriptions. Not only can career counselors help you in the brainstorming phase of your career selection, but they can also put you in touch with important, current resources. They can identify where to begin your search and suggest ways to save you time. Career centers often hold workshops on résumé preparation, which can help you develop a résumé for a particular field. (See pages 689–704 later in this chapter for help on résumé preparation.) Although career centers have their own Web sites, nothing replaces talking to a career counselor about your interests.

Internet Resources

Most traditional resources, such as newspaper and professional journal ads, are also available on the Internet, but specific sources are also useful. For example, Internet discussion groups on topics in your job specialty can provide a useful way to keep up with trends and general employment conditions over time. More immediately, of course, some discussion groups post job openings that may be appropriate for you.

Using the Web can enhance your search in a couple of ways. First, you can make use of general Web sites that give advice to college graduates about job seeking, résumé preparation, and similar topics. For a listing of such sites, see Chart 16–1, Online Employment Resources.

Second, you can visit Web sites created by businesses and organizations that may hire employees in your area. Business sites often not only list job openings but also provide instructions for applicants. Finding an appropriate employer on the Web may involve searching thousands of entries in numerous databases, many of which will be irrelevant to your search. Cyberspace can be as crowded as other settings for finding employment. Employment specialists also suggest that you spend time on the Web later in the evening or very early in the morning so that you can focus on in-person contacts during working hours. (See also the discussion of Internet research on pages 432–443.)

Finally, you might establish your own Web site and post your résumé to attract potential employers. If you post your résumé on the Web, keep in mind the advice given on pages 693–697, Electronic Résumés. If you do not have a Web site or simply don't feel confident in adapting your résumé for the Web, consider using a résumé-writing company that will put your résumé online. Before using such

The following general-interest sites include job-search guidance as well as job listings.

What Color Is Your Parachute?: JobhuntersBible.com
http://www.jobhuntersbible.com/

> *What Color Is Your Parachute?* is a site for job seekers and career changers based on the best-selling book of the same name by Richard N. Bolles. It provides such resources as an interactive test for career counseling, tips for using the Internet, tips for preparing an effective résumé, and links to job postings and other useful sites.

Riley Guide: Employment Opportunities and Job Resources on the Internet
http://www.dbm.com/jobguide/

> The *Riley Guide* contains introductions and annotated links to resources by career field, employer type, and location. There are also sections on résumé preparation and online recruiting.

College Grad Job Hunter
http://www.collegegrad.com/

> *College Grad Job Hunter* is a site for the entry-level job seeker. It has user-friendly design links to sections on résumés and cover letters, interviews and negotiations, what to do when you get an offer, and an E-Zine for job hunters.

America's Job Bank
http://www.ajb.dni.us/

> Sponsored by the U.S. Department of Labor, *America's Job Bank* is a comprehensive listing of job postings categorized by state. It also contains such information as salary and demographic employment profiles for job seekers interested in relocating to a region.

Monster.com
http://www.monster.com/

> One of the best-known sites, *Monster.com* contains such information as career advice and job postings (including international listings). Specialized sites cater to the interests of occupational groups. The following are typical:

Graduating Engineers and Computer Careers Online
http://www.careertech.com/

> This site brings together in-depth company profiles, graduate-school program listings, and entry-level salary surveys as well as special coverage of topics such as "women in technology" and "minority issues."

Copy Editor
http://www.copyeditor.com/

> This site is sponsored by the newsletter *Copy Editor: Language News for the Publishing Profession,* and it provides information on workshops for copyeditors and proofreaders as well as job postings.

Chart 16–1   Online Employment Resources

services, however, browse the Web to learn what types of employers (for example, the health-care industry) look at résumés on the Web. One free service is America's Job Bank (see Chart 16–1). Be aware, however, that commercial services often charge a monthly fee for their posting services, in addition to other fees.

Networking

Networking is communicating with people who might provide useful advice or who might be able to connect you with potential employers in your interest areas. They may be people already working in your chosen field, contacts in professional organizations and volunteer groups, professors and former employers, family members, friends, neighbors, or members of the clergy; any of them might direct you to exactly the job lead you need. Use these contacts to develop even more contacts.

Letters of Inquiry

If you would like to work for a particular firm, write and ask whether it has any openings for people with your qualifications. Normally, you should send the letter either to the director of human resources or to the department head; for a small firm, however, write to the head of the firm. Your letter should present a general summary of your employment background or training. See the section on writing letters of application on page 705.

Advertisements in Newspapers

Many employers advertise in the classified sections of newspapers and on their Internet sites. For the widest selection of help-wanted listings, look in the Sunday editions or the help-wanted Web pages of local and big-city newspapers. Occasionally, newspapers print special employment supplements that provide valuable information on résumé preparation, job fairs, and other facets of the job market. An item-by-item check is necessary because often a position may be listed under various classifications. A clinical medical technologist seeking a job, for example, might find the specialty listed under "Medical Technologist," "Clinical Medical Technologist," or "Laboratory Technologist." Depending on a hospital's or a pathologist's needs, the listing could be even more specific, such as "Blood Bank Technologist" or "Hematology Technologist." So try to read all areas that may be pertinent to your job search.

As you read the ads, take notes on such things as salary ranges, job locations, job duties and responsibilities, and even the terminology used in the ads to describe the work. A knowledge of the words and expressions that are generally used to describe a particular type of work can be helpful when you prepare your résumé and letters of application.

Trade and Professional Journals

In many industries, associations publish periodicals of interest to people working in the field. Such periodicals often contain a listing of current job opportunities. If you were seeking a job in forestry, for example, you could check the job listings in the *Journal of Forestry,* published by the Society of American Foresters. To learn about the trade or professional associations for your occupation, consult the following references at a library: *Encyclopedia of Associations, Encyclopedia of Business Information Sources,* and *National Directory of Employment Services.* Many of the organizations have Web sites where they often list open positions. (See also the coverage of library research in Chapter 11.)

Private and Temporary Employment Agencies

Private employment agencies are profit-making organizations that are in business to help people find jobs—for a fee. Choose a private employment agency carefully. Some are well established and quite reputable, but others have questionable reputations. Check with your local Better Business Bureau as well as with friends and acquaintances or your school's career office before you sign an agreement with a private employment agency.

Reputable private employment agencies provide you with job leads and help you to organize your campaign to find the job you want. They may also provide useful information on the companies doing the hiring.

Often, the employer pays the agency's fee. Before signing a contract, be sure you understand who is paying the fee; if you have to pay, make sure you know exactly how much. As with any written agreement, read the fine print carefully.

Temporary employment agencies and services offer another way of determining the job that may fit you—through experience. For example, if you are interested in—but not certain about—a professional area, consider working in that area as a temporary or part-time employee. Even as a temporary member of a support staff, you can gain valuable experience that can help you decide whether a particular profession is right for you. Temporary work in a professional area will also enable you to network, as discussed on page 687.

Other Sources

Local, state, and federal government agencies offer many employment services. Local government agencies are listed in telephone and Web directories under the name of your city, county, or state. For detailed information on the trends of over 250 occupations, see the 2000-01 edition of *The Occupational Handbook* published by the U.S. Department of Labor at http://stats.bls.gov:80/oco/oco0006 .htm. For information about jobs with the federal government, contact the U.S. Office of Personnel Management at http://www.usajobs.opm.gov/.

Keep records with dated job ads, copies of letters of application and résumés, notes requesting interviews, and the names of important contacts. Such a collection can act as a future resource and reminder.

■ Preparing an Effective Résumé

A résumé is a summary of your qualifications and the key element in the job search. A résumé itemizes, in preferably one page, the qualifications that you can mention only briefly in your application letter. The information in your résumé is key to helping employers decide whether to ask you to come in for a personal interview. If you are invited to an interview, the interviewer can base specific questions on the data the résumé contains. (See also Doing Well in the Interview, pages 709–712.)

Résumés form the basis for a potential employer's first impression, so do not skimp when you create a résumé. Use a high-quality printer and high-grade paper. Take the time to make sure your résumé is attractive, well organized, easy to read, and free of errors. Proofread your résumé carefully, verify the accuracy of the information, and have someone else review it. Experiment with the design to determine a layout that highlights your strengths. Generally, keep the résumé to one page unless you have a great deal of experience. (See also the discussion of designing documents in Chapter 12, pages 496–516, and proofreading on page 281.)

Analyzing Your Background

In preparing to write a résumé, determine what kind of job you are seeking. Then ask yourself what information about you and your background would be most important to a prospective employer in the field you have chosen. On the basis of your answers, decide what details you should include in your résumé and how you can most effectively present your qualifications. Brainstorm about yourself and your background. Answer the following questions:

- What college or colleges did you attend? What degree(s) do you hold? What was your major field of study? What academic honors were you awarded?

- What extracurricular activities have contributed to your learning experience? What are your leadership skills? Do you have any collaborative experience?

- What jobs have you held? What were your principal and secondary duties in each of them? When and for how long did you hold each job?

- What personal and professional experience have you gained that would be of value in the kind of job you are seeking?

Use your answers as a starting point and let one question lead to another.

Organizing Your Résumé

A number of different organizational patterns can be used effectively in organizing your résumé. A common one arranges information chronologically in the following topical categories:

Heading

Employment objective (optional)

Education

Employment experience

Skills and activities

References

Portfolios

Whether you place education or employment experience first depends on which would strengthen your résumé. If you are a recent graduate, you would probably list education first because you may not have much work experience. If you have years of related job experience, you would probably list job experience first because your interviewer will most likely be interested in the skills you gained at your previous jobs. In both cases, list the most recent education or job experience first, the next most recent experience second, and so on.

The Heading

Create a heading that clearly shows your name, address, telephone and fax numbers, and email address. Do not include a date in the heading; if you do, you will have to change it every time you submit your résumé to a prospective employer. Centering your heading at the top of the page usually works best (Figure 16–1).

Employment Objective

If you have a clear employment objective, you can include it in your résumé. If you do, state not only your immediate employment objective but the direction you hope your career will take. An employment objective may be particularly useful in an electronic résumé because it serves both as a screening device and as an introduction to the material in the résumé (Figure 16–2).

Figure 16–1
Heading of a
Résumé

> **CONSUELA B. SANDOVAL**
> 6819 Elm Street
> Somerville, Massachusetts 02144
> (617) 625-1552
> cbsand@cpu.fairview.edu

Figure 16–2
Employment
Objective Section
of a Résumé

> **EMPLOYMENT OBJECTIVE**
> To obtain a position that allows me to use my computer-science training to solve engineering problems with the potential to gain valuable management experience.

Education

List the college or colleges you attended, the dates you attended each one, the degree or degrees you received, your major field of study, and any academic honors you earned (Figure 16–3). Mention the name of your high school only if your attendance was relatively recent, your résumé is very sparse, or you want to call attention to awards you earned in high school or to related programs, internships, or study abroad.

EDUCATION
Bachelor of Science in Engineering (expected June 20--)
Georgia Institute of Technology
Cumulative Grade Point Average: 3.46 out of possible 4.0
　　MAJOR COURSES
　　Calculus, I, II, III, IV
　　Methods of Digital Computations
　　Advanced Computer Techniques
　　Special Computer Techniques
　　Differential Equations
　　Graphic Display
　　Software Design
　　ACTIVITIES AND HONORS
　　Phi Chi Epsilon—Honor Society for Women in Business
　　　　and Engineering
　　Society of Women Engineers—Secretary-Treasurer Junior Year
　　American Institute of Industrial Engineers—Secretary Junior Year
　　Engineering Science Club
　　Doris Harlow Scholarship recipient for two consecutive years
　　Dean's List six of eight semesters

**Figure 16–3
Education Section
of a Résumé**

Employment Experience

List all your full-time jobs, starting with the most recent and work backwards in time (Figure 16–4). If you have had little full-time work experience, list part-time and temporary jobs, including internships. Provide a concise description of your duties for those jobs with duties similar to those of the job you are seeking; if a job is not directly relevant, give only a job title and a very brief description of duties that developed broad skills valued in the position you are seeking. For example, if you were a lifeguard, focus on supervisory experience, or even experience in averting disaster to highlight management and decision making as well as crisis-control skills. If you have been with one company for a number of years, highlight your accomplishments and promotions during those years. List military service as a job, give the dates you served, your duty specialty, and your rank at discharge. Discuss military duties only if they apply to the job you are applying for.

EMPLOYMENT EXPERIENCE
COMPUTER SYSTEMS INTERNATIONAL, ATLANTA, GEORGIA
September 20-- to Present
> As Assistant Training Director, assisted in preparing Professional Training Program for the Design, Data Entry, and Engineering Departments.

VACATIONLAND AMUSEMENT PARK, Toccoa, Georgia
April 20-- to August 20--
As Chief Lifeguard, trained and supervised three other lifeguards.

Some résumés organize work experience by type rather than by job chronology. Instead of listing the positions held in sequence, a functional résumé lists jobs by the functions performed in all jobs. If you were preparing a functional résumé you might group your experience and skills under categories such as "Management," "Project Development," "Training," "Sales," and so on. Organization by function is useful for applicants who want to stress certain skills important to the prospective employer or industry or who have been employed at only one job and want to demonstrate the diversity of their experience in that position. Functional arrangement is also useful if you are changing careers and you want to highlight transferable skills. It can also be useful for anyone with gaps in his or her résumé caused by unemployment or illness. Although functional arrangement can be effective, prospective employers know that it is sometimes used to cover weaknesses, so use it only when you feel it is to your advantage and be prepared to explain any gaps it may reveal.

Skills and Activities

The skills-and-activities category usually comes near the end of the résumé. Include items such as fluency in a foreign language, writing and editing abilities, specialized technical knowledge (such as knowledge of specific computer systems or desktop-publishing programs), student or community activities, professional or club memberships, and published works. Be selective; do not duplicate information given in other categories and include only activities and skills that support your employment objective. Provide a heading for this category that fits its contents, depending on which skills or activities you want to emphasize, such as "Skills and Activities," "Professional Affiliations," or "Publications and Memberships."

References

You can include references as part of the résumé or provide a statement on the résumé that references will be provided upon request. Either way, do not give anyone as a reference without first obtaining his or her permission.

Portfolios

The résumé may also state that a "Portfolio is available on request." Portfolios have traditionally been used by artists and writers to illustrate their work. However, those in other areas can also make use of a portfolio. A portfolio may contain copies of your most impressive work (relatively short reports, proposals, presentations), letters of praise, certificates that attest to special abilities, newspaper clippings, and other items that visually display your accomplishments and potential contributions to a prospective employer. The items should be professionally and attractively displayed in a loose-leaf binder, folder, or other device that makes the material easy to view during an interview. Although advice varies, one authority suggests that for ease of presentation during the interview, the portfolio should contain no more than ten items. For further advice on portfolios, check the Kimeldorf Library Web site at http://www.amby.com/kimeldorf/.

Writing Your Résumé

When writing your résumé, use action verbs (for example, "managed" rather than "was the manager") and state ideas concisely. Even though the résumé is about you, do not use the word "I."

Promoted
■ ~~I was promoted~~ to Section Leader in June 20--.
   ^

Be truthful in your résumé. If you give false information and are found out, the consequences could be serious. In fact, the truthfulness of your résumé reflects not only your personal ethics but also the integrity with which you would represent the organization.

Avoid listing the salary you desire in the résumé. On the one hand, you may price yourself out of a job you want if the salary you list is higher than a potential employer is willing to pay. On the other hand, if you list a low salary, any offer you receive could be less than it might otherwise have been. For further advice on salary negotiations, see page 712.

If you are returning to the workplace after an absence, most career experts say that it is important to acknowledge the gap in your career rather than trying to hide it. That is particularly true if, for example, you are reentering the workforce because you have devoted a full-time period to care for children or dependent adults. Do not undervalue such work. Although unpaid, it often provides experience that develops important time-management, problem-solving, organizational, and interpersonal skills. Figure 16–5 illustrates how you might reflect such experiences in a résumé.

If you have participated in volunteer work during such a period, list that experience too. Volunteer work often results in the same experience as does full-time employed work, a fact that your résumé should reflect, as in Figure 16–6.

Electronic Résumés

In addition to the traditional paper résumé, you can submit a résumé on disk, through email to a potential employer, or to a commercial database service or Web site that functions as an electronic employment agency. Or, you can display and periodically update an electronic résumé at your own Web site.

Primary Child-Care Provider, 20-- to 20--
Furnished full-time care to three preschool children in a home environment. Instructed in crafts, beginning scholastic skills, time management, basics of nutrition, and swimming. Organized activities, managed household, and served as block-watch captain.

Home Caregiver, 20-- to 20--
Provided 60 hours per week in-home care to an Alzheimer's patient. Coordinated medical care, developed exercise programs, completed and processed complex medical forms, administered medications, organized budget, and managed home environment.

Figure 16–5   Employment Experience (Unpaid) Included in a Résumé

A non-Web application of electronic résumés, particularly in large companies, is used to facilitate the screening of many applicants. Although an applicant's paper résumé can be scanned into computer files, employers appreciate receiving an electronic version that facilitates loading the information into their résumé database.

Non-Web electronic résumés differ from paper ones in a number of ways; one significant difference is the abundant use of nouns rather than action verbs (for example, *designer* and *management* rather than *designed* and *managed*). The use of nouns as keywords (sometimes called *descriptors*) is important because potential employers use them to screen candidates for specific qualifications and job categories. Keywords that produce a hit in the search process are critical to the success of an electronic résumé. One way to determine appropriate keywords in your résumé is to read job-vacancy postings and note the terms used for job classifications that match your interests and qualifications.

The organization and design of electronic résumés also vary somewhat from paper résumés. Center the main heading with your name and email address on the first lines on the electronic résumé. Immediately follow the main heading

**Figure 16–6
Employment
Experience
(Volunteer)
Included in a
Résumé**

School Association Coordinator, 20-- to 20--
Managed special activities of the Briarwood Elementary School Parent-Teacher Association. Planned and coordinated meetings, scheduled events, and supervised fund-drive operations. Raised $70,000 toward refurbishing the school auditorium.

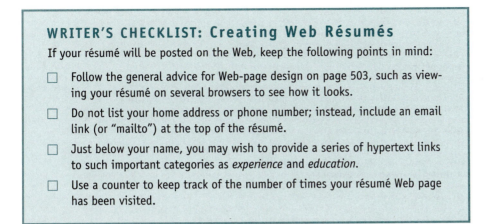

WRITER'S CHECKLIST: Creating Web Résumés

If your résumé will be posted on the Web, keep the following points in mind:

☐ Follow the general advice for Web-page design on page 503, such as viewing your résumé on several browsers to see how it looks.

☐ Do not list your home address or phone number; instead, include an email link (or "mailto") at the top of the résumé.

☐ Just below your name, you may wish to provide a series of hypertext links to such important categories as *experience* and *education*.

☐ Use a counter to keep track of the number of times your résumé Web page has been visited.

with a section of keywords, as shown in Figure 16–7. Following the section of keywords (which can number as many as 50), you can include fairly standard sections discussed earlier, such as "Employment Objective," "Education," "Employment," and "Skills and Activities."

If a résumé is to be sent as an attachment or included on a Web page as a PDF[a] file, you can use the full range of formatting options (boldface, italics, and underlining); the formatting will remain in place. If you submit a résumé on a disk or on paper to be scanned, the document needs to be universally readable in any application. Therefore, either format the résumé as an ASCII[b] file on your disk or use ASCII-compatible features on the paper copy (Figure 16–8). Figure 16–8 shows a résumé in ASCII format. For example, do not use underlining, italics, or boldface

CAROL ANN WALKER
caw@home.com
1436 W. Schantz Avenue
Dayton, Ohio 45401
(513) 339-2712

Keywords: Financial Planner. Research Analyst. Banking Intern. Executive Curriculum. Ph.D. (in progress). The Wharton School. University of Pennsylvania. Computer Model Development. Articles published in "Finance Journal." Written and oral communication skills. Grant writing for Foundation and Government Funding.

**Figure 16–7
Heading of an
Electronic Résumé
with Keywords**

[a]PDF (Portable Document Format) files retain all the original graphic elements of a printed document.

[b]ASCII is an acronym for American Standard Code for Information Interchange and is the most basic format for transferring files between different programs. In terms of word processing, it could be thought of as unformatted text.

DAVID B. EDWARDS
6819 Locustview Drive
Topeka, Kansas 66614
(913) 233-1552
dedwards@cpu.fairview.edu

EDUCATION
** Fairview Community College, Topeka, Kansas
** Associate's Degree, Computer Science, June 2001
** Dean's Honor List Award (six quarters)

RELEVANT COURSE WORK
** Operating Systems Design
** Database Management
** Introduction to Cybernetics
** Computer Graphics
** Data Structures
** Technical Writing

EMPLOYMENT EXPERIENCE
** Computer Consultant: September 20-- to June 20--
Fairview Community College Computer Center: Advised and trained novice computer users;
wrote and maintained Unipro operating system documentation.
** Tutor: January 20-- to June 20--
Fairview Community College: Assisted students in mathematics and computer programming.

SKILLS AND ACTIVITIES
** Unipro Operating System: Thorough knowledge of its word-processing, text-editing, and
file-formatting programs.
** Writing and Editing Skills: Experience in documenting computer programs for beginning
programmers and users.
** Fairview Community Microcomputer Users Group: Cofounder and editor of monthly
newsletter ("Compuclub"); listserv manager.

FURTHER INFORMATION
** References, college transcripts, a portfolio of computer programs, and writing samples
available upon request.

Figure 16–8   Electronic Résumé in ASCII Format

DIGITAL SHORTCUTS: Creating ASCII-Compatible Résumés

ASCII is an acronym for American Standard Code for Information Interchange. The following are the standard ASCII characters that are universally machine readable:

A B C D E F G H I J K L M N O P Q R S T U V W X
Y Z a b c d e f g h i j k l m n o p q r s t u v w x y
z 0 1 2 3 4 5 6 7 8 9 ! " # $ % & ' ( ) * +, - . / :
; < = > ?@ [\ ] ^ _ ` { | } ~

Because your résumé will appear as ASCII text, it should not include special formatting commands specific to your word-processing program. Therefore, consider the following guidelines as you format your document:

■ Avoid special characters, such as "smart quotes," graphic lines, and mathematical symbols.

■ Use the spacebar instead of tabs and column formats.

■ Align everything to the left margin.

■ Use hard returns to insert line breaks, instead of the word-wrap feature.

■ Avoid special fonts because fonts will become whatever a computer uses as its default face and size.

■ Do not use boldface, italics, and various type sizes; these will not appear in the ASCII version.

To create an ASCII résumé in a standard word-processing program, type your résumé and save it as a text-only document (sometimes also called Rich Text Format, or RTF). This option should be available under your *save* or *save as* command. As with any résumé, spell check and proofread before you send the document.

type. Avoid decorative, uncommon, or otherwise fancy typefaces; use simple font styles (a sans serif font such as Ariel) and sizes between 10 and 14 points. For résumés to be scanned, use white space generously; scanners use it to recognize that one topic has ended and another has begun. Although it is best to keep the length of a paper résumé to one page, you need not limit an electronic résumé to a single page. However, keep the résumé as simple, clear, and concise as possible. Use white or beige paper and do not fold a document when you mail it; during scanning, a folded line can produce a misreading.

Sample Résumés

This section includes a number of sample résumés, all of which are formatted for paper, email attachments, or PDF files. These examples are intended to stimulate your thinking about your own résumé, which must be tailored to your own job search. Examine as many résumés as possible and select the format that best suits your goals.

Figures 16–9 and 16–10, respectively, are résumés by a recent community-college graduate and by an applicant who has been employed for many years. The writer of the résumé in Figure 16–9 has only limited work experience and therefore puts the education section first and gives fairly detailed information about his college work. The writer of the résumé in Figure 16–10 has had many years of full-time employment, so he puts his work experience first—his work experience is much more important to a prospective employer than his educational data.

The résumés shown in Figures 16–11, 16–12, and 16–13 are all for the same person. Figure 16–11 is the applicant's first résumé, when she was a student; the résumés in Figures 16–12 and 16–13 reflect work experience later in her career (one is organized by job, the other by function).

DAVID B. EDWARDS
6819 Locustview Drive
Topeka, Kansas 66614
(913) 233-1552
dedwards@cpu.fairview.edu

EDUCATION

Fairview Community College, Topeka, Kansas
Associate's Degree, Computer Science, June 20--
Dean's Honor List Award — six quarters

RELEVANT COURSE WORK

    Operating Systems Design   Computer Graphics
    Database Management   Data Structures
    Introduction to Cybernetics   Technical Writing

EMPLOYMENT EXPERIENCE

COMPUTER CONSULTANT September 20-- –June 20--, Fairview Community College Computer Center: Advised and trained novice computer users; wrote and maintained Unipro operating system documentation.

TUTOR January–June 20--, Fairview Community College: Assisted students in mathematics and computer programming.

SKILLS AND ACTIVITIES

UNIPRO OPERATING SYSTEM: Thorough knowledge of its word-processing, text-editing, and file-formatting programs.

WRITING AND EDITING SKILLS: Experience in documenting computer programs for beginning programmers and users.

FAIRVIEW COMMUNITY MICROCOMPUTER USERS' GROUP: Cofounder and editor of monthly newsletter; listserv manager.

FURTHER INFORMATION

References, college transcripts, a portfolio of computer programs, and writing samples available upon request.

Figure 16–9   Sample Résumé for a Recent College Graduate

ROBERT MANDILLO
7761 Shalamar Drive
Dayton, Ohio 45424

Home: (513) 255-4137   Fax: (513) 255-3117
Business: (513) 543-3337   mand@juno.com

EMPLOYMENT EXPERIENCE

MANAGER, AUTO CAD DRAFTING DEPARTMENT — March 19-- to Present
    Wright-Patterson Air Force Base, Dayton, Ohio

    Supervise 17 Auto CAD drafters in support of the engineering design staff. Develop, evaluate, and improve materials and equipment for the design and construction of exhibits. Write specifications, negotiate with vendors, and initiate procurement activities for exhibit design support.

SUPERVISOR, GRAPHICS ILLUSTRATORS — May 19-- to February 19--
    Henderson Advertising Agency, Cincinnati, Ohio

    Supervised five Illustrators and four Drafting Mechanics after promotion from Graphics Technician; analyzed and approved work-order requirements; selected appropriate media and techniques for orders; rendered illustrations in pencil and ink; converted department to CAD system.

EDUCATION

Bachelor of Science in Mechanical Engineering Technology, 19--
Edison State College, Wooster, Ohio

Associate's Degree in Mechanical Drafting, 19--
Wooster Community College, Wooster, Ohio

PROFESSIONAL AFFILIATIONS

National Association of Mechanical Engineering and Drafting Design

REFERENCES

References, letters of recommendation, and a portfolio of original designs and drawings available upon request.

Figure 16–10   Sample Résumé for an Applicant with an Extensive Work Record

CAROL ANN WALKER
1436 W. Schantz Avenue
Dayton, Ohio 45401
(513) 339-2712
caw@home.com

EMPLOYMENT OBJECTIVE

Obtaining a position in financial research, leading to a management position in corporate finance.

EDUCATION

Bachelor of Science in Business Administration
    (expected June 20--)
Indiana University
Emphasis: Finance   Minor: Technical Communication
Dean's List: 3.88 grade point average out of possible 4.0
Senior Honor Society, 20--

EMPLOYMENT EXPERIENCE

FIRST BANK, INC., of Bloomington, Indiana, 20--
Research Assistant, Summer and Fall Quarters
    Assisted manager of corporate planning and developed long-range planning models.

MARTIN FINANCIAL RESEARCH SERVICES, Bloomington, Indiana, 20-- to 20--
Financial Audit Intern
    Developed a design concept for in-house financial audits and provided research assistance to staff.

SKILLS AND ACTIVITIES

Associate Editor, Business School Alumni Newsletter
    Wrote articles on financial planning with computer models; surveyed business periodicals for potential articles; edited submissions.

President, Women's Transit Program
    Coordinated activities to provide safe nighttime transportation to and from residence halls and campus buildings.

REFERENCES

Available upon request.

Figure 16–11   Student Résumé

**Figure 16–12
Advanced
Résumé
Organized
Chronologi-
cally by Job**

CAROL ANN WALKER
1436 W. Schantz Avenue
Dayton, Ohio 45401
(513) 339-2712
caw@home.com

EMPLOYMENT EXPERIENCE

KERFHEIMER CORPORATION, Dayton, Ohio
November 20-- to Present

Senior Financial Analyst
Report to Senior Vice President for Corporate Financial Planning. Develop manufacturing
cost estimates totaling $30 million annually for mining and construction equipment with
Department of Defense.

Financial Analyst
Developed $50-million funding estimates for major Department of Defense contracts for
troop carriers and digging and earth-moving machines.

Researched funding options, recommending those with most favorable rates and terms.

Promoted to senior financial analyst: 20--

FIRST BANK, INC., Bloomington, Indiana
September 20-- to August 20--

Planning Analyst
Developed successful computer models for short- and long-range planning.

EDUCATION

Ph.D. in Finance: expected, June 20--
The Wharton School of the University of Pennsylvania

M.S. in Business Administration, 20--
University of Wisconsin–Milwaukee
"Executive Curriculum" for employees identified as promising by their employers.

B.S. in Business Administration (*magna cum laude*), 20--
Indiana University
Emphasis: Finance   Minor: Technical Communication

(continued)

Figure 16–12
(continued)

Carol Ann Walker   Page 2

SKILLS AND ACTIVITIES

Published "Developing Computer Models for Financial Planning," *Midwest Finance Journal* (Vol. 34, No. 2, 20--), pp. 126–136.

Association for Corporate Financial Planning, Senior Member.

REFERENCES

References and a portfolio of financial plans are available upon request.

**Figure 16–13
Advanced
Résumé
Organized
by Function**

CAROL ANN WALKER
1436 W. Schantz Avenue
Dayton, Ohio 45401
(513) 339-2712
caw@home.com

MAJOR ACCOMPLISHMENTS

FINANCIAL PLANNING
- Researched funding options to achieve a 23% return on investment.
- Developed long-range funding requirements for over $1 billion in government and military contracts.
- Developed a computer model for long- and short-range planning that saved 65% in proposal-preparation time.
- Received the Financial Planner of the Year Award from the Association of Financial Planners, a national organization composed of both practitioners and academics.

CAPITAL ACQUISITION
- Developed strategies to acquire over $1 billion at 3% below market rate.
- Secured over $100 million through private and government research grants.
- Developed computer models for capital acquisition that enabled the company to decrease its long-term debt during several major building expansions.

RESEARCH AND ANALYSIS
- Researched and developed computer models applied to practical problems of corporate finance.
- Functioned primarily as a researcher at two different firms for over 11 years.
- Published research in financial journals while pursuing an advanced degree at the Wharton School.

EDUCATION

Ph.D. in Finance: expected, June 20--
The Wharton School of the University of Pennsylvania

M.S. in Business Administration, 20--
University of Wisconsin–Milwaukee
"Executive Curriculum" for employees identified as promising by their employers.

(continued)

**Figure 16–13
(continued)**

Carol Ann Walker   Page 2

B.S. in Business Administration (*magna cum laude*), 20--
Indiana University
Emphasis: Finance   Minor: Technical Communication

EMPLOYMENT EXPERIENCE

Kerfheimer Corporation, Dayton, Ohio
November 20-- to Present
        Senior Financial Analyst
        Financial Analyst

First Bank, Inc., Bloomington, Indiana
September 20-- to August 20--
        Planning Analyst

PUBLICATIONS AND MEMBERSHIPS

Published "Developing Computer Models for Financial Planning," *Midwest Finance Journal*
(Vol. 34, No. 2, 20--), pp. 126–136.

Association for Corporate Financial Planning, Senior Member.

REFERENCES

References and a portfolio of financial plans are available upon request.

◼ Writing an Effective Letter of Application

The letter of application is essentially a sales letter in which you are marketing your skills, abilities, and knowledge (see the discussion of sales letters in Chapter 9, pages 334–339). Remember that you may be competing with many other applicants. The immediate objective of an application letter and the accompanying résumé is to attract the attention of the person who screens and hires job applicants. Your ultimate goal is to obtain a job interview.

The successful application letter accomplishes three tasks: It catches the reader's attention favorably; it convinces the reader that you are a qualified candidate for the job; and it requests an interview.

Those who make hiring decisions review many letters of application. To save them time as well as to call attention to your strengths as a candidate, keep your letter to one page and state your job objective directly at the beginning of the letter.

◼ I am seeking a position as a manager in your data center in which I can use my master's degree in information systems and experience as a programmer/analyst to solve business problems.

If you have been referred to a company by one of its employees, a career counselor, a professor, or someone else, mention this before stating your job objective.

◼ During the recent NOMAD convention in Washington, one of your sales representatives, Ms. Karen Jarrett, informed me of a possible opening for a manager in your Data Center. My extensive background in programming and my master's degree in management information systems makes me highly qualified for the position.

In succeeding paragraphs expand on the qualifications you mentioned in your opening. Add any appropriate details, highlighting the experience listed on your résumé that is especially pertinent to the job you are seeking. Close your letter with a request for an interview. Prepare your letter with utmost care, proofreading it closely.

Three sample letters of application are presented here. Figure 16–14, by a recent college graduate, is in response to a local newspaper article about the company's plan to build a new computer center. The writer is not applying for a specific job opening, but he describes the position he is seeking. Figure 16–15 is written by a college senior; the writer does not specify where she learned of the opening because she does not know with certainty whether a position is available. Figure 16–16, by a person with many years of work experience, opens with an indication of where the writer learned of the job vacancy.

6819 Locustview Drive
Topeka, KS 66614
June 14, 20--

Loudons, Inc.
4619 Drove Lane
Kansas City, KS 63511

Dear Human Resources Director:

I read an article in the *Kansas Dispatch* about Loudons' new computer center north of Kansas City. I would like to apply for a position as an entry-level programmer at the center.

I understand that Loudons produces both in-house and customer documentation. I believe my technical-writing skills, as described in the enclosed résumé, are well suited to your company. I am a recent graduate of Fairview Community College in Topeka, with an Associate's Degree in Computer Science. In addition to having taken a broad range of courses, I served as a computer consultant at the college's computer center, where I helped train computer users on new systems.

I would be happy to meet with you at your convenience and discuss how my education and experience will suit your needs. You can reach me at my home address, at (913) 233-1552, or at dedwards@cpu.fairview.edu.

Sincerely,

David B. Edwards

David B. Edwards

Enclosure: Résumé

[handwritten annotations: "Should be Subsidiary — Point — Not main point"]

Figure 16–14   Letter of Application by a Recent College Graduate

2701 Wyoming Street
Atlanta, GA 30307
May 29, 20--

Ms. Laura Goldman
Chief Engineer
Acton, Inc.
80 Roseville Road
St. Louis, MO 63130

Dear Ms. Goldman:

I am seeking a position in your engineering department where I may use my training in computer sciences to solve engineering problems. Although I do not know if you have a current opening, I would like to be part of the department that developed the Internet Selection System.

I expect to receive a Bachelor of Science degree in Engineering from Georgia Institute of Technology in June, when I will have completed the Computer Systems Engineering Program. Since September 20--, I have been participating, through the university, in the Professional Training Program at Computer Systems International in Atlanta. In the program, I was assigned to several staff sections as an apprentice. Most recently, I have been a programmer trainee in the Engineering Department and have gained a great deal of experience in computer applications. Details of the academic courses I have taken are contained in the enclosed résumé.

I look forward to hearing from you soon. I can be contacted at my office (404-866-7000, ext. 312), at home (404-256-6320), or at my email address (vtfrom@aol.com).

Sincerely yours,

Victoria T. Fromme

Victoria T. Fromme

Enclosure: Résumé

Figure 16–15   Letter of Application by a Student

522 Beethoven Drive
Roanoke, VA 24017
November 15, 20--

Ms. Cecilia Smathers
Vice President, Dealer Sales
Hamilton Office Machines, Inc.
6194 Main Street
Hampton, VA 23661

Dear Ms. Smathers:

During the recent NOMAD convention in Washington, one of your sales representatives, Karen Jarrett, informed me of a possible opening for a district manager in your Dealer Sales Division. My extensive background in the office-systems industry makes me highly qualified for the position.

I was with Technology, Inc., Dealer Division, from its formation in 1990 until its closing last year. During that period, I was involved in all areas of dealer sales, both within Technology, Inc., and through personal contact with a number of independent dealers. From 20-- to 20--, I served as Assistant to the Dealer Sales Manager as a Special Representative. My education and work experience are indicated in the enclosed résumé.

I would like to discuss my qualifications in an interview at your convenience. Please write to me, telephone me at (804) 449-6743 any weekday, or email me at gm302.476@sys.com.

Sincerely,

Gregory Mindukakis

Gregory Mindukakis

Enclosure: Résumé

Figure 16–16   Letter of Application by an Applicant with Years of Experience

> ## WRITER'S CHECKLIST: Writing a Letter of Application
>
> When writing a letter of application, keep the following in mind:
>
> ☐ Identify the job by title, and let the recipient know how you heard about it.
>
> ☐ Summarize your qualifications for the job, specifically, work experience, activities showing your leadership skills, and your education.
>
> ☐ Refer the reader to your enclosed résumé.
>
> ☐ Ask for an interview, stating where you can be reached and when you will be available.
>
> ☐ If you are applying for a specific job, include information pertinent to the position that is not included in your general résumé.

■ Doing Well in the Interview

Preparing a professional résumé and writing an effective letter of application are essential to a successful job interview; that preparation helps you articulate your career objectives and understand your strengths as a potential employee. Nevertheless, the interview remains often the most difficult part of the job search because it is so pivotal in the hiring process. A job interview may last for 30 minutes, or it may take several hours; it may be conducted by one person or by several, either at one time or in a series of interviews, by phone, by teleconferencing, or in person. Because it is impossible to know exactly what to expect, it is important that you be as well prepared as possible.

Before the Interview

The interview is not a one-way communication. It presents you with an opportunity to ask questions of your potential employer. In preparation, learn everything you can about the company before the interview. You can obtain information from the Internet, current employees, company literature such as employee publications, and the business section of back issues of local as well as larger national newspapers such as the *New York Times*, the *Los Angeles Times*, the *Wall Street Journal*, and the *Washington Post* (available in the library and on the Web). You may be able to learn about the company's size, sales volume, product line, credit rating, branch locations, subsidiary companies, new products and services, building programs, and other such information from its annual reports; publications such as *Moody's Industrials* at http://www.moodys.com, *Dun and Bradstreet* at http://www.dnb.com, *Standard & Poor's* at http://www.standardpoor.com, and *Thomas' Register* at http://www5.thomasregister.com; and other

> ### WRITER'S CHECKLIST: Learning about Prospective Employers
>
> As you search for information about potential employers, use these questions as a guide.
>
> ☐ What kind of organization is it?
>
> ☐ How diversified is it?
>
> ☐ Is it a nonprofit organization?
>
> ☐ If it is government employment, at what level or sector is it?
>
> ☐ Does it provide a service or product? If so, what kind?
>
> ☐ How large is the business? How large are its assets?
>
> ☐ Is it locally owned? Is it a subsidiary of a larger operation? Is it expanding?
>
> ☐ How long has it been in business?
>
> ☐ Where will you fit in?

business reference sources a librarian might suggest. What you cannot find through your own research, ask your interviewer. Now is your chance to make certain that you are considering a healthy and growing company. It is also your chance to show your interest in the company.

Try to anticipate the questions your interviewer might ask, and prepare your answers in advance. Be sure you understand a question before answering it, and avoid responding too quickly with a standard answer. Be prepared to discuss answers to the interviewer's questions in a natural and relaxed manner. Interviewers typically ask the following questions:

- What are your short-term and long-term goals?
- What are your major strengths and weaknesses?
- Do you work better with others or alone?
- What do you know about our company (or organization)?
- Why do you want to work for us?
- How do you spend your free time?
- What are your personal goals?
- What accomplishment are you particularly proud of? Describe it.
- Why are you leaving your current job?
- Why should I hire you?
- How have you handled an unsuccessful experience?
- What salary do you expect?

Some of these questions are difficult. Give them careful thought, and remember that there is no one correct answer.

Be sure that you arrive for your interview at the appointed time. In fact, it's usually a good idea to arrive early because you may be asked to fill out an application before you meet your interviewer. Always bring extra copies of your résumé and samples of your work (if applicable). Some of the people you meet may not have a copy of your résumé and it contains much of the same information the application asks for: personal data, work experience, education. Read the application form before filling it out, and proofread it when you are finished. Not only does the application form provide the company with a record for its files, but it also gives the company an opportunity to see how closely you follow directions and how thoroughly you complete a task.

During the Interview

The interview actually begins before you are seated: What you wear and how you act make a first impression. The way you dress does matter. In general, dress conservatively and avoid extremes. Be well-groomed. For men, a recent haircut and a clean shave are essential; if you wear a beard or mustache, have a barber trim it. For women, basic clothes with simple jewelry look most businesslike. Avoid heavy perfume and extreme makeup. Remember, you have only one chance to make a good first impression.

Behavior

First, thank the interviewer for his or her time, express your pleasure at meeting him or her, and remain standing until you are offered a seat. Then sit up straight (good posture suggests self-assurance), look directly at the interviewer, and try to appear relaxed and confident. Never chew gum. During the interview, you may find yourself feeling a little nervous. Use that nervous energy to your advantage by channeling it into alertness. Listen carefully and record important information in your memory. Do not attempt to take extensive notes during the interview, although it is acceptable to jot down a few facts and figures. (See also the discussion of listening in Chapter 15 on pages 659–662.)

Responses

When answering questions, don't ramble or stray from the subject. Say only what you must to answer each question properly and then stop, but avoid giving just yes or no answers—they usually don't permit the interviewer to learn enough about you. Some interviewers allow a silence to fall just to see how you will react. The burden of conducting the interview is the interviewer's, not yours—and he or she may interpret your rush to fill a void in the conversation as a sign of insecurity. If such a silence makes you uncomfortable, be ready to ask an intelligent question about the company.

If the interviewer overlooks important points, bring them up. However, let the interviewer mention salary first. In the event that you are forced to bring up the subject, put it into a straightforward question. Make sure that you are aware of prevailing salaries in your field so that you will be better prepared to discuss salary. If you are a recent graduate, it is usually unwise to attempt to bargain. Many companies have inflexible starting salaries for beginners.

Interviewers look for a degree of self-confidence and understanding of the field in which the applicant is applying for a job, as well as genuine interest in the field, the company, and the job. Less is expected of a beginner, but even a newcomer must show some self-confidence and command of the subject. One way to communicate your interest in the job and company is to ask questions. Interviewers respond favorably to applicants who can communicate and present themselves well.

Salary Negotiations

Although it is better to negotiate salary after you have a job offer or certainly late in the interview, you may get the question "What are your salary requirements?" You cannot answer such a question without solid preparation.

First, your goal should be to work toward a win-win situation for you and your prospective employer. Avoid overemphasizing money yourself because it tends to make your potential loyalty to an organization suspect. The issue is not simply one of dollar amounts but of your own job satisfaction and what value you can bring to your employer. Consider the following guidelines:

- Seek advice ahead of time from a professional with relevant experience.
- Determine the lowest salary you would accept, perhaps based on your most recent employment.
- Determine the typical salary ranges for positions in your area.
- Determine possible fringe benefits that would be valuable to you.
- Determine how quickly you expect to be promoted.

If questioned directly about salary, you can give an answer such as, "I was considering a range of $ to $, but that would also depend on the fringe benefits available and the potential or timetable for promotions or salary increases." Remember, it's always acceptable to say to a prospective employer that you would like to think about an offer placed on the table.

Some companies study the market very carefully and give what David G. Jensen, Search Masters International, calls "First Offer, Best Offer"; that is, the offer they make is the best offer they can or will give, and there is no point in negotiating. Jensen offers further advice on negotiating on his Web site at http://www.bio.com/hr/search/negotiation.html.

Conclusion

At the conclusion of the interview, thank your interviewer for his or her time. Indicate that you are interested in the job (if true), and try to get an idea of when you can expect to hear from the company (do not press too hard). Reaffirm friendly contact with a firm handshake.

■ Sending Follow-Up Correspondence

After you leave the interview, jot down the pertinent information you obtained—it may be helpful in comparing job offers. A day or two later always send the interviewer a note of thanks in a brief letter or email. If you find the job appealing, say so and state that you believe you can fill it well, as shown in Figure 16–17.

If you are offered a job you want, call or send a brief message of acceptance as soon as possible—certainly within a week. The organization for such a message is simple. Begin by accepting the job you have been offered. Identify the job by title and state the exact salary so that there will be no confusion on these two important points. The second paragraph might go into detail about moving dates and reporting for work. The details will vary, depending on the nature of the job offer. Conclude with a statement that you are looking forward to working for your new employer, as in the acceptance letter written by a college student in Figure 16–18.

Because you will probably have applied to more than one organization, you will need to write a letter of refusal if you receive more than one job offer. Be especially tactful and courteous because the employer you are refusing has spent time and effort interviewing you and may have counted on your accepting the job. It is also possible that you may apply for another job at this company in the future. Figure 16–19 is an example of a job-refusal letter. It acknowledges the consideration given the applicant, offers a logical reason for refusal of the offer, and then concludes on a pleasant note.

■ Writing a Job Description

Once you are employed, you may be asked to create a description of the duties and requirements of your job. This is a common practice of most large companies and many small ones to ensure that the organization functions efficiently. Sometimes plant or office supervisors are given the task of writing the job descriptions of the employees assigned to them. In many organizations, though, an employee may draft his or her own job description, which is then checked over and approved by the immediate superior.

Job descriptions fulfill several important functions: They provide information on which equitable salary scales can be based; they help management determine whether all responsibilities within a company are adequately covered; they let both prospective and currently working employees know exactly what is expected of them; and, together, a firm's job descriptions present a picture of the organization's structure.

2647 Sitwell Road
Charlotte, NC 28210
March 17, 20--

Mr. F. E. Vallone
Manager of Human Resources
Information Systems, Inc.
3275 Commercial Park Drive
Raleigh, NC 27609

Dear Mr. Vallone:

Thank you for the informative and pleasant interview we had last Wednesday. Please extend my thanks to Mr. Wilson of the Media Group as well.

I came away from our meeting most favorably impressed with Information Systems. I find the position you are filling to be an attractive one and feel confident that my qualifications would enable me to perform the duties to everyone's advantage.

If I can answer any further questions, please email me at pmg@home.com or phone me at 937-964-1955.

Sincerely yours,

Philip Ming

Philip Ming

Figure 16–17   Follow-Up/Thank-You Letter

2647 Sitwell Road
Charlotte, NC 28210
March 26, 20--

Mr. F. E. Vallone
Manager of Human Resources
Information Systems, Inc.
3275 Commercial Park Drive
Raleigh, NC 27609

Dear Mr. Vallone:

I am pleased to accept your offer of $30,500 per year as a junior ACR designer in the Medical Group.

After graduation, I plan to leave Charlotte on Tuesday, June 16. I should be able to find suitable living accommodations within a few days and be ready to report for work on the following Monday, June 22. Please let me know if this date is satisfactory to you.

I look forward to working with the design team at Information Systems.

Very truly yours,

Philip Ming

Philip Ming

Figure 16–18 Acceptance Letter

2647 Sitwell Road
Charlotte, NC 28210
March 26, 20--

Mr. F. E. Vallone
Manager of Human Resources
Information Systems, Inc.
3275 Commercial Park Drive
Raleigh, NC 27609

Dear Mr. Vallone:

I enjoyed talking with you about your opening for a technical writer, and I was gratified to receive your offer. Although I have given the offer serious thought, I have decided to accept a position as a copywriter with an advertising agency. I feel that the job I have chosen is better suited to my skills and long-term goals.

I appreciate your consideration and the time you spent with me. I wish you the best of luck in filling the position.

Sincerely,

Philip Ming

Philip Ming

Figure 16–19   Letter of Refusal

Format for Writing a Job Description

Although job-description formats vary from organization to organization, the following headings are typical:

- *Accountability.* This section identifies, by title, the person or persons to whom the employee reports.
- *Scope of responsibilities.* This section provides an overview of the primary and secondary functions of the job and states, if it is applicable, who reports to the employee.
- *Specific duties.* This section gives a detailed account of the specific duties of the job, as concisely as possible.
- *Personal requirements.* This section lists the education, training, experience, and licensing required or desired for the job.

The typical job description shown in Figure 16–20 never mentions the person holding the job described. It focuses, instead, on the job and on the qualifications any person must possess to fill the position.

Figure 16–20
Sample Job Description

JOB TITLE: Welding Supervisor

ACCOUNTABILITY: Reports directly to the Plant Manager

SCOPE OF RESPONSIBILITIES: Is responsible for supervising the work of 15 welders, for preparing production reports, for maintaining and replacing equipment, and for carrying out such duties as the Plant Manager may specify.

SPECIFIC DUTIES:

Supervises the work of 15 welders. Evaluates, every six months, the performances of the welders assigned to him or her. Instructs new employees in safe working habits. Prepares a monthly attendance report. Periodically checks the quality of work by examining tubes and balls for weld splatters and by reviewing the inspector's quality reports.
Prepares production reports. Prepares a monthly memo itemizing production for the preceding month, including reasons for any failure to meet the production schedule.
Maintains and replaces equipment. Maintains accurate logs for each machine. Makes sure that all equipment is in good operating condition and ready for the start of the next shift. Makes sure that all safety devices function properly.
Carries out such duties as the Plant Manager may specify. Meets each week with the Plant Manager and attends special meetings as requested. Attends in-service training programs and keeps up to date on the latest welding techniques.

PERSONAL REQUIREMENTS: Trade or technical college certification or degree in welding. Six years of welding experience. Ability to interact well with employees and management. Desire to stay up to date in the field.

WRITER'S CHECKLIST: Writing a Job Description

If you have been asked to prepare a job description for your position, consider the following guidelines:

- ☐ Before attempting to write your job description, keep a list of all the different tasks you do in a week or a month. Otherwise, you will almost certainly leave out some of your duties.

- ☐ Focus on content. Remember that you are writing a description of your job, not of yourself.

- ☐ List your duties in decreasing order of importance. Knowing how your various duties rank in importance makes it easier to set valid job qualifications.

- ☐ Begin each statement of a duty with a verb, and be specific about what the duty is. Write "Answer and route incoming telephone calls" rather than "Handle telephone calls."

- ☐ Review existing job descriptions that you know have been successful.

CHAPTER 16 SUMMARY: Finding a Job

Follow these five steps for finding a job:

- ☐ Determine the best job for you.
- ☐ Prepare an effective résumé.
- ☐ Write an effective letter of application.
- ☐ Conduct yourself well during the interview.
- ☐ Send a follow-up message after the interview.

Research the following sources of information for locating jobs:

- ☐ College Career Center
- ☐ Internet resources
- ☐ Tips from friends and acquaintances
- ☐ Letters of inquiry
- ☐ Advertisements in newspapers
- ☐ Advertisements in trade and professional journals
- ☐ Private and temporary employment agencies
- ☐ Local, state, and federal agencies

Plan your résumé carefully.

☐ Determine the type of job you seek and compile a list of prospective employers.

☐ Consider the type of information about you and your background of most importance to those employers.

☐ Determine, based on this information, the details that should be included and the most effective way to present them.

Write an effective letter of application.

☐ Catch the reader's attention.

☐ Create the desire for your services.

☐ Include a brief summary of your qualifications for the specific job for which you are applying.

☐ State when and where you can be reached.

Follow these steps to prepare for a job interview:

☐ Learn everything you can about your prospective employer.

☐ Arrive on time.

☐ Highlight those strengths most useful to the job you are applying for.

☐ Demonstrate your knowledge of your field.

☐ Send the interviewer a brief note of thanks after the interview.

When you receive a job offer, write one of the following letters:

☐ If you plan to accept the offer, send a letter of acceptance as soon as possible after you receive the offer.

☐ If you plan to refuse, send a letter as soon as possible refusing the offer but expressing your appreciation for the organization's time and effort in considering you.

When asked by your employer to write a description of your job, do the following:

☐ Identify the title of the person you report to.

☐ Provide an overview of the primary and secondary functions of your job; include information on any other employees who report to you.

☐ Provide a detailed account of the specific duties of your job, as concisely as possible.

☐ List the education, training, experience, and licensing required or desired for the job.

■ Exercises

1. Write an application letter for a summer job to a corporation; a public-interest group; a research organization; a local, state, or federal agency; or a firm of your choosing. Make a case for yourself as interested in a job because working there will provide valuable experience for your future career. Your letter should be no longer than one single-spaced page. Enclose your résumé only if you think it will enhance your job prospects. Refer to the guidelines for writing application letters in this chapter.

2. Using the guidelines in this chapter, write a letter of application and a résumé in response to an advertisement for a job for which you will be qualified upon graduation. Use high-quality white bond paper and make sure the letter and application are error- and blemish-free.

3. Assume that you have been interviewed for the job in Exercise 2. Write a follow-up letter expressing thanks for the interview.

4. Write a letter to a past or present teacher, an employer, or another appropriate person, asking permission to use him or her as a job reference. Be prepared to explain in class why you think this person is especially well qualified to comment on your job qualifications.

5. Obtain a sample résumé at your school's career-development center or local copy center. Write a brief critical analysis of the résumé for your instructor, pointing out its strong points and how it might be improved in content, organization, or design. Your instructor will determine the length of the analysis.

6. Locate an individual who works in a professional area that might be of interest to you when you graduate. With your instructor's approval, contact that person to arrange an interview in which you learn specific information about the profession. Some questions you might ask could include: What sources did you use to find your first job? Your current job? What are the starting salary ranges for this area? Advanced position salaries? What sorts of skills and abilities are needed to enter this profession? When you have finished, report your findings as your instructor requests, either as a presentation to the class or in a written report.

7. Electronic non-Web résumés differ from paper ones in a number of ways. One significant difference is the abundant use of nouns in the electronic non-Web résumé rather than action verbs in the traditional paper résumé (for example, *designer* and *management* rather than *designed* and *managed*). Make a list of all of the action verbs on your current paper résumé. For each verb, list the corresponding noun. Submit your list to your instructor with a copy of your paper résumé.

8. Following the guidelines in this chapter, on pages 693–697, create an electronic non-Web résumé. You may assume that you are sending your résumé in response to an electronic posting advertising a summer position in your field of study. Your instructor may ask that you also prepare a version to be scanned. Submit your résumé either on a disk or as an email attachment, or both, as required by your instructor.

9. One way to discover if you would fit into a particular job setting or to simply learn more about how a business, company, or office operates is to job-shadow. With

your instructor's approval, call a local job-site and ask if you can job-shadow for a few hours. Many organizations, especially in the government or service sector, are pleased to accommodate students for two or three hours. During that time, you will be assigned to observe closely an employee as he or she follows a regular routine, thus the name *job-shadowing*. Write a brief narrative in the form of a memo to your instructor summarizing your experiences. Within seven days following your visit, send a thank-you note both to the company and to the employee who you shadowed expressing your appreciation for the visit. Your instructor may request a copy of your thank-you note.

10. If your current résumé is prepared by job chronology, prepare a second résumé—a functional résumé—organizing work experience by type. Follow the guidelines in the section of this chapter, Organizing the Résumé. Functional résumés not only are useful to certain potential employers, but they also help you identify important skills, abilities, or experiences. Your instructor may ask you to submit your chronological résumé with your functional résumé.

11. If you are currently employed, write a description of your job according to the guidelines presented in this chapter. If you are not employed, describe your most recent job. Try to reconstruct a typical day at that job, recalling as many particulars as possible.

■ In-Class Activities

1. Prepare a list of at least six job-related assets that you have and explain—as specifically as possible—why and how these qualities would be useful to a potential employer. Include any honors you have received, high grade-point averages, specific skills such as advanced computer knowledge or creative design talent. Include unique work experience. Do not overlook good work habits such as accuracy, dependability, and honesty. If you have held the same job for more than two years, for instance, that indicates you have been a worthwhile employee. Your instructor may ask you to read your list aloud in class. Remember that a degree of self-confidence is a necessary tool in looking for a job, so as you relate your list to your classmates, be proud of your accomplishments. When your classmates read their lists, the class will discover a wealth of talent and potential that they may not have known was present!

2. Divide into groups with classmates who share your major area (or a similar area) of study. For example, business majors would form one group, health sciences another, agricultural interests another, engineering students another, and so forth. If you have more than seven students in your group, divide into two smaller groups. Appoint a group leader and recorder. For the first 30 minutes, brainstorm a list of action words that could be used to describe your collective skills, abilities, and experiences, and which could work well in a résumé to be used in your field. During the next 15 minutes, brainstorm a list of positions that you could apply for when you graduate. Your instructor may ask you to share your information with your classmates.

3. As in Activity 2, divide into groups with classmates who share your major area (or a similar area) of study. As a group, discuss the job-search methods most useful

to job seekers in your field. The purpose of this session is to share information and ideas. Discuss the value of placement services; Internet resources; networking; letters of inquiry; advertisements in newspapers, trade, and professional journals; private and temporary employment agencies; and any other sources you know of. Discuss methods of organizing job-search information and creating workable timelines for job searches.

4. As a class, discuss ways to prepare for your job search when you graduate. For example, what campus organizations would be helpful if you became a member now? What part-time and summer employment would help in your future job search? What other courses besides business writing would help prepare you to find the right job? What networking should you be engaged in right now for future opportunities? During what part of your educational program should you begin to look for a career position? Each person in the class should be prepared to contribute to the discussion.

5. Working in pairs, spend 20 minutes during which you play the role of the job interviewer, while your partner plays the role of the interviewee. Then, switch roles for the next 20 minutes. In preparation for this assignment, refer to the interview section of this chapter. Before the interviews, decide the name and type of company where you are interviewing, the position, and other details about the job. Include the following questions in the interview:
   - What are your short-term and long-term occupational goals?
   - What are your major strengths and weaknesses?
   - Why do you want to work for this employer?
   - How do you spend your free time?
   - What are your personal goals?
   - What accomplishment are you particularly proud of? Describe it.
   - Why should I hire you?

In conclusion, consider what answers you would change in preparation for your next interview.

■ Research Projects

1. After brainstorming about your career goals and career-related assets, search to find what variety of positions you will be qualified for when you complete your current educational program. Use the media resource center, the library, the campus placement center, and networking (with individuals already working in the field) to identify as many positions as you can. Try to discover the following about each of the positions:
   - Detailed job description
   - The future of the job
   - Geographic location
   - Typical working conditions
   - Average salary
   - Other relevant details

Summarize your findings in a brief narrative. Did you learn new information? Which ones appeal to you, and why?

2. Using print sources, find a firm that is rated as "one of the best places to work in the United States." Then write a letter asking whether there is a position available for someone with the qualifications you expect to have either at the end of the present semester or when you graduate.

3. Interview a counselor in your school's Career Development Center to learn what mistakes students tend to make when they seek employment. As directed by your instructor, make a presentation to the class or write a report on what you learn. Share any specific advice or tips that the counselor suggested, providing a print version of relevant information to be handed out in class.

4. Research three major employers in your field and in an outline format answer the following questions about each:
   a. What kind of an organization is it?
   b. Is it a profit or nonprofit organization?
   c. How varied are the organization's operations? (For example, does it produce more than one type of product or service?)
   d. What does its mission statement reveal?
   e. If it is government employment, at what level or sector is it?
   f. Does it provide a service or services? If so, what kind?
   g. How large is the business? How large are its assets?
   h. Is it locally owned? Is it a subsidiary of a larger operation? Is it expanding?
   i. How long has it been in business?
   j. Where would you fit in?
   You can obtain information from the Internet, current employees, company literature such as employee publications, and the business section of back issues of local and national newspapers (available in the library and sometimes on the Web).

5. Beginning your career is important, but knowing what to expect in terms of future advancement and promotion is also important. Choose one career to investigate and find answers to the following questions:
   a. Typically, how often do job-changing promotions come in this career?
   b. Is it important to be geographically flexible to advance in this field?
   c. What kind of travel is expected with promotions?
   d. What salary increases can be expected and when?
   e. Are advanced degrees necessary to remain competitive in this career?
   f. Is continuing education required for advancement?
   g. What kind of schedule do the higher jobs in this field require?
   h. How does a family or how do children fit into this career, once advancements are made?
   Conduct further research on any specific long-term benefits or potential problems that you feel may be involved in this career. Prepare an analysis for your instructor based on your findings. Your instructor may ask you to share your results with your classmates.

6. Interview someone who holds a job in a field that interests you. On the basis of the information you obtain about the job from the interview, prepare a job description of the position, following the guidelines in this chapter.

■ Web Projects

1. Find information about the future employment potential of graduates in your major field of study by using two Web sources, one of which must be the *Occupational Outlook Handbook* at http://stats.bls.gov/ocohome.htm/. You may also refer to the Census Bureau Web site at http://www.census.gov/, which provides data concerning job categories and also other job-related economic data by state and region. In addition, you may check the Web sites of large, well-established employers from your major field. In a brief memo to your instructor, answer the following questions about your major field:

   a. Based on current indicators, what are the job projections in your field in this country?

   b. Is there a worldwide demand for people in your field?

   c. Do employees in your field have an opportunity to advance?

   d. In your field, is there a wide range in salary expectations based on geographic location?

   e. What other relevant information can you provide?

2. Using the Web, find two firms that you would consider working for and compare working conditions and opportunities as presented at their Web sites. To begin your search, you may check the links and resources available at the Library of Congress, Business Reference Services at http://lcweb.loc.gov/rr/business/. Another resource is The Better Business Bureau Resource Library available at http://www.bbb.org/library/. Once you have chosen two company Web sites to review, make a list of important factors to compare as you consider the companies as potential employers. For example, if you choose to compare positions for registered nurses at two different hospitals, look at the size of the facilities, the number of beds, the number of registered nurses employed, the career opportunities and benefits advertised by the hospitals, and so forth. If you are looking at working in the Internet industry, review how old the company is, the qualifications of the president, the working conditions, retirement programs, and so forth. Try to find information about as many items on your list as possible. Write a brief analysis about your findings. Which is the more attractive employer? Explain why. Your instructor may ask that you share your narrative with your classmates.

3. Search the Web to find sites that are specifically appropriate to your career path and area of study. For example, the Small Business Administration, http://www.sba.gov, is available to help small business owners. Or, you may search for links using the Business Library of the Brooklyn Public Library, the nation's largest public library devoted to business and finance, http://www.brooklynpubliclibrary.org/business/business.htm, or the Horn Library at Babson College, http://www.babson.edu/library/index.html, both offering business links to magazine and newspaper articles, library sources, and other electronic sources. Write a brief analysis of at least two Web sites that you would recommend as helpful to you and other students enrolled in your major field of study. Be certain to include URLs. As directed by your instructor, report your findings to the class.

4. Search the Web for positions available in your major field outside the United States. Determine and report on the following:
   a. What language skills are required?
   b. What travel experience is expected?
   c. What cross-cultural experience is expected? Find links to international companies at the United States Council for International Business at http://www.uscib.org, through its membership list, or visit the Argus Clearinghouse site for international business at http://www.clearinghouse.net/cgi-bin/chadmin/viewcat/Business_Employment?kywd++.

5. Review the Web sites of at least three online college or university placement centers, including the one hosted by your school, if one is available. Many centers, such as the Delaware State University Career Planning page at http://www.dsc.edu/updated/special/internetresources.html, and the Center for Career Opportunities, Purdue University at http://www.cco.purdue.edu/, offer links and general job-search information and can be helpful as you plan your own specific job search. Write a brief analysis of at least two career-planning sites you reviewed, including the URLs. Your instructor may ask you to share your results with the class.

6. Review several general job sites to become familiar with job seeking via the Web. Sites may include the following:

   College Grad Job Hunter at http://www.collegegrad.com

   America's Job Bank at http://www.ajb.dni.us/

   Monster.com at http://www.monster.com

   Cruel World (formerly Career Central) at http://www.cruelworld.com/index.asp

   Career Tech.com at http://www.careertech.com/

   Write a brief narrative stating which two sites seemed to be the most helpful for your field of study and why.

7. Review America's Job Bank at http://www.ajb.dni.us/, visiting several Web pages of job candidates. Prepare to establish a site of your own. Design a résumé for the Web by adapting an existing version by following the guidelines in the Writer's Checklist: Creating Web Résumés, page 695.

8. Search the Web to find three to five job descriptions. Write a brief analysis on the effectiveness of these descriptions. Which examples are the best? Why? How would you improve the weaker examples that you found? Bring copies of these descriptions to class and hand them out to your classmates. Give a brief presentation on your findings, supporting your analysis with details from the descriptions.

Writer's Guide

A The Electronic Office

Word Processing

Word-processing software makes it easy for you to create, edit, design, save, and print your documents, including memos, reports, class assignments, outlines, and even books. You can also spell- and grammar-check your text and integrate tables, photos, clip-art images, and spreadsheets into your documents. Word-processing software can help you record your ideas quickly and improve your writing and revising skills.

However, regardless of the benefits of technology, good writing is still the result of careful planning, constant practice, and thoughtful revision. In some cases, word-processing software can initially intrude on the writing process and impose certain limitations. The ease of making minor, sentence-level changes and the limitation of a small viewing screen, for example, may focus your attention too narrowly on surface problems of the text so you lose sight of larger problems of scope and organization. The fluid and rapid movement of the text on the screen, together with last-minute editing changes, may allow undetected errors to creep into the text. Also, as you master the software and become familiar with

> **WRITER'S CHECKLIST: Writing and Word Processing**
>
> ☐ Plan your document carefully by identifying your objective, readers, and scope, and by completing your research. Avoid the temptation of writing first drafts on the computer without any planning.
>
> ☐ Use the outline feature to brainstorm and organize an initial outline for your topic. As you create the draft, you can use the cut-and-paste feature to try alternative ways of organizing the information.
>
> ☐ When you're ready to begin writing, you can overcome writer's block by practicing freewriting on the computer. Freewriting means typing your thoughts as quickly as possible without stopping to correct mistakes or to

complete sentences; concentrate on perfecting your writing when you revise. Before you begin, adjust the monitor brightness so you can't see the text you're typing. Keeping the screen dark will prevent you from criticizing your thoughts before you express them. When you finish the first draft, turn the screen brightness up and review, revise, and reorganize as appropriate.

☐ Use the search-and-replace command to find and delete wordy phrases such as "that is," "there are," "the fact that," "to be," and unnecessary helping verbs such as "will."

☐ Use a spelling or grammar checker and other specialized programs to identify and correct typographical errors, misspellings, and grammar and diction problems. Maintain a file of your most frequently misspelled or misused words and use the search-and-replace command to check and correct them in your documents.

☐ Do not make all your revisions on screen. Print a double-spaced paper copy of your drafts periodically for major revisions and reorganizations.

☐ Always proofread your final copy on paper because the fluidity of the viewing screen makes it difficult to catch all the errors in your manuscript. Print out and distribute or email a copy of your document for your peers to comment on before making final revisions (as Christine Thomas did to good effect in Chapter 1).

☐ When writing a document for readers not familiar with your topic, use the search command to find technical terms and other data that may need further explanation for secondary readers or inclusion in a glossary.

☐ Use style sheets to control your document by defining format standards for different elements (headings, footnotes, pagination, and so on). Style sheets allow you to automate global document changes to ensure that formatting is consistent throughout.

☐ Create effective document design by highlighting major headings and subheadings with bold or italic type, by using the copy command to create and duplicate parallel headings throughout your text, and by inserting blank lines by pressing the enter key and tab-key spaces in your text to allow extra white space around examples and illustrations.

☐ Frequently save your text to the hard drive during long writing sessions, especially if your software does not have an automatic storage backup feature. Routinely create an extra or backup copy of your documents on duplicate disks for safekeeping.

☐ Keep the standard version of certain documents, such as your résumé and application letters, on file so you can revise them to meet the specific needs of each new job opportunity.

its powerful revision capabilities, you may begin to overwrite your documents; that is, inserting phrases and rewriting sentences becomes so easy that you may find yourself generating more text and rewriting more extensively but ultimately saying less. The tips in the Writer's Checklist: Writing and Word Processing will help you avoid these initial pitfalls and will help you develop writing strategies that take full advantage of the software.

The Internet

The Internet is a worldwide computer network connecting millions of computers and users. It is composed of public and private networks that allow people around the world to communicate, find, and share information, and offer commercial services online. The structure of the Internet is often compared to an interstate highway system: To get from one location to another, information travels at high speeds along routes that connect geographically distant sites. Business applications for the Internet include marketing, sales, and collaboration between people in different locations.

The wide range of resources available on the Internet permits users to communicate with others; exchange documents, data, and software; and connect to computers in different locations. These resources include electronic mail (email), discussion groups, chat environments, the World Wide Web (WWW or Web), file transfer protocol (FTP), and Telnet. There are also search engines for most of these resources that make finding information relatively easy. A search engine is software that can locate and retrieve information on the Internet based on words or combinations of words that you specify.

■ Communicating with Others

Email

Email is one of the Internet's most successful and effective services. Using the Internet, you can send an email message to anyone else worldwide with an Internet connection and an email address. (For a definition and discussion of email, see Chapter 8, pages 300–308.)

Email makes it possible to send text messages and to attach files to them that contain documents, pictures, graphics, and even sound and video. These messages may be sent to an individual or to people on a large mailing list. In addition to its speed, email also has the advantage of great cost savings compared with conventional mail, overnight delivery services, the telephone, or fax transmissions.

Be mindful of the need for clarity and completeness in your email messages. Review email messages to non-native speakers of English as carefully as you would written correspondence to them for unambiguous language and for cultural and other conventions used to express, for example, dates, times, and units of measurement. (See Chapter 8, pages 308–315, for more information about communicating in a global environment.)

Discussion Groups

Internet discussion groups provide forums for exchanging information with other users about topics of mutual interest. Some discussion groups are conducted through an exchange of email, while others function as postings on a public bulletin board that anyone can read. Internet Relay Chat (IRC) permits users to participate in discussions in real time. Unless you are using Internet discussion groups for professional purposes, such as gathering information for a report, they are generally inappropriate for the workplace.

Email Discussion Groups

Topic-oriented email discussion groups are relatively easy to locate. The simplest way is to conduct a search using the term "mailing list" in a search service such as AltaVista or Yahoo!. You can also use Liszt at http://www.liszt.com/, a mailing-list directory that is organized into topical areas, such as books, computers, education, humanities, music, news, and recreation (Figure A–1). Each broad topic heading indicates the number of lists found there and shows simple subtopics. The heading Computers (250 lists) includes the subtopics Hardware, Database, and Programming, each of which leads to increasingly specific topics in those categories.

To join an email discussion group (often called "listserv"), send a request to the list administrator asking that your address be added to the list. Thereafter, you will receive all email sent to the group by other members, and your questions and comments will be sent to all other list members. Discussion groups also are often used to distribute information to other members: monthly newsletters, the status of legislation, new developments in a field, upcoming meetings and conferences, and the like.

Newsgroups

Newsgroups are another type of online discussion group in which people exchange ideas, advice, and information. They are part of the Internet distribution network called "Usenet." You can visit a newsgroup site to read and post messages to other people with a shared interest in a specific topic. Unlike email discussion groups, in which messages are sent directly to your email in-box, with Usenet newsgroups, you must actively seek the online bulletin board, where messages are posted. Once you have reached a site, you can bookmark it for future access.

What topics are available? They number in the thousands and for ease of access are organized into broad topic categories: biz (business), comp (computers), sci (science), rec (recreation), soc (social issues), news (Usenet-related topics), and more. Each broad category is subdivided into increasingly specific topics.

Figure A–1   Liszt Home Page

The Liszt Usenet Newsgroup Directory at http://www.liszt.com/news/ provides links to thousands of newsgroups and gives detailed guidance on how to access and participate in newsgroup discussions.

Internet Relay Chat

IRC (or chat rooms) permits online conversations over topic-related channels that take place in real time. That is, the messages are read as they are typed rather than being stored and read afterward, as with listserv and Usenet messages. One advantage of using IRC is that it can function like a telephone conference call by allowing you to carry on simultaneous conversations or interviews with several people in remote locations. The Liszt IRC Chat Directory at http://www.liszt.com/chat/ provides access to over 38,000 IRC topics and gives instructions for participating in a conversation and conducting IRC subject searches.

Other more elaborate chat environments include Multi-User Dungeons (MUDs) and Multi-User Dungeons Object Oriented (MOOs), which are text-based thematic virtual environments. In those environments, users assume online personas, chat with other people, navigate rooms and other settings, and, in more advanced cases, design their own virtual worlds. These environments tend to be used more for recreational chat than for business-oriented activities.

Web Forums

Web forums allow participants to share information directly over the Web. They function as bulletin or message boards similar to Usenet sites in that they permit users to post and respond to messages. Unlike Usenet, Web forums are Web based and do not rely on a separate Internet system. That difference allows Web forums more flexibility to customize their use and to limit solicitations for get-rich-quick schemes and other unwelcome messages.

Most forums require you to register before you can post messages, although they waive that requirement for read-only access. Web forums are not real-time transmissions, like IRC, so you need not be online at the same time as other members to communicate with them.

You can locate Web-forum topics at Forum One at http://www.forumone.com/ by clicking on one of the broad topics listed (Current Events, Society and Culture, Business and Finance, Computers, Health, Science, Education, among others) or by entering a keyword in the search window to retrieve a list of active discussions on that topic. The discussions range from forums for health care, computer, and engineering professionals to forums devoted to hobbies and entertainment.

■ Connecting with Other Systems

Telnet

Telnet is a system that allows you to connect to remote computers via the Internet and run them and their software applications as if you were physically there. For example, if you are on a business trip and want to check your email messages back at the office, you can use Telnet to log on to the computer supporting your account to access your messages. You can also use Telnet to connect to public-access computers and databases, such as those in libraries, to search their bibliographic databases.

File Transfer Protocol

FTP is a resource for moving files around the Internet quickly. Using an FTP client program, you can acquire software applications and data files for your personal computer and download them to your hard drive. Although some FTP sites require passwords, most allow anonymous connections. FTP lets you log on to a host computer, find the files you want, and transfer them to your own computer. FTP does not permit users to view the information before transferring it unless the host computer makes software available online for doing so. Those who create and maintain Web sites also use FTP to send the site's HTML files to the server that hosts the site.

■ Using the World Wide Web

The Web is a system that simplifies navigation around the Internet and combines the capabilities of all the other Internet access systems. The Web supports applications for email, discussion groups, and chat environments, as well as for searching, retrieving, and providing information. The Web is also a multimedia environment: It brings together vast amounts of information—text, graphics, animation, audio, and video—on a global scale by linking information on the Internet. These links, called hyperlinks, are embedded into Web pages when they are created. (A Web page is simply the information visible on your screen. A home page is the first page of a Web site. It identifies whose site it is and often contains a table of contents of the site.) When you point your cursor on certain features displayed on a Web page, such as a button, highlighted words and phrases, or pictures, the cursor changes shape (typically from a pointer to an image of a hand). When you click the mouse on these highlighted features, your browser jumps to (that is, retrieves) a related Web document or image from elsewhere on the Web. (A *browser* is a software program that is necessary to access the Web for viewing Web documents and navigating among Web sites. Netscape and Explorer are two commonly used browsers.) The ability to link to related documents automatically and retrieve them makes hyperlinking a powerful tool. Thus, navigating from page to page and site to site becomes simple and intuitive. For instance, a typical university home-page screen may contain links to the individual colleges and professional schools on campus, the library system's online card catalog, and a brief history of the university and its admissions requirements.

Each page on the Web has a unique address known as a uniform resource locator (URL). The URL is made up of confusing-looking strings of letters and, sometimes, numbers. Fortunately, you do not have to remember URLs for most Web pages. Their addresses are often automated as hypertext links. In fact, when you find a site that you wish to revisit, you need not write the URL for future reference. Instead, you can bookmark the URL and later retrieve it from a drop-down menu, click on it, and go directly to the site. Despite their complexity, URLs make sense if you understand their components. For example, the URL for the Consumer Price Index page at the Bureau of Labor Statistics is typical: http:// www.bls.gov/cpiovrvw.htm. The first element, http://, stands for hypertext transfer protocol, which tells you that it's a Web site. Non-Web prefixes include ftp and telnet. The next component is the host-server or domain name, www.bls.gov, which identifies the root directory of the server (computer) that stores the information. The suffix, gov, is the abbreviation in the domain name that identifies it as a government site. Other distinctive identifiers for Web-page sponsors are edu (educational), com (commercial), and org (often a nonprofit organization). The next element, cpiovrvw, identifies the directory path (the address of this URL) and the file name associated with the page. The final suffix, htm, shows that the file is a hypertext document written in hypertext markup language (HTML).

Web pages are developed using HTML, a set of formatting codes used to tell a Web browser how to display a document on the screen (for example, text fonts, color, and the arrangement of text and graphics on the screen). HTML also permits the creation of hyperlinks to related Web sites.

■ Searching and Using the Internet

Using the Internet for communicating, finding and sharing information, and offering commercial services online is made much easier with the robust search engines provided with many of these resources. On the Web, for instance, there are dozens of search engines that find keywords and phrases, support complex search strategies, and provide extensive categories and indexes. Some of these search engines include Yahoo!, Lycos, Infoseek, AltaVista, and Excite. You can limit a search by specifying which resources you want to examine, for example, only Usenet discussion groups. (See pages 432–444 in Chapter 11 for a discussion of conducting research on the Internet.)

The Internet is not solely a collection of computer hardware and software. It also consists of groups of people learning and working online, some cooperating and some competing. Because the Internet is a social space, conventions exist for both discussions and the design of information on the Web. For example, in exchanging email messages, it is common to quote back the particular part of a message to which you are responding to provide context. (Your software allows you to do so at the click of the mouse.) In creating pages for a Web site, it is common to include a table of contents of what is available at the site and how it is organized. This basic information is located on the site's home page. It is also common to include an automated email link to the person responsible for maintaining the site and answering questions about it.

For a discussion of evaluating and crediting Internet sources and guidelines for using copyrighted material, see Chapter 11, "Researching Your Subject," pages 400–493.

Facsimile

Facsimile (fax) transmission uses telephone lines to transmit images of whole pages — text and graphics — from one fax machine to another at a different location. A fax page takes about 20 seconds to go from coast to coast and costs no more than a phone call to the same destination for the same amount of time. Faxes are used primarily to transmit information to locations without Internet access or to send documents with nondigital elements, such as handwritten corrections and notes, that must be viewed as originally created. A fax is the preferred medium when you have to send a nondigital drawing or diagram or a document such as a contract that contains one or more signatures to ensure its authenticity. Keep in mind that faxes are almost never as clear as the original document. Transmitting text and graphics quickly to others in distant locations facilitates collaborative writing and many other kinds of remote communication tasks, although the Internet is replacing fax technology for collaborative work in many businesses.

When you transmit fax messages, be aware that in many offices they arrive in a central location where they may be viewed by those for whom they are not intended. If you must fax confidential or sensitive messages, alert the intended recipient to be waiting at the machine as you send your information.

B Spelling and Vocabulary

1. Spelling

Human resources managers often reject candidates who make spelling errors on employment applications, résumés, and application letters. Consider, for example, the story of a college graduate who applied for the position of assistant director of human resources and was rejected for misspelling the word *resources.*

Potential employers react strongly to spelling errors because poor spelling reflects negatively on an employee—and, by association, on the employer as well. Everyone makes an occasional error, of course, but a human resources manager may conclude that someone who has overlooked a spelling mistake on something as important as a job application may be careless in his or her work, too. Keep in mind that when you apply for a job, an employer must make a judgment based primarily on your résumé, your letter of application, and your interview.

An even more important reason to learn to be a careful speller is that accuracy in spelling can help you keep the bargain you, as a writer, make with your readers: to assist them in understanding what you are saying. Your job as a writer is to remove roadblocks from the path of communication between you and your readers—and spelling errors, because they can confuse and slow down your readers and create roadblocks.

As you write a first draft, you needn't be concerned about spelling words correctly. At that point, your attention should focus on what you are saying; to worry about spelling when drafting would be a distraction. You can check for and correct spelling errors when you revise; in fact, you should proofread once *just for spelling.* Guard against the natural tendency to concentrate on complex words; pay as much attention to words in common use. It is often the words you use most frequently that can cause you problems.

If your word-processing software has a spellchecker feature, use it as you make your final revisions. Spellcheckers scan the text, stopping at each instance of a misspelled word, a repeated word ("the the"), words with numbers ("wi11" spelled with two *1*'s rather than with two *l*'s), and common errors in capitalization ("THere" for "There"). Most spellcheckers also allow you to create a customized dictionary of acronyms, names, and specialized terms commonly used in your writing but not recognized by the spellchecker's standard dictionary.

Although a spellchecker is an invaluable tool for painless online proofing, you should not rely on it completely for proofing your document. For example, a spellchecker cannot identify in a given context whether you meant *it* or *if*. It recognizes both words as correctly spelled and so will pass over each whenever they occur, regardless of whether you intended one instead of the other. Nor can you count on a spellchecker to help you proof numbers. You still must print a paper copy of a document produced using word-processing software and proof it carefully.

Improving your spelling requires a systematic effort. The following system will help you learn to spell correctly:

- Keep a dictionary handy, and use it regularly. If you are unsure about the spelling of a word, don't rely on memory or guesswork—consult the dictionary. When you look up a word, focus on both its spelling and its meaning. For a more convenient way to check spelling, instead of using a standard dictionary keep a small-format spelling dictionary handy. Usually four by six inches or smaller, these "instant" dictionaries list thousands of words (showing where each can be divided for hyphenation) but give no definitions. Or, consult an online dictionary such as *Merriam-Webster Online* at http://www.m-w.com/, the *Encarta World English Dictionary* online at http://encarta.msn.com/, or *The American Heritage Dictionary of the English Language* available online at Bartleby.com: Great Books Online at http://www.bartleby.com/61/.

- After you have looked in the dictionary for the spelling of the word, write the word from memory several times. Then check the accuracy of your spelling. If you have misspelled the word, repeat this step. If you do not follow through by writing the word from memory, you lose the chance of retaining it for future use. Practice is essential.

- Keep a list of the words you commonly misspell, and work regularly at whittling it down. Do not load the list with exotic words; many of us would stumble over *asphyxiation* or *pterodactyl*. Concentrate instead on words such as *calendar, maintenance,* and *unnecessary.* These and other frequently used words should remain on your list until you have learned to spell them.

- Study the following common sets of words that sound alike but differ in spelling and meaning.[1]

     accept (verb: to agree or receive)
     except (preposition: other than)
     affect (verb: to influence)

----

[1]The meanings given here are for identification only—they are not intended to represent every meaning a word may have.

effect (noun: a result)

all ready (We are *all ready* to go.)
already (Have you finished the work *already*?)

ascent (noun: a movement up)
assent (noun: an agreement)

brake (noun: device for stopping)
break (verb: to crack; noun: period of relaxation)

cent (noun: coin)
scent (noun: smell)
sent (verb: past tense of *send*)

cite (verb: to refer to)
sight (noun: view, something to look at)
site (noun: location)

coarse (adjective: rough)
course (noun: direction of study; adverb in *of course*)

complement (noun: something that completes something else)
compliment (noun: praise; verb: to give praise)

fair (noun: exhibition; adjective: light-hued, beautiful)
fare (noun: cost of a trip, or food served)

foreword (noun: introduction to a book)
forward (adjective and adverb: near or toward the front)

hear (verb: to listen to)
here (adverb: in this place)

its (possessive pronoun: Does the dog have *its* bone?)
it's (contraction[2] of *it is*: *It's* good to see you.)

knew (verb: past tense of *to know*)
new (adjective: not old)

lead (noun: a metal—rhymes with *bread*)
lead (verb: to be first—rhymes with *breed*)
led (verb: past tense of verb *to lead*)

may be (verb: It *may be* true, but it's hard to believe.)
maybe (adverb: perhaps—*Maybe* he will visit us.)

miner (noun: a person who works in a mine)
minor (noun: an underage person)

pair (noun: set of two)

---

[2]In a *contraction,* two words are combined and one or more letters are omitted. An apostrophe (') indicates where the letter or letters have been dropped. Contractions are appropriate in some informal writing, but it is best to avoid them in formal contexts.

pare (verb: to trim)
pear (noun: fruit)

patience (noun: tolerance)
patients (noun: people who are receiving medical attention)

peace (noun: absence of war)
piece (noun: small amount)

plain (adjective: ordinary-looking, simple; noun: large field)
plane (noun: aircraft; verb: to make smooth)

principal (adjective: primary, main; noun: school official)
principle (noun: a controlling idea or belief)

right (adjective: correct, or a direction)
rite (noun: ritual)
write (verb: to create with words)

road (noun: passageway for vehicles)
rode (past tense of verb *to ride*)
rowed (past tense of verb *to row*—to propel a small boat)

stationary (adjective: not moving)
stationery (noun: writing paper and envelopes)

their (possessive pronoun—Do you know *their* telephone number?)
there (adverb: at that place)
they're (contraction of *they are*—*They're* going to meet us at the movies.)

threw (verb: past tense of *to throw*)
through (preposition: by way of)
thru (informal form of *through:* should not be used in business writing)

to (preposition: toward)
too (conjunction: also; adverb: excessively)
two (number)

weak (adjective: not strong)
week (noun: seven days)

weather (noun: atmospheric conditions)
whether (conjunction: if)

who's (contraction of *who is*—Do you know *who's* coming?)
whose (possessive pronoun—*Whose* coat is this?)

your (possessive pronoun—Is this *your* book?)
you're (contraction of *you are*—*You're* a fine friend!)

The following pages contain a number of rules and some advice to help you improve your spelling. Use this section to focus on any specific problem areas in spelling that you may have. (Bear in mind that most of these rules have exceptions.)

> **ESL TIPS: Distinguishing between American and British English**
>
> You may notice a slight difference between the spelling of the English spoken in the United States and that spoken in England. For business writing in the United States, follow the American English spellings of words.
>
> | **American** | **British** |
> |---|---|
> | center | centre |
> | theater | theatre |
> | realize | realise |
> | color | colour |
> | learned | learnt |
> | check | cheque |
> | connection | connexion |

■ 1.1 The Silent-*E* Rule

Words of one syllable that have a long vowel sound usually end in silent *e*. (A *long vowel* is one that is pronounced like the letter's name.) Adding silent *e* to a one-syllable word that has a *short-vowel sound* ordinarily gives the vowel a long sound. (Dictionaries vary in the symbols they use to indicate how a word is pronounced. Examine the pronunciation key in the dictionary you use.)

Compare the words in the following two lists:

Short-Vowel Sounds	**Long-Vowel Sounds**
bit	bite
cut	cute
dot	dote
fat	fate
pet	Pete

The silent-*e* rule also applies to the accented syllable in some longer words.[3]

com·plete′   con·trive′   re·fuse′

The silent-*e* rule does not apply in longer words in which the final syllable is *not* accented.

com·pos′·ite   gran′·ite   op′·pos·ite

---

[3]An *accented syllable* receives the emphasis when the word is spoken. The symbol ′ is used here to indicate the accented syllable. Check your dictionary for the symbol it uses.

If endings are added to the basic word, the silent-*e* rule still holds, even if the silent *e* is dropped when the ending is added.

complete, completed   hope, hoping   late, later

■ 1.2 Hard and Soft Sounds

The letter *c* can sound like a *k* ("hard" *c*) or like an *s* ("soft" *c*). The letter *g* can sound like "guh" ("hard" *g*) or like a *j* ("soft" *g*).

Hard Sound	Soft Sound
attic	ace
cog	agent

1.2.1 Hard C and Soft C

Hard *c* and soft *c* cause problems mostly at the ends of words. The following guidelines will help you to distinguish between hard *c* and soft *c*:

- The sound of *c* is always hard when it is the last letter of a word.
  automatic   economic   electric   spastic   specific

- A long vowel followed by a *k* sound is always spelled with a *k* and a silent *e*.
  eke   fluke   like   take   woke

- A short vowel followed by a *k* sound is spelled *ck* when another syllable follows, except in certain words borrowed from French, such as *racquet*.
  beckon   bracket   picket   pocket   trucker

- An *e* after a *c* almost always indicates a soft *c*.
  ace   ice   piece   place   puce

1.2.2 Hard G and Soft G

Hard *g* and soft *g* cause problems mostly at the beginnings of words. The following guidelines should help you to distinguish between hard *g* and soft *g*:

- Any *g* followed by a consonant is a hard *g*.
  ghetto   gladly   grain   green

- The *g* in the combinations *gu* and *go* is always hard.
  cargo   goblet   guess   guide

- The *g* in the combination *ga* is always hard except in the word *margarine.*

  gale   gape   garage   gate

- The *g* in the combination *gi* can be either hard or soft.

  fragile   giant   gift   give

- The *g* in the combination *ge* is usually soft.

  cage   garage   general   germinate   gesture

- The *g* in the combination *gy* is normally soft. Words such as *gynecology* are exceptions.

  gymnasium   gypsum   gyrate   gyroscope

■ 1.3 Adding to Basic Words

Words may change spelling according to the way they are used in a sentence. The following rules can serve as a guide in choosing the correct spelling of a plural noun, a verb form, an adverb formed from an adjective, and the comparative and superlative forms of some adjectives (*nicer, nicest*).

1.3.1 Plurals of Nouns

You may have no difficulty spelling words such as *tax, brush,* or *ox.* You may encounter some trouble, though, in spelling the plural forms of these and other words. The general rules for forming the plural of nouns are as follows.

- To form the plural of *most* nouns, add *-s.*

  circumstance/circumstances   hat/hats   mule/mules

  pen/pens   tie/ties   tool/tools

- To form the plural of nouns that end in *ch, s, sh, ss, x, z,* or *zz,* add *-es.*

  branch/branches   brush/brushes   bus/buses

  buzz/buzzes   glass/glasses   tax/taxes

- To form the plural of nouns that end in *y* preceded by a vowel, add *-s.*

  boy/boys   monkey/monkeys

  But if the *y* is preceded by a consonant, change the *y* to *i* and then add *-es.*

  filly/fillies   fly/flies

■ To form the plural of most nouns that end in *f* and all nouns that end in *ff,* add *-s.*

reef/reefs   roof/roofs   cuff/cuffs

For a few nouns that end in *f,* change the *f* to *v* and add *-es.*
leaf/leaves   loaf/loaves   wolf/wolves

If a noun ends in *fe,* change the *f* to *v* and add *-es.*
knife/knives   life/lives   wife/wives

Note: If there is a *v* in the plural form of a noun, you can usually hear it in the spoken word.

■ Some commonly used nouns have special plural forms.

child/children	foot/feet	ox/oxen
tooth/teeth	woman/women	mouse/mice

Consult your dictionary for other plural forms that may be troublesome: nouns ending in *o,* foreign words used in English, a number of scientific and medical terms, and so on.

1.3.2 Adding Verb, Adjective, and Adverb Endings

The general rules for adding endings to verbs, for forming adverbs from adjectives, and for adding the comparative (*-er*) and superlative (*-est*) endings to adjectives are as follows:

■ If the word ends in a consonant, simply add the ending.

burn + ing = burning   long + er = longer
small + est = smallest   want + ed = wanted

■ If the word ends in silent *e* and the ending begins with a vowel (including *e*), drop the silent *e* of the basic word.

advise + ory = advisory   base + ic = basic
desire + able = desirable   fine + est = finest
landscape + er = landscaper   note + ed = noted

■ If the basic word ends in silent *e* and the ending begins with a consonant, simply add the ending.

care/carefully   like/likely   use/useless

There are a few exceptions to this rule.

argue/argument   nine/ninth   true/truly

- If the basic word ends in a consonant and the ending begins with the same consonant, keep both consonants.

  cool/coolly   jewel/jewellike   sad/saddest

- If the basic word ends in *y* preceded by a vowel, simply add the ending.

  betray/betrays/betrayed/betraying

  obey/obeys/obeyed/obeying

  Note: There are three important exceptions to this rule:

  lay/lays/laying   *but*   laid

  pay/pays/paying   *but*   paid

  say/says/saying   *but*   said

- If the basic word ends in *y* preceded by a consonant, change the *y* to *i* before adding the ending, *unless the ending begins with j.*

  copy/copies/copied/copying

  try/tries/tried/trying

- If a verb ends in *ie*, add -*s* or -*d* directly to the word.

  die/dies/died   tie/ties/tied

  But change *ie* to *y* before adding -*ing.*

  die/dying   tie/tying

- When you add -*ly* to most adjectives to form an adverb, simply add the ending. The word *truly* is an exception to this rule.

  careful/carefully   complete/completely   dim/dimly

  nice/nicely   sure/surely   useless/uselessly

  When you add the ending -*ly* to most adjectives ending in *cal*, be sure to retain the *a* and both *l*'s.

  magical/magically   practical/practically

- When you add -*er*, -*est*, or -*ly* to an adjective that ends in *y*, change the *y* to *i* before adding the ending.

  happy/happier/happiest/happily

  noisy/noisier/noisiest/noisily

- When you add *-ly* to adjectives ending in *-ble,* drop the *e* and add only the *-y.*

  able/ably   favorable/favorably   incredible/incredibly

■ 1.4 Doubling Final Consonants

Knowing when and when not to double a final consonant before adding an ending is important. Three things affect the decision: (1) whether the vowel in the basic word is long or short, (2) whether the last syllable of the basic word is accented, and (3) whether the basic word ends in more than one consonant.

1.4.1 The Effect of the Vowel in the Basic Word

For most words of one syllable, double the final consonant only if the preceding vowel is *short:*

flop/flopped	ripe/ripen
let/letting	mate/mated
rip/ripped	tune/tuning

Never double the final consonant of a word if the consonant is immediately preceded by two vowels.

appear/appeared/appearing/appearance
treat/treated/treating/treatment

1.4.2 The Effect of the Word's Accent

In longer words, whether the final consonant is doubled depends on which syllable is accented. When the accent falls on the last syllable of a word, double the final consonant before adding the ending.

ad·mit'/admitted/admitting   com·pel'/compelled/compelling

When the accent does not fall on the last syllable, do not double the final consonant before adding the ending.

dif'fer/differed/differing   ex·hib'it/exhibited/exhibiting
fo'cus/focused/focusing   pro'fit/profited/profiting

1.4.3 The Effect of Final Consonants

When a word ends in more than one consonant, *do not double* the final consonant when adding an ending.

confirm/confirmed/confirming

depend/depended/depending/dependence

When a word ends in a double consonant, keep both consonants when adding the ending.

embarrass/embarrassed/embarrassing/embarrassment

enroll/enrolled/enrolling/enrollment

■ 1.5 Prefixes and Suffixes

A *prefix* is a form such as *dis-*, *un-*, or *anti-* that is placed in front of a word to change its meaning. A *suffix* is a form such as *-able* or *-ible* that is placed at the end of a word (or word part) to change its meaning. To avoid making spelling errors when you use words that contain prefixes and suffixes, study the following rules.

- When you attach a prefix such as *dis-*, *im-*, *mis-*, or *un-* to a word that begins with the same letter as the *last* letter of the prefix, be sure to retain the double letters.

  dis + similar = dissimilar   im + movable = immovable

  mis + spell = misspell   un + natural = unnatural

- When you attach a suffix that begins with a vowel to a word that ends in silent *e,* you should usually drop the *e.*

  advise/advisory   continue/continual

  enclose/enclosure   sane/sanity

- When you attach the suffix *-able* or *-ible* to a word that ends in a soft *c* or a soft *g* sound, retain the *e* of the original word.

  change/changeable   manage/manageable

  notice/noticeable   service/serviceable

- When you attach suffixes such as *-ness* and *-less,* do not change the spelling of the original word.

  care + less = careless (retain the *e*—otherwise you are spelling *carless,* "without a car")

  drunken + ness = drunkenness (retain both *n*'s)

  Note: In a word such as *lioness,* the suffix is *-ess* (to indicate female), not *-ness.*

■ 1.6 Words with *ie* or *ei*

Among the trickiest words in the English language to spell are *ie* and *ei* words. The following guidelines should help you to recognize the correct spelling of these words. The jingle "*i* before *e*, except after *c*" covers rules 1 and 2.

1. In most cases, the correct combination following the letter *c* is *ei*.

ceiling	conceive	perceive	receive

2. Many words that are pronounced *ee* are spelled *ie*.

achieve	brief	cashier	field
piece	relieve	tier	yield

3. Many words that are pronounced with a long *a* are spelled *ei*.

eight	freight	rein
veil	vein	weight

4. Words that are pronounced with a long *i* are always spelled *ei*.

height	seismograph	sleight

■ 1.7 Contractions

A *contraction* is a form that combines two words, omitting one or more letters, and uses an apostrophe (') to indicate where the letter or letters have been dropped.

cannot/can't	is not/isn't
it is/it's	they are/they're

Remember to place the apostrophe exactly where the letter or letters are deleted.

Be careful not to confuse contractions with words that have the same pronunciation as the contractions.

its/it's	their/they're	theirs/there's	whose/who's

Do not confuse the presence of the apostrophe to form a contraction with the use of the apostrophe to show possession.

Contraction	**Possession**
can't (can + not)	the woman's voice
don't (do + not)	a student's book

In a contraction, the apostrophe indicates that a letter has been left out. In a possessive form, the apostrophe indicates ownership.

■ 1.8 Abbreviated Spellings

In very informal writing, certain words are sometimes spelled in an abbreviated form: *thru* (*through*), *tho* (*although*), and *nite* (*night*). Such abbreviated spellings should be avoided in all job-related writing.

■ 1.9 Word Groups of Frequently Misspelled Words

■ Words ending in *ery*

creamery	bravery	effrontery
hatchery	imagery	nursery

■ Words ending in *ary*

arbitrary	complementary	complimentary	documentary
elementary	fragmentary	imaginary	library
monetary	necessary	primary	tributary

■ Words ending in *able*

acceptable	agreeable	avoidable	changeable
dependable	manageable	profitable	valuable

Note: Remember to keep the *e* in *changeable* and *manageable*.

■ Words ending in *iable*

appreciable	enviable	justifiable
liable	reliable	variable

■ Words ending in *ible*

audible	combustible	compatible	credible
divisible	eligible	feasible	forcible
illegible	indelible	invincible	negligible
reducible	visible		

■ Words ending in *ise*

advertise	advise	comprise	compromise
excise	exercise	franchise	revise
supervise			

Note: The noun form of *supervise* is *supervisor;* the noun form of *advise* is *adviser* or *advisor*.

ESL TIPS: Using a Bilingual Dictionary

As a non-native speaker of English, you may periodically want to consult a bilingual dictionary. Be careful, because using a bilingual dictionary is not as simple as looking up the word in your native language and copying down the first entry—you could easily end up with the wrong equivalent or an inappropriate form.

Here are some tips for using a bilingual dictionary:

1. Look up the word in your first language.
2. Carefully review the dictionary entry. What part of speech are you interested in? A noun? A verb? A participle? Try to match the part of speech you are looking for with the parts of speech listed in the dictionary entry. If you need help with the abbreviations, you can usually find the legend at the bottom of the page or in the introduction to the dictionary.
3. If your dictionary lists fields of knowledge, scan the entry to see if any field seems particularly suited to your situation. Is the way you want to use the word specifically related to one of the fields?
4. Once you determine that you have located the correct English word, turn to the English section of the dictionary and look up that word. Read the entry carefully. Does the meaning of the definition in your first language match your intended meaning in English? If not, look the word up in your native-language section again and select another word. Repeat step 4 until you find the word that expresses the meaning you intended.
5. As you write, make sure you have used the appropriate form of the new word.

(See also ESL Tips: Selecting Bilingual and ESL Dictionaries on page 753.)

- Words ending in *ize*

authorize	energize	familiarize	magnetize
notarize	organize	specialize	stabilize
standardize	subsidize	summarize	synchronize

- Words ending in *yze*

  analyze   paralyze

  Note: The noun forms are *analysis* and *paralysis*.

- Words ending in *eous*

courteous	erroneous	gaseous
heterogeneous	homogeneous	instantaneous
outrageous	spontaneous	

- Words ending in *ious*

cautious	contagious	curious	laborious
mysterious	nutritious	previous	repetitious

■ Words ending in *ous*

anonymous	callous	dangerous	disastrous
grievous	hazardous	intravenous	mischievous
monotonous			

■ Words ending in *sion*

compulsion	conclusion	conversion	diversion
erosion	expansion	expulsion	extension
occasion	persuasion	propulsion	provision
reversion			

■ Words ending in *ssion*

accession	admission	concession
discussion	omission (note one *m*)	recession
remission	succession	transmission

Note: Be sure to distinguish between *intersession* (the period between two *sessions* of the school year) and *intercession* (intervention on behalf of someone).

■ Words ending in *cede*

accede	concede
intercede	precede (to go ahead of someone or something)
recede	secede

The *-ing* forms of these words follow the silent *-e* rule: *acceding, conceding, interceding, preceding, receding, seceding.*

■ Words ending in *ceed*

exceed	proceed (to go forward)	succeed

The *-ing* forms are *exceeding, proceeding, succeeding.*

Note: The word *supersede,* "to take the place of something that went before," is often misspelled. It is the only word in common use that has a *sede* ending.

■ Words ending in *ence*

magnificence	maleficence	permanence
persistence	pertinence	

■ Words ending in *ance*

dissonance   malfeasance   perseverance

■ Words ending in *scence*

effervescence   luminescence   phosphorescence

2. Vocabulary

Trying to get along with a limited vocabulary is like trying to prepare a five-course meal with only one utensil and a pan. The limited equipment prevents you from dealing successfully with the range of situations you'll find yourself in. A limited vocabulary is a problem, but it is one you can overcome. The emphasis here is on *you* because there is no magic formula for vocabulary building. It must be done because you want it done. It must also be done systematically and over a period of time. This section provides a system; you must provide the time and desire.

If you stop to think about it, you'll realize that you use at least three different vocabularies, perhaps four. Your largest vocabulary is your *recognition vocabulary*, which includes all the words you recognize and understand in your reading. Your next-largest vocabulary is your *writing vocabulary*, which takes in all the words you use in your writing. The third largest is your *speaking vocabulary*; it is smaller than your writing vocabulary because you may consider some words from your writing vocabulary too formal for conversation. Finally, you may have a limited vocabulary, of from 50 to 1,000 words, that are unique to the particular trade or profession in which you are (or will be) engaged.

You will probably have no trouble in learning your trade, or professional, vocabulary, but you may need to work on improving the other three—especially your writing and recognition vocabularies. An excellent way to improve your vocabulary is by increasing the amount of reading you do and keeping a good dictionary nearby for looking up unfamiliar words. The movement of a word from your recognition vocabulary to your writing vocabulary should be relatively easy.

The following are considered good desk dictionaries. (See also the dictionaries listed in Chapter 11, page 416–419.)

- *The American Heritage Dictionary of the English Language.* 3rd ed. New York: American Heritage Publishing Company, 1994.

- *The Random House Webster's College Dictionary.* Indexed ed. New York: Random House, 1999.

- *Merriam Webster's Collegiate Dictionary.* 10th ed. Springfield, MA: G. & C. Merriam Company, 1993.

- *Webster's New World College Dictionary.* 3rd updated ed. Cleveland and New York: Simon & Schuster, 1997.

(See also ESL Tips: Selecting Bilingual and ESL Dictionaries on page 753.)

ESL TIPS: Selecting Bilingual and ESL Dictionaries

Professor Robert Beard of Bucknell University has compiled one of the best and most extensive collections of online bilingual dictionaries and grammars:

DICTIONARIES http://www.facstaff.bucknell.edu/rbeard/diction.html

GRAMMARS http://www.facstaff.bucknell.edu/rbeard/grammars.html

ESL dictionaries are a good source for checking the meaning of a word. Some comprehensive ESL dictionaries include the following:

- *Oxford ESL Dictionary: For Students of American English.* Oxford University Press.
- *Oxford American Wordpower Dictionary.* Oxford University Press.
- *Longman Lexicon of Contemporary English.* Longman Press.
- *Longman Dictionary of English Language and Culture.* Longman Press.
- *Longman Dictionary of American English.* Longman Press.
- *Longman Dictionary of Contemporary English.* 3rd ed. Longman Press.

The following ESL dictionaries specialize in business English:

- *Longman Business English Dictionary.* Longman Press.
- *NTC's American Business Terms Dictionary.* National Textbook Company.
- *Oxford Dictionary of Business English. For Learners of English.* Oxford University Press.

C Handbook of Grammar, Punctuation, and Mechanics

3. Parts of Speech

Part of speech is a term used to describe the class of words to which a particular word belongs, according to its function in a sentence. If a word's function is to name something, it is a noun or a pronoun. If a word's function is to indicate action or existence, it is a verb. If its function is to describe or modify something, the word is an adjective or an adverb. If its function is to join or link one element of a sentence to another, it is a conjunction or a preposition. If its function is to express an exclamation, it is an interjection.

◼ 3.1 Nouns

A noun names a person, place, thing, concept, action, or quality.

3.1.1 Types of Nouns

The two basic types of nouns are proper nouns and common nouns.

a. Proper Nouns

Proper nouns name specific persons, places, things, concepts, actions, or qualities. They are usually capitalized.

PROPER NOUNS	New York, Abraham Lincoln, U.S. Army, Nobel Prize, Montana, Independence Day, Amazon River, Butler County, Magna Carta, June, Colby College

b. Common Nouns

Common nouns name general classes or categories of persons, places, things, concepts, actions, or qualities. The term *common noun* includes all types of nouns except proper nouns. Following are discussions of the basic types of common nouns. Note that many nouns can be placed in more than one of the overlapping categories.

Concrete nouns identify those things that can be detected by the five senses—by seeing, hearing, tasting, touching, or smelling. Concrete nouns can be either count nouns or mass nouns. *Count nouns,* as the term suggests, name things that can be counted or divided; their plurals often end in *s*. (See Writer's Guide Section D, pages 866–867, for an explanation of using count and noncount nouns.)

COUNT NOUNS　　　　human, college, house, knife, bolt, carrot

Mass nouns name things that are not usually counted and do not usually appear in the plural.

MASS NOUNS　　　　water, sand, air, copper, velvet

Many words, of course, can serve either as count nouns or as mass nouns, depending on the context in which they are used. If you were to say "I need one brick," *brick* would be a count noun. If you were to say "The building is built of brick," *brick* would be a mass noun.

Abstract nouns refer to things that cannot be detected by the five senses.

ABSTRACT NOUNS　　　　love, loyalty, pride, valor, peace, devotion, harmony

Collective nouns indicate groups or collections of persons, places, things, concepts, actions, or qualities. They are plural in meaning but singular in form when they refer to groups as units.

COLLECTIVE NOUNS　　　　audience, jury, brigade, staff, committee

3.1.2 Functions of Nouns

Nouns may function as subjects of verbs, as objects of verbs and prepositions, as complements, or as appositives.

NOUN AS SUBJECT　　　　The *metal* bent as *pressure* was applied to it.

[*Metal* and *pressure* are both subjects of a verb, naming the thing about which the verb makes an assertion.]

**NOUN AS
DIRECT OBJECT**　　　　The bricklayer cemented the *blocks* efficiently.

[*Blocks* is the direct object of a verb, naming the thing acted on by the verb.]

**NOUN AS
INDIRECT OBJECT**　　　　The company awarded our *department* a plaque for safety.

[*Department* is the indirect object of a verb, naming the recipient of the direct object.]

**NOUN AS OBJECT
OF PREPOSITION**　　　　The event occurred within the *year*.

[*Year* is the object of a preposition, naming the thing linked by the preposition to the rest of the sentence.]

NOUN AS SUBJECTIVE COMPLEMENT	An equestrian is a *horseback rider.*
	[*Horseback rider* is the subjective complement, renaming the subject of the sentence.]
NOUN AS OBJECTIVE COMPLEMENT	We elected the sales manager *chairperson.*
	[*Chairperson* is the objective complement, renaming the direct object.]
NOUN AS APPOSITIVE	George Thomas, the *treasurer,* gave his report last.
	[*Treasurer* is the appositive, amplifying the noun that precedes it.]

3.1.3 Forms of Nouns

With the general exception of mass nouns and abstract nouns, nouns can show number (singular or plural) and possession.

a. Singular and Plural Nouns

The singular form of a noun refers to one thing; the plural form refers to more than one. Most nouns form the plural by adding *-s.*

■ *Dolphins* are capable of communication with humans.

Nouns ending in *s, z, x, ch,* and *sh* form the plural by adding *-es.*

■ How many size *sixes* did we produce last month?

■ The letter was sent to all the *churches.*

■ Our company supplies cafeterias with *dishes* and *glasses.*

Those ending in a consonant plus *y* form the plural by changing the *y* to *ies.*

■ The store advertises prompt delivery but limits the number of *deliveries* scheduled on a single day.

Some nouns ending in *o* add *-es* to form the plural; others add only *-s.*

■ One tomato plant produced 30 *tomatoes.*

■ We installed two *dynamos* in the plant.

Some nouns ending in *f* or *fe* add *-s* to form the plural; others change the *f* or *fe* to *ves.*

■ cliff/cliffs; fife/fifes; knife/knives; leaf/leaves

Some nouns require an internal change to form the plural.

■ goose/geese; man/men; mouse/mice; woman/women

Some nouns do not change in the plural form.

- Several *fish* swam lazily in the clear brook while a few wild *deer* mingled with the *sheep* in a nearby meadow.

Most compound nouns joined by hyphens form the plural in the first noun.

- He provided jobs for his two *sons-in-law.*

If you are in doubt about the plural form of a word, look up the word in a good dictionary. Most dictionaries give the plural form if it is made in any way other than by adding *-s* or *-es.*

b. Possessive Nouns

The possessive case, indicating ownership, is formed in two ways—either with an *of* clause, as in "the nature *of* the beast," or by adding *'s.* This discussion will address the *'s* construction, which is generally used with animate nouns.

- The *chairperson's* statement was forceful.
- *Henry's* arm was broken.
- The installation of the plumbing is finished except in the *men's* room.

Singular nouns ending in *s* may form the possessive by adding either an apostrophe alone or *'s.* The latter is now preferred.

- a waitress' uniform *or* a waitress's uniform
- a seamstress' alterations *or* a seamstress's alteration

Plural nouns ending in *s* add only an apostrophe to form the possessive.

- The *architects'* design manual contains many illustrations.

With word groups and compound nouns, add the *'s* to the last noun.

- The *chief operating officer's* report was distributed.
- My *son-in-law's* address was on the envelope.

To show individual possession with a pair of nouns, use the possessive with both.

- Both the *Senate's* and the *House's* galleries were packed for the hearings.
- *Mary's* and *John's* presentations were the most effective.

To show joint possession with a pair of nouns, use the possessive with only the latter.

- The *Senate and House's* joint committee worked out a compromise.

- *Mary and John's* presentation was the most effective.

Occasionally you will use both an *of* phrase and an *'s* construction.

- Mary is a colleague *of John's.*

■ 3.2 Pronouns

A pronoun is a word that is used as a substitute for a noun. The noun that a pronoun replaces is called its *antecedent.*

3.2.1 Types of Pronouns

Pronouns fall into several categories: personal, demonstrative, relative, interrogative, indefinite, reflexive, intensive, and reciprocal.

a. Personal Pronouns

The personal pronouns refer to the person or persons speaking (*I, me, my, mine; we, us, our, ours*), the person or persons spoken to (*you, your, yours*), or the person or thing (or persons or things) spoken of (*he, him, his; she, her, hers; it, its; they, them, their, theirs*).

- I wish *you* had told *me* that *she* was coming with *us.*

- If *their* figures are correct, *ours* must be in error.

b. Demonstrative Pronouns

The demonstrative pronouns (*this, these, that, those*) indicate or point out the thing being referred to. They also serve as adjectives. In good writing, demonstrative pronouns are avoided because they can lead to ambiguity. (As adjectives, however, demonstratives are not only acceptable but useful.)

- *This* is my desk.

- *These* are my coworkers.

- *That* will be a difficult job.

- *Those* are incorrect figures.

c. Relative Pronouns

The relative pronouns (*who, whom, which, whose, that*) perform two functions simultaneously. They substitute for nouns or preceding ideas, and they connect and establish the relationships between parts of sentences. (Refer to the discussion of independent and dependent clauses in Sections 4.2.1 and 4.2.2.)

- The human resources manager told the applicants *who* would be hired.

- The supervisor, *whose* office is next door, keeps those records.

ESL TIPS: Understanding Relative Pronouns

A clause that begins with a relative pronoun (*who, whom, which, whose, that*) is a dependent clause. The relative pronoun introduces the dependent clause and also points back to the noun being referred to.

- The warehouse *that* stocks those books is located in Georgia.

Relative pronouns are sometimes "understood."

- The things [*that*] *we know best* are the things [*that*] *we haven't been taught.*

---

d. Interrogative Pronouns

Interrogative pronouns (*who, whom, which, whose, what*) ask questions.

- *Who* went to the meeting in Detroit?
- *Which* copier does two-sided copying?

e. Indefinite Pronouns

Indefinite pronouns do not refer to a particular person or thing. They include *all, another, any, anyone, anything, both, each, either, everybody, few, many, most, much, neither, nobody, none, several, some,* and *such.*

- Not *everybody* liked the new procedures; *some* even refused to follow them.

f. Reflexive Pronouns

The reflexive pronouns (*myself, yourself, himself, herself, itself, oneself, ourselves, yourselves, themselves*) always end with the suffix *-self* or *-selves*. Reflexive pronouns refer to the subject of the sentence, clause, or phrase in which they appear and turn the action of the verb back on the subject.

■ I asked *myself* the same question.

g. Intensive Pronouns

The intensive pronouns are identical in form to the reflexive pronouns, but they perform a different function. They emphasize or intensify their antecedents.

■ I *myself* asked the same question.

h. Reciprocal Pronouns

The reciprocal pronouns (*one another, each other*) indicate relationships among people or things. Use *each other* when referring to two persons or things and *one another* when referring to more than two.

■ Sam and Ruth work well with *each other.*

■ The four crew members work well with *one another.*

3.2.2 Grammatical Properties of Pronouns

a. Person

Person refers to the forms of a personal pronoun that indicate whether the pronoun represents the speaker, the person spoken to, or the person (or thing) spoken about. If the pronoun represents the speaker, the pronoun is in the first person.

■ *I* followed the directions in the manual.

If the pronoun represents the person or persons spoken to, the pronoun is in the second person.

■ *You* should report to Ms. Cooper before noon.

If the pronoun represents the person or persons spoken about, the pronoun is in the third person.

■ *They* followed the procedure that *he* had outlined.

**Table C–1
Identifying
Pronouns by
Person**

Person	Singular	Plural
First	I, me, my	we, ours, us
Second	you, your	you, your
Third	he, him, his, she, her, hers, it, its	they, them, their

Identifying pronouns by person helps you avoid illogical shifts from one person to another. A common error is to shift from the third person to the second person.

INCORRECT USE OF PERSON	*Employees* must sign the guard's logbook when *you* enter a restricted area.
CORRECT USE OF PERSON	*Employees* must sign the guard's logbook when *they* enter a restricted area.
CORRECT USE OF PERSON	*You* must sign the guard's logbook when *you* enter a restricted area.

b. Gender

Gender refers to forms of words that designate sex. English recognizes three genders: masculine, feminine, and neuter (to designate objects considered neither masculine nor feminine). The pronouns *he, she,* and *it* indicate gender; only a few nouns (such as *seamstress*) do so.

Gender is important to writers because they must be sure that nouns and pronouns within a grammatical construction agree in gender. A pronoun, for example, must agree with its antecedent noun in gender.

- Because Wanda Martin supervised *her* sales staff as effectively as Frank Martinez supervised *his,* the company doubled *its* profits.

(See also Section 3.2.3a for a discussion of how sexist language is best avoided.)

c. Number

Number signifies how many things a word refers to. A singular pronoun substitutes for a noun that names one thing; a plural pronoun replaces a noun that names two or more things.

- The manager took *her* break after the employees took *their* breaks.

All singular pronouns (*I, he, she, it*) change form in the plural (*we, they*) except *you.*

- Because *he* organizes efficiently and *she* supervises effectively, *they* are both valuable employees.

Number is a frequent problem with a few indefinite pronouns (*each, either, neither,* and those ending with *-body* or *-one,* such as *anybody, anyone, everybody, everyone, nobody, no one, somebody, someone*). Because these pronouns are normally singular, they require singular verbs and are referred to by singular pronouns.

- *Everyone* at practice that day had *his* blood pressure checked.

- *No one* should leave without returning *her* copy of the test booklet.

d. Case

Pronouns have forms to show the subjective, objective, and possessive cases. A pronoun is in the *subjective case* when it is used as the subject of a clause or sentence, representing the person or thing acting or existing. The subjective case is also used when the pronoun follows a linking verb, such as *to be*. (A linking verb connects the pronoun with the subject it renames.)

- *He* is my boss.

- My boss is *he*.

A pronoun is in the *objective case* when it indicates the person or thing receiving the action of a verb or when it follows a preposition.

- Mr. Davis hired Tom and *me*. (not *I*)

- Between *you* and *me*, his facts are questionable.

To test whether a pronoun is in the subjective case or the objective case, try it with a transitive verb (one that requires a direct object—a person or thing to receive the action expressed by the verb.) *Hit* is a useful verb for this test. If the form of the pronoun can precede the verb, it is in the subjective case. If it must follow the verb, it is in the objective case.

- *She* hit the baseball. (subjective case)

- The baseball hit *her*. (objective case)

A pronoun in the *possessive case* expresses ownership.

- He took *his* notes with him on the business trip.

**Table C–2
Subjective,
Objective, and
Possessive
Pronouns**

Subjective	*Objective*	*Possessive*
I	me	my, mine
we	us	our, ours
you	you	your, yours
he	him	his
she	her	her, hers
it	it	its
they	them	their, theirs
who	whom	whose

If compound pronouns cause problems in determining case, try testing each separately.

- In his letter, John mentioned *you* and *me*.

- In his letter, John mentioned *you*.

- In his letter, John mentioned *me*.

To determine the case of a pronoun that follows *as* or *than,* try mentally adding the words that are normally omitted.

- The director does not have as much formal education as *he* [does].

  [You would not write, "Him does."]

- His friend was taller than *he* [was tall].

  [You would not write, "Him was tall."]

An appositive is a noun or noun phrase that follows and amplifies another noun or noun phrase. A pronoun appositive takes the case of its antecedent.

- Two systems analysts, Joe and *I,* were selected to represent the company.

  [*Joe and I* is in apposition to the subject, *systems analysts,* and therefore must be in the subjective case.]

- The systems analysts selected two members of our department—Joe and *me.*

  [*Joe and me* is in apposition to *two members,* which is the object of the verb *selected,* and therefore must be in the objective case.]

The reverse situation can also present problems. To test for the proper case when the pronouns *we* and *us* are followed by an appositive noun that defines them, try the sentence without the noun.

- (*We/Us*) pilots fly our own planes.

- *We* fly our own planes.

  [You would not write, "*Us* fly our own planes."]

- He addressed his remarks directly to (*we/us*) technicians.

- He addressed his remarks directly to *us.*

  [You would not write, "He addressed his remarks directly to *we.*"]

3.2.3 Usage of Pronouns

Pronouns must agree with and clearly refer to their antecedents.

a. Pronoun-Antecedent Agreement

The noun for which a pronoun substitutes is called its antecedent. A personal pronoun in the first or second person does not normally require a stated antecedent.

- *I* like my job.

- *You* were there at the time.

- *We* all worked hard on the project.

A personal pronoun in the third person usually has a clearly stated antecedent.

- John presented the report to the directors. *He* [John] first read *it* [the report] to *them* [the directors] and then asked for *their* [the directors'] questions.

Agreement, grammatically, means the correspondence in form between different elements of a sentence. A pronoun must agree with its antecedent in person, gender, and number. (See Section 3.2.2 for additional information about these properties of pronouns.)

A pronoun must agree with its antecedent in *person*. If you are describing the necessity of accurate data for laboratory technicians, for example, use either the third person or the second person. Don't mix them. The first sentence following suggests that the technicians are preparing data for someone else (you).

INCORRECT USE OF PERSON	If *laboratory technicians* do not update *their* records every day, *you* will not have accurate data.
CORRECT USE OF PERSON	If *laboratory technicians* do not update *their* records every day, *they* will not have accurate data.
CORRECT USE OF PERSON	If *you* do not update *your* records every day, *you* will not have accurate data.

A pronoun must agree with its antecedent in *gender*.

- *Isabel* was already wearing *her* identification badge, but *Tom* had to clip on *his* badge before they could pass the security guard.

Traditionally, a masculine, singular pronoun was used to agree with antecedents that include both sexes, such as *anyone, everybody, nobody, one, person, someone,* or *student.*

- *Anyone* who meets this production goal will double *his* bonus.

However, because most people are sensitive to the implied sexual bias in such usage, it is more common to use the following alternatives:

INDICATES GENDER BIAS	*Everybody* completed *his* report on time.
FREE OF BIAS	*Everybody* completed *his or her* report on time.
FREE OF BIAS	*Everybody* completed a report on time.

Often, the best solution is to rewrite the sentence in the plural. Do not, however, attempt to avoid expressing gender by resorting to a plural pronoun when the antecedent is singular.

ESL TIPS: Assigning Gender

The English-language system has an almost complete lack of gender distinctions. That can be confusing for a non-native speaker of English whose native language may be marked for gender. In the few cases in which English does make a gender distinction, there is a close connection between the assigning of gender and the sex of the subject. The few instances in which gender distinctions are made in English are summarized as follows:

Subject pronouns	*he/she*
Object pronouns	*him/her*
Possessive adjectives	*his/her(s)*
Some nouns	*king/queen; boy/girl; cow/bull*

When a noun, such as *doctor,* can refer to a person of either sex, you need to know the sex of the person to which the noun refers to determine the gender-appropriate pronoun.

■ The doctor gave *her* patients lots of attention.

[Doctor is female.]

■ The doctor gave *his* patients lots of attention.

[Doctor is male.]

When the sex of the noun antecedent is unknown, be sure to follow the guidelines for nonsexist writing in Chapter 4, pages 119–121. (*Note:* Some English speakers refer to vehicles and countries as *she,* but contemporary and non-sexist usage tends to use *it.*)

INCORRECT	*Everybody* completed *their* reports on time.
	[The antecedent, *Everybody,* is singular, but the pronoun, *their,* incorrectly, is plural.]
CORRECT	The *employees* completed *their* reports on time.
	[The antecedent, *employees,* is plural, and the pronoun, *their,* correctly, is also plural.]

A pronoun must agree with its antecedent in *number.*

INCORRECT	Because the *copier* has been used so much, *they* have been overheating.
	[The antecedent *copier* is singular, but the pronoun *they,* incorrectly, is plural.]
CORRECT	Because the *copier* has been used so much, *it* has been overheating.
	[The antecedent *copier* is singular, and the pronoun *it,* correctly, is also singular.]

In formal English, use a singular pronoun with the following singular antecedents:

anybody	everybody	none
anyone	everyone	no one
anything	everything	somebody
each	neither	someone
either	nobody	something

CORRECT   *Everyone* returned to *his or her* department.

[The antecedent *Everyone* and the pronouns *his or her* are also singular.]

When a plural pronoun mistakenly refers to a singular antecedent, as shown in the following example,

INCORRECT   When *someone* has conducted research, *they* are likely to write an effective report.

[*Someone* is a singular antecedent; *they* is incorrect because it is a plural pronoun and does not agree with the singular *someone*.]

you can use the following options for revision:

1. Replace the incorrect plural pronoun with *he or she* (or *his or her*).

    ■ When *someone* has conducted research _{*he or she is*} ~~, they are~~ likely to write an effective report.

    [*Someone* is a singular antecedent; *he or she* is correct because *he or she* are singular pronouns and agree with the singular *someone*.]

2. Make the antecedent plural.

    ■ When _{*writers have*} ~~someone has~~ conducted research, they are likely to write an effective report.

    [*Writers* is a plural antecedent; *they* is correct because it is a plural pronoun and agrees with the plural *writers*.]

3. Rewrite the sentence so that no problem of agreement exists.

    ■ _{*A writer who*} ~~When someone~~ has conducted research_{*is*}~~, they are~~ likely to write an effective report.

    [The singular antecedent *writer* does not require a pronoun in this revised sentence.]

Collective nouns may be singular or plural, depending on meaning.

CORRECT   The *staff* prepared *its* annual report.

CORRECT   The *staff* returned to *their* offices after the meeting.

A compound antecedent joined by *or* or *nor* is singular if both elements are singular and plural if both are plural.

CORRECT   Either the *supervisor* or the *foreman* should present *his or her* report on the accident.

                 [The antecedents *supervisor* and *foreman* are singular and the pronouns *his or her* are also singular.]

CORRECT   Neither the *stockholders* nor the *executive officers* wanted *their* company to be taken over by Coast International.

When one of the antecedents connected by *or* or *nor* is singular and the other plural, the pronoun agrees with the nearer antecedent.

CORRECT   Either the *receptionist* or the *typists* should go on *their* lunch breaks.

                 [The plural pronoun *their* agrees with the nearest antecedent, *typists*, which is plural.]

CORRECT   Either the *typists* or the *receptionist* should go on *his or her* lunch break.

                 [The singular pronouns *his or her* agree with the nearest antecedent, *receptionist*, which is singular.]

A compound antecedent with its elements joined by *and* requires a plural pronoun.

CORRECT   The *architect* and the *designer* prepared *their* plans.

                 [Because the antecedents *architect* and *designer* are meant to be understood together, and are therefore plural, the pronoun *their*, correctly, is also plural.]

If the two elements refer to the same person, however, use the singular pronoun.

CORRECT   The *architect and designer* prepared *his* plan.

                 [The *architect and designer* are the same individual, and therefore the antecedent, correctly, is singular and the pronoun *his* is also singular.]

b. Pronoun Reference

The noun to which a pronoun refers must be unmistakably clear. Pronoun references may be unclear if they are general, hidden, or ambiguous.

A *general* (or *broad*) *reference,* or one that has no real antecedent, may confuse your reader.

UNCLEAR	He sold plumbing supplies in Iowa for eight years. *This* has helped him in his present job as sales manager.
IMPROVED	He sold plumbing supplies in Iowa for eight years. *This experience* has helped him in his present job as sales manager.

A *hidden reference,* or one that has only an implied antecedent, is another problem.

UNCLEAR	Electronics technicians must continue to study because *it* is a dynamic science.
IMPROVED	Electronics technicians must continue to study *electronics* because *it* is a dynamic science.
UNCLEAR	A high-lipid, low-carbohydrate diet is called ketogenic because it favors *their* formation.
IMPROVED	A high-lipid, low-carbohydrate diet is called ketogenic because it favors the formation of ketone bodies.

The third basic problem is an *ambiguous reference,* or one that can be interpreted in more than one way.

UNCLEAR	Susan worked with Jeanette on the presentation, but *she* prepared most of the slides. [Who prepared most of the slides, Susan or Jeanette?]
IMPROVED	Susan worked with Jeanette on the presentation, but Jeanette prepared most of the slides.

Ambiguous references frequently occur with the pronouns *it* and *they.*

UNCLEAR	The fire marshal examined the stairway and inspected the basement storage room; *it* had suffered extensive smoke damage.
IMPROVED	The fire marshal examined the stairway, which had suffered extensive smoke damage, and inspected the basement storage room.
UNCLEAR	The inspector checked the scales and the time clocks; *they* needed to be leveled again.
IMPROVED	The inspector checked the scales and the time clocks; the scales needed to be leveled again.

Do not repeat an antecedent in parentheses following the pronoun. If you feel that you must identify the pronoun's antecedent in this way, you need to rewrite the sentence.

AWKWARD	The specialist met the patient's mother as soon as she (the specialist) arrived at the hospital emergency room.
IMPROVED	As soon as the specialist arrived at the hospital emergency room, she met the patient's mother.

■ 3.3 Adjectives

An adjective modifies or describes a noun or pronoun.

3.3.1 Types of Adjectives

An adjective makes the meaning of a noun or pronoun more exact by pointing out one of its qualities (descriptive adjective) or by imposing boundaries on it (limiting adjective).

DESCRIPTIVE ADJECTIVE	a *hot* iron
DESCRIPTIVE ADJECTIVE	He is *cold.*
LIMITING ADJECTIVE	*ten* automobiles
LIMITING ADJECTIVE	*his* desk

Limiting adjectives include some common and important categories:

Articles (*a, an, the*)
Numeral adjectives (*one, two, first, second*)
Indefinite adjectives (*all, any, each, no, some*)
Demonstrative adjectives (*this, that, these, those*)
Possessive adjectives (*my, his, her, its, your, our, their*)
Interrogative and relative adjectives (*whose, which, what*)

Of these, the forms of the demonstrative, possessive, interrogative, and relative adjectives derive from pronouns and are sometimes called *pronominal adjectives.*

ESL TIPS: Using Adjectives

Unlike many other languages, adjectives in English have only one form. Do not add *-s* or *-es* to an adjective to make it plural.

- the *long* trip
- the *long* letters

Likewise, adjectives in English do not change to show gender.

- The *tall* man (masculine noun)
- The *tall* woman (feminine noun)
- The *tall* building (neuter noun)

Capitalize adjectives of origin (city, state, nation, continent)

- the *Venetian* canals
- the *Texan* hat
- the *French* government
- the *African* desert

In English, verbs of feeling (for example, *bore, interest, surprise*) have two adjectival forms: the present participle (*-ing*) and the past participle (*-ed*). Use the present participle to describe what causes the feeling. Use the past participle to describe the person who experiences the feeling.

- We heard the surprising election results.

  [The *election results* cause the feeling.]

- Only the candidate was surprised by the election results.

  [The *candidate* experienced the feeling of surprise.]

Adjectives follow the noun in English in only two cases: when the adjective functions as a subjective complement, as in

- That project is not *finished*.

and when an adjective phrase or clause modifies the noun, as in

- The project *that was suspended temporarily . . .*

In all other cases, adjectives are placed before the noun.

When there are multiple adjectives, it is often difficult to know the right order. The guidelines illustrated in the following example would apply in most circumstances, but there are exceptions. (Normally, do not use a phrase with so many stacked modifiers.)

The six extra large rectangular brown Chinese cardboard take-out containers

| determiner | number | comment | size | shape | color | origin | material | qualifier | noun |

3.3.2 Comparison of Adjectives

Most adjectives add the suffix *-er* to show comparison with one other item and the suffix *-est* to show comparison with two or more other items. The three degrees of comparison are called the *positive* (the basic form of the adjective), the *comparative* (showing comparison with one other item), and the *superlative* (showing comparison with two or more other items).

POSITIVE DEGREE	The first ingot is *bright.*
COMPARATIVE DEGREE	The second ingot is *brighter.*
SUPERLATIVE DEGREE	The third ingot is *brightest.*

Many two-syllable adjectives and most three-syllable adjectives, however, are preceded by *more* or *most* to form the comparative or the superlative.

COMPARATIVE DEGREE	The new facility is *more impressive* than the old one.
SUPERLATIVE DEGREE	The new facility is the *most impressive* in the city.

A few adjectives have irregular comparative and superlative degrees (*much, more, most; little, less, least*).

Absolute words (such as *unique, perfect, exact,* and *infinite*) are not logically subject to comparison. After all, something either is or is not unique; it isn't more unique or most unique. Language, however, is not always logical, so these words are sometimes used comparatively.

COMPARATIVE DEGREE	Phase-locked loop circuits make FM tuner performance *more exact* by decreasing tuner distortion.

3.3.3 Placement of Adjectives

When limiting and descriptive adjectives appear together, the limiting adjectives precede the descriptive adjectives, with the article usually in the first position.

- *the ten gray* cars

  [The article *the* is followed by the limiting adjective *ten,* which is followed by the descriptive adjective *gray.*]

Within a sentence, an adjective can precede its noun or follow its noun.

CORRECT	The *small* jobs are given priority.
	[The adjective *small* precedes the noun *jobs.*]
CORRECT VARIATION	Priority is given when a job is *small.*
	[The adjective *small* follows the noun *job.*]

In a larger, more complex construction, an adjective may shift from preceding its noun to following it.

| CORRECT | We negotiated a *bigger* contract than our competitor did. |
| | [The adjective *bigger* precedes the noun *contract*.] |

| CORRECT VARIATION | We negotiated a contract *bigger* than our competitor's. |
| | [The adjective *bigger* follows the noun *contract*.] |

An adjective is called a predicate adjective when it follows a linking verb, such as *to be*. By completing the meaning of a linking verb, a predicate adjective describes, or limits, the subject of the verb.

| PREDICATE ADJECTIVE | The job is *easy*. |
| | [The adjective *easy* follows the linking verb *is*.] |

| PREDICATE ADJECTIVE | The manager was very *demanding*. |
| | [The adjective *demanding* follows the linking verb *was*.] |

An adjective also can follow a transitive verb and modify its direct object (the person or thing that receives the action of the verb).

| MODIFIES DIRECT OBJECT | The lack of lubricant rendered the bearing *useless*. |
| | [The adjective *useless* modifies the direct object *bearing*.] |

| MODIFIES DIRECT OBJECT | They painted the office *white*. |
| | [The adjective *white* modifies the direct object *office*.] |

3.3.4 Use of Adjectives

Nouns can sometimes function as adjectives, especially when precise qualification is necessary.

| NOUN AS ADJECTIVE | The *test* conclusions led to a redesign of the system. |

Frequently, business and technical writing is weakened by too many nouns strung together to serve as modifiers. Therefore, exercise caution when you use nouns as adjectives.

WEAK	The test control group meeting was held last Wednesday.
IMPROVED	The meeting of the test control group was held last Wednesday.
MORE IMPROVED	The test control group met last Wednesday.

Furthermore, you should avoid general adjectives (*nice, fine, good*) and trite or overused adjectives (a *fond* farewell). In fact, question the need for most adjectives in your writing. Often, your writing not only will read as well without an adjective but may even be better without it. If you need to use an adjective, select one that expresses your meaning as exactly as possible.

■ 3.4 Verbs

A verb is a word, or a group of words, that specifies an action or affirms a condition or a state of existence.

■   The antelope *bolted* at the sight of the hunters.

■   She *was saddened* by the death of her friend.

■   He *is* a wealthy man now.

A verb is an essential part of a sentence because the verb makes an assertion about the action or existence of its subject, the someone or something that is its topic. Within a sentence, a verb alone is called a simple predicate; a verb with its modifiers and complements forms a complete predicate. When a subject and a predicate convey a complete thought, they form a sentence (or independent clause). When a subject and a predicate do not convey a complete thought, they form a dependent clause. In contrast to a clause, a phrase is a group of words without the subject-predicate combination.

3.4.1 Types of Verbs

Verbs may be described as either transitive or intransitive; the intransitive verbs include linking verbs.

a. Transitive Verbs

A transitive verb requires a *direct object* to complete its meaning. The direct object normally answers the question *whom* or *what* by naming the person or thing that receives the action of the verb.

TRANSITIVE VERB AND DIRECT OBJECT   They *laid* the *foundation* on October 24.

[*Foundation* is the direct object of the transitive verb *laid*.]

Some transitive verbs (such as *give, wish, cause,* and *tell*) may be followed by an *indirect object* as well as a direct object. The indirect object is usually a person and answers the question "to whom or what?" or "for whom or what?" The indirect object precedes the direct object.

Georgiana Anderson *gave* the *treasurer* a *letter.*

[*Treasurer* is the indirect object and *letter* is the direct object of
the transitive verb *gave.*]

b. Intransitive Verbs

An intransitive verb is a verb that does not require an object to complete its
meaning. It makes a full assertion about the subject without assistance (although
it may have modifiers).

■   The water *boiled.*

■   The water *boiled* rapidly.

■   The engine *ran.*

■   The engine *ran* smoothly and quietly.

c. Linking Verbs

Although intransitive verbs do not have objects, certain intransitive verbs may
take complements. These verbs are called linking verbs because they link the
subject of a sentence to words following the verb. When this subjective complement is a noun (or pronoun), it refers to the same person or thing as the noun (or
pronoun) that is the subject.

■   The conference table *is* an antique.

■   Maria *should be* the director.

When the complement is an adjective, it modifies the subject.

■   The study *was* thorough.

■   The report *seems* complete.

Such intransitive verbs as *be, become, seem,* and *appear* are almost always linking
verbs. Others, such as *look, sound, taste, smell,* and *feel,* may function either as
linking verbs or as simple intransitive verbs.

AS LINKING VERB   Their antennae *feel* delicate.

[*Feel* is a linking verb meaning that the antennae seem fragile to
the touch.]

AS SIMPLE
INTRANSITIVE VERB   Their antennae *feel* delicately.

[*Feel* is a simple intransitive verb meaning that the antennae
have a delicate sense of touch.]

3.4.2 Forms of Verbs

By form, verbs may be described as either finite or nonfinite.

a. Finite Verbs

A finite verb is the main verb of a clause or sentence. It makes an assertion about its subject, and it can serve as the only verb in its clause or sentence. Finite verbs may be either transitive or intransitive (including linking) verbs. They change form to reflect person (I *see*, he *sees*), tense (I *go*, I *went*), and number (he *writes*, they *write*).

- The telephone *rang,* and the secretary *answered* it.

- When the telephones *ring,* you *answer* them.

A *helping verb* (sometimes called an *auxiliary verb*) is a verb that is added to a finite or main verb to help indicate mood, voice, and tense. (See the discussions of voice, mood, and tense in Sections 3.4.3b, 3.4.3c, and 3.4.3d, respectively.) Together, the helping verb and the main verb form a verb phrase.

HELPING VERBS   The work *had* begun.

I *am* going.

I *was* going.

I *will* go.

I *should have* gone.

I *must* go.

The most commonly used helping verbs are the various forms of *have* (*has, had*), *be* (*am, is, are, was, were*), *do* (*did, does*), *can* (*could*), *may* (*might*), *shall* (*should*), and *will* (*would*). Phrases that function as helping verbs often include *to:* for example, *am going to* and *is about to* (compare *will*), *has to* (compare *must*), and *ought to* (compare *should*).

- I *am going to* quit.

- I *will* quit.

- She *has to* get a raise.

- She *must* get a raise.

The helping verb always precedes the main verb, although other words may come between them. (See also ESL Tips: Using Helping Verbs in the Writer's Guide, Section D, p. 882.)

- Machines *will* [helping verb] never completely *replace* [main verb] people.

b. Nonfinite Verbs or Verbals

Nonfinite verbs are the verbals (gerunds, infinitives, and participles) that, although they are derived from verbs, actually function as nouns, adjectives, or adverbs.

When the *-ing* form of a verb functions as a noun, it is called a *gerund*.

■ *Seeing* is *believing.*

An *infinitive,* which is the root form of a verb, can function as a noun, an adverb, or an adjective. Because the word *to* usually precedes an infinitive, it is considered the sign of an infinitive.

■ He hates *to complain.*

[*To complain* functions as a noun and direct object of the verb *hates.*]

■ The valve closes *to stop* the flow.

[*To stop* functions as an adverb and modifies the verb *closes.*]

■ This is the proposal *to select.*

[*To select* functions as an adjective and modifies the noun *proposal.*]

A *participle* is a verb form that functions as an adjective. The *present participle* ends in *-ing.*

■ *Declining* sales forced us to close the branch office.

The *past participle* may end in *-ed, -t, -en, -n,* or *-d.*

■ What are the *estimated* costs?

■ Repair the *bent* lever.

■ Here is the *broken* calculator.

■ What are the *known* properties of this metal?

■ The story, *told* many times before, was still interesting.

The *perfect participle* is formed with the present participle of *have* and the past participle of the main verb.

■ *Having received* [perfect participle] a large raise, the *smiling* [present participle], *contented* [past participle] employee worked harder than ever.

3.4.3 Grammatical Properties of Verbs

Verbs can show person and number, mood, voice, and tense.

a. Person and Number

Verbs must agree with their subjects in *number* (singular or plural) and *person* (first, second, or third). In the present indicative of regular verbs (see Section 3.4.3b), only the third-person singular differs from the infinitive stem. The verb *to be*, however, is irregular: I *am*, you *are*, he *is*, we *are*, they *are*. (See Section 3.4.4.)

- I *see* [first-person singular] a yellow tint, but he *sees* [third-person singular] a yellow-green hue.

- I *am* [first-person singular] convinced, and they *are* [third-person plural] convinced; unfortunately, he *is* [third-person singular] not convinced.

b. Mood

Mood refers to the functions of verbs: making statements or asking questions (indicative mood), giving commands (imperative mood), or expressing hypothetical possibilities (subjunctive mood).

The *indicative* mood refers to an action or a statement that is conceived as fact.

- *Is* the setting correct?

- The setting *is* correct.

The *imperative* mood expresses a command, suggestion, request, or entreaty.

- *Install* the wiring today.

- Please *let* me know if I can help.

The *subjunctive* mood expresses something that is contrary to fact, conditional, or hypothetical; it can also express a wish, a doubt, or a possibility. The verb *be* is the only one in English that preserves many changes in form to show the subjunctive mood.

- The senior partner insisted that he [I, you, we, they] *be* in charge of the project.

- If the salesman [I, you, we, they] *were* to close the sale today, we would meet our monthly quota.

Most verbs other than *be* do not change form for the subjunctive. Instead, helping verbs show the subjunctive function.

- *Had I known* that you were here, I would have come earlier.

The advantage of the subjunctive mood is that it enables you to express clearly whether you consider a condition contrary to fact. If you wish to express a contrary-to-fact condition or a highly doubtful hypothesis, use the subjunctive; if not, use the indicative.

SUBJUNCTIVE MOOD	If I *were* president of the firm, I would change several of its policies.
INDICATIVE MOOD	I *am* president of the firm, but I don't feel that I control every aspect of its policies.

ESL TIPS: Determining Mood

In written and especially in spoken English, there is an increasing tendency to use the indicative mood where the subjunctive traditionally has been used. Note the differences between traditional and contemporary usage in the following examples:

Traditional Use of the Subjunctive Mood

- I wish he *were* here now.
- If I *were* going to the conference, I would room with him.
- I requested that she *show* up on time.

Informal Use of the Indicative Mood

- I wish he *was* here now.
- If I *was* going to the conference, I would room with him.
- I requested that she *shows* up on time.

As a non-native speaker of English, you are faced with a choice: Do you use the subjunctive and, consequently, in some circles sound sophisticated, intellectual, or even weird? Or do you use the indicative and in other circles sound uneducated? The answer might be to master both uses and be able to move freely between the different circles. In formal business and technical writing, however, it is best to use the more traditional expressions.

Be careful not to shift haphazardly from one mood to another within a sentence; to do so makes the sentence unbalanced as well as ungrammatical.

INCORRECT	Put the clutch in first [imperative]; then you should put the truck in gear [indicative].
CORRECT	Put the clutch in first [imperative]; then put the truck in gear [imperative].
CORRECT	You should put the clutch in first [indicative]; then you should put the truck in gear [indicative].

c. Voice

The grammatical term *voice* refers to whether the subject of a sentence or clause acts or receives the action. A sentence is in the active voice if the subject acts, in

the passive voice if the subject is acted upon. The passive voice consists of a form
of the verb *to be* and a past participle of the main verb.

ACTIVE VOICE	The aerosol bomb *propels* the liquid as a mist.
PASSIVE VOICE	The liquid *is propelled* as a mist by the aerosol bomb.

In your writing, the active voice provides force and momentum, whereas
the passive voice lacks these qualities. In the active voice, the verb identifies
what the subject is doing, thus emphasizing the subject and the action. However, the passive voice emphasizes what is being done to the subject, rather
than the subject or the action. As a rule, use the active voice unless you have
good reason not to.

PASSIVE VOICE	The report *was written* by Joe Albright in only two hours.
	[The emphasis is on *report* rather than on Joe and the writing.]
ACTIVE VOICE	Joe Albright *wrote* the report in only two hours.
	[Here the writer and writing receive the emphasis.]
PASSIVE VOICE	Things *are seen* by the normal human eye in three dimensions: length, width, and depth.
	[The emphasis is on *things* rather than on the eye's function.]
ACTIVE VOICE	The normal human eye *sees* things in three dimensions: length, width, and depth.
	[Here the eye's function—which is what the sentence is about—receives the emphasis.]

ESL TIPS: Choosing Voice

Different languages place different values on active-voice and passive-voice
constructions. In some languages, the passive is used frequently; in others,
hardly at all. As a non-native speaker of English, you may have a tendency to
follow the pattern of your native language. But remember, even though business
writing may sometimes require the passive voice, active verbs are highly valued
in English.

Sentences in the passive voice may state the actor, but they place the actor in a
secondary position as the object of a preposition ("*by* the normal human eye").

The passive voice has its advantages, however; when the doer of the action is
not known or is not important, use the passive voice.

■   The firm *was established* in 1929.

ESL TIPS: Avoiding Shifts in Person, Number, Voice, Mood, and Tense

To achieve clarity in your prose, it is important to maintain consistency and avoid shifts. A shift occurs when there is an abrupt change in person, number, voice, mood, or tense. Pay special attention when you edit your writing to check for the following types of shifts.

Person

- *Students* must get financial clearance before ~~you~~ *they* can attend class.

  [This sentence shifted from third-person *students* to second-person *you*.]

Number

- *Everyone* must turn in ~~their~~ *his or her* timecards.

or

- All *employees* must turn in *their* timecards.

  [When possible, it is more concise to make the antecedent plural so a plural pronoun can be used. Using the pairing *his or her* or *he or she* can make writing appear awkward and difficult to follow.]

Voice

- The captain permits his crew to go ashore, but ~~they are not~~ *he does not permit* ~~permitted~~ *them* to go downtown.

  [The entire sentence is now in the active voice.]

Mood

- Reboot your computer, and ~~you should~~ empty the cache too.

  [The entire sentence is now in the imperative mood.]

Tense

- I was working quickly and suddenly a box ~~falls~~ *fell* off the conveyor belt and ~~breaks~~ *broke* my foot.

  [The entire sentence is now in the past tense.]

ESL TIPS: Using the Progressive Form

English uses the progressive form, particularly the present progressive, more frequently than other languages do. Here are some guidelines to help you practice using the progressive form.

The progressive form of the verb is composed of two features: a form of the helping verb *be* and the *-ing* form of the base verb.

PRESENT PROGRESSIVE	I *am rewriting* the memo.
PAST PROGRESSIVE	I *was rewriting* the memo for several days.
FUTURE PROGRESSIVE	I *will be rewriting* that memo forever.

The present progressive is used in three ways:

1. To refer to an action that is in progress at the moment of speaking or writing

   - The conference chair *is* constantly *interrupting* the speakers.
   - The parliamentarian *is wearing* an Oscar de la Renta suit.

2. To highlight that a state or action is not permanent

   - The office temp *is helping* us for a few weeks.

3. To express future plans

   - The summer intern *is leaving* to return to school this Friday.

The past progressive is used to refer to a continuing action or condition in the past, usually with specified limits.

   - I *was failing* calculus until I got eyeglasses.

The future progressive is used to refer to a continuous action or condition in the future.

   - We *will be monitoring* his condition all night.

Verbs that express mental activity, or the senses of sight, smell, touch, sound, and taste are generally not used in the progressive.

   - I *believe* the defendant's testimony.

adore	contain	know	recognize	suppose
appear	corresponding	like	remember	taste
appreciate	exist	love	represent	think
be	feel	mean	resemble	understand
believe	forget	need	see	want
belong	hate	own	seem	
consist of	have	possess	smell	
constitute	hear	prefer	sound	

When the doer of the action is less important than the receiver of the action, use the passive voice.

■ Police Officer Bryant *was cited* for heroism by Chief of Police Colby.

Be careful about shifting voice within a sentence.

INCORRECT	We *worked* late last night, and all the tests *were* finally *completed*.
CORRECT	We *worked* late last night, and finally *completed* all tests.

d. Tense

Tense is the grammatical term for verb forms that indicate time distinctions. The six simple tenses in English are present, present perfect, past, past perfect, future, and future perfect. Each of these tenses has a corresponding progressive form that shows action in progress and is created by combining the helping verb *be*, in the appropriate tense, with the present participle (*-ing*) form of the main verb. (See also Table D–2, Forming Tenses: A Timeline, on page 876.)

Table C–3
Forming the Simple and Progressive Tenses

Simple	*Progressive*
I begin (present)	I am beginning (present)
I began (past)	I was beginning (past)
I will begin (future)	I will be beginning (future)
I have begun (present perfect)	I have been beginning (present perfect)
I had begun (past perfect)	I had been beginning (past perfect)
I will have begun (future perfect)	I will have been beginning (future perfect)

The *simple present tense* represents action occurring in the present, without any indication of time duration.

■ I *use* the calculator.

A general truth is always expressed in the present tense.

■ He learned that "time *heals* all wounds."

The present tense can be used to present actions or conditions that have no time restrictions.

■ Water *boils* at 212°F.

The present tense can be used to indicate habitual action.

■ I *pass* the paint shop on the way to the office every day.

The present tense can be used as the *historical present* to make things that oc-curred in the past more vivid.

- ■ It is 1865, and the founder of our company is pushing his cart through Philadelphia, delivering fish to his customers. He *works* hard, *expands* his business, and *builds* the firm that still bears his name.

The *simple past tense* indicates that an action took place in its entirety in the past. The past tense is usually formed by adding *-d* or *-ed* to the root form of the verb.

- ■ We *closed* the office early yesterday.

The *simple future tense* indicates a time that will occur after the present. The helping verb *will* (or *shall*) is used along with the main verb.

- ■ I *will finish* the job tomorrow.

The *present perfect tense* describes something from the recent past that has a bearing on the present—a period of time before the present but after the simple past. The present perfect tense is formed by combining a form of the present tense of the helping verb *have* with the past participle of the main verb.

- ■ He *has retired,* but he visits the office frequently.
- ■ We *have finished* the draft and are ready to begin revising it.

The *simple past perfect tense* indicates that one past event preceded another. It is formed by combining the helping verb *had* with the past participle of the main verb.

- ■ He *had finished* by the time I arrived.

The *future perfect tense* indicates an action that will be completed at the time of or before another future action. It is formed by linking the helping verbs *will have* to the past participle of the main verb.

- ■ He *will have driven* the test car 400 miles by the time he returns.

3.4.4 Conjugation of Verbs

When a verb is conjugated, all of its forms are arranged schematically so that the differences in tense, number, person, and voice are readily apparent. Following is the conjugation of the verb *drive.* Its principal parts, used to construct its various forms, are *drive* (infinitive and present tense), *drove* (past tense), *driven* (past participle), and *driving* (present participle). Table C–4 shows each conjugated form in both the active voice and the passive voice.

ACTIVE	I *drive.*
	[The subject, *I,* is doing the driving.]
PASSIVE	I *am driven.*
	[The subject, *I,* is being driven by someone or something else.]

3.4.5 Subject-Verb Agreement

Agreement, grammatically, means the correspondence in form between different elements of a sentence. Just as a pronoun must agree with its antecedent in person, gender, and number (see Section 3.2.3a), so a verb must agree with its subject in person and number.

■ I *am* going to approve his promotion.

[The first-person singular subject, *I,* requires the first-person singular form of the verb, *am.*]

■ His colleagues *are* envious.

[The third-person plural subject, *colleagues,* requires the third-person plural form of the verb, *are.*]

Do not let phrases and clauses that fall between the subject and the verb mislead you.

■ Teaching proper oral hygiene to children, even when they are excited about learning, *requires* patience.

[The verb *requires* must agree with the singular subject of the sentence, *teaching,* rather than with the plural subject of the preceding clause, *they.*]

Be careful to avoid making the verb agree with the noun immediately before it if that noun is not its subject. This problem is especially likely to occur when a modifying phrase containing a plural noun falls between a singular subject and its verb.

■ Each of the engineers *is* experienced.

[The subject of the verb is *each,* not *engineers.*]

■ Only Bob, of all the district managers, *has doubled* his sales this year.

[The subject of the verb is *Bob,* not *managers.*]

■ Proper cleaning of the machines and tools *takes* time.

[The subject of the verb is *cleaning,* not *machines and tools.*]

Tense	Number	Person	Active voice	Passive voice
Present		1st	I drive	I am driven
	Singular	2nd	You drive	You are driven
		3rd	He drives	He is driven
		1st	We drive	We are driven
	Plural	2nd	You drive	You are driven
		3rd	They drive	They are driven
Progressive present		1st	I am driving	I am being driven
	Singular	2nd	You are driving	You are being driven
		3rd	He is driving	He is being driven
		1st	We are driving	We are being driven
	Plural	2nd	You are driving	You are being driven
		3rd	They are driving	They are being driven
Past		1st	I drove	I was driven
	Singular	2nd	You drove	You were driven
		3rd	He drove	He was driven
		1st	We drove	We were driven
	Plural	2nd	You drove	You were driven
		3rd	They drove	They were driven
Progressive past		1st	I was driving	I was being driven
	Singular	2nd	You were driving	You were being driven
		3rd	He was driving	He was being driven
		1st	We were driving	We were being driven
	Plural	2nd	You were driving	You were being driven
		3rd	They were driving	They were being driven
Future		1st	I will drive	I will be driven
	Singular	2nd	You will drive	You will be driven
		3rd	He will drive	He will be driven
		1st	We will drive	We will be driven
	Plural	2nd	You will drive	You will be driven
		3rd	They will drive	They will be driven
Progressive future		1st	I will be driving	I will have been driven
	Singular	2nd	You will be driving	You will have been driven
		3rd	He will be driving	He will have been driven
		1st	We will be driving	We will have been driven
	Plural	2nd	You will be driving	You will have been driven
		3rd	They will be driving	They will have been driven
Present perfect		1st	I have driven	I have been driven
	Singular	2nd	You have driven	You have been driven
		3rd	He has driven	He has been driven
		1st	We have driven	We have been driven
	Plural	2nd	You have driven	You have been driven
		3rd	They have driven	They have been driven
Past perfect		1st	I had driven	I had been driven
	Singular	2nd	You had driven	You had been driven
		3rd	He had driven	He had been driven
		1st	We had driven	We had been driven
	Plural	2nd	You had driven	You had been driven
		3rd	They had driven	They had been driven
Future perfect		1st	I will have driven	I will have been driven
	Singular	2nd	You will have driven	You will have been driven
		3rd	He will have driven	He will have been driven
		1st	We will have driven	We will have been driven
	Plural	2nd	You will have driven	You will have been driven
		3rd	They will have driven	They will have been driven

Table C–4   Conjugation of Verbs

Words such as *type, part, series,* and *portion* take singular verbs even when such words precede a phrase containing a plural noun.

■ A *series* of directions *was given* to each branch manager.

■ A large *portion* of most employee handbooks *is devoted* to the responsibilities of the worker.

Subjects expressing measurement, weight, mass, or total often take singular verbs even though the subject word is plural in form. Such subjects are treated as a unit.

■ Ten pounds *is* the shipping weight.

■ Fifty dollars *is* her commission for each unit she sells.

However, when such subjects refer to the individual units that make up the whole, a plural verb is required.

■ If you need to make change, fifty singles *are* in the office safe.

Similarly, collective subjects take singular verbs when the group is thought of as a unit and take plural verbs when the individuals are thought of separately.

■ The staff *is* teaching its decision.
  [The staff is thought of as a unit.]

■ The staff *are* so divided in their opinions that a decision is unlikely to be reached soon.
  [The staff members are thought of as individuals.]

A book with a plural title requires a singular verb.

■ *Monetary Theories is* a useful source.

Some abstract nouns are singular in meaning though plural in form: examples are *mathematics, news, physics,* and *economics.*

■ News of the merger *is* on page four of the *Chronicle.*

■ Textiles *is* an industry in need of import quotas.

Some words are always plural, such as *pants* and *scissors.*

■ His pants *were* torn by the machine.

■ The scissors *were* on the table.

However, a *pair* of *pants* or *scissors* is singular.

- A pair of pants *is* on order.

- A pair of scissors *was* on the table.

Modifiers such as *some, none, all, more,* and *most* may be singular if they are used with mass nouns or plural if they are used with count nouns. Mass nouns identify things that comprise a mass and cannot be separated into countable units; count nouns identify things that can be separated into countable units (see Section 3.1.1b).

- Most of the oil *has* been used.

- Most of the drivers *know* why they are here.

- Some of the water *has* leaked.

- Some of the pencils *have* been used.

One and *each* are normally singular.

- One of the brake drums *is* still scored.

- Each of the original founders *is* scheduled to speak at the dedication ceremony.

Following a relative pronoun such as *who, which,* or *that,* a verb agrees in number with the noun to which the pronoun refers (its antecedent).

- Steel is one of those industries that *are* hardest hit by high energy costs.
  [*That* refers to *industries.*]

- She is an employee who *is* rarely absent.
  [*Who* refers to *employee.*]

- She is one of those employees who *are* rarely absent.
  [*Who* refers to *employees.*]

A subjective complement is a noun or adjective in the predicate of a sentence, following a linking verb. The number of a subjective complement does not affect the number of the verb—the verb must always agree with the subject.

- The topic of his report *was* rivers.
  [The subject of the sentence is *topic,* not *rivers.*]

Sentences with inverted word order can cause problems with agreement between subject and verb.

■ From this work *have come* several important improvements.

[The subject of the verb is *improvements*, not *work*.]

A compound subject is one that is composed of two or more elements joined by a conjunction such as *and, or, nor, either . . . or,* or *neither . . . nor.* Usually, when the elements are connected by *and,* the subject is plural and requires a plural verb.

■ Education and experience *are* valuable assets.

There is one exception to the *and* rule. Sometimes the elements connected by *and* form a unit or refer to the same person. In this case, the subject is regarded as singular and takes a singular verb.

■ Ice cream and cake *is* his favorite dessert.

■ His lawyer and business partner *prepares* the tax forms.

[His lawyer is also his business partner.]

A compound subject joined by *or* or *nor* requires a singular verb with two singular elements and a plural verb with two plural elements.

■ Neither the *doctor* nor the *nurse is* on duty.

■ Neither the *doctors* nor the *nurses are* on duty.

A compound subject with a singular element and a plural element joined by *or* or *nor* requires that the verb agree with the element nearest to it.

■ Neither the doctor nor the *nurses are* on duty.

■ Neither the doctors nor the *nurse is* on duty.

■ 3.5 Adverbs

An adverb modifies the action or condition expressed by a verb.

■ The recording head hit the surface of the disk *hard.*

[The adverb tells *how* the recording head hit the disk.]

An adverb may also modify an adjective, another adverb, or a clause.

■ The graphics department used *extremely* bright colors.

[The adverb *extremely* modifies the adjective *bright.*]

■   The redesigned brake pad lasted *much* longer than the original model.

[The adverb *much* modifies the adverb *longer.*]

■   *Surprisingly,* the machine failed.

[The adverb *surprisingly* modifies the clause *the machine failed.*]

3.5.1 Functions of Adverbs

An adverb answers one of the following questions:

- Where?

  ■   Move the throttle *forward.*

- When?

  ■   Replace the thermostat *immediately.*

- How?

  ■   Add the solvent *cautiously.*

- How much?

  ■   The *nearly* completed report was lost in the move.

  ■   I *rarely* work on the weekend.

  ■   I have worked overtime *twice* this week.

Some adverbs (such as *however, therefore, nonetheless, nevertheless, consequently, accordingly,* and *then*) can join two independent clauses, each of which could otherwise stand alone as a sentence.

■   I rarely work on the weekend; *nevertheless,* this weekend will be an exception.

Other adverbs, such as *where, when, why,* and *how,* ask questions.

■   *How* many hours did you work last week?

3.5.2 Comparison of Adverbs

Adverbs, like adjectives, show three degrees of comparison: the positive (the basic form of the adverb), the comparative (showing comparison with one other item), and the superlative (showing comparison with two or more other items). Many adverbs indicate comparison with the suffixes *-er,* or *-est;* alternatively, *more* or *most* may be placed in front of an adverb to indicate comparison. One-syllable adverbs use the comparative ending *-er* and the superlative ending *-est.*

- This copier works *faster* than the old one.

- This copier works *fastest* of the three tested.

Most adverbs with two or more syllables end in *-ly*, and most adverbs ending in *-ly* are compared by inserting the comparative *more* or *less* or the superlative *most* or *least* in front of them.

- He moved *more quickly* than the other company's salesperson.

- Of all the salespeople, he moved *most quickly*.

- He moves *less quickly* than the other company's salesperson.

- Of all the salespeople, he moved *least quickly*.

A few irregular adverbs require a change in form to indicate comparison.

- Our training program functions *well.*

- Our training program functions *better* than most others in the industry.

- Our training program functions the *best* in the industry.

3.5.3 Adverbs Made from Adjectives

Many adverbs are simply adjectives with *-ly* added, such as *dashingly* and *richly*. Sometimes, the adverb form is identical to the adjective form: examples are *early, hard, right,* and *fast*. Resist the temptation to drop the *-ly* ending from such adverbs as *surely, differently, seriously, considerably, badly,* and *really*.

- The breakdown of the air-conditioning equipment damaged the computer system *considerably* ~~considerable~~.

However, resist the temptation to coin awkward adverbs by adding *-ly* to adjectives (*firstly, muchly*).

- *First* ~~Firstly~~, I'd like to thank our sponsor; *second* ~~secondly~~, I'd like to thank all of you.

3.5.4 Placement of Adverbs

An adverb may appear almost anywhere in a sentence, but its position can affect the meaning of the sentence. Avoid placing an adverb between two verb forms where it will be ambiguous because it can be read as modifying either.

INCORRECT   The man who was making calculations hastily rose from his desk and
               left the room.

               [Did the man calculate hastily or did he rise hastily?]

CORRECT   The man who was making calculations rose hastily from his desk and
               left the room.

An adverb is commonly placed in front of the verb it modifies.

■   The accountant *meticulously* checked the figures.

An adverb may, however, follow the verb (or the verb and its object) that it
modifies.

■   The accountant checked the figures *meticulously*.

■   The gauge dipped *suddenly*.

An adverb may be placed between a helping verb and a main verb.

■   He will *surely* call.

If an adverb modifies only the main verb, and not any accompanying helping
verbs, place the adverb immediately before or after the main verb.

■   The alternative proposal has been *effectively* presented.

■   The alternative proposal has been presented *effectively*.

An adverb phrase, however, should not separate the parts of a verb.

■   This suggestion has ~~time and time again~~ been rejected. *time and time again*

To emphasize an adverb that introduces an entire sentence, you can put the adverb before the subject of the sentence.

■   *Clearly,* he was ready for the promotion when it came.

■   *Unfortunately,* fuel rationing has been necessary.

In writing, such adverbs as *nearly, only, almost, just,* and *hardly* are placed immediately before the words they limit. A speaker can place these words earlier and
avoid ambiguity by stressing the word to be limited; a writer, however, can ensure
clarity only through correct placement of the adverb.

■   The punch press almost ~~costs~~ $47,000. *costs*

■ 3.6 Conjunctions

A conjunction connects words, phrases, or clauses. A conjunction can also indicate the relationship between the two elements it connects. (For example, *and* joins together; *or* selects and separates.)

3.6.1 Types of Conjunctions

Conjunctions may be coordinating, correlative, or subordinating. In addition, certain adverbs act as conjunctions.

a. Coordinating Conjunctions

A coordinating conjunction is a word that joins two sentence elements that have identical functions. The coordinating conjunctions are *and, but, for, nor, or, so,* and *yet.*

- Bill *and* John work at the Los Angeles office.

  [*And* joins two proper nouns.]

- To hear *and* to obey are two different things.

  [*And* joins two phrases.]

- He would like to include the test results, *but* that would make the report too long.

  [*But* joins two clauses.]

b. Correlative Conjunctions

Correlative conjunctions are used in pairs. The correlative conjunctions are *either . . . or, neither . . . nor, not only . . . but also, both . . . and,* and *whether . . . or.* To ensure not only symmetry but also logic in your writing, follow correlative conjunctions with parallel sentence elements that are alike in function and in construction.

- Bill will arrive *either* on Wednesday *or* on Thursday.

c. Subordinating Conjunctions

A subordinating conjunction connects sentence elements of different weights, normally independent clauses that can stand alone as sentences and dependent clauses that cannot. The most frequently used subordinating conjunctions are *so, although, after, because, if, where, than, since, as, unless, before, that, though, when,* and *whereas.*

- He left the office *after* he had finished writing the report.

d. Conjunctive Adverbs

A conjunctive adverb is an adverb that has the force of a conjunction because it is used to join two independent clauses. The most common conjunctive adverbs are *however, moreover, therefore, further, then, consequently, besides, accordingly, also,* and *too.*

■ The engine performed well in the laboratory; *moreover,* it surpassed all expectations during its road test.

3.6.2 Use of Conjunctions

Coordinating conjunctions generally appear within rather than at the beginning of a sentence. There is, however, no rule against beginning a sentence with a co-ordinating conjunction. In fact, such conjunctions can be strong transitional words and at times can provide emphasis.

■ I realize that the project was more difficult than expected and that you have also en-countered personnel problems. *But* we must meet our deadline.

Starting sentences with conjunctions is acceptable in even the most formal Eng-lish. But like any other writing device, this one should be used sparingly lest it be-come ineffective and even annoying.

■ 3.7 Prepositions

A preposition is a word that links a noun or pronoun (its object) to another sen-tence element. (See also Prepositions in Writer's Guide Section D, on page 873.)

3.7.1 Functions of Prepositions

Prepositions express such relationships as direction (*to, into, across, toward*), lo-cation (*at, in, on, under, over, beside, among, by, between, through*), time (*before, after, during, until, since*), or figurative location (*for, against, with*). Although only about 70 prepositions exist in the English language, they are used frequently. Together, the preposition, its object, and the object's modifiers form a preposi-tional phrase, which acts as a modifier.

Many words that function as prepositions also function as adverbs. If a word takes an object and functions as a connective, it is a preposition; if it has no ob-ject and functions as a modifier, it is an adverb.

■ The manager sat *behind* the desk in his office.

[*Behind* functions as a preposition.]

■ The customer lagged *behind;* then she came in and sat down.

[*Behind* functions as an adverb.]

3.7.2 Usage of Prepositions

Do not use unnecessary prepositions, such as "off *of*" or "inside *of.*"

Inside
- ~~Inside of~~ the cave, the spelunkers turned on their headlamps.

Avoid adding the preposition *up* to verbs unnecessarily.

Call
- ~~Call up~~ and see whether he is in his office.

However, do not omit needed prepositions.

to
- He was oblivious ^ and not distracted by the view from his office window.

If a preposition falls naturally at the end of a sentence, leave it there.

- I don't remember which file I put it *in.*

Be aware, however, that a preposition at the end of a sentence can indicate that the sentence is awkwardly constructed.

AWKWARD   Corn was the crop in the field that the wheat was planted *by*.

IMPROVED   The wheat was planted next to the corn in the field.

The object of a preposition—the word or phrase following the preposition—is always in the objective case. Despite this rule, a construction such as "between you and *me*" frequently and incorrectly appears as "between you and I."

him
- The whole department has suffered because of the quarrel between ~~he~~ and Bob.

Certain verbs (and verb forms), adverbs, and adjectives are used with certain prepositions. For example, we say "interested *in*," "aware *of*," "devoted *to*," "equated *with*," "abstain *from*," "adhere *to*," "conform *to*," "capable *of*," "comply *with*," "object *to*," "find fault *with*," "inconsistent *with*," "independent *of*," "infer *from*," and "interfere *with*."

■ 3.8 Interjections

An interjection is a word or phrase of exclamation that is used independently to express emotion or surprise or to summon attention. *Hey! Ouch! Wow!* are strong interjections. *Oh, well,* and *indeed* are mild ones. An interjection functions much as *yes* or *no,* in that it has no grammatical connection with the rest of the sentence in which it appears. When an interjection expresses a sudden or strong emotion, punctuate it with an exclamation mark.

- His only reaction was a resounding *"Wow!"*

Punctuate a mild interjection with a comma.

- *Well,* that's done.

- *Oh, well,* that's done.

Because they get their expressive force from sound, interjections are more common in speech than in writing. They are rarely appropriate to business or technical writing.

4. Phrases, Clauses, Sentences, and Paragraphs

Good writing relies on the writer's ability to put words together that convey a message to a reader in the most effective way. The writer can use a number of tools to help communicate ideas to a reader; among them are phrases, clauses, sentences, and paragraphs.

◼ 4.1 Phrases

Although a phrase is the most basic meaningful group of words, it does not make a full statement. Unlike a clause, it does not contain both a subject (words that name someone or something) and a predicate (words that make an assertion about the subject). Instead, a phrase is based on a noun, a verbal (that is, a gerund, infinitive, or participle), or a verb without a subject.

- *by August fifth*
  [phrase based on a noun]

- *operating the machine*
  [phrase based on a verbal]

- *has been working*
  [phrase composed of a verb without a subject]

A phrase may function as an adjective, an adverb, a noun, or a verb.

ADJECTIVE	The subjects *on the agenda* were all discussed.
ADVERB	We discussed the project *with great enthusiasm.*
NOUN	*Hard work* is her way of life.
VERB	The chief engineer *should have been notified.*

4. Phrases, Clauses, Sentences, and Paragraphs

Even though phrases function as adjectives, adverbs, nouns, or verbs, normally they are named for the kind of word around which they are constructed—preposition, verb, noun, or the three verbals. For definitions of the parts of speech, refer to Section 3 of this Guide.

4.1.1 Prepositional Phrases

A preposition is a word that shows the relationship between the noun or pronoun that is its object and another sentence element. Prepositions express relationships such as direction, location, and time. A preposition, its object, and the object's modifiers form a prepositional phrase, which acts as a modifier.

■ *After the meeting,* the regional managers adjourned *to the executive dining room.*

4.1.2 Verb Phrases

A verb phrase consists of a main verb preceded by one or more helping verbs.

■ Company officials discovered that a computer *was outputting* more data than it *had been asked* for.

■ He *will file* his tax forms on time this year.

4.1.3 Noun Phrases

A noun phrase consists of a noun and its modifiers.

■ *Many large companies* own corporate fleets.

■ Have *the two new employees* fill out *these forms.*

4.1.4 Participial Phrases

A participial phrase consists of a participle plus its object and any modifiers. A participial phrase functions as an adjective, so it must modify a noun or pronoun and must be placed so that this relationship is clear.

■ *Looking very pleased with himself,* the sales manager reported on the success of the policies he had introduced.

4.1.5 Infinitive Phrases

An infinitive is the root form of a verb (*go, run, talk*), one of the principal parts that is used to construct the various forms of a verb. An infinitive generally follows the word *to*, called the sign of the infinitive. An infinitive phrase consists of the word *to* plus an infinitive and any objects or modifiers.

■ *To succeed in this field*, you must be willing *to assume responsibility*.

4.1.6 Gerund Phrases

When the *-ing* form of a verb functions as a noun, it is called a gerund. A gerund phrase, which also must function as a noun, consists of a gerund plus any objects or modifiers.

■ *Preparing an annual report* is a difficult task.

■ She liked *running the department*.

■ 4.2 Clauses

A clause is a part of a sentence that contains both a subject (the word or group of words that name someone or something as a topic) and a predicate (the main verb and its modifiers and complements that make an assertion about the subject).

Every subject-predicate word group in a sentence is a clause. Unlike a phrase, a clause can make a complete statement because it contains a finite verb (as opposed to a nonfinite verb or verbal) as well as a subject. Every sentence must consist of at least one clause. A clause that conveys a complete thought and thus could stand alone as a sentence is an independent clause.

■ *The scaffolding fell* when the rope broke.

A clause that could not stand alone without the rest of its sentence is a dependent or subordinate clause.

■ I was at the St. Louis branch *when the decision was made.*

A dependent clause may function as a noun, an adjective, or an adverb in a larger sentence; an independent clause may be modified by one or more dependent clauses.

■ While I was in college, I studied differential equations.

[*While I was in college* is a dependent clause functioning as an adverb; it modifies the independent clause *I studied differential equations.*]

A clause may be connected with the rest of its sentence by a coordinating conjunction, a subordinating conjunction, a relative pronoun, or a conjunctive adverb. (Refer to Sections 3.2 and 3.6 for discussions of pronouns and conjunctions.)

4. Phrases, Clauses, Sentences, and Paragraphs

COORDINATING CONJUNCTION	Peregrine falcons are about the size of a large crow, *and* they have a wingspan of three to four feet.
SUBORDINATING CONJUNCTION	Mission control will have to be alert *because* the space laboratory will contain a highly flammable fuel at launch.
RELATIVE PRONOUN	It was Robert M. Fano *who* designed and developed the earliest "Multiple Access Computer" system at M.I.T.
CONJUNCTIVE ADVERB	It was dark when we arrived; *nevertheless,* we began to tour the factory.

4.2.1 Independent Clauses

Unlike a dependent clause, an independent clause is complete in itself. Although it might be part of a larger sentence, it always can stand alone as a separate sentence.

■ *We abandoned the project* because the cost was excessive.

4.2.2 Dependent Clauses

A dependent (or subordinate) clause is a group of words that has a subject and a predicate but requires a main clause to complete its meaning. A dependent clause can function in a sentence as a noun, as an adjective, or as an adverb.

As nouns, dependent clauses may function in sentences as subjects, objects, or complements.

SUBJECT	*That human beings can learn to control their glands and internal organs by direct or indirect means* is now an established fact.
DIRECT OBJECT	I learned *that drugs ordered by brand name can cost several times as much as drugs ordered by generic name.*
SUBJECTIVE COMPLEMENT	The trouble is *that we cannot finish the project by May.*

As adjectives, dependent clauses can modify nouns or pronouns. Dependent clauses are often introduced by relative pronouns and relative adjectives (*who, whom, whose, which, what, that*).

■ The man *who called earlier* is here.

[The clause modifies *man.*]

As adverbs, dependent clauses may express relationships of time, cause, result, or degree.

EXPRESSES TIME	You are making an investment *when you buy a house.*

EXPRESSES A CAUSE	A title search was necessary *because the bank would not otherwise grant a loan.*
EXPRESSES A RESULT	Consult an attorney *so that you will be aware of your rights and obligations.*
EXPRESSES DEGREE	Monthly mortgage payments should not be much more *than the buyer earns in one week.*

Dependent clauses clarify the relationships between thoughts. As a result, dependent clauses can present ideas more precisely than can simple sentences (which contain one independent clause) or compound sentences (which combine two or more independent clauses).

IMPRECISE	The sewage plant is located between Millville and Darrtown. Both villages use it.
	[These sentences convey two thoughts of approximately equal importance.]
IMPROVED	The sewage plant, *which is located between Millville and Darrtown,* is used by both villages.
	[Here, one thought, the plant's location, is subordinated to the other, its service area.]
IMPRECISE	He arrived at his office early and was able to finish the report without any interruptions.
	[These sentences convey two thoughts of approximately equal importance.]
IMPROVED	*Because he arrived at his office early,* he was able to finish the report without interruptions.
	[Here, one thought, his early arrival, is subordinated to the other, his completion of the report.]

Subordinate clauses effectively express thoughts that describe or explain another statement. They can state where, when, how, or why an event occurred, thus supplying logical connections that may not be obvious from the context. Too much subordination, however, may be worse than none at all. A string of dependent clauses, like a string of simple sentences, may obscure the important ideas.

IMPRECISE	He had selected classes *that* had a slant *that* was specifically directed toward students *who* intended to go into business.
	[This sentence contains three dependent clauses of approximately equal importance.]

IMPROVED He had selected classes *that* were specifically directed to business students.

[One dependent clause emphasizes the most important of the three points.]

■ 4.3 Sentences

A sentence is a sequence of words that contains a subject and a predicate and conveys a complete thought. A sentence normally has at least two words: a subject (something or someone) and a predicate (an assertion about the action or state of existence of the subject). (See also ESL Tips: Using Common Sentence Patterns, in Chapter 4 on page 95.)

■ Sales [subject] declined [assertion about the subject].

To the basic sentence can be added modifiers—words, phrases, and clauses that expand, limit, or make more exact the meanings of other sentence elements.

■ *Computer* sales declined *in August.*

In most sentences, the subject is a noun phrase rather than a single word, and the predicate is a verb or verb phrase with appropriate modifiers, objects, or complements.

■ A good human resources department [subject] screens job applicants carefully [predicate].

Sentences may be classified according to structure (simple, compound, complex) and intention (declarative, interrogative, imperative, exclamatory).

4.3.1 Structure

A simple sentence is often used to make its content stand out in the reader's mind. A compound sentence is used to show that the clauses in the sentence are of equal importance. A complex sentence is used to show that the clauses in the sentence are of unequal importance.

a. Simple Sentences

A simple sentence has one clause. In its most basic form, the simple sentence contains only a subject and a predicate.

■ Profits rose.

■ The strike ended.

Both the subject and the predicate may be compounded to include several items without changing the basic structure of the simple sentence.

COMPOUND SUBJECT   *Bulldozers and road graders* have blades.

COMPOUND PREDICATE   Bulldozers *strip, ditch, and backfill.*

Likewise, although modifiers may lengthen a simple sentence, they do not change its basic structure.

■   *The recently introduced* procedure works *very well.*

b. Compound Sentences

A compound sentence combines two or more related independent clauses that are of equal importance.

■   Drilling is the only way to collect samples of the layers of sediment below the ocean floor, but it is by no means the only way to gather information about these strata.[1]

The independent clauses of a compound sentence may be joined by a comma and a coordinating conjunction, by a semicolon, or by a conjunctive adverb preceded by a semicolon and followed by a comma.

■   The plan was sound, *and* the staff was eager to begin.

   [The clauses are joined by a comma and coordinating conjunction.]

■   The plan was sound; the staff was eager to begin.

   [The clauses are joined by a semicolon.]

■   The plan was sound; *therefore,* the staff was eager to begin.

   [The clauses are joined by a conjunctive adverb.]

c. Complex Sentences

A complex sentence contains one independent clause and at least one dependent clause.

■   We lost some of our efficiency [independent clause] when we moved [dependent clause].

A dependent clause may occur before, after, or within the independent clause. The dependent clause can function within a sentence as a subject, an object, or a modifier.

---

[1]Bruce C. Heezen and Ian D. MacGregor, "The Evolution of the Pacific," *Scientific American*, November 1973, 103.

SUBJECT	*What he proposed* is irrelevant.
OBJECT	We know *where it is supposed to be.*
MODIFIER	Fingerprints, *which were used for personal identification in 200* B.C.E., were not used for criminal identification until about 1800.

Because complex sentences offer more variety than simple ones, changing a compound sentence into a complex one can produce a more precise statement. When one independent clause becomes subordinate to another, the relationship between the two is more clearly established.

- We moved, *and* we lost some of our efficiency.

   [This sentence contains a compound sentence with a coordinating conjunction.]

- *When* we moved, we lost some of our efficiency.

   [This is a complex sentence with a subordinating conjunction.]

A complex sentence indicates the relative importance of two clauses and expresses the relationship between the ideas contained in them. Normally, the independent clause states the main point, and the dependent clause states a related but subordinate point.

- Although the warehouse was damaged by the fire, all the employees escaped safely from the building.

4.3.2 Intention

By intention, a sentence may be declarative, interrogative, imperative, or exclamatory.

   A declarative sentence conveys information or makes a factual statement.

- This motor powers the conveyor belt.

An interrogative sentence asks a direct question.

- Does the conveyor belt run constantly?

An imperative sentence issues a command.

- Start the generator.

An exclamatory sentence is an emphatic expression of feeling, fact, or opinion. It is a declarative sentence that is stated with great force.

- The heater exploded!

4.3.3 Construction

a. Parts of Sentences

Within a sentence, every word or word group functions as a sentence element. A *subject* names (and perhaps includes words that describe) the person or thing that is the topic of the sentence.

■   *The new machine* ran.

A *verb* describes an action or affirms the condition or state of existence of its subject.

■   The new machine *ran.*

A *complement* is used in the predicate (with the verb) to complete the meaning of a sentence. There are four kinds of complements. The first, the direct object, names the person or thing on which a transitive verb acts. The direct object normally answers the question *what* or *whom.*

DIRECT OBJECT He wrote *a letter.*

DIRECT OBJECT I admire *the boss.*

The second type of complement, the indirect object, names the recipient of the direct object; that is, it names the person or thing that something is done to or for.

INDIRECT OBJECT He wrote *the company* a letter.

The third type of complement, the objective complement, describes or renames a direct object.

OBJECTIVE COMPLEMENT I like my coffee *hot.*

The last type of complement, the subjective complement, describes or renames the subject of a sentence.

SUBJECTIVE COMPLEMENT The director seems *confident.*

A *modifier* expands, limits, or makes more exact the meaning of other sentence elements.

■   *Automobile* production decreased *rapidly.*

A *connective* (a conjunction, a conjunctive adverb, or a preposition) ties together parts of sentences by indicating subordination or coordination.

- I work hard each week, *but* I relax *when* I play racquetball.

An *appositive* is a noun or noun phrase that follows and amplifies another noun or noun phrase.

- Bob, *the human resources director,* just interviewed another engineer.

An *absolute* is a participial or infinitive phrase that modifies a statement as a whole and is not linked to it by a subordinating conjunction or preposition.

- *To speak bluntly,* the proposal is unacceptable.

An *expletive* is a word such as *it* or *there* that serves as a structural filler and reverses standard subject-verb order.

- *It* is certain that he will go.

Because expletives are meaningless, they are best avoided in business or technical writing.

b. Sentence Patterns

Subjects, verbs, and complements are the main elements of a sentence. Everything else is subordinate to them in one way or another. The following are the basic sentence patterns with which a writer works.

- The cable snapped.

  [subject-verb]

- Generators produce electricity.

  [subject-verb-direct object]

- The test results gave us confidence.

  [subject-verb-indirect object-direct object

- Repairs made the equipment operational.

  [subject-verb-direct object-objective complement]

- The metal was aluminum.

  [subject-linking verb-subjective complement]

Most sentences follow the subject-verb-complement pattern. In "The company dismissed Joe," for example, you recognize the subject and the object by their positions before and after the verb. In fact, readers interpret what they read more easily because they expect this sentence order. As a result, departures from it can be effective if used sparingly for emphasis and variety, but annoying if overdone.

An inverted sentence places the elements in other than normal order.

- A better job I never had.

  [direct object-subject-verb]

- More optimistic I have never been.

  [subjective complement-subject-linking verb]

Inverted sentence order can be used in questions and exclamations; it can also be used for emphasis.

- Have you a pencil?

  [verb-subject-complement]

- How heavy your book feels!

  [complement-subject-verb]

In sentences introduced by expletives (*there, it*), the subject comes after its verb because the expletive occupies the subject's normal location before the verb. Because expletives are fillers, they are avoided in concise writing.

Compare the following pairs of sentences:

- There [expletive] are [verb] certain principles [subject] of drafting that must not be ignored.

- Certain principles of drafting must not be ignored.

  [The meaningful verb of the sentence, *be ignored*, which was buried in a relative clause in the expletive construction, becomes the only verb; the meaningless *are* is unnecessary.]

- It [expletive] is [verb] difficult [complement] to work [subject] in a noisy office.

- To work in a noisy office is difficult.

Unusual sentence order, however, cannot be used often without tiring or puzzling the reader. Instead, a sentence that moves quickly from subject to verb to complement is clear and easy to understand. The writer's goal is to preserve the clarity and directness of this pattern while writing sentences that use more complicated forms to present more information. A skillful writer depends on subordination—the relative weighing of ideas—to make sentences more dense. This sentence lacks subordination:

> The city manager's report was carefully illustrated, and it covered five typed pages.

But it can be rewritten in several ways by subordinating the less important ideas to the more important ones, as follows:

ADJECTIVAL CLAUSE	The city manager's report, *which covered five typed pages,* was carefully illustrated.
PARTICIPIAL PHRASE	The city manager's report, *covering five typed pages,* was carefully illustrated.
PARTICIPIAL PHRASE	The *carefully illustrated* report of the city manager covered five typed pages.
MODIFIER	The *five-page* report of the city manager was carefully illustrated.
APPOSITIVE PHRASE	The city manager's report, *five typed pages,* was carefully illustrated.

The effective subordination of words, phrases, and clauses produces varied, concise, and emphatic sentences.

4.3.4 Common Sentence Problems

The most common sentence problems are faulty subordination, run-on sentences, sentence fragments, and dangling and misplaced modifiers.

a. Faulty Subordination

Faulty subordination occurs (1) when a grammatically subordinate element, such as a dependent clause, actually contains the main idea of the sentence; or (2) when a subordinate element is so long or detailed that it overpowers the main idea. You can avoid the first problem, expressing the main idea in a subordinate element, by deciding which idea is the main idea. Both of the following sentences, for example, appear logical, but each emphasizes a different point.

■ Although the new filing system saves money, many of the staff are unhappy with it.

[This sentence emphasizes the staff's unhappiness and downplays the saving of money.]

■ The new filing system saves money, although many of the staff are unhappy with it.

[This sentence emphasizes the saving of money.]

In this example, if the writer's main point is that *the new filing system saves money,* the second sentence is better. If the main point is that *many of the staff are unhappy,* then the first sentence is better.

The other major problem with subordination occurs when a writer puts so much detail into a subordinate element that it overpowers the main point by its sheer size and weight. In the following example, details are omitted to streamline the sentence.

■ If company personnel do not fully understand what the new contract ~~that was drawn up at the annual meeting of the district managers this past month in New Orleans~~ requires of them, they should call or write the vice-president for finance.

b. Run-On Sentences

A run-on sentence, sometimes called a fused sentence, is made up of two or more sentences unseparated by punctuation. The term sometimes includes pairs of independent clauses separated by only a comma, although these are usually called comma faults or comma splices. Run-on sentences can be corrected by (1) making two sentences, (2) joining the two clauses with a semicolon (if they are closely related and of equal weight), (3) joining the two clauses with a comma and a coordinating conjunction, or (4) subordinating one clause to the other.

INCORRECT   The training division will offer three new courses interested employees should sign up by Wednesday.

[run-on sentence]

INCORRECT   The training division will offer three new courses, interested employees should sign up by Wednesday.

[comma fault or comma splice]

CORRECT   The training division will offer three new courses. Interested employees should sign up by Wednesday.

[period]

CORRECT   The training division will offer three new courses; interested employees should sign up by Wednesday.

[semicolon]

CORRECT   The training division will offer three new courses, so interested employees should sign up by Wednesday.

[comma plus coordinating conjunction]

CORRECT   When the training division offers the new courses, interested employees should sign up for them.

[one clause subordinated to the other]

c. Sentence Fragments and Minor Sentences

A sentence that is missing an essential part (subject or predicate) is called a sentence fragment.

■ She changed jobs. (sentence)

■ And earned more money. (fragment, lacking a subject)

But having a subject and a predicate does not automatically turn a clause into a sentence. The clause must also make an independent statement. "I work" is a sentence; "If I work" is a fragment because the subordinating conjunction *if* makes the statement a dependent clause.

Sentence fragments are often introduced by relative pronouns (*who, whom, whose, which, that*) or subordinating conjunctions (such as *after, although, because, if, when,* and *while*). When you use these introductory words, you can anticipate combining the dependent clause that follows with a main clause to form a complete sentence.

■ The accounting department received several new computers. ~~After~~ *after* its order was processed.

A sentence must contain a main or finite verb; verbals (gerunds, participles, and infinitives) cannot replace main or finite verbs. The following examples are sentence fragments because they lack main verbs. Their verbals (*working, to skip, expecting*) cannot function as finite verbs.

FRAGMENT	*Working* overtime every night during tax season.
FRAGMENT	*To skip* the meeting.
FRAGMENT	The manager *expecting* to place an order.

Fragments may reflect incomplete or confused thinking. The most common type of fragment is the careless addition of an afterthought.

■ These are the branch tellers. ~~A~~ *, a* dedicated group of employees.

The following examples illustrate common types of sentence fragments:

INCORRECT	Health insurance rates have gone up. *Because medical expenses have increased.*
	[adverbial clause]
CORRECT	Health insurance rates have gone up because medical expenses have increased.
INCORRECT	The engineers tested the model. *Outside the laboratory.*
	[prepositional phrase]
CORRECT	The engineers tested the model outside the laboratory.
INCORRECT	*Having finished the job.* We submitted our bill.
	[participial phrase]
CORRECT	Having finished the job, we submitted our bill.

INCORRECT	We met with Jim Rodgers. *Former head of the sales division.*
	[appositive]
CORRECT	We met with Jim Rodgers, former head of the sales division.
INCORRECT	We have one major goal this month. *To increase the strength of the alloy without reducing its flexibility.*
	[infinitive phrase in apposition with *goal*]
CORRECT	We have one major goal this month: to increase the strength of the alloy without reducing its flexibility.

Occasionally, a writer intentionally uses an incomplete sentence. This kind of deliberate fragment, called a *minor sentence,* makes sense in its context because the missing element is clearly implied by the preceding sentence or is clearly understood without being stated.

■ In view of these facts, is new equipment really necessary? *Or economical?*

■ You can use the one-minute long-distance rates any time between eleven at night and eight in the morning. *Any night of the week.*

Minor sentences are elliptical expressions that are equivalent to complete sentences because the missing words are obvious to a reader from the context.

■ Why not?

■ How much?

■ Ten dollars.

■ At last!

■ This way, please.

■ So much for that idea.

Although they are common in advertising copy, fictional dialogue, and informal emails, minor sentences are not normally appropriate to business or technical writing.

d. Dangling and Misplaced Modifiers

A *dangling modifier* is a word or phrase that has no clear word or subject to modify. Most dangling modifiers are phrases with verbals (gerunds, participles, or infinitives). Correct this problem by adding the appropriate noun or pronoun for the phrase to modify or by making the phrase into a clause.

■ After finishing the negotiations, ^we relaxed at dinner. ~~dinner was relaxing.~~

■ *As you enter*
   ~~Entering~~ the gate, the administration building is visible.
   ^

A *misplaced modifier* refers, or appears to refer, to the wrong word or phrase. The misplaced element can be a word, a phrase, or a clause.

■ Our copier was used to duplicate materials ~~for other departments~~ that needed to be
         for other departments
   reduced.
         ^

You can avoid this problem by placing modifiers as close as possible to the words they modify. Position each modifier carefully so that it says what you mean.

■   *just*
   We ~~just~~ bought the property for expansion.
              ^

A *squinting modifier* is ambiguous because it is located between two sentence elements and might refer to either one. To correct the problem, move the modifier or revise the sentence.

■ *During the next week, the*
   ~~The~~ union agreed ~~during the next week~~ to return to work.
   ^

or

■   *to return to work*   ^
   The union agreed during the next week ~~to return to work.~~
                    ^   ^

Occasionally, a subject and verb are omitted from a dependent clause; the result is known as an *elliptical clause*. If the omitted subject of the elliptical clause is not the same as the subject of the main clause, the construction dangles. Simply adding the subject and verb to the elliptical clause solves the problem. (Or, you can rework the whole sentence.)

INCORRECT	When ten years old, his father started the company.
	[Could his father have started the company at age ten?]
CORRECT	When *Bill Krebs was* ten years old, his father started the company.
CORRECT	*Bill Krebs was* ten years old when his father started the company.

e. Other Sentence Faults

The assertion made by the predicate of a sentence about its subject must be logical.

■ Mr. Wilson~~'s job~~ is a salesman.

■ Jim~~'s height~~ is six feet tall.

Do not omit a required verb.

■ The floor is swept *^* and the lights *are* out.

■ I never have *written* and probably never will write the annual report.

Do not omit a subject.

■ Although he regarded price-fixing as wrong, he engaged in it until *it was* abolished by law.

Avoid compound sentences containing clauses that have little or no logical relationship to each other.

■ My department is responsible for all company publications *;* ~~, and the~~ *The* staff includes twenty writers, three artists, and four composition specialists.

4.3.5 Effective Sentences

Effective sentences guide the reader and engage his or her attention. They can alert a reader to ideas weighted equally (through parallel structure) or differently (through subordination). In addition, carefully constructed and revised sentences clarify ideas for the reader. Besides highlighting especially significant information, sentences can be varied in length, pattern, and style to avoid boring the reader. Most writers wait until they are revising to concentrate on effective sentences. Then, they can try to eliminate confusion and monotony by building clear, precise, and varied sentences.

a. Sentence Parallelism

Express coordinate ideas in similar form. The very construction of a sentence with parallel elements helps the reader to grasp the similarity of its parts.

■ As a working team, we need to understand that our project is a collaborative effort; as members of a team, we need to recognize that each person's assignment is his or her responsibility.

b. Emphatic Sentences

Subordinate your minor ideas to emphasize your more important ideas.

■ *Because we* ~~We~~ had all arrived, ~~and~~ we began the meeting early.

The most emphatic positions in a sentence are the beginning and the end. Do not waste these spots by burying the main idea in the middle of the sentence between less important points or by tacking on phrases and clauses almost as afterthoughts.

For example, consider the following original and revised versions of a statement written for a company's annual report to its stockholders.

INEFFECTIVE SENTENCE	Sales declined by 3 percent in 2000, but nevertheless the company had the most profitable year in its history, thanks to cost savings that resulted from design improvements in several of our major products; and we expect 2001 to be even better, since further design improvements are being made.
	[The sentence begins with the bad news, buries the good news, and trails off at the end.]
IMPROVED, EFFECTIVE SENTENCE	Cost savings from design improvements in several major products not only offset a 3-percent sales decline but made 2000 the most profitable year in the company's history. Further design improvements now in progress promise to make 2001 even more profitable.
	[The beginning sentence emphasizes *cost savings* and *design improvements;* the ending sentence stresses profits.]

Reversing the normal word order is also used to achieve emphasis, though this tactic should not be overdone.

NORMAL WORD ORDER	I will never agree to that.
REVISED FOR EMPHASIS	*That* I will never agree to.
REVISED FOR EMPHASIS	*Never* will I agree to that.

c. Clear Sentences

Uncomplicated sentences are most effective for stating complex ideas. If readers must unravel a complicated sentence in addition to a complex idea, they are likely to become confused.

CONFUSING SENTENCE	Burning fuel and air in the production chamber causes an expansion of the gases formed by combustion, which in turn pushes the piston down in its cylinder so that the crankshaft rotates and turns the flywheel, which then transmits to the clutch the power developed by the engine.
IMPROVED, CLEAR SENTENCE	Burning fuel and air in the production chamber causes an expansion of the gases formed by combustion. These gases push the piston down in its cylinder so that the crankshaft rotates. Then the flywheel on the end of the crankshaft transmits to the clutch the power developed by the engine.

Just as simpler sentences can make complex ideas easier to understand, so more complex sentences can make groups of simple ideas easier to read.

| CHOPPY, NOT INTEGRATED | The industrial park was designed carefully. A team of architects and landscape designers planned it. It has become a local landmark. |
| IMPROVED, INTEGRATED | The carefully designed industrial park, planned by a team of architects and landscape designers, has become a local landmark. |

d. Sentence Length

Variations in sentence length make writing more interesting to the reader, because many sentences of the same length become monotonous.

Short sentences often can be combined effectively by converting verbs to adjectives.

■ The steeplejack ~~was exhausted. He~~ collapsed on the scaffolding.
       exhausted

Sentences that string together short, independent clauses may be just as tedious as a series of short sentences. Either connect such clauses with subordinating connectives, thereby making some of them dependent, or turn some clauses into separate sentences.

POOR	This river is 60 miles long, *and* it averages 50 yards in width, *and* its depth averages 8 feet.
IMPROVED	This river, *which* is 60 miles long and averages 50 yards in width, has an average depth of 8 feet.
IMPROVED	This river is 60 miles long. It averages 50 yards in width and 8 feet in depth.

Although too many short sentences make your writing sound choppy and immature, a short sentence can be effective at the end of a passage of long ones.

■ As a working team, we need to understand that our projects are collaborative efforts; as individual members of the team, we need to recognize that each person's assignment is his or her responsibility. Put more simply, team members should complete their respective tasks on time and be willing to comment on and advise their teammates' work. Successful collaboration requires that we do our best for each other as a group and for ourselves as individuals. *There is no other way.*

In general, short sentences are good for emphatic statements. Long sentences are good for detailed explanations and support. Nothing is wrong with a long sentence, or even with a complicated one, as long as its meaning is clear and direct. A sentence that is either noticeably short or noticeably long can be used to good effect because its length will draw the reader's attention. When varied for emphasis or contrast, sentence length becomes an element of style.

e. Word Order

When successive sentences all begin in exactly the same way, the result is likely to be monotonous. You can make your sentences more interesting by occasionally starting with a modifying word, phrase, or clause.

ADJECTIVE	*Fatigued,* the project director slumped into a chair.
ADVERB	*Lately,* our division has been very productive.
PARTICIPLE	*Smiling,* he extended his hand to the irate customer.
INFINITIVE	*To learn,* you must observe and ask questions.
ABSOLUTE CONSTRUCTION	*Work having already begun,* there was little we could do.
PREPOSITIONAL PHRASE	*In the morning,* we will finish the report.
PARTICIPIAL PHRASE	*Following the instructions in the manual,* she located and repaired the faulty parts.
INFINITIVE PHRASE	*To reach the top job,* she introduced constructive alternatives to unsuccessful policies.
ADVERB CLAUSE	*Because we now know the results of the survey,* we may proceed with certainty.

Overdoing this technique can also be monotonous; use it with moderation.

Be careful in your sentences to avoid confusing separations of subjects and verbs, prepositions and objects, and the parts of verb phrases. Your reader expects the usual patterns and reads more quickly and easily when they are clear.

CONFUSING	The manager worked closely with, despite personality differences, the head engineer.
	[The preposition and the object are separated.]
IMPROVED	Despite personality differences, the manager worked closely with the head engineer.

This is not to say, however, that a subject and verb never should be separated by a modifying phrase or clause.

■ John Stoddard, who founded the firm in 1963, is still an active partner.

Vary the positions of modifiers in your sentences to achieve variety as well as different emphases or meanings. The following examples illustrate four different ways in which the same sentence could be written by varying the position of its modifiers.

■ Gently, with the square end up, slip the blasting cap down over the time fuse.

■ With the square end up, gently slip the blasting cap down over the time fuse.

■ With the square end up, slip the blasting cap gently down over the time fuse.

■ With the square end up, slip the blasting cap down over the time fuse gently.

f. Loose and Periodic Sentences

A loose sentence makes its major point at the beginning and then adds subordinate phrases and clauses that develop the major point. You express yourself most naturally and easily in this pattern. A loose sentence could seem to end at one or more points before it actually ends, as the periods in parentheses illustrate in the following example.

- It went up (.), a great ball of fire about a mile in diameter(.), an elemental force freed from its bonds(.) after being chained for billions of years.

A compound sentence is generally classed as loose because it could end after its first independent clause.

- Copernicus is frequently called the first modern astronomer(.), and he was the first to develop a complete astronomical system based on the motion of the earth.

Complex sentences are loose if their subordinate clauses follow their main clauses.

- The installation will not be completed on schedule(.) because heavy spring rains delayed construction.

A periodic sentence delays its main idea until the end by presenting subordinate ideas or modifiers first. Skillfully handled, a periodic sentence lends force, or emphasis, to the main point by arousing the reader's anticipation and then presenting the main point as a climax.

- During the last decade or so, the attitude of the American citizen toward automation has undergone a profound change.

Do not use periodic sentences too frequently, however, for overuse may irritate a reader who tires of waiting for your point. Likewise, avoid the sing-song monotony of a long series of loose sentences, particularly a series containing coordinate clauses joined by conjunctions. Instead, experiment in your writing, especially during revision, with shifts from loose sentences to periodic sentences.

■ 4.4 Paragraphs

A paragraph is a group of sentences that supports and develops a single idea. Like an essay in miniature, it expands on the central idea stated in its topic sentence (*italicized* in the following paragraph).

- *For a good educator, there are no stupid questions or final answers.* Educators who do not cut off the curiosity of their students, who themselves become part of the inner movement of the act of discovery, never show any disrespect for any question whatsoever. Because even when the question may seem to them to be ingenuous or wrongly formulated, it is not always so for the person asking the question. In such cases, the rule of educators, far from ridiculing the student, is to help the student to rephrase the question so that he or she can thereby learn to ask better questions.[2]

Paragraphs perform three essential functions: (1) they develop the central ideas stated in their topic sentences; (2) they break material into logical units; and (3) they create physical breaks on the page, which visually assist the reader.

4.4.1 Topic Sentences

A topic sentence states the central idea of a paragraph; the rest of the paragraph then supports and develops that statement with pertinent details.

The topic sentence is most often the first sentence of the paragraph. It is effective in this position because it lets the reader know immediately what subject the paragraph will develop.

■ *Anyone who has been reading the press for the last few years should by now be quite familiar with the shortcomings of "Generation X."* As the *Atlantic* explained in 1992, people under thirty are "more comfortable shopping or playing than working or studying. . . . They watch too much TV . . . , cheat on tests, don't read newspapers." In 1993, the *Houston Chronicle* described today's young people as "poorly educated, politically apathetic, and morally obtuse." The generation's attitude has been summed up by the media in a single word: "slacker." Faced with this chorus of derision, one can easily forget that five years ago the media's concerns about people in our generation—those born between 1961 and 1972—were altogether different.[3]

ESL TIPS: Understanding Paragraph Structure

North American readers expect writers to use a direct strategy when they present ideas. A typical paragraph in English will begin with a topic sentence containing the subject and a claim about the subject that will be developed throughout the paragraph. After the topic sentence, readers expect to find specific examples that support the topic sentence and help to clarify the writer's point.

On rare occasions, the topic sentence logically falls in the middle of a paragraph.

■ It is perhaps natural that psychologists should awaken only slowly to the possibility that behavioral processes may be directly observed, or that they should only gradually

---

[2]Paulo Freire and Antonio Faundez. *Learning to Question: A Pedagogy of Liberation.* New York: The Continuum Publishing Company, 1989, 37.

[3]David Lipsky and Alexander Abrams. *Late Bloomers.* New York: Times Books/Random House, 1994: 33.

put the older statistical and theoretical techniques in their proper perspective. But it is time to insist that science does not progress by carefully designed steps called "experiments," each of which has a well-defined beginning and end. *Science is a continuous and often a disorderly and accidental process.* We shall not do the young psychologist any favor if we agree to reconstruct our practices to fit the pattern demanded by current scientific methodology. What the statistician means by the design of experiments is design which yields the kind of data to which *his* techniques are applicable. He does not mean the behavior of the scientist in his laboratory devising research for his own immediate and possibly inscrutable purposes.[4]

Although the topic sentence is usually most effective early in the paragraph, a paragraph can lead up to the topic sentence to achieve emphasis. When a topic sentence ends a paragraph, it also can serve as a summary or conclusion, based on the details that were designed to lead up to it.

■ Although Merton does construct his book as a delightful romp through the intellectual life of medieval and Renaissance Europe, he does have a serious point to make. For Merton had devoted much of his work to the study of multiple discoveries in science. *He has shown that almost all major ideas rise more than once, independently and often virtually at the same time—and thus, that great scientists are embedded in their cultures, not divorced from them.*[5]

Because several paragraphs are sometimes necessary to develop different aspects of an idea, not all paragraphs have topic sentences. In this situation, transitions between paragraphs are especially important so the reader knows that the same idea is being developed through several paragraphs.

TOPIC SENTENCE   *WordPerfect's style feature lets you insert styles that format your text for an entire document or for specific sections of text within a document.* Because styles contain formatting codes that are grouped under one structure, you can save time and ensure consistency by using styles throughout your document.

TRANSITION   *For example, suppose you write books.* You might want to create several styles that will help you format these books. Here are some examples of the kinds of styles you might want to create:

- A Chapter Heading style. This text could be a centered, 24-point font with italics. You could add extra lines to the style to control the space between the heading and the text that follows.
- A Text style. The text of the book could be formatted in a 10-point font with two columns and a first-line indent for each paragraph.

---

[4]B. F. Skinner, "A Case History in Scientific Method," *American Psychologist* 2 (1956): 232.

[5]Steven Jay Gould. *The Panda's Thumb: More Reflections in Natural History.* New York: Norton, 1980: 47–48.

- A Long Quotes style. The text for long quotes from other sources could be similar to the text style, but in 9-point text instead of 10, single-spaced and indented on both sides.

TRANSITION

When you reach a place in your book where you want to create a chapter heading or a long quote, you can easily apply the style to text rather than reinserting the same formatting codes every time. And if you want to change any of the formatting codes, all you have to do is edit the style, and the change will affect all text to which the style has been applied.[6]

In this example, the idea expressed in the topic sentence is developed in three paragraphs, rather than one, so that the reader can more easily assimilate the two separate parts of the main idea.

4.4.2 Paragraph Coherence and Unity

A good paragraph has unity and coherence. Unity means singleness of purpose, based on a topic sentence that states the central idea of the paragraph. When every sentence in the paragraph contributes to the central idea, the paragraph has unity. Coherence means being logically consistent throughout the paragraph so that all parts naturally connect with one another. Coherence is advanced by carefully chosen transitional words that tie together ideas as they are developed. In the following paragraph, the topic sentence and the transitions are italicized.

- *It turns out to be very difficult to devise a theory to describe the universe all in one go. Instead,* we break the problem up into bits and invent a number of partial theories. Each of *these* partial theories describes and predicts a certain limited class of observations, neglecting the effects of other quantities, or representing them by simple sets of numbers. *It may be that this approach is completely wrong. If* everything in the universe depends on everything else in a fundamental way, *it might be* impossible to get close to a full solution by investigating parts of the problem in isolation. *Nevertheless,* it is certainly the way that we have made progress in the past. The classic example again is the Newtonian theory of gravity, *which* tells us that the gravitational force between two bodies depends only on one number associated with each body, its mass, *but* is otherwise independent of what the bodies are made of. *Thus* one does not need to have a theory of the structure and constitution of the sun and planets in order to calculate their orbits.[7]

A good paragraph often uses details from the preceding paragraph, thereby preserving and advancing the thought being developed. Appropriate conjunc-

---

[6]WordPerfect. *Reference Manual for Windows Version 5.2.* Orem, UT: WordPerfect Corporation, 1992: 500.

[7]Steven J. Hawking. *A Brief History of Time: From the Big Bang to Black Holes.* New York: Bantam, 1988: 11.

tions and the repetition of keywords and key phrases can help to provide unity and coherence among, as well as within, paragraphs.

■ Ten years ago, choosing to educate your child at *home* was a sure sign of crankiness. Today it is a growing *movement*. The department of education estimates that the number of *school*-age children being taught at home has risen from 15,000 at the start of the 1980s to 350,000 in 1992. The *Home School* Legal Defense Association puts the figure even higher, at 500,000 or more. The reason for the discrepancy, according to Scott Somerville, a lawyer with the association, is that *home-schoolers* are not over-keen on owning up to census-takers.

In general, *home-schoolers* have slightly higher incomes and much more stable families than the average American. Apart from that, they are a fairly mixed bunch. In the Northwest, where the *movement* has been growing for 15 years, they tend to be New Age types, intoxicated by the *anti-schooling* ideas of A. S. Neill and Ivan Ilich. Elsewhere, particularly in the South, they are usually evangelical Christians, angry at the constitutional ruling that keeps God out of the classroom.[8]

5. Punctuation

Punctuation is a system of symbols that help the reader to understand the structural relationships within (and the intention of) a sentence. Marks of punctuation may link, separate, enclose, terminate, classify, and indicate omissions from sentences. Most of the 13 punctuation marks can perform more than one function. The use of punctuation is determined by grammatical conventions and by the writer's intention. Misuse of punctuation can cause your reader to misunderstand your meaning. The following are the 13 marks of punctuation.

apostrophe	'
brackets	[ ]
colon	:
comma	,
dash	—
exclamation mark	!
hyphen	-
parentheses	( )
period	. (including ellipses and leaders)
question mark	?
quotation marks	" " (including ditto marks)
semicolon	;
slash	/

---

[8]"Classless Society." *The Economist* (June 11, 1994); 24.

■ 5.1 Commas

The comma (,) is used more often than any other mark of punctuation because it has such a wide variety of uses: it can link, enclose, separate, and show omissions. Effective use of the comma depends on your understanding of how ideas fit together. Used with care, the comma can add clarity and emphasis to your writing; used carelessly, it can cause confusion.

5.1.1 To Link

Coordinating conjunctions (*and, but, for, or, so, nor, yet*) require a comma immediately preceding them when they are used to connect independent clauses.

■ Human beings have always prided themselves on their unique capacity to create and manipulate symbols, but today computers are manipulating symbols.

Exceptions to this rule sometimes occur when the two independent clauses are short and each has a single subject and a single predicate. However, even in such cases, a comma is preferred.

UNLINKED CLAUSES   The cable snapped and the power failed.

IMPROVED   The cable snapped, and the power failed.

5.1.2 To Enclose

a. Nonrestrictive and Parenthetical Elements

Commas are used to enclose nonrestrictive and parenthetical sentence elements. Nonrestrictive elements provide additional, nonessential information about the things they modify; parenthetical elements also insert extra information into the sentence. Each is set off by commas to show its loose relationship with the rest of the sentence.

NONRESTRICTIVE CLAUSE   Our new Detroit factory, *which began operations last month,* should add 25 percent to total output.

PARENTHETICAL ELEMENT   We can, *of course,* expect their lawyer to call us.

Similarly, commas enclose nonrestrictive participial phrases.

NONRESTRICTIVE PHRASE   The lathe operator, *working quickly and efficiently,* finished early.

In contrast, restrictive elements—as their name implies—restrict the meaning of the words to which they apply and cannot be set off with commas.

RESTRICTIVE ELEMENT	The boy *in the front row* is six years old.
NONRESTRICTIVE ELEMENT	The boy, *who is sitting in the front row,* is six years old.

In the first sentence, *in the front row* is essential to the sentence: The phrase identifies the boy. In the second sentence, the nonrestrictive relative clause *who is sitting in the front row* is incidental: The main idea of the sentence can be communicated without it.

Phrases in apposition (which are nonrestrictive and follow and amplify an essential element) are enclosed in commas.

■ Our company, *the Blaylok Precision Company,* is doing well this year.

b. Dates

When complete dates appear with sentences, the year is enclosed in commas.

■ On November 11, 1918, the Armistice went into effect.

However, when only part of a date appears, do not use commas.

■ In November 1918 the armistice went into effect.

When the day of the week is included in a date, the month and the number of the day are enclosed in commas.

■ On Friday, November 11, 1918, the Armistice went into effect.

c. Direct Address

A direct address should be enclosed in commas if it appears anywhere other than at the beginning or end of a sentence.

■ You will note, *Mark,* that the surface of the brake shoe complies with the specifications.

5.1.3 To Separate

Commas are used to separate introductory elements from the rest of the sentence, to separate items from each other, to separate subordinate clauses from main clauses, and to separate certain elements for clarity or emphasis.

a. To Separate Introductory Elements

In general, use a comma after an introductory clause or phrase unless it is very short. This comma helps indicate to a reader where the main part of the sentence begins.

■ *Because many rare fossils never occur free from their matrix,* it is wise to scan every slab with a hand lens.

When long modifying phrases precede the main clause, they should always be followed by a comma.

■ *During the first field-performance tests last year at our Colorado proving ground,* the new motor failed to meet our expectations.

When an introductory phrase is short and closely related to the main clause, the comma may be omitted.

■ *In two seconds* a 20°C temperature rise occurs in the test tube.

Certain types of introductory words must be followed by a comma. One such is a name used in direct address at the beginning of a sentence.

■ *Bill,* here is the statement you asked me to audit.

A mild introductory interjection (such as *oh, well, why, indeed, yes,* and *no*) must be followed by a comma.

■ *Yes,* I will make sure your request is approved.

■ *Indeed,* I will be glad to send you further information.

An introductory adverb, such as *moreover* or *furthermore,* must be followed by a comma.

■ *Moreover,* this policy will improve our balance of payments.

Occasionally, when adverbs are closely connected to the meaning of an entire sentence, they should not be followed by a comma. (Test such sentences by reading them aloud. If you pause after the adverb, use the comma.)

■ *Perhaps* we can still solve the balance-of-payments problem. *Certainly* we should try.

b. To Separate Items from One Another

Commas should be used to separate words in a series.

■ *Basically,* plants control the wind by *obstruction, guidance, deflection,* and *filtration.*

Phrases and clauses in coordinate series, like words, are punctuated with commas.

■ It is well known that plants *absorb noxious gases, act as receptors of dust and dirt particles,* and *cleanse the air of other impurities.*

Although the comma before the last item in a series is sometimes omitted, it is generally clearer to include it. The following sentence illustrates the confusion that may result from omitting the comma.

■   Departments within the company include *operations, finance, mergers* and *benefits*.

  [Is "mergers and benefits" one department or two? "Operations, finance, mergers, and benefits" removes the doubt.]

When adjectives modifying the same noun can be reversed and make sense, or when they can be separated by *and* or *or,* they should be separated by commas.

■   The *dull, cracked* tools needed to be repaired.

When an adjective modifies a noun phrase, no comma is required.

■   He was investigating the *damaged radar-beacon system*.

  [*Damaged* modifies the noun phrase *radar-beacon system*.]

Never separate a final adjective from its noun.

■   He is a conscientious, honest, reliable worker.

  Commas are conventionally used to separate distinct items. Use commas between the elements of an address written on the same line.

■   Walter James, 4199 Mill Road, Dayton, Ohio 45401

Use a comma to separate the numerical elements of a complete date. When the day is omitted, however, the comma is unnecessary. (When a date appears in a sentence, a comma also follows the year. See Section 5.1.2b.)

■   July 2, 1949

■   July 1949

Use commas to separate the elements of Arabic numbers.

■   1,528,200

Use a comma after the salutation of a personal letter.

■   Dear Juan,

Use commas to separate the elements of geographical names.

■   Toronto, Ontario, Canada

ESL TIPS: Punctuating Numbers

The rules for punctuating numbers in English are summarized as follows:
Use a comma to separate numbers with five digits or more into groups of three, starting from the right.

- 57,890 cubic feet
- $187,291
- 5,289,112,001 atoms

The comma is optional in numbers with four digits.

- 1,902 cases or 1902 cases

Do not use a comma in years, house numbers, zip codes, and page numbers.

- The airplane was first flown commercially by United Airlines in June 1995.
- Autotech Industries is located at 92401 East Alameda Drive in Los Angeles.
- The zip code is 91601.
- The citation is located on page 1204.

Use a period to represent the decimal point.

- Their stock values increased at a monthly rate of 4.2 percent.
- The jackpot for last week's lottery was $3,742,097.43.

Use a comma to separate names that are reversed.

- Smith, Alvin

c. To Separate Subordinate Clauses

Use a comma between the main clause and a subordinate clause when the subordinate clause comes first.

- While the test ramp was being checked a final time, the driver reviewed his checklist.

Use a comma following an independent clause that is only loosely related to the dependent clause that follows it.

- The plan should be finished by July, even though I lost time because of illness.

d. To Separate Elements for Clarity or Emphasis

Two contrasting thoughts or ideas can be separated by commas for emphasis.

- The project was finished on time, but not within the cost limits.

- The specifications call for 100-ohm resistors, not 1,000-ohm resistors.

- It was Bill, not Matt, who suggested that the names be changed.

Use a comma to separate a direct quotation from its introduction.

- Morton and Lucia White said, "Men live in cities but dream of the countryside."

Do not use a comma, however, when giving an indirect quotation.

- Morton and Lucia White said that men dream of the countryside even though they live in cities.

Sometimes commas are used simply to make something clear that might otherwise be confusing.

- The year after ‸ Xerox and 3M outproduced all the competition.

If you need a comma to separate two consecutive uses of the same word, rewrite the sentence.

- *We were surprised at the* ~~The~~ assets we had~~, had surprised us~~.

5.1.4 To Show Omissions

In certain coordinate constructions, a comma can replace a missing, but implied, sentence element.

- Some were punctual; others, late. (Comma replaces *were*.)

5.1.5 Conventional Use with Other Punctuation

In American usage, a comma always goes inside quotation marks.

- Although he called his presentation "adequate," the audience thought it was superb.

Except with abbreviations, a comma should not be used with a period, question mark, exclamation mark, or dash.

- "I have finished the project/," he said. [omit period]

- "Have you finished the project?/" I asked. [omit comma]

5.1.6 Comma Problems

The most frequent comma problems are the comma fault and the use of super-fluous commas.

a. Comma Faults

Do not attempt to join two independent clauses with only a comma; this is called "comma fault" or "comma splice." (See also Section 4.3.4b.)

INCORRECT   The new medical plan was comprehensive, the union negotiator was pleased.

Such a comma fault could be corrected in several ways:

Substitute a semicolon.

- The new medical plan was comprehensive; the union negotiator was pleased.

Add a conjunctive adverb preceded by a semicolon and followed by a comma.

- The new medical plan was comprehensive; *therefore,* the union negotiator was pleased.

Add a conjunction following the comma.

- The new medical plan was comprehensive, *so* the union negotiator was pleased.

Create two sentences. (Be aware, however, that putting a period between two closely related and brief statements may result in two weak sentences.)

- The new medical plan was comprehensive. The union negotiator was pleased.

Subordinate one clause to the other.

- *Because* the new medical plan was comprehensive, the union negotiator was pleased.

b. Superfluous Commas

A number of common writing errors involve placing commas where they do not belong. These errors often occur because writers assume that a pause in a sentence should be indicated by a comma. It is true that commas usually signal pauses, but it is not true that pauses *necessarily* call for commas.

Be careful not to place a comma between a subject and its verb or between a verb and its object.

■ The extremely wet weather throughout the country/makes spring planting difficult. [omit comma]

■ The advertising department employs/four writers, two artists, and one photographer. [omit comma]

Do not use a comma between the elements of a compound subject or a compound predicate consisting of only two elements.

■ The chairman of the board/and the president prepared the press release. [omit comma]

■ The production manager revised the work schedules/and improved morale. [omit comma]

Placing a comma after a coordinating conjunction (such as *and* and *but*) is an especially common error.

■ We doubled our sales, and/we reduced our costs. [omit comma]

■ We doubled our sales, but/we still did not dominate the market. [omit comma]

Do not place a comma before the first item or after the last item of a series.

■ We are purchasing new office furniture, including/desks, chairs, and tables. [omit comma]

■ 5.2 Semicolons

The semicolon (;) links independent clauses or other sentence elements that are of equal weight and grammatical rank. The semicolon indicates a greater pause between clauses than a comma would, but not so great a pause as a period would.

When the independent clauses of a compound sentence are not joined by a comma and a conjunction, they are linked by a semicolon.

■ No one applied for the position; the job was too difficult.

Make sure, however, that the relationship between the two statements is so clear that a reader will understand why they are linked without further explanation. Often, such clauses balance or contrast with each other.

■ Our last supervisor allowed only one long break each afternoon; our new supervisor allows two short ones.

Use a semicolon between two main clauses connected by a coordinating conjunction (*and, but, for, or, nor, yet*) if the clauses are long and contain other punctuation.

■ In most cases these individuals are corporate executives, bankers, Wall Street lawyers; but they do not, as the economic determinists seem to believe, simply push the button of their economic power to affect fields remote from economics.[9]

A semicolon should be used before conjunctive adverbs (such as *therefore, moreover, consequently, furthermore, indeed, in fact, however*) that connect independent clauses.

■ I won't finish today; moreover, I doubt that I will finish this week.

The semicolon in this example shows that *moreover* belongs to the second clause.

Do not use a semicolon between a dependent clause and its main clause. Remember that elements joined by semicolons must be of equal grammatical rank or weight.

■ No one applied for the position; even though it was heavily advertised.

A semicolon may also be used to separate items in a series when they contain commas within them.

■ Among those present were John Howard, President of the Omega Paper Company; Carol Martin, President of Alpha Corporation; and Larry Stanley, President of Stanley Papers.

■ 5.3 Colons

The colon (:) is a mark of anticipation and introduction that alerts the reader to the close connection between the first statement and the one following. A colon may be used to connect a clause, word, or phrase to the list or series that follows it.

■ We carry three brands of watches: Timex, Bulova, and Omega.

A colon may be used to introduce a list.

■ The following corporations manufacture many types of computers:
    International Business Machines
    NCR Corporation
    Unisys Corporation

---

[9]Robert Lubar, "The Prime Movers," *Fortune*, February 1960, 98.

Do not, however, place a colon between a verb and its objects.

■ The three fluids for cleaning pipettes are: water, alcohol, and acetone. [omit colon]

Do not use a colon between a preposition and its object.

■ I would like to be transferred to: Tucson, Boston, or Miami. [omit colon]

A colon may be used to link one statement to another that develops, explains, amplifies, or illustrates the first. A colon can be used in this way to link two independent clauses.

■ Any large organization must confront two separate, though related, information problems: it must maintain an effective internal communication system, and it must maintain an effective external communication system.

Occasionally, a colon may be used to link an appositive phrase to its related statement if special emphasis is needed.

■ Only one thing will satisfy Mr. Sturgess: our finished report.

Colons are used to link numbers in biblical references and time designations.

■ Genesis 10:16 (refers to chapter 10, verse 16)

■ 9:30 a.m.

In a ratio, the colon indicates the proportion of one amount to another. (The colon replaces *to*.)

■ The cement is mixed with the water and sand at a ratio of 7:5:14.

■ 7:3 = 14:6

A colon follows the salutation in business letters, as opposed to personal letters, where a comma may be used.

■ Dear Ms. Jeffers:

■ Dear Parts Manager:

■ Dear George,

The first word after a colon may be capitalized if the statement following is a complete sentence, a formal resolution or question, or a direct quotation.

■ This year's conference attendance was low: We did not advertise widely enough.

If a subordinate element follows the colon, however, use a lowercase letter following the colon.

■ There is only one way to stay within our present budget: to reduce expenditures for research and development.

■ 5.4 Periods

A period (.) usually indicates the end of a declarative sentence. Periods also link (when used as leaders) and indicate omissions (when used as ellipses).

5.4.1 Uses of Periods

Although their primary function is to end declarative sentences, periods also end imperative sentences that are not emphatic enough for an exclamation mark.

■ Send me any information you may have on the subject.

Periods may occasionally end questions that are really polite requests and questions that assume an affirmative response.

■ Will you please send me the specifications.

Periods end minor sentences (deliberate sentence fragments). These sentences are common in advertising but are rarely appropriate to business or technical writing.

■ The spreadsheet that started it all is taking it to the next level—via the Internet and all other ways that people work together. *The easiest to use, best-connected spreadsheet. Ever.*

Do not use a period after a declarative sentence that is quoted within another sentence.

■ "The project has every chance of success," she stated.

A period, in American usage, is placed inside quotation marks.

■ He liked to think of himself as a "tycoon."

■ He stated clearly, "My vote is yes."

Use periods after initials in names.

■ W. T. Grant, J. P. Morgan

Use periods as decimal points with numbers. (See also ESL Tips: Punctuating Numbers on page 824.)

■ 109.2

■ $540.26

■ 6.9 percent

Use periods to indicate abbreviations.

■ Ms.

■ Dr.

■ Inc.

Use periods following the numbers in numbered lists.

■ 1.

■ 2.

■ 3.

5.4.2 Periods as Ellipses

When you omit words from quoted material, use a series of three spaced periods—called ellipsis marks—to indicate the omission. Such an omission must not change the essential meaning of the passage.

■ "Technical material distributed for promotional use is sometimes charged for, particularly in high-volume distribution to education institutions, although prices for these publications are not uniformly based on the costs of developing them." [without omission]

■ "Technical material distributed for promotional use is sometimes charged for . . . although prices for these publications are not uniformly based on the costs of developing them." [with omission]

When introducing a quotation that begins in the middle of a sentence rather than at the beginning, you do not need ellipsis marks; the lowercase letter with which you begin the quotation already indicates an omission.

■ "When the programmer has determined a system of runs, he must create a systems flowchart to trace the data flow through the system." [without omission]

■ The booklet states that the programmer "must create a systems flowchart to trace the data flow through the system." [with omission]

If there is an omission following the end of a sentence, retain the period at the end of the sentence and add the three ellipsis marks to show the omission.

■ "During the year, every department participated in the development of a centralized computer system. The basic plan was to use the computer to reduce costs. At the beginning of the year, each department received a booklet explaining the purpose of the system." [without omission]

■ "During the year, every department participated in the development of a centralized computer system. . . . At the beginning of the year, each department received a booklet explaining the purpose of the system." [with omission]

5.4.3 Periods as Leaders

When spaced periods are used in a table to connect one item to another, they are called leaders. The purpose of leaders is to help the reader align the data.

■ *Weight*   *Pressure*
  150 lbs . . . . 1.7 psi
  175 lbs . . . . 2.8 psi
  200 lbs . . . . 3.9 psi

5.4.4 Period Fault

The incorrect use of a period is sometimes called a period fault. When a period is inserted prematurely, the result is a sentence fragment. (See Section 4.3.4c.)

■ After a long day at the office during which we finished the report. We left hurriedly for home.   [correction: ; we]

When a period is left out, the result is an incorrect fused (or run-on) sentence.

■ The work plan showed the utility lines they might interfere with construction.   [correction: . They]

■ 5.5 Question Marks

The question mark (?) indicates questions. Use a question mark to end a sentence that is a direct question.

■ Where did you put the specifications?

Use a question mark to end any statement with an interrogative meaning (a statement that is declarative in form but asks a question).

■ The report is finished?

Use a question mark to end an interrogative clause within a declarative sentence.

■ It was not until July (or was it August?) that we submitted the report.

When used with quotations, the question mark may indicate whether the writer who is doing the quoting or the person being quoted is asking the question. When the writer doing the quoting asks the question, the question mark is outside the quotation marks.

■ Did she say, "I don't think the project should continue"?

However, if the quotation itself is a question, the question mark goes inside the quotation marks.

■ She asked, "When will we go?"

If the writer doing the quoting and the person being quoted both ask questions, use a single question mark inside the quotation marks.

■ Did she ask, "Will you go in my place?"

Question marks may follow each item in a series within an interrogative sentence.

■ Do you remember the date of the contract? its terms? whether you signed it?

A question mark should never be used at the end of an indirect question.

■ He asked me whether sales had increased this year.

When a directive or command is phrased as a question, a question mark usually is not used, but a request (to a customer or a superior, for instance) would almost always require a question mark.

■ Will you please make sure that the machinery is operational by August 15. [directive]

■ Will you please telephone me collect if your entire shipment does not arrive by June 10? [request]

■ 5.6 Exclamation Marks

The exclamation mark (!) indicates an expression of strong feeling. It can signal surprise, fear, indignation, or excitement but should not be used for trivial emotions or mild surprise. Exclamation marks cannot make an argument more convincing, lend force to a weak statement, or call attention to an intended irony—no matter how many are stacked like fence posts at the end of a sentence.

The most common use of an exclamation mark is after an interjection, phrase, clause, or sentence to indicate strong emotion.

■ Ouch! Oh! Stop! Hurry!

■ The subject of this meeting—note it well!—is our budget deficit.

■ The gas line is leaking! Clear the building!

When used with quotation marks, the exclamation mark goes outside unless what is quoted is an exclamation.

■ The boss yelled, "Get in here!" Then Ben said, "Yes, sir"!

■ 5.7 Parentheses

Parentheses ( ) are used to enclose words, phrases, or sentences. Parentheses can suggest intimacy, implying that something is shared between the writer and the reader. Parentheses deemphasize (or play down) an inserted element. The material within parentheses can clarify a statement without changing its meaning. Such information may not be essential to a sentence, but it may be interesting or helpful to some readers.

■ Aluminum is extracted from its ore (called bauxite) in three stages.

Parenthetical material pertains to the word or phrase immediately preceding it.

■ The development of IBM (International Business Machines) is an American success story.

Parentheses may be used to enclose the figures or letters that mark items in a sequence or list. When they appear within a sentence, enclose the figures or letters with two parentheses rather than only one parenthesis.

■ The following sections deal with (1) preparation, (2) research, (3) organization, (4) writing, and (5) revision.

Parenthetical material does not change the punctuation of a sentence. A comma following a parenthetical word, phrase, or clause appears outside the closing parenthesis.

■ These oxygen-rich chemicals, including potassium permanganate ($KMnO_4$) and potassium chromate ($KCrO_4$), were oxidizing agents.

If a parenthesis closes a sentence, the ending punctuation appears after the parenthesis. When a complete sentence within parentheses stands independently, however, the ending punctuation goes inside the final parenthesis.

■ The institute was founded by Harry Denman (1902–1972).

■ The project director outlined the challenges facing her staff. (This was her third report to the board.)

Use parentheses with care because they are easily overused. Avoid using parentheses where other marks of punctuation are more appropriate.

■ 5.8 Hyphens

The hyphen (-) functions primarily as a spelling device. The most common use of the hyphen is to join compound words. Check your dictionary if you are uncertain about whether to hyphenate a word.

■ able-bodied, self-contained, carry-all, brother-in-law

A hyphen is used to form compound numbers and functions when they are written out.

■ twenty-one, one-fifth

Two-word and three-word unit modifiers that express a single thought are frequently hyphenated when they precede a noun (a *clear-cut* decision). If each of the words could modify the noun without the aid of the other modifying word or words, however, do not use a hyphen (a *new digital* computer—no hyphen). If the first word is an adverb ending in -*ly*, do not use a hyphen (*hardly* used, *badly* needed). Finally, do not hyphenate such modifying phrases when they follow the nouns they modify.

■ Our office equipment is *out of date.*

■ Our *out-of-date* office equipment will be replaced next month.

A hyphen is always used as part of a letter or number modifier.

■ 15-cent stamp, nine-inch ruler, e-business, T-square

When each item in a series of unit modifiers has the same term following the hyphen, this term need not be repeated throughout the series. For smoothness and brevity, add the term only to the last item in the sequence.

■ The third-~~floor~~, fourth-~~floor~~, and fifth-floor offices have been painted.

When a prefix precedes a proper noun, use a hyphen to connect the two.

■ pre-Sputnik, anti-Stalinist, post-Newtonian

A hyphen may (but does not have to) be used when the prefix ends and the root word begins with the same vowel. When the repeated vowel is *i,* a hyphen is almost always used.

■ re-elect, re-enter, anti-inflationary

A hyphen is used when *ex-* means "former."

■ ex-partners, ex-wife

The suffix *-elect* is connected to the word it follows with a hyphen.

■ president-elect, commissioner-elect

Hyphens identify prefixes, suffixes, or syllables written as such.

■ *Re-, -ism,* and *ex-* are word parts that cause spelling problems.

Hyphens should be used between letters showing how a word is spelled (or misspelled).

■ In his letter, he spelled "believed" b-e-l-e-i-v-e-d.

To avoid confusion, some words and modifiers should always be hyphenated. *Re-cover* does not mean the same thing as *recover,* for example; the same is true of *re-sent* and *resent, re-form* and *reform, re-sign* and *resign.*

A hyphen can stand for *to* or *through* between letters, numbers, and locations.

■ pp. 44-46

■ The Detroit-Toledo Expressway

■ A-L and M-Z

Finally, hyphens are used to divide words at the ends of typed or printed lines. Words are divided on the basis of their syllable breaks, which can be determined by consulting a dictionary. If you cannot check a word in a dictionary, pronounce the word to test whether each section is pronounceable. Never divide a word so near the end that only one or two letters remain to begin your next typed line. If a word is spelled with a hyphen, divide it only at the hyphen break unless this division would confuse the reader. In general, unless the length of your typed line will appear awkward, avoid dividing words.

■ 5.9 Quotation Marks

Quotation marks (" ") are used to enclose direct repetition of spoken or written words. Under normal circumstances, they should not be used to show emphasis. Enclose in quotation marks anything that is quoted word for word (direct quotation) from speech.

■ She said clearly, "I want the progress report by three o'clock."

Do not enclose indirect quotations—usually introduced by *that*—in quotation marks. Indirect quotations paraphrase a speaker's words or ideas.

■ She said that she wanted the progress report by three o'clock.

Handle quotations from written material the same way: Place direct quotations within quotation marks, but not indirect quotations.

■ The report stated, "During the last five years in Florida, our franchise has grown from 28 to 157 locations."

■ The report indicated that our franchise now has 157 locations in Florida.

Material quoted directly and enclosed in quotation marks cannot be changed from the original unless you so indicate by the use of information in brackets. (See Section 5.13 for how to use brackets.)

When a quotation is longer than four typed lines, indent each line two tabs from the left margin. Do not enclose the quotation in quotation marks.

Use single quotation marks (the apostrophe key on a keyboard) to enclose a quotation that appears within another quotation.

■ John said, "Jane told me that she was going to 'hang in there' until the deadline is past."

ESL TIPS: Using Quotation Marks and Other Punctuation

You may find that the use of quotation marks and other punctuation in North American English may differ from usage in your native language.

- Style of quotation marks
  "exceptional" *not* „exceptional" or <<exceptional>>

- Comma with quotation marks
  "as a last resort," *not* "as a last resort",

- Period with quotation marks
  "to the bitter end." *not* "to the bitter end".

- Semicolon/colon with quotation marks
  "there is no doubt"; *not* "there is no doubt;"

Slang, colloquial expressions, and attempts at humor, although infrequent in business and technical writing in any case, seldom rate being set off by quotation marks.

- Our first six months in the new office amounted to little more than a ⁄shakedown cruise⁄ for what lay ahead.

  [omit quotation marks]

Use quotation marks to point out that particular words or technical terms are used in context for a special purpose.

- What chain of events caused an "unsinkable" ship such as the *Titanic* to sink on its maiden voyage?

Use quotation marks to enclose titles of short stories, articles, essays, radio and television programs, short musical works, paintings, and other art works.

- Did you see the article "No-Fault Insurance and Your Motorcycle" in last Sunday's *Journal?*

Titles of books and periodicals are *italicized.*

- Articles in the *Business Education Forum* and *Scientific American* quoted the same passage.

Some titles, by convention, are neither set off by quotation marks nor underlined, although they are capitalized.

- the Bible, the Constitution, the Gettysburg Address

Commas and periods always go inside closing quotation marks.

■ "We hope," said Ms. Abrams, "that the merger will be announced this week."

Semicolons and colons always go outside closing quotation marks.

■ He said, "I will pay the full amount"; this was a real surprise to us.

■ The following are his favorite "sports": eating and sleeping.

All other punctuation follows the logic of the context: If the punctuation is part of the material quoted, it goes inside the quotation marks; if the punctuation is not part of the material quoted, it goes outside the quotation marks.

Quotation marks may be used as ditto marks, instead of repeating a line of words or numbers directly beneath an identical set. In formal writing, this use is confined to tables and lists.

■ A is at a point equally distant from L and M.
  B " " "   "   "   "   " S and T.
  C " " "   "   "   "   " R and Q.

■ 5.10 Dashes

The dash (—) is a versatile, yet limited, mark of punctuation. It is versatile because it can perform all the functions of punctuation (to link, to separate, to enclose, and to show omission). It is limited because it is an especially emphatic mark that is easily overused. Use the dash cautiously, therefore, to indicate more informality, emphasis, or abruptness than the conventional punctuation marks would show. In some situations, a dash is required; in others, a dash is a forceful substitute for other marks.

A dash can indicate a sharp turn in thought.

■ That is the end of the project—unless the company provides additional funds.

A dash can indicate an emphatic pause.

■ Consider the potential danger of a household item that contains mercury—a very toxic substance.

Sometimes, to emphasize contrast, a dash is also used with *but*.

■ We may have produced work more quickly—but our results have never been as impressive as these.

A dash can be used before a final summarizing statement or before repetition that has the effect of an afterthought.

■ It was hot near the ovens—steaming hot.

Such a thought may also complete the meaning of the sentence.

■ We try to speak as we write—or so we believe.

A dash can be used to set off an explanatory or appositive series.

■ Three of the applicants—John Evans, Mary Stevens, and Thomas Brown—seem well qualified for the job.

Dashes set off parenthetical elements more sharply and emphatically than do commas. Unlike dashes, parentheses tend to reduce the importance of what they enclose. Contrast the following sentences.

■ Only one person—the president—can authorize such activity.

■ Only one person, the president, can authorize such activity.

■ Only one person (the president) can authorize such activity.

Use dashes for clarity when commas appear within a parenthetical element; this avoids the confusion of too many commas.

■ Retinal images are patterns in the eye—made up of light and dark shapes, in addition to areas of color—but we do not see patterns; we see objects.

A dash can be used to show the omission of words or letters.

■ Mr. A— told me to be careful.

The first word after a dash is never capitalized unless it is a proper noun. When keying in the dash, use two consecutive hyphens (--), with no spaces before or after the hyphens.

■ 5.11 Apostrophes

The apostrophe (') is used to show possession, to mark the omission of letters, and sometimes to indicate the plural of Arabic numbers, letters, and acronyms.

5.11.1 Possession

An apostrophe is used with an *s* to form the possessive case of many nouns. (See Section 3.1.3b.)

■ A recent scientific analysis of *New York City's* atmosphere concluded that a New Yorker on the street inhaled toxic materials equivalent to 38 cigarettes a day.

Singular nouns ending in *s* may form the possessive either by an apostrophe alone or by *'s*. The latter is now preferred.

■ a waitress' uniform, a seamstress' alteration

■ a waitress's uniform, a seamstress's alteration

Use only an apostrophe with plural nouns ending in *s*.

■ a managers' meeting, the technicians' handbook, a motorists' rest stop

---

ESL TIPS: Indicating Possession: *'s* or *of?*

English expresses possession in two ways: apostrophe*s* (*'s*) and *of*.
    Use *'s* with personal names, personal nouns, collective nouns, and animals. (Use just an apostrophe for plural nouns and multisyllable singular nouns that end with *s*.)

■ Ms. *Corrales'* stock portfolio
■ the *secretary's* lunch hour
■ the *government's* pension plan
■ the *dog's* tail
■ the *cows'* milk

You can also use *'s* (or just an apostrophe) with some inanimate nouns: geographical and institutional names, nouns that refer to time, and nouns of special interest to human activity.

■ the *company's* investors
■ *today's* agenda
■ a *week's* rest
■ *business'* influence on politics

Use *of* with inanimate objects and to express measure.

■ the title *of* the monthly report
■ a cup *of* coffee
■ the length *of* the memo

ESL TIPS: Indicating Possession: Parts of the Body and Personal Belongings

English uses possessive pronouns to express possession of parts of the body and personal belongings.

- Ms. Winters broke *her* leg skiing.
- Mr. Sommers leaves *his* briefcase in the boardroom after every meeting.

English also uses apostrophes to express possession of parts of the body and personal belongings.

- Ms. *Smith's* arm was broken in a car accident.
- Mr. *Gonzalez's* briefcase was lost in the shuffle.

English gives you the option of using the definite article *the* in prepositional phrases that refer to the object of a sentence.

- Dr. Meehan led me by *the* arm into the conference room.
  [*by the arm* is a prepositional phrase]
- The stockroom clerk was struck on *the* leg by a box that fell from the shelf.
  [*on the leg* is a prepositional phrase]

However, it would also be correct to write *by my arm* and *on her leg*.

When a noun ends in multiple consecutive *s* sounds, or when the word following the possessive begins with an *s,* the possessive is often formed by adding only an apostrophe. Your ear should tell you when you are stacking up too many sibilants.

- Jesus' disciples, Moses' sojourn, for goodness' sake, Euripides' plays

With word groups and compound nouns, add the *'s* to the last noun.

- The *chairman of the board's* statement was brief.
- My *daughter-in-law's* business has been thriving.

With a series of nouns, the last noun takes the possessive form to show joint possession.

- Michelson and *Morley's* famous experiment on the velocity of light was made in 1887.

To show individual possession with a series of nouns, each noun should take the possessive form.

- *Bob's* and *Susan's* promotions will be announced Friday.

The apostrophe is not used with possessive pronouns. (*It's* is a contraction of *it is*, not the possessive form of *it*.)

■ yours, its, his, ours, whose, theirs

In names of places and institutions, the apostrophe is usually omitted.

■ Harpers Ferry, Writers Book Club

5.11.2 Omission

a. Contractions

An apostrophe is used to mark the omission of letters in a word. Omission of letters in a word and their replacement with an apostrophe produce a *contraction*. Contractions are most often shortened forms of the most common helping verbs. In addition, contractions can reflect negation, combining elements of the word *not* with elements of the helping verb (*don't* for *do not*, for example). Although contractions are in no sense wrong, they are less formal than the longer forms and should therefore be used with caution in writing.

b. Abbreviated Dates

An apostrophe can also stand for the first two digits of a year when these digits can be inferred from the context. This device is most common in alumni newsletters and in informal writing; it should be avoided in formal situations.

■ the class of '61

■ the crash of '29

5.11.3 Plurals

An apostrophe and an *s* may be added to show the plural of a word as a word. (The word itself is underlined or italicized to call attention to its use.)

■ There were five *and*'s in his first sentence.

However, if a term consists entirely of capital letters or ends with a capital letter, the apostrophe is not required to form the plural.

■ The university awarded seven Ph.D.s in engineering last year.

■ He had included 43 ADDs in his computer program.

Do not use apostrophes to indicate the plural forms of letters and numbers unless confusion would result without one.

■ 5s, 30s, two 100s, seven I's

■ 5.12 Slashes

Although not always considered a mark of punctuation, the slash (/) performs punctuating functions by separating and showing omission. The slash has various names: slant line, virgule, bar, shilling sign.

The slash is often used to separate parts of addresses in continuous writing.

■ The return address on the envelope was Ms. Rose Howard/62 W. Pacific Court/Claremont, California 91711.

The slash can indicate alternative items.

■ David's telephone number is (504) 549-2278/2335.

The slash often indicates omitted words and letters.

■ miles/hour (for "miles per hour")

■ c/o (for "in care of")

■ w/o (for "without")

The slash separates the numerator from the denominator of a fraction.

■ 2/3 (2 of 3 parts); 3/4 (3 of 4 parts); 27/32 (27 of 32 parts)

In informal writing in the United States, the slash is also used in dates to separate day from month and month from year.

■ 2/28/98

■ 5.13 Brackets

The primary use of brackets ([ ]) is to enclose a word or words inserted by an editor or writer into a quotation from another source.

■ He stated, "Wheat prices will continue to rise [no doubt because of the Russian wheat purchase] until next year."

Brackets are also used to set off a parenthetical item within parentheses.

■ We have all been inspired by the energy and creativity of our president, Roberta Jacobs (a tradition she carries forward from her father, Frederick Jacobs [1910–1966]).

6. Mechanics

Certain mechanical questions tend to confound the writer on the job. Such questions as whether a number should be written as a word or as a figure, how and where acronyms should be used, whether a date should be stated day-month-year or month-day-year, and many others frequently arise when you are writing a letter or a report. This section of the Writer's Guide is provided to give you the answers to those and other perplexing questions concerning the mechanics of writing on the job.

■ 6.1 Numbers

6.1.1 When to Write Out Numbers

The general rule is to write numbers from zero to ten as words and numbers above ten as figures. There are, however, a number of exceptions.

Page numbers of books, as well as figure and table numbers, are expressed as figures.

■ Figure 4 on page 9 and Table 3 on page 7 provide pertinent information.

Units of measurement are expressed in figures.

■ 3 miles

■ 45 cubic feet

■ 9 meters

■ 27 cubic centimeters

■ 4 picas

Numbers that begin a sentence should always be spelled out, even if they would otherwise be written as figures.

■ One hundred and fifty people attended the meeting.

If spelling out such a number seems awkward, rewrite the sentence so that the number does not appear at the beginning.

■ *Last month, 273* ~~Two hundred seventy-three~~ defective products were returned ~~last month.~~

When several numbers appear in the same sentence or paragraph, they should be expressed alike regardless of other rules and guidelines.

- The company owned 150 trucks, employed 271 people, and rented 7 warehouses.

When numbers measuring different quantities appear together in the same phrase, write one as a figure and the other as a word.

twelve

- The order was for ~~12~~ *twelve* 6-inch pipes.

Approximate numbers may be spelled out but are more often written as figures.

- More than 200 people attended the conference.

In business or technical writing, percentages are normally given as figures, with the word *percent* written out except when the number appears in a table.

- Exactly 87 percent of the stockholders approved the merger.

On manuscript pages, page numbers are written as figures, but chapter or volume numbers may appear as figures or written out.

- page 37
- Chapter 2 *or* Chapter Two
- Volume 1 *or* Volume One

6.1.2 Dates

The year and day of the month should be written as figures. Dates are usually written in month-day-year sequence, but businesses and industrial corporations sometimes use the European and military day-month-year sequence.

- August 24, 20--
- 24 August 20--

The month-day-year sequence is followed by a comma in a sentence.

- The November 24, 20--, issue of *Smart Computing* has an article . . .

The day-month-year sequence is *not* followed by a comma.

- The 24 November 20-- issue of *Smart Computing* . . .

The slash form of expressing dates (8/24/00) is used in informal writing only.

6.1.3 Time

Hours and minutes are expressed as figures when a.m. or p.m. follows.

- 11:30 a.m., 7:30 p.m.

When not followed by a.m. or p.m., however, times should be spelled out.

- four o'clock, eleven o'clock

6.1.4 Fractions

Fractions are expressed as figures when written with whole numbers.

- 27 1/2 inches, 4 1/4 miles

Fractions are spelled out when they are expressed without a whole number.

- one-fourth, seven-eighths

Numbers with decimals are always written as figures.

- 5.21 meters

6.1.5 Addresses

Numbered streets from one to ten should be spelled out except where space is at a premium.

- East Tenth Street

Building numbers are written as figures. The only exception is the building number *one*.

- 4862 East Monument Street
- One East Tenth Street

Highway numbers are written as figures.

- U.S. 70, Ohio 271, I-94

6.1.6 Writing the Plurals of Numbers

The plural of a written number is formed by adding *-s* or *-es* or by dropping *y* and adding *-ies*, depending on the last letter, just as the plural of any other noun is formed. (See Section 1.3.1.)

- sixes, elevens, twenties

The plural of a figure should be written with *s* alone.

■ 5s, 12s

6.1.7 Redundant Numbering

Do not follow a word representing a number with a figure in parentheses that represents the same number.

■ Send five ~~(5)~~ copies of the report.

■ 6.2 Acronyms and Initialisms

An acronym is an abbreviation that is formed by combining the first letter or letters of two or more words. Acronyms are pronounced as words and are written without periods.

■ radar (*r*adio *d*etecting *a*nd *r*anging)

■ LAN (*l*ocal *a*rea *n*etwork)

■ scuba (*s*elf-*c*ontained *u*nderwater *b*reathing *a*pparatus)

An initialism is an abbreviation that is formed by combining the initial letter of each word in a multiword term. Initialisms are produced as separate letters. When written lowercase, they require periods; when written uppercase, they do not.

■ e.o.m. (*e*nd *o*f *m*onth)

■ COD (*c*ash *o*n *d*elivery)

In business and industry, acronyms and initialisms are often used by people working together on particular projects or having the same specialties—such as, for example, engineers or accountants. So long as such people are communicating only with one another, the abbreviations are easily recognized and understood. However, if the same acronyms or initialisms were used in correspondence to people outside the group, the acronyms or initialisms might be incomprehensible to those readers.

Acronyms and initialisms can be convenient—for the reader and the writer alike—if they are used appropriately. Business writers, however, often overuse them, either as an affectation or in a misguided attempt to make their writing concise.

6.2.1 When to Use Acronyms and Initialisms

Two guidelines apply in deciding whether to use acronyms and initialisms.

1. If you must use a multiword term an average of once each paragraph, introduce the term and then use its acronym or initialism. (See Section 6.2.2.) For example, a phrase such as "primary software overlay area" can become tiresome if repeated again and again in one piece of writing; it would be better, therefore, to use PSOA.

2. If something is better known by its acronym or initialism than by its formal term, you should use the abbreviated form. The initialism a.m., for example, is much more common than the formal *ante meridiem*.

If these conditions do not exist, however, always spell out the full term.

6.2.2 How to Use Acronyms and Initialisms

The first time an acronym or initialism appears in a written work, write out the complete term and then give the abbreviated form in parentheses.

■ The Capital Appropriations Request (CAR) controls the spending of the money.

Thereafter, you may use the acronym or initialism alone. In a long document, however, you will help your reader greatly by repeating the full term in parentheses after the acronym or initialism when the term has not been mentioned for some time. This saves the reader the trouble of searching back to the first time the acronym or initialism was used to find its meaning.

■ As noted earlier, the CAR (Capital Appropriations Request) controls the spending of money.

Write acronyms in capital letters without periods. The only exceptions are those acronyms that have become accepted as common nouns; these terms are written in lowercase letters.

■ laser, scuba, sonar

Initialisms that do not stand for proper nouns may be written either uppercase or lowercase. In general, do not use periods when the letters are uppercase; always use periods when they are lowercase. Two exceptions are geographic names and academic degrees.

■ COD/c.o.d., FOB/f.o.b., CIF/c.i.f., EOM/e.o.m.

■ CIA, FBI, NASA

- U.S.A., U.K.

- B.A., M.B.A.

Form the plural of an acronym or initialism by adding an *-s.* Do not use an apostrophe.

- PACs, CD-ROMs

■ 6.3 Abbreviations

An abbreviation is a shortened form of a word, formed by omitting some of its letters. Most abbreviations are written with a period; however, in technical and business writing, abbreviations of measurements are generally an exception. In cases where an abbreviation of a measurement might be confused with an actual word, the period is used.

- Mister/Mr.

- Avenue/Ave.

- September/Sept.

- centimeter/cm

- inch/in. (the abbreviation *in* could be misread as the word *in*)

Abbreviations, like symbols, can be important space savers in business writing, where it is often necessary to provide the maximum amount of information in limited space. Use abbreviations, however, only if you are certain that your readers will understand them as readily as they would the terms for which they stand. Remember also that a memo or report addressed to a specific person may be read by others, and you must consider those readers as well. Take your reader's level of knowledge into account when deciding whether to use abbreviations. Do not use them if they might become an inconvenience to the reader. A good rule of thumb is: When in doubt, spell it out.

In general, use abbreviations only when space is limited. For example, abbreviations are often useful space savers in charts, tables, graphs, and other illustrations. Normally you should not make up your own abbreviations, for they will probably confuse your reader. Except for commonly used abbreviations (U.S.A., p.m.), a term to be abbreviated should be spelled out the first time it is used, with the abbreviation enclosed in parentheses following the term. Thereafter, the abbreviation may be used alone.

- The annual report of the National Retail Dry Goods Association (NRDGA) will be issued next month. In it, the NRDGA will detail shortages of several widely used textiles.

6.3.1 Measurements

When you abbreviate terms that refer to measurement, be sure your reader is familiar with the abbreviated form. The following list contains some common abbreviations used with units of measurement. Notice that, except for *in.* (inch), *bar.* (barometer), and other abbreviations that might be mistaken for other words, abbreviations of measurements do not require periods.

amp	ampere	hr	hour
atm	atmosphere	in.	inch
bar.	barometer	kc	kilocycle
bbl	barrel	kg	kilogram
bhp	brake horsepower	km	kilometer
Btu	British thermal unit	lb	pound
bu	bushel	mg	milligram
cal	calorie	min	minute
cm	centimeter	oz	ounce
cos	cosine	ppm	parts per million
ctn	cotangent	pt	pint
doz or dz	dozen	qt	quart
emf or EMF	electromotive force	rad	radian
F	Fahrenheit	rev	revolution
fig.	figure (illustration)	sec	second or secant
ft	foot (or feet)	tan.	tangent
gal	gallon	yd	yard
gm	gram	yr	year
hp	horsepower		

Abbreviations of units of measurement are identical in the singular and plural: 1 *cm* and 3 *cm* (not 3 *cms*).

6.3.2 Personal Names and Titles

Personal names should generally not be abbreviated.

INCORRECT	Chas., Thos., Wm., Marg.
CORRECT	Charles, Thomas, William, Margaret

An academic, civil, religious, or military title should be spelled out when it does not precede a name.

■ The *doctor* asked for the patient's chart.

When it precedes a name, the title may be abbreviated.

■   Dr. Smith, Mr. Mills, Capt. Hughes

Reverend and *Honorable* are abbreviated only if the surname is preceded by a first name.

■   The Reverend Smith, Rev. John Smith

    (but not Rev. Smith)

■   The Honorable Commissioner Holt, Hon. Mary J. Holt

An abbreviation of a title may follow the name; however, be certain that it does not duplicate a title before the name.

INCORRECT	Dr. William Smith, Ph.D.
CORRECT	Dr. William Smith
CORRECT	William Smith, Ph.D.

The following is a list of common abbreviations for personal and professional titles.

Atty.	Attorney
B.A. or A.B.	Bachelor of Arts
B.S.	Bachelor of Science
B.S.E.E.	Bachelor of Science in Electrical Engineering
D.D.	Doctor of Divinity
D.D.S.	Doctor of Dental Science
Dr.	Doctor (used with any doctor's degree)
Ed.D.	Doctor of Education
Hon.	Honorable
Jr.	Junior
LL.B.	Bachelor of Law
LL.D.	Doctor of Law
M.A. or A.M.	Master of Arts
M.B.A.	Master of Business Administration
M.D.	Doctor of Medicine
Messrs.	Plural of Mr.
Mr.	Mister (spelled out only in the most formal contexts)
Mrs.	Married woman
Ms.	Woman of unspecified marital status

M.S.	Master of Science
Ph.D.	Doctor of Philosophy
Rev.	Reverend
Sr.	Senior (used when a son with the same name is living)

6.4 Ampersands

The ampersand (&) is a symbol sometimes used to represent the word *and,* especially in the names of organizations.

- Chicago & Northwestern Railway

- Watkins & Watkins, Inc.

The ampersand may be used in footnotes, bibliographies, lists, and references if it appears in the name of the title being listed. However, when writing the name of an organization in sentences or in an address, spell out the word *and* unless the ampersand appears in the official name of the company.

An ampersand must always be set off by normal word spacing but should never be preceded by a comma.

- Carlton, Dillon, & Manchester, Inc.

   (omit comma)

Do not use an ampersand in the titles of articles, journals, books, or other publications.

- Does the bibliography include Knoll's *Radiation Detection & Measurement?*

   and

6.5 Capital Letters

The use of capital letters (or uppercase letters) is determined by custom and tradition. Capital letters are used to call attention to certain words, such as proper nouns and the first word of a sentence. Care must be exercised in using capital letters because they can affect the meaning of words (march/March, china/China, turkey/Turkey). Thus, capital letters can help eliminate ambiguity.

6.5.1 First Words

The first letter of the first word in a sentence is always capitalized.

- Of all the plans you mentioned, the first one seems the best.

ESL TIPS: Understanding the Rules of Capitalization

The rules of capitalization vary from language to language. English capitalizes

days of the week

- Every *Monday* we have a meeting at noon.

months of the year

- The fiscal year ends in *June.*

the pronoun I

- My sister and *I* went grocery shopping last week.

The first word after a colon may be capitalized if the statement following is a complete sentence or if it introduces a formal resolution or question.

- Today's meeting will deal with only one issue: What is the firm's role in environmental protection?

If a subordinate element follows the colon, however, use a lowercase letter following the colon.

- We had to keep working for one reason: pressure from above.

The first word of a complete sentence in quotation marks is capitalized.

- He said, "When I arrive, we will begin."

Complete sentences contained as numbered items within a sentence may also be capitalized.

- He recommended two ways to increase sales: (1) Next year we should spend more on television advertising, and (2) Our quality control should be improved immediately.

The first word in the salutation or complimentary close of a letter is capitalized.

- Dear Mr. Smith:
- Sincerely yours,
- Best regards,

6.5.2 Specific People and Groups

Capitalize all personal names.

■ Walter Bunch, Mary Fortunato, Bill Krebs

Capitalize names of ethnic groups and nationalities.

■ American Indian, Italian, Jew, Chicano
■ Thus Italian immigrants contributed much to the industrialization of the United States.

Do not capitalize names of social and economic groups.

■ middle class, working class, ghetto dwellers

6.5.3 Specific Places

Capitalize the names of all political divisions.

■ Chicago, Cook County, Illinois, Ontario, Iran, Ward Six

Capitalize the names of geographical divisions.

■ Europe, Asia, North America, the Middle East, the Orient

Do not capitalize geographic features unless they are part of a proper name.

■ In some areas, mountains such as the Great Smoky Mountains make television transmission difficult.

The words *north, south, east,* and *west* are capitalized when they refer to sections of the country. They are not capitalized when they refer to directions.

■ I may travel south when I relocate to Delaware.
■ We may build a new plant in the South next year.
■ State Street runs east and west.

Capitalize the names of stars, constellations, galaxies, and planets.

■ Sirius, Leo, Milky Way, Saturn

Do not capitalize *earth, sun,* and *moon,* however, except when they are used with the names of other planets.

- Although the sun rises in the east and sets in the west, the moon may appear in any part of the evening sky when darkness settles over the earth.

- Mars, Pluto, and Earth were discussed at the symposium.

6.5.4 Specific Institutions, Events, and Concepts

Capitalize the names of institutions, organizations, and associations.

- The American Management Association and the Department of Housing and Urban Development are cooperating in the project.

An organization usually capitalizes the names of its internal divisions and departments.

- Faculty, Board of Directors, Accounting Department

Types of organizations are not capitalized unless they are part of an official name.

- Our group decided to form a writers' association; we called it the American Association of Writers.

- I attended Post High School. What high school did you attend?

Capitalize historical events.

- Dr. Jellison discussed the Boston Tea Party at the last class.

Capitalize words that designate specific periods of time.

- Labor Day, the Renaissance, the Enlightenment, January, Monday, the Great Depression, Lent

Do not, however, capitalize seasons of the year.

- spring, autumn, winter, summer

Capitalize scientific names of classes, families, and orders, but do not capitalize species or English derivatives of scientific names.

- Mammalia, Carnivora/mammal, carnivorous

6.5.5 Titles of Books, Articles, Plays, Films, Reports, and Memos

Capitalize the initial letters of the first and last words of a title of a book, article, play, or film, as well as all major words in the title. Do not capitalize articles (*a, an, the*), conjunctions (*and, but, if*), or short prepositions (*at, in, on, of*) unless they begin the title. Capitalize prepositions that contain more than four letters (*between, because, until, after*). These guidelines also apply to the titles of reports and to the subject lines of memos.

- The author worked three years writing the book, *The Many Lives of an Organization.*

- The article "Year After Year" describes the life of a turn-of-the-century industrialist.

- The report, titled "Alternate Sites for Plant Location," was submitted in February.

6.5.6 Personal, Professional, and Job Titles

Titles preceding proper names are capitalized.

- Ms. March, Professor Galbraith, Senator Kennedy

Appositives following proper names are not normally capitalized. (The word *President*, however, is usually capitalized when it refers to the chief executive of a national government.)

- Frank Jones, senator from New Mexico (but Senator Jones)

The only exception is an epithet, which actually renames the person.

- Alexander the Great, Solomon the Wise

Job titles used with personal names are capitalized and those appearing without personal names are not.

- John Holmes, Division Manager, will meet with us on Wednesday.

- The other division managers will not be present on Wednesday.

Use capital letters to designate family relationships only when they occur before a name or substitute for a name.

- One of my favorite people is Uncle Fred.

- My uncle is one of my favorite people.

- Jim and Mother went along.

- Jim and my mother went along.

6.5.7 Abbreviations

Capitalize abbreviations if the words they stand for would be capitalized. (See also Section 6.3.)

- OSU (Ohio State University)

- p. (page)

- Ph.D. (Doctor of Philosophy)

6.5.8 Letters

Certain single letters are always capitalized. Capitalize the pronoun *I* and the interjection *O* (but do not capitalize *oh* unless it is the first word in a sentence).

- When I say writing, O believe me, I mean rewriting.

- When I say writing, oh believe me, I mean rewriting.

Capitalize letters that serve as names or indicate shapes.

- vitamin B, T-square, U-turn, I-beam

6.5.9 Miscellaneous Capitalizations

The word *Bible* is capitalized when it refers to the Judeo-Christian Scriptures; otherwise, it is not capitalized.

- He quoted a verse from the Bible, then read from Blackstone, the lawyer's bible.

All references to deities (Allah, God, Jehovah, Yahweh) are capitalized.

- God is the One who sustains us.

A complete sentence enclosed in dashes, brackets, or parentheses is not capitalized when it appears as part of another sentence.

- We must make an extra effort in sales this year (last year's sales were down 10 percent).

- We must make an extra effort in sales this year. (Last year's sales were down 10 percent.)

When certain units, such as chapters of books or rooms in buildings, are specifically identified by number, they are normally capitalized.

- Chapter 5, Ch. 5, Room 72, Rm. T7A1

Minor divisions within such units are not capitalized unless they begin a sentence.

- page 11, verse 14, seat 12

When in doubt about whether to capitalize, check a dictionary.

■ 6.6 Dates

In business and industry, dates have traditionally been indicated by the month, day, and year, with a comma separating the figures. (See also Section 5.1.2b.)

- October 26, 20--

The day-month-year system used by the military does not require commas.

- 26 October 20--

A date can be written with or without a comma following the year, depending on how the date is expressed. If the date is in the month-day-year format, set off the year with commas.

- October 26, 20--, was the date the project began.

If the date is in the day-month-year format, do not set off the date with commas.

- On 26 October 20-- the project began.

The strictly numerical form for dates (10/26/00) should be used sparingly, and never in business letters or formal documents because its meaning is less immediately clear. When this form is used, the order in American usage is always month/day/year. For example, 5/7/00 is May 7, 2000.

Confusion often occurs because the spelled-out names of centuries do not correspond to the numbers of the years.

- The twentieth century is the 1900s (1900–1999).
- The nineteenth century is the 1800s (1800–1899).
- The fifth century is the 400s (400–499).

▇ 6.7 Italics (Underlining)

Italics are a style of type used to denote emphasis and to distinguish foreign expressions, book titles, and certain other elements. *This sentence is printed in italics.* You may need to italicize words that require special emphasis in a sentence.

- ▇ Contrary to projections, sales have *not* improved since we started the new procedure.

Do not overuse italics for emphasis, however.

OVERUSE OF ITALICS	This will hurt *you* more than *me.*
IMPROVED	This will hurt you more than me!

6.7.1 Titles

Italicize the titles of books, periodicals, newspapers, movies, and paintings.

- ▇ The book *Applied Statistical Methods* was published in 1999.
- ▇ The *Cincinnati Enquirer* is one of our oldest newspapers.
- ▇ The *Journal of Marketing* is published monthly for those engaged in marketing.

Italicize abbreviations of such titles if their spelled-out forms would be italicized.

- ▇ The *WSJ* is the business community's journal of record.

  (The reference is to the *Wall Street Journal.*)

Put titles of chapters or articles that appear within publications and the titles of reports in quotation marks, not italics.

- ▇ The article "Does Advertising Lower Consumer Prices?" was published in the March 20-- issue of the *Journal of Marketing.*

Do not italicize titles of holy books and legislative documents.

- ▇ The Bible and the Magna Carta changed the history of Western civilization.

Italicize titles of long poems and musical works, but enclose titles of short poems and musical works and songs in quotation marks.

- ▇ Milton's *Paradise Lost* (long poem)
- ▇ Handel's *Messiah* (long musical work)

- T. S. Eliot's "The Love Song of J. Alfred Prufrock" (short poem)

- Elton John's "Candle in the Wind" (song)

6.7.2 Proper Names

Italicize the names of ships, trains, and aircraft, but not the names of companies that own them.

- Years ago, they sailed to Africa on the Onassis *Clipper* but flew back on the TWA *New Yorker.*

Exceptions are craft that are known by model or serial designations, which are not italicized.

- DC-10, Boeing 777

6.7.3 Words, Letters, and Figures

Italicize words, letters, and figures that are discussed as such.

- The word *inflammable* is often misinterpreted.

- Word-processing spellcheckers will stop at each instance of words containing numbers ("*will*" with two *1*'s rather than two *l*'s).

6.7.4 Foreign Words

Italicize foreign words that have not been assimilated into the English language.

- *sine qua non, coup de grâce, in res, in camera*

Do not italicize foreign words that have been fully assimilated into the language.

- cliché, etiquette, vis-à-vis, de facto, siesta

When in doubt about whether to italicize a foreign word, consult a current dictionary.

6.7.5 Subheads

Subheads in a report are sometimes italicized.

- There was no publications department as such, and the writing groups were duplicated at each plant or location. Wellington, for example, had such a large number of publications groups that their publications effort can only be described as disorganized. Their duplication of effort must have been enormous.

Training Writers

We are certainly leading the way in developing first-line managers (or writing supervisors) who not only are technically competent but can train the writers under their direction and be responsible for writing quality as well.

■ 6.8 Symbols

From highway signs to mathematical equations, people communicate in written symbols. When a symbol seems appropriate in your writing, either be certain that your reader understands its meaning or place an explanation in parentheses following the symbol the first time it appears. However, never use a symbol when your reader would more readily understand the full term. Table C–5 contains a list of symbols and their appropriate uses.

Symbol	Meaning and Use
£	pound (basic unit of currency in the United Kingdom)
$	dollar (basic unit of currency in the United States)
O	oxygen (for a listing of all symbols for chemical elements, see a periodic table of elements in a dictionary or handbook)
+	plus
−	minus
±	plus or minus
∓	minus or plus
×	multiplied by
÷	divided by
=	equal to
≠ or ≒	not equal to
≈ or ≐	approximately (or nearly equal to)
≡	identical with
≢	not identical with
>	greater than
≯	not greater than
<	less than
≮	not less than
:	is to (or ratio)
≐	approaches (but does not reach equality with)
‖	parallel
⊥	perpendicular

Table C–5   Symbols and Their Uses

Symbol	Meaning and Use
√	square root
³√	cube root
∞	infinity
π	*pi*
∴	therefore (in mathematical equations)
∵	because (in mathematical equations)
( )	parentheses
[ ]	brackets
{ }	braces (used to group two or more lines of writing, to group figures in tables, and to enclose figures in mathematical equations)
°F or °C	degree (Fahrenheit or Celsius)
′	minute *or* foot
″	second *or* inch
#	number
*	asterisk (used to indicate a footnote when there are very few)
&	ampersand
♂	male
♀	female
©	copyright
%	percent
c/o	in care of
a/o	account of
@	at (sometimes used in tables, but never in writing; also used in email addresses)
´	acute (accent mark in French and other languages)
`	grave (accent mark in French and other languages)
^	circumflex (accent mark in French and other languages)
~	tilde (diacritical mark identifying the palatal nasal in Spanish and Portuguese)
¯	macron (marks a long phonetic sound, as in *cāke*)
˘	breve (marks a short phonetic sound, as in *brăcket*)
¨	dieresis or umlaut (mark placed over the second of two consecutive vowels indicating that the second vowel is to be pronounced separately from the first—*coöperate*)
¸	cedilla (mark placed beneath the letter *c* in French, Portuguese, and Spanish to indicate the letter is pronounced as *s*—*garçon*)
∧	caret (proofreader's mark used to indicate inserted material)
FR	franc (basic unit of currency in France)
Mex $	peso (basic unit of currency in Mexico)
$	peso (Philippine peso)
R	ruble (basic monetary unit of Russia)
¥	yen (basic unit of currency in Japan)

Table C–5   (continued)

■ 6.9 Proofreaders' Marks

Publishers have established symbols, called proofreaders' marks, which writers and editors use to communicate with compositors in the production of publications. A familiarity with these symbols makes it easy for you to communicate your changes to others. Proofreaders' marks are listed in Table C–6.

Mark in Margin	Instruction	Mark on Manuscript	Corrected Type
ℓ	Delete	the ~~lawyer's~~ Bible	the Bible
lawyer's	Insert	the bible	the lawyer's bible
(stet)	Let stand	the ~~lawyer's~~ bible	the lawyer's bible
(cap)	Capitalize	the bible	the Bible
(lc)	Make lowercase	the Law	the law
(ital)	Italicize	the lawyer's bible	the *lawyer's* bible
(tr)	Transpose	the bible lawyer's	the lawyer's bible
⊂	Close space	the Bi ble	the Bible
(sp)	Spell out	2 bibles	two bibles
#	Insert space	the Bible	the Bible
¶	Start paragraph	¶ The lawyer's . . .	The lawyer's . . .
(run in)	No paragraph	. . . marks. Below is a . . .	. . . marks. Below is a . . .
(sc)	Set in small capitals	the bible	the BIBLE
(rom)	Set in roman type	the (bible)	the bible
(bf)	Set in boldface	the bible	the **bible**
(lf)	Set in lightface	the (**bible**)	the bible
⊙	Insert period	The lawyers have their own bible	The lawyers have their own bible.
↗	Insert comma	However we cannot . . .	However, we cannot . . .
‿=⁒=‿	Insert hyphens	half and half	half-and-half
⊙	Insert colon	We need the following	We need the following:
↑	Insert semicolon	Use the law don't . . .	Use the law; don't . . .
∜	Insert apostrophe	Johns law book	John's law book
↲/↲	Insert quotation marks	The law is law.	The "law" is law.
(/)/	Insert parentheses	John's law book	John's (law) book
[/]/	Insert brackets	(John Martin 1920–1962 went . . .)	(John Martin [1920–1962] went . . .)
─ⁿ	Insert en dash	1920 1962	1920–1962
─ᵐ	Insert em dash	Our goal victory	Our goal—victory
∨	Insert superior type	3² = 9	$3^2 = 9$
∧	Insert inferior type	HSO₄	H_2SO_4

Table C–6   Proofreaders' Marks

D English as a Second Language (ESL)

Learning to write well in a second language takes a great deal of effort and practice. The best and easiest way to improve your written command of English is to read widely beyond reports and professional articles: Read newspaper and magazine articles, novels, biographies, short stories, or any other writing that interests you.

This section is a guide to some of the common problems nonnative speakers experience when writing English. For specific help when you are writing a memo or report, ask a native speaker or refer to earlier sections of this Writer's Guide.

Persistent problem areas for nonnative English speakers include the following:

- distinguishing between count and noncount nouns (see pages 866–867)
- using articles (see pages 867–872)
- using prepositions (see page 873)
- distinguishing between gerunds and infinitives (see pages 873–874)
- forming adjective clauses (see pages 874–875)
- determining verb tenses (see pages 875–881)
- using modal helping verbs and writing conditional sentences (see pages 881–884)
- using idioms (see pages 884–886)

Count and Noncount Nouns

Count nouns refer to things that can be separated into countable units: *tables, pencils, boys, dentists.* Noncount nouns identify things that comprise a mass that cannot be counted: *electricity, water, oil, air, wood.* Noncount nouns also describe abstract qualities: *love, loyalty, pride, harmony.*

The distinction between whether something can or cannot be counted is important because it determines the form of the noun to use (singular or plural), the kind of article that precedes it (*a, an, the,* or no article), and the kind of limiting adjective it requires (*fewer* or *less, many* or *much,* and so on). This distinction can be confusing with words such as *electricity* or *oil.* Although we can count kilowatt hours of electricity or barrels of oil, counting becomes inappropriate when we use the words *electricity* or *oil* in a general sense, as in "oil is a limited resource." When you learn a noun in English, you need to learn whether it is count, noncount, or both. Some ESL dictionaries will provide this information. Use the following rules to help you determine between count and noncount nouns:

1. *Count nouns* refer to things that can be separated into countable units. Count nouns have plurals:
   - *tables, pencils, boys, dentists*

   A concrete noun may be countable:
   - There are *six cats* in the apartment complex.

   A collective noun is countable:
   - There are many baseball *teams* in the United States.

2. *Noncount nouns* refer to things that comprise a mass or collection of items that cannot be counted separately. Noncount nouns do not have plurals:
   - *electricity, water, oil, air, wood*

   An abstract noun is uncountable:
   - *Honesty* is the best policy.

   Many concrete nouns are uncountable:
   - *Rice* is a popular food item in China.

3. Many uncountable nouns can be made countable, but a change in meaning takes place:

Uncountable	**Countable**
■ *Life* is full of surprises. [Here, *life* is an abstract noun.]	■ A *life* is a long time. [Here, *life* refers to a specific life and is countable.]
■ *Art* can be thought-provoking. [*Art* is meant in a general sense.]	■ A cat has nine *lives*. [*Lives* are distinguished as countable.]
	■ The *arts* can enrich a person's life. [*The arts* refers to components of art as a whole, such as literature, music, painting, etc.]

Articles

Most count nouns are preceded by an article (*a, an, the*), a demonstrative adjective (*this, that, these, those*), a possessive adjective (*my, her, their,* and so on), or some expression of quantity (such as *one, two, several, many, a few, a lot of, some*). The article, adjective, or expression of quantity appears either directly in front of the noun or in front of the whole noun phrase.

- Mary read *a* book last week.

  [The article *a* appears directly in front of the noun *book*.]

- Mary read *a* long, boring book last week.

  [The article *a* precedes the noun phrase *long, boring book*.]

- *Those* books Mary read were long and boring.

  [The demonstrative adjective *those* appears directly in front of the noun *books*.]

- *Their* book was long and boring.

  [The possessive adjective *their* appears directly in front of the noun *book*.]

- *Some* books Mary read were long and boring.

  [The indefinite adjective *some* appears directly in front of the noun *books*.]

▧ Indefinite and Definite Articles

A and *an* are indefinite articles. *A* is used with singular nouns or adjectives that begin with consonant sounds.

- *a* dog, *a* long walk, *a* cat

An is used before a singular noun or adjective that begins with a vowel sound.

- *an* hour, *an* apple, *an* ill patient

A and *an* do not precede a plural countable noun or an uncountable noun.

- Women are a large group in the workforce.

  [You would not write "*An/a women*," because *women* is a plural countable noun.]

The articles *a* and *an* are used with nouns that refer to any one thing out of the whole class of those items. The article *the* refers to a specific item.

- Bill has *a* pen.

  [Bill could have *any* pen.]

- Bill has *the* pen.

  [Bill has a *specific* pen and both the reader and the writer know which specific one it is.]

The only exception to this rule occurs when the writer is making a generalization. When making generalizations with count nouns in English, writers can either use

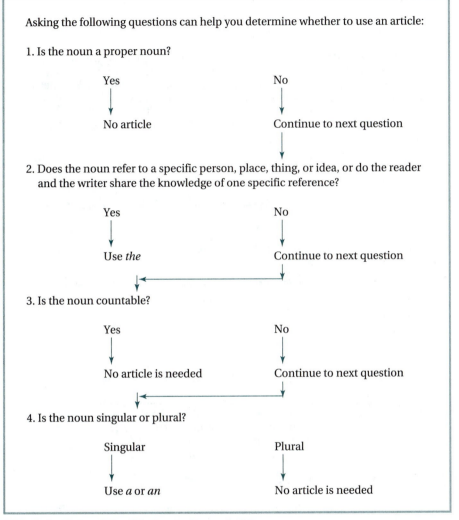

Asking the following questions can help you determine whether to use an article:

1. Is the noun a proper noun?

Yes → No article

No → Continue to next question

2. Does the noun refer to a specific person, place, thing, or idea, or do the reader and the writer share the knowledge of one specific reference?

Yes → Use *the*

No → Continue to next question

3. Is the noun countable?

Yes → No article is needed

No → Continue to next question

4. Is the noun singular or plural?

Singular → Use *a* or *an*

Plural → No article is needed

Table D–1 Determining Whether to Use an Article

a or *an* with a singular count noun or they can use no article with a plural count noun (see Table D–1). Consider the following generalization using an article:

■ *An* egg is a good source of protein.

   [*Any egg, all eggs, all in general*]

However, the following generalization uses a plural noun with no article.

■ Eggs are good sources of protein.

   [*Any egg, all eggs, eggs in general*]

ESL TIPS: Choosing Definite or Indefinite Articles

Whether to use a definite or an indefinite article is determined by what you can safely assume about your audience's knowledge. Do your readers have enough information—either from their knowledge about the world *or* from the context of your writing—to identify the noun that will be modified by the article? If the answer is yes, use a definite article; if no, use an indefinite article.

In each of these sentences, you can safely assume that the reader can clearly identify the noun.

- *The* sun rises in the east.

  [There is only one *sun.*]

- Did you know that yesterday was *the* coldest day of the year so far?

  [The modified noun refers to *yesterday.*]

- *The* man who left his briefcase in the conference room was a very bright man.

  [The relative phrase *left his briefcase in the conference room* restricts and, therefore, identifies the meaning of *man.*]

In the following sentence, you cannot assume that the reader can clearly identify the noun:

- *An* ice storm is on the way.

  [It is impossible to identify specifically which *ice storm* is meant.]

The principles for using definite and indefinite articles appropriately are rather detailed. In fact, most native speakers of English cannot explain the rules for using articles, even though they may use the articles correctly. Definite and indefinite articles are small words that are frequently used, but they are extremely difficult to master. It may help to keep the following in mind:

Using the Indefinite Articles *a* and *an*

Use *a* when a singular count noun is indefinite and the article is followed by a consonant sound.

- *a* cat, *a* delicious apple

Use *an* when a singular count noun is indefinite and the article is followed by a vowel sound.

- *an* apple, *an* appetizing apple

Do not use *a* or *an* with plural nouns.

- *Women*
  A women

Do not use *a* or *an* with noncount nouns.

>   *Electricity*
> ■ ~~An electricity~~
>   ^

Using the Definite Article *the*

Do not use *the* with plural or noncount nouns that mean "all" or "in general."

>   *Power*
> ■ ~~The power~~ corrupts.
>   ^
> [This sentence means that all power corrupts, in general.]

Use *the* with the following phrases:

> ■ in *the* afternoon, in *the* evening, and at night

but not with

> ■ at ~~the~~ night

Use *the* when the noun that follows has been previously mentioned.

>   *the*
> ■ A van filled with circus performers cut in front of our car. When van
>   turned left, we followed it.   ^

Use *the* when a phrase or clause that follows the noun restricts its identity.

>   *the*
> ■ The scientist warned me that beaker on the top shelf was filled with
>   poison.   ^
> [The phrase *on the top shelf* identifies the beaker.]

Use *the* with the superlative form.

>   *the*
> ■ His report was best the board ever read.
>   ^

Do not use *the* with the comparative form.

> ■ Which of these two restaurants is ~~the~~ better?

Use *the* with the word *same*.

>   *the*
> ■ She works same shift as her husband.
>   ^

Use *the* with plural names.

>   *the*
> ■ She went to visit Smiths.
>   ^

(continued)

ESL TIPS (continued)

Do not use an article with the names of streets, avenues, roads, lanes, boule-vards, squares, cities, states, counties, most countries, bays, single lakes, single mountains, or islands.

■ ~~the~~ Miami, ~~the~~ Trafalgar Square, ~~the~~ Mt. Everest

But do use *the* for united countries, large regions, deserts, peninsulas, oceans, seas, gulfs, canals and rivers, mountain ranges, and groups of islands.

■ *the* United Arab Emirates, *the* Sahara, *the* Iberian Peninsula, *the* Dead Sea, *the* Panama *the* Canal, *the* Alps, Solomon Islands

Use *the* with the names of hotels, motels, theaters, bridges, and buildings.

■ *the* Park Plaza Hotel, *the* Golden Gate Bridge, *the* Empire State Building

but do not use an article with the names of hospitals.

■ ~~the~~ Albert Hall, ~~the~~ Mt. Sinai Hospital

Use *the* with the names of zoos, gardens, museums, and institutes.

■ *the* Bronx Zoo, *the* Museum of Modern Art

Use *the* when the noun refers to something that is the only one that exists.

■ *the* Eiffel Tower

Do not use an article with the names of most diseases.

■ ~~the~~ AIDS, ~~the~~ heart disease, ~~the~~ osteoporosis

but do use an article for

■ *the* flu, *the* measles, *the* mumps

When making generalizations with noncount nouns, do not use an article in front of the noncount noun.

■ Sugar is bad for your teeth.

Prepositions

Prepositions are words that help connect nouns or pronouns to other parts of a sentence. They help to specify a relationship between items.

■ Prepositions of Time

on is used with days of the week.

- ■ We have staff meetings *on* Mondays.

at is used with hours of the day

- ■ We leave work *at* 5:00.

and with noon, night, and dawn.

- ■ Lunch will be served *at* noon.

in is used with other parts of the day

- ■ I check email *in* the morning.

and with months, years, and seasons.

- ■ I started to work for the firm *in* May.

■ Prepositions of Place

on indicates a surface on which something rests.

- ■ The files are *on* the desk.

at refers to an area or to a place.

- ■ My secretary is *at* her desk.

in indicates a place that is in an enclosure.

- ■ The documents are *in* the file.

Gerunds and Infinitives

Non-native writers are often puzzled by the form of a verbal (a verb used as a noun) to use when it functions as the direct object of a verb. No consistent rule exists for distinguishing between the use of an infinitive or a gerund after a verb when it is used as an object. Sometimes a verb takes an infinitive as its object, sometimes a gerund, and sometimes it takes either an infinitive or a gerund. At times, even the base form of the verb is used.

◼ Using a Gerund as a Complement

- ◼ He enjoys *working*.

- ◼ She denied *saying* that.

- ◼ Did Alice finish *reading* the report?

◼ Using an Infinitive as a Complement

- ◼ He wants *to attend* the meeting in Los Angeles.

- ◼ The company expects *to sign* the contract soon.

- ◼ He promised *to fulfill* his part of the contract.

◼ Using an Infinitive or a Gerund as a Complement

- ◼ It began *to rain* soon after we arrived. [infinitive]

- ◼ It began *raining* soon after we arrived. [gerund]

◼ Using the Base Form of a Verb as a Complement

- ◼ Let Maria *finish* the project by herself.

- ◼ The president had the technician *reassigned* to another project.

To make these distinctions accurately, you must rely on what you hear native speakers use or on what you read to determine the proper choices. Many ESL texts contain chapters on infinitive and gerund usage that list verbs with their appropriate complement.

Adjective Clauses

Because of the variety of ways adjective clauses are constructed in different languages, they can be particularly troublesome for non-native speakers. You need to remember a few guidelines when using adjective clauses in order to form them correctly.

First, place the adjective clause directly *after* the noun it modifies.

- ◼ *who is standing across the room*
  The tall man is a vice-president of the company who is standing across the room.

[The adjective clause *who is standing across the room* modifies *man*, not *company*, and thus comes directly after *man*.]

Second, do not omit the relative pronoun when it is in the subject position of its clause. If, however, the relative pronoun is in the object position in its clause, it may be omitted. Notice the difference in these two sentences.

■   The man *who sits at that desk* is my boss.

[The relative pronoun *who* is in the subject position.]

■   The man *whom we met* at the meeting is on the board of directors.

[The relative pronoun *whom* is in the object position.]

■   The man we met at the meeting is on the board of directors.

[The relative pronoun is omitted.]

Finally, avoid using a relative pronoun with another pronoun in an adjective clause.

■   The man who ~~he~~ sits at that desk is my boss.

■   The man whom we met ~~him~~ at the meeting is on the board of directors.

Verb Tenses

There are many verb tenses in English that are similar. When you are determining which verb tense to use, think of the time in which the action you are describing occurs in relation to other actions. (Using the verb-tense timeline in Table D–2 will help you choose which tense to use.)

The **present** tense expresses activities that occur on a regular basis

■   Ms. Sanchez *takes* her break at 10:15 in the morning.

and indicates facts.

■   The meeting *is scheduled* for tomorrow at noon.

The **past** tense describes a completed action.

■   My boss *left* for the airport two hours ago.

The **future** tense describes an action that will occur in the future.

■   Leaven Corporation *will hire* two financial consultants at the beginning of the year.

The "X" marks on the timelines of this chart indicate points in time when action takes place. Arrows extending from the past and future labels further identify the activity of the verb. For example, the first timeline indicates that the accounting department presently works late, has worked late in the past, and will work late in the future.

Present Tense (base + -*s* or -*es*)

■ The accounting department *works* late every Tuesday.

[The accounting department does work, has worked, and will continue to work late every Tuesday.]

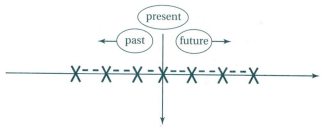

Present Progressive Tense (*am/is/are/* + base + -*ing*)

■ Mr. Greczek *is speaking* to the new employees.

[The speaking is taking place in the present.]

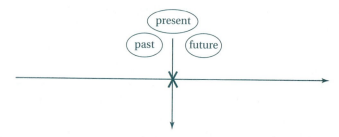

Past Tense (base + -*ed* or irregular form of verb)

■ The file clerk *worked* in the new office on Monday.

[The working took place in the past.]

■ The assistant *ran* to answer the phone.

[The running took place in the past.]

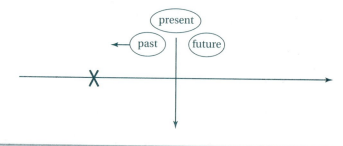

Table D–2   Forming Tenses: A Timeline

Past Progressive Tense (*was/were* + base + *-ing*)

■ My assistant *was typing* the report when I walked in the office.

[The typing took place in the past, when something else also took place.]

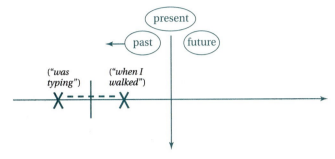

Present Perfect (*have/has* + *-ed* or irregular form)

■ Mrs. Carols *has decided* to take early retirement.

[The decision was made in the past and also applies to the present.]

■ The manager *has* already *made* his decision.

[The decision was made in the past and also applies to the present.]

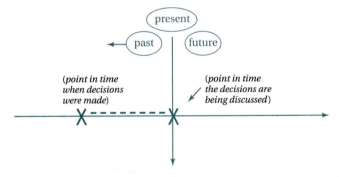

Present Perfect Progressive Tense (*have/has* + *been* + base + *-ing*)

■ I *have been working* on the fiscal-year report for two weeks.

[The working began in the past, and continues into the present and future.]

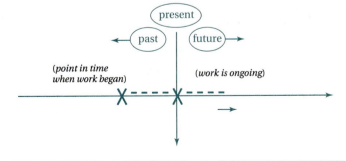

Table D–2 **(continued)**

Past Perfect Tense (*had* + *-ed* or irregular form)

■ The chairperson *had* already *started* the meeting when Celia arrived.

[The meeting began; Celia arrived some time later (both in the past).]

■ James *had taken* the client out to dinner to discuss the project before he offered her the job.

[The client was taken out to dinner and later offered the job.]

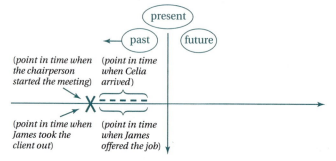

Past Perfect Progressive Tense (*had* + *been* + base + *-ing*)

■ The assistant manager *had been working* for three hours before anyone else arrived.

[The working took place; others arrived some time later (both in the past).]

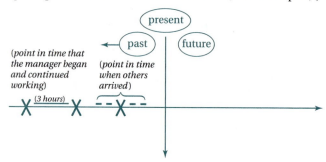

Future Tense (*will* + base) or (*is/are* + *going to* + base)

■ Mr. Williams *will coordinate* this year's conference.

[The conference will be coordinated in the future.]

or

■ Mr. Williams *is going to coordinate* this year's conference.

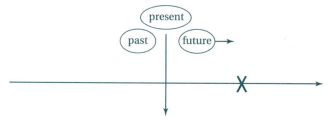

Table D–2 (continued)

Future Progressive Tense (*will* + *be* + base + *-ing*)

■ He *will be working* when we arrive.

[The working will already be taking place when they arrive.]

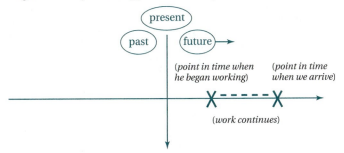

Future Perfect Progressive Tense (*will* + *have* + *been* + base + *-ing*)

■ Mrs. Stuart *will have been speaking* for two hours by the time you arrive.

[The speaking will already be taking place (will have been going on for some time) before you arrive.]

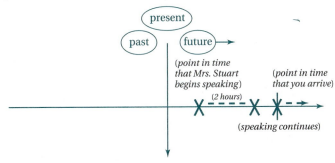

Future Perfect Tense (*will* + *have* + *-ed* or irregular form)

■ Because Mr. Santiago arrived at work early, he *will have finished* his work before noon.

[The working, which began in the morning (past), will be finished before noon (future).]

■ Because of the company's use of flextime, Mr. Santiago *will* already *have left* when Mrs. Patrick arrives.

[The leaving by Mr. Santiago will take place before the arrival of Mrs. Patrick.]

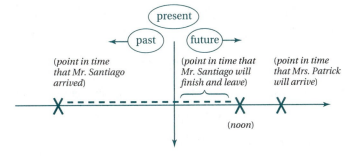

Table D–2 **(continued)**

ESL TIPS: Forming the Present Perfect Tense

Because it is so closely related to the past tense, the present perfect tense in English remains one of the most problematic of all tenses for non-native speakers. A few guidelines, however, will help you remember the correct use of this tense. As a general rule, use the present perfect tense when referring to events completed in the past, but at unspecified times. When a specific time is mentioned, use the simple past tense. Notice the difference in the following two sentences.

- ◼ I *wrote* the letter yesterday.

  [simple past tense *wrote*. The time when the action took place is mentioned.]

- ◼ I *have written* the letter.

  [present perfect tense *have written*. No specific time is mentioned; it could have been yesterday, last week, or ten years ago.]

Also use the present perfect tense to describe actions that were repeated several or many times in the unspecified past.

- ◼ She *has written* that report three times.
- ◼ The president and his chief technical advisor *have met* many times over the past few months.

Finally, use the present perfect tense with a *since* or *for* phrase when describing actions that began in the past and continue up to the present.

- ◼ This company *has been* in business *for* ten years.
- ◼ The company *has been* in business *since* 1983.

The **present perfect** tense describes an action that occurred at an unspecified time in the past and continues into the present moment. (See ESL Tips: Forming the Present Perfect Tense, above.)

- ◼ The accounting staff *has started* on the new budget plan for next year.

The **past perfect** tense is used to specify that an action occurred in the past before another past action occurred.

- ◼ I *was typing* the report when the phone rang.

The **future perfect** tense is used to specify that an action will occur in the future before another future action occurs.

- ◼ I *will have* the report *completed* before the next meeting starts.

The **present progressive** tense describes an action that is occurring at the moment of speaking.

■   Now I *am reading* the financial section of the paper.

The **past progressive** tense is used to specify a continuous action in the past that was interrupted by another action.

■   I *was finishing* my lunch when the client walked into my office.

The **future progressive** tense is used to specify a continuous action in the future that will be occurring when another action takes place.

■   He *will be asleep* by the time I get home.

The **present perfect progressive** tense specifies a continuous action that started in the past and continues to the present.

■   Daniel *has been working* at his desk all day.

The **past perfect progressive** tense specifies an action that occurred for a time in the past but was completed before another action in the past.

■   When I saw Mr. Smith this morning, he *had been jogging*.

The **future perfect progressive** tense specifies an action in the future that will be finished before another action occurs in the future.

■   The secretarial assistants *will have been working* on the project for three hours before the secretaries will begin.

Helping Verbs and Conditional Sentences

Modal verbs are helping verbs that have a variety of meanings. After using a modal helping verb, use a base form of the verb. (See ESL Tips: Using Helping Verbs, in this section.)

In *conditional sentences,* clauses that follow the words *if, when,* and *unless* show whether the result is possible or real, depending on other circumstances. Conditional sentences have two parts: a subordinate clause—that begins with *if, when,* and *unless*—and a main clause that expresses a result. The following are types of conditional sentences.

A *prediction* foretells something based on conditional circumstances. To form a prediction, use a present tense verb within the *if* clause. The clause that expresses the result is formed with a modal helping verb (usually *will*) and the base form of the verb.

■ *If* you treat employees fairly, they *will be* better workers.

A *fact* explains a factual relationship between two or more occurrences. To form a fact, use the same verb tense in both the conditional clause and the result clause.

■ When it *snows,* I *have to leave* an hour earlier for work.

■ When the chairperson *started* the meeting, he *welcomed* all new employees.

ESL TIPS: Using Helping Verbs

In English there are twenty-three helping verbs (forms of *have, be, do*) that may also function as main verbs. There are also nine modals (*can, may, would,* etc.; see below) that function only as helping verbs. The main difference between modals and the forms of *have, be,* and *do* is that *have, be,* and *do* change form to indicate tense; the nine modals do not.

Can

■ He *can* type fast. [ability]
■ Bill, you *can* still improve. [possibility]

Could

■ He *could* type fast before he broke his wrist. [past ability]
■ Bill, you *could* still improve. [possibility]

May

■ Juanita *may* show up for the meeting. [possibility]
■ You *may* come and go as you please. [permission]

Might

■ Juanita *might* show up for the meeting. [possibility]
■ *Might* I go home early today? [very formal; permission]

Must

- We *must* finish this report by the end of the week. [necessity]
- You *must* see his new office. [recommendation]
- You *must* be hungry; you haven't eaten all day. [inference]

Shall

- *Shall* we go? [intention]

  [In American English, *shall* is used only for questions seeking agreement.]

Should

- You *should* apologize immediately. [advisability]
- Prentiss *should* be here any minute. [expectation]

Will

- Greg *will* finish as soon as he can. [intention]

Would

- *Would* you excuse me? [permission]
- He *would* review his work incessantly when he first started working here. [habitual past]
- That *would* be a good guess. [probability]

The following guidelines will help you determine the proper use of modals.

One-word modals do not change form to show a change in subject.

- I could quit. She could quit.

Most two- and three-word modals do change form, like other helping verbs.

- I have to finish the project. She has to finish the project.

Never use *to* between a one-word modal and the main verb.

- Can type, *not* can to type.

  [Most of the two- and three-word modals include *to*, as in, *ought to drive.*]

Never use two one-word modals together.

- I will be able to work tomorrow.

When several auxiliaries occur simultaneously, they must be in the following order:

  modal perfect progressive participle

- He may have been being defrauded for several years.

A hypothetical sentence explains that a result is impossible, did not happen, or is unlikely to happen. To form a hypothetical sentence, use a past tense verb within the *if* clause, and *would, could,* or *might* in the result clause.

■ *If* I were CEO, I *would take* three months' vacation every year.

Idioms Used in Business

An *idiom* is an expression that means something different from the literal translation of each of its words into another language. An idiom such as "it's raining cats and dogs" (meaning much rain is falling) is not understandable from the individual meaning of each word. Some idioms are considered *colloquial,* meaning they are typically used only in informal English.

The following are common idioms used in North American English.

bottom line	the last figure on a financial balance sheet; the result or final outcome or ultimate truth
break down	to stop working properly
break up	to separate into smaller parts
bring about	to cause
bring up	to raise in a conversation
brush up on	to review (informal English)
call back	to return a phone call
call off	to cancel (informal English)
call on	to visit
call up	to telephone
carry out	to obey orders
check on	to inquire
come up with	to imagine; to think up (informal English)
count on	to depend on
cut down	to decrease the consumption of
cut off	to abruptly stop
deal with	to negotiate with; to take care of
decide on	to choose
do over	to repeat an action usually with corrections
do without	to manage without
drag on	proceed slowly (informal English)
drop off	to deliver (informal English)

fall behind	to not keep up with a job or a project (informal English)
fall through	to fail
figure out	to solve; to understand
fill out	to complete by writing
find out	to discover
finish up	to finish completely
get away with	to commit a bad act without being punished (informal English)
get by	to manage (informal English)
get in touch with	to call or to contact
get through	to finish (informal English)
go out of business	to stop doing business forever
go over	to review; to look over (informal English)
hang up	to replace a telephone receiver or to place an article of clothing on a hook
help out	to assist
hold on	to wait (informal English)
iron out	to solve a problem (informal English)
keep up	to maintain
lay off	to fire
lay over	to be delayed because of an airplane problem
lock up	to lock completely
look into	to investigate
look over	to examine carefully
look through	to search
make up one's mind	to make a decision (informal English)
on the table	open for discussion
pass around	to hand around to a group of people
pick out	to select
point out	to indicate
pull out	to break an agreement
put off	to postpone
run across	to find unexpectedly; to meet by chance
run into	to meet by chance
run up	to increase a bill
see about	to consider

send out	to mail
shape up	to improve (informal English)
size up	to analyze (informal English)
sort out	to classify
speak of	to mention
speak out	to say aloud
stand by	to wait for
stick with	to stay with (informal English)
switch off	to turn off
switch on	to turn on
take charge of	to assume responsibility for
take place	to occur
talk over	to discuss
think up	to imagine or to invent
try out	to test
turn down	to reject
wear out	to use until old; to exhaust
wrap up	to complete (informal English)
zero in (on)	to focus in on (informal English)

Comprehensive dictionaries of North American idioms include

NTC's American Idioms /Dictionary, 2nd ed. NTC Publishing Group.

A Dictionary of American Idioms, 3rd ed. Barron's.

Cambridge International Dictionary of Idioms. Cambridge University Press.

Longman's American Idioms Dictionary. Longman Publishing.

Retrieval System), including truncated (250 words) abstract from M. Gausche et al., "Vital signs as part of the prehospital assessment of the pediatric patient: A survey of paramedics," from *Annals of Emergency Medicine* 19, no. 2 (February 1990). Reprinted with the permission of Mosby, Inc.

Figures 11–16, 11–17, and 11–18: Initial Yahoo! Search Screen, Yahoo! Search Screen showing scope of business information available, and Yahoo! Search Screen showing scope of e-commerce information. Text and artwork copyright © 2000 by Yahoo!, Inc. All rights reserved. Yahoo! and the Yahoo! logo are trademarks of Yahoo!, Inc.

Figure 11–19: NTRG "Network Payment Mechanisms and Digital Cash"

screen from http://ntrg.cs.tcd.ie/me peirce/project.html. Copyright © 1994–2000 by Michael Peirce, mepeirce@cs .tcd.ie. Reprinted with the permission of the Networks and Telecommunications Research Group (NTRG) and Michael Peirce.

Figures 13–1 to 13–5, and 13–7 to 13–11: Susan Litzinger, "Reported Ethics Cases, Annual Report 1997" (a student's sample formal report about a corporation's ethics program). Adapted and reprinted with the permission of Susan Litzinger.

Figure 14–6: Eric Shoop, Short sales proposal (a student's sample sales proposal). Adapted and reprinted with permission of Eric Shoop.

Index

Mark in Margin	Instruction	Mark on Manuscript	Corrected Type
_e_	Delete	the ~~lawyer's~~ Bible	the Bible
lawyer's	Insert	the bible	the lawyer's bible
stet	Let stand	the lawyer's bible	the lawyer's bible
cap	Capitalize	the bible	the Bible
lc	Make lowercase	the Law	the law
ital	Italicize	the lawyer's bible	the *lawyer's* bible
tr	Transpose	the bible lawyer's	the lawyer's bible
⊂	Close space	the Bi ble	the Bible
sp	Spell out	2 bibles	two bibles
#	Insert space	theBible	the Bible
¶	Start paragraph	¶ The lawyer's . . .	The lawyer's . . .
run in	No paragraph	. . . marks. Below is a . . .	. . . marks. Below is a . . .
sc	Set in small capitals	the bible	the BIBLE
rom	Set in roman type	the *bible*	the bible
bf	Set in boldface	the bible	the **bible**
lf	Set in lightface	the **bible**	the bible
⊙	Insert period	The lawyers have their own bible	The lawyers have their own bible.
⌄	Insert comma	However we cannot . . .	However, we cannot . . .
⁼/⁼	Insert hyphens	half and half	half-and-half
:⊙	Insert colon	We need the following	We need the following:
⁏	Insert semicolon	Use the law don't . . .	Use the law; don't . . .
⌄	Insert apostrophe	Johns law book	John's law book
⌄/⌄	Insert quotation marks	The law is law.	The "law" is law.
(/)/	Insert parentheses	John's law book	John's (law) book
[/]/	Insert brackets	(John Martin 1920–1962 went . . .)	(John Martin [1920–1962] went . . .)
⊥N	Insert en dash	1920 1962	1920–1962
⊥M	Insert em dash	Our goal victory	Our goal—victory
∨	Insert superior type	3²= 9	3² = 9
∧	Insert inferior type	HSO₄	H₂SO₄

Writer's Checklists, Digital Shortcuts, and ESL Tips